LETTERS
OF
FRANCES HODGKINS

Sept 1st - 39
Corfe Castle
Dorset -

My Dearest Willie

I must write you a quick line
all is confusion - we have been very
near war for six vital days & now
it is war - Germany is bombing
Poland - I am filled with hatred
of Germany and filled with hatred
of Russia - but even now, at
this flash point - I still hope for a
solution and still dare hope for
the miracle to happen

Don't worry about me

I beg you not to worry -
I can't help wishing I were with
you all - & you with me - I am
well enough thank goodness, & strong enough
to go and fetch my own gas mask

Letter to William Hodgkins, 1 September 1939 (Letter 495).

LETTERS
OF
FRANCES HODGKINS

Edited by Linda Gill

AUCKLAND UNIVERSITY PRESS

To E. H. McCormick

First published 1993
Auckland University Press
Private Bag 92019
Auckland, New Zealand

ISBN 1 86940 081 X

Publication is assisted by the Literature Programme
of the Queen Elizabeth II Arts Council

Typeset in Garamond by Deadline Typesetting Ltd
Printed by Kings Time Printing Press, Hong Kong

Distributed outside New Zealand by Oxford University Press

Contents

As in mountaineering so in art — there is only a very narrow edge of safety on which we can walk.

Letter from Frances Hodgkins to Jane Saunders, September 1924

The art historian may sometimes regret that Vasari did not give us more of the aesthetics of his time; but Vasari knew his business, knew, perhaps, that the aesthetics of an age are quickly superseded but that the human document remains of perennial interest to mankind.

Roger Fry, *Vision and Design*

Acknowledgements

In preparing this book, I am indebted in every possible way to Dr E. H. McCormick. He gave me dated transcriptions of the letters of Frances Hodgkins, additional information and photographs, a treasure trove of material representing years of research. Though I have had the pleasure of his friendship while working on the manuscript and have been guided by the example of his scholarly dedication, Dr McCormick carries no responsibility for the use I have made of his gifts. He has refrained from advice and enquiry and left me free to make my own decisions.

The late Peter Field, nephew of Frances Hodgkins and trustee of her estate, gave me permission to publish the letters, which are still under copyright. I am most grateful to him and his wife Dorothy for their generosity and encouragement.

Jim Traue of the Turnbull Library and his successor Margaret Calder supported the publication and I have appreciated the help of David Colquhoun, David Retter and Penelope Feltham of the Manuscripts and Archives Section. I am also grateful for assistance from: Ron Brownson (Auckland City Art Gallery), Rosemary Entwisle and Peter Miller (Hocken Library), Oliver Stead (Dunedin Public Art Gallery), Jennifer Booth and Susan Breakell (Tate Gallery Archive). Dr Francis Pound, Priscilla Pitts and Alexa Johnston made suggestions about the introduction, as did Gretchen Albrecht, whose comments on early drafts of the manuscript were invaluable. Iain Buchanan drew my attention to an important letter in the Art Gallery of New South Wales. For various combinations of information, friendship and hospitality I would like to thank: the late Sir Colin Allan, Maurice and Beverley Allen, Dr Roger Collins, Jetta and Bruce Cornish, Elizabeth Eastmond, Sarah Hillary, Bill and Marjorie Hursthouse, Louis Johnston, Roberta and Brian McKeon, James Ross, Peter Scholes and Elizabeth Steiner.

From the beginning I have been sustained by the enthusiasm and advice of Elizabeth Caffin of Auckland University Press and, more recently, by similar encouragement and assistance from Dennis McEldowney.

I gratefully acknowledge the generous assistance of the Literature Programme of the Queen Elizabeth II Arts Council.

To my husband Mike, my thanks for much material help as well as the greater kindness of being a patient listener.

Editorial Note

The extant letters of Frances Hodgkins contain over half a million words. The informal nature of the letters contributed to the decision to publish a selection rather than a complete edition of this extensive correspondence. Comments and enquiries about friends and relations, the chronicling of small daily events (often the most engaging parts of a letter for its recipient) diminish in interest the further a reader is removed in time and kinship. The flavour of these exchanges may be adequately conveyed by samples. Sometimes FH passed swiftly from one subject to another and some of those fragments may be omitted without misrepresenting her style. At other times she dwelt repetitively on one topic and again little violence is done if the discussion is condensed.

The outstanding quality of these letters is their completeness as a record of a life and the selection has been made with a view to retaining that quality. Of the 992 surviving letters 616 have been selected, and nearly all of these have been abridged. Overall, the correspondence has been reduced by half. I was concerned to show FH at her best as a letter-writer but not at the expense of biographical information, especially where that was relevant to her development as an artist. Footnotes have been kept to a minimum; artists mentioned by FH are briefly identified if they are not well known or if their life and work had some bearing on what she was doing at the time.

FH's letters are visually interesting documents, expressive in ways that are lost when they are rendered in print. Her handwriting has something of the calligraphic variety of her paint strokes and is a supple instrument for revealing mood. The relation between word and space is also eloquent: the length of the gaps between words may vary, suggesting pauses, the lines of writing may run almost diagonally across the page, the final sentences wind round the margins of preceding pages. There has been no attempt, beyond this brief note and one or two comments later, to indicate idiosyncrasies of this kind. Other idiosyncrasies have been retained: FH's abbreviations; her casual use of apostrophes; her paragraphing; her varying ways of writing the date. Most inconsistencies in spelling, including that of names, have been left without comment. Some errors have been silently corrected: those that were obviously the result of a momentary lapse or, very occasionally, where too pedantic an insistence on fidelity might interrupt the larger truth of a passage, introducing, for example, a touch of humour into what was deeply felt by the writer.

I have taken some small liberties with punctuation, especially in the later letters. As time went by, FH's punctuation was increasingly reduced to the dash, varying in length from a flick to an emphatic line more than two centimetres long. Even her question marks regularly have dashes as their base. I have interpreted some of these dashes as full stops. I have also supplied full stops and the occasional comma when lack of punctuation seemed inadvertent and prevented fluent reading. I have standardised the punctuation of the addresses and completed brackets and quotation marks.

Square brackets indicate material supplied editorially within the letter. Ellipses, never used by FH herself, indicate omitted material, three stops . . . for a passage between the beginning and end of a sentence, four stops . . . . for a longer omission.

Sources of the letters
Nearly all the letters of Frances Hodgkins, either the original documents, photocopies or transcriptions, are lodged in the Alexander Turnbull Library, Wellington. The editor and publishers gratefully acknowledge the library's permission to publish this selection.

Grateful acknowledgement is also made to: Maurice and Beverley Allen (David Brynley), the Art Gallery of New South Wales (H. V. F. Mann), The Lefevre Gallery (Dr Honeyman, Duncan Macdonald, A. J. McNeill Reid), the Sarjeant Gallery (Edith Collier), the Tate Gallery (Jane Saunders, Arthur Howell, Arthur Lett Haines). The letters to Karl Hagedorn and some to Eardley Knollys were collected and transcribed by Peter Millard.

Introduction

'I do so enjoy your letters', wrote Dorothy Kate Richmond to Frances Hodgkins when the two women were in Europe in 1903. 'You write in the same style as you paint, with brilliant patches of colour and any amount of snap and go.'

Over sixty years later Katharine West, another close friend, spoke of the pleasure Frances Hodgkins's letters had given her in the 1940s: 'Most painters write well . . . . The whole person comes in the paintings and in the writing and this is particularly true of Frances . . . . Her letters were an absolutely spontaneous outpouring of the person she was.'[1]

Frances Hodgkins's letters span almost six decades of her life, from her twenties to her seventies, 1892 to 1946. They document a remarkable journey in the course of which an amateur painter, glad to earn a few guineas with her paintings of 'livestock', was transformed into a distinguished modern artist. Her first exhibition was with the Canterbury Society of Arts in Christchurch in 1890 where she showed a watercolour, *Girl Feeding Poultry*. One of her last exhibitions was a group show in London at the Lefevre Gallery in 1945: *Recent Paintings by Francis Bacon, Frances Hodgkins, Henry Moore, Matthew Smith, Graham Sutherland.*

From provincial, Victorian New Zealand Frances Hodgkins went, by way of Edwardian England and sketching grounds in Europe, to live in Paris in 1908 at the height of its influence as the art centre of the western world. Her life in France, and with it the possibility that she might become a French painter, was brought to an end by the First World War, and from then on she was regarded as a British painter. The full flowering of her talent occurred in the 1930s and 40s and, in spite of failing health and a second world war, her last paintings were some of the best she had ever done.

The letters come from a multitude of addresses. Frances Hodgkins had no permanent home after leaving New Zealand in 1901. She lived in cheap hotels, in rented rooms and studios, in borrowed cottages and flats. Occasionally, she luxuriated in comfortable living, hot baths and good food, as a house guest of wealthy friends. Her travels took her as far south as Morocco, to Holland and Italy, to France, Spain and all over the British Isles. She twice returned to New Zealand.

Frances Hodgkins did not marry, nor, after her second departure from New Zealand in 1906, did she live closely with other people for any length of time. She remained separated by half a world from her closest relatives. It was through her letters that she kept alive the links with her family in New Zealand and sustained the friendships made in England. Many of these letters preserve material that would have been conveyed by the spoken word in a less solitary life. They are like conversations with a trusted companion at the end of a day's work and they have the vivid impromptu quality of speech, being swiftly written, with no rough drafts, no phrases carefully hammered out with at least some thought of future publication. Those written to Frances's mother, Rachel Hodgkins, have the narrative continuity of a diary. Sometimes there are long descriptive accounts, of new places, new people. Scattered among the day to day reporting are remarks that hindsight seizes upon as significant in the development of her career. Many of these have already been quoted in publications about the artist. Read within their context they no longer stand out like clear signposts and the reader moves with the artist along an unmapped path criss-crossed with trails of doubt and uncertainty.

The letters are full of information about the practical side of the painting life: the need to make sales, the difficulty of finding models and studio space, the discomfort of working in public places while keeping street urchins at bay, the incessant problem of the weather ('never quite right for artists or farmers'). Those who cling to romantic illusions about the lives of artists may be disappointed by the businesslike attitudes revealed. The language is down to earth and concrete, varying in tone and topic according to recipient. Writing to Miss Richmond, a fellow painter, about Morocco, she describes the colours in careful detail: 'no gorgeous east here – no oriental riot of colour – all browns & whites & muddy creams with here & there a splash of crimson & orange & the better class Moors making blots of indigo in their handsome blue cloaks.' To her mother she stresses practical matters: 'I am revelling in this place – such sumptuous colour & I feel sure if I can get a good portfolio of sketches it will pay me over & over again.'

There is very little theorising. In 1926 she related to her sister an incident involving a professor of philosophy who 'was very keen to get out of me *what* went on inside me when I painted a picture. He is writing a thesis on Art. I couldn't tell him much more than that I painted a picture much as a hen lays an egg – that it was inevitable – which seemed to please him – though he would have preferred some philosophic abstractions on the subject. Artists are too engaged "doing" it to analyse their emotions.'

Such comments imply a belief in an intuitive, almost naive approach to painting and the corresponding desire to refrain from formulating theory. And this was the position from which Hodgkins eventually painted, a sophisticated and chosen naivety. If her mature paintings look awkward or childlike, it is because she has knowingly discarded the signs of forethought and control –

careful finish, smooth transitions, conventional colour harmonies, spatial logic. She was well-informed about current art movements. Her letters and comments from friends make it clear that she visited art galleries assiduously, studying the established collections in public galleries as well as the work of contemporary artists to be seen in the private galleries. Earlier in her life she used art language fluently when it seemed necessary. In 1913 for example she gave a press interview about her exhibition in Sydney, spoke of the Futurists and the Post-Impressionists and concluded that 'the abstract pervades all modern art'.[2] There are no records of such public statements later in her life. In the letters clues to her ideas about painting are gained mainly from her comments about other artists, but these are uncertain guides, since artists do not always acknowledge the influences that have most powerfully stirred them.

Frances Hodgkins herself set little store by her letters. Her paintings were the focus of her intellectual and emotional energy, testifying to her increasing engagement with modernism, and it was by them that she hoped to be remembered. 'Such tin-pot letters written in my light minded moments must be kept strictly in the family', she wrote to her mother in 1907. When she discovered that Dorothy Richmond in 1903 was copying her letters to send back to relatives in New Zealand, she cheerfully offered to make duplicates and then more seriously remarked, 'It seems to me that a letter that is good enough to publish should be either whimsical enough to treat as a joke or thoughtful enough to take seriously & mine are neither – better let them rest in peace with the family archives.'

Her mother and later her elder sister, Isabel Field, stored most of a lifetime's correspondence though they were forgetful archivists and the story grew up in the family that the letters from Frances had been inadvertently thrown on the fire by Mrs Hodgkins. Scholarly instincts took Dr E. H. McCormick to the family home in Wellington just after Isabel Field's death in 1950 and hundreds of letters from Frances Hodgkins came to light. Half of the extant letters, of which there are just under a thousand, come from this source.[3]

Her close friends also valued and kept Frances Hodgkins's letters. The fact that three quarters of the surviving letters are written to women is a true reflection of the importance of women in Frances Hodgkins's life. But it may also suggest that women are more likely than men to keep informal letters. Frances Hodgkins had many loyal men friends and only some of them are represented. Her long friendship with the English painters Cedric Morris and Arthur Lett Haines, who used their influence to advance her career in the late twenties and early thirties, is commemorated by only three letters, a postcard and a telegram, all to Lett Haines. She wrote to Ben Nicholson and to the French artist Maurice Garnier, and kept in touch with two Australian patrons, George Rich and Peter Waite. The painters Norman Garstin and Moffat Lindner were good friends during the first years in Europe and it is inconceivable that she did not occasionally write to them. There was some correspondence with the critic Frank Rutter and also with

Paul Nash, when he invited Hodgkins to join his avant garde group Unit One in 1933. These letters, along no doubt with many others to both men and women, have not survived.

Over three hundred letters are addressed to Frances Hodgkins's mother Rachel, with the intention that they be passed round the family. In these she had the chance to talk honestly about her difficulties as well as her achievements, unconstrained by the need to keep up a public appearance of success. At the same time her reluctance to cause her mother anxiety led her to minimise the times of greatest hardship until she had overcome them. After Mrs Hodgkins, her sister Isabel and Dorothy Selby, the close friend of the last part of Hodgkins's life, are the most important correspondents, each receiving around a hundred letters. Of the remaining forty-four correspondents eleven are immediate family members and thirteen are close friends.

A significant aspect of the artist's life is revealed in the correspondence with the dealers who from 1929 onwards looked after her work. Most of the letters of 1928-31 to Arthur Howell of St George's Gallery were published in 1951 in his book *Four Vital Years*. 'These letters are intriguing,' wrote the critic of the *New Statesman*, who clearly had rigid ideas about what constituted a 'good' letter. 'Underneath the inarticulate descriptions, the rather schoolgirlish slang and the conventional remarks about holidays and the weather, the sympathetic reader can begin to sense her erratic, passionate, naive – and yet in some ways very shrewd – personality.'[4]

There is a more sustained correspondence with Duncan Macdonald and A. J. McNeill Reid of the Lefevre Gallery, lasting from 1934 to 1946. Never entirely formal, these letters provide an insight into the complex relationship between dealer and artist with its highly charged mixture of financial, aesthetic and emotional considerations.

Frances Hodgkins's letters bear witness to the warmth of her affections and tributes from her friends after her death are unanimous in their description of her as a marvellously witty and stimulating companion. But let there be no mistake: Frances Hodgkins was not a 'nice' woman, if by that one means gentle and unassuming. She was, in the words of one of her relations, a 'small, strong-willed, sharp-tongued creature'.[5] The writer Greville Texidor who met her in Spain in 1936 wrote: 'I was entertained and alarmed by her sometimes rather summary summings up. She noticed so much and drew such amusing conclusions.'[6] Frances Hodgkins had all the singlemindedness and ambition needed to nurture a major talent, though it was some time before she accepted those qualities in herself. Soon after her arrival in Europe in 1901 she wrote to her mother: 'I feel as if I was possessed by a painting devil which is devouring me body and soul & claims all my brains & energy, & leaves me with no wish or inclination for anything else. I must not give way to it I know.' It is a sad commentary on the internalised prohibitions Frances Hodgkins had to overcome as a Victorian woman artist that she should respond to the discovery of her vocation, not with joy, but with a guilty sense of satanic visitation. It was not until October 1910, at the age of forty-one, that she felt free to speak openly to her mother: 'I wish you were as *terribly* ambitious for me as I am for myself.'

It will probably never be known whether Frances Hodgkins was absolutely the celibate woman she appears to be. There are no love letters in the conventional sense of the term. Her brief engagement to the writer Thomas Wilby remains mysterious because the letters they wrote to each other have not survived and she did not talk about it later to other friends. What does emerge from the letters is her passionate delight in the beauty of women and her enjoyment of the company of intelligent, well-informed and adventurous people, men and women. Whether these emotions were ever given sexual expression is less important than the fact that they were experienced with such pleasurable intensity. In Dorothy Richmond she found a person who combined many of the qualities she admired, and the time spent painting with her in France and Italy was the most exuberantly happy period of her life. She wrote of and to Miss Richmond in the language of love, a usage sanctioned by the tradition of romantic friendship between women, and not necessarily indicative of any closer relationship. Part of her joy at this time undoubtedly came from the satisfaction of being at last in Europe, free to travel about and do her own work, after spending over two years accumulating the necessary money. Although Dorothy Richmond was the more experienced painter, she deferred to Frances Hodgkins's talent and this pattern was repeated with all Hodgkins's later friendships with women.

That a person capable of such intense feeling for others lived much of her life alone may be explained by another aspect of her temperament, the vein of solitariness and eccentricity that runs in the Hodgkins family. But an equally compelling explanation is to be found in the nature of her calling as a woman artist.

Frances Hodgkins had to look no further than her own family to see the effect of family ties on a woman artist. If family obligations limited her father's artistic achievement, the duties of wife and mother all but stifled her sister Isabel's considerable gifts. Frances Hodgkins accepted that a woman artist, if she was serious about her work, must remain free from such obligations, and sacrifice the pleasures associated with them. The renunciation of the normal human satisfactions associated with home and family was complete only after the death of her mother in 1926. It is noteworthy that the paintings on which her reputation chiefly stands were begun only after that date. Was there, one wonders, some undercurrent of mingled love, guilt and anxiety that, allied with more obvious difficulties, distracted her from the intensity of focus that ultimately brought her work to fruition? The overwhelming social expectation of the time was that an unmarried daughter should care for a widowed mother, and the inhibiting effect of this on a woman as dutiful and affectionate as Frances Hodgkins can be judged from the anguished tone of the letters in which she discussed with her mother her desire to remain in England. Though she continued to write from time to time to other members of her family after her mother's death, the letters have none of the intensity of those earlier communications.

Frances Hodgkins found in friendship an alternative to family satisfactions. All the friendships commemorated in her letters grew out of her activity as an artist and remained subservient to it. The boundaries between friends, pupils, fellow artists, patrons and dealers became blurred because there was finally no separation between the woman and the artist. Friendships did not last if people failed to keep up with the intellectual adventure she had embarked upon. Nothing provoked more irritation than to hear someone express a preference for her early work and the wish that she had not 'changed her style' to accommodate modernism. Even those who were entirely sympathetic to her artistic goals were kept at a little distance. Towards the end of her life she felt comfortable only with people like Dorothy Selby, a former pupil and amateur artist, a practical, sensible woman who made no demands, or Eardley Knollys, a man of 'infinite kindness and perfect manners' whose 'great talent for friendship' was 'combined with an almost fierce independence'.[7] Lucy Wertheim was a generous benefactor and admirer of her work, but she ignored the boundaries Hodgkins had drawn and was sharply, even harshly rebuffed. Frances Hodgkins did not allow financial dependence to imply any other kind of dependence and was aggressively protective of her right to paint her pictures and organise her life on her own terms. While she could never be called an amenable, compliant person, her combativeness was exaggerated by a social order that more readily granted to men the right to singlemindedness.

Frances Hodgkins's physical appearance is documented in a sequence of photographs and descriptions by her friends. Short in stature, with a large mouth and a sharp, intense, amused look in her eyes, she did not conform to prevailing standards of feminine attractiveness, though it is easy now to call her a handsome woman. She loved clothes and, given the necessary large income, would have dressed in the height of fashion all her life. Betty Rhind, a New Zealand friend, spoke of the comparison between Dorothy Richmond and Frances Hodgkins when they both returned to Wellington in 1904: 'Miss Richmond with her long skirts and her flat men's shoes and mushroom hat and Miss Hodgkins looking so "Frenchy".' Betty Rhind became a pupil of Frances Hodgkins at Concarneau in 1911, and described her at that time: 'She would wear perhaps a bright jacket, even two bright jackets under a dark coat, and several scarves of the very best quality, probably hand woven and beautiful, a little bit of oriental jewellery, always a jaunty hat and always high heels.'[8] Another friend and pupil, Madeline Williams commented in a letter of 1919 on Miss Hodgkins's 'very finished & dainty appearance in London'. Frances Hodgkins was well aware of the part played by dress in her role as an artist and, as time went by and lack of money prevented her from maintaining anything like a fashionable appearance, she opted more and more for distinctiveness bordering on eccentricity. Where conventional observers noted only the strangeness, artist friends appreciated the quality and design of the fabrics and the skill with which pattern and colour were juxtaposed. 'She looked like her own paintings,' commented Douglas Glass, 'sometimes the most incredible colours put together.'[9] 'She was small, and heavily made up, like a bright tropical bird,' wrote Peter Davis, who met Hodgkins in the 1930s.[10] Edna Holland, who knew her in Corfe Castle towards the end of her life, remembered a 'small, straight-backed, dignified woman, eccentric in dress, always wearing a jaunty beret.'[11]

There was something of a theatrical flair in Frances Hodgkins, evident in the photographs taken for publicity purposes. As she grew older, the normal dislike of ageing was heightened by the knowledge that an elderly unmarried woman would lack credibility as a serious artist, and she did her best to disguise her age. She wore a wig and shortened her skirts. There is a telling photograph reproduced in E. H. McCormick's *Portrait of Frances Hodgkins* (p.111). Taken at Flatford Mill in 1930, it was part of the publicity for an important exhibition at the St George's Gallery and shows the artist sitting on the bed in her studio, looking at one of her paintings. Leaning casually on one arm, with shapely legs stretched out and stylishly crossed, her feet in elegant shoes, Frances Hodgkins at sixty-one succeeded in making herself look as if she were half that age. At seventy, she tried to avoid photographers altogether.

Much has been written about Frances Hodgkins's slow beginnings as an artist and the overshadowing influence of her sister Isabel's precocious talent. Her father William Mathew Hodgkins belonged to the first generation of New Zealand artists who settled in the towns and made painting excursions to places of spectacular scenic beauty. He created images of the wilderness in the romantic tradition of British watercolour and believed that landscape was the obvious theme for New Zealand art.[12]

Isabel Hodgkins was content to follow her father's example. She became a landscape painter in watercolour, using the medium with great skill to produce appealingly poetic pictures which were more generalised and perhaps less deeply felt than her father's work. She also painted flowers, a traditional subject for the woman artist. She had a professional attitude towards painting and was rewarded with financial and critical success, but she understood her limitations: 'I know just enough to show me how very far short my painting falls of what it ought to be. For . . . I have absolutely no artistic education what ever and I can never expect to be a good artist without that.'[13] Her education had been informal, gained while accompanying her father on sketching excursions.

Equally lacking in formal training, Frances was more independent and in a sense more ambitious. Within the limits of watercolour she tried her hand at a variety of genres. She painted at least one competent mountain landscape, but the combination of landscape with evidence of human activity interested her more than the empty wilderness. And people interested her far more than landscape, so that much of her earliest work consists of portraits, figures and genre studies.

In attempting portraits and figures in the 1890s at the very beginning of her career Frances Hodgkins had to be measured, in her own mind as well as in the eyes of her New Zealand contemporaries, against the very high standard of three dimensional draughtsmanship gained from academic training at the Royal Academy or the Slade School where particular emphasis was placed on the study of the living model. Coming from a family of self-taught artists, she was at first untutored in these disciplines. Only with the arrival of the Italian artist Girolamo Nerli in 1893 did the kind of teaching she needed come her way. There followed two years of drawing study at the Dunedin School of Art in 1895 and 1896. She concentrated on portraits or single figures, clothed, standing or seated, with emphasis on the face. Once embarked, she made rapid progress, winning a prize for a portrait head from life at the New Zealand Academy of Fine Arts in 1895.

She became skilful at depicting Maori women, young women alone and mothers with children. These paintings were unusual at the time in Dunedin and highly regarded by her contemporaries. Today they are seen as making an interesting contribution to the Pakeha representation of Maori women.

Frances Hodgkins painted female subjects almost exclusively and the treatment ranges from single to group studies, with double portraits providing some of the more memorable images. There are mothers with babies and family groups including other young children and female adults; there are small girls, adolescent girls, young women and old women. Some of these were commissioned, most were not. The number of women and girls in Hodgkins's paintings reinforces the sense of her affection for women, but the availability of models and a painter's response to a traditional subject must also be taken into account. Some of the notable images of men in her work are the portraits of her friends, Moffat Lindner with his family, Cedric Morris, Lett Haines and David Brynley.

In the last two decades of her life she returned to some of the subjects that had interested her as a young woman, buildings in the landscape, the barns, machinery, implements and livestock associated with farm life. In the end, people disappear and their artefacts remain. She painted china ornaments and a wonderful array of containers, sometimes standing empty, sometimes filled with flowers, leaves or fruit, set often with startling effect in the midst of landscape, or arranged over the picture surface without regard for the laws of gravity and perspective. There was a context for such work among modern painters, among the post-impressionists and cubists who revitalised still-life, among those who were interested in the formal qualities of naive art; it was very close to the neo-romanticism of the late 1930s that celebrated English rural life and it fitted, too, into the kind of landscape-based surrealism that was a British response to the exploration of the subconscious. Perhaps this meditation on earlier motifs, on the apparatus of the domestic life she had left behind in New Zealand has some distant similarities with Katherine Mansfield's return to the beloved scenes of her childhood, evoked with the dream-like intensity of early memory.

An expatriate like Frances Hodgkins loses the sweet familiarity of the homeland and becomes sharply, even painfully aware of the strangeness of the adopted country. The sensation has something in common with the dream, for everything is at once familiar yet altered and one feels disconnected, alienated. The dislocation brings its rewards in terms of poignancy of vision. There are practical reasons that explain why Frances Hodgkins kept moving – the need to find cheap lodgings, to get away from the cold of the English winters – but she turned herself again and again into an alien and endlessly recaptured the flavour of strangeness. She finally found a pictorial language that would convey the extraordinariness of everything she laid eyes on, so that her later paintings of, say, a cat basking in the courtyard outside her front door, or clumsy jugs on a table, or a barrel and a tangle of barbed wire outside a barn arouse in the viewer sensations that are as difficult to describe as the atmosphere of a dream.

In these later paintings, Frances Hodgkins distorts and simplifies shape, plays with scale, juxtaposes near and far, multiplies viewpoints. An impression of freshness and spontaneity comes from the freely drawn calligraphic lines that dance around areas of colour and from the inventiveness of her patterning. For all these painterly manoeuvres there were precedents in modernist practice; her achievement was to evolve an intensely personal synthesis of what was relevant for her. And the most personal, the most original element in this synthesis was colour. Frances Hodgkins's colour was never simply expressive, never entirely divorced from the physical world, because it changed in response to local conditions. Her unique colour harmonies presented critics with more than the ordinary challenge faced in the attempt to describe the indescribable. In his review of her exhibition at the Leicester Galleries in October 1941 the critic Eric Newton wrote: 'To call her colour "delicious" is merely to praise it without giving an inkling as to its quality: but, for want of an adequate vocabulary, one must leave it at that. Titian's colour glows, but it lacks acidity: Matthew Smith's is luscious and exuberant, but it is simple like tropical sunshine. Frances Hodgkins needs a finer adjustment. Hers is a twilight colour. It is queer and surprising. Moreover it continues to be surprising. Looking at her best gouaches, the eye, long after the first impact, goes on receiving little subsidiary shocks of delight.'[14] Five years later, in his foreword to the major retrospective exhibition at the Lefevre Gallery, he returns to the topic: 'She can . . . make certain colours 'sing' as they have never done before – in particular a certain milky purplish-pink, a most unpromising colour: she can make greys and browns look positively rapturous: she can juggle with colour, orchestrally.'[15] In 1970 the critic Bryan Robertson wrote: 'Her colour is unique and unforgettable: chocolate bluish-brown, coloured whites, riverweed greens, French blue and mauve-grey.'[16] Winifred Nicholson who used both words and paint with poetic simplicity, wrote of her 'dusky, honeyed sequences'.[17] Henry Moore said simply, 'One could recognize a Frances Hodgkins from a long distance purely by colour alone.'[18]

Frances Hodgkins remained always something of an outsider. Her colonial background and lack of money prevented her from fitting into the established middle and upper middle classes in England, from whose ranks many artists and patrons came. But her outsider status was not entirely a disadvantage. Indeed it probably contributed to her success by providing her with a particular kind of freedom, which was added to the freedoms being claimed by English women during the 1890s and the early years of the twentieth century. One result of her colonial upbringing was that she felt herself to be more robust physically and psychologically than the equivalent English woman. In September 1907 she wrote to her mother: 'English ladies are so sensitive & I sometimes feel the superiority of a hardy Colonial over these gently nurtured dames.' She could put up with living conditions that would have been intolerable to middle class English women. As she grew older she drew about herself a protective cloak of eccentricity and moved even more freely, living alone in studios in London and frequenting humble cafés in France and Spain.

Her colonial inheritance gave her a degree of independence and confidence. Victorian social patterns, while still oppressive enough, had undergone modification in the colonial environment where the demands of pioneering life had been felt by some middle class women as a liberation from inactivity and uselessness. The enfranchisement of New Zealand women in 1893 was symbolic of altered attitudes. In Dunedin, the southern town where she was born, women had access to the newly established university and art school and a few made good use of their opportunities. Frances Hodgkins was one of a generation of women who became professional artists and teachers. Two of the best of them, Dorothy Richmond and Margaret Stoddart, returning to New Zealand after study abroad, found a place in the art history of their country.

As an artist, she could remain detached from the insular attitudes that inhibited many British painters. She was never beholden to any school or group, never suspicious of foreign influences. She readily assimilated the important lessons of modernism and all her life remained open to new ways of seeing and doing. Anne Kirker wrote of her: 'Probably Frances Hodgkins's most impressive quality was [the] ability to recharge her artistic vocabulary, to search continually for a more meaningful way to express her vision. She approached most of her paintings, whether in oil, watercolour or gouache, as though facing unexplored territory.'[19] Graham Sutherland, who came upon her work in the 1930s, said later that 'she had . . . a moral effect on artists of that day . . . she was 'virtually the only [woman artist] who was artistically emancipated and was already speaking the language which gradually spelt freedom in art . . . . She just seemed to know exactly what she wanted to do and there appears to be no question in her mind that she was being anything particularly pioneering.'[20]

Frances Hodgkins became one of the foremost artists of her day in Great Britain, honoured in 1952 with a memorial exhibition at the Tate Gallery in the company of Gwen John and Ethel Walker. She was awarded a Civil List Pension in 1942 for her services to art. Just after her death in 1947 a letter came from the British prime minister asking if he might submit her name in the birthday honours as a CBE. Hodgkins was glad of the money that came with the pension, wryly remarking how useful it would have been fifty years earlier. About the civil honour she would have had something crisp to say. What mattered to her was her work and the opinion of the artists she admired. She was one of the few women painters associated with the British artists who in the wake of Roger Fry's Post-Impressionist exhibitions of 1910 and 1912 gradually broke down the insular conservatism of late Victorian and Edwardian British art and opened the country up to the ideas that were to dominate twentieth-century art. She belongs with the group of British artists which includes David Jones, Paul Nash, Cedric Morris, John Piper, Ivon Hitchens, Graham Sutherland, Matthew Smith, Winifred Nicholson, Ben Nicholson, Alfred Wallis and Christopher Wood. The reciprocal influences that link her with these artists have yet to be disentangled by art historians. The other question that awaits analysis is the level of her indebtedness to European painters – first to the Dutch painters, the Maris brothers and Anton Mauve, and later and overwhelmingly to those associated with Paris – Lucien Simon, Jongkind, Manet, Monet, Cassatt, Morisot, Laurencin, Cézanne, Bonnard, Vuillard, Van Gogh, Gauguin, Matisse, Derain, Dufy, Picasso, Braque.

Art historical study of Frances Hodgkins's paintings has been difficult. She was a prolific artist and her work is spread widely through private collections on both sides of the world. Always on the move, she kept no records herself; many works are undated, some unsigned. Frances Hodgkins did not attach much importance to titles and these often failed to distinguish, say, one 'Still life, Landscape' from another. Titles were sometimes given by others, sometimes changed. Subject matter is a reasonably reliable guide to dating, but not absolutely secure, for studies done in the field were regularly worked up in the studio later. Stylistic evidence can also be confusing, especially during the period 1913-27, when she was coming to terms with modernism.[21]

The life divided between two hemispheres was the theme of E. H. McCormick's classic study of Frances Hodgkins, *The Expatriate*, published in 1954, and the reversal of reputation that has taken place since her death continues that theme. In Great Britain she is represented in the Tate Gallery, in the Victoria and Albert Museum and in regional galleries throughout the country. But her work has slipped out of sight much as she disappeared from the New Zealand art scene after her final departure in 1913. She was not, for example, included in the 1987 exhibition *A Paradise Lost, the Neo-Romantic Imagination in Britain, 1935-55* at the Barbican, a re-evaluation of the British painters with whom she was chiefly associated. While comparable artists like Cedric Morris and Winifred Nicholson have been given major retrospectives at the Tate Gallery (in 1984 and 1987 respectively) she has received no such recognition. However, she is described in two recent reference books, the *Oxford Companion to Twentieth Century Art*, 1981, and the *Oxford Dictionary of Art*, 1988. A provincial touring exhibition initiated by the Minories Gallery in Colchester at the end of 1990 may signify the beginning of a reappraisal of her work. In his foreword to the catalogue, the director of the Minories wrote: 'I hope the exhibition will prove illuminating for those who, like me, had never heard of this unjustly neglected artist.'[22] Critical response to the exhibition also emphasised the welcome rediscovery of a neglected or forgotten painter. Similar attitudes greeted the New Zealand sesquicentennial exhibition at the Whitford and Hughes Gallery in London organised by the UK/NZ 1990 Committee.[23]

Her invisibility in Great Britain may account for her absence from some important feminist studies. The catalogue of the landmark American exhibition of 1978, *Women Artists 1550-1950*, does not include her, though Laura Knight is mentioned in the list of artists regretfully omitted, while Gwen John and Vanessa Bell were included. Frances Hodgkins was not mentioned in Germaine Greer's *The Obstacle Race*, 1979, an exhaustive account of women artists. Germaine Greer's explanation of this omission shows an astonishing lack of information: 'I myself have never seen a Hodgkins original. The reason that she wasn't included . . . was that I didn't know where to put her. . . . I think she must be a painter who is very badly served by reproduction.'[24]

Frances Hodgkins re-entered New Zealand art history when painters like Colin McCahon, Gordon Walters and Milan Mrkusich were at the beginning of their exhibiting lives. In 1949, two years after her death, the controversy surrounding the gift of her 1933 painting *Pleasure Garden* to the Robert McDougall Gallery in Christchurch contributed to the same process that she had already been part of in Great Britain – the breaking down of the prejudice against modernism. The controversy served as a rallying-point for the growing number of New Zealanders who were dissatisfied with the parochial conservatism that dominated many art institutions.

The choice of Frances Hodgkins to represent New Zealand in the 1990 sesquicentennial exhibition in London is indicative of the standing she now enjoys in her native country. No other expatriate artist has been so enthusiastically reclaimed, with many of her paintings and drawings being brought back to New Zealand.[25] There are few painters whose works inspire as much interest and affection. All major New Zealand galleries now have substantial holdings of her work. As early as 1953, Eric Westbrook, the first professional director of the Auckland City Art Gallery, established a buying policy of which one part laid down that a 'truly representative collection of the works of Frances Hodgkins should be built up.'[26] It was unusual, if not unique, for an artist to be singled out in this way. There have been several exhibitions of which the most comprehensive took place on the centennial of her birth in 1969. Organised by the Auckland City Art Gallery under the directorship of Gil Docking, the exhibition toured the four main centres and travelled to Melbourne and London. Of this exhibition Charles Brasch wrote: 'It is probably the biggest enterprise which the Arts Council has yet initiated, and for us in some ways the most important exhibition of painting ever to have been held in New Zealand. . . . [It rests] on Dr McCormick's long-continued, patient, scrupulous work . . . it is fitting that the country's finest painter should have won the devotion of its foremost scholar. . . .'[27]

Belated recognition in New Zealand of Frances Hodgkins's achievement as a painter accounts for this activity, but she has an additional hold on the imagination through Dr McCormick's account of her life, which makes the artist into something of a symbol for the conflicts inherent in the cultural history of New Zealand and gives a legendary resonance to the story of her long struggle. She has personal significance for many artists. Colin McCahon, the most eminent modern New Zealand painter, wrote of his childhood in the 1920s: 'There was one painting in the [Dunedin Public Art] Gallery I loved above all else, Frances Hodgkins's *Summer*. It sang from the wall, warm and beautiful, beautiful faces beaming from summer blossoms. It was strong and kind and lovely.' A few years later, McCahon wrote, he left high school with 'a profound loathing for several of the masters and for their utter failure . . . to communicate anything as important as . . . *Summer*".[28] Frances Hodgkins's life and work has been particularly relevant to women. Even when she was fully involved in her European life, she encouraged a number of her New Zealand contemporaries whose paths crossed hers – Edith Collier, Maud Burge, Gwen Knight, Betty Rhind, Cora Wilding, May Smith. Present day artists as diverse as Gretchen Albrecht, Christine Hellyar, Joanna Paul and Merylyn Tweedie cite her as an influence on their life or work. It is not going too far to suggest that the importance of women in the art history of New Zealand has much to do with the example of this dedicated and courageous woman.

For E. H. McCormick, writing in the early 1950s, there is something bordering on the tragic in the story of Frances Hodgkins. Born before her time, before there was in New Zealand a cultural life that could support so large a talent, she had no choice but to leave. She suffered because of this exile and the loss to her country was also great. She stands for all those New Zealanders, including Dr McCormick himself, who felt the allure of Europe and had to make an often painful choice between the two hemispheres. In the epilogue to *The Expatriate* McCormick wrote: 'In spite of the example of a few courageous artists, one must conclude that New Zealand does not yet provide the setting in which a Frances

Hodgkins of our time could reach full artistic maturity. For the visual artist, at least, the era of the expatriates is not over.'

Artists still leave New Zealand and make their reputation overseas, but expatriation is no longer surrounded by the heightened feelings that found expression in words like 'rejection', 'abandonment'. New Zealanders are secure in their own culture, and there is a longer perspective which notes that artists are itinerant beings, that artists from other countries have come to New Zealand, and that art builds on art as much as on locality. There are ironies that bridge the gulf that once separated 'here' from 'there'. The visiting British artist Christopher Perkins, for example, provided New Zealand in the early 1930s with two of its most potent regionalist images, *Taranaki* and *Frozen Flame,* and Frances Hodgkins created on occasion a sense of quintessential Englishness. Both knew Paul Nash and were following formal interests that were current at the time and independent of location. It is not entirely coincidental that both Frances Hodgkins and Christopher Perkins spent time painting and drawing at the Maori village of Ohinemutu on the shores of Lake Rotorua.

Frances Hodgkins is a New Zealand heroine and her story takes on new meanings as time passes. Her dilemmas as a woman have as much to suggest as those associated with being an expatriate, and the long journey of her life with all its movements through time and place is as absorbing as that major shift from colony to 'home'. Her story loses its tragic overtone and becomes instead an inspiriting account of challenges met and success achieved.

[1] June Opie, *Frances Hodgkins – The European Years*, Radio New Zealand, 1969.
[2] Reprinted in *Evening Post*, 30 April 1913. See also E. H. McCormick, 'Frances Hodgkins: The Path to Impressionism: 1892-1912', *Art New Zealand* 16, 1980, p.33ff.
[3] For a full account of the finding of the letters see the Introduction to E. H. McCormick, *The Expatriate*, 1954.
[4] *New Statesman and Nation*, 16 February 1952.
[5] Interview quoted in a letter from Helen Laing to E. H. McCormick, 26 April 1951.
[6] Unpublished memoir to Frank Sargeson, 8 December 1951.
[7] Frances Partridge, Obituary, *Independent Gazette*, 11 September 1991.
[8] *Recollections of Frances Hodgkins*, Radio New Zealand Sound Archives.
[9] June Opie, *Frances Hodgkins – The European Years.*
[10] Dr Peter Davis, the nephew of Amy Krauss, in a letter to E. H. McCormick, 20 February 1967.
[11] Personal communication, November 1990.
[12] 'A History of Landscape Art and its Study in New Zealand', 1880, quoted in full in Peter Entwisle, *William Mathew Hodgkins & his Circle*, 1984, p.156.
[13] Letter to Will Field, 18 October 1892.
[14] Eric Newton, 'Frances Hodgkins', *Listener*, 2 October 1941, p.473.
[15] *Frances Hodgkins, Retrospective Exhibition*, Lefevre Gallery, November 1946, Foreword by Eric Newton, p.3.
[16] Bryan Robertson, 'With flying colours', *Spectator*, 17 January 1970.
[17] Winifred Dacre, 'Liberation of Colour', *World Review*, 1944, reprinted in *Unknown Colour, Paintings,*

Letters, Writings by Winifred Nicholson, an anthology compiled by Andrew Nicholson, Faber and Faber, 1987, p.128.

[18] June Opie, 'The Quest for Frances Hodgkins', *Ascent,* December 1969, p.50.

[19] Anne Kirker, *New Zealand Women Artists,* 1986, p.50.

[20] June Opie, 'The Quest for Frances Hodgkins', p.61.

[21] The New Zealand paintings are meticulously documented in E. H. McCormick's *Works of Frances Hodgkins in New Zealand,* 1954, and Mary Chamot's Appendix to *Four Vital Years* provides some information about solo exhibitions and owners in Great Britain.

[22] Richard Stokes, *Frances Hodgkins, the Late Works,* 1990, p.5.

[23] Tony Warner, 'Frances Hodgkins', *Arts Review,* 25 January 1991, p.49; Max Wykes-Joyce, 'Frances Hodgkins', *Arts Review,* 27 July 1990, p.417; John Russell Taylor, 'An Odd Couple Plus One', *The Times,* 3 August 1990, p.16.

[24] Letter to *Art New Zealand* 18, Summer 1981, p.12.

[25] She has become a popular artist with New Zealand investors and a profitable trade in her paintings has developed between England and New Zealand. The 1935 gouache *Ruins, Cadaquez, Spain,* for example, was sold at Sotheby's in 1988 for £17,000 and reappeared in a New Zealand dealer gallery in 1991 priced at $125,000.

[26] *Frances Hodgkins and Her Circle,* Auckland City Art Gallery, 1954, p.3.

[27] Charles Brasch, 'Frances Hodgkins at One Hundred', *Landfall,* September 1969, p.265.

[28] Colin McCahon, 'Beginnings', *Landfall* 80, December 1966, pp.362-3.

Frances Hodgkins's Family

These are the principal members of Frances Hodgkins's family who appear in the letters:

Her father, *William Mathew Hodgkins* (1833–98). Born in Liverpool, the son of a brushmaker, he emigrated to Melbourne in 1860 before moving on to Dunedin, probably in 1862. His father, mother and sister, *Jane Brotherton*, remained in Melbourne.

Her mother, *Rachel Owen Hodgkins* (1838–1926). Born in New South Wales, a daughter of John Skottowe Parker, the District Coroner of Sydney. Rachel married William Mathew in 1865 while on a visit to Dunedin.

Her aunt and uncle *Isabella* and *Alexander Carrick (Aunt Bella* and *Uncle Sandie)*, who lived in Christchurch. Isabella was Rachel Hodgkins's sister.

Her five siblings:
Her elder brother *William John Parker (Willie)* (1866–1945).
Her elder sister *Isabel Jane (Sis* or *Sissie)* (1867–1950).
Her three younger brothers:
   Percy D'Esterre (1873–1956)
   Gilbert Graham (Bert or *Bertie)* (1875–1943)
   Frank Parker (1877–1932)

Her brother-in-law *William Hughes Field (Will)* (1861–1944), a Wellington lawyer. He and Isabel were married in 1893.

Her nieces and nephews, the five children of Isabel and Will Field:
   Isabel Hughes (Girlie) (1894–1973)
   Lydia Helen Hughes (Ba) (1895–1971)
   William Geoffrey Hughes (Geoff) (1897–1973)
   John Hughes (Jack) (1899–1980)
   George Alexander Hughes (Peter) (1905–92)

PART ONE

1869-98

Family and Friends

Frances Mary Hodgkins was born in Dunedin on 28 April 1869 and spent the first thirty-one years of her life there with her family. Eighty letters survive from that time, nearly all of them written to her sister Isabel when both women were in their twenties.

The only earlier letters provide two glimpses of FH's childhood. The first, to her father, is the only letter to him in the entire correspondence, a curious distortion of the importance of W. M. Hodgkins in the life of his daughter. A lawyer by profession, he was a dedicated and gifted watercolourist, the centre of a private Art Club, a founding member and later President of the Otago Art Society and prime mover in the establishment of the Dunedin Public Art Gallery in 1884. Northcote was the family home from just after FH's birth until 1878. A one-storeyed, rambling wooden house set in spacious grounds on the northern outskirts of the city, it represented middle-class comfort rather than elegance.

[1] To William Mathew Hodgkins, 11 June c.1875
[Northcote, Cumberland St, Dunedin] Juen the 11

My dear papa
    I am very glad to see you again
     And I wish you many happy returns of the day
       With love dear papa
         from your affactionate daughter
         Fanny Hodgkins
          love and 000000000.

The other letter was written just before FH's twelfth birthday. This was the most prosperous period in the Hodgkins family life. In 1878 W. M. Hodgkins had bought Claverton House, a substantial dwelling which may still be seen at 30 Royal Terrace, then as now one of the most attractive and desirable residential streets in the heart of Dunedin. It is the only Hodgkins house to survive. In 1881 William Mathew and his wife were able to afford a holiday in Melbourne, visiting his Australian relations and viewing the International Exhibition. They left their children in the care of Aunt Isabella Carrick who came to stay in Dunedin from her home in Christchurch. The Royses were neighbours and family friends.

[2] To Rachel Hodgkins, c.12 April 1881
[Claverton House, Royal Terrace, Dunedin] Tuesday

Dearest Mother
    I am so sorry that I have not written to you before this, but I really could not

help it. I was going to write on Sunday night, but just as I was going to do so some gentlemen came in. I forgot to tell you that this was down at Mrs. Royse's. . . . I am sorry to say I have broken a little bit off my tooth, in a tumble I had. I will tell you how it happened – On Monday morning we were all playing in the garden, when Mr. Royse came out and went into the conservatory to water the plants, then we went in too, Mr. Royse began to water us instead of the plants then all of a sudden he dodged and ran after me, and I bolted [out] of the door, but just as I was going through my foot skipped and I fell on my face and knocked half of my tooth out, and cut my lip a little. I did not go to school that day because my mouth hurt a little. You must not think it much because it is not.

I hope you are enjoying yourself very much. Will you be back for my birthday. Willie is coming down on the 22 of this month & not going to wait for you. Give my love to all our cousins and dear Grandpapa[1] and everybody.

Aunt Bella let us all go to the Beach on Saturday because it was such a fine day. The little Royse's went with us. I must not write too much, because I have to go to bed directly or else I will get a bad mark. Although I think Aunt Bella is only pretending to give us bad marks, because I found out that she only puts down all the money she spends, and the things she buys. I trully must say goodnight now because I am afraid of a bad mark, so good night darling mother give my best love to papa and tell him I am going to write to him next time, all the little ones are exceedingly good and send their love.

I remain your

Very goodest daughter

F Hodgkins.

P. S. Did you have a nice voyage over and make haste and come home –

FH was now twenty-three and in the preceding eleven years the family had moved house twice. W. M. Hodgkins's prosperity declined as the boom years following the discovery of gold in 1861 gave way to the depression of the 1880s. In order to economise he sold Claverton House and in 1884 moved his family into a much humbler house, Waira, in the suburb of Ravensbourne. Then, declared bankrupt in 1888, he rented Cranmore Lodge, a large thirteen-roomed house closer to the city where the family lived from 1889 to 1897. In the eight and a half acres of grounds they kept a cow and poultry, which provided FH with some of her earliest subject matter. They retained one servant, Phemie, who served as a model for FH's first attempts at genre painting.

W. M. Hodgkins's financial difficulties did not interfere with his continued leadership in Dunedin art circles and may even have enhanced the artistic life of his gifted daughters, motivating them to push their talents beyond mere accomplishment.

[1] Frances Hodgkins's grandfather, William Hodgkins, died in Victoria, Australia in 1888.

Isabel had exhibited regularly since 1884 and in 1888-9 financed an eight-month visit to Australia from the sale of her paintings. There she visited the Centennial Exhibition in Melbourne at which both she and her father were represented. By 1892, when she became engaged to William Hughes Field, she was an established artist in watercolour with a considerable reputation in Wellington, Christchurch and Dunedin. FH had first exhibited in 1890 in Christchurch and Dunedin. Like Isabel she was now painting seriously, preparing work for sale at the annual exhibitions of the art societies in Dunedin and Christchurch, and the Academy of Fine Arts in Wellington.

In 1892 Isabel Hodgkins went to stay with Aunt Bella in Christchurch to be nearer her fiancé, a young Wellington lawyer, and the sisters corresponded.

[3] To Isabel Hodgkins, 25 April 1892

Cranmore Lodge. April 25th '92.

My dearest Sissie

I am scribbling a few lines before going to bed to keep you from feeling yourself neglected. I have just come home from the Scotts[2] where Father and I have been dining and am very tired. This morning I went for a long tramp over the hills with Mr. Cherry.[3] I took him down the N.E. Valley and up as far as the Upper Junction. He seems to have an insane desire to climb every hill he comes across . . . and my condition at present is of the chewed string description. However it was a lovely morning & I enjoyed the ramble tho I grudged the time. I am hoping there will be a letter tomorrow from you, but I must not build my hopes too high for likely as not I will be disappointed.

Mrs. Scott is a good deal annoyed at the romantic Katie.[4] She got married without consulting anyone and has gone out to Oregon – and Mrs. S. doesn't foretell the future married bliss that Katie has such ideals of – nothing like an old maid for romance & sentiment is there! . . . Dr. S. gave me a lively description of the Chch pictures, mine included, they were very funny at my expense tonight over the head[5] and made scathing remarks about carved out turnips and beetroot ears, expressions more agricultural than artistic I think. I paid Dr. S. out however by forgetting to ask to see his Rotorua sketches and he had to offer to show them much to Mrs. Scott's amusement. . . .

---

[2] Dr John Halliday Scott was a close friend of W. M. Hodgkins. He combined a serious interest in painting with his work as professor of anatomy and physiology at the recently established Otago Medical School.
[3] Mr Cherry was the husband of Alice, an Australian cousin, daughter of W. M. Hodgkins's sister Jane Brotherton.
[4] Mrs Scott's sister, Katherine Bealey.
[5] FH exhibited a portrait at the Canterbury Society of Arts April exhibition in Christchurch.

[4] To Isabel Hodgkins, 3 May 1892

Cranmore Lodge. May 3rd 92.

My dearest Sissie

It is getting too dark to paint any more, so I have stopped and am going to have a yarn with you. It has been such a miserably wet day and I am glad to light the lamps and pull the blinds down and shut out the dreary outlook. How am I to thank you for the very generous "trifle" you sent me for my birthday as if you had not already given me enough. I felt such a brute taking it from you, especially now when you want all you have. Ungracious tho' it sounds it would give me a great deal more pleasure to return it to you than to spend it. So Aunt Bella has bought my ducks,[6] her kindness has indeed outweighed her choice and artistic judgement, surely she has got enough of my livestock on her walls. I met Miss Ross[7] in town today and she said "Anything here in the way of feathers?" I told her I had turned my attention to pork! Dont you think pigs are very paintable?. . . I went with Miss Ross to see her studio – what a lot of pottering things she does paint, and yet she makes it pay, and talks quite cheerfully about selling at the Chicago Ex. to which she is sending some things. Your description of the Meeson[8] lunch was killing and your flow of bad language cheered me up considerably. It showed me that you had not set about that "revised edition" of yourself that you talked of so earnestly after your engagement do you remember?

Miss Marshall's trip to Japan didn't come off after all; when she got to Sydney, the Rosses cabled for her to come back as Mrs. R. was ill & couldn't manage without her. A trifle selfish don't you think! Fancy coming back to vegetate in Ravensbourne after having been half way on one's way to the Land of the Rising Sun.

. . . . You say you find Chch. dull without Will, it's nothing to the dullness I feel here without you, it's a good thing I have got a painting fit on me, or I might find these wet days a trifle long. . . .

Bertie has been playing the Dead March in Saul for the last half hour and Boss is howling outside the door. Bertie with both pedals down refuses to hear my shouts so I will end this scribble and go and stop the awful racket.

With best love from us all, ever your loving sister Fanny. . . .

[6] *Tanks and Ducks,* watercolour, c.1892.
[7] Dagmar Ross, an animal painter, who exhibited with the OAS, 1885-93.
[8] The Meeson family of Christchurch included the painter Dora, who left New Zealand in 1893 and studied in both London and Paris.

[5] To Isabel Hodgkins, 14 May 1892

Cranmore Lodge. May 14. 92

My dearest Sissie

Before this reaches you, you will have seen Father, poor old man. He must have had a miserably cold journey up. We seem to have suddenly plunged into the middle of winter, and the cold today & yesterday has been intense. . . .

. . . . I spent the evening at Joe's and Clara's[9] last night. How I do dislike that worthy couple! They asked me to tea so I started at half past five mindful of the last evening you & I spent there but to my horror I found tea half over and Clara as sulky as a bear and very nasty – I had a cold reception in every sense of the word, tomatoes and bread & butter for tea on a winter's night are not to quote Miss Holmes[10] "grateful & comforting", so you may imagine I had a cheerful evening. They were quite regardless of my presence & spooned in the most disgusting manner. Clara said with a mawkish smile "dont we look the picture of happiness?" I said "I think you both make a much better caricature."[11] Clara stiffened at once and behaved herself for the rest of the evening! She has a wholesome dread of me, I am glad to say and tried to make me promise before I came away that I will not draw her but I shall.

May[12] came over this afternoon she was going to the Cumines so I arranged to meet her there at six o'clock and we would come thro' the bush together. When I got there I found she had trotted off with the youngest Cumine youth and left me to go home by myself. Wasn't that a shabby trick and for an old fossil like that too. I was very angry for she has served us that way so often. . . .

[6] To Isabel Hodgkins, c.25 May 1892

[Cranmore Lodge]

. . . . Did I tell you about the Lecture on Ancient Statuary Prof. Sale[13] gave in aid of [the] Art Gallery Fund. It went off splendidly and the dem'd total raised was £30, which as the Mayor said in his speech, would buy a "few good pictures". I collected nearly £4. One place I went to I discovered my little washing girl on

---

[9] Joseph Webb was a cousin on Mrs Hodgkins's side of the family.

[10] Katherine Holmes, twenty years older than FH, was a family friend and former member of W. M. Hodgkins's Art Club and the Otago Art Society. She became a leading figure in the Academy of Fine Arts in Wellington. It was while visiting her that Isabel Hodgkins had met Will Field.

[11] Both FH and her father enjoyed drawing caricatures. One of her sketches, *How Jean-Francois Millet would have painted the influenza,* demonstrates a flair for parody. It also indicates familiarity with the Barbizon school treatment of peasant life, an important influence on FH's work in New Zealand and during her early years in Europe.

[12] May Kenyon, daughter of a lawyer, was a close friend, fellow painter and model.

[13] G. S. Sale was professor of classics at the University of Otago.

the walls. They gushed a bit when they heard I was the artist and next day sent me 10/. Wasn't it handsome of them! The lime-light views were splendid but in spite of their beauty when the gas was turned up, several people were found fast asleep. The lecture was too long, so when Father got up to make a few remarks nobody listened, but poured out in a mass, and he was left on the platform with his neat little prepared speech with several apt quotations in it echoing round an empty building. It was very funny but it took him some time to see the joke . . . . I am going up the Valley again tomorrow to do some sketching. The Rattrays, Dinah McNeill, the Scotts and Nellie Haggitt & Mrs. Stilling came up today. You see my news has come to an end when I have to fall back on the visitors hasn't it? So I will stop before I write any more twaddle. So goodbye, dear old girlie With best love to everybody, ever yours most lovingly

Fanny.

[Letter incomplete]

[7] To Isabel Hodgkins, 22 June 1892

Cranmore Lodge. Wednesday.

My dearest Sissie

. . . . I was so awfully glad to hear of your success at Fisher's,[14] tho' I wish I could have seen the picture before it was sold. I too have had a small stroke of luck. Mrs. Woodhouse has given me a £2.2. commission for a picture. She prefers a duck subject so I will not have to waste any time on an idea hunt. . . .

The Savage last night was at the Rattrays.[15] I went to dinner at the Spences and went with them. Maudie Butterworth was chair-woman and got together a very good programme. Maggie Gilk[ison] was there & sar plain she looked too. Manie Reynolds and Mrs. McKenzie both gave recitations, respectively of the milk-and-water and fire-eating types and Miss Cumine gave a chapter from Pickwick deliciously, & for the rest the entertainment was mostly vocal.

I hope you are having fine weather for Will's visit. We have had snow & heavy frosts, & the ground has been frozen hard for some days. My poor old cow has been almost starved. Yesterday Phemie lost a kerozene-tin stopper and couldn't find it anywhere, but tonight it came to light in the most wonderful manner. Frank rushed in and said the cow had got a fit, and I ran out to find the poor animal choking violently in the stable. Presently it opened its mouth and with a final convulsion out shot the long lost stopper, and the cow of course recovered

---

[14] A dealer gallery in Christchurch.

[15] The Savage Club, exclusive to men, had its origins in London in 1857 when a group of authors, journalists and artists began to meet with a view to fostering all forms of artistic talent in a convivial atmosphere. The name 'savage' was chosen in a spirit of irony. Savage clubs were formed in New Zealand in the 1880s. In Dunedin the women set up a female equivalent, usually called the Kahanga Club, which met once a week.

rapidly. Mother's vivid imagination discovered a kerozeny flavor about the milk tonight but as the cow refused to digest the stopper that could hardly be so. You say nothing about coming home, dear. Your sorrowing relatives ask for news. If I wasn't so busy I would miss you horribly. I spend all my spare time with Miss Wimperis[16] and as yet I despair of ever being able to draw in a fairly decent manner.   She is a cheerless little lady & it is like swimming against the tide without you to jog along with. Mother is very well and sends her best love . . . .

[8] To Isabel Hodgkins, 1 July 1892

Cranmore Lodge.

My dearest Sissie
    . . . . I am so glad dearest you have made up your mind to come home, we are prepared to kill the fatted calf at a moment's notice. How frightfully disappointed you must have been at Will's hurried return. It did seem cruel after all those delays and worries, but cheer up dearie and remember that worse things happen at sea. According to Miss Holmes in a letter to father, this is the last time you will see each other for six months, it does seem hard doesn't it. Kate Rattray has returned and asked after you at the Savage on Tuesday. It was a very good meeting . . . . There was a vast deal of amusement created by Manie posing as Helen of Troy, while Mrs. Melland spouted Tennyson's Dream of Fair Women, and then Rachel came on as Iphigenia, and I felt that my ideals of classical beauty had sustained a severe shock. Miss Annie Cargill made a buxom and countryfied Cleopatra and frollicked thro' her part successfully, and Lulu Roberts as Joan of Arc looked splendid in tinsel and silver paper. . . . I went to lunch at the Scotts' yesterday. . . . Dr Scott has given me a £2.2 commission to copy an old picture, or rather print. He wont hear of my doing it as a "labor of love" as I wished, so I have consented to accept a "slight remuneration". It is a gruesome subject of a surgical operation for his dissecting room[17]. . . .

    The new Academy Notes[18] have just come in and I have promptly sat upon them to prevent them being rushed by the rest of the family so I must stop and have a look at them before Father comes in. . . .
P.S. Tell Will when you write that I hope his next visit will be to Dunedin!

---

[16] A. Jane (Jenny or Jeannie) Wimperis (1838-1927) had studied in Munich and Antwerp and was a member of the Art Club. She came from a painting family which included her brother Edmund Wimperis in England and her sisters Frances and Susannah (Joachim).
[17] The painting still hangs in the Otago Medical School.
[18] The Royal Academy published a catalogue illustrating in black and white the principal pictures exhibited at the annual summer exhibition which ran from May to August.

FH's future brother-in-law Will Field became a good friend. Early in 1892 she had painted for him a portrait of Isabel which had convinced him of her talent: 'I trust that you will persevere in this kind of work, for if you do there must surely be a brilliant future before you.'

[9] To WILLIAM HUGHES FIELD, 4 OCTOBER 1892

Cranmore Lodge. October 4, 92

My dear Will

I am afraid you long ago have voted me a fraud but I really am going to begin a letter to you tonight and if possible finish it before morning even if I have to sit up all night with a wet bandage round my head. I know that sister of mine has given me away so completely that I will make no excuses but go straight ahead with this epistle. I am surrounded with books of reference, and I daresay I will be able to worry thro with the help of them and the dictionary.[19]

Many thanks for the Parson and the Painter. The vulgarity for which Sissie says you apologised I am afraid in my opinion only added a decided piquancy to the book. The illustrations are wonderfully clever and far in advance of the letterpress which seems little better than a peg to hang them on. I know you now want me to tell you something about Sissie don't you Will? She has been painting a good deal lately and rather knocked herself up. The long tramps she took with her sketching class were too much for her I think but now they are nearly over I am glad to say and she is quite her old self again. . . .

Did Sissie tell you I have been rusticating in the country?[20] I had glorious weather but it was very lonely work there all by myself and at the end of a week my resources gave way and I made tracks for town with enough sketching material to last me for some time.

Sissie read me aloud today your description of the new frame Mr. Pearse has put my picture into. I only hope I may never see it. I daresay I am very obstinate but I intend to persevere with those white frames. I know you dont approve of them but some day, Will I hope to persuade you personally that they are suitable to some pictures which gold would only kill. Do not worry about changing my poultry frame. Sis has made up her mind to annex it so I suppose it had better leave McGregor Wrights[21] and adorn your walls in the meantime.

I think after our Exhibition[22] is over, I will give my painting a rest. I am beginning to hate the sight of a brush, and feel inclined very often to put them

---

[19] Both sisters considered themselves poor spellers.
[20] At Brighton, on the coast some twenty kilometres south of Dunedin.
[21] A dealer gallery which had started in Dunedin and moved to Wellington.
[22] The November exhibition of the Otago Art Society.

in the fire. However I daresay if anyone else offered to perform that kind little action for me I would be the first to object.

Has your Boating Season opened yet.[23] I suppose it has. The Otago Rowing Club had their opening day last Saturday. Neither Sis or I were able to go but I hear it was very successful. . . .

Yrs very affectionately
Fanny Hodgkins

After her marriage in April 1893 Isabel moved to Wellington. Her departure was immediately followed by the arrival, in May, of the Italian artist Girolamo Pieri Nerli (1860-1926). In touch with modern developments in European art, notably aspects of impressionism, he was primarily a figure painter. He recognised FH's talent, reinforced her interest in portraiture and encouraged her to paint more broadly.

[10] TO ISABEL FIELD, 9 JUNE 1893

Cranmore Lodge. Friday evening

My dearest old Girlie

I am afraid that you will think I have neglected you sadly this week, but really dearie I have been so busy that I have scarcely had any time for writing . . . . I want to make the most of Nerli's lessons and have been painting hard all the week and the evenings always find me more ready for bed than for letter writing. . . .

Did the two Holbeins arrive safely that I sent by Archie Bartleman? I think so often of your house and how it will look with all your pretty things in it. . . .

I don't think I have any special news to tell you since my last letter. . . . Today Maggie Gilkison and the Spences gave Daisy afternoon teas. It was a bitter day, one of the wildest snowstorms I ever remember, but I braved the elements and went to them both. . . . That is all my gaiety for the week I think with the exception of the Savage on Tuesday. . . . It was a splendid evening and I enjoyed it immensely. Next night May is going to do a little dialogue piece (out of Black & White) with Miss Issy Cargill and great things are expected of them. I am down for the programmes and May Burnes is going to play. Doesn't that strike you as a fine display of talent?. . . The Roberts are giving a "bal poudre" next Thursday week. It is Amy's idea and everyone seems to think it is a very good one. I went to see Mr. Cole's[24] studio today. I admire his work and his method tremendously but I think compared with Nerli his work is lifeless. What an artist a judicious blending of the two would make! Nerli has been most awfully good to me and

---

[23] Will Field was captain of the Star Boating Club in Wellington.
[24] F. Tennyson Cole was an English watercolour artist recently arrived in New Zealand.

gives me an extra lesson on Saturdays at his studio. Lulu Roberts & Peep Gibson
are learning and I think Rattie Neill is going to have lessons.

. . . . I told you I had been to the Gaiety Company, didn't I. I suppose you
heard of the horse-whipping the chorus girls gave the Editor of the Workman.
Mr. Mason Mabel Maitland's husband, has been fêteing them in a royal style
much to the disgust of his relations. This is pure gossip isn't it and take it for what
it is worth. Ethel McLaren is going to sit for me, I think I told you, and she is
coming for the first sitting on Tuesday. . . .

. . . . Write to me soon dearie, you don't know how I long for your letters,
there is never an hour in the day that I don't think and long for you, and it is a
very good thing for me that I have my painting as a rival in my affection for you,
otherwise I think I should be a very unhappy creature. . . .

*During the second half of the year FH went to stay with Isabel in Wellington. It is
possible that she painted the first of her studies of Maori women during this year, an
informal study of a woman with a pail.*

*In April 1894 Mrs Hodgkins was preparing to visit Isabel who was expecting her
first child.*

[11] To Isabel Field, c.15 April 1894

Cranmore Lodge. Sunday Afternoon.

My dearest Sis

It is raining as if it never meant to stop and I have settled down by the kitchen
fire to have a yarn with you. Winter weather has set in with a vengeance – it will
be horribly damp here in the winter if we don't get something done to the roof.
Scoular refuses to spend a penny on the place so I expect our only remedy is to
move into another house as soon as we can, but of course that is quite out of the
question till Mother comes back again. Mother has really made up her mind to
start next week on her travels, she is quite ready & has done all her sewing and
is only waiting for a good boat. She told me to tell you on no account to send
down the rug . . . she has bought herself a very warm sealette mantle and a fur boa
so she will be quite warm enough. . . . I have become most domesticated and
havent as much as looked at a brush for months. Aunt Bella sent me a £1 for a
birthday present the other day. She is good to her impecunious neices & no
mistake. . . . I went into the dining room a minute ago to get another pen and
found Mother & Willie arguing in the most spirited manner over Frank's
affection for Percy. Mother asserted that Frank would go thro' fire and water to
save Percy so great was his love for him!! Willie said he didn't doubt he would
go thro fire but he didn't believe Frank would go near water for anyone. Frank

came in at this opportune moment in time to defend himself and then the argument got lost in general abuse, so I retired.

. . . . The White Art Union[25] still drags drearily on and the tickets are not going off very well. Mrs. Scott has bought some of their white table cloths so you see they are selling everything they can to raise the wind. We are going to part with the cow this week. We havent so much ground as formerly, so it is just as well to part with her. Two ugly little tin roofed houses are springing up, one at the back and the other just below the tennis lawn so our privacy is invaded at last. I wish I had more news to tell you dear old girl. Keep up your spirits, and don't fret darling. With heaps of love from Mother & myself to you both ever your loving sister

Fanny.

FH was now running the household in Mrs Hodgkins's absence.

[12] To Isabel Field, 29 April 1894

Cranmore Lodge. Sunday afternoon

My dearest Sis

. . . . Thank you so much for your dear letter and the stockings how thoughtful of you to remember my birthday, as you say it will save darning and you could not have sent me anything more acceptable and useful. I can't realise that I am 25. After this you must cease to remember my birthdays. Last Thursday was the anniversary of your Wedding. I am so glad you have got safely over that date before the infant arrived. Poor old Alice[26] isnt half as lucky as you were. . . .

. . . . For several evenings Father has gone out ostensibly on business but has always returned with a large portfolio which he instantly secreted in the most mysterious manner in the study. I was most curious and yesterday I solved the mystery and I confess it gave me a bit of a shock. It turns out that he is attending a *nude* class at Nerli's Studio and he is much too ashamed to own it.[27] His drawings were most angular and looked as if they had been drawn with a T. square. He has quite made up his mind that he is a figure painter and I am terribly afraid he will exhibit a figure subject at the next exhibition

---

[25] Annie Julia White was Katherine Holmes's married sister, also an artist. Art Unions were originally an ingenious form of art patronage that enabled less wealthy people to acquire paintings by buying a ticket in a lottery run either by the artist or a gallery.

[26] Alice Spence, the daughter of family friends, was married to Robert McGowan.

[27] Entwisle points out that there had been a life class at the Dunedin School of Art as early as 1880 (*William Mathew Hodgkins and his Circle*, p.22).

. . . . Mrs. Finker[28] and her cousin Mr. Harris came in last night, I think curiosity to see how I was managing prompted the visit, she said she came down to say goodbye to Mother and brought her a "lovely bottle of scent" but when she found out she had gone, she said "of course I took the scent away again," and I rudely said, "yes for there was nobody here who would have accepted it". She was perfectly insufferable the questions she asked.

I am asked to a small dance at Bishopscourt tomorrow night and to another at the Farquhar's the next night but I don't think I will go to either. There was a dance at Girton Hall the other night given by some of the batchelors and I believe 17 girls sat out each dance. May Kenyon went home after the 3rd. dance. . . .

Well, dear old Girlie, I must say goodbye for the present. Willie has asked Mr. Mitchell to supper so I must fly round. I never realised how much there is to be done in this house till Mother went. The cooking is the hardest part. Agnes is after all a very primitive cook and savours a little too much of the boarding house, but otherwise she is a very nice girl. . . .

[13] To Isabel Field, 5 May 1894

Cranmore Lodge. May 5th 94.

My dearest old Girl

You can imagine how delighted we all were to get Will's telegram with the news that your trouble was safely over and that you and the baby are getting on so well.[29] I hope dear old girl you will be soon well and strong again. I can hardly realise that you are a Mother but I expect I will understand the situation better when you and the baby come down at Christmas. . . .

I am getting quite used to the house keeping now and things are going on very smoothly. I find Agnes is anything but a strong girl and it does not do to leave too much to her. I always manage to get everything done by the afternoon so I can trot round and see my friends. Mrs. McKenzie is getting up the "Seasons" again do you remember and you took the part of November. They came to me for your dress the other day, but I told them you never had a regular costume and that it consisted mostly of borrowed plumes. . . . Mrs. Scott's portrait by Nerli is finished and Father says it is lovely. I havent seen it myself yet. I went down to see her on Thursday she was very anxious to hear all about you . . . . Her children have the whooping cough but mildly I think. . . .

Mrs. Kenyon has lost her father and they are all in mourning. May went in to black very grudgingly

---

[28] Mrs Finker was a neighbour, of German Jewish origin, whose daughter Dulcie was the subject of FH's painting *Brown Eyes*.
[29] Isabel and Will's child, Isabel Hughes Field, known as Girlie, was born on 2 May 1894.

Now dear old Girlie I will say goodbye. I will write again in a day or two. In the meantime I hope to have good news of you. . . .

[14] TO RACHEL HODGKINS, 15 MAY 1894

Cranmore Lodge. Tuesday morning.

My dearest Mother

I am adding a few lines to enclose with Frank's letter. I was so glad to get your welcome letter last night and to hear such good news of Sissie. How glad she will be to have you with her and you to be with her. I am longing for further news about the baby and what they are going to call her. . . . We have not had another letter from Percy[30] since the last I forwarded to you. . . . Things still go on very smoothly. Willie still complains of want of originality concerning breakfast dishes. I manufactured a new sort of pâté and gave it him this morning, it evidently pleased his somewhat critical palate for he forthwith presented me with ½ a sovereign for a birthday present. Eggs are 2/4, ought I to buy them at that costly price. The fowls are not laying at all, tho well taken care of by Frank.

. . . . Has May ever written to Sissie? She comes over to see me occasionally, on Sunday she brought a funny little German Doctor in and he and Mrs. Finker who also dropped in got on famously together, talking German in the most animated fashion.

I am looking after your ferns and they look very healthy. . . . Father has developed into a figure painter and has actually persuaded Dr. Scott to join the life class they are both quite enthusiastic about it.

I must not write any more or else I will need an envelope all to myself. . . .

[15] TO ISABEL FIELD, 20 MAY 1894

Cranmore Lodge. May 20th 94.

My dearest Sis

. . . . I am waiting anxiously for news of you and the baby – tell Mother I think she might have written knowing how anxious I am to hear how you are. . . .

We have been having the most glorious weather these last three weeks clear frosty days without a breath of wind. If the weather holds fine Father and Dr. Scott and I are going up the Otago Central on the Queen's Birthday. I went down to see the Scotts today. . . . I saw her portrait for the first time . . . and I must say I was horribly disappointed. I don't think it either resembles or flatters her tho

---

[30] Percy had gone to the North Island where, apparently with help from Will Field, he was making a career in farming.

they are very pleased with it. It is about 3 times the size of Miss Richardson's portrait of Mrs. Holmes[31] and Nerli has only charged £6 with a self designed frame thrown in. On Saturday I went out to an afternoon tea given by the Stephenson's on the Racecourse. We had an awfully jolly day, they had shooting with rifles and Mrs. Hosking made the top score. Everybody was there I think and there were many enquiries after you. I was greeted everywhere as "auntie". . . .

Mrs. Scott showed me Dr. S's drawings from the nude model today, they were hidden at the back of her wardrobe; they are very good indeed and very modest.

Frank and Bert are ardent footballers this winter. Last night they potted goals in the bedroom and this morning the wreck was dreadful to see, for the future their goals must be potted outside.

. . . . May Kenyon has been having a very heavy time with Poggy who is in town just now. On Friday night I happened to be all alone in the house and about ½ [past] 8 May stalked in looking very excited and mysterious and it turned out that she had been loafing on the [town] belt since ½ [past] 5 with Poggy, and when it got too cold they came and sat under our pine trees. I was horribly disgusted with her and told her what I thought of her servant's behaviour and after I had relieved my mind she coolly demanded something to eat and a boy to take her home. . . . Did you ever hear anything so unladylike and nasty. Has she ever written to you?. . .

[16] To Isabel Field, 16 December 1894

Cranmore Lodge. Sunday 16th 94.

My dearest Sissie

Mother has the only available ink so I am reduced to pencil. My wishes for your birthday would have looked better in ink, tho' not more sincere than in pencil. . . .

[Alice McGowan's] baby is getting much fatter but not prettier. I dont think Alice amuses it half enough. May spent the evening developing its latent playing powers and it showed great intelligence much to Alice's surprise. May said she didnt think Alice ever did anything else but kiss it on its soft little brain and call it "ducky". I havent been out at all since you left tho' certainly there has been nothing to go to. Father has had a letter from Aunt Bella (which I havent seen or I could have given you more definite information) in which she says there is a lady who is writing an article on the N.Z. lady artists for an English magazine and she wants some [information] as to your career etc This lady (name unknown) got

[31] Mary Elizabeth Tripe née Richardson (1867-1939) was associated with James Nairn and the Silverstream group. She became a successful portrait painter, exhibiting at the Royal Academy and the Paris Salon.

Miss Stoddart[32] to write to Aunt Bella. Father at once sent off all particulars as to your birth and art education and also I expect if the truth were known a biography of the whole family. I am not mentioned which is a nasty jar for me!
[Letter incomplete]

[17] To Isabel Field, 30 December 1894

Cranmore Lodge. Dec. 30th 94.

My dearest Sis
    . . . . We have spent the quietest Christmas! a tour round the neighborhood our only disapation. I have done a tremendous lot of painting and have had a model nearly every day.
    The McLean's had a blustery cold kind of day for their fête, but a great crowd went out in spite of the bad weather. The Royse's have some sort of a garden entertainment at the end of the week with games freshly introduced from Adelaide. I think May must be away somewhere I haven't seen her for nearly a fortnight. We had a billy tea together one night. I entrusted the tucker to her and she nearly killed me with a vile concoction of parsely and onion and red herring sandwiches. . . .

[18] To Isabel Field, 30 January 1895

Cranmore Lodge. Wednesday, 30th '95.

My dearest Sissie
    . . . . I must tell you about the two dances, my red dress did service at both and I certainly can boast of attracting much attention – of a kind. . . . It was very carefully made but I can assure you I didnt feel at all happy in it. May assures me I never looked better but I don't believe her. Mother incautiously asked Alice McGowan what she thought of it and Alice's desire to stick to the truth and at the same time not hurt my feelings was very comical, however she compromised matters and said with much tact that it would look "all right at à euchre party" which was consoling. In the meantime I will pray for a euchre party. Alice herself looked a sketch but that of course I couldn't tell her. . . . Alice told me to tell you that vaccination isnt half such a terrifying performance as she thought it was, her baby has got over it splendidly. . . .

[32] Margaret Olrog Stoddart (1865-1934), a distinguished painter among FH's contemporaries, had trained at the Christchurch School of Art and been elected to the council of the Canterbury Society of Arts in 1885. Her main interest at this time was in flower painting, though she later became a noted landscape painter. After study abroad, when she and FH met on several occasions, she returned to New Zealand in 1906 and became an influential teacher at the Canterbury School of Art.

The famous Miss Hill[33] is staying next door with Mrs. Adams. Father is very anxious for me to call but I am prejudiced against the lady. She told Mrs. Adams she hoped she wouldn't be lionised! and after that I don't think I will trouble her.

I am so glad you have joined a library. You can always find time to read books if one can only get them. The ones I have read most recently are Katherine Lauderdale, M. Crawford. Ships that pass in the night "Fantasy" get it if you can. "Marplot" very good. A Lilac sunbonnet, Crockit "A Human Document" clever. Mother is devouring the Heavenly Twins and enjoying it. Tell me what you think of it. Do you remember what you said about the woman who wrote The Yellow Aster.[34] I saw your opinions echoed in a London paper the other day. I can't take the Twins seriously I think it is an awful story. I mustn't write any more tonight dearest Sis I have been painting all day and my eyes are nearly tumbling out of my head . . . .

[19] To Isabel Field, 18 February 1895

Cranmore Lodge. Feb. 18th. 95.

My dearest Sissie

Please excuse pencil, Mother has got the ink. . . .

. . . . Did I tell you Dr. Scott has a nephew staying with him, he has been on a Station in the N. Island for a few months, but he was not strong enough for the life so Dr. Scott is trying to get him into a bank here. His father died leaving them very badly off so he came out to try and get something to do out in the Colonies. He is a very good looking young fellow about 24 tall and rather distinguished and enough polish to satisfy Dr. Scott which goes a long way with him as you know. I went to supper with them on Sunday. Mrs. Scott has her new teeth in and strange to say it has quite altered the expression of her face, it has made her mouth very small and her face slightly nut cracking. Her mouth, tho it was faulty, was very sweet and I couldnt help noticing a difference in her face. . . . I have commenced at the Art School and am going in for the South Kensington exams[35] so that I can teach properly later on, it will be pretty hard for me, for I hate that kind of work. Father has undertaken to coach me in geometry with Willie's

---

[33] Mabel Hill (1872-1956) married John McIndoe in 1898 and is referred to thereafter as Mrs McIndoe. Widowed in 1916, she continued to paint while raising her family of four children.

[34] The books were all works of popular fiction, published in both England and the United States and successful enough in most instances to be reprinted. *A Human Document* by William Hurrell Mallock, first published in 1892, was reprinted in 1975 in the series, *Victorian Fiction: Novels of Faith and Doubt*. *Katherine Lauderdale* by Francis Marion Crawford was first published in 1894, and reprinted in 1968 under the Scholarly Press imprint. *A Yellow Aster* (1894) was written by an Australian, Kathleen Mannington Caffyn, who based one of her characters on the painter Charles Conder.

[35] In 1894 the Otago School of Art had affiliated with the art department of the South Kensington School of Science and Art, London, and was renamed the Dunedin School of Art and Design. Dunedin students could now send work for assessment to England as well as presenting themselves for internal examinations.

assistance. (Willie studied it while at the S. of Mines).[36] I am just wondering how much I will learn between the two, both being about as clear as mud in their explanations. I have given up all idea of taking pupils this year, tho' I have had several promised me beside Lulu Roberts. . . . Did Mother tell you about my children's party. I had little Boy Moore down and all the neighboring children. They had a grand time in the orchard and we all wished we could have had your babs to laugh to them all. . . . We are all very anxious to hear about Percy. . . .

[20] TO ISABEL FIELD, 27 MARCH 1895

Cranmore Lodge. March 27th. 95

My dearest Sis
    . . . . What a dreadful shock you have had over this burglary. I can think of nothing else, and the fright you must have got when you found the man in your room. . . . I got a fright last night small as it was compared to yours that makes me pretty well understand your feelings. I was awakened by somebody violently pulling my hair, I sat up too terrified even to scream and heard somebody knock against the foot of the bed and go out of the door, and a second afterwards I heard the indian clubs in the boys' room clatter on the floor – then I found my voice and yelled, then I heard Frank in a very terrified voice say "Don't be frightened Fanny it's only me!" He was walking in his sleep and was quite as terrified as I was. The family in the meantime behaved most heroically. Annie got up dressed and locked her door on the inside.   Mother who sleeps alone lit a candle and nearly fainting with palpitation waited for the end, and Father snored on in blissful ignorance, and Willie didn't even hear a sound, so I think if there is ever a burglary in this house, we mustn't depend on mutual help. . . .
[Letter incomplete]

[21] TO ISABEL FIELD, 5 MAY 1895

Cranmore Lodge. Sunday morning

My dearest Sissie
    Just a line or two, altho' I have no news to tell you. I expect you have heard all

---

The subjects offered included Freehand Drawing, Model Drawing, Drawing in Light and Shade (from the plaster cast), Painting in Monochrome, Painting from Still Life, Geometrical Drawing, Perspective, Principles of Ornament, Machine Construction and Building Construction. In the July exams of 1895 FH gained first class passes in elementary Freehand Drawing, Model Drawing, Drawing in Light and Shade and Geometrical Drawing. In 1896 she gained first class passes in advanced Freehand Drawing, Model Drawing and Drawing in Light and Shade. There is no record of her having passed any painting subjects, either in oil or watercolour. Of the eight students who entered Painting from Still Life in 1896 only five passed.
[36] Students from the School of Mines were taught technical drawing at the Art School.

news past and present from the Spences.[37] I went up and sat with Alice the afternoon they left. She is wonderfully cheery but after all it isn't such a wrench for her for she is awfully happy with her hubby and child. . . .

. . . . [May] has befriended Miss Cumine's nephew to an alarming extent and he spends most of his time there. I see very little of May for I am away all day bar Mondays from 1/2 past 9 till 5, so I havent much time for gadding. I had a note from Capt. Garsia asking me if I would sell one of my heads for a 1£ less. I said yes, of course. Aunt Bella is most snubby on the subject of my pictures and the only paper she has sent me is a very vulgar comic paper holding me up to great ridicule, but in the select company of Messrs Nairn, Nerli and Miss Joel.[38] I would send it you, only I have given it to Nerli. I also figure in a leading article so tho' condemned by Aunt Bella and Mr. Rhind (who wrote to Father and said he thought I was completely spoilt by Nerli) I still hold up my head. You know the portrait of R. L. Stephenson[39] in McGregor Wright's in Wellington. I wonder if you could find out if the Mrs. Turnbull who has bought it for £40 to present it to the Edinburgh National Collection is the mother of that girl we met one night at the Bethunes. I know she comes from Fielding and she wrote Nerli such an awfully kind letter about it. . . .
[Letter incomplete]

[22] To Isabel Field, 19 June 1895

Cranmore Lodge. June 19th. 95.

My dearest Sissie
. . . . Mrs. D. Roberts gave a big euchre party on Wednesday and Mrs. Paston a musicale on Thursday both I believe in honor of Miss Ziele. I was much surprised to receive a note from that young lady asking me to her wedding and apologising for not giving me a formal invitation on the score of not knowing me well enough! Of course I am not going. I believe they are giving a most pretentious wedding and asking a number of people they scarcely know.

---

[37] The Spence family called in at Wellington on their way to England.

[38] FH exhibited six pictures, portraits and figure studies, with the Canterbury Society of Arts in April 1895. James Nairn (1859-1904), the Scottish impressionist, had visited Dunedin in 1891 on his way to Wellington where he became an influential teacher. His work would have been familiar to FH: it was exhibited at the Otago Art Society and her father owned at least one work. G. P. Nerli was Visiting Master for Art at the Dunedin School of Art and Design from 1895 to October 1896, when he abruptly left. Grace Joel (1865-1924) was born in Dunedin but left to study art in Melbourne 1891-93, returning in 1894. A member of the Easel Club founded in 1895, she left for England round the beginning of 1901. A friendship between Frances Hodgkins and Grace Joel might have been expected, but the Joel family belonged to the wealthy cosmopolitan Jewish community in Dunedin, while the Hodgkinses moved in middle class professional and commercial circles, more conventional and provincial in outlook.

[39] Nerli's portrait of Robert Louis Stevenson, possibly his finest work, was painted during his stay in Samoa in 1892.

I have entered for that £2 competition in Wellington, hope I wont be plucked this time. Mr. Luke gave me a commission to illustrate a story for the "Leader" but I dont think it is much in my line tho I will have a shot at it. . . .

Now dear old girl I will say goodbye. I will write whenever I can but you don't [know] what a quiet life I lead and there is very little to write about. My painting absorbs me more & more every day. I am slowly settling down to an oldmaidship, and I have only one prominent idea and that is that nothing will interfere between me and my work.

[23] To Isabel Field, 26 June 1895

[Cranmore Lodge] Melrose. June 26th, '95

My dearest Sis

Just a few lines before bedtime to thank you for your cheery letter which was hailed with delight. . . .

Lillie Grummitt . . . told us all about the Ziele wedding. . . . I went to see the wedding with the Rattrays . . . . Miss Ziele made the most self possessed bride ever seen here. She managed and directed everything up till the last moment and Willie said he heard her say, when saying goodbye to her mother whom she wont see again as they went straight to Sydney, "well goodbye Mother dear – oh! where's my mackintosh!". . .

. . . . I have got my competition head finished at last and Father is quite excited about it and has hunted up an elaborate title for it and a verse of poetry, which he is going to get inscribed on a plate to be put on the frame! I havent the heart not to agree with him so for once he is going to get his own way. He says that if I call it a "Head of an Old Woman" which it is, he will forbid me sending it[40]. . . .

I hope you will find a use for the gaiters, they are scarcely worth sending you but they will keep [the baby] warm while creeping about. I have got a pattern of a dutch hood and I am going to try and worry out one, but I expect it will be about ready for the "next of kin"[41]. . . .

---

[40] W. M. Hodgkins's title: 'Thinking of the Olden Time –
      Of days long vanished,
      Of years gone by.'
Father and daughter appear to have compromised. The work was given FH's title in the Academy of Fine Arts catalogue but the poetry appeared on the frame and was used as the title when the work was exhibited with the Otago Art Society in November.
[41] Isabel was now expecting her second child.

[24] TO ISABEL FIELD, 23 JULY 1895

Cranmore Lodge. July 23rd 95

My dearest Sis

. . . . It is so cold I can hardly hold my pen. If the frost holds good Mr. Pasco is going to take a party of us out to Outram to have some skating (skates provided) and drive back the same night. . . . but as I write I can hear the rain coming on so our little trip is as good as knocked on the head.

We had a great night at the Savage Club on Monday night. It was guest night and we had a bumper house at Mrs Ritchies. . . . I took Mrs. Finker as my guest and she put me to the blush by openly cleaning her nails with a knitting needle at the drawing [room] door.

I got up a little play called the "Ticket Office". I daresay you have read it in the Press. My part of the performance was the Giddy girl for which I got quite an ovation and was recalled amid loud applause.[42] The Websters gave a little sketch called "A Row in the Pit", which was screamingly funny. I took a small part in it. It reminded me very much of that night we sat behind that woman and her hat. Rosie Webster had a hat quite 3 yds. in circumference and the polite Savage Club ears have never before listened to such language as came from behind that hat. Mrs. Scott was there looking lovely in a new English teagown.

The Otago Rowing Club is going to have a huge ball on the 8th August in celebration of its coming of age. Willie wants me to go so I am having a dress furbished up.

I suppose you haven't seen anything of my pictures yet. I have taken great care not to send any Nerli work. Dr. Belcher has asked me to paint a head of his son Frank, only dont mention it till it is an accomplished fact. . . . Mr O'Keefe[43] has returned from Paris and is shocking the proprieties by exhibiting a number of nude studies. Father won't let me go and see them! Boo hoo! . . . .

Will Field sent a telegram announcing that FH's Head of an Old Woman *had been awarded the prize for the best painting from life at the New Zealand Academy of Fine Arts in Wellington.*

Sunday evening.

I have just come home from the Scotts and must close this letter in time for tomorrow's mail. Please thank Will for his telegram and kind congratulations, how thoughtful of him to wire at once. I was pleased – but won't be jubilant till I hear who the other competitors were. Mother was most surprised and Father

[42] '. . . . the chief praise must be awarded to Miss Hodgkins who was a decided hit.' *Otago Witness*, 1 August 1895.
[43] A. H. O'Keeffe (1858-1941) returned from study at the Académie Julian in Paris in 1895 and established a teaching studio.

said, "It was the title that did it!" and Willie said "What did you get, £2, good big treat!" Father at once sent the unfortunate Frank unknown to us down to the [Otago Daily] Times and next morning it appeared, he ought to have waited till it was officially announced to me. Suppose there is some mistake, horrible thought! I would feel as if I had been jilted and sue the N.Z.A. for breach of promise. I got quite a number of congratulations and this afternoon the neighbors came in in a most uncongenial mass. Finkers – Cargills – Kenyons – and all hate each other. . . .

[Letter incomplete]

[25] To Isabel Field, 10 August 1895

Cranmore Lodge. Aug. 10th 95

My dearest Sissie

. . . . Now for a bit of news that I know will surprise you – May Kenyon is engaged!! and to the most awful little tadpole I have ever set eyes on. I think I told you about the Cumine's nephew Mr. Garden, commonly called the Garden Goat a name I gave him when first he came. To begin with he is as ugly as they make them small and has a big nose, and is altogether a most unprepossessing little man. He is scrupulously neat and clean so he will tidy May up a bit. It is the biggest bit of luck for him getting such a girl as May, for I am sure nobody else would have looked at him. . . . I have said the hardest & nastiest things about him to May, and now you can imagine how I feel, but she bears me no ill will. . . . Mother smelt a rat sometime ago, and advised me to hold my tongue but I never in my wildest moments dreamed she could care for him, much less marry him. He has just come into an estate in Aberdeenshire which leaves him very well off, and I sincerely hope it has not influenced her, for it is a good match looking at it from that point of view. . . . One thing I must say, May has always stuck up for him. . . . About a month ago he disappeared into the country and the other night at the Boating Club Ball, I found him at my elbow asking me for a dance. I positively shuddered as I looked at him and dodged him behind May. He had grown a stubbly beard and looked like a Gorilla. It now turns out that she advised him to rusticate awhile and grow a beard, for as she said the poor boy has an "expansive mouth and a defective chin". He took May home from the dance and proposed to her at 3 o'clock in the morning in the Fergusson's garden, isn't that all in keeping with her character? and the next morning, he called for her and kissed her before Mrs. Fergusson. May says his kisses are "elementary, a sure sign he has never spooned before." I would just give anything to have you here at present, there are so many funny things I can't very well write down, as it is I feel I have said a great deal too much but I know you won't give me away. . . . He has very good brains but he is so agressive and puts you down and sets you right in such an irritating fashion, his cleverness quite loses its charm. I can't imagine she is in love with him . . . . Anyway, he is a very lucky fellow for she is a good girl and awfully sweet tempered and if she makes him half as good a wife as she does a daughter they ought to be very happy. She came in this morning, I was very busy making pastry, Saturday morning so you can imagine I wasn't overjoyed to see her. She said – "Fan dear I want to be kissed," well you know how I hate being kissed in the first place so I snapped out "Oh bother your kisses!" then she said, "Congratulate me, I am going to be Frank Garden's little wife" you could have knocked me down with a feather and I tried hard to make my congratulations sound sincere tho I could hardly realize it till she showed me the ring, a very pretty hoop of diamonds. . . .

Well I think I have pretty well exhausted that subject. . . .

The Boating Club Ball was a great success. . . . The lion of the evening was Mr. F. Villiers,[44] who came in after his lecture. I had the honor of being introduced to him and we had a long talk, he remembered dining with us at Royal Terrace when he was here before and asked if we lived in the same house. He quite startled me by his strong resemblance to Will, and Willie saw it too – perhaps that is why I admire him so much. I have always taken a great interest in him, and have read his life and know a good deal about him, so you can imagine how glad I was to meet him. He was so natural & unaffected and had a most delightful voice. . . . I have never been so fascinated by anyone before. . . .

[26] To RACHEL HODGKINS, 18 AUGUST 1895

Cranmore Lodge. Sunday Evening

My darling Mother

What can I say to comfort you in this dreadful trouble.[45] We have just received the telegram and my heart is aching for you and Uncle Sandie. You must not grieve darling but be your own brave self, and when you come home we will show you how much we love you and how good we shall be to you dear little Mother. I feel as if we could never make your loss up to you. How glad I am you were with her at the last, and when I think I shall never see her dear kind face again it comes upon me with a terrible pang what you and Uncle Sandie are feeling. . . .

Do not worry about anything at home, everything is going on smoothly, all the

---

[44] Frederic Villiers (1852-1922), Royal Academy trained war artist and correspondent, was on a world lecture tour, fresh from covering the Chinese-Japanese War of 1894-5. His two volumes of memoirs, *Villiers: His Five Decades of Adventure*, 1921, give a lively account of a lifetime's involvement in all the wars of the day, including the relief of Khartoum and World War 1.

[45] Isabella Carrick died on 18 August 1895. Mrs Hodgkins had gone to Christchurch some days earlier to be with her.

neighbors have been so kind, especially Mrs. Cargill who has been in every day

You will see Father before this letter reaches you, I am so glad you have sent for him, for he feels terribly lonely without you.

Goodnight darling Mother you may be sure we are all thinking and sorrowing with you tonight ever your loving daughter Fanny.

[27] TO RACHEL HODGKINS, 25 AUGUST 1895

Cranmore Lodge. Sunday morning.

My darling Mother,

. . . . I am so glad you are going up with Uncle Sandie to Wellington. There is nothing to bring you home, Mother dear, for everything goes on splendidly . . . . Everybody says I keep everything in apple-pie order and even the boys dont grumble. The first week I got into great difficulties over the boys' undergarments but by a superhuman effort I got them right and now everybody is at peace with each other. Yesterday morning Mrs. Meeson turned up and is here now, but goes down to Port [Chalmers] tonight. She is a funny little thing and makes great love to Father who I think rather likes it. . . . She pranced down to breakfast and began gushing about the spring and the flowers and the sunshine etc when Father said, "Yes! Yes! but don't you think you had better eat your sausage before it gets cold," and she did promptly. . . .

I had a letter from Miss Holmes on Saturday in which she sent her love and sympathy to you. She wants to buy my "Marguerite" picture[46] and would I knock off a guinea! rather hard lines isn't it but I suppose I must.

[Letter incomplete]

[28] TO RACHEL HODGKINS, 19 SEPTEMBER 1895

Cranmore Lodge. Sept. 19th. 95.

My darling Mother

. . . . You seem to think from your last letter that we have got influenza in the house but I can assure you Mother dear, we are all in the best of health, and please don't worry yourself about that and cut your holiday short and come home on our account. Bert has bought a safety bicycle for which he gave £30 I believe and is tremendously proud of himself. I feel very tempted to learn but Bert is a perfect Turk and wont let anyone touch it. Father with his usual youthful enthusiasm

---

[46] A portrait of a young woman at the New Zealand Academy of Fine Arts Exhibition which opened on 27 July 1895.

tried it and you may as well make up your mind to a cricked back or a dislocated shoulder, for he certainly will have one or the other before he is done.

I had a letter from Miss Holmes this morning enclosing the welcome £2-10. Now that I have got the money I must tell you that when that picture left Dunedin it had only £2-10 marked on it and either thro some mistake of the framemaker's or a mixing up of labels or perhaps one of Father's muddling directions it had got changed to £3.10. Anyhow when Miss Holmes offered £2.10. I was more angry at the principle of the thing than at the actual loss of the Guinea. But when I told Dr. Scott, he strongly advised me to close with Miss Holmes and he rather enjoyed the joke against Miss Holmes and my getting the full value for my picture after all for in the first place he had advised me not to put more than £2.10 on it. . . .

[29] To Isabel Field, 6 October 1895

Cranmore Lodge. Sunday evening.

My dearest Sissie

Just a few lines to tell you of Mother's safe arrival. I was so glad to get her home again and thought her looking wonderfully well and cheerful. . . . Mrs. Martin came down on Friday and stayed for 3 long hours and harrowed poor old Mother by talking over everything, but Mrs. Finker came in in the evening and I never liked her so much as I did that night and could have hugged her for her cheerfulness.

I rather neglected the garden when Mother was away, so there is lots to do to keep her occupied and she is never so happy as when she is in the garden. I asked her how Will's garden was looking and she says he is much too fond of investigating the roots to make a successful gardener. Does he still stalk snails by candlelight?

Yesterday we went for the last of our walking parties, we crossed in a boat to Vauxhall and climbed the hill to Larnach's Castle and had tea in the bush. The party consisted of the Grahams Rattrays McLarens and myself, and a man apiece. It has always been the same party so we ought to know each other. Willie and Issy Rattray are flirting mildly and I think like each other, but there are no other flirtations afoot.

It was most awfully good of you to send me that beautiful piece of tapestry, you don't know how I prize it and I cant thank you enough and also for the dress which will make up beautifully later on. . . .

[30] To Isabel Field, 11 February 1896

Cranmore Lodge. Tuesday 11. 96

My dearest Sis

I feel that I have treated you very badly never writing to you all these weeks and I have still to thank you for the stockings you sent me at Christmas. I wore them at Cannington[47] and was very glad of them . . . . I have been home now for more than a week. I found Mother looking the picture of health and as brown as a berry being so much in the garden. I brought back a fine tan myself and am now in the peeling stage. The best news I have heard for a long time was that you were so much better and stronger. Mrs. Finker wrote many complimentary things about you & the babies. . . . I came back to find Willie gone[48] and much as I miss him I cannot help enjoying the entire peacefulness that reigns. Father doesnt know himself, he hasnt been once contradicted and I am not so sure that it is altogether good for him. He is now his own master in his own study and his native spirits are returning. The Congress Gaieties[49] are all over and the last of the doctors have gone. It was a memorable week one whirr of excitement and perfect weather. I contented myself with three garden parties, The Reynolds, Cuttens and Mr. Russells, at all 3 of which Vice Royalty was present. . . . Alice McG[owan] does not seem to be any stronger and the doctor is again in attendance . . . . I think Robert ought to feed her up and give her wine & beer and give her a proper chance. I am sure Mrs. Spence would insist on it if she saw how delicate she is looking. The baby is of the stodgy and extremely healthy order and has a face devoid of any expression save a penetrating stare. . . .

[31] To Isabel Field, 1 April 1896

[Cranmore Lodge]

. . . . [May] is hoping to come and see you on her way thro Wellington. I will miss her very much. . . . Last night Frank went down to Henley and inaugurated the opening of the duck Season by sitting in a swamp all night, shooting from all accounts many hundreds of duck but bringing home none, and now he is snuffling up sympathy for a cold. The John Roberts are going home again this month, Mr. Roberts fancys he will get better more quickly if he takes another sea voyage, so they are going home and coming out again in the Gothic. I wish I was

---

[47] Cannington was a sheep station near Timaru where FH had just spent a month's holiday with a large house party.

[48] Willie had gained a position as accountant in the Bank of New South Wales in Invercargill. He had been working in the Dunedin branch.

[49] The Australasian Medical Congress took place in Dunedin, 3-11 February 1896.

in their shoes. Miss Sievwright[50] has just sent out portraits of Aggie and Lulu in pastel for which she got the tidy sum of £35 each. I havent seen them yet but Father thinks they are very feeble tho' other people gush over them.

I have just finished a pastel of Alice McGowan to send home to [her mother] Mrs. Spence. Dr. Scott likes it so much he has asked me to do Mrs. Scott. Alice was frightfully difficult to do as she is very ugly and grows scraggier every day, but I drew her bones anatomically and covered them as she ought to be covered. Mrs. Cargill says I am a Court painter, I flatter so fulsomely. The Spences will only think Alice has improved. . . .

[Letter incomplete]

The sisters' lives continued to diverge. Isabel's second child, a daughter, had been born on 9 November 1895 and Isabel was again pregnant. FH rented a studio in town and sent out cards advertising art classes from 7 September 1896.

[32] To Isabel Field, 2 September 1896

Cranmore Lodge. Wednesday

My dearest Sis

I have been reproaching myself for leaving you so long without a letter, but I must send you a line tonight to show you I have not quite forgotten you all. Poor old girl you may be sure you have my deepest sympathies about present and future worries, it does all seem a peice of the most unfortunate ill-luck that ever befell a girl. If it is any comfort to know it, Alice McG. is in the same box and both she and Robert are cussing fate as they had planned a trip home at the beginning of the year. Dont breathe a word of this to any Dunedinites for of course it is early days yet and Alice keeps herself very much to herself . . . .

Just fancy having Mrs Scott next door, she came up last week and has been over once. She already seems better for the change and rest from those naughty boys. They are perfect little wretches and worry their mother terribly and I am sure she would never have got better lying in bed with those whiny children round her . . . . Mother and I are very anxious to hear how you both are. We have been worrying about you and are so afraid you will knock yourself up. I enclose you a card which will explain itself. It is a bit of a venture to start a room, but the rent is not deadly, only 2/6 a week and furnished at that. I have £5 capital to start with and already 2 pupils so I will not run into debt yet awhile. I advertised in the "Star" and I start teaching next week. I have been asked so often to take pupils so thought it wise to commence in time for spring sketching.

[50] Miss Sievwright exhibited at the Otago Art Society from 1885-90 and was a prizewinner at the New Zealand and South Seas Exhibition in Dunedin in 1889.

Daisy Fitchett[51] has started a Studio, but so far has no pupils. She is frightfully lackadaisical and about as unpractical as they make them.

Tell Will he would see a marked improvement in me re. money matters and [I] pride myself that I know exactly how many beans make five.

Reading this letter over there seems to be a good deal about myself in it.

Mrs. Finker is back and has brought Mother an elagant butter cooler of frosted silver and cut glass which reposes on the sideboard and I am glad Mother has decided it is only to be looked at! How glad you will be to have a yarn with old Dunedinites. Kate Rattray left covered with honor and carrying the championship with her.[52] There is a cocksureness about her that is sure to carry something before it. . . .

[33] To Isabel Field, 5 September 1896

Cranmore Lodge. Sept 5th 96

My dearest Sis

You cannot think how glad I was to get your letter this morning, and lose no time in answering it. I have been in bed the three last days with this wretched influenza, and still feel very weak and shaky. I could not go out to Warrington as I intended and now it is too late as I begin teaching next week. Mother has told you I expect that I have heard from May, there is nothing special in it or I would send it on. The only things she bought in Paris were a pair of *corsets* and a pewter pot! Isn't that like May?. . .

That was rich about Mr. Nairn, you must show him the extent of your "powers" later on when you take to painting again. I hear he has done a good portrait of Miss Grace [Joel]. Have you seen it?

I am frightfully disatisfied with my own work. I would like to give myself a rest from painting for a time but now must tackle my Exhibition work, and with anything but a fresh brain! I miss having someone to consult and talk over things, for now that May has gone I have nobody who takes any real interest in my work, except Dr. Scott and one's ideas have to be of the first water before one submits them to his critical judgement, and Signor Nerli, although he may have a very nice opinion of me, behind my back, is absolutely useless as far as advice goes.

Father paints away as much as ever, and the "old Study" is given over to innumerable busts of Dr. Stuart[53] in various stages. He is working up for another clay revival and several Dr. Stuarts are melting in kerozene tins and I know that he meditates another "statoo" for the Exhibition. . . .

---

[51] Dunedin-born Margaret or Daisy Fitchett studied in Dresden and Paris and returned to teach in Dunedin in 1895 before going to live permanently in England.
[52] Kate Rattray became the lady golf champion of New Zealand.
[53] Reverend Dr D. M. Stuart was Chancellor of the University of Otago.

[34] To Isabel Field, c.21 April 1897

[Cranmore Lodge] Melrose. Wednesday.

My dearest Sis

I am afraid I have very selfishly left all the writing to Mother since you left, but I seem to have done nothing but paint since you left, the brush has scarcely been out of my hand. I had no sooner finished my work for the Auckland Exhibition[54] than an art dealer from Chch. appeared on the scene and ordered 3 pictures of mine and 3 of Fathers and also bought the 2 Giffords.[55] Of course I was sorry to part with your old friend the Otira Gorge, but "£10 is £10". By this time I suppose Annie has left you. How are you faring without her, poor old Girl, I hope Jessie is a comfort to you. I am so glad you finally fixed on Geoffrey for a name.[56] The McGowans are going to call their child Jack and have asked me to be its godmother . . . . Poor Alice is still on her back and will be for another month . . . .

. . . . Father has been much better these last few days and he and Mr. Finker are dissipating at Carl Hertz[57] tonight. I went last night with Bert and Charlie Robinson (awful bore that boy) and your innocent sister's maiden cheek was on the blush most of the evening. I was warned in a letter from Georgie Wilford that it was vulgar, but that was putting it mildly.

. . . . Dr Scott comes over every evening to sit with Father. He has been a good friend to him since he has been seedy, and insists on him changing boots and socks whenever it is damp. Father wouldn't do it for anybody else, but is meekness itself in Dr. Scott's hands. . . . I think it is just as well that you did not leave Girlie behind for Mother's time is a good deal taken up looking after Father and cooking for him. His appetite failed him very much at first but now he is picking up again and if he does not get a chill tonight he will be quite well in a day or two.

Mrs. Finker has gone to Melbourne . . . and Mr. Finker remains where he is and is going to economise and live on Passover bread and smoked fish. I was nearly forgetting to tell you that I am going to Timaru for a fortnight to stay with Edith McLaren. I am going next Thursday, if I can get my pupils, pictures and – ahem! underclothes – ready. At present I am in a high old muddle and have a bad cold into the bargain and I feel as much like going to Timaru as going to the moon. To make matter worse I have weakly promised to take part in some theatricals up there. I dont know a word of my part and I am due at a rehearsal

[54] G. P. Nerli left Dunedin towards the end of 1896 and was exhibiting at the Auckland Society of Arts in April 1897. McCormick suggests his presence in Auckland may have led FH to exhibit there for the first time. (*Portrait of Frances Hodgkins*, p.29)

[55] E. A. Gifford RA (1819-94) arrived in New Zealand in 1877 and exhibited at the Otago Art Society until 1893. He was admired by W. M. Hodgkins as a landscape painter.

[56] Isabel's third child, William Geoffrey Hughes, was born on 2 January 1897.

[57] A visiting illusionist.

tomorrow at Mrs. McKenzies who has promised to coach us. . . . I cant possibly stay more than a fortnight and I am beginning to feel that it won't be the best preparation for my Wellington work. I am anxious to send up some good work and my head is like a pumkin at present. Did you get the sketch I sent you by Mrs. Blair? I haven't forgotten my promise to copy Girlie's and Baba's heads for you: you might mention in your next letter how the pastel travelled. I would like to know in case I send to Wellington.

With much love from Mother and myself and hoping the kiddies are all well your ever loving sister Fanny.

[35] TO ISABEL FIELD, C.17 JUNE 1897

Cranmore Lodge. Thursday.

My dearest Sis

. . . . Mother wants you to send [a photograph of the baby son] to Willie, he has been enquiring several times lately for news of the Christening and wants to know when it is to take place! . . . Now for a bit of news! We have notice to quit this house in a month, it being sold to Mr. Stephenson (Irvine & Stephenson) a gentleman with 10 children all young! . . . It came as a great shock to me after all for I never really thought we would leave this house. Of course I am glad and Mother is delighted, but all the same there will be many regrets at leaving the old home, especially as I am afraid from the way the wind is blowing at present in the maternal mind that it will be a case of out of the frying pan etc. Mother as you know has a sneaking regard for Roslyn in general and for a house up there in particular and you know what Mother is once she takes an idea into her head & how quietly obstinate she is. I have a positive aversion to Roslyn and the very idea of going up there makes me shudder. I have been hoping to get nearer town for many reasons and the boys want to too so I only hope combined resistance will have a desired effect. Mother has been twice up to see a house up there and steadily refuses to see any good in any other place. Mind you write soon and express yourself *strongly* on the subject, and say you will never come down to Dunedin again if we perch ourselves up on a hill Roslyn especially. I wish you were here to give advice. Mother is so obstinate, but I think she might move nearer town if only for her children's sake. She is so frightened of not getting a garden, but a garden should be made quite secondary to a house. However it is no use grumbling and I only hope it will pan out all right, and to everybody's satisfaction. One thing I am very glad we are moving away from this house for Father's sake. I think on the whole he is better tho' he is really far from well. I wish Frank was a greater comfort to him. Frank is so anxious to please, yet office work seems to be so irksome to him. . . . If we are to turn out in a month we will have lots to do. I have already sorted all the magazines & sketches and am making a bundle of pictures up for you. . . . I have had a veritable fit of inspiration this week, & have painted no less than 3 pictures. Father seems much pleased and they are going to the man in Chch I told you about where they ought to have gone long ago. Will you ask Will if he happens to have any Maori snapshots or photos, & tell him I will be very grateful if he can give me some he ought to have plenty of opportunities of getting photographs of them[58]. . . . Mrs. Finker is home again. While in Melbourne she consulted a "leading doctor" about the state of her health. He knowing his case advised a strict course of dieting and Melbourne becoming *un*bearable under such conditions she hurried home a month before she was expected and much inconvenienced Mr. Finker who was teaching Dulce "How doth the little busy bee" as a surprise for her mother and in consequence there was an ignominious break down when Dulce stood forth to recite it. Dulce cried & Irene laughed spitefully and Irene was smacked and put out of the room, and altogether the home coming was not a success. . . .

[36] To Isabel Field, c.29 August 1897

Nevada. [Roslyn]. Sunday evening

My dearest Sis

. . . . Mother has not been at all well since my last letter . . . . Indeed she has never been well since we moved into this house, she has had her old enemy intergestion and internal pain with sleepless nights and in consequence she is looking thin and far from well. . . . She has not been over working herself either in the house or the garden and she stays in bed to breakfast and takes porter so you see she gives herself every chance of getting better. Poor Mother I hate to see her ailing she is such a stoic with it all too and so different from our other parent in the matter of endurance. Father on the other hand is much better both in health and spirits and actually asked me for a piece of stretched paper today. You can imagine I was pleased for he has taken no interest in painting for a long time and several times has said he would never touch a brush again. I have every hope that if he weathers this winter safely that he will with care be as strong as ever he was. . . .

[Postscript] Dont worry about Mother, for I am sure she will be quite well again in a few days . . . .

[58] From the 1890s onwards, Will Field was engaged in buying land in the Waikanae district north of Wellington from its Maori owners.

[37] To Isabel Field, c.19 October 1897

Nevada. Tuesday evening.

My dearest Sis

. . . . I have not much news to report from home. Father is better I think on the whole. He has actually started a picture and a big one too but whether it will be finished in time for the Exhibition or not remains to be seen. I have got nothing of any importance I feel artistically played out and am longing for a change of scenery and pastures new. I squirmed when I saw my two pictures from Wllgtn. anything so deplorably weak and feeble I couldn't imagine. I think I shall go on the teaching ticket for a little time, it seems to promise well and is a rest from painting. I had letters arranging for two new pupils today. I hear great things of Miss Hill's work this year. I wish she could manage to send her big picture down here. I havent felt in a painting mood since we have been in this house. I had hoped for an inspiration at the eleventh hour such as you used to have, but it failed me and here I am, the last week and minus a picture worth mentioning. However, everybody will have the satisfaction of remarking how much I have "fallen off" which after all pleases people better than success sometimes! Frank has such a depressing influence on us all. . . . he is so selfish and hard to get on with, he has made this winter a very trying one for us all, and goodness knows we have been patient enough hoping things would brighten. He doesn't take an interest in anything and seems to be thoroughly morbid and low-spirited. Bert on the other hand is such a comfort and so good to Father who is devoted to him. Just fancy old May coming over again. I shall be glad to see her again *and* the child. . . . I have started a market garden in the backyard, and have quite a decent plot with cabbages, cauliflowers, peas and lettuces. Growing cabbages is quite a fine art and is not the simple thing it looks by any means. I had many difficulties to wrestle with in the shape of cats and fowls but now I have so successfully wirenetted them in that I find the greatest difficulty in getting anywhere near them myself. . . . Willie's friend Miss Dalgleish[59] has been staying with the Rattrays and I had a few girls to meet her at lunch on Friday. . . . I have very little news for you socially. I go out very seldom, and never at night. Did you see Mrs. Finker? I believe she is in Wllgtn. . . .

[38] To Isabel Field, 17 November 1897

Nevada. Wednesday.

My dearest Sis

It is a deadly hot and deeply unwholesome afternoon so take it not amiss if this

---

[59] Jean Dalgliesh, Willie's future wife.

is a scratch of a letter. . . . I am going out to Brighton for a week on Monday, and am hoping to get some sketches. I am going to stay at Bert's diggings, a one-roomed cottage . . . . The Exhibition has been open a fortnight now and a matter of 3 or 4 small and very dreadful pictures have been sold. It is a rather poor show but the loan collection is a good one and leavens the rest. Daisy Fitchetts work is splendid but there is no work especially outstanding. Mr. Nairn's and Miss Richardson's pictures seem to have faded, one of Nairns is almost black. It must be the paints they use, for one cannot help contrasting them with Mr. Gouldsmith's[60] beautiful fresh oils hung beside them and with the color as fresh as when he first painted them. I touched up the lilac bonnet and altered it considerably and took out the purple and it looks quite a different picture. If it does not sell here or at Chch. you are to have it eventually for the new house. It does not sound a very generous gift does it but you know how necessary it is for me to sell my pictures. I have a little scheme on for the winter if I can only run it and that is to go down to the Islands on that excursion the U.S.S co is running. Mrs. Hocken is going and is very anxious I should go with her. I feel sure I could make something out of it for that kind of scenery and native life appeals to me tremendously. I believe £25 would cover expenses and my classes so far promise to pay, so it is just on the cards I will go. . . .

[39] To Isabel Field, c.13 January 1898

Nevada. Thursday.

My dearest Sis

. . . . I had hoped to have better news for you dear. We have all been so sad and anxious about Father, and I am greived to have to tell you that he is in a very critical state. The Doctor has just been and he has told us that Fathers symptoms are very grave.

Mother would have written to you herself, but she does not feel able. I wish you were with us dear . . . but I hope and trust the dear old man will soon be better and as strong as ever he was. Until quite lately he has driven to and from the office for a few hours, but now he is too weak to get out of bed. He suffers from intense drowsiness and sleeps nearly all day. . . . Percy is not going back for a few days yet, he is a great comfort so thoughtful and unselfish. Frank, I am glad to say is out camping. Mother wants me to write to Aunt Jane by this mail. I am dreading it but I suppose it must be done. . . .

---

[60] Edmund T. Gouldsmith RBA, RWA (1852-1932), an English artist, was in New Zealand 1886-9 and had visited the Hodgkins family. He had proposed marriage to Isabel Hodgkins.

[40] To Isabel Field, c.16 January 1898

Nevada. Sunday morning.

My dearest Sis,

I know how anxious you will be for news so I am writing you a few hurried lines. There has been no improvement since I last wrote and we can hope for none. Dr. Hocken[61] had a consultation yesterday with Dr. Roberts and they hold out no hope of his recovery.[62] They say he may go off in a state of coma any time or linger on for weeks which I pray from the bottom of my heart may not be so. Our only comfort is that he does not suffer tho' the poor darling has had a good deal of pain up till quite lately. He sleeps most of the time and Dr. Scott comes backwards and forwards and chats to him whenever he feels well enough to see him. I can't tell you what a comfort Dr. Scott is. . . .

I feel as if I hardly realized things and yet I have known for a long time that this has been hanging over us. I shall write again in a few days and hope to have better news for you.

[41] To Isabel Field, c.18 January 1898

Nevada. Tuesday morning.

My dearest Sis

. . . . Mother thinks that if you came down you might alarm Father & much as she would like to have you she thinks it best for you to wait and if there is any change we will wire you. . . . Until he was taken ill Father was very busy over the Finker business. The poor Finkers are in great trouble, Mr. F. having made a terrible muddle of his affairs, and about Christmas time slipped off to Melbourne, where Mrs. Finker is following him next week. . . . I am so dreadfully sorry for Mrs. Finker she has been coming here for the last month every day, and sits in a broken hearted way talking of her troubles. We are the only friends she cares about, and of course we can do so little for her. . . . I will write again tomorrow and tell you how Father is. . . .

---

[61] Thomas Morland Hocken (1836-1910), a surgeon and, for twenty-two years, Dunedin coroner. Like J. H. Scott and W. M. Hodgkins, his interests and influence extended beyond his professional activities: he wrote wide-ranging scholarly articles, published in 1909 the *Bibliography of the Literature relating to New Zealand* and bequeathed to the city an invaluable collection of manuscripts, books and maps,

[62] They accurately diagnosed cancer of the bladder, complicated by interstitial nephritis.

[42] To Isabel Field, c.19 January 1898

Nevada. Wednesday morning

My dearest Sis

Just a line to tell you there is no improvement or change. Father has had a bad night but is sleeping easily now. . . . Willie is coming up tomorrow . . . .

No more, dear Sis in great haste,

Yours

Fanny

W. M. Hodgkins died on 9 February 1898.

PART TWO

1898-1901

Mother and Daughter

After the death of W. M. Hodgkins Mrs Hodgkins was left with little to live on. She moved with Bert and Frances to a six-roomed rented cottage in Castle Street. Frank was living at Otokia south of Dunedin.

FH was now twenty-nine and destined, it would seem, to settle into the supportive role of unmarried working daughter. That she eventually resisted conventional expectations may be due in part to the independence of mind that so often found expression in the satiric tone of her letters. They leave no doubt about her dissatisfaction with the preoccupations of Dunedin society and many of its artists. Her ambition found a spur also in the rivalry that existed, in equal measure with their affection, between FH and Isabel, two sisters so close in age and interests.

FH adapted quickly to the altered family circumstances and continued to earn her living in a business-like way. Some time in 1898 it was decided that she would go 'home' for a period of study. The next two and a half years were devoted to accumulating enough money to do this, with an art union of her own as the final effort.

[43] To Isabel Field, 8 May 1898

Castle Street. May 8th. '98.

My dearest Sissie

. . . . Thank you so much for the gloves and veiling, they were most acceptable and are just what I want. You must not send me anything more please, Sis, you have been so very generous to us all that I feel we can never pay back all your kindness. You must let me return you the £5 you lent me to pay Robb. I have been a long time sending it you but I have only just got my money. . . . At the end of this month I will have made £30, the result of two months' teaching. My sketching classes are nearly over and I have an indoor class of six who are coming to me for the winter. After all bills are settled I think I will take out an insurance policy I think it is a good investment and it will make me put by a little every year which otherwise I would spend. I have got the prospectus of all the different companies and I think I will insure in the A.M.P. they give the biggest bonuses. . . . I hope to paint hard during the winter and try and reap a harvest at our Exhibition and the only way is to stay here quietly by myself and perhaps in the spring go for a sketching trip somewhere. . . . on Friday night I go to a nude class at the Art School, one of Mr. Nairn's models sits. We are going to the [Industrial] Exhibition tomorrow we havent been yet and it closes very soon. . . .

At Will Field's suggestion it was decided that Frank would join Percy on his farm in the North Island. Over the next two years it became clear that Frank's difficulties in adjusting to adult life were abnormal. After many efforts by the family to find a place

for him he was in 1901 committed to Seacliff Asylum north of Dunedin where he
remained until his death in 1932.

[44] TO ISABEL FIELD, C.30 MAY 1898

[Castle Street] Monday Evening.

My dearest Sis

It was indeed generous of you to send back that check. . . . I hope some day
I will be able to repay your & Wills kindness. You must accept the little Maori
head I am sending up by Frank in place of the one you sold. . . . Do not try to
sell it for I want you to keep it. . . . I was *very* pleased that Dr. Fyffe bought the
[other] little head. It was good of you to give it up. I have undertaken to illustrate
the stories in the Xmas number of the Otago Witness. I am to do 20 small wash
drawings for which I am to get £10. I sent in a specimen to Mr. Fenwick and the
next morning I got the commission. . . . If it is a success it may lead to more work
of the same kind. It pays. . . .

Frank is most likely going up to Percy on Thursday by the Wakatipu but will
wire you if he leaves that day. There is no news to tell you, we lead such
uneventful lives. Mother is very uncertain when she will be able to go up to you,
she does not seem to like the idea of leaving me alone. But of course, I can manage
by myself and I hope you will write and persuade her to go to Wellington before
the worst of the winter sets in. It is bitterly cold now and tho' she is keeping very
well, I am sure she would be all the better for a change. It is very dull for her as,
of course, I have my work and have no time to think of anything else, and tho'
we are never a day without visitors, I often think how much more lonely it must
be for her than it is for me. . . . No more at present dear Sis

With love from Mother & myself, your loving sister
Fanny.

[45] TO ISABEL FIELD, C.1 AUGUST 1898

[Castle Street] Monday Evening

My dearest Sis

. . . . [I have had] a letter from May Kenyon, and such a hard unsympathetic
caddish letter it was. . . . She must have changed very much or rather she is
showing herself in her true colors: she shall never see my hand writing again. I had
to pay 6d. on the letter too. . . .

I have never written to congratulate [you] on your taking up your brush again and so successfully[1]. . . . That must be a most charming friendship you have made with Lady Ranfurly.[2] It does one good to strike a congenial spirit now and then, it lifts one out of the ruts. Dr. Scott said "Sissie will do her Ladyship a great deal of good". Artistically she is not up to much, I believe. Tell us what her pictures are like – dont forget – and also to whom you sold your tenpounder. I wish I could steal your secret of painting like that and selling like that too! My pictures are what you would expect.[3] I rarely touched a brush till after dark, except in the case of the little old man which as you notice has a very different tone about it to any of the others. It is not that I am so busy after three but we seldom have a day pass without visitors and it is impossible in a small house like this to isolate oneself, and besides one fire has to do for all and that I think is the greatest hardship.

I am hard at work on the black & whites just now; they must be in at the end of the month. I feel fagged out my brain wont work and I am going to be very selfish and go out to Miss Jeanny at Puketeraki for 3 days. I am going in self-defence, for I am feeling so wretchedly seedy that I think a few days change is the only thing that will do me good. Bert has promised to do all he can for Mother and stay in every night, and the work wont be very much for two persons. We will get safely over the washing day (tomorrow) and I will go out on Wednesday and be home again by Saturday. All the neighbors have promised to look after Mother so I dont think she will be very lonely. . . .

We have been thinking and worrying a great deal about Frank since you wrote. Do for Mother's sake tell us everything you hear about him. She can not induce him to write to her tho' she has written and sent him paper and stamps. It is most distressing to think he has gone back to his old morbid ways. . . .

I must close now dear Sis it is late and I am writing on my knees before the fire. . . . Be sure and tell me what *your picture was like,* and about the Exhibition generally, especially Mrs. McIndoe she is very "hors de combat" at present which however didnt prevent her writing to ask Dr. Scott to come out and criticise her work before she sent it to Wllgton. Needless to say he didnt go. She has not made the most favorable impression here among the artists.

FH visited Willie in Invercargill in January. The Estuary, *one of her rare early landscapes, was painted at that time. Mrs Hodgkins was staying with Isabel whose fourth child and second son had been born on 3 January 1899.*

[1] After several years away from painting Isabel exhibited with the New Zealand Academy of Fine Arts 1898-1904. She had always intended to resume her painting career 'a year or two' after her marriage (Letter to Will Field, August 1892), but her duties as wife and mother absorbed her and her work did not develop. She ultimately gave up all thought of being a serious artist, while continuing to paint attractive watercolours that sold readily.

[2] The Governor's wife.

[3] FH sent six works to the Academy of Fine Arts exhibition that opened on 30 July 1898.

[46] To Isabel Field, 12 February 1899

Castle Street. Sunday afternoon

My dearest Sis

. . . . I have some dreadfully sad news for you if you have not already heard it. Poor Mrs. Scott is dead, it has all been so sudden I feel shocked and stunned and I can hardly realise it all. . . . [She] died at 7 o'clock on Friday evening a year and a day after poor Father. . . . I can't get her out of my mind and I feel quite unerved for my work, dear gentle creature, how we will all miss her. I went up there this morning and Dr. Scott seemed glad to see me. I think it was a relief for him to talk to me. He was quite cheerful and calm you would hardly expect him to be anything else, but you can see how deeply he feels it all. We went up to see her and he broke down for a minute, poor lonely man, he said "We were all so happy at Christmas, Fanny". She was so changed I hardly knew her. . . . Dr. Scott said sadly "I shouldn't complain Fanny: we have had many happy years together and I was luckier than most men." The children are a great comfort to him. I am going up again tomorrow . . . . Dr. Scott said he had missed Father so much in this trouble, and he kept referring to the fact of our trouble & his falling at the same time. It is such a comfort to think of those three weeks I spent with them [at Christmas], they were very happy ones and I shall never forget them. I feel quite brokenhearted about it all and I know what a shock it will be to you and Mother. I have lost a very good friend and I realise now how fond I was of her and what a blank it will make in my life. . . . I cannot write any more just now dear Sis but I will write again in a day or two.

With dearest love
Yours lovingly,
Fanny.

[47] To Isabel Field, 28 April 1899

Castle Street. 28th. April

My dearest Sis

. . . . Today *is* my birthday (I don't mean it as a hint) and I am 30. I found Bert clearing a space on the shelf for me this morning, but I don't feel so much on the shelf now as I did 10 years ago. Dr. Scott came down this afternoon to look at the portrait I am doing of Mrs. Scott, he was pleased with it and seemed to think it a good likeness. . . . He came and approved of my studio one day.[4] I left the sign writer emblazoning my noble name on the windows today. I crossed the road to see how it looked but it didnt seem to alter the look of the street in any way or

---

[4] FH set up a teaching studio on a first floor premises in George Street in the heart of the city.

collect a crowd, but what did collect a crowd last week was poor Egeria[5] with her naked back in full view of the street. The smaller boys used to gather and hoot at her, as I found out later, and it was a splendid if somewhat immodest ad. for me. Mr Dunne[6] at last asked me to remove Egeria to a less public place, and today Dr. Scott asked Mother to tell me to be sure and take her out of the window so he has evidently seen her too, in fact, I have heard on all sides of the nood hussy mid nodings on to be seen at my window. I now understand why the top deckers used to grin as they passed, the very horses seemed to smile. I am very busy, my last advertisements bringing in quite a number of pupils. I have been promoted to a seat on the O[tago] A[rt] S[ociety]'s Council. . . .

[48] To Isabel Field, c.4 June 1899

Castle St. Sunday Evening

My dearest Sis

We were so sorry to hear you have had such a sick house but hope by this time that you are all well again . . . . We have all been well but are feeling the cold horribly, it is such a wretchedly damp little place and it is a marvel we have all been so well. Willie[7] is agitating a move, he finds it rather comfortless and inconvenient. Willie's return to the bosom of his family is not altogether an unmixed blessing . . . . as we three were very happy together before he came, his was rather a disturbing influence. . . . It is a mistake for a man to come home to live I think after being away so long. I find I have to give up little luxuries like flying round in the morning in nondescript garments. I find it upsets Willie to meet me in anything less than a dressing gown, and I find also that I am generally the odd man out in the fireside scenes, two arm chairs will not accomodate three people. I suppose giving up your pet chair ought to have a chastening effect, but I am afraid I don't feel particularly amiable.

. . . . Mr. Hanson has been and gone, and I feel I have benefited much by seeing his work.[8] He wrote from Chch. to say he was coming and duly turned up at the Studio and I have seen a good deal of him on and off during his stay. Personally of course, I thought him rather a rough diamond but still a man who paints like he does couldn't help but be interesting. . . . I think he has succeeded in teaching me what "quality" means, he complained that my work lacked it altogether and certainly as shown by him it was an unknown quantity to me entirely. However

[5] A partially draped Greek statue owned by the family.
[6] Mr Dunne occupied the shop below.
[7] Willie was now accountant in the Bank of New South Wales in Dunedin, joining the household at Castle Street.
[8] Albert J. Hanson (1866-1914), a Sydney artist, was on a sketching tour of New Zealand, one of several visits during the 1890s. He had exhibited at the Royal Academy in 1893 and settled in Dunedin from 1899 to about 1905, exhibiting and teaching.

he said if I gave him a Maori Head he would show me how to get quality and he promptly did. He gave me an afternoon's lesson and he used to drop in after Classes and put me up to many cunning little dodges. "Quality" it seems can only be got by rubbing, scrubbing, scratching, sandpapering and otherwise ruining the surface of your paper. Anything like direct straightforward brush work doesn't appeal to him. He wanted to take some of my sketches over to Sydney with him, but I prefer to send something good over for the Exhibition if I can get something done in time. He did not sell well here at all, 3 small things one of which Dr. Scott bought. I daresay you remember it the "East Gleam" sunset effects and horses. His Mt. Cook & Wakatipu sketches were very fine. I wish you could have seen them. He tinkered up one of my pictures for me and it now has a fine Hawaiian effect. He left me some nice paper and all my spare time I employ scrubbing & scratching with the awful result that I have lost all my crispness and freshness and as yet not a sign of "quality"! Even Dr. Scott is on the warpath after "quality"! and he flattered himself he has got it into one of his pictures he has just finished.

Willie has come in and is fussing for the ink, so I had better stop this scrawl. Mother and I have decided to come up to you for Xmas if you will have us, she says she will look after the house for you while we take the children out to the farm.[9]

My hands are simply frozen and I can hardly hold my pen for chilblains so goodbye for the present with much love to yourself, Will and the children.

Yours ever lovingly
Fanny.

Does Will know a young Mr. Fildes, he comes from Wellington and is a nephew of Luke Fildes. He comes to me for drawing and is very clever. He has studied under Mr. Nairn.

Mrs. McIndoe has started taking pupils. I wonder what she got married for. I should have thought she had had enough of that kind of thing. She is a perfect demon for work and gets through a tremendous amount. I like her! she is so practical and energetic, if a trifle vulgar! I don't know whether I told you I sold a picture in Chch at the Exhibition, sales are few and far between nowadays and I would starve if I depended on them.

[49] To Isabel Field, c.1 July 1899

Castle St. Sunday.

My dearest Sis

What on earth has happened to you all that you havent written to us for such an age. . . .

---

[9] Will Field was farming his land at Waikanae.

Since last I wrote you I have had a lot of worry & trouble over my studio. I got a few hours notice to turn out, a regular Irish eviction. I got legal advice but it was no good. I had to go, being illegally on the premises I could not claim a week's notice. It was a complication of sub-leases. Dunne had no power to sublet the room to me . . . .

Before resuming classes on 1 October at a new studio in George Street, this time over a jewellers shop, FH spent time at the Maori settlement at Moeraki, on the coast north of Dunedin.

The period between 1870 and 1900 was the lowest point in the history of Maori-European contact when the Maori seemed destined to die out. In the South Island they lived in poor coastal settlements, largely ignored by Pakeha society. FH found models for her studies of Maori women and children in the villages at Moeraki and Puketeraki, seeing them with eyes attuned to the picturesque values of exotic subject matter. The paintings appealed to European taste and sold well. Her work is different from that of other artists who painted the Maori at this time. Charles Frederick Goldie expressed in his work the compassion and nostalgia evoked by the apparently inevitable decline of the Maori, while Gottfried Lindauer sought to document a way of life that was already a thing of the past. Louis John Steele used Maori subject matter in an attempt to create a tradition of historical painting in the colony. All three included details of ethnic interest. FH painted attractive young Maori women in European dress, occasionally posed against a background of work. All her interest focused on the face and attitude and there is an appealing informality and liveliness in her treatment, as well as keen observation of skin tone and features. As in much of FH's figure work at this time there is also an element of sentimentality.

[50] To Rachel Hodgkins, 18 September 1899

Moeraki. Monday morning

My dearest Mother,

I have left Effie [Spence] toasting scones for a very belated breakfast and I am sending you a few lines to let you know how we are jogging along. . . . She couldn't have come at a better time to see the Maoris, the old Chief died on Tuesday and they have been holding a tangi ever since over at the Kaik.[10] We go over there every day, fleas notwithstanding. They have already eaten about £100 worth of food, and if they can find the old chiefs money which he buried somewhere in his back-yard they will prolong the festivities till all is blue, chief

---

[10] Kaik, the present name of the settlement near Moeraki, is derived from the South Island Maori word *kaika*, an unfortified village.

included. They are the filthiest lot and I am disgusted, tho none the less interested. They have hired the hall over at the Kaik and covered the floor with straw, and there they squat and eat and sing and you could dance a jig on the smell. The old chief lies in state at the head of the room, partly covered with a cheap counterpane, partly with [a] Maori mat a truly incongruous covering and with his photo in a cheap Oxford frame hanging over his head against a colored glass window, it is a most inartistic and conventional setting for the old warrior. I persuaded Mrs. Hosking to venture in and take a photo of it: what made it more impressive was the squatting figure of an old woman beside the coffin, the very personification of broken hearted grief – she has sat there all thro I believe a silent dignified figure. The Maoris have come from all parts and I have renewed acquaintance with a lot of old models, they are mostly a rather degenerate lot I think but still hugely interesting from an artistic point of view. Saturday we had an adventure which might have been a serious one. Effie and I had borrowed a baby and we had taken it a little distance from the pah and with a little girl to hold it I was painting it. I happened to look up and I saw some men herding a number of cows into a corner of a field without a fence between them and us, next minute a shot rang out then another and before I could realise what had happened a cow covered in blood came tearing towards us with all the others in full cry after it. I was conscious of a wild uproar from the Maoris and somehow Effie and I got under the barbed fence nearest us, quite forgetting the baby, and when I looked round I saw it rolled up on the wrong side of the fence and the little girl crying on the right. I am glad to think now I got over my cowardice sufficiently to go back for it, and somehow between us we got it further up the hill and when we unrolled the blanket we found the poor little thing upside down and perfectly breathless. We looked round once and we saw the cow with its head between the wires and finding it couldnt get through, it tore up the road with the other cows after it. The Maoris came and took the baby back and Effie & I made our way home cautiously along the beach. When we got to the top of the hill we heard five more reports and they told us the next day they had shot it seven times and eventually had to rope it to a fence and put an end to it there.   For inhuman brutality I never heard anything to equal it, and the next day when I went over boiling with rage they simply laughed at us and I might have saved myself the trouble. This is quite a true story and Effie is prepared to swear to it. The weather still holds good, yesterday it blew a good deal but it is gloriously fine today and we are going to take our lunch over to the Kaik and sketch Maoris. Effie said you were looking very well, we both wish you were out here with us, but never mind we will have some good days together with Sis in the Summer. . . .

[51] To Isabel Field, c.1 October 1899

Castle St. Sunday.

Dearest Sis

I was so distressed when I got home last night to hear you have been so unwell, poor old girl I felt so selfish enjoying myself out at Moeraki when you were in bed and much more in need of a change than I was. Mother says she has written to ask you to come down to us for a month she thinks it is [a] sea trip and a rest from the children that you want more than anything. . . . I know the great difficulty is leaving the Chicks, but think it over and try and make some arrangement that would leave you free to get away. . . . I can't bear to think of your suffering in the way you do and getting gradually more run down. . . . I wish you could have been with me out at Moeraki. I saw heaps of things that would have suited your brush. I hope you are proud of yourself, you certainly have wiped everyone's eye this time and no mistake. It must have been a genuine inspiration that made you do so well and we were all very proud of you. Mr. Walsh[11] said no one could equal you for broad clean washes and he said that Mr. Gouldsmith had once said if you had gone home you would have made a sensation. However you have compensation haven't you and you must allow me to make the sensation instead! only fair. . . . Poor Mrs. McIndoe came in one day nearly crying and read me a letter from Dr. Fyffe with the cruellest slashing in it she had ever received. Of course he meant it kindly but it hurt nevertheless. It is not in human nature to suppose I was very sorry for she has been cock of the walk so long and it was lovely to think how you walked in without an effort and scooped the pool. He condemned her work all through as trashy and feeble – was it so bad?

Naturaly we are very upset at the news about Frank, and I am glad that I am home again to be with Mother. Where can the poor boy have got to, if he will not stay with Percy what is to become of him . . . . it is so heart breaking just when everything seemed to be improving and he was writing so cheerfully and more sensibly. . . .

[52] To Isabel Field, 24 October 1899

[Castle St] Tuesday Evening

My dearest Sis

You are much too good and generous. I dont know how to thank you for the lovely dress you have sent me. . . . Mother is delighted with her dress and it is just what she wanted too, in fact we were both getting rather shabby, and were going

[11] Alfred Wilson Walsh (1859-1916) was born in Australia and went to Dunedin as a child. He was a fine watercolour artist and taught at the Canterbury School of Art from 1886 to 1910.

to get a new rig out for Wellington. We have all fallen in love with Baba, she is the sweetest pet and certainly a much more tractable child than Girlie, tho I was very fond of Girlie and her odd little ways. It is so nice to see Baba's dear little face when I come home at night, and she is a godsend to Mother and you couldn't have sent her down at a more opportune time. . . . She recited for us tonight and Bert and I are teaching her some new things she is letter perfect in all her recitations but her prayers want a good deal of prompting. . . .

It is good news to hear you are sending some pictures down.[12] It was announced the other night at the council meeting that you were going to exhibit and much pleasure was expressed. Lulu Roberts came in today to tell me she had seen some of your work somewhere & that it was "just lovely". I wish I could say the same of mine. I find 30 odd pupils as much as I can manage comfortably without killing myself over painting – that I hope will come. . . .

[Postscript] Shall I bring my bicycle up with me. . . .

[53] To Isabel Field, c.12 November 1899

[Castle St] Sunday.

Dearest Sis

Your pictures are splendid! and I am glad to be able to tell you that one is sold. . . . It is simply wonderful to me how much you have improved . . . you must have been storing it all up and the result is beyond all expectations. I was prepared to be critical but I must confess I could only admire when I saw them. Of course Tranquill Waters is the best and after that a "Bush Track" which is quite majestic in its simplicity and solitude. The "Hutt Road" strikes me as being a little out of proportion and in need of a little more work. They are wonderfully rich in coloring and the skies atmospheric. . . . We are all very proud of you! Personally, what I feel now about your work is that you want to do more work direct from nature; that added to the strong poetic feeling which you put into your pictures ought to make a combination that very few of us can hope to attain to. . . . My work is . . . mostly the rough Maori sketches I got out at Moeraki. I had no time to do anything with them. The Sydney work is splendid. I like Cofley's[13] Maori things tremendously and they suggest new treatment. . . .

FH and her mother spent the Christmas of 1899 in Wellington, in Isabel's new house on The Terrace. FH sketched the Maori at Otaki and visited the artists' colony centred on James Nairn's Pumpkin Cottage at Silverstream. She helped canvass for Will Field

---

[12] For the 23rd annual exhibition of the Otago Art Society.
[13] The Australian artist Alfred Coffey (1869-1950).

who was elected in 1900 to represent Otaki for Richard Seddon's Liberal Party, beginning a thirty-two year parliamentary career. While her mother prolonged her stay in Wellington, FH returned to Dunedin and prepared to move the family into the accommodation above the Bank of New South Wales. In a February letter FH mentioned Willie's engagement to Jean Dalgliesh. Bertie had joined Percy on his farm.

[54] To Rachel Hodgkins, 30 March 1900

Castle St. Friday.

My dearest Mother

Your welcome letter arrived today. You must not think of coming home till after we have moved in. It will be quite a simple matter. . . . the Bank is in such perfect order there wont be much cleaning to do. If we have no garden we will have compensations in the way of hot water and cupboards galore and I think we will manage to spend a very comfy winter there. . . .

Couldn't you take a run up to see the boys before you come home. I enclose a £1, for I know your pocket money must be running short. . . .

Mr. Hanson has settled into a big studio which he has taken for a year. He is going over to Sydney to get his goods and chattells then he will settle here indefinitely. . . . I met Mrs. Hooper the other day, I was on my bicycle and I got off and affably asked her how she had enjoyed her trip. She drew herself up haughtily and said "Before I can answer any questions Fanny, – when is your Mother coming to see me!" I said that you would be charmed to go and see her were you at home: – then she melted and said – "That of course quite alters the case, thank you! I enjoyed my trip home very much". . . .

We had a tremendous day on Saturday[14]. . . We began the day very early and watched the procession pass from the P.O. Buildings then we made a dash for a train and with great difficulty got [a] foothold on one. When we arrived at Port [Chalmers] we retired to the only quiet place we could find and eat our lunch on a drainpipe at the side of the road and after we had fortified ourselves with buns and unripe pears, we took up our position in a cattle truck on the wharf and sat there from 2.30 till 5 o'clock, and all we saw in that time were more or less excited roughriders rolling down to the Monawai followed by troups of girls, some of the men were boisterously kissing every girl they could reach. It was a most disenchanting scene and after the well managed Wllgtn departure it was a very poor show. . . . One of Willie's Invercargill friends in the 5th. Contingent was with us part of the time, poor fellow, he had been on duty all day on the wharf and he was very grateful for the remains of our lunch, and we filled his nose-bag, or whatever you call that white thing they wear with cake and fruit. . . .

[14] On Saturday 24 March 1900 the Fourth Contingent of New Zealand soldiers departed for the South African War on board the *Monowai* from Port Chalmers.

[Postscript] Mr. Hanson hasn't sold a single picture but he has a night class with 10 pupils. There are two rivals in the field in the shape of an artist from Home a Miss Eller-beck who has taken my old room at Dunne's and an Australian girl who also is teaching. I havent written to Bert yet, but I send him all the papers I can muster. . . .

[55] To Isabel Field, c.6 May 1900

[Bank of New South Wales]

My dearest Sis

I am indeed glad to hear you are thinking of paying us a visit. I shall love to have you and I think you will be very comfortable at the Bank. . . . While you are here I think it would be a very good thing to try a course of massage, there is a splendid woman here a Mrs. Booth who simply works wonders where nervous pains and aches are concerned. . . .

. . . . Mr. Tom Roberts the Sydney artist has been in Dunedin for this last week and I had the honor of his company on several occasions at the studio.[15] He greeted me as a brother brush which was flattering. He went home via Melbourne, otherwise I would have given him a letter to you. I have been doing a great deal more gadding this week than is good for me and wound up on Sat night by standing at Jacob's corner and collecting for the [Indian] Famine Fund with Mrs. Butterworth – caught a chill and feel anything but bright today. . . .

[56] To Isabel Field, c.31 October 1900

B.N.S.W. Wed. afternoon

My dearest Sis

We have just received Will's telegram and are so sorry to hear that poor little Jack has been so unwell, but hope the poor wee chap is better now. I am afraid you have had a very anxious and worrying time and I wish I could spare Mother to you for a month or two, but I feel if she leaves me now that I will not feel equal to getting my Art Union together. As it is I feel so thoroughly worn out with the

---

[15] Thomas William Roberts (1856-1931) was a leading Australian artist who had studied in London and travelled on the continent. In 1885 he had returned to Australia with some knowledge of impressionism. Called by Arthur Streeton 'the father of Australian landscape', he was the leading figure among the Heidelberg School painters, whose landmark '9 x 5 Exhibition of Impressions' in Melbourne in 1889 had presented to the Australian public a series of small oil paintings mostly done on cigar-box lids. Roberts was also a portrait-painter and well known for his ambitious figure paintings like *Shearing the Rams* (1890), enshrining the heroic myths of the pioneering days. A studio visit from an artist of his stature is an indication of the level of professionalism FH had reached before she left New Zealand. It is interesting to note too the degree of cultural interchange between New Zealand and Australia.

long strain of teaching & painting that it takes me all my pluck to start painting again for it, and if it is to come off at all it must be ready by Dec – and if you only knew how out of conceit I am with my own work you would realise what an effort it requires to produce any more of it. I wish you were getting your strength back a little faster, it is very weakening and depressing lying in bed. . . . It may cheer you up to know that your pictures are much admired by the powers that be, Mr. Hanson included – and we are all very sorry there are so few of them – not much fear of me getting them for my Art Union. They are sure to go. We finished the hanging this morning and I am going back presently to help Dr. Scott with the catalogue. The show is a very fair one Mr. Worsley[16] & Hanson being the biggest & most important exhibitors. Mr. H. was on the hanging committee this year and was quite useless except for finding excellent places for his own pictures – no one could accuse him of being unselfish – I can't say I think you improved my picture by touching it up. I think it is a mistake for one artist to touch another's work. You wouldn't have liked me to turn those little white blobs on your water into ducks. . . .

[57] TO ISABEL FIELD, c.9 DECEMBER 1900

[Bank of New South Wales] Monday morning

My dearest Sis

I simply don't know how to thank you for the pictures, you have been far too generous and I don't know how I shall ever repay you for all your kindness. I had felt so very despairing about my Art Union but now your pictures have given me pluck to carry it through. I shall frame the large picture handsomely and make it a £15 prize. . . . I do hope by this time Frank has left you and that your domestic arrangements are more settled. . . .

On 6 February 1901 the long preparation was over. FH embarked on the Moana *at Dunedin for the first stage of the journey to Europe. She was sharing a cabin with Mrs Turton, a Dunedin acquaintance. The first port of call was Christchurch, where she visited the Carrick household.*

---

[16] C. N. Worsley, RBA, d.1923, a professional watercolourist who arrived in New Zealand c.1898 and exhibited with the art societies.

[58] TO RACHEL HODGKINS, 8 FEBRUARY 1901

[Christchurch] Friday morning, 11.30.

My darling Mother

Here I am at Park Terrace, having come up by the 9.30 train after a record trip, the sea was like glass and I had two good meals out of the Company. The Troops are here and the town is in a turmoil. . . . I felt very sad at saying goodbye to you, darling, but the year will soon slip by and I will be back again with you before you have time to miss me. I hope Mrs. Bartleman went home with you and that you had a cosy dinner together. Mrs. Turton and I retired early both feeling very sad, but neither of us slept much, our cabin is just over the screw and next to the steward's pantry, and there was much "sound of crockery by night". I expect we will get used to the ship's noises before long. . . . I do hope Willie's cold is better. I felt so worried leaving him looking so seedy . . . .

Goodbye, darling, I shall write again from Wllgton . . . .

[59] TO RACHEL HODGKINS, 9 FEBRUARY 1901

The Terrace [Wellington]

My darling Mother

Just another short line to report myself. I arrived here at 8.30 this morning after a record trip of 12 hours. . . . We sail at 8.30 so will have a good long day with Sis. I found her looking very well but quite toothless and on enquiring after the missing molars she said she always kept them in her jewel case and never wore them. . . . She had a cosy breakfast waiting for me when I arrived and has been so good to me and would give her head away, she is so generous.

afternoon.

. . . . I am rather dreading going to sea tonight and feel very shaky breaking my last tie with N.Z. It is blowing a pretty stiff breeze and I expect we shall get a good old rolling tonight. I cant help feeling a little sad and I am so glad I have dear old Sis to say goodbye to me. I am wondering how you and Willie are getting on without me. Is Willie's cold better, send me a line to Melbourne to cheer me up and tell me how you both are. Goodbye darling God bless you and take great care of yourself till I come out again. Sis is looking forward to having you with her and I shall feel much happier when you are with her tho' I know how good Willie will be to you. Goodbye your loving Fanny. . . .

PART THREE

1901

The Voyage Out

[60] To Rachel Hodgkins, 12 February 1901

S.S. Moana. Tuesday.

My darling Mother

Just a short line to post to you directly we land to tell you we have had a glorious passage and I have proved myself a first rate sailor. It has been a record run so the Captain says, and we will be in Sydney by nine tomorrow morning. . . .

While waiting to board the Arcadia *in Sydney FH stayed with her mother's cousin, Lydia Rolin. Formerly Lydia Bowker, she had visited her New Zealand relatives in about 1886, when FH sketched her profile in pencil, one of the earliest portraits to survive. Something of a 'society beauty', Lydia was now married to a wealthy lawyer.*

[61] To Isabel Field, 15 February 1901

Turramurra [Sydney]. Friday evening.

My dearest Sis,

Lydia has a perfectly insane habit of retiring to bed at eight o'clock so here I am enveloped in a mosquito net with my brand-new blotter and my brand new pen writing to you. I no sooner commence an interesting conversation with Mr. Rolin than Lydia suggests bed which to me is a perfect nightmare as I am nearly eaten alive . . . . Lydia . . . gets deadly bored when she is not talking herself. It seems such ages since I said good bye to you in Wellington . . . . I found Lydia waiting for me and after a lot of fuss and bother over my luggage finally got it stored in the P&O shed where it will wait till the 'Arcadia' is ready to receive it. I took the precaution to insure it. I have already lost my deck chair, it must have been stolen for I saw it safely on board at Lyttleton and on looking for [it] after we left Wllgtn it was nowhere to be seen. . . . [Mrs. Turton and I] have both developed that furrowed and anxious look that marks lone females looking after their own luggage. . . . [Today] we went to the Soc. of Artists show in Pitt St with a few exceptions was much disappointed especially with Tom Roberts' work. Lambert is quite the coming man, his work is wonderfully strong and virile. "The Black Soil Country" is magnificent[1] I havent seen any local work I like as well as Mr. Hanson's. Sid Long and J. Ashton[2] one would tire of very quickly. After an

[1] George Lambert (1873-1930) painted *Across the Black Soil Plains* in 1899. It was a large picture, three by ten feet, dignifying the pastoral subject of a team of horses dragging a load of wool bales. Lambert had left Australia in 1900 to study in Europe and returned in the 1920s.
[2] Sydney Long (1871-1955) is remembered for his symbolist paintings in the art nouveau idiom. Julian Ashton (1851-1942) was an early advocate of plein air painting and founded the Julian Ashton School of Painting of which Lambert was a student.

hour in the gallery we had another meal, this time at the A.B.C., beastly, and then bought some grapes (2d. a lb) and eat them in the Domain then went to the National Gallery and had a hurried glimpse at all the pictures. I am going again on Monday and by myself – fatal to go with anyone not interested. . . . I like Mr. Rolin, he amuses me with his excessive politeness of which he seems to have got a perfect disease. He should have been a family doctor his manner is so very soothing. Lydia is much the same except for an extraordinary click which she winds up all her sentences with. She is very sweet to me. . . . [Her] children are not beauties by any means, their old little faces with their huge blots of eyes are decidedly uncanny. . . . The streets are a constant marvel to me, the way the traffic is managed is wonderful. I am much impressed with the beauty of everything and am enjoying everything tremendously. I hope dear old Mother is well, be sure and write me a line to Melbourne. I am longing for news of you all. . . .

[62] To Rachel Hodgkins, 21 February 1901

R.M.S. Arcadia. Thursday morning.

My darling Mother,

I hope Sis posted you my letter written from Sydney. I thought it best to wait till I was comfortably settled on board before writing again. . . . We are now half way between Sydney & Hobart spanking along with a good stiff breeze behind us. . . . So far our voyage promises to be a very dreary one, the passengers are 2nd. class in every sense of the word. . . . Our cabin is small . . . and the washing arrangements primitive in the extreme, and cockroaches & fleas hop about gaily. I am bitten badly and am a most unlovely object, last night I peppered everything with insect powder and managed to ward off night attacks. . . . I saw a good deal of Mr. Roberts while in Sydney, he was most awfully good to me and showed me round. I had a kind note from his wife asking me to stay with them but of course it was out of the question. He got me a ticket for the conversazione at the Society of Artists and introduced me to all the artists, introducing me to the men as the cleverest girl in Australia, and to the women as the "best artist in N.Z." – modifying it slightly to suit the sex – naturally they all looked skeptical and I felt rather a fool – but it was all very jolly and they made it very nice for me. It sounds horribly conceited repeating this twaddle but it is the last chance I shall have of suffering from swelled head. The further I get from NZ and the nearer I get to England the more & more humble I feel. So far the women artists in Australia are not up to much. . . . Tell Dr. Scott when you see him that Mr. Sid Long is going to Dunedin next month to try his luck. I persuaded him that there was a big opening for him now that Mr. Hanson is laid aside. He is an ugly little man with a Phil May face but tremendously clever. I met Mr. Ashton, Souter, and a host of sister brushes, they all seem a poverty stricken lot & would hardly believe I had made enough by my brush to go Home. . . . Mr. Rich[3] & Mr. Rolin gave us a lunch at the Australia the day before I left it was very swagger . . . . Betha has such a pretty home far prettier than Lydia's, her husband is a dear little man and very jolly. Mr. Rolin is the soul of propriety and would suit Willie down to the ground. He keeps Lydia in check and is most particular what she does and whom she knows. . . . Goodbye darling, take care of your dear self, and be sure and tell me always exactly what you are doing and how you feel. . . . I hope Willie has not had much bother with my Art Union. I hope to hear of its successful conclusion. I feel a wretch leaving you all to do my dirty work. I feel the most heartfelt gratitude for all you dear people have done for me. . . .

[Postscript] Mr. Roberts came down to see me off and brought me a budget to [call] out to artists all along the line so I am in well. . . .

In Melbourne FH met her father's sister Jane Brotherton and her daughter Winnie.

[63] TO RACHEL HODGKINS, 27 FEBRUARY 1901

R.M.S. Arcadia. 27.2.1901

My darling Mother,

There was no time to write from Melbourne, so I am writing you a few lines now to post in Adelaide. The boat is rolling so it is hard to keep one's writing materials together. . . . We reached Melbourne on Monday morning at day break . . . . We had only till noon the next day so I wanted to see as much as possible. . . . The [National] gallery itself is a far finer one than the Sydney one, but the collection of pictures not nearly so good, tho there are some very fine examples of British art. There is some fine statuary, a bronze figure of Circe by McKennal[4] is a masterly thing, it is a full length figure of a woman, upright on tiptoe with outstretched hands drawing everything towards her with such compelling vampire-like force that it was almost too strong to look at. He is a young Australian who has now attained quite a European reputation. He has other work, mostly marbles and they are all fine. Amy then took me to Mr. McCubbins[5] studio I had a letter to him, but he was out so did not see him. By this time I felt more like sitting down & howling with sheer tiredness and heat & grime. It was a dust storm of the very dustiest, and it had got into my eyes and I was quite miserable

---

[3] George Edward Rich (1863-1956) was married to Betha, a cousin of Rachel Hodgkins. He was appointed a Justice of the High Court of Australia in 1913 and knighted in 1932.

[4] Bertram Mackennal RA (1863-1931) spent most of his life from 1882 in Europe, exhibiting at the Royal Academy and the Paris Salon. He returned to Australia for three years, 1899-1901.

[5] Frederick McCubbin (1855-1917), one of the Heidelberg School painters, was dedicated to the development of a national art and spent all his life in Australia apart from a visit to England in 1906.

with the pain in them, so we made for the railway station and fortified ourselves with a lemon squash and were sitting waiting for our train when a quaint looking oldfashioned girl in an unmistakeably homemade dress stopped in front of me and said "I know you are Fanny, I'm Winnie." She said she recognized the family jaw and my P.&O labels confirmed her suspicions. She took me to see Aunt Jane who is staying with old friends in Auburn (very worthy but decidedly common-place people) and I straight way fell in love with Aunt Jane. She is such a dear courteous old lady, and when she said "Welcome my love" I felt proud to think I was her neice tears were never very far from her eyes and she evidently lives a great deal in the past and she enjoys to its fullest the luxury of grief. She reminds me of one of the dear old ladies in "Cranford" quite of the old school who is yet quite in sympathy with the girls of today. She thought me very like Father, but I could see not the slightest trace of a resemblance in her to him. . . . We went up to the cemetery to see the famous Springthorpe monument which has just been erected. It is by McKennal and he has just brought it out from Home & supervised its erection. It is a magnificent piece of statuary under a canopy of blood red leaded glass supported by granite pillars. The figure is recumbent and a protecting guardian angel hovers above while the living figure of grief crouches beside the dead, the difference between the dead, living and the spiritual figures being wonderfully suggested.

Winnie is a delightful girl and I should like to have her as a travelling companion she is a trifle oldfashioned and prim but there is such a sweetness and sincerity about her that one can't help liking her. She is pretty too in her way, but dresses badly, with a fine disregard to stays and pointed toes. She has all her Brotherton brains and gift of expression and she made me feel a very ignorant and ill-educated person. . . . Thanks for enclosing Mr. Roberts' letter I quite agree with Willie he is a bounder but for all that he has been of very great assistance to me and Willie mustn't forget that I have my way to make and also that I am more than capable of looking after myself and that I hope I never lose my dignity. My Sydney & Melbourne friends think me so very lucky to have been befriended by Mr. Roberts, but for him I should not have seen half as much as I have seen. Thank Willie for his letter. I am glad to hear Excelsiors are on the rise, you may yet make your fortune.

. . . . We are pleased with everything except the company which still continues hopelessly impossible. I fancy most of them are bound for Freemantle, the men in search of nuggets and the girls of husbands – Freemantle being a happy hunting ground for both. . . . I must go for a walk on deck it has been an intolerably long day made longer by putting the clocks back and I feel much brighter now I have had a chat with you. I shall never feel that we are really off till we leave Australia. . . .

[64] To Rachel Hodgkins, 3 March 1901

R.M.S. Arcadia, off Cape Darwin. 3.3.1901

My darling Mother,

. . . . We had two hours in Adelaide and two very hot and thirsty hours they were. We caught an early train to town and . . . . wearily made for the Nat. Gallery. All my fatigue vanished when I saw the pictures . . . . they have a splendid collection, a Rossetti made my heart beat and I positively ached with pleasure when I found myself in front of some of the more modern pictures. Byam Shaw, La Thangue and Brangwyn, all old Academy note[s] friends and it was joy indeed to meet them in the flesh.[6] We ran ourselves short of time & had to fly for our train . . . . Adelaide is a good place to turn one's back on and once seen I never want to see it again. . . .

[65] To Rachel Hodgkins, 11 March 1901

R.M.S Arcadia, The Equator. 11.3.1901

My darling Mother,

We are now two days sail from Colombo and today are crossing the line so you can imagine the temperature. . . . I shall be glad when we reach Colombo, *more glad* when we reach Marseilles and *most* glad when we reach London. I find shipboard life most irksome and am wearying to get to work. . . .

. . . . Our Equatorial menu today is worth recording, pea soup, boiled mutton and plum pudding, with ices in semi liquified form. . . .

We spent a long and very hot day in Perth . . . [we] journeyed up to town thro a tract of the most barren dusty infertile looking country that it has ever been my ill luck to traverse. I was hot & thirsty and could see no beauty in anything and the Swan river they are so proud of I thought a wretched little dried up ditch – the want of vegetation is almost painful to N.Z. eyes. When we reached Perth we were astonished to find such a pretty well laid out town, with fine buildings and a most up to date electric tram service. . . . There is no doubt about its prosperity and now that Freemantle harbor is finished and the big boats call there they prophecy a big future for it.

I have now reached the stage when I am holding blotting paper under my chin. Oh the heat! I have quite changed my mind about living in a hot climate and would give worlds for a cool southerly wind from Dunedin.

14.3.1901. I am finishing this in the train returning from Kandy. The last two

[6] The paintings were: *The Comforter* by James Byam Shaw (1872-1919), *Harrowing* by H. H. La Thangue (1859-1929), *Harpooning a Whale* by Frank Brangwyn (1867-1956). The Rossetti (1828-82) was probably the gouache, *The Loving Cup.*

days I have been suffering from an attack of cholera brought on by the heat and the ship's water. . . .

FH's illness lasted for twelve days. It seems to have been a combination of severe diarrhoea and the dyspepsia that was to trouble her intermittently until she underwent surgery in 1941. The following letter was shakily written in pencil.

[66] To Rachel Hodgkins, 24 March 1901

Sunday, off Suez

My darling Mother

Mrs. Turton is writing you to let you know how I am. I am really on the mend now tho' still very weak. I am still in bed but they promise me I am to get up tomorrow to see the canal. They are all so good to me . . . . Oh how I wish I was home with you all. I am so homesick but I am better so I mustn't grumble. It has been bad luck. I wonder if I shall ever feel like work again? Goodbye dear, don't worry shall write from Pt. Said

Your loving Fanny.

Those nightgowns have been a boon and a blessing.

[67] To Rachel Hodgkins, 29 March 1901

Mediterranean, R.M.S. Arcadia. 29.3.1901.

My darling Mother,

. . . . Heigh ho! what a queer world this is, who would have thought I should have had such bad luck. I have had a wretched time and as long as I live I shall never forget that journey across from Colombo to Aden, and up the Red Sea. Fortunately for me the Dr. gave me a good deal of morphia to deaden the pain so I slept a great deal of the time. . . . I have consumed an amazing amount of stimulant and I was rather staggered to get in my bill today. I had to have brandy every hour and am still taking it. Everyone has been most awfully kind and I have been given as much claret and Port as will see me thro' to London. . . . They put me in a top berth coming thro the canal but it was unsatisfactory work seeing Egypt thro' the porthole. They carried me on deck for the first time 3 days ago just in time to see the straights of Messina and Stromboli. . . . Talk of the Sunny South! it is most bitterly cold and I cant pile on enough warm clothing. We have had very rough weather since we left Pt. Said and I have had to alter my ideas about the blueness and beauty of the Mediterranean. Our Pacific seas can claim much more cobalt. The peep we had of the Italian coast passing thro' the straights was very beautiful in spite of grey skys and at night we saw Stromboli with its red night cap flaming away, it was very weird and impressive. This is a very feeble little scrawl but you will understand it is all I can do to hold my pen. I shall be so glad to get to London, I have lost all my pluck and simply dread being left alone. . . . Mrs. Turton has written to Mrs. Spence to look after me so I shall be all right . . . . How I am wearying for a letter from you, are you taking care of yourself and not working too hard. I wonder if Willie and Jean will be married by the time this reaches you?

Goodbye darling little Mother with heaps of love to you both your loving, Fanny.

[68] To Rachel Hodgkins, 4 April 1901

R.M.S. Arcadia, Bay of Biscay. 4.4.1901

My darling Mother

. . . . We are due in London on Easter Sunday, three days from now, and tomorrow morning we reach Plymouth. I shall be heartily glad to reach my journeys end. . . . I had cheery letters of welcome . . . from the Spences and Ethel McLaren and a wildly excited one from Issy – dear old friends . . . . Effie was very busy doing up my room, putting up new curtains etc. . . . I am almost well again now . . . . I feel so thankful I was well enough to go ashore at Marseilles, I wouldn't have missed it for worlds. . . tho' I did collapse and return to bed for two days . . . Marseilles is the most beautiful old town imaginable. I thought I had never seen anything so picturesque as it looked as we approached it in the early morning under a sky of true mediterranean blue, blue-green water, white quays, colored craft of all nations and the red-tiled flat roofed houses. I began to understand the witchery an old continental town must have for artists. . . . Marseilles was out on strike and had been for the past month. The military had been called out and a few days previous to our arrival had fired on the rioters. Broken windows and sullen looking groups of workmen drinking outside the cafés were the only signs of any disturbance – otherwise the town was quite quiet . . . patrols of Cuirassiers gorgeously mounted and equipped rode up and down the streets and at the corners pickets of gendarmes and queer brigand like little soldiers slouched in most unmilitary attitudes. They may have inspired the Marseillaise with awe and respect but to us they looked for all the world like supers in a comic opera. We prowled round the streets mostly in the old quarter of town. I loved the steep, uneven, badly paved streets plentifully strewn with every kind of rubbish and the quaint, dingy, discolored buildings with emerald green latticed shutters and dark haired women hanging over the balconies and the orange stalls making vivid blots of color at the street corners. Some day I must go back to Marseilles and paint. . . .

UPPER LEFT: Rachel Hodgkins, née Parker, c.1875, Australian-born mother of Frances Hodgkins. Auckland City Art Gallery.
UPPER RIGHT: Frances Hodgkins, aged about twelve. Auckland City Art Gallery, photograph Burton Bros.
LOWER RIGHT: Isabel Field, née Hodgkins, in her early twenties. Auckland City Art Gallery.
LOWER LEFT: Rachel Hodgkins, c.1895. Alexander Turnbull Library.

ABOVE: Frances and her father, William Mathew Hodgkins, at Waira, Ravensbourne in 1888. Auckland City Art Gallery.
RIGHT: Frances Hodgkins shortly after the move to Cranmore Lodge in 1889. Hocken Library.

ABOVE: Cranmore Lodge, the rented home of the
Hodgkins family, 1889–97. Auckland City Art Gallery.
RIGHT: May Kenyon, 1890, friend, fellow artist and
occasional model. Photograph F. L. Jones.
BELOW: Frances in the drawing room at Cranmore
Lodge. Alexander Turnbull Library.

UPPER RIGHT: Frances and Will Field, taken at the time of his engagement to Isabel, February 1892. Alexander Turnbull Library.
LOWER RIGHT: W. M. Hodgkins at work in his study at Cranmore Lodge. Alexander Turnbull Library.
BELOW: Dr and Mrs John Halliday Scott at early breakfast. Hocken Library.

Walking in the hills, 1895. Frances is in the centre with folded hands, Rattray sisters to the left, Lily McLaren (partly obscured) below her. Alexander Turnbull Library. The younger brothers, Bert (left) and Percy, on their farm at Mangatainoka in the North Island, c.1901. Photograph W. Jeffery.

RIGHT: The Hodgkins
sisters in Wellington,
1901, before Frances's
departure for England.
Isabel was now the wife of
a Member of the House of
Representatives and
mother of four children.
BELOW: Dorothy Kate
Richmond (right) and her
sister, Ann Elizabeth
(Alla) Atkinson, Otaki,
1898. Courtesy of the
Atkinson family,
Wellington.

UPPER: Norman Garstin and members of his class on the way back from the Helston Furry Dance, May 1902. Maud Nickalls second from left, Rosamond Marshall with face obscured.
LOWER: Frances Hodgkins and Maud Nickalls at Lingfield near Patteson Court, Surrey, c.1902.

RIGHT: Maud Nickalls (left) and Gertrude Crompton at Patteson Court, c.1903. BELOW: Rosamond Marshall, Dorothy Kate Richmond and Frances in Holland, 1903. Auckland City Art Gallery.

Part Four

1901-2

Two Artists Abroad

Frances Hodgkins arrived in London just before her thirty-second birthday and ten weeks after the death of Queen Victoria. She had £100, which would last for about a year. Still weak from her illness she went at first to stay with old Dunedin friends, the Spences, who lived at Upper Norwood, some way out of central London south of the Thames.

She was a watercolourist coming to a country with a long tradition of watercolour painting. The Royal Academy had admitted watercolours since its first exhibition in 1769 and there were several institutions for watercolour painters, the most important being the Royal Society of Painters in Watercolours (RWS) and the Royal Institute of Painters in Watercolours (RI). Oil remained the medium for 'important' work, however, and watercolours destined for exhibition in the Royal Academy strove after the size, finish and significance of traditional oil paintings.

During her first stay in Europe FH painted only in watercolour, content to join the group of artists who made a living recording picturesque scenes. Such work catered for English taste and for the even more pressing colonial nostalgia for Europe which she herself felt and wanted to express. She painted old houses and streets, market places, fishing harbours, village squares. She continued to paint figures, either within a setting or as single studies, finding subjects among village people who were part patronised, part idealised by the wealthy middle-class patrons who bought pictures of them. By the end of the three years, the illustrative aspects of this subject matter were becoming secondary to more formal concerns, particularly an interest in colour and the effects of light. She had also gained some success as a portrait painter.

FH went to England equipped with some useful information. She had probably made up her mind before leaving New Zealand to study at the artists' colony at Newlyn, the fishing village on the south coast of Cornwall near Penzance. Two Newlyn artists, Norman Garstin (1847-1926) and Stanhope Forbes (1857-1948), had exhibited in the 1889-90 New Zealand and South Seas Exhibition in Dunedin, and the latter's Preparations for the Market, Quimperlé, Brittany *had been bought for the Dunedin Art Gallery in 1890 when William Mathew Hodgkins was active in gallery affairs. FH's Maori studies were distantly related to the Newlyn pictures of rural life, for the Maori were as exotic and picturesque to New Zealand painters as the Cornish and Breton villagers were to English artists. Most of the Newlyn artists, like those of St Ives a few miles away on the north coast, worked towards acceptance at the annual exhibition of the Royal Academy, where their work became accessible to wealthy patrons. The artists moved regularly across the channel to sketching grounds in Brittany and Normandy.*

In 1886 Stanhope Forbes had been one of the founding members of the New English Art Club, formed by a group of progressive English artists, most of whom had studied in Paris. They rejected the conservatism and privilege of the Royal Academy and organised annual exhibitions of their own. The American-born John Singer Sargent, who had spent ten years studying in Paris, was another founding member, as was Philip Wilson Steer, a contemporary of FH, who had been strongly influenced by

81

Monet in the late 1880s and early 1890s. By the turn of the century the gap between the NEAC and the RA had narrowed and many artists exhibited at both.

Less important institutions, like the Royal Society of British Artists (RBA), also held annual exhibitions; and it was mainly through these recognised channels that an artist gained exposure. There were in addition private galleries of varying degrees of prestige, increasing as one approached Bond Street in the West End, but access to them was difficult without some reputation gained through exhibiting in the large annual exhibitions. When FH first arrived in London her aspirations were humble enough, but her work won the respect of the Newlyn artists and she was encouraged to try for an exhibition in London.

In Norman Garstin she found an excellent mentor. An articulate, well-informed Irishman of great personal charm, he had painted in Belgium, Paris, and Morocco, admired Manet, tolerated the French impressionists, who never completely appealed to English taste, and loved Japanese art. Unlike many English painters he had only a very small private income and had to rely on selling paintings, teaching and writing to support his family.

[69] To Rachel Hodgkins, 19 April 1901
20 Lunham Rd, Upper Norwood, S.2. 19 April 1901.

My darling Mother,
.... Well dear I have been in England nearly a fortnight and this is my first letter home. My first week, sad to relate was spent in bed, same old trouble brought on by the excitement of arriving I suppose .... [The Spences] have been so good to me. I shall never forget their kindness. . . . [the Doctor] has put me back to strict milk diet again and threatened me with chronic trouble if I did not take care of myself – he advises me not to start work for another month. I shall wait for May Garden who is to join me for a week on the 3rd. and shall then go down to Newlyn in time for the summer term. It seems such ages since I arrived no wonder one's first impressions of London are disappointing, it was a thick yellow fog and pouring in torrents as we steamed up the Thames and we threaded our way slowly thro' all kinds of craft, the bright brown sails of the barges making ripping pictures against the peasoup background. Then the long weary wait at the Docks and the long train journey up to London thro forests of houses and chimney pots with peeps of very sordid humanity. Then change at London Bridge, bus to Victoria and down to Norwood. Effie and Mr. Spence were waiting for me, Effie looking hopelessly dowdy in a last century circular waterproof, and Mr. Spence very bent and feeble. Mrs. Spence I thought looking younger than ever, she is the only smart one of the family .... Effie and I went to town for the first time on Monday .... We took a bus and rode up some of the principal streets. I caught sight of the New English Art Club in Picadilly so in we went –

such daubs, with the exception of a few good things there was nothing worth looking at, so we went on to the R[oyal] B[ritish] Artists which was better tho' I was much surprised at the average standard of work. The best water color in the room was one by Gouldsmith, a freshly painted coast scene vigorous and strong. Most of the modern watercolors are tremendously worked up, miniature work seems to have influenced the style – and it is quite a relief to see crisp un-worried looking canvases. Some work I saw by a man called Proctor[1] I was tremendously taken with and I asked the Sec. about him & if he took pupils, it was beautiful work, figure in landscape and just what I wanted both color and style but alas he didnt teach. I saw a lot of work very like Hansons but not so good: there was a lovely portrait by Shannon[2] but beyond this there was nothing particularly outstanding. There was a little side room quite like our own Chamber of horrors at the O.A.S. with some dreadful potboiling atrocities – altogether, I came away not particularly impressed with the R.B.A's. We retired very tired and hungry to an A.B.C. and stodged buns and tea then up into Regent St where we glued our noses to the shops which are simply ravishing. How Sis would revel in them, once into Liberty's you would never get her out again. It is simply impossible to live economically in London. You cant move without spending money – and the sooner I am out of it the better for my purse. It has been pay, pay, pay ever since I arrived starting with £1.3. simply for getting my luggage down to Norwood which I thought most excessive, then train fares and busses which are nothing in themselves, but when you multiply them by 6 they soon mount up. I got a very decent hat, black tulle and roses for £1.1 and a mackintosh for the same price then shoes and gloves and that I think is the extent of my purchases. Mr. Spence took me to the Bank N.S.W. where I deposited my draft and opened an account. I am not going to get any clothes but am going to make my N.Z. things do so do not be surprised if I arrive home again in the same coat & skirt as I set out in. . . .

Last Sunday was your birthday I thought of you dear and wished you many happy returns. I wonder where you spent it – put the little lace mats on your dressing table I got them in Colombo.

The last few days have been gloriously fine, and I am glad to see the sun can shine in England. One day Effie and I took our lunch and went to Croydon, sketching, we camped in a queer old cobbled street with a policeman as body-guard to shoo off the small boys and a flower girl posed in the middle distance and a coster & his donkey cart consented to stand in the foreground for the handsome gratuity of 3d. It was great sport and I brought home my first English sketch (which was really a wretched daub) as proud as if I had painted an Academy picture. Talking of the Academy it opens early next month so I shall see it before I leave town. . . . I have been up to town once by myself. I went to the Institute

[1] Adam Proctor (1864-1913), RI, ROI.
[2] Sir James Shannon (1862-1923) RA, NEAC, president of the Royal Society of Portrait Painters.

of Water Colors, it was very fine and oddly enough one of the first things I lighted on was a design by Flor Broome[3] – good – and well hung – the only thing of its kind in the gallery. I wonder how it got there?. . . Everybody is beginning to leave off their mourning which was everywhere general when I first arrived. There is hardly anything worn but purple & heliotrope and one gets sick to death of the color.

Since last writing I have seen Mrs. C[unningham] Smith – she is just the same as ever, rather more portly and breathless. It was nice seeing her again and she gave me such a warm welcome. She has such a cosy little flat and it was good to see the wall full of old friends, a black and white sketch of Father's greeted me as I came in the door. . . .

How is Sis? I do hope she is strong and well, and the chicks, give them a kiss and a hug from me and dont let them forget me. . . .

[70] To Rachel Hodgkins, 15 May 1901

10 Selwood Terrace, Kensington, S.W. May 15th 01.

My dearest Mother,

Here I am still in London, and feeling every day more disinclined to leave it – I have rather altered my plans since last writing. For the last fortnight I have had a room in Kensington quite close to Mrs. Cunningham Smith, and have been having my meals with them, and have found it most comfortable and convenient. Mrs. S. has been such a trump and you can't imagine what a good friend she has been to me. . . . I find that the sketching class in Brittany does not start till the first week in July, so I have decided to take advantage of the cheap classes at the Polytechnic and draw from the nude for the next month. . . . I shall keep on this room for which I pay 10/6 and board myself. The "Poly" is quite close, so I shall be able to go in the evenings as well. I am joining Norman Garstin's sketching class, they are going to Caudebec in Brittany[4] and probably I shall go on to Paris in the autumn and study there for some months and come back to England for the spring again. . . . May has been and gone, I saw a good deal of her and her "little hublet" as she calls him. She is just the same only *more* so, especially as regards clothing. Shall I ever forget the morning when I met her at Victoria? There she was clad in a severely plain and very dusty blue serge with a bright yellow leather courier bag slung over her shoulder and a hat which she fondly tried to persuade me was a Paris model (same old May, same old deceptions) but was in reality a pure Aberdeen production and consisted of the entire breast of a

[3] Florence Broome, a Wellington painter, who went to study at the Slade in 1900 and returned to New Zealand about 1903.
[4] Caudebec-en-Caux, a small picturesque town on the lower reaches of the Seine in Normandy, popular with English artists as a sketching ground.

very red and very ugly bird – being very thin and gaunt she looked like a huge macaw. I thought her very little changed the same bright alert old May with perhaps a dash more of the lemon in her remarks. . . . [We went] to Hertford House, such a treasure house, room after room filled with priceless pictures and curios. May got bored in the middle and faint so wandered off and I found her later chatting affably to a dissipated looking old gentleman. No wonder Mr. Garden won't trust her alone in London, the idea of speaking to strange men! She said "Dear old General, he was so good to me Fan". I said very crossly "Dear old fiddlesticks" so ended our first day! The next day . . . . we started to go to the Nat. Gallery and going down Regent St. May said "Fan my petticoat is coming down" and before I could prevent her she hopped into a big fashionable flower shop and said to the man who came forward, "Sir, I am shedding an underskirt". The man couldn't have looked more horrified if she had started shedding petals. . . . It all sounds very amusing on paper but when you are part and parcel of it it does not strike you as being quite so funny . . . . May's "hublet" arrived in due course to take her home and one night they took me to "Twelfth Night", dined sumptu-ously first of all off silver plate at the Burlington Hotel, then off to the theatre May in black silk, beautifully made looking very smart Fanny also in black silk neither smart or beautifully made – oh! the dresses one sees. Except for one's own satisfaction it does not matter what one wears in London, it is so hopelessly impossible to be fashionable, to be neat is all one can ever hope to be. When May and her husband come to town they neither seem to see anything or do anything – they spend their evenings at music halls and I dont think May trys to improve her husbands taste. She had not been to a single gallery till she came with me and she knew absolutely nothing about London. They talked a great deal about their poverty but whether it is real or fancied I dont know, but people who can afford £500 for a motor can't be very badly off. There is no doubt as to who is master, the little man has a very strong will and a very bad temper of his own and May is very subdued in his prescence, he holds her in check which she wants badly, he is very proper and correct. I liked him a great deal better than I did in N.Z. I think they are very happy and he is evidently very proud of her . . . . Last Sunday I lunched with the Olivers, she is just the same, a most odious and uncomfortable woman, all sniffs and grunts and purse pride. They have a lovely house, and live in great style. Mrs. O. & Mrs. C. Smith have been putting their heads together and trying to persuade me that my best plan is to study in London. I am equally determined I wont. Mr. O. in his consequential way talked "at" me all lunch about the beauties of good drawing etc. I am quite aware that I want drawing but I have quite made up my mind I shall not get it in London. Mrs. Turton & Miss Marchant arrived last week. . . . and [I] heard all their experiences. They simply seethed with Madonnas, Churches and statues – it was dull, madonnas never did interest me. On the fol. day we four had a day in London together, went first to the Guildhall to see a lovely collection of Spanish pictures, ancient & modern

Velasquez, Fortuny, Madrazo and a host of other less celebrated but all good.[5] I did not know what painting was till I saw these. British art cannot compare with it. This is a loan collection and thrown open free to the public, the free provision in art and music that is made for the public is wonderful – there is no need to be ignorant in London – the Tate gallery and Hertford House are both free, the latter was bequeathed by Sir Richard Wallace to the nation and has the most costly collection of pictures, arms, bronzes tapestries and cabinets of priceless china. I could spend days there. I wish you and Sis could see half what I have seen lately. I have a pang sometimes when I think of all you dear people and wish I could transplant you here to enjoy things with me. The Academy is open and I have been several times, there is nothing particularly exciting, it is not a good year. The most impressive picture is the Queen's funeral by Wylie, the Royal Yacht with its stately escort of battleships against a brilliant sunset. The portrait of the Queen by Constant occupies the whole of one wall draped in black & purple. I looked at it, gasped and passed on – as a portrait it is bad and as a picture it is worse. I gasped pretty often as I met old friends in the shape of Leader, Waterlow, Parsons, McWhirter, Herkomer & co. one and all disappointing, but the younger men such as Abbey, La Thangue, Stanhope Forbes, Stott, Clausen & Brangwyn were all delightful. With the exception of Sargent[6] & Shannon the portraits were all poor – Sargent is wonderful masterly in treatment & color – he flings his subjects on the canvas in the most audacious manner no attempt at ellaboration you stand back and behold meaningless blobs shape themselves into the most perfect modelling and form – A wonderful picture of his a full length of two Jewesses in all their blatant vulgarity, red velvet and white satin and a vast expanse of flesh – painted with an utter disregard to all flattery and refinement. They are the daughters of a man called Wertheimer the richest picture & curio dealer in London. On the opposite side of the wall is [a] portrait of a very different type a thin emaciated patrician looking woman painted with exquisite grace and refine-ment. Shannons things are all lovely – beautiful duchesses with their offspring in picturesque attitudes grouped gracefully. Last but not least there is a fine oil by Gouldsmith, hopelessly skied, it is almost a replica of the watercolor in the Institute. . . . One day last week I started off for a prowl round Lincoln's Inn Fields, a very old part of the City, most of the old places are being pulled down now and rebuilt and old London is disappearing very fast. Everywhere new streets are being opened up and the grimy and crooked old thoroughfares enlarged. At the back of Chancery Lane I came upon the genuine Old Curiosity Shop a queer little old place with a collection of Dickens prints & portraits and some genuine old Barnard watercolor illustrations of Dickens books. The Shop and the

[5] This exhibition included Goya and Murillo.
[6] John Singer Sargent (1856-1925) painted sumptuous portraits of wealthy sitters using an impressionist-influenced freedom of brush stroke and responsiveness to light. He was an American, born in Italy, trained in Florence and Paris, who had settled in London about 1884.

neighborhood was so picturesque that I came back the next day and made a careful sketch of it. I spent the whole day there sketching and got some fairly good studies of the old houses. . . .

17.5.01

Since last writing your letter has arrived. So Frank is with you. I am glad he is improved, foolish boy not to realise how impossible it is for him to stay in Dunedin. I do hope you have persuaded him to go back to the farm now that Bert has left. He will be really wanted to help Percy. . . .

. . . . Miss Robertson has arrived at the Spences after a most dreadful voyage . . . . a terrible rabble who got so rowdy one night that they threw 200 deck chairs overboard . . . . Mrs. S[mith] had a big NZ. levée today, all the New Zealanders congregate in her little drawing room. I am not at all anxious to rub noses with any of them. Last night I helped Mrs. S. rehang her pictures, it was a great business doing her bedroom with her two sets of husbands. I had to keep them separate. . . .

The next letter sees the beginning of FH's friendship with Dorothy Kate Richmond (1861-1935), an experienced artist and traveller. Her mother had died when she was four and at the age of eleven she had been taken to Europe by her father, the artist James Crowe Richmond, to be educated. Showing an early artistic vocation, she studied at a drawing academy in Dresden in 1875. 'She looks so splendid when she comes home from . . . her drawing lesson, she glows out of every pore', reported a cousin at the time.[7] Dorothy Richmond won a scholarship to the Slade School at the age of seventeen and studied under Alphonse Legros for two years. Returning to New Zealand in 1881, she was appointed to teach art at the newly opened Nelson College for Girls in 1883. There followed two further periods in England in 1885 and 1888. Both William Mathew Hodgkins and James Crowe Richmond died in 1898 and in 1900 Dorothy Richmond returned to study at the Newlyn School of Art under Elizabeth Stanhope Forbes. There is no record of Frances Hodgkins and Dorothy Richmond having met in New Zealand, though their fathers knew each other.

[71] To Rachel Hodgkins, 2 June 1901

10 Selwood Terrace, Kensington S.W. June 2nd 1901

My darling Mother,

. . . . I have been very homesick this last week and am just longing for the

---

[7] Letter from Margaret Richmond to Arthur Samuel Atkinson, 23 December 1875, quoted in Frances Porter, *Born to New Zealand*, Wellington, 1989, p.305.

Frisco to come in. . . . I expect by this time [Willie and Jean] are married and comfortably settled in the Bank and you are with Sis. Tell me everything about the wedding and the arrangements at the Bank. . . . I have nothing very exciting to tell you about myself. I have been working hard at the Polytechnic, too hard. I am afraid I knocked up again and had to take some days in bed to recover. It is so terribly hot and London heat isn't pleasant. I shall be glad when I go abroad and work out of doors. Did I tell you my master is Mr. Borough Johnston,[8] tell Sis to look in the last Studio[9] and read an article of his on pencil work & methods. His pencil work is beautiful. I have two days a week working under him in pencil and am already feeling much benefited, and the rest of the week I draw from the nude – oh what a humbling process it all is and I realise only too well there are to be no shortcuts to fame for me, if I am to do anything at all good I must work for a year or two at my drawing. They all give me praise for what I have got already and say if I can succeed in adding good drawing to it I shall be all right, but without it I can hope to go very little further. I knew that this kind of work would unsettle me terribly and I was rather dreading it. I feel I shall be all right out of doors or with my pencil but put me down in front of a nude figure and I am at a loss. Of course, I know it is only time & practice that is required it is very silly of me to be depressed. I want to go ahead in leaps and bounds and not to "hasten slowly". I have not been to the studio at all this week but have been sitting out of doors a great deal in some gardens quite close to my room, trying to get strong again. . . . I am leaving this room tomorrow and going into a cheaper one at the back of the house for 8/. I provide my own breakfast, tea & a roll and I get my lunch at the Polytechnic, and I always dine with Mrs. S. She likes me to go and we talk over our day together. She has been such a brick to me, a somewhat bossy brick, but most awfully good never the less. . . . I had a letter today from Miss Dorothy Richmond, she is in Paris and very anxious that I should go too. Also one from Miss Stoddart whom I am to meet tomorrow. . . . I find it rather distracting working here, there are so many people to see and it is really rather a nuisance when you are busy – and thro' Mrs. C. Smith everyone knows my whereabouts so it is no good trying to evade people. Mrs. S. is a N.Z. directory and can put her finger on any New Zealander in London at a moment's notice. . . . I am getting quite fond of Mrs. O[liver], in spite of what I said about her in my last letter which I take back. I have been there a good deal and one always meets nice interesting people there. She has a dear old sister Miss Courtenay who lives in Penzance and is a great friend of the Stanhope Forbes, she has promised to befriend me when I go down there. . . .

I am getting a lot of sketches together to send out to McGregor Wright, tho'

[8] Ernest Borough Johnson RI, RP, RBA (1867-1949), a former pupil of Hubert von Herkomer.
[9] The art magazine *The Studio* was founded in 1893 by Charles Holme and ran for ninety-five years. Using the new halftone reproduction process, it was well illustrated and sought to disseminate images of both art and craft throughout England and the colonies.

of course I can send nothing really good till I go abroad and get some lessons –

Here is a riddle I heard yesterday, ask Bert – Why did the barmaid wine and champagne? Because the stout porter bitter –

I have just heard from Mr. Garstin. I am to join them on the 1st July and cross with them to Caudebec, it is a lovely spot I believe, on the north bank of the Seine with as much variety as you can get anywhere. I must stop now dearest, it is getting late. Tell Sis I mean this letter equally for her. I hope the dear old girl is well and Will and the chicks, be sure and write to me every Frisco mail you don't know how I count the days till your letter arrives

With fondest love to you all

Your loving daughter

Fanny.

Be sure and tell me all about the wedding.

[72] TO ISABEL FIELD, 28 JUNE 1901

10 Selwood Terrace, Kensington S.W. June 28th.

My dearest Sis

. . . . Frank has been a sad source of worry and expense to you all. I have been puzzling my brains thinking what you would arrange to do for him. It is only too evident that the boy is utterly incapable of helping himself and the only thing left to do is to keep him out of further mischief. I have written to Willie insisting on my sharing the expenses and I want him to use whatever money he has of mine in hand. I cant bear to think that I am having this splendid trip and spending my money entirely on myself while an unfortunate brother the other side of the world is being supported by the other members of the family. I can earn money and he can't so it is my duty to help him. . . . Poor old Mother writes most sorrowfully about him. I am so glad to think she is with you. I like to think of her sitting up in that bright window watching the shipping. Oh! the contrast between your window and the one I am sitting in front of now. Nothing can be more hideous in the world than London backyardom sooty clusters of chimney pots and an indescribable look of grime over everything. I shall be very glad to leave this poky little room. . . . I have had quite as much as I want of London (and Mrs. C. Smith) . . . . unless you fall in with her views & ideas she is a bit tiresome. . . . [She] bicycles a lot tho I really think she is getting too big a girl for that kind of thing – it is a marvel to me she is not run over. She rides in and out of the trafic in the most reckless manner generally. When I am with her I hug the shore, otherwise the gutter, it is a sight sometimes when there is a block in Picadilly to see the cyclists hanging on like limpets to the bus wheels. The thing is to ride slowly. The perfect control of the London trafic is wonderful. You never see an accident or an unruly horse, it is like a marvellous mechanical toy to see the tide of vehicles moving at an even pace thro some of the crowded thoroughfares . . . . in & out between the horses feet move an army of workers constantly sweeping & cleaning the streets – its a wonderful world this London but a cruel place for those who can't afford it. There is such lavish display of wealth on all sides and it is hard to live a quiet & contented life in the midst of so many distractions. I feel I have benefited much by my 2 months with Mr. Borough Johnston, he has been most good to me and I have learnt much from his pencil work. . . . His painting is a long way behind his pencil work, it is very correct & academical, he says he would give much to possess what I have in my work & which I dont value, his is knowledge and mine is instinct – none of the water color work I have seen comes up to yours either in color or strength. You would be surprised at the low level of the water color work lots of things in my line little figures & genre subjects are exquisitely painted but for any important work it falls a long way short. Arthur Melville whom Dr Fife admires so much is a strong painter, at first sight you laugh, then out of a chaos of blots comes wonderful form & color & you finally end by admiring very much indeed.[10]

I had a very happy jaunt to High Wycombe in Bucks last week. I met a very clever artist a Mrs. Chas Hobbs . . . and I went down to stay a week with her, such a nice woman, very clever with her brush, she reminded me in many ways of you she adores old things and her house is full of old treasures oak furniture, china & pictures which she picks up in pawn shops. Old jewellery is her latest craze & she gave me a lovely rope of old Roman pearls. I got some fairish sketches. . . . The Hobbs are anxious I should go with them to Holland they are off to Amsterdam next month. I will probably join them there. Holland is not the best place in the world for English people to go to just now, we are in very bad odour there and they do all they can to annoy tourists & the street children are unequalled for their mischief & rudeness it is also rather a dear place. I met a nice old Dutch thing who was staying at the Hobbs when I was there, and she asked me to stay with her in Amsterdam. She is a sister of Van Wisslinghe the owner of the Dutch gallery in Bond St who is regarded as one of the best judges of pictures in London. You see Corots & Greuzes & pictures by the best Continental artists at his gallery. She knew Van de Welden well.[11] I want to see Miss Richmond before making any Dutch plans. She is to join me at Caudebec, she seems anxious we shld paint together, and she is certainly the only person that I am at all keen to throw in my

[10] Arthur Melville RWS (1855-1904), a Scottish impressionist and member of the Glasgow School, was later singled out by FH as the British watercolourist from whom she had learnt most: 'In England – with what delight I discovered Arthur Melville!' (*Otago Witness*, 28 May 1913). Melville travelled about Great Britain, Europe and the Middle East painting scenes and people.

[11] The Dutch artist Petrus Van der Velden, who had arrived in Christchurch in 1890 and exhibited at the Otago Art Society. W. M. Hodgkins was instrumental in buying for the Dunedin Art Gallery Van der Velden's paintings, *The Otira Gorge* (1892) and *Old Jack* (1893).

lot with. I think it is much better to be by yourself unless you get a really congenial companion. . . . I spent a week-end with Mrs. Inglis at Hampstead lately & while with her called on Mr. Arthur Streaton[12] (Mr. Roberts gave me a letter to him) both Mrs. I. & myself were very charmed with both artist & studio & spent a most delightful hour chatting with him – he came to supper next night – he is devoted to T. Roberts & expects him home quite shortly. I have posted you a linen cushion cover – will you be sure & let me know when it arrives also whether you had to pay duty. . . . I do not suppose I shall come back to London again till I return to N.Z. I shall go wherever I can get good sketching & get a good folio to bring back with me. Mr. Johnston doesn't advise me to study under anyone, he thinks I should work alone. Oh! Sis if you were only here, what jaunts we could have together. I longed for you when I was in Bucks, the beauty of the English lanes is beyond all description. We simply dont know what green is out in N.Z. The endless sloping fields with every imaginable & unimaginable shade of green & yellow & over all a wonderful blue haze which mellows all – then to see glorious masses of poppies foxgloves & countless red white & yellow wildflowers nodding at you from the side of the road – it was like fairyland to me and I began to wonder if these things really were or whether I was walking in a dream. I really think I came as near being really happy as I can ever hope to be in this world – during that short week in High Wycombe – amidst such beauty one seemed to get more at the heart of things. . . .

I mustn't prose on any longer, the mail goes out in the morning so I must slip out and post this. Thank you so much dear old girl for all your kind letters & thoughts for me. I am nearly all right again now, but I am very much afraid I have been left with that [most] uninteresting of all complaints, a feeble interior – over fatigue or undue indulgence in meat brings on an attack wh. invariably means milk puddings & bed for a day or two. I have a very good prescription wh. always sets me right again (tear off this page if letter is circulated). . . .

[73] To Rachel Hodgkins, 14 July 1901
Hotel de France, Caudebec en Caux, Seine Inferieure. 14.7.01

My darling Mother
Here I am settled down at last in Caudebec . . . . I found Miss Richmond already installed when I arrived and winning all hearts by her sweetness & beauty, it is a kind of link with Wellington having her here, we talk about our respective neices, her little nephew who goes to Miss [Mary] Richmond's school seems to be

[12] Arthur Streeton (1867-1943), member of the Heidelberg School and one of the exhibitors at the 9x5 exhibition in Melbourne. He spent some twenty years in England, returning to Australia in 1920, where he remained loyal to the landscape tradition he had helped to establish.

just such another odd little interesting mortal as Girlie. . . . Time is slipping by, nearly 6 months since I left N.Z. I wonder what this time next year will bring forth. I feel now as if I had really started to work in earnest, conditions are all favorable to work and I am living in an atmosphere of art, it is a very pleasant life, we are leading and I wish time could stand still for a while. This is a charming spot full of quaint old streets & buildings and subjects in plenty for every day in the year. This is an anyhow sort of hotel, but we cheerfully put up with all discomforts provided our meals are regular and plentiful. We are a very jolly party of 12, spread over the town in detachments. Miss R[ichmond] & self & several others are with the Garstins at the Hotel de France. We rise betimes and are out by 6.30, work till midday then back to déjeuner, a comprehensive meal consisting of many courses mostly vegetables & very under done meat, puddings never, and copious libations of cider. . . . After déjeuner we rest till 3, when we all meet in a large room & have afternoon tea and criticise each other's work, then out again for evening effects & at 8 30 we have another huge meal which lasts till 10 o'clock & we end the evening with a stroll & so to bed. I wish you could see my room, very small room very large mahogany bedstead small table which serves as both dressing table & wash stand, a pie dish & milk jug to wash in and a looking glass whose face is cracked in three places, in my best French I asked for a chest of drawers or failing that for some pegs. The landlord looked at me blankly, ruminated aloud with hand on brow then disappeared and after some time reappeared staggering with two other men under a huge sideboard, it now fills up all the available space in my room and is better than nothing. For all these luxuries we pay 5 frcs a day equal to 30/- a week in English money. Baths are unheard of and are looked upon as one of the many idiosyncrasies of the Britisher abroad. You can get them if you like to pay a franc each time but ones weekly washing bill would soon run up at that rate. Miss Richmond has a rubber bath and I manage to keep fairly cleanly. . . . Miss Richmond and I are never tired of congratulating ourselves on our good luck in coming abroad with such delightful people as the Garstins. She is a nice woman, very practical and clever and manages her husbands business for him. She knows nothing at all about painting & never knows her husband's sketches from one of ours. They have two jolly little children and are a most devoted couple – Mr. Garstin refuses to accept me as a pupil & will not let me pay a penny he seems to think I have nothing to learn which is absurd and any help he gives me he says is merely from one brother artist to another. He wants me to work here for a while and then go down to Spain for the winter, get plenty of material there then go back to Penzance & take a studio there for a while & get all my sketches in order & then have a show in London in the Spring – he has promised to write me up in the "Studio", he writes a lot for that paper & has influence – it is a very attractive programme and the most delightful part of it is that Miss Richmond is coming with me. We are at present studying

Spanish guide books and making plans. There is a Mr. Moffat Lindner[13] here just now (you probably have seen his work in the academy notes) and he knows Spain well and he has given us much help & advice on the subject. . . . Miss Richmond has to go to England at the end of August so I shall go to Paris & wait for her to join me there at the end of Sept. She is an old campaigner & knows her way about thoroughly. I am a lucky beggar to have her for a travelling companion. She is so restful & sweet and I think we suit each other very well. She has been wintering in San Remo so knows that part of Italy well. She is not very strong & has to be very careful of herself. How I wish you & Sis could be here with me. When I make my fortune (you would think it a very simple matter to hear them talk) you must come home & live with me in one of these quaint old towns. The life is so different, it would interest you tremendously – at present you stumble up against easels wherever you go & you meet depressed looking figures sitting in shadows at all the street corners, the old town is being most thoroughly painted. Mr. Garstin & Mr. Lindner are doing some fine things and it is a great help & stimulus to see them work – I have been out once or twice with Mr. Lindner & today I have been for a long tramp with him to a place called Duclair where I discovered a lovely subject, an old man & woman in their garden and am going back to paint it tomorrow. I never thought I could feel so happy & light hearted, it is the lovely fresh air and perfect weather & congenial surroundings – after the stifling depression of London it is delightful to lead a simple & rather elemental life like this. There is nothing sordid to meet the eye at least it is a happy country all smiles & gaiety, & their light heartedness affects your spirits like champagne.

. . . . We have been for several picnics. Miss Richmond & I showed them how to make billy tea, the poor things always took a spirit lamp & silver teapot & gave themselves endless bother. The first day the water was smoked badly & we got much abuse and ridicule for what they called our "kippered tea" but the next time we took bricks & built a proper fire & had a prime brew. We spend our spare time telling them tall stories about N.Z. which they try hard to cap. . . . Tell Sis Mr. Garstin was tremendously taken with her Trentham sketch, he thought it very strong & clever, & shook [his] head sadly when I told him she was married!

I hope you are keeping well & strong and not feeling the cold very much do write me fully about yourself & all the home news and about the chicks. Is Sis painting? & what. I am anxious for news of Frank. Thank Will for the photos, I showed them with great pride. Goodbye darling, with heaps of love to you all

Your ever loving Fanny.

---

[13] Peter Moffat Lindner (1852-1949) was a member of the St Ives art community, a successful painter in the English impressionist tradition who exhibited regularly at the Royal Academy. With his wife and young daughter, Hope, he is the subject of a painting by FH, now in the Dunedin Art Gallery. Begun in 1916, it is evidence of the friendship that developed between the two artists.

[74] To Rachel Hodgkins, 7 August 1901

Hotel de France, Caudebec-en-Caux, Seine Inferieure. 7.8.01

My darling Mother,

. . . . So Bert is thinking of settling in Wllgtn, it is good & sweet of him to want
to have a little house again. Of course dear I should rather live in Wllgtn and be
near Sis & the children, from a business point of view it would be better too – it
is impossible to say definitely when I shall return if all goes well with you darling
and I can manage to sell some work between now & then I hope to stay at Home
for another year at least. Does Bert see his way to taking a house at once, it will
make a great difference to me going back to you & Bert. I have lost all wish to go
back to Dunedin, it would be unbearable there without a home of one's own
. . . . Frank is a sore trial to you, poor thoughtless boy, it is something at least to
know he is safe from temptation down at Stewarts Island. . . . Miss Richmond
has decided not to go to England so we shall not lose sight of each other even for
a few weeks. I have grown so fond of her, I dont know how I am ever going to
let her go, she is one of those people whom you want always with you. This kind
of existence is too too happy to last. What a gay time you must have had with the
Duke & Duchess.[14] There was a very funny description in the "Telegraph" of the
Royal arrival at Auckland described as "an industrious thriving little townlet."
. . . Our sketching party has increased this month and we now number nearly 40,
there are some very nice girls, no one particularly clever, Miss Richmond is a long
way ahead of them all. Molly Sale is here for a month.[15] I am proud of my two
countrywomen, they are both so nice looking. Last night I dined with Mr. & Mrs.
Garstin at the Hotel Marine with some English friends of theirs. We all love Mr.
& Mrs. Garstin. Miss Richmond & myself are quite hopelessly in love with the
former and both agree we have met our ideal artist & man at last. . . .

[75] To Rachel Hodgkins, 26 August 1901

Hotel de France, Caudebec en Caux. Aug. 26th. 1901

My darling Mother,

. . . . I have been selling some of my sketches which has brought me in £20,
not bad is it it will more than cover my two months expenses here & it will help
to build up that slowly diminishing little fund of mine. I have had qualms
sometimes at night when I think of all I want to do with that £100 there is really
no need to worry for I can always teach if the worst comes to the worst. I am quite

[14] The Duke and Duchess of Cornwall and York, the future George V and Queen Mary.
[15] Molly Sale was the daughter of the classics professor at Otago University. She had studied under Borough
Johnson in about 1898.

ready to go back to N.Z. after I have had a show in London but certainly not before. It has been a very precious time to me these last two months, full of friendship & sympathy. Mr. & Mrs. Garstin have been such good friends to me apart from the great help I have got from him artistically. . . . A rather distinguished French artist has just come & gone. He brought his work up to the Hotel one day and all he had to show . . . after a fortnight's stay was a dead pig in a butcher's shop painted with a sickening regard to detail – curious perversion of mind dont you think that prompts a man to overlook such beauties as the Cathedral & the market place & the quaint old streets & paint instead a faithful portrait of a dead cochon – very French & quite incomprehensible. The Headmaster of the Leicester School of Art has been painting here, he gave me a commission to paint his portrait, which much to their satisfaction & my delight turned out all right. This led to another commission from my friend Miss Nicolls,[16] she is a very pretty girl, not unlike Mrs. Hosking I am working at it now and I think [it] is fairly good. I hate these portrait commissions, they are such anxious work and never somehow go where you want them. There is a dear little widow lady who is staying at the Marine whom we are all very fond of, Mrs Ashington. She has bought one of my sketches & given me an order for a second, a replica of one I am sending out to N.Z. She has asked me to spend a month with her next Spring when I return to England and give her some lessons & she will pay my fees & my travelling expenses wherever we decide to sketch. I have been asked over & again to teach but I don't want to start that little game just at present, it will pay me much better to make pictures & work for my show in the Spring. I have also sold a Maori head. I wish I had brought more with me, they seem to have caught on. I am sending some work out at the end of this month and will send some more later on in the month for the Nov. show in Dunedin. I am only sending out small things, will you give them to McGregor Wright to sell & forward to Dunedin when Sis sends her work down for Exhibition. . . . I had a paper from Willie with his marriage notice I hear from so many that they are very happy. . . . I do hope the Dunedin people will be nice to Jean. Heigh ho, I should not like to lead the life some of those good people in Dunedin do. Monday – High St calls – Tues. – Queen St. & Heriot Row – Wed – guild – Thursday – University & Chingford – Friday Andersons Bay – Sat – what *can* we do. Sunday – why was I born! looking back on it now it strikes one as awful but what can one do, it is inevitable and part of the awful social tyranny of a small town. This kind of life quite unfits one for a colonial hereafter – everything is given up to painting we think & talk of nothing else which in itself is a tremendous stimulus & which of course I shall miss most dreadfully but on the other hand I could not live on this side of the world happily without you & Sis – I pine for my own "bits" and

---

[16] Maud Nickalls and her sisters, Grace and Una, were to become friends, FH staying with them later in England.

shall not feel really happy till I see you all again. You are always in my thoughts & the last thing at night I send you a goodnight kiss across the waters. When I am particularly down Miss Richmond comes & tucks me up – like Sis her unfailing remedy for all evils is whisky & a hot bottle, the latter I have the moral courage to refuse. . . . Miss Richmond goes to England today it is very sad saying goodbye to a face like hers even for a short time. I wish you could see her as she looks sometimes at night with a black dress with a crimson fichu falling off her shoulders & corals & a suggestion of old lace at her throat – I discovered it one day when she was rummaging in her boxes & have since insisted on her wearing it every night. She is a dreadful person & insists on clothing herself abominably – and it is a marvel that she looks as beautiful as she does, did I tell you the girls call her the "Divine Lady", but my dear divinity is the most human person I have ever known with an adorable sense of humor and perfect appreciation of other people's shortcomings. She and I spent a profitless day yesterday having our photographs taken by the numerous cameras by special request. We posed in various artificial attitudes against various backgrounds, against brick walls, olean-der trees, pumps vegetable stalls & finally languished against a brocaded back-ground in an entwined & graceful attitude. They call us the "enterprising New Zealanders". We have earned rather a shocking reputation for drawing the longbow, it is our greatest joy whenever anyone tells a story to immediately cap it with what they call a "New Zealander" & many & marvellous are the stories Miss Richmond tells. I enclose two snapshots of me. I will send out the others later.

Last Sunday I bicycled with Miss Nicolls to a place called Jumièges about 12 miles from here famous for its old abbey & its cherries & plums. It was the first time I had seen an old ivied ruin, very beautiful, these old churches take hold of one, the R.C. churches are all so tawdry and the beauty of the buildings so spoilt by the cheap fripperies, banners & hideous saints covered with ribbons & flowers. We had a great church fête here last week, the feast of the Assumption, one of the three great R.C. feast days of the year – for several days before there were great preparations all the saints in the church were taken down & cleaned & garnished with new ribbons & fresh flowers the night before. I saw a wheelbarrow with no less than 3 saints sitting bolt upright & looking very clean & frivolous so covered were they with flowers & ribbons. The next day commenced with much bell ringing and after High Mass there was a grand procession through the old town headed by the priests in their gorgeous vestments proceeded by acolytes and after them came a number of young girls in their snowy communion dresses looking so spotless & pure against the background of grimy old houses. . . . It is certainly a most picturesque religion. You would love the Calvarys and the Piétas along the roads. The Piétas are generally little railed in monuments of a recumbent figure of the dead Christ rudely modelled and sometimes colored. It is very beautiful country all round this neighborhood and the peasants are a real joy. I would like to buy a few and take them out with me as properties – some of the old men wear such beautiful blue corduroy bags that make me ache to paint them, it is a great sight to see them on Market day (every Saturday) the whole town is covered with little canvas booths and with the different goods displayed and the babel of noise that goes on, each stallholder crying up their own particular wares. It is useless trying to paint a market scene, we have all tried and then sadly turned our backs on its facinations. We found we always came home so cross & irritable after a morning spent in the market that Mr. Garstin mildly suggested that we should cease wrestling with it. I think French people are most charming, they are so smiling and gracious and wherever we go we always meet with the greatest civility and kindness, they are certainly very dirty and have many nasty little tricks, but for all that they are a very lovable people with the most charming manners in the world. I havent heard from the Rattrays for some time . . . . I cant keep up a big correspondence; there is so little time for anything but painting and as I have come home to paint & not to write I cannot be expected to answer all the letters I get every mail. I feel as if I was possessed by a painting devil which is devouring me body and soul & claims all my brains & energy, & leaves me with no wish or inclination for anything else. I must not give way to it I know.

I am leaving this open in case your letters come before the mail closes. I want a letter from you badly darling, write me always everything you are doing & tell me about Frank. With heaps of love to you all Your loving Fanny

Tell me what Sis is painting

Do the children ever talk of me, dont let them forget me. I have bought the boys two white berries, a kind of tam o'shanter which French boys wear and look so nice I must send a line to Jean by this mail so goodbye

[76] To Kate Rattray, 27 August 1901

Hotel de France, Caudebec en Caux, Seine Inf. Aug. 27

My dear Kate

I shall not attempt anything like an excuse for not writing before this. . . . It is the same old trouble I am afraid the fatal little habit of putting off, in this respect only have I not improved since leaving N.Z. Thank you all so much for your letters, it was real joy getting them . . . . I howled over your description of Mrs. Denniston's adventures with the Duke and Duchess. I lay on my bed and kicked my feet in pure joy and laughed so loud my neighbor requested me thro' the wall either to stop or tell the joke, needless to say I did neither. What luck your being presented. I hope you are not comporting yourself with undue arrogance in consequence. . . . I have been here now nearly two months, very glad indeed to get away from London & its many distractions. . . . I have vowed a vow not to return till I have written the name of Frances Hodgkins in capital letters across – is it the scroll of fame or what that we are all so anxious to sign I am getting a trifle mixed, anyhow I am afraid my return will be somewhat delayed in consequence. . . .

[77] TO ISABEL FIELD, 15 SEPTEMBER 1901

21 Av. de la Grande Armée, Paris. Sept. 15.9.01

My dearest Sis

I would have given worlds if you could have been with me this last week in Paris . . . . You must certainly paint & save up and come Home with Will some day soon & leave the chicks for Mother & me to look after. Molly & I have been here now for 10 days & had a glorious time & yesterday morning I saw Molly off for England . . . . Both of us have spent far more than we intended, instead of £5 it is much nearer £10 . . . . We are in a very nice pension kept by an English lady and they are mostly all Americans here. They do us for 5 frcs a day which is really cheap for Paris, everywhere you go in Paris you meet Americans, you sit beside them in the trams & in cafés and you bump up against them in galleries and you hate the whole clamjamfry, with their shrill nasal voices & their pinched in over dressed figures. They ape the Parisians in dress and come over here in swarms. I dont admire the French figures a scrap, squeezed in waists with abnormal hips & busts and a wobbely look about their shoulders which is very ugly. For a nation who uphold the Venus of Milo as the highest type of beauty, they seem to be curiously lacking in a sense of beauty & form. Oh those marbles at the Luxembourg & the Louvre they send you crazy with their beauty, modern French sculpture is magnificent and contrary to all expectations I thought the sentiment in both pictures & sculpture far less degrading than I was led to believe, on the contrary I found much that was ennobling & uplifting in most of the pictures. I confess with much disappointment that I have not had *one single shock* since I came to Paris.

Molly & I stood for quite a long time the other day in front of what they call a "shocking machine" which undertakes for the price of 1d. to shock any person disposed to put a penny in the slot. As Molly was about to succumb I dragged her away & have regretted it ever since. . . . We went to the opera which is the only place open. . . . Molly & I took seats in the 10th. tier & at 7 o'clock found ourselves tucked away under the roof. Such a place, I never saw anything so gorgeous in all my life. It was Wagner's Tannhauser with one of the leading orchestras in Europe. Nearly all the parts were taken by musical celebrities, there was something so weird & uncanny sitting so high up and listening to this grand volume of sound coming from below and seeing little fore-shortened pin-head figures acting on the stage. There is something wicked about Wagner's music I think which seemed heightened by the gorgeous staging & magnificent surroundings . . . . You can have no idea of the beauty of Paris. There is a white glamour about it which is dazzling, the wide open streets & the almost silent trafic on the wooden pavements. The buildings are truly magnificent & everything is built with a view to beautifying the city. . . . In spite of all this I infinitely prefer smoky grimy old London. Between you & me . . . I get so tired of sight seeing. I am longing to settle down again in some quiet place where I can get my spirit lamp out & make my own afternoon tea and darn my stockings and sew on all those buttons which have come off since I left N.Z. . . . I am looking forward to a long peaceful winter with Miss Richmond who has a rooted objection to over exertion and abhors sight seeing. If Molly's & my private opinions were only known I think we would confess our happiest moments were spent in the cafés. We had to tramp about a good deal so as to economise . . . and in consequence we were always in a state of intense weariness . . . . I shall never forget how we dropped into Notre Dame & eat an orange in a back pew then had forty winks with our feet up on a prie Dieu. There is really some excuse for me for I have been getting up at 5.30. every morning to finish my sketches which I was unable to finish at Caudebec as the last week I was seedy & could not paint so I brought them with me to Paris and much to my relief got them posted safely away . . . . I am afraid they will only just arrive in time for the 9th,[17] if they should be late please use all your influence with Dr. Scott to admit them. . . . I wonder what you will think of them. I am not a bit pleased with them myself and wld far sooner not have sent any out except for you & Mother to see. It is too soon to expect any great wonders and I feel myself I shall paint much better when I am by myself. Too much advice is just as bad as too little & only bewilders one. I felt the whole time a desperate feeling that it was necessary to send out so as to keep the pot boiling and it is not conducive to good painting. Get McGregor Wright to frame them for me. I expect you have got some lovely things yourself ready for the Dunedin show, price mine as you think fit.[18] I had to send them off in such a hurry I had no time to put prices on them. I was packing them up in the dining room and a little American woman came in & was seized with a wild desire to possess the sketch of the old buildings. She was on her way to the train and there was no time for me to think over her offer and I particularly wanted you to see it so I decided not to sell it, it was a most amusing interview in which she guessed many times I was on the right trail sure enough and that my work reminded her strongly of Phineas B. Shipley of Buffalo (have you ever heard of him) and if I came right out to Chicago I would do real well. She finally wound up by shaking me warmly by the hand and saying "I reckon dearie, you're a genius!". . . I was sorry I had not

---

[17] 9 November, the opening date of the Otago Art Society exhibition.
[18] The prices ranged from 3 to 8 guineas.

produced my work before. I am so glad that Mother & Bert think of setting up a little house together. I shall be quite ready to come out by the middle of next year if I can manage to hang out till then. I have still got a £100 & with management I should make it last (with fresh supplies from N.Z.) till then. I have got plenty of clothes and have never ceased being thankful I got such a good outfit in Dunedin. The only mistake I made was in getting too many washing things – prints are a luxury and are only worn on very special occasions. Tell Mother my light blue cloth skirt has seen champion service, my brown tweed is quite new & I am keeping it for the winter. Tomorrow I am off to a place called Les Andelys about 60 miles from Paris where Miss Nickalls is to join me for a fortnight. If we report very favorably on it Mr. Garstin will most likely join us and I will wait there for Miss Richmond. I have bought a bicycle for £5, a really good one and I think a bargain the gay Parisiennes all ride men's bikes & "bicyclettes pour dames" are not in demand in consequence. . . . They all wear bloomers here, so hideous tho' I confess they have points. . . . It is rather exciting going off by myself. My French is hardly what you wld call fluent but I can get along. I shall be two days by myself, but I shall not mind that if the place is pretty as I am told it is, & I shall have my bicycle. If I do not like the place I shall go further on to a little town called La Bouilli[19] wh Mr. Garstin says is beautiful. I have not managed to see any of the Paris studios which are unfortunately all closed. Give dear old Mother my love I am longing [to see] you both again. I have had such a good time I shall be quite glad to settle down in N.Z. again after my year's wanderings and I am looking [forward] to having a home of our own again. I hope you have good news of Frank and that the poor boy shows some signs of improvement. . . .

[Postscript] . . . . Tell me all about your pictures when you write & any art gossip you can pick up.

[78] To Rachel Hodgkins, 9 October 1901

Hotel du Forum, Arles, Bouches du Rhone. 9.10.01

My darling Mother

Since my last letter I have jumped from the North of France to the South and am back again in the middle of summer – such delicious air – so warm and mild and we intend to stay here as long as it remains warm. I think my last letter was from Paris just before I left for Les Andelys. Les A. proved a capital sketching ground and three weeks didnt half exhaust its beauties . . . but the cold weather drove us South. Miss Nickalls & Mr. Garstin joined me there and we were a very merry party and it was a very happy wind up to our summer's sketching. Les A. would have suited Sis such beautiful landscape, the Seine at its very best which

[19] Les Andelys and La Bouille are both in the Seine valley in Normandy.

means a lot – tall poplars and sedgy banks that Sis would have painted deliciously. How I wish she and her clever brush were here with me. She would make their hair curl with her color and technique. I have not seen any water color landscape as good as hers anywhere. Be sure and tell me about her pictures when you write, it was good news to hear she was painting so hard. Well dear, to go back to Paris. Miss Richmond and I met each other last Sunday morning . . . . and spent the rest of the day discussing plans & consulting trains & guide books, also bank books (dismal reading) finally deciding to catch the early train next day & come down here. Spain we abandoned neither of us caring to wrestle with the language or go to the expense of grammars & Baedekers. We turned in soon after dinner as we were to make a very early start, our train leaving at 7 o'clock. The weather was anything but promising, pouring with rain and blowing a perfect gale. We were up by 5, quite dark but fine and by six we were driving across Paris with the sun rising, a sensation not to have been missed for worlds. By 7 we were snuggled up in a 3rd class carriage, prepared to spend the next 16 hours as comfortably as we could on wooden seats (it is very unusual for ladies of any quality at all to travel 3rd. class in France but as Miss Richmond says "we are such very poor devils what can we do?") We raced all day thro beautiful country vineyards mostly sheets of gold and purple, picking up the river Rhone from time to time, all very beautiful & good to paint. Finally at 11.30 very sleepy and dirty we found ourselves sitting on our baggage on the Arles platform, feeling much more inclined to go to sleep there & then than make an effort to find an hotel. Rather foolishly we had forgotten to wire for rooms, but had taken Baedekers word for it that the busses belonging to the two hotels met every train. We had settled it all very nicely that we would take the least ostentatious & smaller of the two busses, it being more likely to be cheaper. Imagine our confusion & blank despair on finding no bus, no vehicle of any description and everybody in Arles with the exception of a sleepy porter or two in bed. We swallowed our tears & explained the situation to the porter who in turn explained to a besotted looking individual who afterwards turned out to be the village idiot, who undertook to guide us to the Hotel if we would graciously condescend to follow him, on the contrary we ungraciously refused, whereupon he disappeared, and just as we were making up our minds to sleep in a railway truck for the night, he turned up this time with an open fiacre & we set out for the hotel, how we ever got there I dont know we corkscrewed in and out of winding cobbled streets, inky blackness everywhere & picturesque smells which promised well for painting purposes (it is a safe maxim follow your nose & you get a good sketch). Once he stopped to ask the way of three villianous looking ruffians & we clung to each other nervously quite sure our last moments had come & we were going to be garrotted. How it all ended I dont remember. I think we got into bed with the help of the waiter and we slept till late next day. The next thing was to see about terms, so we approached the proprietor on the subject there & then. He couldn't think of taking us for less than 7 frcs 50c. a day which was much more than we could afford. At this point Miss R. said very pathetically in a voice that would have melted a stone "You see we are such very poor devils of artists and we have come all the way from N.Z. to paint your beautiful country" The proprietor, quite overcome made a low bow & said "Madam there is nothing dishonorable in either being poor or an artist," and immediately reduced his tariff to 5 frcs merely stipulating that we should introduce his hotel as often and as large as possible into our sketches. Pennell the artist had been here before us illustrating a book of travels in these parts. It is all ever so nice here, quite what I want & plenty of stuff to paint for months to come. Such color! but there I can never make you understand how beautiful it all is. The Provençal women are famed for their beauty, rather a classical type, straight features with clear olive skins. There is a wonderful Roman amphitheatre where they have bullfights on Sundays in the summer, it sounds pagan enough! I shall write more fully when I have explored a bit, my bicycle has been such a comfort and I am feeling so well & fit since I have had it. Next week a friend of Miss R.s, a Miss Astley is coming from England to join us for a few weeks. She is an invalide and has a villa in San Remo. She wants to take lessons from me before going on there so will break her journey here for that purpose. I have also a commission to paint a £10 picture from a cousin of Miss R.s so my little artistic pot is kept boiling gently, is it not? I am wondering how you all are and if you & Bert have managed to find a house that will suit us. What about that new suburb Kilburnie on the hill, is it not possible to get a house there? I am anxious for news of Frank & wish my letters could have come in before finishing this. . . . Goodbye darling

[79] To Rachel Hodgkins, 29 October 1901

> Hotel du Forum, Arles, S. Rhone. 29.10.01

My darling Mother,

I had hoped for a line from you before posting this. I have been feeling very anxious and unhappy about Frank since your last very disheartening account of him. I think if he is as bad as you say Bert should try and arrange to stay in Wellington & take a small house and I shall arrange so that I shall be out with you again by the middle of next year. It frets me dreadfully to think of Willie being burdened with him and it is not right or good for him to be alone by himself among strangers. I do not know what to suggest, I feel much tempted to come out to you by Xmas and help start a home where we can look after him. If Bert feels he cannot undertake the expense by himself, I am *quite* willing to come, do write fully all you think – it does not seem right that I should be away from you when you have this trouble & responsibility to face. At least we could share it and perhaps lighten it. It will be no hardship to come back, much as I love this life I feel it is a one sided & very selfish existence and directly I have finished what I

have set myself to do I shall make tracks for N.Z. with all possible speed . . . .
Mother, where does the time go to? To think I have been at Home 7 months and
it feels like 7 weeks. I have had 3 weeks hard work since last I wrote and have
managed to turn out quite an unprecedented amount of work, it is a land of
enchantment you can't help painting, everything & everybody is a picture. Alas,
today we have had the first warning note to move on in a cold northerly wind
which has changed into a steady downpour and we are sitting in our respective
bedrooms with hot bottles at our feet. . . . Miss R.s friend Miss Astley stayed with
us for 10 days during which I gave her sketching lessons. She is very delicate &
has to spend the winter abroad. She reminded me so of Mrs. Scott both in looks
& manner. We are to join her at her villa in San Remo on the 15th. and give her
more sketching lessons. She sends pathetic postcards for me to come to her rescue
as soon as possible and save her from committing more artistic atrocities. This
gives me another month in Europe and is an excellent arrangement for me. If I
can only continue to pay my way in the same satisfactory manner all through!

Horrors! Wait a minute! My hot water bottle has burst! ! that's a dirty little
trick to play one at the beginning of winter isn't it and in a foreign land where
everything is 3 times as dear as it should be. Oh! well I shall have to use Miss
Richmonds flannel petticoat & my own stockings – I certainly can't afford
another one . . . . Talking of stockings mine are in sad need of a little darning
wool. I am glad you are spared the distressing sight. Some day Miss R. & I are
going to have a day off and do a little mending. I had a paper from Willie today
– which recorded among other news that Mrs. W. Hodgkins was visiting her
Mother. What does this mean? explain! Yours and Sissie's letters are much too
short & sweet I swallow them like oysters at one gulp. . . . You never tell me
anything about the children & what they say and do. Now for a few questions
which I insist on your answering. Are you well? do they give you plenty to eat? Are
they kind to you? DO YOU MISS ME ! ! ! Is Bert sober and industrious and *have*
you given up that pernicious habit of sitting in the grate? That reminds me how
cold my poor feet are. Last night I was nearly eaten alive by mosquitoes, left off
the net & the wretches got in & today the modelling of my features is somewhat
lost. We have been for two or three picnics to different places, it is all flat country
round about, vineyards mostly. The canals are very paintable with tall poplars on
either bank & flat bottomed looking craft. Sis would love them. The river is our
greatest joy, the old houses toppling over into it and the washer women lining the
banks – they look like a chattering line of magpies they nearly all dress in black
& white. There is not much shipping but . . . the queer flapping lateen sailed
boats are good things to paint. I regret I am unable to tell you about the Roman
remains – we are much too busy to go and see them. Did I tell you we had a nice
little slab of Forum sandwiched in between our hotel and a barbers saloon next
door. . . . Goodbye dear I am sorry this is such a scrappy letter, more next time.
Scrape all the news about the Dunedin show together for me & be sure & tell me

exactly what people say about my pictures, it is too soon to expect any improvement but ahem! there are people on this side of the world who seem to think there is no need for any improvement. As there is no possible chance of your seeing my present work I can safely say it is a long way better than anything I have done so far. . . .

[80] To Isabel Field, 6 November 1901

Hotel du Forum, Arles, S. Rhone. 6.11.01

My dearest Sis

. . . . I do sympathise with you dear so much in your painting I know that old familiar pain – growing stale and losing one's freshness of ideas – but wait awhile old girl and dont try & force your brush – the children are growing older every day now and will soon cease to want your attention so much – and in the meantime what better work can you do than bring up four beautiful children? My work is as nothing compared to it – we poor spinsters must embrace something, if it is only a profession – I snapped at Mr. Garstin when he said this but in my heart I know it is true – my art is everything to me – at least at present – but I know it is not the higher life or the right life for a woman. The older I grow the more convinced I am that after all love is everything and one's own people become more precious & needful to one than all else in the world. To be without ties seems to me awful beyond words. When I think of Miss Richmond I feel sad – everyone wanting her – no one needing her – no niche, no reason why she should go home. Some good man has missed a great happiness. It is the tradition of her family to bring happiness when they give love and I do not wonder at it knowing her. It was sweet of Mrs. Atkinson[20] to read you her letters. What has she been saying about me? She has far too exalted an opinion of my work & too little of her own – she will never be a great painter, she has nice taste & judgement but lacks fire & originality. So Will thinks my letters are not long enough greedy cormorant, I knew Miss R's would spoil you, her letters are poems compared to my uninteresting scribbles. She writes as she speaks, wittily and to the point. She is the dearest piece of perfection I have ever met and unlike most perfection not in the least tiring to live up to. With all her poetical nature she has a solid backbone of fact which is good for us both and keeps us from any inclination to drift. There has been a sudden snap of cold weather this last week, the mistral

---

[20] Miss Richmond's elder sister Ann was married to Tudor Atkinson, reinforcing in the second generation the links between the Richmond and Atkinson families who had settled in New Plymouth in 1853 and played so prominent a role in the political and cultural life of the new colony. Harry Atkinson, Tudor's father, was the Premier who lost to the Liberals in the 1890 elections. The political differences between the Field/Hodgkins and Richmond/Atkinson families became the subject of teasing between FH and Miss Richmond.

roaring like a thousand lions burst down upon us from the mountains in the most offensive manner – stripped the trees bare and sent the barometer down almost to freezing point and has quite banished any regrets we may have felt at leaving Arles, and our one idea now is to quit it as quickly and as warmly as we can. We are both fighting colds – Miss Richmond in her room with a cold water compress (made out of her sponge bag and a woolen vest) me in my room with an Elliman plaster on my lower chest. We were to have started for San Remo today but I felt too seedy to travel so we have postponed it till next week. . . . in cases like this we congratulate ourselves we have no husbands to consider – they would never let you change your mind at the 11th. hour. Think of Will or Willy, how cross they would have been, they would have insisted on your going and very probably you would have died on the way! Two days ago we made our farewells to our beautiful Arlesian friends – in the market where we paint nearly every day. We had a touching and imposing scene. To the poulterer who was our best & most intimate friend we presented a photo of ourselves with a suitable inscription. She was a nice woman and we were grateful for little attentions in the way of chaufrettes to keep our feet warm, cups of black coffee on cold days & various little kindnesses. Her profession was the one thing against her. She was *always* killing a bird or an animal of some description but with such a light heart and deft fingers we forgave tho' we did not approve – I must tell you, this market is a huge white washed building lighted from above round which the different tradeswomen have their stalls, imagine the color with the sun overhead – the butcher's stall, made to look as red as possible with crimson colored tables & awnings to help out the illusion of a plentiful supply of meat – this stall is flanked by the poulterer on the left who is always in a cloud of feathers and distressed cackling & gurgling from the strangling victims. Then comes the green grocer with her two pretty daughters always beaming from behind a barricade of pumpkins, melons, pomegranates, figs and green stuff. This is my favourite stall and I have made many studies of it. Then there is a corner given up to pottery & earthenware of many colors & shapes. These are a great temptation to my purse, but I have learned to deny myself, partly because of the expense, partly because they are so brittle & wont travel. I remember my first day in Caudebec, I bought as many as I could carry away – delighted to get so much for so little but alas when it came to packing them it was quite another pair of shoes. . . .

Villa Solaro, San Remo, Italy. 19.11.01

We have been here a week today and these are quite the most comfortable quarters we have struck yet. Just recovering from a bad cold and am not feeling quite fit, not sick you know, but out of sorts and not able for any work and it is so jolly having a nice comfortable "homey" house where one is not paying 5 frcs daily and where they make me stay in bed for breakfast. . . . I am afraid we will be horribly spoilt by the time we leave here . . . . The villa itself is delightful it belongs to an American artist & has a lovely studio & is most artistically furnished. . . . By the bye, I have just received a paper from Willy with a perfectly idiotic account of my prowess in the art line – it is really just a little too strong and if Miss Richmond told her sister all that rubbish I can only say it is not true. The paint is laid on a little too thick & wants lifting a trifle. To read in cold print that "I have nothing to learn" & "Mr. Garstin says so" is too much. Why make a fool of me. . . .

[81] To Rachel Hodgkins, 2 December 1901

Albergo Mont Allegro, Rapallo, Italy. 2.12.01

My darling Mother,

It was so nice getting your last letter written from the little cottage on the hill – how sweet of Sis to do it up so cosily for you and I am longing to see it . . . tell me in your next letter if you find the work hard – have you got a gas stove? Also do you get a charwoman for the rougher work. I know how helpful & good dear old Bert is so I am not afraid he will let you over work yourself. How well it has all panned out has it not and I now feel for the first time there is no reason why I should not prolong my stay at home a few months longer – and give myself a fair chance of making the most of my opportunities. . . . We had a very happy fortnight [at San Remo] . . . . We did appreciate the home comforts, olive wood fires, hot baths, good plain English cooking and plenty of books & magazines. The studio was a perfectly delicious place, top light, oaken furniture, old masters, Eastern rugs and all the rest of it with a window opening onto a sunny loggia with marble steps down to the garden. We had our meals out of doors and that in itself made everything taste much nicer. Miss Astley is supposed to spend 22 hours out of the 24 out of doors . . . . It is a very wonderful treatment and how widely opposed to the old methods of treating tubercular troubles. . . . Fancy in my wanderings one day on the hill I found a gnaio tree. I could hardly believe my eyes & was glad when Miss R. bore me out & verified our old N.Z. friend. . . . The Italians are a small wizened toil worn looking lot – they are so desperately poor – poor souls, ground down by heavy taxation to support army & navy . . . . When the olive crops are good all goes well but when they fail there is much hunger & distress . . . . It is nearly a fortnight since we left San Remo . . . and took an early train for Genoa en route for anywhere, in a deliciously vague mood as to future destination. All we wanted was to find a nice cheap little inn in an equally nice warm little corner, somewhere, anywhere away from obnoxious silklined English tourists – how I *hate* them and I no longer marvel at the intense dislike they inspire abroad wherever they go. There is a particular British aggressiveness & smugness about them that is indescribable, & yet do you wonder at it? There is something of pride to stiffen one's back in belonging to a nation whose gold, bank notes, & cheques are worth more than any other country. It is nice to be in a country again which is friendly to England, no longer are our ears vexed by nasty little boys singing a disgusting little ditty beginning "Vive les Boers" I have boxed many French ears for this insult – thereby helping to avenge my country. At Arles we strongly suspected our first confectioner of strong Pro Boer tendencies, mainly founded on the fact that she frequently gave us stale cakes . . . .

We started from the Villa Solaro last Friday week, our luggage piled high on a voiture, Miss R & self intending to ride down the hill to the station on our bicycles. As luck wld have it half way down I struck glass & got badly punctured. I signed to Miss R to go and see after our baggage while I walked my poor disabled bike to the foot of the hill where I got a cab, and putting the machine on top drove to the station, just in time to catch our train . . . . On our arrival [at Genoa] we took the most unpretentious hotel omnibus we could find and drove to what we discovered to be a small & very clean German Inn . . . . We went to bed but not to sleep – our hotel was situated somewhere between the railway station & the docks a thin slip of a house with streets on 3 sides of it & the noises were ceaseless, shrieking trains, electric trams, barrell organs street cries & belated revellers and just as we were dropping off to sleep . . . it all started all over again and finally a particularly disagreeable noise thro the keyhole advised that it was eight o'clock and time to get up. On cross examining Miss R at breakfast I discovered that *she* had heard none of the noises that *I* had heard and *I* had heard none of the noises *she* had heard, which led me to believe that we had both slept a good deal more than we had imagined. . . .

. . . . Miss R. is a most capital traveller, calm and very un-fussy. She does all the ticket-taking & registering & I am generally told off to sit on our luggage and see that no one molests it, and keep a tally of accounts which we generally square up in the train. I find sightseeing more wearing than weeks of painting. . . . it was with a sigh of relief I said goodbye to Genoa and waved my hand to Christopher Columbus, standing chilly & dignified in scanty garments in the Place near the railway station – it is the statue, you remember, that Mark Twain is so funny about in Tramp Abroad.

Arrived at Rapallo, (we were the only passengers) . . . . we left our luggage & proceeded to make a tour of inspection of the town & if possible find a place cheap enough for our purses. These winter resorts are so expensive, 8, 9 & 10 frcs. being the lowest they will take you for. We went to at least 6 hotels, all laid out to attract tourists – none of which wld look at us under 8 frcs and just as were getting quite hopeless we spied a modest looking little Inn, quite unpretentious but very clean looking – it looked more in our line so we ventured in and we were so impressed by the kindliness & hospitality of the padrona and his wife and liking our rooms so much we decided at once to stay where we were & send for our luggage. They do us for 5.50 – & we are really very comfortable indeed. We have two bedrooms opening on to a sitting room the use of which they have given us. . . . Today is our first wet day and we are indoors both writing, our feet on delicious hot Scaldinos (charcoal stoves). . . . At first they only gave us one Scaldino between us, but I found that Miss R's feet were so much ahem! larger than mine that I came off very badly indeed as regards heat so I petitioned for another and now we have ceased quarrelling and have one apiece. . . . Rapallo is not as beautiful as we had hoped to find it – altogether too much like a well painted drop scene – but then I think the whole Riviera rather gives one that impression – the houses here are painted to represent palaces and the spaces between the windows are often filled in with life size figures of madonnas, old masters, sculptors & poets – there is too much Villa-dom for my taste, and the gay Casinos palm trees and all the gay continental riff-raff you meet with in every town helps the illusion of a bright colored scene painting however there are ample compensations in the crowd of beautiful models that are to be had here. The lacemakers who sit outside their doors in the older part of the town are charming, a postcard I am sending you will describe them better than any words of mine. They make all sorts of lace, but principally Torchon, for which they get 8d a day & can make no more no matter how hard they work – compare this wage with a colonial sewing girl who gets 4/- & her keep. . . .

6th. Dec.

Fancy, a little more than a fortnight to the shortest day. We are having wonderful weather, clear bright days, fiercely hot sun but a cold wind which tempers it . . . . I am busy at present on a biggish picture of some gipsies I have discovered outside the town. They are camped in an old green caravan, and are a disreputable tho picturesque lot. I have made friends with them . . . . The father gipsy has a wooden leg, the father's friend has one eye but the donkey, the two eldest daughters of the house and the sons are beautiful and it is them I am painting, lighting a fire while the blue smoke curls across the green caravan and a bright jumble of color in which donkey and all their bright colored clothes help to join a harmonious whole. It is so good for one living in a house where they talk nothing but Italian – one is forced to try & learn it. Miss R. very kindly gives me a lesson every night. I find it much easier than French or perhaps my French has made it much easier for me to understand it.

Dec 7th.

. . . . How are Jean & Willie. . . . I dont write to them as often as I would like to . . . painting takes up all my strength & time, and it is very disappointing to find I am not nearly as strong as I hoped to find myself, free from studio work & the strain of teaching. I had hoped to be a tower of strength by this time with the steady, regular out of door life but that tiresome illness coming home has left me subject to attacks whenever I get overtired or chilled. I am in good hands so dont have a moments uneasiness about me. Miss R. is a dragon of discretion & watchfulness and takes the greatest care of me. I am well & fit for anything between whiles and am turning out pictures at a great rate. You would think at the rate at which we are spinning that our web would soon be exhausted but there is such infinite variety of material in a land like this it wld be impossible to paint oneself out. Thank Sis for her letter and tell her that her idea about the Maori photos is a very good one – but I think it would be a mistake to waste time faking heads when my time is so precious and a live dog is better than a dead lion any day – a copy is always dull & lifeless and I think it would be wiser to wait till I return to N.Z. before tackling any more Maories tho I regret as much as she does that I shall have none of my dear beautiful people in my show. I wonder if my sketches have reached you yet. I am so anxious to hear what you all think of them. I wish you could see my present work it seems to me to be much stronger fresher & original. I am nervous about their being late for the Dunedin show & not selling in consequence. Be sure and send them round the Colony till they sell. Surely I must sell after that very flattering notice in the "Times"![21] Prices might safely be doubled! I find on looking at my bank book tonight that I have spent £100 up to date, that leaves me with £80 to my balance at the Bank, which will keep me going for some time longer – I had hoped to afford a trip to Florence from here but I am afraid it cannot be managed, tho it seems such a great pity to miss such a chance of seeing it when I am so near, but if I am to have a Show in London I must have enough money to keep me going while there – it is appalling the way the money goes – we live as cheaply as we know how – & yet somehow it flies. . . .

10th. [December]

I have left finishing this to the last as I hoped your letters might come before the mail closed. No such luck, tho Miss R. had hers two days ago. Is it possible you have forgotten to write? if so this letter should heap coals on your head.

Much love to you all from your ever loving Fanny.

[82] TO RACHEL HODGKINS, 20 DECEMBER 1901

Albergo Mont Allegro, Rapallo, Riviera de Levante, Italy. 20.12.01

My dearest Mother,

Very little has happened since my last letter – except rain – it has rained more or less steadily for the last fortnight and we are beginning to despair of ever seeing

---

[21] 'Mr Garstin was . . . struck with the originality, strength and colour of her work . . . . He states that she has nothing to learn, and he predicts a brilliant future for her.' *Otago Daily Times*, 28 Sept. 1901, p.7. This was the article that had earlier aroused her indignation.

the sun again. . . . Miss R. is worse off than I am as she cannot work away from nature or the model & has no taste as she says for "making pictures in the dark" which she rudely calls my creations from my imagination. Our room is a poky little place, very dark & gloomy. Yesterday I went forth & scoured the streets & brought home a bedraggled little model, very like a wet hen, but good enough to keep us busy for a few days. . . .

21st. [December] Wet again – the shortest day – but owing to the rain & our low spirits generally it has been the longest day I ever remember – have thought seriously of catching the next steamer home – the weather was bad last week but the last two days it has been simply immoral – painted all the morning, washed it out in the afternoon – Miss R. went out and brought home a pot of honey to sweeten my temper – she says I am ungrateful because I said it was the kind of stuff prisoners would be given as a great treat on Sundays – late in the afternoon I was struck by a happy thought that we should give each other Christmas presents & that we should go out straight away & choose them. . . . I wanted a maltese tie badly & so did Miss R. so we hied ourselves to the lace shop – greatly sustained by the thought that we were doing a kind & generous action – we chose two very nice ties, (good lace is a kind of thing that justifies itself over & over again & is not really a bit extravagant) and formally presented each other with them & returned home much more cheerful & light-hearted & quite pleased with ourselves.

22nd. [December] It has been finer today – this morning I painted some old houses with the silver olive trees as a background . . . . I had an old Italian artist looking over my shoulder as I painted – you never saw such excitement he applauded every stroke & got so worked up I thought he would have a fit, & whenever I put on color he didnt approve of he ground his teeth & snapped his fingers with disgust – finally I entered into the spirit of it & feeling I was on my mettle I turned out quite a smartish thing. He acted as an excellent bodyguard & kept all the small boys off, threatening them in violent language whenever they attempted to approach – he was a nice old man, & we had a little polite conversation in French after he had calmed down a bit – & with many compliments we said goodbye. I have found several splendid models – on closer acquaintance I have found the people improve tremendously – they are naturally rather stern & serious looking, at least the Northern Italians are – & want knowing. In our wanderings one day on the hill we made friends with a peasant family – & I have since painted one of the children, they are a family of extraordinary beauty – and I love going up there merely to gaze at them.

Xmas Day. It cleared up yesterday for a short time & the sun came out & went

down in a fiery sky – giving us great hopes of a fine day today – not a bit of it –
it is raining harder than ever . . . . We had a big budget of letters which have
cheered us up considerably . . . . Letter from Dora Meeson announcing her
engagement to a fellow student – poor foolish girl – her career done for . . . . We
spent most of the day looking forward & speculating on our dinner so low have
we fallen! This morning we were presented with a beautiful bouquet of flowers &
many pretty wishes in Italian – "Buona Festa" is their "Merry Xmas". We read the
service had lunch, slept all the afternoon & at 7 went down to dinner very curious
as to what they wld give us – a special bottle of Malaga wine was given us, then
came turkey – devoid of trimmings of any kind but good, then an Italian
imitation of plum pudding with a holly tree planted in the middle of it & flaming
furiously . . . . A paper arrived yesterday from Willy with a description of the
O.A.S. It gave me a bad pang to think they had had a show without my illustrious
name in their catalogue. Sis has amply atoned, just fancy 12 pictures, how did she
manage it, I see she is re-painting her Manapouri sketches – good line! and good
luck to them. . . . It was a great blow my pictures not arriving in time, it will
hinder their sale considerably I am afraid. . . .

San Remo 31st. [December] We couldn't stand Rapallo any longer – it refused
to clear so *we* had to. . . . As Miss A[stley] was so ill I thought it wiser to come
to this hotel where I am comfortable, not to say luxurious, rather lonely but too
busy to think much about it. . . .

*Dr Scott had arranged for FH's paintings to be included in the Otago Art Society's
exhibition. The* Otago Daily Times *of 19 November reported: 'An additional
attraction to the exhibition is now to be seen in 12 pictures forwarded by Miss F. M.
Hodgkins, at present studying in France, and these pictures alone are worth a visit.
These only arrived yesterday, and no time was lost in hanging them, a couple of screens
in front of the stage being utilised.'*

[83] To Isabel Field, 20 January 1902

Grand Hotel, Oneglia, Italy. 20.1.02

My dearest old girl

Words can't tell you how happy your last two letters made me. Such dear
letters full of warm generous sympathy, tho' far, far too much praise. It rejoiced
my heart to hear that you approved of my work. I care so dreadfully for your &
Dr. Scott's opinion and I hardly dared open your letter. I was so frightened you
might think I had fallen off. Oh! my dear such a load is lifted from me, I never

dreamed of their getting such a reception & selling so well, and I am full of gratitude & thankfulness for all you have done for me. How good of Dr. Scott to get them into the gallery. I have written to thank him. Your letters came one morning when I was at San Remo. I swallowed them at a gulp, then took them up to a quiet place among the olives and read them over again, gathering up all the crumbs I had overlooked at my first hasty glance. . . . Later I showed your letters to Miss R. & she thought them so beautiful she asked to be allowed to show them to Miss Astley who pronounced them "fine literature" How dare you say all those absurd things about your own painting. . . . dont let me hear any more nonsense about "house painting" & want of quality. I wouldn't for worlds have you exchange that cunning slickness of yours for the more "worried" look that striving after quality sometimes gives. Many can worry quality into a picture but few can run up a tree with that magical touch of yours & sell said tree for £14. My only fear for you is that you are too clever and facile which rather takes the place of a more subtle insight into nature. I take it there can be no abiding pleasure in a picture which lacks truth – it is so easy for an unshackled free-lance like myself to talk – if *I* had a husband and four children, divil a bit would I bother about quality – quality wont always help to buy the baby a new frock, while smart chic – ahem! *devilishly* clever work will.

What luck my not pricing my pictures, & by the merest chance too, if I hadnt been in such a hurry I should have named them properly & priced them, my lucky star must be looking up – poor Miss R. I hope they will manage to knock off some of the £5. What an iniquitous duty it is! & what a way to encourage local artists to send out their work. By the way how did Will as an upright Government member reconcile his conscience to defrauding the customs & smuggling his sister-in-laws pictures thro.

. . . . For the last four days we have had a Miss Welton, a friend of Miss Astley's we met at San Remo, & whom we liked so much & found so entertaining we asked her to join us here for a few days which she did. She wanted to take lessons from me but I did not care to bother, but promised if she would come to us I wld drop pearls which she could have for the picking up. She has now gone & Miss R & I have just gone over a list of all the articles we fleeced her of before we wld let her go – items, tin of cocoa, ditto tea, ditto bull's eyes hot water bottle (cost her 17/6 bought it for 2/6) all her literature, novels, papers etc. cobalt (all she had) a priceless tube of rose madder and her methylated spirits. She said she had never fallen among such thieves & considered herself lucky to have escaped with her skin. . . . *Dont* read my stupid letters to Mrs Tudor Atkinson – tell her thro' the telephone some night that her sister is looking well – ever so much *better* than when she joined me in Paris don't forget for I fancy she worries a good deal about D.K.R's health – tell her also we have instituted cocoa suppers & we dont spend quite all our money on paints & models as she seems to think. Tell me on a private sheet what you think of Miss R's pictures if you see them. I think she has gone ahead in leaps & bounds & is painting a great deal now in water color & very cleverly too. . . .

[Postscript] Be sure & deduct all expenses from my account.

[84] TO RACHEL HODGKINS, 8 FEBRUARY 1902

Grand Hotel, Oneglia, Italy. 8.2.02

My darling Mother,

Your last dear letter has only just reached me – nearly 3 weeks late – you must have missed the Frisco dear. . . . I didnt take to drink as some people might have done – I merely gave way to fit after fit of violent irrittibbillitty and Miss R. humbly asks you for her own sake that you will see & not miss another mail. I have been thinking a great deal of what you said about Bert feeling unsettled & wishing to go off to S. Africa.[22] I can quite understand him wanting to go but I think now that he has taken up the house he ought to stick to it for at least a year. I have quite made up my mind that I shall be back with you at Xmas – but if he leaves you I shall come home at once. The year will soon pass & once I am back with you he will be free to go where he likes. I know how he feels – poor old boy – & I know how bad it feels to see an opportunity slipping from one, but I feel most strongly that he should consider himself bound to you for at least this year till I come out again. Tell him that as soon as my wander year is over he will be free to start on his . . . . I am afraid you often feel lonely dear – I am glad you see so much of the children – I loved hearing about them, & am looking forward to seeing their photos. Is Bert often out at night? You dont say anything about neighbors – and is Devon St in the new suburb of Kelbourne? if so haven't they started their new trams? Do you get plenty to read? . . . I have hardly seen a book since I left England – we get the Spectator & Punch sent on from the Villa Solaro & that with a volume of Shakespeare & an Italian grammar is all our literature. We do Italian every night & Miss R. when ever I let her reads Shakespeare aloud. . . . I am getting impatient to get back to England & see about my exhibition. Mr. Garstin writes urging me to go at once as he thinks I am leaving it too late & will find a difficulty in getting a gallery . . . . He is sanguine that if I can but get them to look at my work I will have a success but who knows! things do go so very cronk & contrariwise in this very inferior planet, and I am nervous & low spirited about my work. I want some criticism badly and I fancy I am a bit stale. I have worked at too high a pressure & suddenly things have grown uninteresting and insufficient. Another thing, it has been raining on & off for for nearly a fortnight & everything looks ugly & dirty & cold & eastwindy & foggy & muddy & fishy

---

[22] Both Bert and Percy were thinking of volunteering for the South African War. Percy joined the 9th Contingent in April 1902, but Bert remained at his job with the Civil Service in Wellington.

& smelly & altogether beastly. . . . So next Wed, if we can get our things finished by then we are going to San Remo en route for England. . . . . We hope to be in London about a week. Imagine me during that time tramping round to different art dealers & agents inducing them to make their fortunes by running a show for me. I anticipate nothing but rebuffs but intend to enjoy it all the same. Miss R. is a great standby, always cheerful & sanguine & very business like – & I do not know what I should do without her. Mr. Garstin has promised me help & letters but I know I must stand or fall on my own merits . . . . We are looking forward to going down to Penzance & meeting the artists there. We have mapped out a rough sort of plan for the year – we thought we should go abroad again in July, either with the Garstins or Mr Stanhope Forbes, this time to Brittany, and then about Sept make our way slowly South to Venice & paint there for a month or two & I should catch my boat from there & Miss R. wld either come with me or return to England. This wld give me a chance of getting plenty of material to bring back & work from . . . . Our last plan is to come home again when we have made our fortunes & take a villa somewhere in Italy & have our respective neices to live with us – & introduce them to the advantages of continental life. Poor Will I was so sorry to hear of the sad accident to his camera. What wretched bad luck. Sis will have to paint a picture & sell it & buy him another for his birthday. I've started a camera myself – I thought I was sadly neglecting my opportunities so I thought I wld spend the £1 Sis sent me & buy a Kodak – I got it last week . . . & I've snapped unceasingly ever since . . . .

. . . . I want you in your next letter to tell me more about Frank who he is with & what he does with himself [23]. . . .

[85] TO WILLIAM HODGKINS, 11 FEBRUARY 1902

Grand Hotel, Oneglia, Italy. 11th-2-02

My dearest Willie

Many thanks for your kind letter, also for forwarding draft to the Bank. I shall feel much happier with an extra £42 to my credit, my funds were getting uncomfortably low . . . . What about my insurance premium, which I think falls due some time in May? I don't think you have any funds of mine in hand so it had better come out of the next sale of pictures – I shall be sending out again quite shortly – also, my bill for frames – you should have deducted it from my picture money – however please do so next time. . . . We leave here on the 14th for S. Remo where we shall get vaccinated before going to England . . . . It is a precaution everyone should take these small-poxy times . . . . There is a scare all

[23] The family had apparently concealed from FH the news that Frank had been committed to Seacliff Asylum in 1901.

along the Riviera, it has appeard at Nice & S. Remo & yesterday two cases were reported from here. . . . We went for a walk in the woods this morning and the first signs of an Italian spring gave me some idea of how beautiful it must be here later on – the pink & white almond blossom among the olive woods – & the ground just beginning to show the color of violets, hyacinths & anemonies – I wish we could see the spring thro' but it is better to go back to England & see what can be done about my pictures . . . . Have I ever thanked you for all the papers you sent me? Would you like me to send you on the Spectator when we have read it? a kind friend sends it to us. I send you one by this post & if you like it I will continue to send it. It is always good reading. Mother will send you on my home letter I expect – this is only a scrap to thank you for all the trouble you have taken about my money affairs. This is my 5th letter this mail so goodbye. I am quite warped with sitting so long in the same position.

Love to Jean & much to yourself
Yours lovingly
Fanny.

PART FIVE

1902

'Little Mother Pulling at My Heart Strings'

1 Wellington Terrace, Penzance. 7.3.2.

My dearest Sis

. . . . It is a long cry from the North of Italy to the South of England but somehow we have managed it & here we are – arrived two days ago – very comfortable – but still uncertain whether we like ourselves better on the Riviera or in Cornwall. If it were only a little warmer! and of course I caught influenza in London and am feeling rather shivery & limp in consequence. We are housed two doors from the Garstins with a friend of theirs a Miss Parks, a kind old thing who treats us very well . . . . we are paying 30/- this week but after that by foregoing late dinner & having tea instead she is taking us for 25/. Of course we could do it cheaper than this by boarding ourselves but neither of us feel equal to it just at present – later on we may experiment & try and reduce expenses. To hark back to Oneglia . . . . on the train we fell in with some English ladies who . . . . told us some exciting stories of ladies travelling on the night trains being chloroformed & robbed so we determined to take all precautions & if necessary fight for life dearly, so accordingly towards evening we arranged a deadly sort of mantrap of string & hat boxes & umbrellas & having strapped up the door securely we lay down to sleep & had no sooner composed ourselves when the guard came round for the tickets & wanted to know in good strenuous French what we meant by tying up the door – so we had to knock down our barricades, & we spent a sleepless & interminable night – waiting for the burglar who never came. Towards dawn a phantom guard appeared & told us we wld stop for coffee at the next station – and red-eyed, sleepy & dishevelled we crept out & drank in gloomy silence the most delicious cup of coffee that ever warmed the heart of man. We had gone to bed under blue skys & woke up under low grey ones hanging over long reaches of red ploughed land broken by hedges & little clumps of leafless trees looking like delicate etchings against the skyline. They are so beautiful these leafless trees, you wld paint them gloriously with your nimble brush – I hate the idea of spring with its foolish green leaves & sentimentality everyone here is babbling about it, the first primrose etc – never was a young person so disinclined to welcome the billing & cooing and all the other foolishness that is supposed to come at this time of year. The beech trees are brown with bud & in a week or two the wretched leaves will be out. They are to me infinitely more beautiful in their present state and I must hurry up & get some sketches before they turn.

. . . . My head reels now when I think of all we did in the first 3 days in London . . . . The first morning I met Miss R. a foggy dirty morning, everything looking like a big inkpot and we proceeded to Dowdeswells with a portfolio of sketches under my arm. I now find out I made a grave mistake not mounting & framing a few before I showed them to the dealers – I was told they were fools and – now

I know it – not because they wouldn't touch my sketches but because – well – because they are fools. We swam into Dowdeswells heads high – crimson pile carpet & damask hangings costing at least £10 a foot – Dowdeswell Senior received us, a benevolent looking old man – & he liked my things so much that I was deceived into thinking he meant business – however he said he wld like to show them to his son – who was then out & wld we leave them & return in an hour. We did so – but alas when we returned the benevolent old man had disappeared & in his place was a dreadful person with a brutal jaw and a shark like expression – cad – cad – cadissimo! He said my work was *very nice* but not what *his clientèle* wanted – now if I had brought flower gardens for instance it wld have been quite another matter. The general public *must* have flower gardens just now at any cost & he didnt think there was any demand for my kind of work. Early Italian work was also very popular & if I could show them any decorative sketches à la Botticelli he thought they would stand a better chance. By this time I began to grasp that until I had made some kind of a name I could hope to get no dealer to run a show for me – they wont take the risk until they are assured of a success – and they accordingly make all sorts of excuses to get rid of you. We next went on to the Fine Arts – I had two letters to the proprietor Mr. Huish, one from Mr. Garstin & another from his Mr. H's brother in law whom I met in Dunedin before I left. Mr. Huish however was ill & we could not see him – I was sorry for I heard he was a gentleman and a very artistic man. His gallery is considered even better than Mr. Dowdeswells – but oh! the rubbish I saw on his walls – it made me sad – & ever so many sold – they were nearly all flower gardens – there is a horticultural wave passing over the Art world just now Parsons[1] leading & many followers following a long way after. Our next visit was to the Editor of the "Studio" Mr. Holme, he is a busy man but I had a letter from Mr. Garstin which proved an open sesame – I send you a copy of it. I thought it was so charmingly expressed –

Dear Mr. Holme,

This is to introduce Miss Hodgkins a friend of mine and I think you will agree with me a very clever & interesting watercolorist. She comes from N.Z. where all her art training has been gained. Well! it is no disparagement to N.Z. to say that this is very wonderful! I have had a good deal of experience in the training of art students and I feel that this case upsets my ideas very much – but I expect Miss H. is the exception that proves the rule – that art does not come spontaneously but is the product of pains & labor & not a little conscious & unconscious imitation anyhow let me have the pleasure of introducing her to you & you can judge for yourself.

. . . .

[1] Alfred Parsons RA, RI, PRWS (1847-1920), a painter of pastoral scenes, landscapes, gardens and plants.

Mr Holme was delightful & soothed my ruffled feelings with judicially administered praise which was as "oil unto my bones" after Dowdeswell & Co's treatment, & he told us much concerning wicked hardhearted dealers & their little ways – he advised me strongly to exhibit at the different galleries before trying to have a show & he offered me any letters I wanted to enable me to do so – however I find I am too late for them all but the Academy and the NEAC. He was much taken with my Maori work – of wh I had one or two, & would have reproduced them had they been in black & white & has asked me to send him some typical Maori work for reproduction – & if he approves he will print it. This is a good thing, too good to be spoiled by shoddy work faked from photos this side of the world so I am going to reserve it till I come out at the end of the year & get some genuine native studies. Mr. Holme showed me some beautiful black & white work, the originals of many old "Studio" friends, Mortimer Menpes' etchings, charcoals by that clever Frenchman Dupuis & many others. I told him how much we prized the "Studio" in the Colonies & how it was a source of much help & inspiration to us all – after this we went on to lunch with Mrs. Walter Sickert at her rooms in Grey's Inn. She is an old friend of Miss R's & has just published a book which has been very well reviewed – it is called "Wistons" I havent read it yet but they say it is very clever – she is a daughter of Richard Cobden & last year she divorced her husband the gay Walter who I daresay you know is an eccentric & decadent artist who prides himself on never painting anything which is obvious – & who is always figuratively of course, trying to stand on his head[2] – after lunch we hied West to Leighton House there to see Miss Eleanor Brickdale's pictures. They were beautiful – about 40 smallish sized water colors – illustrating allegories & proverbs treated decoratively, not unlike Miss Broome's things in design, The Vain Lady & Pride Goeth before Destruction, you remember, color flashed jewel-like from every frame – oh! happy woman to paint like that & give such pleasure – it was a refreshment of the soul to see them – some years ago she took her things to Dowdeswells who flouted them – finally however he gave her £10 for each sketch then proceeded to sell them for five times the amount, now she is famous & London is raving over her – look up her work in the "Studio" & see for yourself how beautiful her designs are[3]. . . . Next day we tramped round some more galleries – Graves & Clifford's in the Haymarket, this time without my sketches, merely enquiring their terms, which in most cases was about the same – 25 per cent on the profits & in some cases a deposit –

[2] Ellen Cobden, daughter of the liberal politician and founder of the Anti-Corn Law League, married Walter Sickert (1860-1942) in 1885. They were divorced in 1899, after which Sickert settled in Dieppe where he remained until 1905. He exhibited with the NEAC 1888-1912, so FH may have seen his work. He was one of the leading English impressionists, who found his subject matter in the working-class environment of modern urban life, the music halls, shabby interiors and humble streets.

[3] Eleanor Brickdale RSW (1872-1945) exhibited at the RA from 1896. Her work was unlike FH's in its concern for precise rendering.

passing up the Haymarket we caught sight of a long queue outside "Her Majesty's" pit door so we took our place on the pavement, dumped our half crowns & in an hours time were following "Ulysses"[4] – not by any means spellbound through his perilous adventures & home by way of hell to the arms of his faithful Penelope. It was all wonderfully well done & we wondered why we weren't thrilled – but we weren't a little bit, it wasn't simple & elemental enough & throughout the whole play there wasn't one touch of real nature – it seemed nothing but a brilliantly staged set of tableaux . . . . The part I liked best was the crowd of suitors outside Penelope's house, for all the world they were like Maoris at a tangi feasting & squatting & singing & full of extraordinary purposeful strength to get what they had come for – it was the only bit that was primitive & convincing. . . .

    . . . . By the way . . . I think you all treat me very shabbily about writing. Mother does her best but her best never runs to more than a sheet & a half, as I told you before it goes quicker than any oyster – cant she be induced to scollop it or do it up in batter so to speak. Miss R. gets rheems from her sister nothing is too small to chronicle – how many colds the baby has had in a month down to how they did up last week's cold meat, & mind you it is all good literature . . . .

[Penzance] 27th March [1902] We have been here now three weeks & it has blown & rained & drizzled & fogged in what the Cornish people try to make us believe is an unprecedented manner but we know better – we have had two or three fine days and everyone seemed so inordinately proud of them & swaggered so much that we saw at once how unused they are to good weather. Penzance is not beautiful tho' they try to make you believe it is – but Newlyn a mile away along a muddy road is charming – it is a fishing village (but your nose tells you that long before you reach it) – & the queer uneven streets & the forests of trawlers in the harbor make it a much more interesting place than Penzance – on the other coast 10 miles away is St Ives. We went over there one day to see the Moffat Lindners – he had his academy things on view, very fine – he paints in a nice fat, flat comfortable way full of richness & juice – he had his show earlier than the other artists as he is on several hanging committees in London & has to be there. . . . Mr. L. sent me an invitation to exhibit at the New English Art Club, also a note explaining that his being on the Hanging Committee wont insure my things being hung – the jury are a queer Slade School clique who pride themselves on their chucking out propensities & slay unmercifully even their own members. The same day we looked Miss Stoddart up at her lodgings. She was in & showed us her work. It struck me as being hopelessly dowdy & uninteresting or rather most of it did, some things were splendid – but her old vigour & freshness has given place to wooliness & want of form – which she seems to have lost in her

___

[4] By Stephen Phillips.

searchings after tones & values. It is the rock on which so many of the Newlyn people have split – they see nothing but tones & they miss everything else. She is a wonderful girl & she tells me she manages to live on a £1 a week – I am going over to share her sitting room with her next month when the spring blossom comes out – & St Ives is a paradise of beauty and I shall try & learn the art of keeping down expenses. On the 24th. we went over again to St Ives – it was a dreadful day – raining in sheets & wretchedly cold but nothing daunted we set out, for we had 15 studios to visit before dark. It was show day, the great day of the year[5] – & it wld never do to miss it – of the 15 studios occupied by 32 artists I dont think I saw more than 10 good pictures. Arnsby Brown & Julius Olsson were the best, their work was splendid, especially the latters – Louis Grier was good I believe but unfortunately by the time we reached his studio it was shut. It was great fun going round – the Studios were hidden in the queerest places – down dark subterranean passages, up chicken ladders – in old boat houses up sail lofts – anywhere where they could get a whitewashed wall & a top light . . . .

The next day was *our* show – that is Newlyn. *We* have a gallery of *our* own, & are very proud of it. It was a brave show & the Stanhope Forbes work raised it to a much higher level. Her work was magnificent – much better than her husbands – they were mostly Shakespearian, mediaeval things – but they simply sang with color & light & brilliancy – no one could touch her – she is head & shoulders above them all down here or in fact in England. I think she is pretty generally regarded as the first woman artist in England – she together with Mrs. Adrian Stokes.[6] I had 5 things on the walls 3 for the Academy & 2 for the N.E.A.C. & they all said nice things about them – & seemed to think I painted like Arthur Melville, which is rubbish – or if it is [true] it is quite unconscious. I went down in the morning with Mr. Garstin and was introduced to Mr. & Mrs S. Forbes – W. Langley, Rheam R. I., Lamorna Birch & several others, it was all very nice & interesting. Mrs Stanhope has asked me to go & see her & I am to go this Saturday . . . . I am at Mrs. Forbes feet – she wins one with her strength of color & design – tho I dont want to be influenced by her – merely seeing her work helps one. I had a try for the Academy tho it is quite hopeless I am sure – it is not the place for water colors in the first place – but they all thought I should send something & try my luck – I am looking out for a room for a studio. In the meantime I am working in the afternoon at the studio where Mr. Garstin's pupils work. They are seldom there in the afternoon & I have it to myself. Do forgive me for rambling on talking so much shop – but it is all part of ones life here – one absorbs it

---

[5] Artists opened their studios to friends and fellow artists on Show Sunday, the Sunday before work had to be sent in to the Royal Academy.

[6] Elizabeth Armstrong Forbes had made her début at the Royal Academy in 1883. Like Marianne Stokes (née Preindlsburger), the wife of Adrian Stokes RA (1854-1935), she was usually seen as the less important artist in the husband and wife grouping. 'It is as indicative of British aesthetic conservatism as of Victorian sexual politics that the French-inspired painting of Elizabeth Armstrong Forbes . . . was not more approved than it was.' Nunn, *Victorian Women Artists*, p.220.

unconsciously. . . . It was so nice to get a really decent [photo] of dear old mother
– I hope she is well – & not finding the work too hard – with Percy down & a
prospect of having Frank with her. . . .

[Postscript] Havent time to read this over I *do* hope I havent bragged unduly –
I really feel humble enough – wait till my 5 pictures are returned from London!

[87] To Rachel Hodgkins, 13 April 1902

1 Wellington Terrace, Penzance. 13.4.02

My darling Mother,

. . . . So Percy has gone in the 9th – how splendid for him & except for leaving
you I could have wished for nothing better than that dear old Bert could have
gone with him – it will be a grand life & the dicipline & experience tremendously
good for him – his going makes my prayer like yours, more ardent than ever for
peace. These last few days the nation has been holding its breath in anticipation
of the great longed-for news – but nothing has come of it & all this conference
has passed without any definite result.[7] I wish I could have seen Percy before he
sailed – I like to think of him in Khaki. . . .

Bert's promotion was good news . . . . I suppose the census work would not
have lasted much longer, but there is a nice substantial kind of permanency about
births & marriages . . . . Its no good – in spite of all I've said you can't help
gushing & raving over Spring in these parts – the glories of fruit blossoms & the
wild flowers in the woods all catch hold of one – and blue bell groves &
primrose dells (in spite of Miss Stoddart's pictures) are the most beautiful things
in the world – & I only wish you were here with me so that we could rave
together. . . . So Maggie Gilkison went to see you – I am sorry she feels hurt I
have not written to her, at that rate there must be rows of hurt friends in
Dunedin. . . . The old Mariner's albatross never weighed more heavily round his
neck than does the weight of my unanswered letters weigh round mine. . . . If they
would only understand that painting by itself is the most exhausting, brain
wearing nerve destroying, temper spoiling, spirit depressing work there is and it
takes me all my time & all my brains and you know oh! my mother that they are
not inconsiderable to keep the artistic fires going much less write letters to N.Z.
. . . I work hard all day and in the evenings I am slack & tired . . . . We had a merry
time at Easter in spite of bad weather. . . . One day we drove to Land's End . . .
it was truly wonderful – the cliffs not a bit more beautiful than our own coast but
the sentiment & mystery of the place thrilling, the sense of space & air and the
ocean coming straight at one & the wind so strong that we could not have thrown
ourselves down if we had wished. . . . Give Girlie the little bit of enclosed moss
from one of the rocks & point it out to her on the map . . . . Now to tell you the

[7] The South African War ended with the signing of the Treaty of Vereeniging on 31 May 1902.

fate of my pictures – first of all I am quite out of the running for the Academy owing to a foolish mistake on the part of my London frame maker who failed to get my frames ready in time for the last day for receiving water colors. . . . There was a contumelious passage (good word that) between us . . . . I had chosen some particularly choice mouldings which he specially designs & gilds in imitation of the color wh. gilt gets with old age – it is called "dirty gold" & it is very becoming & refined. All this was very annoying but no doubt saved me the greater humiliation which would undoubtedly have come later – as to the N.EAC – *REFUSED REJECTED* spurned – flouted and returned – and now the only comfort I get is from reading Miss Richmond's diary which exactly expressed my feelings – I quote extract by permission – "D— 'em and B— 'em for dunderheaded idiots – serve them right if Miss H never touched a brush again!". . . To go back a few days I quote another extract from Miss R's diary – which has a more triumphant ring about it – it was after the Newlyn show – and we were a little more sanguine & light hearted than we are now – "March 25th – Miss H. famous at last – all the artists crawling at her feet licking her little tan boots – &, to think that I produced her! my old bosom glows with pride". . . . Our visit to [Mrs Stanhope Forbes] came off in due course interesting but by no means satisfying she is much too self absorbed a lady to waste time in sympathy for others. She is a great worker – the only one in this lazy little colony – I think – & never wastes a minute. She & her husband are great comrades & devoted to each other & to their only child, a charming little boy. . . . Mr. Forbes for all the world like R. L. Stevenson as he walked into the room is a genial talkative man with a most heart whole admiration for his wife's talent – & it was charming to see the way he effaced himself & his work as he took me round the studio showing me all she had painted – it was inspiring seeing her sketches and I realised her great powers also her limitations, for great painter tho' she is, she has her boundaries. They have now gone to London & the little colony after its mighty effort has become once more inert & sleepy and at St Ives they will continue to play golf till it is time to paint more Academy pictures. Miss Stoddart wants me to join her at a small village St Erth a few miles from here & paint spring blossoms, but I have already committed myself to a studio & feel more inclined to work indoors for a bit. . . . This studio is at Newlyn and I am paying 10/- a month for it furnished the artist is away till June. It is a nice little room & has as one of its properties the old table which Frank Bramley put in his famous "Hopeless Dawn"[8] & next door

---

[8] Painted in 1888, the picture shows in naturalistic detail the interior of a fisherman's cottage, with the first light of day playing on the table laid for the homecoming meal of the man who will never return. Among the shadows of the foreground sit two women in the attitudes they have probably been in throughout the night, the younger on the floor, her head resting on the lap of a seated older woman who leans over her, half comforting, half drowsing. Cottage, table and women are 'real', but everything is arranged and posed. This combination of artifice and naturalism is typical of Newlyn painting, as is the interest in the lives of humble people and careful observation of the effects of light. Bramley's large painting of a child's funeral, *For of Such is the Kingdom of Heaven* (1891), is in the Auckland City Art Gallery.

is the identical cottage in which he painted it. . . . I enjoyed Sissie's description
of old King Dick – has the great man gone mad or does he actually give speech
to the idiotic bombasities that are cabled from N.Z. . . . Did Sis ever go down to
Dunedin to see Frank. How is he? *do* tell me something about him when next you
write – I am sending out a number of sketches . . . there will be enough to have
a little show at Wright's & later I can send out more for the Wllgtn Exhibition.
I shan't forget to leave them unpriced. . . .

No more dearie – it isn't much of a letter but it will keep you going till I write
again – *dont pass it on to Willie* – I am afraid my unbridled remarks re my pictures
would unnerve him. . . .

[88] To Rachel Hodgkins, 8 May 1902

1 Wellington Terrace, Penzance. 8.5.02

My darling Mother,

Forgive a short & scrappy letter this mail. I am just recovering from a rather
sharp attack of influenza . . . . It has been so cold & wintry, just heart breaking
from a sketching point of view – of course I didnt come Home for the climate
but I should be glad if we had a little more sun & a good deal less wind from the
East. . . . We go up to town the first week in June – I have written to the agent
general to see if I can get a seat for the Coronation on their stand. . . . There is
no news to record save one small item – sold a picture a small four pounder – at
the Gallery here – sales are of rare occurrence in these artistic parts . . . . What does
Sis think of the R.A. pictures? arent they dreadful – bar a few – dont Mrs Forbes'
& Mrs. Young Hunter's stand out? & isn't there a tremendousness about
Sargent's Wertheimer's[9] – Oh! my, when shall I paint like that – and oh! my what
a bad head I've got & I wonder if I shall ever paint again – goodly or badly – or
anyhowly. Miss Richmond says it is far worse than having a drunken husband –
in fact wld infinitely prefer one to nursing me thro' another attack of influenza
– so you see oh! my mother how unkind everyone is to me – no wonder I am low
& like to die. Yesterday – like Mrs. Dombey I made an effort – & went with a
party or rather they bicycled & I went in the train, to a place called Helston, some
13 miles from here, to see a curious old ceremony which takes place every year on
what is called Flora day. . . . The day starts at daybreak when the village maidens
turn out gotten up all in their best & bravest & with their partners dance –
accompanied by a band – thro the village. All the houses, spring cleaned &
garnished for the occasion are thrown open & the dancers pass in & out wherever
they like, in at the front door, out at the side, thro' a garden, or wherever their

[9] A reference to the portrait by Sargent, mentioned in Letter 70, of Ena and Betty, daughters of Mr and Mrs
Asher Wertheimer, 1901.

fancy takes them – this goes on till breakfast when they adjourn – and at midday & this is what we saw – the ladies of quality with their partners, all in top hats & frock coats & the ladies gayly dressed also in their best come out & trip thro the town to the accompaniment of a gay tune called the Fairy dance.[10] The gentry of course dance much more sedately . . . but they go thro exactly the same performance & it is a pretty sight to see them keeping time to the music in a long swinging step & disappearing quite suddenly, like a will o' the whisp, into a house & for the time throwing us completely off the scent & emerging again with a blast of music two or three doors down the street. It was a mad frolic & I longed to take part in it. I said to an imposing looking master of ceremonies – "May I join in" & he said – "Well you may have a little twirl miss, but you be'ant allowed to go far" so thus permitted I seized Miss Nickalls & together we danced down the street in the aristocratic company of the county families & greatly to the delight of the rest of our party. . . . People are pouring into London every day now – it will be a marvellous year – the Court will be the most brilliant one in Europe & very rightly so. The King is bent on having princely display everywhere & everything now is being done in the most magnificent style – & descriptions of London social gaieties sound like a modern Babylon – such a barbaric display of wealth & jewels – such a change from the frumpish & dowdy court of the dear old Queen. . . .

[Postscript] I wrote to Maggie G. last week, hope she will feel less hurt.

[89] To Rachel Hodgkins, 29 May 1902

1 Wellington Terrace, P.z. 29.5.02

My darling Mother,

   It was a grumbly, whiny sort of a letter I sent you off last mail of which no sooner posted, than I was ashamed. Thanks be I am all right again now & once more in my usual serene & sunny temper – and very busy painting the Spring before it turns into redhot mad midsummer ugliness. It is all mad green just at present but very beautiful and I am 'that driven' trying to make the most of it before we leave next week – I am a bit hustled just this week getting my pictures off to N.Z. paying bills, mending clothes etc before I leave – also wiping out a few of my accumulated letters – 6 have already gone this mail & tho my hands are stiff & my brain a bit addled my conscience is of a virtuous whiteness. . . . Thanks for photos . . . . *You* look very sweet and younger than ever. How do you manage it Mother dear & your daughters rising forty. Girlie has . . . a dear little sweet & thoughtful face – & Baba is just as beautiful as ever . . . . They are pets all of them & quite the best pictures Sis has ever painted . . . . Mr. Seddon is talking a good

[10] Properly the Furry Dance.

deal on his way Home & Europe is listening. The papers are full of the doings & sayings of our great Jingo and he is evidently going to enjoy himself very much indeed. . . .

Now for news – which is really nil. We leave here next week. Miss R. on the 2nd. to pay a visit, & I on the 5th for London & for the next month we "dwell sundered" the first time for nearly a year. I am going to share Miss Robertson's doll's house flat with her in Chelsea for such time as I am in town. It will be a bit of a squeeze but women can always manage when there are no men around. There is only one bedroom & that Miss M. Cargill inhabits. Miss R[obertson] therefore sleeps *in* or *under* the kitchen table. I am to be coyly & chastely tucked away behind a curtain in the drawing room . . . . Miss Robertson like other London landladys is making the most of her opportunities in Coronation week. . . . I will be very little there. I merely want headquarters & a safe harborage for my luggage – I *cant* ask the Spences to take any more – their bathroom is bulging with mine already . . . . I am going to spend a fortnight with the Nickalls in Surrey – they have a lovely home I believe & it will be jolly, they are such good sorts, rather like the Rattrays. . . . I have just enough [funds] now with careful living to see me thro' till I get another remittance from N.Z., I hope in 3 or 4 months from now. The pictures are all ready to go & should reach you about the middle of July. Do with them what Sis thinks best. I suggest keeping a few of the best out for the Wllgtn Show and exhibiting the rest at Mr. Wrights. Show him the white mount I have enclosed with them & see if he can copy it. The artists here use it a great deal for their water colors & with a putty-colored white frame it is most becoming. It is not as deep a one as I wld like to send – the bevel can be cut any depth the deeper the better – I have kept some of my more important sketches by me & some are in the gallery here.

We are very sad at leaving Penzance . . . . You and I will have to come back here & live some day. They never die in these parts – nearly everyone lives to over a 100. How do you like this story? An old woman up the road, aged 95 is doing some sewing for Miss R. & doing it jolly well too – without specs – she is as upright as a dart . . . so full of pluck & nature it does one good to go & see her. Our first visit we were in doubt as to her state married or otherwise & hazarded a Miss thinking she wouldn't notice. "Law! my dear dont 'ee go for to call me an old maid – you wldn't b'lieve but I 'ed two husbands, & the last a widow-man & 'e earned nawthen to spake of for the 4 years of his life – a matter of 16/4 was all 'e gave me – I wuddn't ha' married en ef I'd ha knawed, I wuddn't indeed". We comforted her & then she told us she had been feeling rather poorly & how the doctor had been to see her & she wound up cheerfully reflecting that she supposed it must be old age creeping on – creeping on at 95 sounds rather good doesn't it – and I hope the life of Emily Polfew may be spared just as long as she has health to enjoy it. . . .

We are reading Robt. Louis Stevenson's Letters just now – dear man – every day I fall more & more in love with him – & could I but have seen him I wld cheerfully have married him at sight – get them if you can, not Vailima letters but a later lot edited by Colvin. I enclose a snap shot of myself – the smug & portly look arises from a successful sketch. What do you think I weigh (I'll just whisper it – 9 stone only dont tell anyone) this is pretty good considering I was only 8 stone when I left Sydney.

Later – This letter should have been finished this morning, but the sun came out with a rush . . . & I went out with another paint box in hand so Mother dear instead of writing to you I have been doing a ripping fine sketch – I *have* I tell you I have, so stop smiling at once. . . .

[90] To Rachel Hodgkins, 27 June 1902

21 Chelsea Gardens. June 27th.

My darling Mother,

I was so glad to get your dear letter with news of the safe arrival of the Bank baby. . . . I got a delightful letter from Willie simply bubbling with bliss and I could hardly believe that the dear sedate man could expand so heartily. . . . Many thanks for Percy's spirited letter – wh I return – I know how much you rejoiced at the news of peace. . . . I came up to London on the 5th. & for two days Miss R. and I did picture galleries till we dropped – & then she went up to Scotland and I went down to Redhill to the Nickalls for 10 days. . . . London is in a turmoil . . . . The rain had spoilt all the decorations, at least as much of them as are up – & things generally were looking very gloomy for the great event next week. The Indian troops in camp at Hampton Court . . . are full of sympathy not for themselves but for the unfortunate people who live in England & have to put up with such a climate. The curious thing is that all loyal colonials ie. Seddonites claim that the weather began to break from the moment the great man set his foot in England which was last Sat & upon my word it looks as if there was something in it. The English papers hail him as all-powerful & claim that his Government has all N.Z. & all that therein is, weather included, under perfect control. . . . On Monday when he was banqueted by the Colonials in London he made a very telling speech, not too long, tremendously Imperialistic & very much to the point. . . . He has had a good innings, none of the other Premiers having arrived . . . .

Friday 19th [June] . . . . I have arranged for a seat on the A[gent] General's stand for the 27th. & have had to pay 10/- for a ticket . . . . Today I went to see where the stand was & went carefully over the course so as to know my way on the 27th. for it will be no easy thing to get through the crowd. . . . I cant afford a new dress just now so am wearing a pink muslin I had last year – and I am getting a new hat – everything is frightfully expensive . . . . I have refused all these N.Z. functions I can't dress up to them & it is best not to go unless one can look smart. . . .

Tell Sis there is a Colonial show on at the Institute for water colors just now run by Wadham & Sinclair,[11] she will remember them – I went to see it this afternoon & blush to think how badly the Colony is represented – most of them are truly awful. N.Z. is represented by Miss Meeson, Miss Joel & Wadham & Sinclair – all the rest are Australian & Canadian artists. Miss Stoddart & I were feeling a little annoyed at being missed over but I now feel so no longer – the papers are all very down on it and it will only do Colonial art more harm than good I fear . . . . Miss Joel has a big canvas representing "Maternity" – it is fine color but too clumsily painted. Dora Meeson's work is not good – but the man who she is engaged to has rather a nice portrait of herself. . . . I have not seen much of Mrs C. Smith but am going there to supper on Sunday. She is fussing round with New Zealanders & is very important – & busy. . . .

. . . . I am very homesick for a sight of you dearie and I shall not be sorry when my year is up. . . . I hate the racketty life I am leading now . . . I am only fitted to be a dull old worker – I have had an ideal time with Miss Richmond who is as much in earnest as I am – and when I am away from her I realise all her friendship has been to me. She wants me badly to stay another year & wait for her but my dear old mother I think you will see me back at the end of the year or very soon afterwards. I am so sorry Sissie is so unsettled with her servants – tell her not to worry so much & take life more easily – & not wear herself out with needless cares – real ones come soon enough, goodness knows. . . .

[Postscript] . . . . Best love to dear old Bert – you never tell me anything about Frank.

[91] To Rachel Hodgkins, 8 July 1902
                    Hotel des Voyageurs, Dinan, Cote du Nord. 8.7.02

My darling Mother,

Here I am back in France once more & very glad to start work again after my months gadding in London. The sudden stop to all the Coronation festivities was a great blow – how wonderfully dramatic the whole thing was – could you imagine a more impressive setting aside of all the pomps & vanities than this has been. . . . the sense of consternation & anxiety was so great & for the first day or two until the King was out of danger people did not begin to realise all they had lost. Tuesday was a never-to-be-forgotten day – I spent the morning on the tops

---

[11] Alfred Sinclair (1866-1938) and William Joseph Wadham (1863-1950) were brothers, founding members of the Adelaide Easel Club. Wadham visited New Zealand in the 1890s.

of busses following the line of decorations & seeing all that was going on. . . . People were pouring into London in thousands soldiers were everywhere & the sense of excitement was intense. . . . St. James was the gem of the streets, leading from Picadilly into the Abbey. It was one long arcade of festooned wreaths stretching from one side of the road to the other broken only by a huge arch made entirely of Canadian grain-sheaves of corn & wheat supporting the proud legend "Britain's Granary" in red letters. . . . At one oclock I found myself in an A.B.C. in the Strand . . . . I shall never forget the thrill that ran round the room as a new's boy put his head in the door & shouted "Coronation postponed, King danger-ously ill."[12] There was a wild rush for papers & the sense of calamity in the air was oppressive. . . . I spent the rest of the day in reading bulletins & following the crowd. . . . everybody seemed at loose ends & didnt quite know what to do with themselves. On Thursday, which was to have been the greatest day of the century, I spent moved my things from the Chelsea flat to my friend Miss Weltons place in High St. Kensington . . . . At the end of my month I was a faded, jaded, washed out piece of humanity. . . . The beautiful shops & well dressed people rouse wicked feelings of envy & malice & your little soul yearns for the unattainable with wild hankerings. The simpler country life suits me better, also my purse & when I am working I lose the haunting fear of running short of funds. If my things do not sell in Wllgtn I shall get Will or Willie to advance me my passage and I shall come out after the summer's sketching is over – funds are at rather low water just as present but I have enough to keep me going for a month or two longer. There is really no need to worry. Miss Richmond has kindly offered to be my banker till fresh supplies arrive & I shall not in the least mind letting her help me if I should need it. She has ample for herself & it would not inconvenience her to advance me some in case of need – & of course it gives me a much more comfortable sort of feeling having her as a standby. . . . [Dinan] is charming in all respects – a cheap homey clean sort of hotel and the old town full of good things to paint – & quite up to our Caudebec standard. . . . We are a jolly party, smaller than last year but on that account much nicer.

I have just been out to the post and to my great joy found a dear letter waiting from you . . . . I was glad you mentioned Frank, I was beginning to fear you were keeping something from me . . . I quite agree darling about your wish to have him with you . . . but as long as you are in town I fancy it wld not answer – a country life is the only one possible for him, & I for one should be quite glad to make a home somewhere out of town where we cld have him with us & look after him. I must say the idea of a town life when I return does not attract me – I am more than ever set on painting Maoris & the thought that I am going back to a whole island full of them gives me infinite comfort – they are still to me so much more beautiful than anything I have seen on this side of the world – I am looked upon

[12] Edward VII was operated on for appendicitis and the coronation took place in August.

as a sort of mad crank & my "niggers" as they will call them here are held up to unseemly ridicule & contumely. . . .

[92] To Dorothy Richmond, c.27 July 1902

Patisserie Taffatz, Rue de l'Apport, Dinan. Sunday morning.

Dearest Miss Richmond

Just a line to greet you before you leave London. Are you really coming on the 4th. It seems too good to be true. I was indeed sorry to hear of the return of Miss Astley's trouble . . . . It does not look as if Scotland was quite the best place for her does it? Please give her my love when you write or if you are with her still & tell her I didnt in the least grudge you to her. At first I felt a little furious & thought if I wrote to you at all I should begin it with a d—n then I had thought of hurling an ultimatum at your head – & then of a warrant for your arrest & forcible abduction but slept over it & calmed down & decided to let matters take their own course. . . . I moved in here last Monday – and am most comfortable *but lonely* – and I shall be very glad when I shall have you sitting opposite me again at meals. . . . I feel that I should be living much more frugally than I am – my bank account is alarmingly low – and I am afraid I shall have to ask you for a loan when you come. Are you quite sure you can let me have a little to tide me over till I get a fresh supply – I hate asking you for it. I feel I have managed badly running myself short in this way. I have told my brother if my pictures dont sell, to remit me my passage money & I shall go out at once – in any case I shall go out by the end of the year – I have a feeling in my bones that my little Mother is very lonely & misses me. The winter is a trying time for her I fear – she can get out so little & she is so dependant on her garden & fresh air. . . . Mrs. Garstin & family arrived last Monday & are installed at their pension, the poor Prof. has had another attack & is at present very feeble & limp. . . . I dont see over much of Maud [Nickalls] nowadays. She is very much taken up with Miss Crompton[13] & they ride & paint a lot together. Miss C. is such a nice girl & paints very well. I want you to see her oils which are really clever – she handles her color in a fine dashing style – a little too impetuous perhaps but full of spirit. I think I told you about the Studio which we have taken. It is no good telling you about the new pupils & who's who – you will never remember – so I will wait till I see you. . . .

Yrs lovingly Fanny.

[13] Gertrude Hall (née Crompton) (b.1874) studied in Paris, exhibited at RI and IS and the Paris Salon. She became a close friend of FH until her marriage later in life.

[93] To Rachel Hodgkins, 28 July 1902

Rue de l'Apport, Dinan. 28th. July

My darling Mother,

. . . . I feel very bad and wicked to have stayed away from you so long – but try & wait till the end of the year dear & then I shall be with you again and then no more long lonely days for the dear little brave Mother perching all alone on the top of a mountain. We will always be together after this darling, no more separations if I can help it. I feel it just as much as you do and I never forget for a moment how good & brave you have been to spare me for so long – I try not to worry or think about it too much for nerves play the very deuce with your work, but I never forget how good & unselfish you & Bert are . . . . I shall make it up to you both when I come out, you see. . . . I must abandon all idea of my having a show in London it can't be done without money, & also it is difficult to get enough work together. N.Z. exhausts my supply & I can't feed two markets. To give you an idea of how long most artists take to get sufficient work together for a show, Mr. Garstin has been working 3 summers & has not yet got enough to fill a small room – he is not a slow worker either, but you can never count on doing tip top work straight on end . . . inspirations are coy ticklish sort of things & dont come too often! There is always a lot one has to tear up – & cheerfully start again. How funny it will seem to start teaching again – ye gods how shall I ever do it? & if I do do it will the Ada Sinclair's & the Ella Morrises of Wellington rally round my colors. Heigh ho! it is not an inspiring thought. Will there be room in the little house for me? You have never said how many rooms there are. . . . I have been very industrious up at 6. & out working by 7.30. The French are early birds & the streets are just as busy then, in fact busier than later in the day. Dinan is a first rate place – a variety of everything – old streets, peasant women, fruit stalls, river scenery, feudal castles & 2 "dashing" cavalry regiments. . . .

Miss Richmond is still in Scotland – nursing her sick friend Miss Astley. . . . It is horrid without her. I have left the Hotel Voyageurs and am now living over a facinating confectioner's shop. I found the big party at the hotel rather distracting & didnt get enough quiet time to myself. With the exception of Miss Richmond & a very few others I have never met anyone who is really serious about their work – most of the girls who come to a class like this come to amuse themselves & pass the time, but very few work earnestly. I keep reminding myself I must do 5 francs worth of painting every day to pay my daily board – but I am afraid there are many days when I dont paint 5 sous worth. . . .

The great event of the week is the Thursday market, more especially the cattle market – cows, pigs sheep etc. pour in from the country & muster in great force in the Place. The cows stand in tight rows flank to flank (from a painting point of view it is disappointing – heads or tails). . . . The Bretons are notoriously unkind to their animals, & ill-treat & overwork them to a cruel extent. . . . I am in a fury of indignation the whole time, which is stupid & futile & does no good whatever. I have got a big thing on at present of the pig market (my swinish tendency is considered low) with pink & black satin piglets wallowing happily in a sea of straw – they make a good picture. . . . We couldn't have come at a better time, the town has been en fête for 3 successive Sundays in celebration of the erection of a new statue of Bertrand du Guesclin. It was his birthplace & from the old castle he made many stands against the English – sometime in the 13th. century. . . . The day the statue . . . arrived the excitement was intense – I heard one Frenchman say to another "Il est arrivé" and kissed each other excitedly on both cheeks. I think one of the chief reasons of his popularity is because he helped to drive the English out of France. For a whole week after his arrival Mr. Du Guesclin sat in the Place enveloped in a black shroud veiling him from the public eye. . . . Sunday was a great day. . . . We put on our gayest & best & took up an early stand on the nearest pavement facing the Statue. There was a murderous looking thunder cloud sitting overhead, making up its mind to burst & we saw at once that it wld be a race between it and the inaugural ceremony. The Minister of War, General André was to open it & presently he drove up with an escort of cavalry, looking very martial & imposing. . . . with him was the distinguished sculptor M. Fremiet[14] & a little French Academician wearing his Academy orders – he was to recite an ode but this ode alas! never came off. There were a few warning drops of rain, a hint to hurry up the ceremony, so in rather undignified haste (the cloud by this time was literally sitting on poor Du Guesclin's head) – the veil was drawn off & Bertrand stood revealed in all his glory to a wildly cheering crowd. He certainly is magnificent a dull bronze, warlike mailed figure, sitting squarely in his saddle with a defiant throw back of his head – every inch a soldier, & we forgave him for wanting to turn "us" out of France & cheered wildly with the others. By this time it was pouring . . . I never saw such rain it came down in sheets, as it does in the tropics – we made for the trees – so did 5,000 others – the trees poured on the umbrellas & the umbrellas poured on us, or rather other peoples did, so we decided to make a rush for a café awning opposite . . . & I found myself carried off my feet & lifted on to a table, but anything was better than the drenching rain outside. . . . It was an hour and a ½ before we could leave our shelter. . . . It has been a very unsettled month, hardly a day without a little rain. . . . Fortunately the old houses have arcades underneath them where we can sit & paint when it rains. . . .

No more tonight dearest, it has struck 11 and I must get to bed. Take great care of yourself & do not work too hard, long nights & short days remember. . . .

---

[14] Emmanuel Frémiet (1824-1910), a pupil of Rude, who worked on public commissions in Paris.

[94] To Rachel Hodgkins, 21 August 1902

Patisserie Taffatz, Rue de l'Apport, Dinan. 21st or thereabouts.

My darling Mother,

I intended making an early start with my letter to you tonight when the postie came in with a big budget, 12 letters & a paper – imagine the joy – yours and Sissie's came first & then a very sweet one from Jean all about the baby. . . . All the Dunedin letters written with frosty fingers & a slightly snippy tendency on account of the cold. . . . One comfort the worst of it is over now and our turn is coming. Not that we have had any summer so far. It has been odious weather . . . so different from last year & its glorious 2 months of hot days. I suppose the Snt. Pierre eruptions must have something to do with it . . . . The class altogether has not been as brisk this year as last. Mr. Garstin poor man has been far from well & really not equal to the strain of teaching. We are a very nice party but not an exciting one – I mean as far as painting goes – no artists have joined us this year . . . . Miss Richmond came a week ago looking beautifully well & brown after her 2 months in Scotland . . . she hates the idea of my going back to N.Z. without her. She is as disappointed as I am not having a show in London. The difficulty of course now is that I have no work, even if I had money. I am sending out next week all I have for the Nov. show[15] – which leaves me with an empty portfolio – & it will be several months before I can hope to get some decent work together again. We are going to have a final try before I leave however to see if something might be managed – I wish the shekels weren't so scarce, it wld be a very slight matter indeed if one could only pay for it all – but please understand clearly that whatever I do, I must do off my own bat so don't for a moment let anyone think I am whining for help. It was good of Willie & so like him to arrange with the Bank should I run short but I can hold on till fresh supplies come – some of the pictures are sure to sell. . . . After my N.Z. work is off next week I am going to tackle some peasant studies out in the country – women herding their sheep & cows etc. I shall be glad when they are safely despatched – the last few weeks are always poisoned a bit for me before I finally pack up my sketches, doubts & fears & disgust of one's own work & finally a great peace of mind and relief when they are once really off – I am much calmer about my work now I am thankful to say – this calm un-fussy atmosphere & the serene & leisurely way Miss R takes life has done much to dicipline me – she is a great philosopher & like the Garstins takes the rough with the smooth smilingly & cheerfully – that's rather like you dear little Mother, isnt it?. . .

. . . . We had a mad dog scare here the other day – 3 unfortunate people were bitten – & hastily sent off to the Pasteur Establishment in Paris – and all the dogs, & there are legion are now in muzzles – I trust for the rest of my stay. They can never hope to stamp out hydrophobia as long as they allow such numbers of ill-

[15] At the Otago Art Society, where sixteen works were exhibited.

conditioned curs to over run a town as they do here – one of the pupils was attacked the other day by a huge Dane hound & her dress torn badly – but she herself was fortunately not bitten. The fear of hydrophobia is a very real & menacing one with people on this side of the world – it seems so strange to me coming from a hemisphere where such a thing is unknown . . . .

[95] To Rachel Hodgkins, 10 September 1902
                    Patisserie Taffatz, Rue de l'Apport, Dinan. Sept 10th. 1902

My darling Mother,
    Your dear letter of the 5th. Aug reached me last night, with the good news of Percy's safe return. . . . Why did he come back so soon? was he under orders to return with the contingent? Personally I prefer him in N.Z – but as far as seeing life & making opportunities are concerned I should think S. Africa was the place to be in at the present time. . . . I should like the Brothers Hodgkins to have a place somewhere in the country where their Mother & sister could keep house for them. I wish I didnt dislike the idea of town life in Wllgtn so much but I do – but wherever it is we are to live, I shan't grumble I shall be so glad to be with you all again. I was much troubled to hear of the bad time Sis has had with her children, poor old girl, she must be quite worn out by nursing . . . . we know the anxiety of one whooping child, you remember Baba. What must it have been with three poor little choking things. . . . whooping cough & servant worries are a combination of trials one feels unable to bear – the former, thank heaven, is over for once & all but the latter, like the poor, seems to be always with us. . . . I am so sorry that Sis should have the trouble of arranging with McGregor Wright about a show. She has quite enough worries of her own without having this added to them. I sent off a small packet of sketches (7) on the 30th. of last month which I hope will arrive in time for the Nov. show – if by chance they dont – will you see that the best of the unsold ones of the first batch are sent down to Dunedin. I am keeping my best work by me. I shall probably send to some London galleries when the next watercolor shows come on in the spring. In a month or two I hope to be in funds again & then I shall not feel so cramped. I can make no plans or look ahead till I hear how my pictures have sold. The anxiety of mind is affecting my work a little, and I feel I am working in a feverish sort of way making the most of my time. The weather has been agin' us too – & the class has been tearing its hair in despair . . . . On Monday a Miss March Phillips comes & is going to share our rooms with us. She has rather a celebrated brother who has written some of the best articles yet published on the war.[16] Strangely enough we had read extracts

---

[16] Lisle March Phillipps (1863-1917) had wide-ranging interests. Among other titles, he wrote *With Rimington [in the Boer War]*, Edward Arnold, London, 1901; *In the Desert: the Hinterland of Algeria*, London, 1905, reprinted 1985; *Form and Colour*, London, 1915.

from them in the Spectator & straightway fell in love with the author of them, they were so vivid & picturesque & smacked of the veldt in a most convincing manner. We little thought we should so soon have a chance of telling his sister how much we admired him. . . .

We had a day at Dinard one day last week. It is one of the most fashionable of French watering places about 2 hrs rail from here. . . . We found the tide most depressingly & vulgarly low, nothing but crabs & children & stranded bathing machines & indecent looking bathing gowns hanging out to dry. I especially wanted to see them bathing & whether they wore as preposterous looking costumes as one sees in pictures. It seems high life & low tide are never seen together, & it is only when the tide is full that they come out & crowd together on the beach. It was disappointing so we went for a scramble over the rocks instead & by the time we got back we were ready for tea – & fashion failing us, we turned into the Casino – it also was empty or nearly so – and a beautiful band which deserved a better audience was playing to a few inattentive gossipy women . . . . It was all very gorgeous & rather wicked looking & very much like a scene out of a novel. . . . After this another walk on the beach, the tide was beginning to creep in & the pretty ladies were appearing one by one like so many beautiful & fantastic colored birds – they were mostly Americans in gorgeous Paris clothes. There was no time to sit & watch them, we had to run for our train which we barely caught. We sat in a 3rd. class carriage & moralised all the way home on the vanity of human nature and the awful boredom of being a professional pleasure seeker –

. . . . The Garstins have had rather a combination of worries & ill luck this year . . . . he has had bad luck with his pictures & far from good health & the final blow came the other day in the news of his son's failure to get into the Navy. He is such a clever spirited boy just suited for the sea & with a perfect passion for it, but the stiff exams proved too much for him & he was plucked badly . . . . They are such dear delightful people but I do wish they had a little more of this worlds goods – living on pictures is a dog's life – I dont want much, quite a modest little competence would satisfy me, but I do want enough to keep me from looking at my coppers six times before I spend one. Well darling this is a silly letter. . . .

[96] To Isabel Field, 30 September 1902
                    Patisserie Taffatz, Rue de l'Apport, Dinan. 30.9.02

My dearest Sis,
    This has been an exciting day – your letter arrived this morning with news of the arrival & sale of pictures. Thanks ever so much dear for all the trouble you have taken for me. . . . I wish I could drop in to Wright's with you & have a talk – letters are poor sort of things – can't say half what one wants to. You must have

blessed me & my old pictures turning up when you were feeling so weary & played out . . . . I wonder if you went off to Dunedin – I hope so – sans babies – & with plenty of nice clothes – and had a nice time with old friends. Will will want all your spirits & energy for the elections – so rest while you can & reserve yourself for Otaki canvassing later on. I wish I were going to be with you – do you remember the last campaign – you & I in a milkcart & Mrs Tudor A[tkinson] flashing round in a spanking yellow dogcart, & your conquest of the burly barman & every wife & mother in the district. . . . I am so glad you are pleased with the pictures – I did not know whether to laugh or cry when I got your letter – & have felt unstrung & rather shattered all day – of course I am touched & proud that they have sold so well but was it wise dear to let them go for so little? A lump rises in my throat when I think of 12 pictures selling for £40 and Suzanne & the San Remo market among them. Oh! my poor little brains, is that all you can do for me. Surely without undue vanity I could have got more than £8 for Suzanne. Have you any idea of the work that was in her? or in the others for that matter. I blame myself for not giving you some idea of the prices I hoped to get – for after all surely these two years of hard work & experience should go for something – and I am sure people would have given more & at least there is always the chance of coming down in price if they didn't sell. Suzanne was the outcome of two months hard work at Penzance – & like a fool I refused an offer of £15 for her – wishing instead that you should all see her & never dreaming you would sell her for less. It is my fault entirely dear and I dont blame you for one moment but I cant help feeling a little sad & sore that you didnt think my work worthy of bigger prices – or at any rate of trying for them. Of course it is urgent that I should have money but it wld have done no harm to have waited a little while to see how far people would go. Taking Suzanne at £8 as an average the others must have sold for a little over £3 each and when I hear of Miss Richmond selling her "lacemakers" the same day for £6.6 it did seem a little unfair – she cried for me, dear thing, & couldn't enjoy the news of her own good luck. You see dear it is my last chance of getting together such a collection again and naturally I valued them more – and expected that the public should too. Dont think that because my work looks easy that it is so – remember what Sheridan said when a friend complimented him on the easy style of his books – "Then all I can say [is] that easy reading is damned hard writing" Those market scenes are the outcome of great mental strain, with nerves at a tension & eyes bewildered with an ever moving crowd & ones senses all alert & linx eyed for effects & relations one thing to another. This all sounds so peevish & cross & ungrateful – perhaps I am a little tired and overwrought – I have been working under pressure for this last fortnight getting together some things to send to John Baillie[17] who is showing some of

---

[17] John Baillie was a New Zealander who had established an art gallery in London. He later organised exhibitions of overseas artists into New Zealand.

Miss Stoddart's things & wants me to join with her. He has nice rooms in Bayswater & fairly large clientèle of his own besides many New Zealanders . . . there is little to lose & much to gain. I packed off some this afternoon with more to follow tomorrow – I put on swinging big prices as a balm to my wounded feelings with instructions to drop if required. . . . Miss R. & I go to London in a fortnight & after that our ways be seperate – I dont know what I am going to do without her – we have taken a long time to consider what was best for us both. She has only another year & must make the most of it & she feels she must get more studio work – so Mr. Garstin with the knowledge full upon him that he was breaking up our happy home conscientiously advised [her] to go back to Penzance & have a solid winter's grind from the model – I conscientiously backed him up – I am sure it is for her good – & she wld be unselfish enough to give her time up to me & go wherever I wanted if we didnt put pressure on her and insist on her considering her own interest. So back she goes to [Penzance] in November & I shall be alone once more. I am beset with anxieties to do the right thing – & feel much puzzlement as to whether to come home or stay another winter & get more work together before coming out. If I come now I come empty handed which seems a foolish proceeding. On the other hand there is little Mother pulling at my heart strings. I do not feel so bad now that Percy has returned – it will be brighter & jollier for them in every way – but of course it means more work for her – when Percy gets something to do perhaps they will get a little maid. Oh! I do want to do the best for everyone, & surely it is the hardest thing of all to make your choice between duty & affection. Miss March Phillips who has been with us for this last fortnight has taken a great fancy to my work & wants me to join her in a show – or rather exhibit as many as I can get together in a gallery (Doré) in Bond St. in November. It is an attractive offer – for many reasons – she pays for the rooms & my only expenses would be the 15 percent commission on sales. The only crumple in the rose leaf is the extreme badness of her work or rather it is not so bad as banal & commonplace & I do not quite relish the idea of hanging cheek by jowl with so many inartistic & frightening daubs. However beggars cant be choosers. We did hope we should discover something of her brother's brilliant witty touch in either herself or her pictures – but alas there is none. She is only a well-dressed handsome complacent English woman with a fine belief in her own powers. . . . We like her all the same – she is so genial & nice to talk to when we keep her off the subject of her own exploits. She has a large circle of friends literary & artistic who will rally round her no doubt. She intends giving a reception the first day & wants me to be there & introduced as the "talented New Zealander" I fancy she feels rather like a variety show manager who has got hold of a new weird human freak for an attraction . . . . The thing is now to get as much work together as possible . . . . We have had a very happy fortnight – in spite of struggling with pictures & elements – we were a jolly little party – Mr. Garstin, the Col: & Mr. Legge & we three – ours was the only sitting room & they spent their evenings round our log fires . . . . The Prof. was always so gay & amusing & the other two men were travellers & had lots of tales. What a queer little world, getting to know people so well & then saying goodbye – it is the way of life but a sad way I think. Mr. Garstin went off today . . . . He has gone to London to see about his show. He is going to try & pave the way for me . . . in case there is a chance of my running one later on myself. I want you to talk to Mother seriously about my staying through another winter & write & tell me exactly how she feels about it. . . . Miss March Phillips wants me to go with her to Sicily for the winter, but I do not yet know whether I could stand being so long with such an inartistic person. She would be a good friend to me & is a most capable business like woman. . . . Sicily would do beautifully & is one of the few places in the South you can keep warm during the winter. I feel rather at loose ends – I hate deciding & making plans – & Miss R. has entirely spoiled me for anyone else. She has been too good to me & thought for me & cared for me like ten mothers – I am glad she is going back to the Garstins, they will look after her – & not let her feel lonely – they all love her down there – as indeed everywhere. . . .

I insured my pictures for £40 in case of loss – but didnt value them at that. Tell Will he must get that iniquitous duty on pictures knocked off by the Gov. Thats not the way to encourage Art in the Colonies. Mind and put decent prices on my pictures for Dunedin & leave it to Dr. Scott to alter them if they are too much. . . . Goodnight dear old girl – forgive this grumbling letter – it sounds ungrateful but I am not really so – I never thank you half enough for all your kind thoughts for me – & all you have done for me. . . .

[97] To Rachel Hodgkins, 23 October 1902

24 Gordon Place, W. 23rd. Oct.

My darling Mother,

. . . . Sis tells me you have had neuralgia – dear I am so sorry – why didnt you tell me yourself – I *insist* on knowing all your pains & aches – do you hear?. . . It sounds as if you wanted a rest & change. If I was worth my salt I would pack up & be off home next mail – but I want you to be patient & unselfish a little longer and spare me for a few months more. Sometimes I feel, especially after your letters come in, that it wld be better for me to give up this struggle and rush & restless yearning after the unattainable & come out and take care of you – then comes Miss Richmond's sane, calm, common sense, urging me to stop worrying & make the most of this golden chance that has been given me & which I know will never come again. She feels as much as I do how lonely you must often be – but she also feels that you wld be the last to grudge me these few extra months – each month seems to make a difference in my work – to harden strengthen & drive home any knowledge & experience I may have gleaned these last 18 months

– and also there seems as if at last I was going to get in the thin end of that obstinate old wedge. Before I tell you of our plans I must tell you how relieved & grateful I felt this morning on going to the Bank to find they had only just received the cable remitting £80. I felt I should be living on charity before the end of the week & I almost fell on the cashier's neck when he told me the good news. I felt like rushing off & spending some of it on riotous clothing but resisted all temptations & got on the top of a bus & got safely past the shops . . . . I have not yet settled the problem as to whether your friends prefer you shabby & honest or well-dressed & in debt! Sis has been very prompt getting in my money so quickly, & I feel so grateful to her for managing it all so well for me. At first I had thought she had underpriced them too much, but I now think she was after all quite right to let them go for small sums. She couldn't consistently have sold them for more after having got thro' the customs so lightly. Don't think I over value my own work. I only know the pains & labor with which I evolve each picture – some cute commercial brother brush said somewhere he made the public pay for what he tore up – not for what he painted. How very kind & flattering of Lady Ranfurly to want to see my pictures – & what a business sending them all up to Gov. House. . . . So much has been packed into these last 3 weeks. We are back in this giddy vortex once more – & all is rush, bustle, dirt, fog, rain, fag, busses and fusses. We had an awful crossing last Thursday (16th) – a howling N.W. gale right in our teeth & 16 hours of misery – we *did not* contain ourselves – I dont want to swagger about it but it was the unhappiest 16 hours I have ever spent in my life – not even excepting that short period in my early middle life when Mr. Collins in exchange for £12.6 or something took away my own teeth & gave me instead those dazzly pearls of more than human whiteness. . . .

 . . . . Naturally the first thing we did after we reached London was to go and see our pictures at Mr. Baillies studio – mine did not look well . . . they were hung opposite a window & the light blazing right in their poor faces – however it was the only place there was so there was nothing to be done – & I couldn't grumble seeing I had sold one for £12.12. Miss Stoddart had hers upstairs in a room by herself – they were only mounted & didnt look their best – poor girl she has had rather bad luck I am afraid – only 4 small £4.4 sold – one of which Miss Richmond had bought. . . . She works so hard – it seems so sad she should be so little appreciated. She got very good Press notices I believe tho' I have not yet seen them. . . . It was odd to find oneself flanked, as in the old Dunedin days by Miss Joel & Annie Black – Miss J. showed some flowers, old friends, & Miss B. a frightening sort of figure thing – quite in her old style. Dora Meeson's painting is a fraud. Miss March Phillipps show opens on the 15th. – we lunched with her on Wed at the Sesame Club & she showed us her sketches. They were not half bad I am glad to say – big bold blottings, rather empty but fearless & with nothing at all tentative about them. She then took us on & introduced us to the manager of the Doré Gallery who was affable & more civil than most of his race. Walter

Crane[18] is having a show at the same time . . . . I wont have more than a dozen to show, but anyway it will do to introduce myself. . . . It is really most awfully kind of Miss M.P. to do all this for me – she is anxious I should have a show of my own later on & thinks this may possibly lead to one. She has been so kind – dinner & theatre last night & innumerable picture galleries – and Miss Eleanore Brickdale's Studio next week. "Quality Street" last night by Barrie was charming . . . witty, pretty pathetic & humorous, like everything of Barrie's and so sweetly acted. We went on Sat to the private view of the R[oyal] Institute of Water Colors. It was very crowded, there were some nice things tho nothing wildly exciting, mostly sketches. . . .

I went to see Mrs. Cunningham Smith one night . . . . she had been seeing too many Canadians & New Zealanders these last few months I think & her voice sounded hoarse from much talking. We are to dine with her next Tuesday. . . .

I have left the most exciting piece of news for the last – I am going to Tangier for the winter or rather for the next 3 months . . . . Do you remember me telling you about Mrs. Ashington. I met her at Caudebec last year & we have always kept up our friendship. She is so very nice & I couldn't have found anyone who could be more suitable. . . . Miss R. will join us later – and remember darling – Tangier is on the way home if you should want me – it is just across the Straights from Gibraltar. You can live very cheaply there – and the passage P.&O. is only £6.10. . . . I shall get heaps of work – there are plenty of English people there so dont be frightened that I shall be carried off into the heart of Africa by some dusky Arab sheik. . . .

[98] TO RACHEL HODGKINS, 14 NOVEMBER 1902

24 Gordon Place W. Nov. 14th.

My darling Mother,

It is very good & sweet of you to say I can stay till Miss Richmond comes out. You dont know how much it will mean to me, after all it wont be quite 3 years. I dont think one ought to stay away longer than that if one ever means to go back again . . . . I wish I could keep this letter back till tomorrow night & let you know how I get on at the Doré Gallery. I have got a new dress for the occasion, a navy blue cloth with silk strappings rather neat I think and only £3.10. I have a little tailor who makes for me and I have got a green & blue toque to wear with it. The Agent Gen's wife gave a reception on Wed. I meant to have gone & looked up all the New Zealanders but I was busy getting my pictures off & didn't go – however I have sent cards to all who are in town. . . . Effie Spence has retired from this

---

[18] Walter Crane (1845-1915), a decorative artist and designer associated with the Arts and Crafts Movement and the flowering of Art Nouveau in Britain.

world into a training home for nurses – rather a hard life for the poor old girl I am afraid – but she has grit enough for anything & if only her strength will hold out so will her spirit. She is really a fine girl Effie – quiet & purposeful with a fine idea of making herself useful in this world. . . . I am so glad Percy is making a garden for you – I shall keep my eyes open for seeds. I wish he cld find some work to do . . . . Well dearest I must stop I am doggy tired, have been on the wing all day . . . . I shall be gone in a fortnight on the 27th. Shall you mind if I join a harem?. . .

[99] To Isabel Field, 14 November 1902

24 Gordon Place. Nov. 14th.

My dearest Sis

I am dreadfully worried about you dear – of all the wretched luck surely this is the worst, measles on the top of whooping cough is killing work & too much for human flesh & blood to stand. . . . I feel rather a villain going off on this glorious jaunt while all you dear people are having such a wretched time. . . . I hope most earnestly you have got over the worst of the trouble now & that the chicks are once more spotless & convalescent. I am afraid you wont have much surplus energy left for the elections. Dont kill yourself, that's all. Will is sure to go in with a spanking big majority . . . . I suppose the Richmond-Atkinson faction is very active – what rabid opponents they are – I have had a riotous morning choosing some toys for the children . . . . I have sent them a family of Gollywogs – hardly remarkable for good looks but a very loveable lot. I can hardly bear to part with them. I said to the attendant "Do children really love these" she said "Indeed Madam no well-brought up Kensington child evah goes to bed without one" so thus assured I purchased the family. . . .

Tomorrow will be the fateful 15th. at the Doré Gallery – I feel horribly nervous as to results. I have been at it pretty hard this last fortnight getting my work ready for review order. They are an odious 10 & I very nearly sent them over the Embankment & went after them myself. It is going to be a big function – a sort of combined Walter Crane-March Phillipps affair with a mustering of all the New Zealanders I can get together. I have sent cards to the Agent Gen: & all the Col[onial] press men and I have several kind friends who are sowing cards broadcast for me and acting trumpeter. I have 3 Maori things and the others are Dinan sketches – Mr. Crane said some kind things about them yesterday & said it was remarkable work . . . . For Heavens sake dont repeat this foolishness – I look upon you all as my safety valve so you must just put up with my harmless vanity. . . . I have been very busy arranging about the Tangier trip – it is not quite like taking an ordinary journey. It is a primitive sort of a place & we must stock for the summer – also there are passports letters to the Consul – money arrangements & numberless small things which have to be seen to . . . . I knocked up against Mr. Theomin[19] in Bond St. the other day. They are off on a long tour thro' Spain & Morocco so we may meet again on a foreign strand. . . .

[100] TO DOROTHY RICHMOND, 20 NOVEMBER 1902

24 Gordon Place, W. Thursday evening

My dearest Miss Richmond

. . . . I feel a wretch not writing before to tell you of the Show. . . . It has *not* made the commotion in art circles I thought it wld in fact so far has been entirely overlooked by the Press. Business was bad – Miss March P. sold 3 the first day (2 aunts and a friend were the purchasers) & Mr. W. Crane only sold 2 small things, wretched little landscapes both of them, in body colour on brown paper – & Mr. Fletcher-Watson (he of the Cathedral interiors) & I nil. I had a wretched bad head & cld. hardly rouse myself to going at all but finally Miss Welton & I got up there some time before 3 – the rooms were packed with people & Bond St. with carriages but they were not a buying lot. I was furious to find my pictures almost obscured in the tea-room . . . . I spoke to the manager & in 5 minutes he had them down & a wall cleared for them in a small room opening out of Miss M.P.'s. . . . Very few New Zealanders turned up. Miss Welton & her family mustered strong . . . . All your news about the Studio was vastly interesting. The posing sounds wearing work, but what a most excellent rule to allow no one to raise objections to each others choice of pose. Clearly understand I wont have you making up to Mrs. Salmon. You needn't tell me you can't help it – *I* had no difficulty in making myself disliked. It was nice seeing Miss M. Nickalls on Sat., I didnt mind how many duchesses circled round the M.P. as long as I had her & Miss Crompton to talk to. . . . I had a lesson in drawing from a distinguished architect, name unknown, who said he wouldnt have lived in any of my houses for a hundred pounds. He was very nice – and a friend of William Morris's who prints Mr. Crane's wall papers told me a lot of interesting Pre-Raephelite gossip – all very interesting – also forgotten his name – may the gods prevent them from forgetting mine. Miss Welton was so ardent a supporter & admired my pictures so industriously & ostentatiously that the manager mistook her for a likely purchaser & nearly, to her horror, landed her with the cabbages & onions. Walter Crane received homage posing in front of his own beautiful portrait by Watts evidently borrowed for the occasion from the Nat. Gallery. His wife received at the door . . . got up in early Victorian style – very smiling & bland. The room was a tight pack all the afternoon with a miscellaneous crowd – from Paisley shawls

---

[19] The Theomins lived in Dunedin, one of the group of wealthy Jewish families whose enlightened patronage of the arts contributed to the cultural life of the city. They had bought FH's prizewinning *Head of an Old Woman* in 1895.

& poke bonnets & ladies with Pre-Raephaelite countenances & long haired artists to ultra fashionable theatrical people – but out of all that crowd, as the manager said, he only succeeded in "pulling off" two small pictures. . . .

Goodnight my onliest. Love to Miss Parks & all the studio and Mrs. Garstin. Are these photos any use to Mr. G. in finishing his pictures?

Part Six

1902-3

Winter in Morocco

In 1902 Morocco was in a state of turmoil that eventually opened the way for the French to take over in 1912. In 1900 a strong regent, Bou Ahmed, had died, leaving in nominal control of the country the young, well-intentioned Sultan Abd El Aziz. Abd El Aziz was diverted from affairs of state by his Grand Vizier who encouraged him in his ruinously expensive acquisition of European goods, a course of action that alienated him from his people and strengthened the position of those who challenged his supremacy. He faced two main rivals: the notorious but aristocratic brigand Raisuli, whose stronghold was about twelve miles from Tangier, south of Tetuan; and a pretender, Bou Hamara, who, at the end of 1902, had defeated the Sultan's army at Taza near Fez. Frances Hodgkins, like the other artists who included North Africa in their repertoire of sketching grounds, could rely for protection on the prestige of the Empire backed up by the British presence in Gibraltar, but there was an element of personal danger. The Greek-American poet, Ion Perdicaris, who appears in FH's letters, was kidnapped by Raisuli in 1904, and it took the presence of four American warships and a telegram from President Roosevelt's office, 'Perdicaris alive or Raisuli dead', before the Sultan's ministers secured his release by agreeing to Raisuli's terms: a $70,000 ransom and the appointment of Raisuli himself as Governor of Tangier in place of his enemy, the 'Basha' referred to in Letter 103. The fighting FH witnessed in January 1903 was part of the quarrel between Raisuli and the Basha, who was supported by the Sultan's government. The 'weird and grizzly stories' mentioned by FH would have included the display of the severed heads of opponents and other mutilations routinely practised by the Moroccans.

[101] To DOROTHY RICHMOND, 3 DECEMBER 1902

Hotel Bristol, Tangier, 3.12.02

My dearest Miss Richmond

Salaams from Morocco! We've arrived – and considering what we've passed thro its an achievement to be proud of. . . . Heavens! how beautiful it is! Why aren't you here you foolish and misguided woman. . . . I am never going back to New Zealand – I am going to turn Moslem – I am going to wear a haik – I am going to lie on a divan for the rest of my days with a handmaiden called Fatima to wait on me. I am going – but I must wait till the Sultan returns before I can become one of the faithful. He is away at present, on march with a rabble army at his heels devastating the country & quelling tribal risings in the interior. We have heard some weird & grizzly stories of the treatment of rebels at Tetuan & Fez – but here it is all quiet & peaceful & people only laugh at the exaggerated accounts of things that have got about. To hark back to last Monday – did you get a letter from me posted at Gib?. . . I couldn't sufficiently abuse the old "Rome". . . she was the vilest old tub . . . . & we parted from her with the same feelings of relief that one has when saying goodbye to one's dentist. . . . There were two Englishmen on board going to Tangier, one a doctor at the mission station here, so we arranged to share a boat with them & row to the Tangier boat. It was barely light when we left the ship – a lovely rosy dawn, with the Rock in a crown of clouds . . . On the Tangier boat I found Mr. & Mrs. Theomin – N.Z. friends. Do you remember we met him one day in Bond St.? They were travelling in great style, courier, & a luncheon basket bulging with good things. We had tea on deck and I sat fairly close to the luncheon basket. They seem to be buying up the whole of Europe – but doing it in such a delightful light-hearted fashion that one doesn't mind in the least. We had a splendid crossing – a delicious warm sun & just enough wind to let us know we were at sea. Directly the boat stopped – some way from the landing pier – a thousand or so Moors hurled themselves on deck & began fighting violently over our baggage – some of them such magnificent looking men, bronze giants, others wizened up, wicked looking little brigands and a few coal black Nubians with plunging eyes. It was the first day of the Rama-dhan (cant spell it) & they were fiercely peevish with long fasting. We had 10 pieces of luggage & each piece was in a different boat, & the boat we were in had no luggage at all – but we clung together & hung on for dear life to our nice missionary's coat tails & trusted in Heaven. Three waves took us to the pier – where the rest of the populace stood waiting [for] us, hungrier, if possible & fiercer than the first lot & all very keen on helping us thro the Customs with our luggage. . . . Our missionary whom all the natives seemed to love, cheered us on & led the way to the Customshouse which Mr. Garstin will remember is under the arches at the entrance to the town. We found our luggage obstructing the archway & two sets of muleteers engaged in a free fight as to who should take it up to the hotel. Three turbaned officials sat in a recess in the archway – & to them we delivered our keys . . . . Things became so riotous at this stage between the muleteers that Abraham (one of the turbaned 3) arose & scourged the crowd in fine style with a leathern thong & scattered them to right & left, just as the buyers & sellers might have been driven out of the Temple. . . . Finally our ten packages . . . were seized & piled on to one small donkey's back . . . . The unfortunate little animal struggled up a dreadfully steep little street with us at its heels & after us a ragged brown rabble which we were thankful to leave behind at the hotel door. I dont think much of Mrs. Ashington's little Marquis sending us to a commercial hotel . . . it is in the centre of the town & the noises & smells are awful . . . . We are shaken out of our beds at gunfire in the morning – it is fired from a battery just below us – & what with the Ramadaming all day & feasting all night it is hardly the place for two peacefully inclined artists to be. . . . Mr. McLeod who has the English stores here . . . . recommended the Villa Valentina on the hill . . . & we shall go up there this afternoon after tea.

Friday evening – Villa Valentina
   This letter has had to stand over for a few days – we moved up here early this

morning & are now settled in & unpacked & very comfortable indeed. It is a big new place on the Fez Rd. just beyond the large Soko (market). . . . We have two rooms leading out of each other – & Mrs. A. is paying 7/ for hers & I 6/ for mine – rather more than I wanted to give but it is difficult to get any place for less at this time of year. It is quiet & just far enough out of the town to give us some exercise. We are beginning to shake down & get more accustomed to things – at first we felt bewildered & a trifle nervous at the crowds of lean, brown fierce looking men but they are so busy coming & going & farthing splitting in the market that they never turn a head to look at us. The Soko is a wonderful place, indescribably dirty . . . . It is on the hillside just outside the walls & the principal street leads out of it right thro' the town down the hill to the sea. . . . Apparently there is no method in the market – donkeys saddled & unsaddled are ubiquitous & anyone with anything to sell sits down & sells it. There is a corner devoted to cobblers, dwellers in tents who seem to eke out a miserable existence patching each others old shoes. Then there is a row of Arab women squatting like Sybills with their impenetrable leathern looking faces peering out of their white burnous – they sell pottery & I hope to get some pictures here if I have any luck. It is all so crowded that I dont expect to get much done in the streets. Mr. East said he had to take his models in to court yards & quiet places. Mr. Garstin was right, no gorgeous east here – no oriental riot of color – all browns & whites & muddy creams with here & there a splash of crimson & orange & the better class Moors making blots of indigo in their handsome blue cloaks. . . . The predominant odour is morocco leather & olive oil – not at all disagreeable. Do you remember Miss Talbot . . . putting her nose into a homespun shawl & exclaiming "What a delicious stink!" Well its something like that. . . . We haven't bought anything yet, much too frightened of being taken in – Mrs. A. prays pathetically that she may not cheat the natives – *I* pray that the natives may not cheat *me*. . . .

Sunday evening 7th.

Will this letter ever get finished? It must go in the morning. . . . We have got a boy to shepherd us about & he is coming tomorrow morning at 8.30. Our missionary doctor sent him, he is one of his servants & thoroughly trustworthy & good looking to boot – & we are to pay him a franc a day. Yesterday we had a model – a ducky little Arab girl who we captured & painted in an aloe grove just behind the Soko – rather prickly but private & peaceful. First hour she was flattered, second, bored & finally she went off after an unseemly haggle over payment. We paid her same as Dinan models & plied her with chocolate. She is coming back tomorrow however so she evidently likes it. . . . Had tea with the Theomins this afternoon . . . . He has given me a £15 commission for a Tangier picture.[1] He has been a most kind friend to me & a most generous patron. We

[1] *Orange Sellers, Tangiers* and *Head of an Old Woman* are still hanging in Olveston, the Theomins' home in Dunedin, now an historic house open to the public.

are going to leave our letters tomorrow on Mr. Perdicaris. He seems to be an uncrowned King of Tangier. . . . No more, goodnight & goodbye – come soon & rejoice the heart of your loving

Frances Hodgkins

Give all sorts of kind messages to everyone, & tell Mr. Garstin Tangier is a pearl of a place & I am borne down with the responsibility I have taken on myself of trying to represent ever so feebly its wondrous charm & beauty.

[102] To Rachel Hodgkins, 12 January 1903

Villa Valentina, Tangier. 12.1.03

My darling Mother,

I posted a letter to Miss Richmond today which will go on to you but this is just a little supplementary one for your private ear . . . things are going on very quietly & calmly here – I dont want you to feel alarmed or anxious about my being here – it is perfectly safe in Tangier & a long way from the disturbed district where they are fighting. There are always more or less inter tribal rows going on in the interior & this particular one is over the appearance of a young fanatical Pretender to the throne who claims to be a descendant of Mahomet & therefore elect of God. The present Sultan is in rather bad odour with some of the tribes owing to his European tendencies & his strong leaning to progress & reform generally – hence the trouble but he is a strong young man & is showing himself equal to the occasion. He has done a lot of rather foolish things, which have displeased his people – played tennis & ridden a bicycle in English dress & drunk whisky with dogs of Christians . . . . no one knows how it will all pan out but all agree that it will be a bad day for Morocco if the Sultan gets killed & the Pretender reigns in his stead. There has been some pretty sharp fighting at Fez but all this part of the country is quiet & normal. Fez is 150 miles south nearly a weeks journey over very rough country. Be quite sure at the slightest sign of uneasiness I shall make tracks – I have no desire to risk my skin – I am much too big a coward – I am revelling in this place – such sumptuous color & I feel sure if I can get a good portfolio of sketches it will pay me over & over again. We have had a splendid spell of fine weather & have got a goodish amount of work done. I am posting a little Normandy sketch for you dearest get it framed & give it to Wright to sell & keep what you get for it as the first installment for the little girl I want you to get to help you during the winter. . . . I was so glad they liked my work in Dunedin the press was very kind & Willie was a brick sending all the papers on to me. . . . Alice sent me a Maori bag on which I had to pay 1/6 but I was so glad to see the little flax friend I forgave her. . . .

[103] To Dorothy Richmond, 24 January 1903[2]

Villa Valentina, Tangier. Jan. 24th. 1903

My dearest Four & Twopence.

How do you like this for a nice little pet name? short for Dollar[3] you know. I think it is rather neat if mercenary, a dollar in these parts is a douro and a douro is five pesetas and five pesetas is 2/6, English money, dont mistake it for the almighty coin of the same name, tho' I have given you the benefit of the American quotation, as you are well worth the extra money. . . .

So you want to know the latest from the front – last week when the battle was raging 1½ miles along the shore, within sight of our windows, I wrote you a long account (from under the bed) but decided not to send it, when peace was declared in a few days. It sounded rather lurid, and smacked too much of gun-powder and dead Moors and burning villages. For four days it was all very exciting, and tho' I wasnt exactly nervous . . . the fighting was altogether too near for comfort and it badly interfered with work. The town was disturbed & excited, we were warned off the beach and sand-dunes (our favourite walk) and the Fez road was not considered safe, so we were rather thrown on our own resources for a few days . . . . It all hung on the doings of a wicked Basha or Native Governor – one tribe wanted him dismissed, the other to keep him – so they fought one fine afternoon . . . in a valley running up from the beach, quite near the Salt-pans . . . . Three or four Moors were killed, and some women taken prisoners, and deposited, for safety in Mr Harris's garden (The Times correspondent) he promptly sent into Tangier for the troops to be sent out . . . . Nothing happened till the next afternoon, when the fighting re-commenced, and the troops went out followed by half the town amidst the greatest excitement. They marched along the sands with the fife & drum band tootling merrily, and almost drowning their war-cry to Allah, invoking Him to send them victory. . . .

They look an undiciplined, out of hand lot, and so they proved during the afternoon, for after they had sent the enemy to the right-about (the enemy being the tribes opposed to the Government Basha) they started looting, and towards evening, they rollicked home across the sands, driving asses, goats, cattle, chickens (no I forgot, you cant drive chickens) anyway they were laden with plunder . . . . We were all rather excited and nobody knew what to believe . . . . I consulted my guide book & seriously considered Algekiras, for I saw no point about being stuck here if things were going to get fussy. Next day Friday being their Sabath, they rested. On Saturday they were at it again and about mid-day the troops turned out once more, with their mules and their guns . . . . This time they all

[2] This letter exists only in a dubious transcript which has been slightly modified in keeping with the other letters of this period.

[3] Miss Richmond was known in her family as Dolla.

passed our hotel, and we looked down on them from the balcony. It was supposed
to be a two days campaign . . . . however the rain came down in sheets before they
had got very far and whether it damped both their ardour and their gun-powder
no one seems to know, anyhow back they marched to Tangier in the morning,
and there were great tales of surrender, and peace making, and sacrifices made by
the enemy, and now thank goodness all is quiet, and things go on in their serene
and normal manner, and we are painting peacefully in the market once more.
Dont believe half you read in the papers, there is a storm of lies raging in the press
. . . . Do you remember what the Ruddy Kip says somewhere. "No news – Kill
a correspondent in the Soudan, – the B[ritish P[ublic] *must* be kept interested"
    . . . . I grow more and more facinated with [the Moors] and their wonderful
religion, there is an old Colonel here who is more than half a Mahomedan, and
spends his time pottering round among the people, for whom he has an intense
admiration, and I fancy he reads his Koran a great deal oftener than his Bible –
the old sinner – anyway he's my great stand-by and the source of all my
information, reliable and otherwise.
    But our real channel of Tangier gossip is Absolom the trustworthy our guide
etc and friend – he knows everything, and what he doesnt know he guesses
at. . . . Mrs. A. is enjoying herself . . . . She is as gay as I will let her be, but I keep
her nose to the grindstone pretty constantly, and won't let her have more than
three tea-parties a week. We are pretty pally with the Austrian Count just at
present. . . . Last night he had a whist party, that is to say, he and Mrs. A., and
Mr Dodd and dummy played whist, and I looked at a lovely collection of
engravings, such beauties – Rembrandts, Albert Durers, Bartolozzis, and ever so
many others. I just knew enough to know they were jolly good – they were all
muddled together in an untidy confusion in a drawer, and I couldn't resist tidying
them up for him, it seemed like old times with my father's sketches, and I did
enjoy it. . . . You may think I have forgotten to mention your delightful letter,
received yesterday. . . . It's difficult to believe we are enjoying two such different
surroundings, your tall spidery spindly trees, and east winds, and snow and hail
and frost and fog and dirt and mud and mist – but there I'll spare you – while I
am all sharp shadows and color and sunshine and noise . . . . We have our east
winds too – the first two days you think what a heavenly, cool, refreshing breeze,
but after that it begins to wither you up, and takes the life out of you, and you
feel that nothing is worth while and everything is a bore, but thank goodness, they
dont last long, and the rain comes and gives us fresh energy and clear skies once
more, and with them the great longing to rise early and paint Brangwyn pictures
in the market. . . .
    Well Miss Richmond dear, I cant stop any longer gossiping here with you; my
hot bottle is getting cold, and the electric light is showing signs of going out. I
think you had better send this on to Mother if you dont mind. I write her little

intermediate letters but save most of the news to send through you. . . .
Ever your loving

Frances.

[104] To Isabel Field, 27 January 1903

Villa Valentina, Tangier. 27th. 03

You poor dear old Sis

Will your troubles never end? I have been very unhappy about you since Will's
letter telling me how ill poor little Jack has been. . . . It must have been agony to
watch the poor mite's sufferings. . . . You poor mothers do go through a lot of
trials, & there is a good deal more difficulty in the bringing up of children than
meets the eye. . . . I am beginning to dream of the time when I shall see you all
again – you & Mother & Will standing waiting for me on the wharf & old Bert
shedding tears of welcome in the background. I dont expect we've changed much
– a few more grey hairs – every picture I paint brings a new grey hair, & every
picture that doesnt sell brings a dozen! . . . I enclose you a letter from Miss
Richmond with an amusing description of Mrs Oliver's opinion of my painting.
She is a lady who considers that nothing good can come from N.Z. but what can
you expect from a lady whose ancestor was a Cornish pilchard. She thinks with
a few other of my friends that nothing can be learnt out[side] of a Paris Studio –
but I find Nature good enough for me & less expensive – my experience of Studio
pupils is that they can never do anything once they leave it, without a top light
& a master at their backs to tell them what to do – & I doubt if many of them
could have supported themselves in Europe for 2 years on what they earned from
their easels – I get fierce when people tell me I should be in a studio & personally
cant see any more reason why I should be in a studio than that they should be in
an asylum. I have put all my news in Mothers letter – there is nothing new here,
all quiet & safe – weather lovely – work mediocre, spirits equable & health A.1.
Take care of yourself. Love to all Your loving Fanny.

[105] To Dorothy Richmond, 7 March 1903

Villa Valentina, Tangier. 7.3.03

Dearest D.K.R.

. . . . I had to read your letter over twice before I could decide to take it
seriously. In the first place I am horrified to think of you wasting your precious
time copying out my stupid letters – I cannot allow it for a minute, if you really
want a copy I shall buy some transfer paper & write a duplicate letter – but they

are not worth it dear lady – to see them in print without the intime touches would rather take the color out of them – besides it seems to me that a letter that is good enough to publish should be either whimsical enough to treat as a joke or thoughtful enough to take seriously & mine are neither – better let them rest in peace with the family archives – it is enough for me to know my letters please you & the Garstins & my mother. I am really terribly proud to think you like them – how do they compare with Miss Astley's for instance – but of course I know that you wld rather nurse one of her empty envelopes than read the outpourings of my innermost soul – however I mustnt expect too much. Oh! bye the bye which part of Italy did you think of going to – San Remo? Oh! the cunning of you, the transparent guilelessness!

There is three weeks arrears of news to make up – I really mustn't dawdle . . . . I have put Mrs. Ashington forcibly on the other side of the door, she wants to discuss the washing list & the fate of a manqué nightgown, there is none like her – none – with such an aptitude for thoroughly investigating affairs of this sort & if there's anything lost from one's temper down to a diamond brooch she will find it or know the reason why – she is really an angelic person & we are very happy together, her virtues & my faults leaven each other & prevent each from becoming tiresome –

About the pictures – I expect they will have arrived before this reaches you – I thought perhaps it might be as well to have another try for the R.A. You see I have my frames at Miss Parks & if you & Mr. Garstin wld be kind enough to choose the most suitable one Peak wld do the rest, get me a form etc & forward them. . . . The rest of the sketches had better go out to N.Z. at once tho' I feel rather loath to send out more while so many of the last lot are still unsold. It seems a futile sort of thing sending to the Academy & will only end in disappointment but at least one may try. I wish I could have sent you my large picture of the market – it is the apple or rather the onion of my eye – much the same sort of subject a jumble of onions melons & oranges. It is going tomorrow to Mr. Theomin – I am going to eschew vegetables after this with a comfortable feeling I have done my duty by them – I have got rather into the way of thinking I cant paint a picture without an onion in it, quite forgetting they are things not quite to everyone's taste – but they do wake a picture up a bit don't they? You see great shining pink satin masses of them with a row of feminine haiks with one eye apiece sitting behind them . . . . I had a little show of my sketches on Sunday . . . . Mr. Perdicaris wanted to buy one but unfortunately did not mention it till after they were posted the next day – however I am to let him see some others later on. They have been so very kind to me & are just the most delightful people in the world – they said as I wouldnt go to the dances I should have a party of my own up at Aidonia, their beautiful place up in the mountain so one morning last week a long cavalcade of us set out on mules headed by a radiantly beautiful soldier & after him Mrs. Perdicaris looking like the Queen of Sheba on a black satin Barb. . . . We climbed about 30-000 ft. up the side of the mountain – sitting on our animals tails. . . the meaning of words is to convey ideas & the idea I wish to convey is that it was a high mountain . . . after 2 hours [we] found ourselves on the top – we turned into a long drive running thro an orderly sort of a wilderness of olives & aloes & golden genesta & palmettos & mauve masses of starry periwinkle. There was a sumptuous lunch ready for us in the cool verandah overlooking the sea, & I dont know which appealed to my senses most the turkey on the table or the peacocks on the terrace – they strutted insolently up & down opening & shutting their tails with the click of a fan & looking superb in the blazing sun. The house is a regular eagle's nest built high on a rock with Gibraltar & Tarifa on their northern horizon & nothing human in sight but a little Spanish smuggling village tucked almost out of sight at their feet. . . . Mr Perdicaris is a poet – looks & speaks like one, but Mrs. Perdicaris never allows him to get too exalted & brings him down with a rush from no matter what height with something deliciously banal & pert & so keeps the balance . . . . She has a large heart & queens it royally over Tangier. After lunch we wandered round the garden – there was a temple of Vesta arranged classically over the garden pump & a moorish mosque concealed the mysteries of the tool house & further on in a hallowed spot there was a thatched mausoleum sacred to the memory of a dead St. Bernard – it was all very interesting & instructive & I came home full of information about the cork oak and the puff adder. Do try & remember dear if you are ever bitten by the former no, I mean the latter to at once administer a red hot poker or failing that apply carbolic acid internally. As death generally results in 20 minutes you will have to look sharp – they say it is never really safe to picnic in the bush without either of these two remedies at hand. . . .

[106] To Dorothy Richmond, 23 March 1903

Hotel Calpe, Tetuan, Morocco. 23rd March 1903.

My dearest D.K.R.

Come to Tetuan – come – catch the next steamer, cancel all engagements, chuck the studio let everything go to the winds only come without a moments delay & realise for yourself all your dreams of beauty color & sunshine. I have been in an ecstatic state of joy for one week – this beautiful white town is a vellum bound collection of exquisite poems compared with which Tangier is as a doggerel rhyme to a Browning sonnet. There is only one crumple in the rose leaf & that is that you are not here to enjoy it with me – but you must come – we must make a pilgrimage some other time & you shall go over in oil where I have floundered in watercolor. It seems to me as near perfection as needs be for a sketching ground – & after noisy shreiking Tangier it is a haven of rest & quietness – its altogether different, more Moorish, less civilised, more bazaars &

mosques fewer donkeys & English people . . . . I wish we could have come here in the first place I think I have done more in this one week than in two months in Tangier . . . . I have broken the onion & orange spell & have struck out in a new line and am painting wonderful little shops aglow with color under the shadow of vine pergolas supported by long spidery props, the whole emphatically repeated in clear purple on the pavement. It is really very Japanesy & Mortimer Menpes figures flit about in filabs of radiant hue – the little junior moors all wear bright colors – the soberer browns & blues are reserved for their dads – the royal shereefian green is a favorite color & catches the eye with an imperious insistance – it turns everything upside down in a picture & has to be dealt with warily but it is a gorgeous color & I have populated two of my pictures with little green gnomes. The whiteness & pearliness of the town simply defies you – you cant get it pure & brilliant enough & the shadows drive one silly – you race after them, pause one frenzied moment to decide on a blue mauve yellow or green shadow – when up & over the wall & away & the wretched things gone for that day at least & you are gazing at a glaring blank wall & wondering why on earth you ever started to sketch it. Cubes & domes are the general outline of things & the intoxicated pergola props take off the stiffness of things & help out compositions & foregrounds in a wonderful way. I had to cut short my last letter & so never told you why we decided to come here. Mrs. A. had arranged to come with Miss Thackeray & her friend but a £6 trip for the inside of a week was too expensive for me so I gave up all idea of seeing Tetuan – however we happened to meet the missionary doctor who asked us to go with him (Mrs. A. & me) & he would lend us his tent, camp bedsteads & all the other impedimenta necessary – & all we should have to pay for wld be the hire of our mules, 8 shillings. This was too good an opportunity to be lost so we decided to come over & stay for a month – no sooner said than done . . . it seemed too good to be true to find ourselves one sunny morning sitting on a tableland of rugs & shawls & sheep skins on our respective animals & keeping the balance true between two bulging panniers of tents & portmanteaux & easels & bedsteads & bundles & various oddments of sorts . . . . We swam out of Tangier like large brown swans thro a sea of yellow sand – into an open valley & up into the hills – the first 10 miles was heavenly then I began to feel as if I was in a water logged vessel & a raking sun & an east wind blowing in our faces blistered & burnt us but we were very jolly and the sensation of travelling in Morocco thro' country which a few weeks before had been impassable on account of the rebellion was quite enough to keep one alert & interested no matter how tired. When we reached the fôndak at 5 it was blowing too hard to put up our tents so we decided to sleep in one of the little rooms which they let to travellers. The fôndak is perched high up on a ridge of the Ape Mnts a spur of the Atlas & which terminate at Tangier in one of the grand old Pillars of Hercules . . . . It is a hollow square, the walls forming arched mangers for the cattle & on one side up a tiny narrow staircase are two attics about 10ft.

square, white-washed, bare & tolerably clean – while the men were cooking our dinner, we performed our ablutions on the roof . . . & then having scraped off some of the dust we sat huddled up in rugs & waited for the full moon to rise over Africa – up she came a ball of gold & lit up the deep mysterious wind swept gorge at our feet and the vastness & loneliness beyond – the yard below was full of cattle & mules all keeping a cheerful sort of munching hoofy sound which never ceased all night. A brown ghost came out of the attic door & clapped hands & in two minutes we were sitting Moorish fashion round a brown earthern-ware pot smelling as no pot has ever smelt before or can again . . . . there was one pang for the tender little chicken that had travelled alive with us all day then our better feelings were smothered & we fished voraciously for drum sticks & wings with our own forks & sopped up the gravy in a way you would have particularly disliked . . . . we only left off eating because there was nothing more in the pot – then the debris was cleared away & Mrs. A. & I made our beds & retired there & then – we didn't get much sleep – our little room was a temple of the winds & frightfully cold. Not having taken anything off there was nothing to put on, so we lost no time in the morning over our toilet & by 6 a.m. were once more on the march. . . . At a point where you first catch sight of Tetuan weary wayfarers have erected a cairn of stones each traveller casting a stone on it – then you lose sight of it & dont see it again till you find yourself riding up to its walls thro a long valley with magnificent rocky hills on either side. The compactness of these old walled towns is delightful, no straggling villages & outskirts, everything snug & trim within the walls and at night when the bugles ring out at 10 o'clock there is a comfortable sort of good night All's well sound about it & you know the gates are closed & all is safe from brigands & jackals & other fearsome prowlers of these dark & lawless nights

We rode into Tetuan under a mid day sun, very stiff & tired & [with] eyes that wld hardly keep open – we could just see enough of the town to know it was beautiful – & were glad we had come. . . . Next morning we . . . started to explore the town with the Vice Consul Mr. Bewicke. . . . He is the only Englishman here & is a lonely man bored to death & glad to see any English faces – or even a Colonial one. We had to do our sight seeing under umbrellas & in the afternoon the rain came down in buckets – Mr. Bewicke sent round to ask us to tea – so we waded round to the Consulate – a square white house set in a lovely garden – he gave us a good tea & plenty of barley sugar & was most entertaining & amusing – he has been here 7 years & has plenty to say about the Moors – I think he must have been forgotten by the Foreign Office . . . . Saturday morning we started to paint in the market & entered into competition with a snake charmer beating a tom-tom & doing his best to collect a crowd – we completely spoilt his show & in five minutes had a crowd round us that he would have given his eyes to possess. Absolom not being in his own forest failed to roar as loudly as usual & wasn't much good. So we gave up the market . . . & found a quiet place in one of the little streets – & have been painting there ever since in perfect peace & quietness. The week has gone by quickly & I am beginning to realise that my time in Morocco is drawing to a close. We have dined with Mr. Bewicke & we have lunched with Mr. Bewicke & Mr. Bewicke has dined with us likewise tea'd & we have walked with Mr. Bewicke & talked with Mr. Bewicke & painted in Mr. Bewicke's garden & there never seems to be an hour in the day or a street in the town in which we dont meet Mr. Bewicke . . . . Did I tell you Mrs. A. is taking Absolom to England with her . . . . she thinks life would be an insupportable blank without Absolom and a donkey so she is taking the former & getting the latter in England when she gets there – at present she is deep in the intricacies of Moorish clothes – & is fitting Absolom out like a young prince. . . . What she is going to do with the boy when she gets him to England I dont know – & what her two maids will say to such a foreign innovation remains to be seen – I chaff her life out about . . . the awful responsibility she is taking upon herself . . . . We are only fairly comfortable at this grubby little hotel . . . . The landlady is one of those hardworking daughters of toil who are always scrubbing & cleaning & yet at the end of the day never have a clean spot to stand on – our landlord is a terrible looking brigand – if I didnt know what a respectable couple they really are in spite of their looks nothing would induce me to come to such a place – they have no children but they have adopted a goat who holds up the stairs sometimes & will allow no one to pass & has other playful little ways with it such as eating the tablecloth & going to sleep in the only chair fit to sit in. . . . How desperately hard you are working . . . still life from 7.30 to 3.30 is a good days work – on Sunday too – keep everything to show me – dont paint over & tear up too much before we meet. I feel rather pleased with *my* work – the first time for many a long day – the subjects facinate me – & dont demand many figures . . . in fact models of any sort are [out of the question] – you cant get man, woman, or child to stand for love or money. . . .

 . . . . Have I succeeded in making you thoroughly sorry & unhappy that you didnt come to Morocco – I hope so – Goodbye – goodbye – love to all kind friends.

[107] To Rachel Hodgkins, 28 March 1903
Hotel Calpe, Tetuan, Morocco. 28th March, 1903.

My darling Mother,
 . . . . I am getting very weary for a sight of you – I am really too homesick to enjoy much more of Europe – you are always at the back of my thoughts & I often wonder at my own selfishness and hardheartedness in staying away so long. . . . We shall be here about 3 weeks longer I think. The Beuider tribe are still troublesome & have cut the road between here & Tangier . . . . The Sultan has

threatened to send an army against them to punish them & "eat them up" as the Moors put it . . . . We are very safe here within these high walls . . . dont worry about me dear – your daughter is much too much of a *cur* ever to run any danger – dont believe anything you ever read in the papers . . . . it is an unhappy country steeped in wickedness & corruption & tyranny – the vindictive oppression of the poor & the cruelty to animals & the fanatical ignorance on all sides makes one very sad & Tetuan needs all its personal beauty to make up for its lack of virtue. . . .

[108] TO RACHEL HODGKINS, 31 MARCH 1903

Tetuan – March 31st.

Just a line to enclose with Miss Richmonds letter which I thought you might like to see. . . .

. . . . We are going on very quietly here – the Beuider have stopped raiding & have retired to the hills & the road to Tangier is open again . . . . The weather is perfect & I am getting lots of work & feel in excellent health & spirits. I am painting a beautiful Jewess in full dress – wonderful coif of pearls & emeralds & massive ear-rings reaching to her shoulders – dress of cloth of gold & black velvet with all sorts of barbaric jewels & ornaments & ropes of pearls & unset emeralds hung about her neck – it makes a splendid study & I am delighted to get such a chance – the Jewesses here are beautiful – descendants of the Jews that were driven out of Spain by Ferdinand & Isabella – they are immensely wealthy & it is their quarter in Tetuan that the Beuider want to come & "eat up". We went for a walk tonight round the walls & found them bristling with cannon. I daresay the Beuider have done the same & thought better of any little idea they may have had of attacking the town. . . .

. . . . I hope next letter to hear you are going down to Ashburton[4] – I shall be glad to hear of you having the rest & change for I know how badly you must want it. Goodbye darling

[109] TO DOROTHY RICHMOND, 11 APRIL 1903

Hotel Calpe, Tetuan. 11th.4.03, Easter Eve

My dearest D.K.R.
. . . . As you see we are still in Tetuan – & how to get out of the wretched place (slightly different tone this to my last letter when I remember I almost wept with enthusiasm) is troubling us greatly. We want to get back to Tangier and as no

---

[4] Willie was now manager of the Bank of New South Wales in Ashburton.

boat goes for a fortnight we have decided to go by the road, Beuider or no Beuider – & trust to getting thro' all right. It is in a wobbly sort of condition neither safe nor un-safe. . . . Before I say any more about our friends the enemy I must thank you for your delightful letter all about the Newlyn Show. . . . I glowed with pride to hear I had hung in such close intimacy with Mr. Stanhope Forbes . . . . would that we might continue our pleasant companionship on the walls of Burlington House – I am deeply grateful for all you have done for me . . . . I only hope all your labor will not be in vain – & that we may live to blushingly greet Fatima in the Gem Room of the R.A. – I dare not hope – it brings such bitter disappoint-ment. . . . Mrs. S. Forbes' picture sounds thrilling – her things have a magnetic charm for me which I know you dont share – her manner is too jolly clever & electric to give one much peace of mind – but its a wonderful inspiring sort of genius which braces slovenly minds like mine & shames them out of scamped drawing & chancey effects. . . . We have been leading a quiet uneventful painting-every-day sort-of-life . . . & trying hard to paint the whole of Tetuan before we leave it. Mr. Bewicke comes in to give us the news at tea time & after that we either get an evening sketch or go for a walk – we still love Tetuan as ardently as ever & discover new beauties in it every day – likewise new smells – lately we have been painting in the slipper quarter, hard by the tanneries & the whole process of turning harmless innocent goats into red & yellow slippers is unfolded before our eyes & nose. . . . The event of the week has been a visit to Absolom's uncle's harem – it was really a most delightfully quaint & picturesque experience. We left Absolom & our slippers on the front doorstep & followed an ebony slave thro' a tiled courtyard where a fountain was playing & 4 tall orange trees grew up into the sky – all round this courtyard were arched recesses, cool little cushioned retreats with rich rugs & divans & draperies. In one of these we found the 4 ladies of the house and the husband their lord. He came forward fat & smiling & pleasant & then we shook hands all round kissing our fingers each time Moorish fashion after each shake which considerably lengthens one's greeting if the room be full – then we all sat down & an hysterical giggle went round which helped to clear the air and two of the youngest & prettiest of the women sat down close on either side of Mrs. A. & proceeded to thoroughly investigate her clothes . . . they were specially interested in her silk & lace front which had a calico back which they soon discovered – they were like babies, only not so well behaved over a new doll – pretty clothes & jewellery delight them . . . . They were very beautiful to look at, quite young & I think must have been Circassians they were so fair, their complexions I mean, which were dazzling, but their hair was blue black – their eye brows were connected in one deeply marked arch of Kohl & their eyes blackened to a tremendous size. Two or three different colored silk handkerchiefs were fastened around their heads, & coquettish bunches of flowers tied at their ears from which hung huge silver rings – they were like beautiful children quite unselfconscious & full of pretty ways. They evidently thought Mrs. Ashington would be greatly improved with a little more eye brow & produced the Kohl sticks & for the fun of the thing she let them paint her. It was really a startling sight to see my respectable chaperone being turned into a "Light of the Harem" or the "White Jewel of Tetuan" or some such person. . . . Then the tea came in brought by [the] same slave & was put down on a low table in front of the master. A large brass urn boiled the water & while it was boiling a silver bottle containing orange water was handed round – I took 3 drops on my handkerchief – & was then rushed at & dowsed & soaked, up my sleeves down my neck & on my face till I was thoroughly damp all over & horribly uncomfortable – & then having wet us thoroughly they proceeded to dry us with incense burning in a little silver brazier – this was swung in front of us & held under our jackets & as far up our sleeves as the fashion would permit. Having been thoroughly fumigated & smelling like a spice box we were prepared for tea – which the master was making very prettily & [with] a great deal of ceremony – first green tea 3 or 4 tea spoons, then a bunch of green mint & half a dozen lumps of sugar like small ice bergs & then boiling water – this brews into a thickish syrup & tastes more of fragrant mint than anything else. It is very nauseous when one tastes it for the first time but you soon get to like it very much indeed . . . . They make a loud sipping noise when they drink, a washerwoman & her saucer is nothing to it. . . . Moorish etiquette requires you to drink 3 cups which we did & then we sat in a deathly silence for 10 minutes & munched peanuts – then the ladies were all sent out of the room & Absolom was called in from the front doorstep & given some tea & then we got up to go & once more Absolom was banished & the ladies came back & we said goodbye as gracefully & gratefully as we could & retired. This is the kind of life that all the women in Morocco lead who are not toilers & workers in the field – they are quite ignorant & untaught with nothing to occupy their minds but intrigue & dress – they can neither read or write & the better class ones never go outside their garden walls . . . . It is a dreadful condition of affairs & one feels the hopelessness of any good ever coming out of a country where such a wrong & iniquitous system of treating their womenkind prevails. . . .

[110] To Rachel Hodgkins, 19 April 1903

Hotel London, Gibraltar. 19.4.03

My darling Mother,

As you see we are on our way back to England – safely back from Tetuan – & now waiting here quietly for our boat which sails tomorrow. After all we did not risk the road, but happily found a boat sailing from Tetuan so we cancelled our mules & soldiers . . . & packed up and were off at a few hours notice. . . . It wld have been a great risk to have run going by the road – the Beuider have terrorised the neighborhood & our last news of poor little Tetuan was that the Sultan's soldiers had arrived & that there were disturbances going on – so we are well out of it. We got back to Tangier touching first at Gibraltar & then across the Straits to the familiar little white town & we went thro' the same noisy struggle to get our luggage and ourselves ashore – but the novelty had worn off & it was merely tiresome & stupid. . . . It was a great wrench & uprooting saying goodbye to that dear country . . . & now it is all a thing of the past & we have left Tangier behind that blue haze on the other side of the Straits & all that remains of Morocco for me is in my portfolio, precious shreds & remnants that must suffice –

Your nice long letter reached me just before I left Tetuan – I was going for a ride with the Consul & just starting as the postie came up – so it had to burn in my pocket for 2 hours before I got a chance of opening it. It was such a bright letter, & cheered me so to read it. Oh! I say what's this about Edith McLaren? She is a stupid old thing – her fiancé is an old McLaren family friend or flame, youngish for ordinary people but infantile for persons of Edith's age. . . . Issy wrote last mail but said nothing about Gertrude's love affairs. I have heard plenty about that particular flirtation from other people but not that one precisely important item that seems to be so ardently desired by her friends. . . .

[111] TO RACHEL HODGKINS, 1 MAY 1903

52 Lower Sloane St., London, S.W. 1st May.

My darling Mother,

I know you will all rejoice over the joyful news that I am on the Line at the R.A.[5] Tra-la-la-la-la! it seems all right & quite natural like somehow – I enclose official statement in case you dont believe me – I arrived in London on Sat. 26th & found the news waiting for me. I also had a 2nd. one accepted but not hung – they accept about a 1000 more than they can find room for – the one on the line is a ¾ length figure of an arab girl more elaborate & more highly finished than my usual work. Mr. Stanhope Forbes wired to Mr. Garstin & he sent the news on to me – the latter, poor man, is out himself, at which he is very sad – it is a chancey sort of lottery & monstrously unfair in its favors. I had your letter last night written just before you left for the South. I was *so* glad to hear you & Sis were really off together for a holiday, only I wish it were a longer one for her . . . . We are going to the R.A. tomorrow, the first day. I did not get a ticket for the private view but I believe I shall get one for the Soirée later on. It was very delightful to see Miss Richmond again – we are very comfy here & have 2 bedrooms & the use of Miss Weltons cosy sitting room. It is a sort of ladies club & most convenient & comfortable. It has been foul (no other word will do)

[5] The Royal Academy exhibitions were gigantic affairs, with about 10,000 pictures submitted and a ten to one chance of being selected. Selected pictures were hung one above the other, the best of them in an honoured position 'on the line', at eye level, as opposed to being 'skied'.

weather since I arrived rain – rain – wind – a little grey sun, then rain & mud & by way of being thoroughly disagreeable, a hail storm. . . . We came back from Gib: in a North German boat, most comfortable & commodious, infinitely finer than P.&O. food better, better service & altogether vastly superior. I shall probably come out in one of them. . . . For goodness sake muster all the Hodgkins you can get together to come down & meet me at the wharf. I hear there are 300 Richmonds & Atkinsons strong going to line up to welcome their beloved Dorothy back again . . . . We have had a busy week . . . paying visits & seeing galleries & doing a little necessary shopping. Has Sis heard anything of my pictures – *did she send* to the Chch show – I am longing for news – dont think because I am on the Line I am any less of a pauper – so do try all you can to sell if it is possible – I think the pictures should be taken away from Dunedin – they dont seem to be doing any good there. . . .

[112] To Rachel Hodgkins, 11 June 1903

2 Rudolph Terrace, Bushey, Herts. 11.6.03

My darling Mother,

. . . . As you see I am at Bushey – I came down here a fortnight ago – it is a dear little village inhabited chiefly by Prof. Herkomer's pupils[6] – it is all very nice & pretty, not in the least exciting, just like an Xmas card . . . nothing calling out specially to be painted. I found Miss Stoddart here also & like myself – very disappointed with the country, we both agree that after Cornwall it is a poor place. She has applied for an art teacher's post at a school in Pretoria at a salary of £300 a year and she is hoping daily to hear she has been appointed. I hope so too, it will be a great relief & rest to have a fixed salary after 5 years precarious struggle with one's brush – she has splendid pluck & is always so cheery & purposeful & un-downcast. I wish her painting had been a greater success – it doesn't seem to have caught on – with all its cleverness & knowledge it just lacks that charm without which good work is so often uninteresting. After our work is over we go for long walks & talks in the evening. She is full of theories and I have none at all, which leaves me all the freer to disagree with hers – she thinks I am suffering from want of teaching & *I* think her chief fault lies in *too* much teaching – it is so easy to paint like your master & to think other peoples thoughts, the difficulty is to be yourself, assimilate all that is helpful but keep your own individuality, as your most precious possession – it is one's only chance. I have had a long quiet fortnight working hard at my Morocco pictures & have almost got them ready to send up to the Fine Arts next week[7]. . . . I was feeling a good

---

[6] Professor Sir Hubert von Herkomer RA (1849-1914) opened an important private art school in Bushey in 1883.

[7] The Fine Arts Gallery in Bond Street had invited FH to show ten pictures.

deal crumpled up & tired after my month in town and was glad to get into quiet quarters once more. London wears me to death . . . . The poorer I get the more I want to dress like a duchess – dont ever send me home again Mother dear under £1000 a year. I was asked to go to Scotland for this month – to Arisaig where Miss R. is right up in the Highlands – it wld have been lovely but my horrid pictures had to be finished, so instead of heather & moors & deer & porridge & gillies & crofters & other Highland joys, here I am in a little back bedroom in Bushey painting Morocco pictures in anything but appropriate surroundings . . . the difficulty I had in getting this room endears it considerably in spite of its pokiness . . . . When Miss Stoddart calls on me I put my head as far out of the window as possible & her feet she disposes of in the fireplace – & so we manage it – my meals I have down stairs in the back parlor & for all these luxuries & comforts I only pay 15/- a week – it is quite comfortable & my landlady is kind & garrulous – she is a sheaf of Bushey memories & flows on like a gentle stream quite without malice or scandal – it is most diverting & I only wish I could keep a record of all she says, her quaint phrases & homely way of putting things. I know all the village gossip for years back – how the Vicar's wife wore red roses in her bonnet 3 months after her mother in laws death & why Borough Johnstone married the girl he did, & the perfidious behaviour of the village postmaster who kept back Nellie Simpson's love letters & so nearly broke two loving hearts & all because he was so useful in the choir nothink was said by nobody – one moral she invariably deducts from all her stories & that is that artists are a canny lot & always marry girls with money . . . . I look out on homely scenes from my window – I have an un-interrupted view of 20 backyards or so with their cabbage plots & ladies in déshabille with babies in their arms gossiping across the fences to their neighbors also with hips out & babies in their arms – it is interesting but hardly inspiring . . . . [I was taken] to a reception at [Prof Herkomer's] last Sunday – the great man had hoisted a flag which intimated that he was at home & would receive from 4 till 5. We went first to the Studio, a large room with 3 unfinished portraits (one of Chamberlain) at one end with flocks of students whispering & tiptoeing in front of them & then we passed into the music gallery where we found the Prof: standing with Mrs. Herkomer with a resigned let-'em-all-come sort-of expression – as we approached he said in a loud German voice "Are there any more? do I know any of these?" And as we shook hands & filed past he sank into a seat with a martyrised air & began talking to a lady about pianolas & motor cars in a loud voice that all could hear – I made a flank movement & observed that his collar was old & frayed & his hair long & grizzled & his face full of force & fire but hard & unsympathetic. I had been warned not to shake his hand too hard or squeeze his fingers no matter how inadvertently as he greatly objected to overtures of this kind, so I tried not to be too affectionate in my greeting. He presently got up & went up to the music loft and played a piece of his own composition on the pianola – he is a musician as well as an artist & I believe plays the zither beautifully – in fact he does most things, wood carving, metal work, enamelling, engraving & on all sides you see his handiwork he is a many sided genius & seems to have a giant's capacity for work. Leading out of the music gallery, up a rose plush-lined staircase was the gold bed-room – walls of gilded wood – bed gold – furniture gold – gold everywhere, reeking of money & just such a room as Mammon might have built in a fit of golden exuberance. A little piece of Pear's soap in a golden soap dish seemed the one alloy in the room – it was glaringly vulgar & the one jarring note in the whole house. The other rooms were beautiful with oak ceilings & panelled walls & recessed fireplaces wonderfully carved & plenty of copper relief work about – all very severe & simple, no flippant ornaments or bowls of flowers. The nicest room in the house was the study, it looked the most lived in & human, & out of it opened a large gallery in which a lot of his pictures hung – three portraits in a sub-divided frame, of his father & his two uncles, were magnificent types of artisans – just such men as Adam Bede grew into – one a weaver, another a builder & the 3rd. a carver – & underneath the central figure was written the proud inscription "The makers of my House" – it was really a fine monument to genius & family pride & affection. I couldn't help thinking what a decadant the son looked beside these grand old toilers. There were a number of his earlier pictures here & it is by these he should be judged – some of them are beautiful & so different from his present vulgar portraits. . . . The other evening I discovered the fol. interesting epitaph in the church yard – it is to H.V.H.'s second wife & runs like this

Lulu
Wife of H.V.H. died Nov. 22 1885 aged 30.
Perfect as wife, as mother, as friend, as hostess, as an inventor of life's ways & means, ready, high minded upright, she magnetised by her presence, she corrected by her example she elevated by her fine sense of goodness all those who came within the circle of her charm, ever watchful, ever steadying them in their giddiest moments of happiness by the splendid balance of her mind. She lived & may she live in the hearts & in the lives of all those who loved her.

This seemed very beautiful but somehow the point of this loving eulogy was lost when I heard he had married Lulu's younger sister only six months after that poor lady's death. Lulu had been the first Mrs Herkomer's maid & had caused much unhappiness to that unhappy lady who finally died & Lulu reigned in her stead, but not for long & she died too, evidently there are more trials in mating with a genius than meet the eye. . . .

[113] To Rachel Hodgkins, 3 July 1903

2 Rudolph Terrace, Bushey, Herts. July 3rd.

My darling Mother

. . . . I have just finished & packed up my pictures for the show & they are to go to the framers in the morning. I am glad to see the last of them, as is usual on such occasions I thought them looking feeble & evil & hate to think I am their parent. I am sorry you cant see them dear – it spoils half the pleasure not showing them to you & Sis . . . . We have had a fortnight of glorious sunshine – which has quite made us forgive & forget the heavy rains & floods at the beginning of the month. . . . I walked over . . . to a small village about 1 mile from here to see what damage was done – it was very lowlying & the water was up in some parts to the windows of the houses – carts were carrying people to & fro, & I heard one man telling another that he hadn't had a wink of sleep all night as he had taken the chickens to bed with him. I shouldn't suppose the chickens slept much either. . . . I dont want to be premature in announcing the sale of my Academy picture – Mr. Soord an artist here . . . came to ask me this morning if I wld sell "Fatima" to a friend of his for £12.12 (£15 catalogue price) of course I said yes and it now remains to be seen if the gentleman will clinch the bargain . . . .

. . . . I wish Sis would commission me to get her some things for the children at Libertys – if she sent me the measurements I could easily get anything she wanted – the childrens clothes are too beautiful for words & I long for Girlie & Baba to have some of the pretty things.

I haven't seen any New Zealanders, but tomorrow I am going to meet Mrs. C. Smith in town. . . . I wish I could have been at Percy's turkey party. I can't believe he's thirty, why I have been 30 ever since I came Home & next year I was going to be 29, there must be some mistake. . . .

[114] To Rachel Hodgkins, 22 July 1903

Hotel St. Armand, Bruges. 22.7.03

My darling Mother,

It was delightful getting all your dear letters – they have been read many times, with tears not very far off – it was really the best part of it all, getting your letters – it never seemed quite right somehow not having you all to rejoice with me – now that "Fatima" is sold I feel I can return to N.Z. with the feeling that my 3 years in Europe has had some good result & that all the hard work hasn't been in vain. . . . I am glad she "Fatima" went off in her first season, and £12.12 will come in very handy to her needy & hard-up parent. I feel in a small degree that flutter of joy & pride which mothers feel when they have successfully married their last

remaining daughter. I havent heard yet if I have had any luck at the Fine Arts –
people seem to like them very much & I have had a great many kind things said
about them. I enclose some of the newspaper clippings, which tho' short are
satisfactory – could you send them on to Dr. Scott when you have finished with
them. . . . I was very proud of Mr. Seddons message – it was read aloud by Miss
R. at supper that night amid loud applause – two German girls were present &
got rather mixed up as to whether New Zealand or my picture was on the line –
& it took some time to explain the differences between islands south of the
Equator & pictures below the Line. . . . I met the Nickalls in London . . . & early
next morning went down to Henley . . . . It was the gayest scene – I couldn't have
believed England had so much color – everyone wore the brightest colors with
parasoles of every shade & hue . . . . I wish Will & Willie could have been there
– they would have enjoyed the racing more than I did, especially Kelly's sculling
which everyone said was magnificent. . . . I had a delightful lazy week [at Patteson
Court] & got very fat & brown – sat all day in the garden & sewed & darned &
got my clothes ready for the Dutch campaign – it is a heavenly place like
Bishopscourt only five times larger – the strawberries I eat would have kept us in
jam for the rest of our lives & I found it hard to set my mind on the duties of life
amid such luxuriant surroundings. We went up on the 11th. to the opening of the
little show at the Fine Arts – a good many London friends were there but no
fellow countrymen. . . . Altogether it is a long way ahead of the Doré Show of last
Nov: & my artistic friends consider it is the thin end of the wedge. The Fine Arts
confers a certain cachet on one's work which I hope may prove valuable. I am now
busy on some things for the Liverpool Exhibition in August – I have been invited
to send – I must get some things off soon for the Nov. Show in Dunedin – I find
it much less easy to paint & choose subjects than when I first came Home – one
gets more fastidious I suppose – & things satisfy one less easily. I am quite aware
that the more one improves in this direction the narrower your circle becomes,
the buying public falls off & the puzzlement is how to pamper them with cheap
attractive work & yet be true to one's self!

Well, to return to our muttons. I persuaded the two Nickalls girls to come to
Holland with me so we all three started one fine morning for Dover – it was quite
the most comfortable journey I have ever taken, all I had to do was to sit still, no
running after porters, finding one's luggage & scrambling for tickets & cheap
meals at railway restaurants – it was all done for me with the leisurely ease &
comfort which makes travelling a joy & pleasure for the rich & for the impecunious a harrassing time in which everyone & everything combines to annoy &
thwart one. . . . We waltzed gaily up to Bruges [on] the railway thro rich pasture
land intersected by the inevitable canals & stiff lines of poplars marking out the
landscape. The whole party was down at the station to meet us – & it is only on
such occasions as these re-unions that one realises how much one loves ones
friends & the big gulf they will leave in one's life when we say goodbye for good.

We had a merry dinner Miss Richmond in great form & Mr. Garstin very witty & amusing & much obliged to me for bringing the Nickalls – who are special pets. . . . We are very pleased with our nice quiet cheap hotel . . . . The "patron" is the chef & as you enter the front door you get a homely glimpse of his nice kind face & portly figure enveloped in a white apron stirring a savory mess on the large shining stove with the white-tiled walls catching all the coppery reflections of the pots & pans. We dine in a long salle à manger which is also the bicycle stable, 16 bicycles recline against the walls & they are generally inextricably mixed up when one comes to get one's own. I occupy a garret 3 stories up & for which I pay 3.50 a week which is just under a 1£ in English money . . . .

[115] To RACHEL HODGKINS, JULY-AUGUST 1903
Eben Haezer's shop, Rijsoord bij Rotterdam.

My darling Mother

Holland is a low damp country where it rains all day . . . . Eben Haezer is a grocer and we are living over his shop not exactly because we like it but because there is nowhere else to go. You see Rijsoord is quite a small place and we are a very large party, growing larger every day and its accomodation is taxed to its uttermost. . . . We all have our meals together [at the Hotel Warendorf] – and the party . . . comes together at 7.30 in the morning for breakfast – it is a most entertaining meal – everyone makes their own toast on little earthenware chaufrettes placed down the centre of the table, then Minchie the Vrouwe's daughter comes in with a blue apron full of boiled eggs & hands them round, just like helping yourself out of a warm nest, delicious! . . . Rijsoord itself is a dull little place, & I cant quite understand the Prof: pitching on it for a camping ground . . . . Windmills and cabbages & large white sabots seem to be the principal features of the country . . . . On days when it hasnt rained it has been too windy to paint with any comfort but the cloud effects have been magnificent tho' not any better than the beautiful Invercargill Estuary effects. . . . [Miss Richmond] has been so good & unselfish looking after the class in Mrs. Garstin's absence . . . . I would have come back howling with loneliness & homesickness long ago if it hadn't been for her – I owe any success I have had to her sympathy & support. Goodnight dearest everybody. We are just going out to post our letters – and a good deal of our hearts go with them. Mr. Eben Haezer is reading a chapter of the Bible in a loud voice just before putting out the lights. So it is time for us to put out ours too. . . .

[116] To Rachel Hodgkins, 4 August 1903

House of the Eben Haezer, Rijsoord bij Rotterdam. 4.8.03

My darling Mother

. . . . Do you realise that in less than 4 months I shall be back with you all once more, it's a distractingly joyful thought . . . . I wonder I have been able to stay away from you all so long and I certainly shall never go away again. This has been a most trying month, storm and wind & rain and so cold we have been living in our mackintoshes and winter clothes & I have got a most miserable show of work to show for my summer in Holland. . . . I had the greatest difficulty in getting off my things for the Dunedin show . . . . I must have dodged a hundred showers at least before I finished those two small pastorals – there was a large pig & a calf in the orchard one, & in rough weather I used to get behind them & use them as a breakwind – they always lay down side by side close to my easel & the calf liked sharpening his young horns on my easel & the pig in a ruminating sort of way got very fond of biting my boots. This peaceful sort of farm yard life suits me so well I should almost be inclined to wed a Boer & naturalise as a Dutchwoman if it hadnt been for my promise to dine with you on Xmas day. Its my idea of heaven to live on a farm & wake up at sunrise with cows & calves & sheep & pigs & ducks & geese & turkeys, all crying out to be fed – tho' probably I should be more interested in painting them than feeding them. . . . There is a very pleasant party of American artists staying here & on Sunday they invited us over to see their work . . . . The Garstin boys are now getting up a regatta Union Jack v. Stars & Stripes . . . & the two crews are now in practice for the great event on Saturday . . . . I am cox of one of the trial crews, having inadvertently mentioned to anyone who liked to listen that I wasn't much of an oar myself but I had a brother & brother-in-law who had held the honorable positions of captains respectively of the O[tago] R[owing] C[lub] & the Star Boating Club Wellington. Mr. Garstin immediately lifted a loud voice & said "Miss Hodgkins says her brother-in-law is Admiral of the Australian Squadron & if anyone should know how to row she should" & thereupon I was unanimously elected . . . . I started them fairly well but fouled the eel pots & then ran them into a mud bank & then the rudder got tangled up in weeds . . . and finally one of the crew when told to "put more back into it," caught a crab & the oar went over board & she rolled into the bottom of the boat. . . . Miss Richmond is one of my crew & is a capital oar but it is difficult to take things seriously. . . .

. . . . I am going to arrange with an agent to look after my pictures for me when I get back to London and it will be the easiest matter in the world to send Home. About money for my passage out I am sorry to report there are no sales at all at the Fine Arts . . . but there is still another month to run & I may have some luck yet. . . .

We shall be leaving early in Nov. so I think if Percy can manage to raise another loan for me like the last you had better cable me £50. . . . I can't bear borrowing & there will be a heavy day of reckoning but still it is the only way to get home. I do hope my pictures will reach [you] in time. . . . Will Sis kindly price them – tell her to put on them what she thinks they will fetch & I shant grumble ungratefully like I did on a former occasion. . . . Dont forget to get a black kitten into the house against my return if you havent already got one. . . .

[117] TO RACHEL HODGKINS, 23 SEPTEMBER 1903
Hotel Central, Delft, Holland. 23.9.03

My darling Mother,

. . . . Miss Richmond . . . has taken our tickets in the Orient S.S. Ophir – inner cabins £43 – sailing from London 6th. Nov. . . . This will just land us in N.Z. for Christmas. There is only one sale so far at the Fine Arts £7.7. but I hear of someone who wants a picture & will probably buy. . . . Delft is a dear little town abounding in artistic bits but the people are not very friendly . . . . I sat down in front of a fish stall this morning to paint & the old fishwife came up & shook her fist at me and said "You dont paint me, you Englander" & she collected such a crowd I thought it wiser to move on. The boys have been dreadfully trouble-some throwing things at us & one day I was mobbed & had to appeal to the police. . . .

[118] TO RACHEL HODGKINS, 16 OCTOBER 1903
24 Gordon Place W. Oct.16th

My darling Mother

. . . . only another 3 weeks now – I can hardly realise it. . . . There are such hosts of people to be seen, I never knew I possessed so many friends in London . . . . The Fine Arts show is still running . . . . I have sold 4 pictures up to date about £50 worth but a monster commission comes off that which reduces it consider-ably. . . .

. . . . I have just been requested by H.R.H. the Prince of Wales & Council of the R.A. to do them the favor of exhibiting "Fatima" at the St Louis Exhibition in 1904. I should have been charmed to send the dear child but fortunately or unfortunately she is sold – I am sorry of course for St. Louis but these things will happen. . . .

I have got you some real Dutch bulbs – tulips & hyacinths, nothing very special I am afraid & not even a black tulip . . . the best sort (black) cost about £2000 but an inferior kind can be had for 2d. I have packed them in wool & tissue paper & I hope the little wretches wont go & sprout in the Tropics.

I shall write again before I start. I am full of joy at the thought of seeing you all so soon . . . .

Part Seven

1904-6

'A Futile and Useless Weariment'

Frances Hodgkins and Dorothy Richmond arrived in Sydney in mid-December 1903 and reached Wellington just before Christmas. In February 1904 they held a successful joint exhibition of their European paintings at McGregor Wright's Gallery in Lambton Quay. Miss Richmond spent the rest of her life in New Zealand, mostly in Wellington, a leader in artistic circles as painter, teacher and council member of the New Zealand Academy of Fine Arts.

Early in 1904 FH set up a teaching studio in Bowen Street but it did not flourish as her Dunedin classes had. Wellington lagged behind the southern city in its cultivation of the visual arts, but it is also likely that FH did not throw herself into teaching with her former dedication. Nor did she produce many paintings. She was at some sort of crossroads. Success in England had reinforced her faith in her talent and held the promise of achievement in that larger sphere. On the other hand she had before her the possibility of turning aside from the challenge of her painting career and for a while at least she gave way to the desire for the comforts of a more conventional life. On the voyage out from England she had met Thomas W. B. Wilby and some time at the end of 1904 became engaged to him. The courtship was carried out by letter, for Wilby had left the Ophir in Cairo and afterwards travelled on to New York. It was decided that they would be married in Europe in 1905. FH prepared to leave New Zealand in April 1905, making a farewell visit to the South Island in March, to see Willie in Ashburton and her Dunedin friends. At about this time the engagement was broken off and the passage to Europe cancelled. FH did not see Wilby again and his name does not appear anywhere in her correspondence. Among the few possessions found in her studio after her death was one of Wilby's letters, a friendly but formal note that had accompanied the gift of a scarab. It had been sent from Cairo and was probably the first she had received. We must assume that she destroyed the rest of the lengthy correspondence.

The details of the broken engagement are unlikely ever to be known, but Wilby's character and career indicate why FH was attracted to him. Born in Norwich, Thomas Wilby (1870-1923) was a talented journalist, a linguist and ardent traveller, who had worked in various European cities before settling in the United States. After his friendship with FH, he married, in 1908, an American woman, Agnes Andrews, and in 1912 wrote with her On the Trail to Sunset, a novel based on a pioneering car journey they had undertaken, claimed to be the first crossing of the United States from east to west. A similar journey across Canada was recorded in another book A Motor Tour through Canada, 1913. In 1914 Wilby wrote The Rise of Menai Tarbell, a short story satirising modern art, his only other piece of fiction. He was remembered by his employer[1] on the Christian Science Monitor, where he worked from 1918-20, as 'enormously self-confident. In his own way he had a certain distinction, and stood out in a crowd. . . . He gave the impression of being

---

[1] Walter W. Cunningham, formerly foreign editor of the *Christian Science Monitor*. (Unpublished material supplied by E. H. McCormick.)

a good husband, but he was at the same time, the man of the house.' Mrs Wilby was 'very much in the background.' There was an element of showmanship and eccentricity in Wilby – in the office he always wore spats and a monocle, and carried a walking stick, he grew hot-house tomatoes in his back garden and successfully marketed them, eventually demolishing the glasshouses and making a profit from the sale of the glass. For all its flair and excitement, it is hard to imagine Frances Hodgkins sharing Wilby's life.

During the second half of 1905 she was unsettled and unhappy, and did not find any alleviation of these feelings within the family circle. Isabel was busy with her children – her fifth child, George Alexander (Peter) was born in November 1905 – and her responsibilities as the wife of a prominent Member of the House of Representatives. She moved in a wealthy and fashionable section of society, which had only a perfunctory interest in the arts. It was a life that divided her from her younger sister and prevented a return to the intimacy of earlier years. The two younger brothers, Percy and Bert, were both married during this period and as a result Frances and Mrs Hodgkins moved house twice. Throughout this difficult time FH was sustained by the friendship of Miss Richmond and her circle. There was also the encouraging news that in both 1904 and 1905 her pictures had again been hung in the Royal Academy.

In June 1905 the two women went to paint in Rotorua.

[119] To Rachel Hodgkins, 5 June 1905

Lake House, Rotorua. June 5th

Dearest Mother

Just as well you didn't come, it was a long & fatiguing journey & you would have been half dead before you got to Rotorua. The journey from N[ew] Plymouth to Onehunga was the pleasantest part, quite smooth & a cabin to ourselves. . . . We came straight to this hotel in Ohinemutu which is one mile from Rotorua & right among the Maoris. Their tariff in the summer is £2.10 a week but they obligingly reduced it to 30/- after a little persuasion – we thought it better to stay a shorter time at a place like this than at a cheaper house out of reach of the Maoris. . . . Poor Miss Richmond lost every stick of her luggage; it stayed behind at N. Plymouth . . . but tonight we have had a wire to say it was coming on tomorrow. Rotorua is a most amazing place & one has to step lively to avoid being scalded to death. The Maoris are coy and greedy – but we have managed to get two good models already & have spent a busy day. There is a hot bath at the foot of the garden, free, & we are told it will renew our youth & make us very sleek & smooth.[2] I would love to have you here but I fear you would find

---

[2] The bath house, now a private dwelling, can still be seen at Ohinemutu, as can the Lake House Hotel though changed beyond recognition and all hope of restoration. Built in the 1870s to cater for the visitors who came to take the waters and view the thermal wonders, Lake House Hotel in 1905 was an elegant double-storeyed wooden building.

it cold – the sun is hot during the day but an icy wind blows off the hills which are sprinkled with snow. To see icebound gutters & an inch or so away boiling springs is a weird sight. Will write a longer letter in a day or so. Much love dearest to you all

Your loving
Frances.

In January 1906, aged thirty-six, Frances Hodgkins set off for England, leaving Mrs Hodgkins in lodgings with a Mrs McIntosh.

[120] TO RACHEL HODGKINS, 13 FEBRUARY 1906

S.S. Tongariro. Feb: 13th

My dearest little Mother

So far the voyage has been one long dulness, first a cold one & now a hot one & I dont know which is hardest to bear. . . . [We had] a fortnight's run to the Horn which we passed in bright clear sunshine about 10 miles off. The air had such a tang & a lash in it that we could hardly stay on deck to watch it. . . . . As soon as we got round the corner we were met by warm North winds which warmed & comforted us & in 5 days from then we were at Montevideo where we spent a long hot & rather expensive day ashore. . . . We landed in a blazing sun about 11. Miss Myers (the only other young lady passenger & a nice quiet girl) and Mr. Loving (Miss England's friend[3]) & myself made straight for the nearest café where we had sandwiches & wine – this merely made us more hungry & thirsty so we moved on in search of a more substantial restaurant where we were given a menu of 20 or so courses to choose from all in Spanish. I have forgotten to mention that by the time I arrived at Montevideo I was a *1st Class* Spanish scholar owing to the kindness of an Argentine gentleman on board who formed a class for anyone wishing to learn Spanish; we had an hour's lesson morning & evening . . . . We had a magnificent repast which rather disabled us for sight seeing so we had what Miss Myers would call a "sinesta" in the seclusion of the Cathedral. Forty winks under the eye of good St Francis set us up wonderfully & then out again into the white glare, found a fat Vigilante (policeman) half asleep in a deep shadow poked him up & after much exertion & a great deal of action with his little wooden sword we understood him to say the way to the gardens was 10 squares straight on, 4 to the left, change trams (if there *was* a tram but he rather thought there was a tram strike on) wait 20 minutes at a place called the Prado

---

[3] Maud England, educated in Dresden and Oxford, a friend of Dorothy Richmond, was well-known in Wellington as a teacher and scholar.

– but beyond this we couldn't follow him so we went into an English hotel & got a plan of the town & found out that the tram to the gardens was the only one running on account of the strike & that it *might* stop at any moment. We decided to risk it as we heard the gardens were very pretty & worth seeing – the tram was in charge of 2 policemen & the driver lashed the 3 mules into a terrific galop & we rocked & pitched & rolled & Mr. Lovings hat flew off & he jumped out amid a great uproar, the mules stood on end, the tram stopped & the driver gurgled queer noises & everyone stood up & talked, then on we went again with a jerk & at last were dumped down at the Prado where we waited ½ an hour in a tram shelter till a 2nd. tram drawn by the skeletons of 2 brown mules came along. . . . Our first thought was tea. . . . A large jug of hot milk & a very small pot of tea & stale ladies fingers with which we fed the gold fish who were more grateful than we were – I could have lingered on & on sitting under the thick plane trees watching the pretty Spanish ladies feeding the fish & lazily moving their fans never speaking except with their eyes which are *most* conversational. The glamour of a continental town was beginning to come back to me & all the mystery & charming color & light that we know nothing of in N.Z. & I began to slowly wonder if after all the painting of pictures was quite such a futile & useless weariment – as I have lately found it. In fact we lingered so long that we just got down to the wharf as the last tender was casting off. We were very disgusted on getting back to the boat to find the 2nd Saloon filled up with a lot of rowdy Argentine harvesters mostly Australians returning to the colony. The N.Z. passengers who were gold dredgers mostly from Otago going out to Patagonia prospecting were a nice quiet set of men if somewhat dull & they all left the boat at Montevideo leaving only 6 of us in the 2nd. class & we had hoped to fill up with a more interesting set of people but alas we have fared very badly. They are a noisy rough lot & at nights it is very unpleasant on deck. . . . Fortunately we have Mr. Loving to look after us – he is very large & kind & is prepared at any moment to lay down his life should any lady so desire it. . . . Tell Sis I plunged into the seedcake almost before she was out of sight with my usual greed & the last caraway I shared with the 2nd. Officer who is Irish enough to make you weep with joy. I was sitting forlornly watching the last of Wellington when he appeared suddenly & said with so much sympathy that I almost fell on his neck Are you very lonely? I said Yes. All he said was "I'm sure" & then vanished into thin air but never before have I received so much sympathy in so few words. The next night he re-appeared & deepened my admiration for him by saying "That was a nice little chat we had last night." My best friend on board is the Chief Steward cum Purser – his more than paternal kindness touches me & in this hot weather effects me almost to tears. "If you look under the cushion behind your dorr Miss you'll find a plum cake." "We planted a bottle of lime juice behind your hat-box Miss" "Did you get the chocolates under the wash stand Miss?" & so on & yesterday he hinted that if either Miss Myers or myself could manage to fake up a birthday between us he would see that we had a cake suitable to the occasion. Miss Myers thereupon fixed next Sat: night as the evening of her 22nd. birthday & has issued invitations for a party. . . .

Feb 20th.

We have now passed through the worst of the heat & are clear of the tropics & four more days will see us abreast of *Europe* climbing up the coast of Spain & into the Bay of Biscay & round the corner into Plymouth Sound. . . .

I have read a prodigious amount & extracted what nourishment I could from the very meagre skinny book shelf they call the Library – Savage Landor in Thibet, Mary Kingsley in W. Africa, Leslie Stephen in a Library, Kiplings Traffics & Discoveries (which bothered me) & a pile of dime novels that an American bequeathed to me before he left at Montevideo . . . . This has helped to keep me awake. In the Tropics I felt more of a dormouse than a living woman & there was one awful day when the marrow in my bones melted & I besought the Capt: should he see a grease spot on the deck not to kick it or tread on it as it was ME. . . .

Feb 21st.

This morning I made the unpleasant discovery that my chair (price 9/6 at every shop in Wellington you will remember) had been thrown overboard by these hoodlums – so much for Bertie's branding! . . . I have rained down fire & brimstone on them, the curs, but of course one can do nothing. . . . No. 3 chair I have lost. This sort of thing can't go on. I have just been listening to the Stewards woful tale of ravage & destruction in the cabins & smoking room; basins broken, taps wrenched off cushions torn "And worse than this, miss my two dear little brass spittoons that I was so proud of thrown overboard". . . . It has been a deadly time boxed up with these creatures. Even Miss Richmond would find it hard to discover any "Soul-Sides"[4] to these *anthropoid apes*. . . .

I do so wonder how you & Mrs. McIntosh are settling down together & whether you find it bearable or unbearable. Do tell me dearest Mother *very* fully & truly just how it answers. I shall know in an instant if you are not speaking the truth so do not try & deceive me. . . . Tell me all about your room & if you had too much or too little furniture. . . . and once more let me exhort you dearest Mother not to live on air but to cook a solid square meal once a day & *hang the expense*. . . .

How is George Alexander? Has he got a nurse yet or is he continuing to break his Mother's back – I do pray Sis has got help & that she is well. Much love to

[4] God be thanked, the meanest of his creatures
   Boasts two soul-sides, one to face the world with,
 One to show a woman when he loves her!
     Browning, *One Word More*

you dearest little Mother & may the 14th be a bright & happy day with you. Many happy returns –

Your loving Frances. . . .

PART EIGHT

1906-7

Return to Europe

Wispers, Sussex. March 4th. 1906

My dearest Mother

England at last & a very warm & balmy England at that & we are going about the country in our blouses & prayerfully gazing up at the blue sky & wondering what it all means. . . . Well to go back to where I left off at Tenerife. We reached Santa Cruz too late at night to land but spent an absorbing evening watching the various vendors of shawls & drawn linen & fruit & tobacco bargaining with the passengers. I bought you a little shawley thing for your shoulders . . . . I am afraid it will not reach you by the 14th. as I wld like it to. We were off again by daylight & in 5 days from then we were sailing into Plymouth Sound after a monotonously smooth voyage of 41 days. We anchored at 4 a.m. & before it was scarcely light Grace Nickalls was on board, she & the pilot, & by 7 oclock I was on shore & soon afterwards eating a large British breakfast & trying to realise that my Tongariro martyrdom was at an end. . . . We caught the 10 o'clock train up to London where Gertrude Crompton (an artist friend) met us & drove across London with us & had tea with us at the railway station where we caught the train for Wispers & which took 2 hours to get here & then a half hour drive . . . & I can tell you I was glad to tumble into a hot bath & have some dinner. Wispers is very very pretty, the house not so grand as Patteson Court but much cosier & has a charming old world chintzy-mullioned-window-oaken look & it is all quite true about the woodpeckers & the pheasants on the lawn . . . & the woods round about are full of primroses & daffodils just bursting into bud. You will hardly believe that though I have only been 4 days here I have painted for 2 long mornings out of the 4 & tomorrow I am starting a big thing of a little cottage girl & a baby & trust my laggard muse will come back to me. The R.A. pictures have to be in about a fortnight & I am anxious to get something done . . . . At the end of the month or the 1st. week in April I hope to start for Venice with Grace & Maud & Rosamond Marshall & perhaps Gertrude Crompton – anyway if all these nice people cannot come at once with me they will join on later. A Miss Abernethy is also most likely coming as my pupil at £5.5. for 12 lessons & it is thus my personal entourage has grown! Never fear I shall not go abroad alone or stay alone. I will contrive to have someone with me till Miss Richmond comes, if she does come but I do not want to ask or persuade her. It is for her to decide & I think if I were in her place I should stay where I was. . . .

7th March . . . . Next week we are going up to town for a night or two & before I come back here I shall probably go down to Norwood to see the Spences. . . . This life of leisure & pleasure is debilitating but I am abandoning myself to all the petting & cossetting for I know I must go back to my frugal living quite soon & high living once in a way can do no harm. I shall feel more at rest when I have a letter from you. I dreamt last night that Mrs. McIntosh was found pummelling you with cushions & that you were rescued by Sis in an exhausted condition. I woke in a wretched state of mind about it. . . . I know I am not a bit necessary to the family comfort but still I always feel that directly my back is turned all sorts of calamities may happen to you all. . . .

[122] To Rachel Hodgkins, 15 March 1906
Thriplands, Kensington Court. March 15th.

Very dearest Mother

    . . . . It was a great relief to hear from you but I gasped with terror at the thought of your stove exploding. . . . I am so glad & thankful that you like Mrs. McIntosh. . . . You see by the above address I am in London. I came up yesterday for 2 days & am staying with Gertrude Crompton with the express object of seeing as many pictures as we can crowd in today & tomorrow. . . . It was strange finding oneself back in London with the same old sensation of wonder & fright, the same old grey mirk, red sun, & mud slop. Many more motors, busses size of trams smelling vilely & the din deafening. This morning I went up to see my framer-agent-man [Mr Taylor]. He had the good news for me that I have a picture in the Institute which is a step forward. . . . Today we go to tea with Mr. & Mrs. Blake Wirgman who have a beautiful house. He was in Tangier when I was there & didn't draw camels nearly as nicely as I did but in London he has a 1st. rate standing as a 2nd. rate portrait painter. . . . I have been for a ride in a motor bus – you might have been inside a kerozene tin as far as smell was concerned with a vibrating screw that jarred your spine. . . .

[123] To Rachel Hodgkins, 29 March 1906
20 Lunham Rd, Upper Norwood. March 29th.

My dearest Mother

    I came here yesterday from Wispers & found all these good people well and flourishing. Mr. Spence so well & his beautiful hair whiter & silkier than ever. Mrs. Spence rather thinner & greyer but just the same cheery little mother, waiting on everybody, warming their boots & brushing their clothes & keeping belated breakfasts hot for the sluggish Effie & her guest! . . . Alack and alas my R.A picture came to nought. All went merrily till 2 days before sending in time when I cracked my finger in the door & it gave me a good deal of pain of a nervous sort & I foolishly tried to paint & only succeeded in undoing in a few minutes all my 3 week's work. I hurried up to London to collect what other pictures there were & selected 3. I was much concerned to find that 2 of my pictures were quite ruined. Some pernicious colour had been used which had blackened like black-lead & quite spoilt the pictures. I have since heard that a similar fate overtook some of Mr Garstin's water colours – I must eschew all fancy foreign pigment after this no matter how tempting. I consulted Newman about it & he advised me in future to use no other paints but his own!

I am starting for Venice on the 6th [April] with Miss Abernethy. I was hoping the Simplon tunnel wld be open for traffic about the same time that I was ready to pass through it but it will not be open for some months yet. . . .

31st. [March]

I had a day in London with Effie yesterday. I spent most of it choosing a new camera. I feel that my Art requires all the extraneous help that these things give. The young man who sold it me told me that every artist of any standing had one, in fact one lady had her negatives enlarged (secretly) by them & then painted over them. Such moral laxity is appalling! . . .

[124] To Rachel Hodgkins, 18 April 1906

Casa Frollo, 50 Guidecca, Venice. 18th April 06

My dearest Mother

To put Venice into words is impossible likewise is it impossible to put it into paint. . . . There is a fairy enchantment about it, a sort of Wizardry that cant be expressed. It is better to be silent about it all than to use the wrong word or the wrong color. The Casa Frollo is a palace & the pretty signorina who lives in it pays exactly the same rent for it as I did for my Bowen St Studio. But the size of the rooms, & the number & the loftiness thereof, & their statlieness & beauty are beyond compare. All day & all night there is the laplap of the water trying to get in the front door and opposite my window is the Salute, & beyond again the Doge's Palace & the blue domes of St Marks. I have done no painting yet. The beauty of things overrules & frightens. Also I am with a most uncongenial companion. Why scholarly ladies like Miss Abernethy with a Greek & Latin & Mathematical mind want to waste their time making wretched little water color daubs puzzles me. She is very learned & elegant & worldly & cold & unpunctual & practical & selfish & rich & Scotch & I detest her, & if she offered to adopt me tomorrow & leave me all her money when she died I wld say NO thank you. At the present moment she is doing a pastel head of a little Italian girl & she has given the poor child a pale mauve nose with gamboge cheeks & a squint. If she had a grain of humour she would break down but there is no levity in her. A lady of Celtic austerity is not an ideal companion in Venice! . . . Of course it is a great privilege to be with such a clever woman. She knows things thoroughly from a purely historical & archaeological point of view which of course is enormously instructive for me. She has that final air of having said the last word about everything which leaves one pumped of ideas & very flat. We have spent most [of] our time since we came in a sandola which I take it is a female gondola. It is smaller & less handsome & there is more of the punt about it than seems strictly in keeping with Venice . . . . Like the gondolas it is painted a hearse-like black. This is in accordance with a law passed in the XV Century to prevent undue extravagance & over decoration of gondolas. The artistic effect is perfect & makes a very telling & effective foil to the delicate opalescent colors of the houses. . . . A scorpion visited Miss A. in the night. The signora has set a mouse trap for it against its return. . . .

20th. April. Since last writing Miss Crompton & Maud Nickalls & 3 of the latters pupils have arrived & are billeted here for the moment & in a week Rosamond Marshall comes & she & I will probably go off somewhere to some smaller country place. I have been doing a great deal of sight seeing, pictures & churches but have got very few sketches. It is a great education seeing this beautiful city which until now has existed only in my imagination. This is horrible news about the earthquake at San Francisco. I wonder if it will effect the mails. The horrors of it do not bear talking about. . . . I have *not* communicated yet with Miss Jeannie [Wimperis]. Oh dear I suppose I must. . . . Goodbye now dearest Mother. I will try & write every Sunday – tho' the desire to write nice letters has gone from me. I seem to have written my heart out on paper & nothing has come of it & writing letters makes me rather dread putting pen to paper. I want you to keep my letters only for yourself & the family & on no account let them go to outsiders. Much love to you all from

Your very loving Frances.

[125] To Rachel Hodgkins, 29 April 1906

Casa Frollo, Venice. April 29th

My very dearest Mother,
    A letter from Miss Richmond brought a first warning that you had been ill & after a very miserable & anxious day came one from your dear self brave & cheerful as you always are. It is impossible not to worry about you dear if you go & catch any more liver chills. Of course it was the worry & anxiety of moving & you over-tired yourself . . . . I felt much more like catching the first boat home this morning instead of starting out with my paint box. Miss Richmond told me she had seen you & that Sissie was feeding you up & that you were getting back your strength again. She said your room was very pretty & that you looked forward to being very comfortable. Of course as you say it is a more wholesome

& useful life than living alone but remember dear that quietness is also very necessary to you & that much as you love Sis & the dear children it is not always that your strength is equal to the bustle that 5 children naturally make in a house. I feel that I have no possible right to disapprove of anything that you think right & expedient to do as I have been the one to leave you alone & homeless but you must not blame me altogether for I have been through a very wretched time but I hope now that I have succeeded in resolutely putting past things from me & am setting my face to the future as bravely as I can. It is far better for me to be away from N.Z. for a year or so & I will come back a much more contented & rational being I hope. Miss Abernethy left yesterday & we have been feeling much brighter & more cheerful. They celebrated my birthday with a teaparty & a gondola fête in the evening on the Grand Canal. I have now taken another pupil at £5.5 a lady staying in this house, she is a much pleasanter person. On Friday I was asked to tea with Miss Montalba.[1] She paid me many compliments on what she seemed to have heard of my work from the few people who have seen it & has asked to see it. She is a kindly creature, markedly Jewish & quite elderly & lives with her sister & a large and corpulent brother who housekeeps for them. Their house is very handsome & interesting full of pictures of course – & on the afternoon that I called her large studio was full of English visitors all paying homage to her. I have now started painting in a very beautiful old garden called the garden of Eden. It is so called from the owners whose name is Eden & there has been a book written about the garden of the same name. It is a bower of fragrant flowers irises & tulips & oleanders & roses & in & out & about among the flower beds are fountains & sundials & statues & well-heads. I have had two little children there today posing for me among the irises. Mr. Eden is a beautiful looking old man & very kind & I am in great good luck to have permission to paint in his garden. . . . Goodnight dearest Mother. To spend the day in a beautiful garden of flowers gives me such nice thoughts & I am feeling better tonight than I have for ages past. Tell Girlie I am sending her some p. cards & I shall buy her & Ba a necklace of Venetian beads. . . .

[126] To Rachel Hodgkins, 10 May 1906

Casa Frollo, Venice. May 10th.

My very dearest Mother

. . . . I have spent a very quiet & uneventful fortnight since my last letter to you. I have settled down to my jog-trot old painting habits & the days slip by & soon we will be moving on in search of fresh fields. The mosquitos arrive on the 26th.

[1] Clara Montalba (1842-1929) RWS, the most famous of four artist sisters, lived in Venice for many years and was noted for her landscapes and coastal scenes in oil and watercolour.

June on which day it is said the swallows fly southwards unable to cope with the incoming hordes of mosquitos. This may or may not be true. . . . I have just heard that I am out of the R.A. this year worse luck. Butler[2] & Miss Stoddart are in though so N.Z. is still represented. They say it is a worse than usual bad year & that there is very little good work. Still bad as it is I should like to be there. The Miss Montalbas came to see me one day. They were very kind & encouraging & seemed to like my work. I have had a letter from Dr. Fell asking me to be one of 3 to select some pictures for the Wellington Art Gallery.[3] I dont quite know what to do as I shall not be in England for at least a year I hope. I should very much like to help choose. He mentioned Miss Montalba as an artist whose work it would be well to enquire about. I did not see anything of hers I greatly coveted but I fancy all her best work is in England. Mr. Garstin is to be one of the choosers and a Mr. Fletcher[4] the other.   Rosamond Marshall is with us now & will probably spend 2 or 3 months with me. I feel much happier now she is here; she is such a dear devoted kind little friend & she makes me feel much less alone in the world. . . . Sometimes at night we go out on to the lagoons in our sandola which is very restful & soothing after the day spent vainly trying to represent a little of the beauty of Venice. . . . Rosamond is very keen about our going over to Croatia on the other side of the Adriatic. It is very cheap there & the food is good & life very picturesque & unhackneyed . . . . Let me know Mother dear when next you write what month the Chch exhibition opens.[5] I must have some work ready for it. . . . I hope Sis has a nice kind servant to help her with wee George Alexander. Does he keep well & strong?

[127] TO RACHEL HODGKINS, 6 JUNE 1906

Casa Frollo, Venice. June 6th. 06

My dearest Mother

    . . . . I have just made a gruesome discovery, well this is hardly the right word but to cross it out will but attract more attention. Miss Jenny [Wimperis] is in Venice! I have peered under every white umbrella for weeks past fearing whom I should discover & the other day I . . . sent a letter to her address asking her where

---

[2] G. E. Butler (1870-1936), a pupil of James Nairn, who had studied in Paris and London, returning to New Zealand round 1900.

[3] Dr Walter Fell (1855-1932), a Wellington surgeon and physician, was president of the New Zealand Academy of Fine Arts, 1900-9. In 1900 the Academy put forward the idea of acquiring works of art that would be the foundation of a national collection. In 1906 £800 was raised by public subscription, to which the government added a subsidy of £500. £800 was to be spent on paintings purchased in London. The National Art Gallery finally opened on its present site in 1936.

[4] Frank Morley Fletcher (b.1866), a portrait painter and engraver.

[5] The New Zealand International Exhibition held in Christchurch 1906-7. The Academy spent £500 on paintings from this exhibition.

she was & quick as quick came back the answer, "I am here near you in Venice!" That was 3 days ago & I have been too seedy to make a sound or a move but today sometime I must . . . go over & see her. Woe is me! This has helped me to decide that I must go to Chioggia on Saturday taking with me a Miss Gordon who is taking lessons from me. I am in that state of mind that I feel that everybody is a vampire sapping all my ideas & vitality & leaving me nerveless & limp. If only I could get some of the inspiration from them that I seem to give them. And after Miss G. leaves me another pupil is coming & I am seeing to it that they pay me passing well. I will leave Rosamond behind in Venice to follow when her etching lessons are finished. Chioggia is about 17 miles to the E. of Venice on the Adriatic & it is famous for its handsome women & its fishing fleet. . . . Your poor daughter is not painting at all well or happily & she hates the sight of her brushes. I am wondering what I can take up instead to rest my weary painting nerves. A change of medium might do it. I fear it is too late to take to the stage or go in for dressmaking or good works. What is Miss Richmond doing? I will write from Chioggia. I am in hopes it will prove the turning point in my career & give me fresh impetus. . . .

[128] To RACHEL HODGKINS, c.27 JUNE 1906
                    Chioggia nr. Venice, June 27th. *I am guessing at the date*

My dearest Mother
    I have been in Chioggia nearly a fortnight now and I think it is about time I wrote to tell you all about it. You will remember I hadn't seen Miss Jenny when I last wrote. The very worst has happened. She is now with me & a more depressing & tiresome little woman you can scarce imagine. It is most wretched bad luck to have fallen in with her – & short of being rather brutal it is difficult to get free of her. I found her in a small room in Venice doing most of her own cooking, looking a picture of abject misery & poverty & helplessness. I found out she was spending far more living like this than she wld spend in a pension where she wld get good food besides cheerful companionship which we all require so I persuaded her to go to a very good pension I knew of & having done this I departed for Chioggia with my pupil feeling fairly happy about her. But in 4 days she turned up here & means to stay as long as I do & she is a very serious *Incubus* indeed to put it mildly. She is not fit for this kind of life & much too old to stand the fatigues and discomforts of painting in public places. It requires enormous nerve & courage especially in Italy where the street children give one a very bad time and literally persecute a timid person. And her painting is bad, very very bad. I shall not be able to stand much more of her. It is grumble grumble the whole time & her whining voice & her fretful old face are too depressing for words & in the matter of small debts she is not punctilious & a constant practice of

this sets up irritation. Rosamond came down for a few days but simply couldnt stand it & cleared back to Venice this morning & I think I will follow her in a few days. . . . I fear Miss J. may follow me there in which case there is nothing to do but to flee Italy. It certainly is a most unfortunate affair. She is utterly unfit to live alone & she has hardly any Italian & judging from the poor little lady's frugality I should think George has allowed her barely enough to live upon. . . . I heard quite casually of Mr. Seddon's tragically sudden death & naturally felt much shocked & later I read in a paper of his homecoming that cold winter night & how they all met their dead chief's body & conducted it at midnight through silent streets to his residence. I felt very moved & my thoughts wandered to that election night when I saw him in the fullness of his powers triumphing over his enemies. I know how deeply the blow will fall on his party & how individually Will will suffer the loss of his friendship. I know nothing of what has followed or who has taken his place in Sir J. Ward's absence – I am hoping you will send me papers. How does it effect Percy & Bert? I am most anxious for news.

There is really very little to tell you dear. It is very hot & there isnt a square inch of shade in Chioggia so I have made friends with the matron of a nice cool old work house where I take my models & paint in the shady quadrangle. Forty-two old dames sit round & knit & net & make lace & it is very peaceful & quiet. My model is a redhaired girl with a baby – real Venetian red hair which frames her olive face & black eyes enchantingly. The baby is very fractious & fidgetty but I have managed to make something of him. The red & yellow sails of course are the feature of Chioggia, otherwise it would be quite uninteresting. . . .

FH returned to Venice, leaving Miss Wimperis in Chioggia.

[129] TO RACHEL HODGKINS, c.1 AUGUST 1906
                          Hotel de la Poste, La Bouille, Seine Inférieure, France.

My darling Mother
    It is a long cry from Venice to La Bouille a funny little village on the Seine not very far from our beloved Caudebec. It is cool and green & very quiet & I am slowly getting back my strength & health on a stern milk diet & already I feel much much better in this bracing Northern air. It was foolish of me to have stayed in Venice so long but I thought if I could bear the heat of July & August it would be better for me to stay on in Italy for the winter but I got so weak & lowspirited from the continual affliction from which I suffered in the Red Sea[6] (you understand?) that I thought it safer & wiser to . . . get away from the heat for a while.

───────────────
[6] A euphemism for menstruation.

It was the heat of a hothouse more than an oven with the added torment of malevolent mosquitoes which ceased not night or day. . . . I can hear their devilish trumpetting in my ears now even from this distance & the thought of them softens the pang of regret at leaving the most beautiful & most enchanting & alluring city in the world. . . . We spent our time while in Paris on expeditions to Barbizon & Fontainbleau but neither of these places seemed very attractive apart from their historical & artistic associations so we decided to come on here, a place approved of by Mr. Garstin as a sketching camp & very cheap. . . . Though quite a short journey from Paris it took us hours & hours to get here, finally we were dumped down at a little station at 8 in the evening & told we had 4 miles to walk to La Bouille but that it was a pleasant road through the forest . . . . It was very lonely & beautiful in the forest with not a sound or light to disturb the solitude; glow-worms were our lamp posts & Girlie will like to know that the only living thing we met were two toads which croaked across the road in front of us. . . . On Sunday Rosamond hired a little chaise & we took our lunch & drove up the hill to the same forest through which we passed the night before & there we spent the day. We meant to write long letters to our respective Mothers but the spell of the slumbrous old forest sent us to sleep & all the time that was left was spent in inducing the spirit lamp to boil for tea. . . . While we were in Paris I showed my work to a well known dealer there[7] & he offered to arrange a show for me on moderate terms for October if I could produce 60 pictures of the same quality as the ones I showed him. . . . At first I thought I could do it & Rosamond wanted to stand all expenses & take the risk of any debt I might incur but on thinking it over it seemed a Herculean task to undertake as I have only about 20 pictures ready & some of these must go out to N.Z. to supply the sinews of war . . . . However I hope to secure a footing in Paris by sending to the International Society for Watercolors[8] held in this man's galleries in Nov. The French paint so little in watercolor but they are very appreciative. I was so glad to get a dear letter from you while in Paris & to hear you are well. It always heartens me up & stiffens my backbone to get a letter from you & I feel I am not quite alone in the wide world as long as I have you to think of & care for & love. . . .

[130] To Rachel Hodgkins, 29 August 1906
Hotel de Lion D'Or, St Valery-sur-Somme. August 29th.

Very dearest Mother
    Your letter telling me of poor Eveline[9] has just come & I am feeling much

[7] Maurice Guillemot of the Galerie Georges Petit, 8 rue de Sèze.
[8] Société Internationale d'Aquarellistes of which Maurice Guillemot was president. FH exhibited with them at the end of 1906 and in 1910.
[9] Bert's wife Eveline was dying of tuberculosis.

distressed. Poor girl what a short ill fated marriage it has been & one cannot blind one's eyes to the grave risks of a union like that & one can only hope that no further harm will come of it & that Bert's fine health will safeguard him. Poor boy . . . my heart aches for him for I know he will suffer, he is so loving & loyal.

I came here two days ago & it has been very nice seeing the Garstins again . . . . I found here also a nice elderly woman I knew in Penzance a Miss Hill rather resembling Miss Richmond in face & manner & she & I have decided to join forces for a while & winter in the South together somewhere. . . . This place is not very attractive & I find it rather difficult to get subjects. . . . I have just received a nice note from M. Guillemot whom I told you of, President of the Society of Watercolours congratulating me on my work & apparently he has selected nearly all of it either to show or to submit to the council of his Society which meets in Nov: I take this as a great honour as he is a man of reputation & the Society is a very select one – so in this letter I am unable to tell you just what work goes out to N.Z. . . . It is better of course to take every opportunity of showing my work while I am in Europe though I must look to my sales from N.Z. I hear Miss Richmond is wintering in Nelson. . . .

[131] To Rachel Hodgkins, 9 September 1906
Hotel Lion D'Or, St. Valery-sur-Somme, France.

Very dearest Mother
. . . . Tomorrow Sept 10th I am moving on to Paris with Miss Hill en route for Avignon. . . . She is very nice, elderly, grey haired . . . quite willing to go wherever it suits my brush. I find the Northern colour very difficult to deal with after Venice & picture making not nearly such a simple matter as in the South, not that it is ever simple but there is greater choice of subject. . . . Avignon is not far from Arles you remember where I went before & found such good subjects. I have had some luck in sales since I came here & have sold £20 worth in all one to a French artist who kisses his hands in ectasy when he mentions my sketches . . . . I dont quite like coming to Mr Garstin's stronghold & selling pictures where he does not but he is so large & generous & unstinting in his praise & he says I have helped him by coming: he certainly has helped me, steadied me & given me a fresh start & re-kindled the desire to paint. He is a good man with a fine gallant heart & the wittiest tongue as ever I've heard. . . .

[132] To Rachel Hodgkins, 15 September 1906.

Hotel Luxembourg, Avignon, Vaucluse. Sept 15th. 06

My darling Mother,

Its a long jump from St Valery in the North to Avignon in the South but we took it slowly & cheaply & without great pressure on purse or constitution managed it in fair comfort. . . . I sent off 6 pictures to Wellington which I trust in Heaven to see that they reach N.Z. in time for the Chch Show. I fear they will not meet with much approval for I have had to keep my best work for Europe but of course I do not wish N.Z. to think I have only sent them the leavings which I rather fear they are. Perhaps Sis will give an eye (if she has an unoccupied one for the moment) to the framing of them or if she cant do it perhaps she will ring up Miss Richmond & get her to kindly see to them. I have kept back some pictures for other shows in England for if I am only going to be in Europe for a short time it is as well [to] distribute my work as freely as possible. I have just had notices from Liverpool & Birmingham that 2 pictures have been accepted by each of these societies & now I am going to make a bid for the much coveted honour of membership of the R.W.S[10] which is the blue ribbon of the artistic world – I can't help feeling the futility of it all if in the end it only takes me back to N.Z. which must always remain my lode star as long as you are in it dear little Mother. There is no human tie on this side nothing but the call of my brush & one side of me is very lonely & forlorn. Miss Richmond says she will come when I say the word but I hesitate to ask her. I really believe she is happier in the simple country life she is now leading in Nelson. . . . Oh yes poor Miss Jenny she is a leaded weight on my conscience but had I stayed with her she wld have to have buried me so wearied to death was I by the poor little thing. Sometimes I thought I might be looking at myself a long way off in a mirror so great was the morbid depression she had upon me – Oh oh the pity of her and such as she. Well from Paris we departed early one morning with a large basket full of provender to eat by the wayside. The so-called Express was nevertheless a slow one & took all day about getting to Avignon . . . . [The Hôtel Luxembourg] is an old old house built in the days of the Popes . . . & we are tucked away in two nice rooms right in the middle of the house & no sound or murmur of the outside world reaches us. The rooms open on to a sunny courtyard . . . . They do us for 5 francs a day & we are well fed on plain food & an abundance of fruit & vegetables. It really seems as though it were the fountain head of all fruits of the earth so rich is the supply in the market: melons seem to gush out of the ground & lie in heaped up piles of ripeness & grapes in riotous Bacchanalian profusion make you giddy as the wine they are destined for – Oh I wish instead of writing these tasteless words about

[10] Royal Watercolour Society. The letters RWS, like RA, were added to an artist's name as a mark of status. The society was originally the Society of Painters in Water-Colours formed in 1802 by artists dissatisfied with the treatment of watercolours at the Royal Academy. It received royal recognition in 1881.

them I could send instead an argosy laden with these lush fruits but I fear you wld all have bad pains in your little insides as I have as a consequence. . . . We are quite close to the Rhone which slides oilily past on its way to the sea & at night we sometimes walk on the ramparts high above the river & before the light goes out can see the Alps & the Cévennes & the flat map of the Rhone valley at our feet & a space so great that it might be the whole of Europe in sight. . . .

. . . . I wld like so much to know what cure Eveline is trying . . . . I fear open air, night & day is the only thing that would save or rather prolong her life. Dear Bert . . . I know he is bearing it like the true philosopher that he all unconsciously is. I hear that the McGowans were to arrive last Sunday . . . . Poor little Mrs Spence was nearly dead with excitement & joy & running up & down stairs & putting up new curtains & painting the bath oh! dont we know – but joy never kills –

[133] To Rachel Hodgkins, 10 October 1906

Hotel du Luxembourg, Avignon. Oct 10th 06

My very dearest Mother

. . . . A terrific thunder storm burst over Avignon in the night & today it is raining & very cold & if I were at home I should probably be sitting over a fire with a good book Sissie wld: probably be tidying drawers & mending things. Now you know the sort of day. . . . The vintage is over & the last grape converted into wine. It has been a plenteous year . . . . I have spent many mornings making studies & still life drawings of the grapes for my big picture which is now well on towards completion. It was an interesting & primitive scene watching the men, who might easily have belonged to any century, handling the grapes with purple stained hands, weighing them & sending them off in laden lumbring carts generally painted the brightest blue, drawn by white mules already much over burdened by heavy but very picturesque harness in which bells play a part. To follow them would be disillusioning for they end up in a prosaic factory. . . . I sent some of my work to Rosamond the other day & she took it all to Mr Patterson a Bond St dealer, a big man in his way & he has consented to show 20 of my pictures in March. This will give me 4 months in which to produce 20 biggish things besides getting things ready for other shows. I heard from Miss Stoddart that she is leaving for N.Z. in Nov. . . .

[134] To Rachel Hodgkins, 18 November 1906

Hotel National D'Alsace, Antibes, Alpes Maritimes. Nov. 18th.

My darling Mother

. . . . My love & warmest wishes to you all. May you all be merry and comfortable and may Sis *not* have to cook the Christmas turkey herself. We shall spend our Christmas here, perhaps go to Nice or Monte Carlo for the day. . . . We came here from Avignon last Wednesday 14th. We travelled 1st. class in comfort – it was quite a short journey from 8a.m. to 2p.m. We took hard boiled eggs & rolls with us to keep off the faintness. In the same carriage were a fine lady & gentleman [who] obviously had been awake all night. . . . We succoured them with eggs & half our rolls & they were grateful & friendly. Presently the lady asked if she might look at my Maori Tiki (given me by Will & Sis & which I am never without) Did it come from New Zealand? She had been to N.Z. the year before and thought it the most wonderful & beautiful country. Did I know Dunedin? I was born there. Was I then an Old Identity or a New Iniquity? How she had come by this old legend I dont know but I explained to her she mustn't ask respectable Dunedinites if they were New Iniquities for it wasnt polite & told her the reason[11]. . . . They lived in Rangoon & were going to winter at Nice. I said when I went to Rangoon I wld: go and stay with them!

Antibes is a nice little 1 horse place and I think I shall find all that I want here – the little harbour is full of picturesque craft & there are lots of nice brown faced people about. It is unfashionable and very very quiet although connected by train with Cannes . . . . We are comfortable here & the food is good and plentiful. . . . The staff consists of a small boy in long swallowtails who does the waiting, a large sized chef and Eugénie the femme de chambre all smiles & blessings & curtseys. As far as amicability can take anyone it has taken Eugénie. The first morning she brought me my coffee while I was yet à la pantaloons. The coffee all but dropped & her eyes went up "Blessed Virgin what small feet, what shoes! ma foi but you should hang them up on a nail!" & next morning when she took the same shoes off to be cleaned I could hear her murmuring endearments over them – The sort of kind old dear I wld: like Sis to have for the children.

. . . . Yesterday was cold & windy so we took a day off & went by train to Cannes. . . . Miss Hill took me to the famous Rumplemayer's to have a cup of chocolate. Such chocolate – best described as a sensation. Twenty years ago Miss Hill was in Cannes & the memory of her cup of Rumplemayer chocolate has never left her. Perhaps some day I may bring Girlie & introduce her to Rumplemayer as Miss Hill did me. . . .

My painting goes steadily on. I am working hard but with what sort of success

[11] The Old Identity were the settlers from the Free Church of Scotland who first arrived in Otago in 1848. The New Iniquity were the very different people who arrived after the discovery of gold in 1861.

I cannot judge. I am to be nominated by two Associates of the R.W.S in Feb: but it is not likely I shall win an associateship for many years to come. Last year there were 110 candidates 40 of whom were good men & they could only elect 3 – however it is a good thing to try for. . . . I would like to write you a longer letter if I had any more news, which I havent, so with much love to you all & a very great deal to your dear self I will say goodnight

Your loving Frances.

[135] To Rachel Hodgkins, December 1906

[Hotel National D'Alsace, Antibes, Alpes Maritimes]

. . . . I am sorry none of you have liked my pictures. I didnt think you wld though of course it would have been nicer if you had. Mr. Von H[aast] was very frank & insinuated my work had gone off – indeed I wish it only would! I shall be up a tree if my London work doesn't sell. The French artist tells me . . . pictures are a drug & everybody's money is spent on motors & so it seems – it is really astonishing how many people can afford them. . . . I would like a year or two more in Europe free of anxiety to try what I can do with my talent and see if I really have a future before me as the French papers put it. . . .

Goodbye now dearest & may your New Year be one of peace & happiness

Love me always & keep well

Your loving Frances.

[Letter incomplete]

[136] To Rachel Hodgkins, 12 January 1907

Hotel National D'Alsace, Antibes, Alpes Maritimes. Jan 12th. 07

My dearest Mother

An armful of papers arrived yesterday & were very much enjoyed. Many thanks to all the kind senders. . . .

I dont feel very uplifted over the purchases of Dr. Fell & the Hon. R. MacDonald[12] . . . . Harcourt is a first-rate man I believe & I have been hearing of him lately as doing good work – but the others . . . Why buy pictures for a young colony by derelict artists of byegone time & taste?. . . I am trying to arrange with my London dealer to run my show without Miss Hodgkins being there in the flesh – I want to avoid the expense of the long journey if possible & all the other inevitable expenses of a month in London. . . . But of course if Mr. Paterson

---

[12] These were the purchases made by the Academy from the Christchurch International Exhibition. They included *The Wanderer* by George Harcourt RA, RP (1868-1947), a portrait and figure painter in oil, and *Poor Motherless Bairns* by Flora Reid.

thinks it unwise of me not to come then I shall make the effort to be there. I am in the final throes of my pictures & not feeling too happy about them – the usual depression overtakes one at this stage & it is heavy going – things baulk & thwart one & you feel as though all the forces of Nature were in league to annoy you – its blue when you want it grey, windy when it should be calm, wet when you have prayed to all your Gods that it may be fine – & as for the behaviour of models, they are past praying for, one & all, male & female, are an abandoned dishonourable lot & what I have suffered at their perfidious hands is beyond words. . . .

. . . . I am working extremely hard doing in 5 months what most people take a year to do or more & letters are sometimes more than one's tired painting brains can manage. Will Life always be a tussle like this I wonder?. . .

[137] To Rachel Hodgkins, 3 February 1907
Hotel National D'Alsace, Antibes, Alpes Maritimes. Feb. 3rd. 07

My darling Mother

This will be my last letter to you from Antibes as we are leaving for London on the 8th. . . . Mr Paterson thinks it would be so much to my advantage to be present that I am reluctantly taking his advice. It is the expense, of course . . . one can rub along so nicely abroad with old clothes but London means new boots gloves hat, everything! I have had my old green dress cleaned & it really looks like new & I am going to wear it at the Show with a new hat. . . I shall have to dress up to my frames which I believe are very fine. . . . I have practically finished my pictures though of course one keeps on keeping on at them till the last possible moment. I'm very tired & the train journey will be almost a rest after the constant strain & excitement of these past few weeks – I hope Mr Paterson will like them – I am to have lunch with him on Monday . . . and afterwards he is to see my drawings[13] – I shall be glad when the ordeal is over. . . . A deep hot bath is what my soul is craving for – I have plunged with splendid courage into my cold tub every icy morning but it is not the same thing – though I am sure it keeps one from taking chills. . . . I wonder if you saw the McGowans on their way home – they wont like Effie going over to the Holy Romans at all. . . . Some months ago she wrote & told me she was contemplating it . . . . I wrote & argued & cajoled & expostulated but in vain. She was absolutely certain that it was the true religion & was very much in earnest. . . . I never thought a well-brought up daughter of Mrs Spence, dear & conventional little church woman that she is, wld ever strike out like this. She waited till after Robert & Alice had left and then she went to a little French convent in Normandy & here she has been prepared by the nuns

---

[13] Watercolours were called 'watercolour drawings' or 'drawings' and sometimes 'sketches'. The word 'painting' refers to oil paintings throughout FH's correspondence.

& priests & yesterday she was received into their religion. I feel deeply sorry for poor Mrs. Spence . . . . I am very fond of Effie she is full of character & spirit & has more spunk than all of them & lately she has shown signs of developing into a really fine woman – in spite of this religious lapse of hers. . . .

It has been most bitterly cold here these last few weeks, like everywhere else, & I am all chilblains & chaps – but . . . in a short time the wild flowers will be out & in this lovely land of flowers that is a sight worth seeing. It really is a great pity I have to leave it all for that frosty old ink pot London – how I dread it – the cold & the mud & the slop-slop in & out of busses! . . .

[138] To Rachel Hodgkins, 7 March 1907
Alexandra Club, 12, Grosvenor Street, W. March 7th 07

My darling Mother

Well the great day has come and gone and the only little shadow on it all was because I had none of you with me. New Zealanders indeed did *not* rise to the occasion & except for my faithful Spences there wasnt a sign of one – plenty of others though but not a crowd, and I was blessed with a beautiful bright sunny day and the Gallery looked charming hung in a dead rose velvet & with a soft yellow light very becoming to the pictures. One picture £15.15 sold on Press Day but nothing on the first day.[14] I send you the only notice that so far has appeared. Mr. Humphrey Ward is the critic of the Times[15]. . . . Mr. Paterson hung my 22 pictures with great taste & effect leaving large spaces between each greatly to their advantage – some of the illustrated papers are going to reproduce one or two of them . . . . It is very comforting that people like them & it repays one for all the anxiety & worry that has gone before. The NZ Press people turned up in force so I expect you may hear something of it before this reaches you. I got no time for any calls only got as far as the Spences one Sunday & found them very cheerful & well Mr. Spence making anti-papal jokes at Effie's expense & all quite reconciled and amiable over it. . . . Tomorrow I am to meet the two gentlemen appointed as co-choosers for the Wellington Art Gallery. One of them Mr. Morley Fletcher came to my show, a very nice man with a fine thoughtful face & evidently a man whose taste & judgment can be trusted. Tomorrow he & Mr. Devitt the other man, are to meet me at the Bond St Gallery to look at some

---

[14] Exhibitions began with a Private View (P.V.) and Press Day, before being open to the public.

[15] 'At Mr Paterson's Gallery, 5, Old Bond-street, a young artist from New Zealand is holding a first and a very promising exhibition. This is Miss Frances Hodgkins, who, like everybody else, has been to Venice, but who has occupied herself almost more with the people than with the place. She uses her brush with force and distinction, and, while thoroughly modern and actual, paints with a certain regard for style. The example called "Purple and Black" – a group of figures passing by an open shop-front – is extremely clever and shows an unusually keen sense of colour.' *The Times*, 7 March 1907, p.15.

PLATE 1: *Summer*, c.1912, watercolour, 586 x 498 mm, Dunedin Public Art Gallery.

PLATE 2: *Double Portrait*, c.1922, oil, 610 x 764 mm, Hocken Library, Dunedin. Mentioned in Letter 363.

PLATE 3: *Three French Children*, 1924, oil, 565 x 660 mm, Private Collection.

pictures Mr Paterson has got together for us and on Saturday we are going to Brangwyn's studio to see some smaller pictures that he has offered to show us & off which he has consented to knock £50 which wld make them about £250. Fortunately Mr. Morley Fletcher is on my side & thinks it far wiser to get together a good nucleus of 3 or 4 good pictures rather than a number of minor ones. Mr. Garstin dear man has been buying some things on his own account which seems hardly fair but I dont think much harm is done. . . . Dont murmur a word of all this Mother dear. I am writing to Dr. Fell this mail telling him what progress we are making. . . . Miss Jenny writes from Rome & bears me no malice, in fact wishes to return to NZ with me in the same boat Ai Ai Ai! . . . We went to a French play the other night – the acting was superb, such finish & perfection – another night to a Bernard Shaw piece called "You never can tell". Acting jerky & affected after the French people but the dialogue as clever as ever it could be – perfectly moral but all heresy & unconvention one's dearest faiths shattered & ridiculed – human foibles & fads held up [to] withering scorn & you come away [with] all your little pet gods smashed & broken but never a word of help or counsel how to set them up again & that is where his weakness as a teacher & reformer lies. He knocks down but he fails to build up –

. . . . This week end I am going to the Nickalls. I feel worn out with excitement & this filthy London air all smuts & sulphur & am pining for some country breezes. The streets are simply murderous nowadays with the motor traffic – ugh! . . .

[139] To Rachel Hodgkins, 21 March 1907

Thriplands, Kensington Court. W. March 21st

My darling Mother

I send you in another envelope some Press cuttings. They are not very exciting though they are considered good as Press clippings go. The reproduction of one of my pictures is such a cruel libel I hardly like sending it – I am feeling rather despairing about my show – no sales at all save the 2 I told you of in my last letter, which is dreadful. Times are so bad – I don't quite know what to do. I was counting so much on selling that this is rather a staggering blow. In the meanwhile till I have collected my wits a little & laid out a plan of action, I shall go to Rosamond for a few weeks & when I return in May I shall most probably take a sketching Class abroad somewhere perhaps to Bruges or Normandy – Gertrude might come with me & help me get rooms etc for the pupils. Several people have asked me to give them lessons – so perhaps I may be able to work up something out of it. For the present I am so much in need of a spell of some sort that I feel I must get away somewhere for a few weeks quiet before starting work again. I must get what comfort I can from the thought that I have established myself artistically if nothing else – made people talk a little & surprised them a little which is the first slow step on the road to success. Mr Paterson still has faith in me in spite of my bringing him in so little & he has been most kind all through & encouraging. The Show has still another five days to run so perhaps my luck may still turn. I went down to Wispers for a few days but it was the home of many gales & I caught a chill out driving & was pretty seedy so didn't get much pleasure out of my visit. . . . .

[140] TO RACHEL HODGKINS, 28 MARCH 1907

Priorsgate, St. Andrews N.B. March 28th.

My darling Mother

. . . . I left London yesterday morning in a thick yellow fog, groping my way to King's Cross in a hansom & all but missed my train so blocked was the traffic. . . . The country as far as York was uninteresting as is most of English scenery, smooth & tidy & groomed & for ever the same, but north of York it grew more rugged & from there onwards to the Great Forth bridge it was all beautiful country. . . .

In this old house once lived Mary Queen of Scots & the garden wall is part of the old Abbey – it is a most romantic spot full of old memories & traditions; the garden is a mass of bursting bulbs, trim little beds surrounded by tall leafless trees full of chattering rooks. Mrs Riddle Webster, Rosamonds Mother is a great gardener & like you dear spends much of her time among her flowers.

Things were looking up a little at the Gallery before I left. Miss Abernethy, my Venice friend you remember, had been in & desired two pictures one £25 & the other £30 but only having ½ an hour on her way through London decided to see them again on her return in 5 days time. She is a lady who knows her own mind on most subjects so I feel fairly confident that this means business. Mr. Paterson has treated me with the greatest generosity – besides allowing my pictures to remain on his walls another fortnight he has refused either to charge me for the gallery or to take a penny of commission – which is really most handsome of him. It wld have been to my advantage if I had had a number of smaller pictures, but I thought it wiser to paint more important ones which have certainly made more of an impression though they are too large for ordinary people's pockets. It is a difficult game I am playing but I must play it my own way though it is hard sometimes to keep one's head level & ones heart brave – but I *feel* my work must win in the long run. I have the artists on my side which gives me strength & courage. The prizes seem so unfairly & capriciously distributed in this world! One must just keep on & if the public understand nothing else they at least can understand & appreciate persistance! . . . Thank you dear for offering the £100 but I am all right for the present . . . .

[Postscript] I have not forgotten your birthday dearest. Many happy returns and next April will I expect see me back with you again famous or otherwise! The R.W.S. elected *no one* this year – they are generally supposed to be off their heads by those whom they have rejected!

[141] To Rachel Hodgkins, 4 April 1907

Priorsgate, St Andrews. April 4th.

My darling Mother

Of all icy, cold, east windy haggard dreary climates poor St Andrews has the worst. . . . Yesterday . . . we drove to a place called Hospital Fields the home of Mr. & Mrs. Harcourt who are in charge of an endowed home for 10 young men who are being trained as artists. It is a delightful place, a fine old house set in pretty country, or alleged pretty country for I could see little of anything through the teeming rain. I found Mr. Cecil Jameson[16] here looking very well & happy & very pleased with his comfortable quarters. The young men stay for 4 years & study both landscape & figure painting under Mr. Harcourt – who is a very able painter and a thoroughly nice man into the bargain. Why is there not a similar place for we poor women artists? Think of what one wld be capable of in 4 years under such conditions, a healthy open-air life, peace of mind & no anxieties and one's creature comforts not overlooked. The suffragettes may see to this – I hope so. Pegasus was never any the better for being put in the plough of that I am certain. Miss Abernethy has bought her two pictures & seems pleased with herself – thereby heaping many burning coals upon my head I did so cordially dislike her but I must from now onwards be for ever silent. This should bring me in about £50 after my expenses are paid, framing will no doubt come to £25. This should keep me going for some time & lift me out of penury & the shadow of the workhouse. I have been specially invited to send 3 pictures to Manchester to a water-colour show there & the remainder I shall distribute among various shows in the hope that they may not return. The Australasian Women at Home & Abroad are having a Show of their work first in London & later in Melbourne to which I am invited to send. The Princess of Wales [is] to contribute some of her own sketches. Talking of this great lady tell Girlie I was walking one day in St James Park when I came to a road where there was a notice that no vehicles except Royal carriages were permitted to pass. . . . I walked up it past some very grim important looking houses & presently sure enough there was a carriage with red ribbons on the horses ears and in a twinkling past flashed the Princess of Wales looking very pretty in a mauve toke and the 2 little Princes sitting very good &

[16] Cecil Jamieson (b.1884) studied under J. M. Nairn in Wellington and was possibly a pupil of FH in 1904 before going to England.

prim opposite their august Mama. I bowed & the little Princes saluted & the Princess just waved slightly in her seat & as there was absolutely no one but ME and the sentry opposite who was terribly busy saluting . . . I can honestly say I was for the time fairly well in it. . . .

Are you well dear & with Bert at Kelburne. How is Evelyn? I hope she is getting daily stronger & a stage nearer recovery. . . .

FH and Rosamond Marshall travelled to Edinburgh in April to meet the Scottish artist James Paterson (1854-1923), a member of the Glasgow School. FH admired his work; one of his watercolours, Moret, *was bought for the New Zealand Academy collection.*

[*142*] To Rachel Hodgkins, 19 April 1907

The Graines, Moniaive N.B. April 19th

My darling Mother

. . . . It was very sweet & good of you to send me that cheque – I hardly liked cashing it thankful as I was to have it. I know you have denied yourself to send it to me – you must *never* do it again dearest. Mr. Paterson hasnt yet paid up & I have been rather hard up not liking to seem too anxious . . . . I was contemplating selling or pawning my silver backed brushes to pay this weeks washing bill but you have saved me from that humiliation. I almost wish I had brought Home my Rembrandt head[17] – it might have sold for quite a lot. . . .

Moniaive is still cold & very windy & sketching is out of the question – I found a sheltered burn the other day – sheltered that is from the wind, but the children found me out as children do in any country – an artist is fair game – these children however were different – Scotch children are well brought up & God-fearing & respect their elders. A silent little group roundeyed & very shy stood behind me, not a word or a sound for nearly an hour – then a chubby little boy with profound solemnity said "I'm away to ma tea but I'll be back" and the others took the hint & also dispersed. They came back no doubt but I in turn "was away to ma tea". . . . I am so glad you have bought yourself some nice clothes – they *do* give one a certain satisfaction dont they? I wish I had all the money I spent on foolish clothes before I left Wellington. What a squandering of good gold it all seems now. Does Life ever cease to hold regret? Is Happiness always a mirage? It sometimes seems so. One comes to look back on a certain little oasis in ones life, that short happy courting – days of illusions & ideals – and your thoughts wander back to it & speculate endlessly why it ever came into your life to leave it so soon.

---

[17] FH inherited this from her father's collection.

Painting is too maddening & perplexing & precarious to ever give one a stable or lasting happiness. This morning I went for a long walk & found under hedges little cushions of primroses & wood anemonies. Primroses & lambs and all young spring things are a great refreshment to one's soul – its really the eternal hope that springs ever in our Nature, which really shows that we are a good deal happier than we think. The Colonial Premiers are having high junkettings, dining with the Prince of Wales, lunching with the Lord Mayor & other high notabilities – General Botha is the pet of them all – and there certainly [is] something whimsically attractive in the thought of he & Lord Roberts drinking each others health across a dinner table – 1200 yards was the nearest they ever got to each other in olden days.[18]

I am sending Will some papers with an account of their doings. Much love to you dearest Mother – and a kiss & many many thanks for the cheque – I loved you for sending it & thinking of my birthday. What did you get for yours?

[143] To Rachel Hodgkins, 2 May 1907

20 Lunham Rd, Upper Norwood. May 2nd

My darling Mother

Choice weather for May let me tell you – cold & windy & wet. Its really the fault of the poets no rational being would have expected fine weather in May if they had not talked so much about it. I have had a busy week since I came to town & very little have I seen of these dear kind Spences except to say goodnight & good morning. . . . On Monday I met Mr Garstin at Thriplands & laid out a plan of campaign, starting the next morning in drenching rain on a round of the picture galleries. . . . With the small sum that we have at our disposal the difficulty is in getting good pictures at a low figure – our game is to hunt up the younger men whose work is on the upward grade & whose work is likely to increase in value – this takes time and an infinity of patience. . . . We went to 5 galleries that day and we saw about the same number of pictures that we might have bought . . . out of all those hundreds we looked at. . . . . Next morning . . . . we went to see Mr Stott's[19] studio – a dirty little hole tucked away in a Mews . . . the man himself is not attractive but his work is . . . full of true feeling & poetry. Where *does* it come from? Such a face . . . . poets & artists should after all remain invisible if we are to retain our illusions – not all I hasten to say – for after this we went on to see Mr Fred Hall,[20] quite another pair of shoes – & just as full of art. . . .

[18] Lord Roberts and General Louis Botha commanded the British and Boer armies in the South African War of 1899-1902. Botha was prime minister of Transvaal, which became a British colony at the end of the war; he was attending the Imperial Conference.
[19] Edward Stott (1859-1918) had been a founding member of the NEAC.
[20] Frederick Hall (1860-1948) was another Newlyn painter.

He is an old friend of Mr Garstin & was glad to see us & insisted on sharing a beef bone & some wine & biscuits with us . . . . It was great fun & they told long yarns about themselves & brother brushes & old times. . . . In between whiles I am busy with arrangements for my class. I leave for Dordrecht on the 22nd with 2 pupils – I hope more will follow. . . .

[144] To WILL FIELD, 15 MAY 1907
Totara, 20 Lunham Road, Upper Norwood, S.E. May 15th 07

My dear Will

I wonder if you will do something for me, your poor absent far away little sister-in-law – but first let me say how very sorry I was to hear of that disastrous fire at your office . . . . Mother tells me Old Cole was burnt (this of course is a futeling loss compared to other things) but all the same I can't help shedding a tear for that early unlovely Pre-Raphaelite effort of mine[21]. . . . I have been getting a great deal of pleasure out of a picture by Sis in this house, one of her Pre-Matrimonial pictures astonishingly good & clever. If they would only swop it for something else I would send it out to you as a balm for your recent losses but they wont part with it the dears & wretches!

But what I mostly and very particularly want to say is this – will you please open my packing case which lies in your cellar & take therefrom my Rembrandt Head & have it packed carefully & well & sent Home to me as soon as possible – I want to try & sell it – I hate suggesting this & I know the family wont like the idea but you will easily realise that it is better for me to have the money I may possibly get from the sale of it so as to enable me *now*, this year to make a last stand & rally in Europe before I come back to you all – I dont want to do as the poor Premiers are doing, return with unrealised hopes & schemes. I want to do a little more with what talent I have & try and consolidate all these minor successes into something firmer & more lasting. And to do this one must "hold on" a little longer. . . . So please, dear Will, get out that Rembrandt & raise no difficulties or even suggest anything else – I *particularly* do not want Mother to send me what small sum of money she has – & I wish to refuse any other form of help – I shall come back at once if I can't get on without borrowing. I am all right for 4 or 5 months ahead & there are my pupils of course but they are uncertain . . . and I want to safeguard myself from that crippling anxiety of mind that prevents one from working ones best & hardest. . . .

[21] During the 1890s Frances Hodgkins painted a number of studies of elderly men, paying great attention to detail.

PART NINE

1907-8

A Year in Holland

Pennock's Hotel, Dordrecht. May 29th.

My darling Mother

Here I am only 4 miles from that little village of Rijsoord where you remember I spent a summer nearly 4 years ago. History repeats itself. I had a perfect crossing to Flushing . . . . I discovered Mr Moffat Lindner on board whom I had met many years ago at Caudebec. He comes twice a year to Dordrecht . . . . Almost his first words to me were "Do you know we have got a baby?" This is really a more than ordinary occasion for rejoicing for they have been many years without. Tell Miss Richmond if you happen to see her, she will be interested. This is a nice quiet homey old hotel where I can live for less than 30/- a week . . . . There are not many people here – the ubiquitous Yank of course, two of them an elderly etcher & his friend nice old boys who very nearly emigrated to N.Z. when they were young . . . . They know a thing or two about art & we have great old talks over dinner in the evening –

This morning early 2 of my pupils arrived by the night boat & they are now asleep so I have not had much opportunity of judging what they are like. They are both elderly & the sort I associate with board schools & the suburbs. It is evident they are infants in art. Two more arrive on Sunday from Paris & these I know are more promising. It hasn't been too warm & I still keep on all my woollies. I am going to do a lot of little sketches for Wellington. If I knew of anything that would pay better than painting I would do it. . . . I hope my Rembrandt will turn up trumps. Mr. Paterson told me of a small head (girl's head) by him that was sold the other day for £1000. . . .

[146] To Rachel Hodgkins, 12 June 1907

Dordrecht. June 12th. 1907.

My darling Mother

. . . . It has been a really busy time settling my Class & getting things into working order . . . . One pupil has been ill ever since she came . . . scared me by a high temperature & an ominous swelling in her throat – I sent for a doctor who spoke English & the sister arrived in a few days for which I was thankful . . . . This reduces my modest little class to 2 pupils which represents £6 a month . . . . Pupils are an uncertain quantity & one cannot build on them. But I do build on the Rembrandt. . . . I hear the Curator of the Hague Museum is one of the great authorities on Rembrandt . . . & I shall suggest to Mr Paterson who is coming to Holland sometime during the summer that he should show my head to him. . . . Yesterday I had tea with Mr Moffat Lindner at his hotel & saw his beautiful sketches – he does know what to do with water colour – today he is coming in to see mine. It has been nice having him here to fling an occasional word to. . . . I am sorry Sis was servantless when you wrote . . . . I wish I could export a stout Dutch wench or so with good strong arms & a perfect passion for cleaning in their honest souls – they dont look happy unless they are beating a carpet or hosing the windows. The family cat of Pennock is sitting 3 parts over my paper – it is playful & scratchy. . . .

Since beginning this luck has looked up a bit – for one thing I have heard of another pupil arriving shortly . . . . and then last night I sold a picture for £5 – a little Dutch head . . . . I was so excited at the rarity of this sale that I didn't sleep a wink for thinking how rich I was & wondering what I should do with the money – then add to this that I have saved 1½ by posting this in England I feel amost a multi-millionairess. It does buck one up – in the evening Mr Lindner came in & took me for a walk to look for nocturnes but the only tangible result so far is a cold in my head the result of getting my feet wet. . . .

[147] To Rachel Hodgkins, 23 June 1907

Pennocks Hotel, Dordrecht. June 23rd.

My darling Mother
    . . . . This house has been full of Americans this last week or so – they come in a hurry & leave in a hurry with a Baedeker under their arms but these people have stayed longer than most of them. Two of them sat opposite me at lunch today strangers to each other & I overheard this conversation. Large lanternjawed stranger with kindly eyes to livery person who passed every dish with a sickly smile – My! you do look snuffed out. Guess you've got stomach trouble.
Lean and livery person – Reckon you're right
Lanternjawed stranger Come right up to my room after lunch and Ill fix you up got most everything for stomach trouble thats in the market –
I heard no more but I would like to have gone upstairs with them & seen the matter through. The lanternjawed one said to me later on – "Wall I know Mrs Ro-bison the mother of your Agent-General and I know Prof Rutherford[1] and I know you and I think you seem a real live lot of people out there!" Praise isnt it.
. . .
    I have just written to Dr Fell to tell him of our latest purchase a fine oil by Mr Moffat Lindner a nocturne of Amsterdam. While he was here he offered it to me for £60 which is £100 less than his catalogue price. It is extremely generous of him for it is a really fine picture. . . . The pictures go out to NZ in August . . . and they

---

[1] Mary Robison was the mother-in-law of William Pember Reeves, who became New Zealand's Agent-General in London in 1896 and first High Commissioner in 1905. Ernest Rutherford was awarded the Nobel Prize in 1908.

should reach Wellington about the end of September I think. . . . Dear I have been thinking of Frank since your letter came with such [a] re-assuring account of him. How wonderful if he gets better after all – one can only hope. . . . I would like to hear Dr King's[2] opinion of his case now – Have you written? . . .

[148] To Rachel Hodgkins, 10 July 1907

Pennock's Hotel, Dordrecht. July 10th.

My darling Mother

. . . . I have at last met a really nice American – a charming creature from Ohio who is a cultivated & most attractive person – terribly well informed on any subject, Maeterlinck, ice creams, bugs, & Russian politics not to mention Greek philosophy whatever that may be, she is equally interested in *and* a voice that would make an angel weep. Her clothes play a part: such pretty things, a judicious mixture of Liberty and a smart Paris bonnet shop. She kindly sat for me for a week & besides the pleasure of painting her I was greatly entertained. The French artist thinks I should send it to Paris – the American to New York – it is interesting I think but I fear it is not finished enough for Exhibition purposes – she went away rather unexpectedly and it did not get finished. She told me before she left that she was going to spend the summer with the Maxim Gorkis at their villa in Capri. I hope he wont turn her into a bomb-throwing Revolutionist – she has fire enough for any great cause – a fine heart & mind I think – I would like the friendship to have gone further – I miss sitting opposite her pretty face. She had blue eyes like Rosie Day's with a lovely honest look in them very good to see. . . . One afternoon I went to tea, escorted by Mr Rijkens who is much more a patron & friend of artists than strictly speaking a hotel Proprietor – though I believe he does nearly all the cooking which is excellent – where am I? – to tea with a Dutch artist Mr Moll[3] who owns a beautiful house & garden – he paints very well in a rather bad style – he presented me with some roses explaining cautiously that he was engaged to an English lady which evidently quite excused the impropriety of such a proceeding! He is an effeminate looking creature with eyes as big as saucers & inclined to cultivate a fringe. . . . We have all got rain on the brain just at present . . . . there are certainly compensations in the wonderful atmospheric effects one sees – the clouds are full of lovely surprises . . . .

[2] Frederick Truby King, better known as the founder of the Plunket Society in 1907, had become Superintendent of the Seacliff Mental Asylum in 1899.
[3] Evert Moll (b.1878), a painter of land and seascapes who worked in London, Paris and Dordrecht.

[149] To Rachel Hodgkins, 12 July 1907

Hotel Pennock, Dordrecht. July 12th. 07

My darling Mother

. . . . Poor old Bert I do feel for him he will miss his little wife & feel very lonely without [her] but his brave bright nature will help him through this bad time. He could not wish her to live suffering as she did – poor little lady. . . . I am glad Sis was able to be with Bert. She is so good and wonderful when there is trouble & has a big comforting way with her. . . . Thank Bert for his kind thought and offer of a home.[4] I feel pulled to pieces between you and my painting. If Rembrandt sells as well as I hope he will Bert must come Home for a trip while I am still here and we would come out together. . . . It would give him such a spurt and a new interest in things and it would give me an awful lot of pleasure to show him round. . . .

FH was invited to send work to autumn exhibitions in Liverpool, Manchester, Leeds and Brighton.

[150] To Rachel Hodgkins, 3 August 1907

Pennock's Hotel, Dordrecht. August 3rd. 07

My darling Mother

The sky looks threatening & showery so I have settled my pupils in the studio before a bowl of roses & now I can have a chat with you . . . . Our little flying trip to Amsterdam came off last week & it was a great enjoyment seeing for the 2nd. time all those fine pictures at the Rijks Museum – you may remember I went there with the Garstins last time I was in Holland. . . . We spent all day with the pictures – ancient & modern, & saw many of my old friends again . . . . We spent the evening at a music hall which was more amusing than edifying, mostly consisting of a Biograph[5] & acrobatic performances – but we were not critical having seen nothing in Dordrecht for so long – this lasted till midnight & then we walked back to the hotel & it brought back Venice to me – it was so beautiful. When you see Mr Moffat Lindner's picture which we have bought for Wellington, you will understand what it was like. The next morning we went on to Haarlem to see the Franz Hals & I liked them infinitely more this time than the 1st visit 4 years ago – they are like Sargent in their wonderful freshness & vigour – or rather he is like Hals – frightfully human & living men – such painting – a tingling vividness

[4] Mrs Hodgkins continued to keep house for Bert.
[5] An early form of cinematograph.

about them that sets one on fire – I remember disliking them when I first saw them – I am wiser now –

. . . . It wasn't a very expensive little trip about 15/- altogether which had been well earned. It proved a tremendous stimulus & inspiration & I have been painting several things almost equal in merit to anything by Rembrandt or Hals. . . . I have 3 pupils at present – a pleasant nice woman Miss Winthrop being the most interesting of them. I knew her in Venice. She is one of the right sort to have, rich & generous & my only regret is that she is one of Mr Garstin's old pupils & I hate taking any of his – he needs them almost as badly as I do. He wrote me yesterday that he was sending one of his pupils on to me which is nice of him. I believe in time I should soon make a connection for I find that one pupil invariably sends others along which is a good sign – & they seem pleased with their lessons which is a comfort. I wonder if you have seen any notice in the papers of my winning a prize at the Australasian show[6]. . . . I hope it may be a money prize. Please keep all my cuttings for me dear – put them in a little clippings book if you happen to see one. . . .

. . . . I expect you are all swaggering about & putting on no end of side now that you are a Dominion. It does sound fine & grand. Have you got Sir Joseph back safely? There have been great doings here in little Dort – a circus, no less! and a real stunning one. Mr Moll, my Dutch artist friend of whom I told you took Miss Winthrop & me last night – it was a beautiful affair of the hippodrome sort – lovely horses who performed wonderful & graceful things under the skilful management of airily clad equestriennes. It looked a heavenly thing to do – to ride on a satin white horse with nothing on but a chiffon frill & a diamond star – not the horse of course but the girl. . . . When I came back from Amsterdam I found that Mr Moll had sent to the hotel a beautiful free-wheel bicycle for my use while I am in Dordrecht and he took me for my first ride after 4 years the other afternoon. It was like flying & I felt I would go on for ever, there was so little exertion required – to think I might have died & never known the joys of a free wheel! one ought never to be without a bicycle – it *is* good for one. I get a lot of sailing & rowing too on the river & often in the evenings we go out snipe shooting. It is great sport creeping up the backwaters of the river in among rushes nearly 12 feet high & waiting for the birds to fly over . . . . Mr Moll is arranging for me to send 2 watercolours to the big Amsterdam exhibition opening next month. I hope I shall get in . . . it is an important show which takes place every 4 years. Brangwyn wants to send the picture we have bought for NZ. & we have agreed – though it will mean at least 5 months before you see it in Wellington. I want to write to Miss Richmond this mail so will stop now dear. I sold a £5 picture today so am feeling pretty well. I like having Miss Winthrop with me –

[6] The exhibition of art and craft by New Zealand and Australian women mentioned in Letter 141. FH's *Place Massena, Antibes* was awarded first prize for watercolour.

she is so nice & a lady – I can't bear being alone among strangers though people
are so kind. . . .

[151] TO RACHEL HODGKINS, 20 AUGUST 1907
Hotel Pennock, Dordrecht. Aug 20th.

My darling Mother
    . . . . Thank Bert for attending to the Rembrandt for me – you alarm me by
casting doubts on its genuineness – I always understood that it *had* been identified by the British Museum – & that it was declared to be a replica of the
Burgomaster Six. . . . It will be a horrid sell if it is a spurious thing . . . . I am
working hard. I do toil for my bread & butter & strain every nerve short of pot
boiling & that I can't do. As long as the summer lasts I shall be all right for I can
count on pupils till the end of October and an occasional sale. It seems useless
sending out more work to Wellington. It doesn't seem to catch on at all – & it
only depresses one to hear nothing but adverse criticisms – both Dr. Scott & Mr
Von Haast apparently delight in pointing out mistakes & repeating facetious
remarks which isn't an amiable thing in an overseas letter – Dr. Scott is turning
sour in his old age or maybe it is only the effect of choosing pictures at the Chch
exhibition that has temporarily upset his temper – every one of our mutual friends
came under his lash. . . . Miss Richmond is ever kind & sweet & cheering in her
wholesome sympathy. She knows what up-hill work it is – for a woman, alone
very up-hill work. Fortunately I have had good friends near me all the summer
anxious to help me up another rung of this old ladder – I do want to come back
to you & Bert dear but give me a little longer in which to achieve something. I
can't come back to N.Z. feeling a failure. This summer has taught me much I feel
– there never was a more beautiful country for atmosphere – I love Holland & I
will leave with many regrets. The weather itself is quite abominable – a most ill-
conducted summer – there are two big classes of ladies conducted by Ludovici a
handsome Italian & the other by the less romantic Robinson of Bruges. I
recognise the futility on my part or on the part of any mere woman artist to attract
a large following of her own sex. It can't be done. It *must* be a man – & an
Eyetalian for choice. Lady artists are the feeblest people on earth – the ground in
Dordrecht is simply strewn with them mostly painting insipid watercolours
under the protection of a large policeman. The policeman keeps all comers off
even your friends in return for backsheesh in the shape of 2 cent cigars. I have
never yet wanted a policeman – but that [is] because I have other protection of
a more adequate & agreeable kind – I dont even carry my things – I am
thoroughly spoilt – all I have to do as Miss Richmond once said, is to lay the paint
on. I teach in the mornings & the afternoon I have quite to myself. Miss
Winthrop is still with me I am glad to say & will stay on during Sept: she is very

pleased with her lessons & she should be a good judge having learnt from nearly every teacher in Europe – full to the brim of excellent theory but quite unable to put any of it on to paper – I have not yet heard from Amsterdam about the fate of my pictures. . . . Last Sunday was a lovely day after a week's almost continuous rain & we were tempted into a picnic. Mr Moll took dinner & we took afternoon tea & started off in the boat which is a great flatbottomed Dutch affair, about 3 & worked our way up one of the backwaters where we boiled the kettle in Sunday silence – nothing but sea gulls & snipe about us & an occasional heron overhead, then we painted till the sun dropped & then had dinner which Mr Moll's man had set out for us – it got frightfully dark all at once & hideously cold so we boiled eggs to warm us up as we had only cold meat & salad & a sort of iced blancmange which gave one the shivers – we gave the eggs 10 minutes but when we tried to eat them they werent even warm – so those who could drank them & those who couldn't threw them away – then in the same pot we made a claret punch which set us on our legs & then we groped about with matches & collected the plates & silver spoons etc & got home as quickly as possible with our teeth chattering – the men of course were rowing & were all right but 2 motor coats & a rug hardly kept the cold out of me. No more picnics till next Mid-Summer Day!

Thank you so much dear for offering to lend me money. . . . I am all right, my expenses are not great & one never spends anything except at the paint shop. But if I am in need of any money I will cable through the Bank. Suppose I settle on the code word "POST" that will mean that I am hard up & [in] need of money – but all this I hope won't happen . . . . I wont stay in Europe & starve dear – dont be frightened. . . .

[152] To Rachel Hodgkins, 5 September 1907

Pennock's Hotel. Sept 5th.

My darling Mother
. . . . Since my last letter to you I have paid a little flying visit to a small village called Overschie not very far from here & reached by a canal steamer. I have been feeling rather tired & headachy & I thought a few days change of scene would put strength into me for the rest of the Autumn – one gets a trifle stale staying a summer through in one place though in every other way it is a very wise & good thing to do – better for one's work certainly. . . . The Hotel got so full of noisy Americans I thought it would be a lovely thing to find some quiet spot where the ubiquitous Yank had never set foot – for you never find them off the beaten track – so Miss Winthrop & I escorted by our faithful friend and ally Mr Bryce set out one morning in a canal boat on a voyage of discovery & before very long we came to Overschie a quaintish little place with a good supply of windmills & bridges & barges & a very agreeable sense of remoteness about it that made

[a] strong appeal to us. . . . We arranged to come back on the following day which we did making the journey a 2nd. time in the funny little canal boat. When we came to a bridge down came the funnel, the rails, the chairs on deck & finally down went we on our knees noses on the ground flat as we could make ourselves & the little boat fizzed & hissed itself under the bridge & instantly up went the funnel the rails & the chairs & not quite so automatically & gracefully up went we. . . . Three times this happened. If you ever have an uncontrollable desire to go a journey on a canal boat in Holland take my advice & go by rail instead. . . . The first night at Overschie was hardly a success – Miss Winthrop & Mr. Bryce spent a maddened night with fleas & in the morning said they had literally been chewed up by them & were indignant with me for having slept through it all. I certainly did wake up once to find Miss W. with a candle looking *in* the bed & *under* the bed & round the room generally for the offending insect & I got up & with great swiftness caught the nimble one on a piece of soap & went back to bed & as I thought making it quite comfortable for the poor afflicted lady. At breakfast Miss Winthrop red-eyed & severe said she would have to return to Dordrecht but I persuaded her to give it one more chance & sent Mr Bryce off to the village chemist to buy up stores of insect powder & then went out & did the best sketch of the season – which was pleasant for me of course but hardly so soothing to my smarting friends. Fortunately it was glorious weather & we were able to be out of doors all day & by the time we got back to the Hotel in the evening we were so tired that we were able to sleep without much disturbance – not that I was troubled the whole time but poor Miss Winthrop suffered a good deal. English ladies are so sensitive & I sometimes feel the superiority of a hardy Colonial over these gently nurtured dames. . . . I am sending a few things out to N.Z. for the Dunedin show in November. I believe I will send them straight to Dr. Scott to get framed for me as time is short . . . .

[153] To Rachel Hodgkins, c.8 September 1907

Pennock's. Sunday.

My darling Mother

Since my letter a few days ago I have heard from Mr Paterson of the safe arrival of the Rembrandt. He says he is almost certain it is genuine though it has unfortunately been scrubbed & cleaned to death by someone which has greatly injured it & lessened its value. This of course was not done by any of us – it must have happened in a previous existence before it fell into Father's hands. Dealer-like he depreciates its value – thats their little game. . . . Thank dear old Bert for seeing about it for me – I hope something will come of it – I sold a £5 picture this morning to a departing tourist & what with my teaching fees I am quite in funds. I am also feeling particularly bolstered up at having weened one of Ludovici's

PLATE 4: *The Green Urn*, 1933, oil, 630 x 540 mm, Private Collection.

PLATE 5: *Double Portrait No. 2 (Katharine and Anthony West)*, 1937, oil, 695 x 1588 mm, The Museum of New Zealand Te Papa Tongarewa, Wellington.

pupils away for some future time. Ludovici, the great Ludovici friend of Whistler, who paints bad little pictures & has a huge following of adoring Ladies!! It will not break him. This particular girl saw me painting & asked if I would give her lessons – not this year – but some other time. . . . The Editor of the local paper is reported to have said that there were 42 ladies making pictures of Dordrecht but only one artist. Modesty forbids me mentioning names. . . .

I will write again when I have more to tell you of the Rembrandt. Fancy Rembrandt across all these ages being such a factor in my destiny & Fate. That little picture that he knocked off sometime in 1600 to play a part in the fortunes of a worshipful little admirer 200 years later.

[154] To Rachel Hodgkins, 20 September 1907

Hotel Pennock, Dordrecht. Sept 20th.

My darling Mother

Was there ever such a vale of tears? Wasn't I babbling last letter of the joys of life & how much I was enjoying the late Indian Summer of my youth so to speak and such like vanities & now here I am down with an attack of that vulgar & sorry complaint shingles. Do you know it? extremely painful & uncomfortable. I feel as if I had boiling oil & melted lead poured in me and over me & my poor body is one hot burn . . . though I am easier today & on the sofa & the doctor says I'm on the mend – he says it has been a rather virulent attack how come about I dont know, for I was feeling so particularly fit just before. . . . Dont be anxious about me dear – it is not the least serious – only very painful and uncomfortable . . . . Fortunately for me there are staying in the hotel two kind & charming English-women one of them a nurse who was out in S. Africa as head of a big nursing hospital – and she has been mothering me in the most angel kind way. She and her sister are taller than the tallest lamp-lighter and if I were up, which I'm not, I should look very much like a small pea does beside a French bean . . . . They are pupils of Ludovici the Great – and next year they intend coming to me – but I have stipulated I can only teach them on condition that they take their lessons lying down. They are extremely nice looking & would make a good Sargent portrait. . . . Mr. Moll came back last night from the Hague with the cheering news that I had 2 pictures hung in the big Show at Amsterdam. This is really very good news & quite the best thing that has happened to me artistically for a long while. The Show is one of a certain international importance & men all send their best. . . . so do rejoice with me over this Mother dear – I think Will had better put this in the paper if he will. They have also hung 2 of my things at the Walker Art Gallery in Liverpool which isnt to be despised. If only a sale or two would appear on the horizon. . . . Nothing more has been settled about the Rembrandt . . . . Christie of course would value it for me – & it might go for [a] song or it might fetch £1000 but if they condemn it as spurious then it is a marked & valueless picture for the market & you can never hope to realise a penny on it. . . . Mr. Paterson says I can show it to anyone I like. He is quite generous & honest about it I think – but how can a simple artist woman probe the workings of a cunning dealer's mind?. . . I had a letter this morning from Mr. Lindner saying he would be here next week. Everyone has been so good to me. I have 3 bowls of beautiful roses & my room is quite gay & enough peaches & grapes to stock a stall. . . .

[155] To Rachel Hodgkins, c.30 September 1907

Pennock's Hotel.

My darling Mother
    . . . . I am much better I am thankful to say . . . . I feel heart-broken when I think of the past 3 weeks of glorious weather wasted on the sofa. . . . It is still a painful affair to get my clothes on & off and effort of any kind is a burden. Dear kind Grace Nickalls is with me for 4 days – she cannot stay longer as her Mother is ill & wants her but she is coming back in a fortnight by which time I, too, hope to be up & about and all right again. . . . Grace arrived early one morning & walked in with the breakfast tray – it was a good sight to see her kind strong face – she is one of the sort to lean upon & so full of cheer – she bristled with safety pins & ointments of which I was very glad. She is now sketching out of the window with the Black Cat purring beside her. I have a cat in every port but this particular cat has qualities of a very endearing nature. Like Kitchener[7] it talks continuously and is a warrior where dogs are concerned. . . .

[156] To Rachel Hodgkins, 8 October 1907

Overschie. Oct 8th. 1907

My darling Mother
    . . . . Gertrude Crompton arrived just 2 days after Grace left me & then, after giving her time to recover from the journey I whisked her off here. . . . This time we have come to a more comfortable hotel – a tea garden it really is – a large thin house made of papier maché, very much maché since the rain has come on, & inhabited by the biggest spiders I have ever seen in or out of New Zealand. . . . Thanlow the Norwegian painter often came here. Have I forgotten to mention that Mr Moffat Lindner & Mr Moll are here with us. It is most unfortunate. Every day it has rained – heavy stormy rain & cold as winter – we meant to do

[7] Mrs Hodgkins's cat, named for the hero of the South African War.

such great things – but we have only played Patience & knocked billiard balls about & guessed Limericks & gone for damp walks & as best we could tried to pass the time innocently & happily, but it has been hard work. We all keep an eye on the great man (which is Moffat) to see how he is taking it & we all play up to him for all we are worth. He & Mr. Moll are very fond of each other & the latter . . . is an excellent mimic & has a graphic way of saying & doing things that never lets one get dull. I am sorry for poor Gertrude who has only come for a fortnight & wants to get some work for winter consumption. . . .

There goes the sun – the first we have seen of him for days – the fields look as if the flood had just subsided & left all manner of teeming animal life behind it – cows & cows & cows – hundreds of them & sheep grazing in fields ever so far below the level of the canals . . . . I must go out and paint a windmill. . . .

[157] To Rachel Hodgkins, 20 October 1907

Pennocks Hotel, Dort. Oct 20th.

My darling Mother

. . . . Since my last letter from Overschie I have decided to go back to England with Maud Nickalls for a fortnight & while there I shall try & come to some arrangement about the Rembrandt . . . . Then I shall come back here & settle down for the winter & get something big & important ready for the R.A. I believe I shall paint in oils[8]. . . .

Mr Lindner has gone back to England. . . . He taught me to play a mightily interesting game called Miss Milligan – I have always thought Patience players were a poor lot of people but I now see my mistake – it is an enormous rest to ones painting nerves. . . . Today is as wet as yesterday was beautiful & warm – it was real summer & in the afternoon Mr Moll drove us to a place called Willemsdorp. It took 3 hours along a long straight road lined on either side with dotted silver rows of willows. . . . We passed woolly flocks of sheep browsing along the dykes & there were always mills to be seen on the sky line – dykes & willows & spotted cows & mills make up the sum of Holland – you have the big elemental sense of Nature & the eternal repetition of the work of man rolled in to one fine whole. . . .

[Postscript] Oh do tell me what the inhabitants of a Dominion call themselves. Am I a Domino or just a plain Dominican? It is a point I would like settled –

---

[8] The first mention of a desire to enlarge the scope of her work. If she did use oils while in Holland, the paintings have not survived.

[158] To Rachel Hodgkins, 27 October 1907

Hotel Pennock, Dordrecht. Oct 27th.

My darling Mother,

There have been many cold winds and not many glints of sunshine since my last letter . . . . Maud is a stout hearted woman & isnt dismayed by an East wind if she wants to get a sketch but I am cottered up into knots of blue misery & prefer having a model indoors beside a nice stuffy warm stove. . . . I hate the winter coming on – if I could find some nice cosy hole somewhere lined with fur I would creep into [it] & hybernate. I had a real treat this morning, a nice long letter from you & a merry little one from Miss Richmond – oh what a wicked indiscreet little Mother you are letting her have my silly old letters which she reads to her family & the Von Haasts & God only knows who else – such tin-pot letters written in my light minded moments must be kept strictly in the family. You are really *very* naughty. You alarm me dreadfully when you talk of influenza – what will I do if you go and get it. . . . *do do* be careful and dont run risks or get cold. My poor old Kitchener – I was very fond of the little grey boy and I dropped a few tears in to my egg as I read of his death at breakfast. . . .

You needn't be anxious about my Dutch friend even though his engagement has been broken off and I am certainly not surprised. His heart is not broken whatever hers may be – but I am sorry, there is always one who cares, he is too good a fellow to treat a girl badly. His mother came over from the Hague a few weeks ago anxious to see what her dear son was up to . . . . He brought her to dine at the Hotel, a solid kind faced old Dutch lady very dignified & calm – rather like Rembrandt's Mrs. Bas. I sat between them & looked prodigious small I'll be bound – though I vastly enjoyed the situation & looked as innocent as I knew how. . . . The good lady departed I think quite satisfied in her mind that I was no globe-trotting adventuress anxious to entrap her son but a very homely little artist woman whose hair shows signs of turning grey – not in the least dangerous. Now you know the whole situation & when I tell you he is 5 years my junior & that neither of us is at all likely to forget that no matter how much we may be attracted by each others painting. He is extremely clever & has a future before him – and so I hope have I – but it must be alone. A woman has no future otherwise. . . . The International[9] is coming on in Nov: & I am going to have a shy at it. It is the great show in London for artists. I have quite a lot of pictures at different shows in England, all invitations & no expenses. It all helps. . . .
[Postscript] They have sent me a cup for the 1st Prize – what rot! Why couldn't they have sold one of my pictures & given the cup to someone else –

---

[9] The International Society of Sculptors, Painters and Gravers was founded in 1898 to challenge the conservatism of the Royal Academy and draw attention to contemporary foreign art. Its first president was Whistler and works by Degas, Monet, Manet and Renoir were shown at the first exhibition. FH became a regular exhibitor between 1910 and 1919.

[159] To Rachel Hodgkins, 22 November 1907
20 Lunham Rd, Upper Norwood. Nov 22

My darling Mother

. . . . I have been in England a week – a week of fogs . . . London is a city of Dreadful Night & one just gropes about in a helpless sort of way & keeps underground as much as possible in order to get anywhere. . . . I have been mainly occupied looking at pictures by what light there is, with Mr Morley Fletcher for Wellington. I will be most truly thankful when this business is through – the money is nearly all spent now[10]. . . . The Spences are all as usual – very well . . . . Effie is very busy doing good deeds from morning till night & very much given up to the Church – the house is strewn with Catholic Times & Tablets & similar signs of her recent conversion – or perversion – the family are quite cheerful about [it] & they really love her so much that if she chose to become a Parsee or a Hindoo they would not much mind provided she stayed at home & bullied them all in her kind & motherly way. . . . I am going to stay 2 nights with Gertrude next week & then go down to Wispers – I am feeling rather too shabby for polite society – ones clothes do not last for ever & I *detest* looking impecunious. Its the worst form of policy I know especially when one has business to transact, so the sooner I get back to my oldfashioned little Dordrecht the better for me though I will not stay there any longer than needs be. . . .

[160] To Rachel Hodgkins, 29 November 1907
Thriplands, Kensington Court, W. Nov: 29th

My darling Mother

A nice letter came from you this morning telling me you were well which is the best of all news to me. . . . I am so glad Bert is getting so much exercise and enjoying life once more. . . . I have been leading the life of a harried toad this last week flying about London in the fog & mud & carefully considering all the likely pictures that are under consideration for Wellington. . . . I wish it were a little more easy to sell my own pictures or even Rembrandts. I have had no luck at all at all! You seem to be right about it after all . . . . Mr. Paterson says my Rembrandt is of no value – Sir Charles Holroyd the Keeper of the National Gallery says the

[10] For the New Zealand Academy collection, FH and her friends bought works by: Robert Anning Bell, Frank Brangwyn, Lamorna Birch, Joseph Crawhall, Elizabeth Stanhope Forbes, Frederick Hall, Harold Knight, Laura Knight, Moffat Lindner, Frederick Mayor, H. I. Norris, James Paterson, Bertram Priestman, Charles Sims and Philip Wilson Steer. 'What was bought was a fine collection by the standards of any British influenced art gallery of the time' (Jane Vial, *National Art Gallery Newsletter*, 1/1989). Since the choice of pictures reflects FH's attitudes in 1907 it is worth noting that there was no thought of buying the work of contemporary French artists.

same thing . . . . The gods are all against me. . . . Its only a fool who might buy
it. Lord send me a rich fat fool – thy servant badly needeth one. My only asset
after all must be my own sketches & my brains such as they be. Paterson has my
drawings at his place in Bond St now & thinks well of them . . . .

[161] To Rachel Hodgkins, 5 December 1907
Wispers, Stedham. 5th. Dec

My darling Mother
   . . . . To flop into a big family after having lived a celibate's life so long is no
easy thing & at times life seems a little beyond one. These gay Nickalls have all
such merry wits I feel a dull dog beside them . . . . They are fearfully good to me
& pet me & utterly spoil me for the sparse & frugal life that awaits me in Holland.
Fires in one's bedroom hot baths, high living & other little indulgences are not
good training for the likes of me – I fly from these voluptuous pleasures next week
before my liver gets too disordered & turgid (this may not be quite the right word
but let it pass) Let me see what news have I? My heart is lighter by several pounds
since my last letter – and at the same time my pocket is heavier by the same. Mr
Paterson to the rescue – Best of men & most astute of Dealers. He has bought 2
of my largest pictures. I did not put a very stiff price on them remembering past
kindnesses £30 for the two but it is quite a tidy little sum & will keep the wolf
at bay for some time to come. So you see my prayer has been answered – "Oh!
Lord if you can't sell my Rembrandt for me at least sell thy servants unworthy
little water colours". . . . Life is full of knocks & blows – For example – A rich man
from Park Lane who owns a fine collection of pictures saw my sketches the other
day . . . & said he would like to buy two. His wife however must be consulted.
His wife *was* consulted. Damn her! She said he had more pictures than he could
possibly hang or words to that effect. He had probably stacks of them under his
bed . . . so what difference could one or two more have made to him – but oh the
difference was to me! Did I tell you about the cup & how I "popped" it? I mean
the cup the Australian ladies presented me. When I saw it my first idea was how
to get rid of such a common & ugly thing. . . . It had no inscription, nor yet any
diploma sent me – just a dirty p.c. asking for a receipt of same – gracious wasn't
it? I took it to a silversmith who gave me £2.10 for it & asked no questions & I
went out from thence thinking myself a jolly smart woman – I beg of you not to
mention this to anyone. . . . Yesterday, being one of the worst days of the year,
the Nickalls family said Let us go to town. It takes ¾ of an hour to drive to the
station, & 2 hours from the station up to London. Before we had any chance of
getting into the train the engine broke down just before it arrived at Stedham –
& for 2 long icy hours we waited for it . . . . At last it came on & 3 famished &
shivering creatures crawled into it. The sleet was coming down & the wind was

blasting & as we neared London the fog was like greasy potage. Oh! we were miserable – Grace got a taximeter at the station, which is the latest thing in motor cabs . . . quite cutting the cabbie's throats. This bore us to a restaurant where we satisfied the inner woman & then we tore off again in another taximeter to Daly's Theatre where "The Merry Widow" is holding high revel. It was one long scream of fun & the music most taking. If I had my own way in such matters I would go to a Theatre 365 times every year. . . .

There is only just time to lick the envelope if I am to catch this post. It is cold, cold, and I am colder than any frog sitting at the bottom of a damp & muddy pond

Your Frozen Frances

[162] To Rachel Hodgkins, 19 December 1907

Pennock's, Dordrecht. Dec 19th. 07

My darling Mother

. . . . The kind Nickalls wanted to keep me over Xmas but I couldn't muster courage to face a rollicking family party of I dont know how many sisters & brothers & respective progenies – I can barely keep up with them in their quietest moments I am certain I haven't sufficient dynamic force to see me through a Christmas orgie. . . . I should want to be under the sofa all the time or up a tall tree . . . .

. . . . Did I tell you I painted a portrait of Maud & Una at Wispers – in evening dress pale mauve & blue, in the window seat by lamp light & faintest moonlight – a very good thing I say & Mr. Paterson says ditto & advises me to send it to the International which I have done. I think, when Christmas expenses are over that the Nickalls would like to buy it. I left Wispers early last Friday morning before it was light & had a frozen drive to the station. I had a terrific day in town & did a multi-million different things including lunch with Miss Winthrop & tea with Mr Paterson & finally flopped on to Gertrude Cromptons bed at 5.30 & vowed I wouldn't cross to Holland that dirty night for all the powers on earth. I slept myself into a more courageous frame of mind and at 8.45 after a hot bath & a comforting dinner I set off for my train – teeming rain – cats & dogs . . . . Lo at Queenboro' at 11 o'clock I found it cleared & starry & every sign of a fair crossing . . . . It was so smooth I slept & dreamed sweetly that I was the consort of the King of Spain & could hardly realise it when I heard a whisper in my royal ear that it was 4 30 & time to get up & wash . . . . I got through the customs, drank a scalding cup of coffee & snuggled into the train, which I seemed to have to myself & turned on the warm pipes & settled down to thaw & incidentally to sleep if I could be certain that old Fischer would haul me out of the carriage at Dordrecht in case of not waking up in time. It was sleeting & hailing & the whole of Holland seemed under water. Fischer was there, large, red, important like a German crown Prince (but not always perhaps quite as sober) & the tribulations of the night were over . . . . What ever do you mean by burning down our beautiful Parliament Buildings the one architectural beauty of Wellington. This will upset the Parliamentary dovecot pretty badly. You are all breathing prayers of thankfulness that the Assembly Library has been saved – *that* would have been irreparable. . . . I am full of heart just at present with my bank account in a little more secure condition. We must see what the next Spring will bring. . . . I have two large rooms, a Studio & a bedroom & stove to keep me warm & I hope to get through a lot of work – though of course it will be frightfully dull – Gertrude is going to try & come over after Xmas some time – in the meantime there is always Mr. Moll to talk to when I am tired of my own society & there's the black cat whom I converse with a good deal during the day & also an English speaking Dutch lady is going to call on me & there are the 2 talkative green parrots downstairs always keen on a chat – so it will be my own fault if I'm lonely. . . . I am going out for a walk now for my health's sake. I wish I had you here – one has to keep moving this snappy weather to keep one's blood a-jigging. The frost this morning was as thick as any snow & the boats in the canals, packed away for the winter, looked beautiful. . . .

[163] To Rachel Hodgkins, 29 December 1907

Pennocks, Dordrecht. Dec 29th

My darling Mother

Christmas is passed and I know you thought of me as often as I thought of you. . . . It is impossible not to feel pensive and lonely at such a time and I did both . . . .

The principal thing about my Christmas was the presents. What did you get in your stocking? the usual thing? the latest novel and a bottle of old Scotch? both to be eked out as long as possible. I had as many things as ever came out of a bran pie. The Swan pen with which I am writing is one of them. He is not quite broken in yet . . . but I know he is going to be a trusty little friend to me. Largest and warmest and most useful and most welcome was a full length fur lined coat from the Nickalls – this they gave me while I was in England. It is a boon & a blessing – and I defy the coldest wind in Dordrecht to get through me. It is a coat that one might die in and not be ashamed. Perhaps I shall wear it like a Russian moujik does his sheepskin until the day of his death when it is cut off him. They also ministered unto my inward needs by sending me a hamper with a cake & biscuits & other goodies & by the same post came a little volume of Plato from my more spiritual minded Gertrude who no doubt was warned in a dream of wanton excesses and thought a little purging of the Soul might be in season. And from Mr

Paterson I had a little antique silver hair ornament that looked as if it might have been picked up at the seige of Troy – and from Mr. Garstin the first fruits of a woodcut. From the kind people in the hotel I got quite a crowd of small offerings – mostly things to put in my mouth. . . . I thought we were going to have a white Xmas. It was so piercingly cold the day before but it was not till Xmas night that the snow came down. It was wonderfully beautiful – Dordrecht was like a new world and I was glad I had stayed on to see the snow. It was quite a new experience, a northern winter. The canals all froze over & the children brought out their little sledges & everybody went about muffled up in furs. The Dutch people in winter are much more picturesque than in summer – curiously it didnt feel very cold, only when the wind caught you & then it was like a surgical operation without chloroform and you were afraid to blow your nose for fear of it breaking off. . . . I have been painting furiously out of the window & get some funny things. One big sketch I am rather pleased with. I dont really think it is any colder than the South of France in spite of the snow. The rooms are so much warmer and indoors it is possible to keep warm which never seemed the case in either France or Italy. There are one or two artists in the Hotel . . . . A large Frenchman a mountain of a man, came down with the first snow flake & has been spending his days coming in & going out, muffled up like Nansen, making rapid sketches. . . . I have been having two little girlies staying in the hotel for models – sitting on the floor playing with dolls – rather nice little persons & tomorrow a Dutch mother and her baby are coming to sit for me. Here I am half way through my letter and I have never thanked you for that very acceptable £5 that arrived . . . most opportunely on Xmas morning. It was thoughtful & kind of you dear to send it me . . . . Don't worry about my funds – things always right themselves somehow – though I sometimes come rather too close up to the edge of my last penny. . . . I am living far more cheaply here with more comfort than I could anywhere else. . . . it is lonely of course but I am not sure that it does not help to make my work realise itself better. Everybody thinks my work has made strides this year – I *have* slogged. I do want to make all these years worth while and make you all proud of me. . . . It is such a joy to me to get your letters & hear that you are well & all about the children. How they have stretched out. Girlie's legs make me green with envy. And such clever capable hands I can see even in the small photograph. The enfant George [Peter] looks like a small imp of mischief very cuddlesome & sweet. . . .

[164] To Rachel Hodgkins, February 1908

Pennock's Hotel, Dordt.

My darling Mother

This isn't a tear to raise your sympathy – it is a drop of orange juice that has sourly squirted over my paper –

I am feeling rather slipped up and ill used this morning & not in the best of moods to write a cheerful letter. You remember my telling you of a commission I had from Mr. Heywood of Manchester – I was rather counting on this as I had every right to, and only posted off some sketches and awaited results, which were not long in coming. Yesterday I had a p.c to say he liked the sketches immensely and would make up his mind which he would keep & send me a check. A blessed night of anticipation – at least £15 and an easy mind for a month or so – counting chickens! This morning came a note to say he had kept one small one £3 – the smallest & cheapest – and perhaps later I would send some more and he would give himself the pleasure – etc etc. Most beastly fraud – it was hardly worth the trouble & expense of sending. He wrote in such a lordly patron's way – to come down to this – after especially asking me to send a certain sketch – Said he would keep it and another – Bah! it makes me furious. He is a wealthy old batchelor who lives with his Mother and I always notice when there is a woman in the case they invariably advise their husbands or sons *not* to buy pictures – I can hear this old dame saying – No dear dont get any, or only keep the little one, they are *so* impressionistic. Everything they dont understand is put down to impressionism. If he didnt send me papers (for which I am always thankful) twice a week I would like to send his dirty old cheque back. Moral never put in a cheap picture if you want to sell the others. Truly life is a most perplexing & difficult affair. By the time you have made a living there is no more life to live. I know your answer to this. Come back but if I come back now it means turning my back on all my chances. I will come back if you really want me and feel the need of me if you are lonely. Dont think for a moment that I forget that you are very often alone I am too lonely myself not to know how forlorn one can feel at times, but as long as you are well and happy I feel I have the heart and courage to go on with the fight. I shall have my sketches ready by the end of the week to post. I will write directions to Butler about them. I want the cheapest of frames and I dont care what you sell them for – only sell – I think the small ones ought to go if you put reasonable prices on them. Do you think you can arrange this for me – to let me borrow from you either £15 or £20 till some of them sell. I have only £8 in the bank now and nothing coming in and in March I shall want to advertise for pupils and after that it should be quite smooth sailing. You must pay yourself back from the pictures ticklish security I hear you saying – but I think you will make £20 out of them at least which is not saying much. I loathe and hate having to ask you for this dear but if I didnt write it down now I wouldn't sleep either tonight or any other night for worrying. The Rembrandt has been a disappointment – I am going to have a last try on Friday & see what can be done at the Hague – but I wont get a twopenny offer for it I fear in its present state –

Get Bert to arrange with the Bank N.S Wales to *cable* the money & not to send it by draft. . . .

[165] To Rachel Hodgkins, 11 February 1908

Dordrecht. Feb 11th. 1908

My darling Mother

I was much cheered to get a bright letter from you this morning . . . . I also had letters from Girlie & Ba which I greatly enjoyed. . . . They are dear children & I wish I wasn't missing so much of their childhood – I hope they may never grow into artists but marry young & happily & only know enough about art to appreciate their mother's & their grandfathers & their aunties pictures. No woman can be an artist happily unless she has £100 a year to live on. As my wise friend Gertrude says nearly 75% of the clever people of this world have endured poverty & hardship but a woman comes through bad times less easily than a man if that ugly parasite, nerves, settle upon one then it is all up with her. I cant believe that I shall be so continuously unlucky in selling my pictures. . . .

I can't reproach myself that it is through slackness or want of energy on my part – times are just dam bad. I know you will help me willingly dear till I get things going again so I am not ashamed to ask you for a small loan. I know you know I have tried my best – I told you in my last letter of the mean behaviour of the Manchester man – dastardly bastardly behaviour – his conscience evidently pricked him painfully for he wrote again to say he thought he would like another sketch for £5. This will keep me going till your £5 you sent at Xmas arrives. . . . Six sketches have already been posted to Will's care & I am sending a few more larger ones this week. I can't afford to part with the best & most important as they are wanted for London shows. I have just posted 3 large ones to Taylor for various shows. It is quite useless sending out any of the pictures I had in my show – they would not sell. . . . I am now putting my energies into something for the Salon which comes on in March. Miss Richmond tells me that Miss Stoddart used a very cheap & effective frame for her sketches – ask Sis if she can spare the time to consult with Richmond about it. I particularly want *white* mounts. I hope for your sake dear, they will sell & that you will recover your loan quickly. Wait till all the pictures arrive before showing them. . . . It is such a long time since I have sold anything that I have lost confidence in my work. Sis will know best how to frame the big ones – white mounts & narrow gold frames are very popular in England just now & I think it is the best thing for water colours which are not heavy in tone. Anyway I leave it to you – only get the cheapest & best you can. It is most lovely warm spring weather here – quite unusual for February. . . . There has been a lovely pink barge in the canal in front of my window & I have been painting it. I sent Pete, the waiter, over to find out how long it was going to remain & to tell the Captain I was painting it & to stop as long as he conveniently could. The Captain, much pleased, ran up a little Dutch flag & saluted me at the window. . . . I haven't been to the Hague yet. Mr Moll has been in & now he is waiting to hear from a man he is going to consult about the Rembrandt – we may go tomorrow. . . .

[Postscript] So the boys are going to a boarding school. Hurrah! how splendid – it will be *so* good for them & good for Sis too. . . .

The visit to The Hague confirmed that the Rembrandt was worthless. In February 1908 FH found 'a good subject in the sewing room' at the Orphan House and early in March sent the picture off to the Paris Salon. It was not accepted.

[166] To Rachel Hodgkins, 10 March 1908

Dordrecht. March 10th. 1908

My dearest Mother

I have very little news for you this week – it has been wet & cold & I have spent most of my time indoors or at the orphanage painting. Mr Garstin forwarded a letter this morning from Dr. Fell very full of thanks & delight at the pictures – alas there will be no bonus for us much as we deserve or desire it . . . I had notice yesterday that the Society of Women Artists have elected me an Associate. I am quite pleased at this as it all shows recognition & that I am not standing still – it has increased my expenses by 30/- per annum but one must pay for these little honours. I am hard at it for the R.A & 2 or 3 other Spring Shows. I hope I shall have luck. I would like some nice Spring clothes there is always a tingling in one's blood at this time of the year for a new dress hat & boots. I am longing to be out sketching again they say March has 5 days of summer – yesterday I thought was one of them . . . I took my things & went across the river where I saw some beautiful boats – the clouds were glorious, stupendous piles of them. I said the Spring has come . . . I will paint a beautiful sketch to commemorate the glad event – how happy I am & how beautiful everything is etc etc. Down I sat – a tug came & took away the boats – rude Boreas began to blow from the East – the clouds vanished & over everything a yellow grey mist settled & before I quite grasped the situation I was in a snowstorm & before I could reach shelter was white from head to foot – such is the treachery of March in Holland. . . .

[167] To Rachel Hodgkins, 8 April 1908

Veere, Zeeland. April 8th. 1908

My darling Mother

I am now at Veere & have been here for 3 days. I think it is going to repay me as there are lots of models all willing to be painted and quite one half of the people wear costume. . . .

. . . . [Veere is] really rather an absurd little town. It was originally intended to be a very large town as the Cathedral & Town Hall indicate but all that there is of it now is a handful of tiny redroofed houses cuddling round the Cathedral. There is a minute harbour & a dozen or so fishing boats & for the rest it is as dead a little townlet as ever you could see. . . . I have been taken round to some of the farmhouses & cottages by my landladys daughter and now I have as many models as my heart can desire. This morning I was out by 8 to paint a churning scene – none of your ugly modern churns but a large blue barrel with a piston like arrangement that the women moved up & down for an hour without once stopping. . . .

This morning I got an invitation to compete for a £50 prize in connection with this British-Franco Exhibition shortly to be held in London.[11] The competition is for Australian womens work, the same people who awarded me the cup, so I may have a chance of winning this. I hope so – in fact I *must*. I have written off to Taylor to send in my very best picture available – what a spree it would be if I won it. . . .

[168] To Rachel Hodgkins, 14 April 1908
Nieuw Hotel Roland, Markt Veere, Veere. April 14th 1908

My darling Mother

This is your birthday and I have drunk to your health & now I am going to write you a little line – not a very long line dear, for there is really nothing to hang on it – but my love & good wishes. A welcome letter came from you this morning and a paper full of terrible bush fires. It is tragic to think of our beautiful bush being destroyed like that. Poor little scarred & blackened New Zealand – it will take a long time to recover from these dreadful burns. . . . It is a hard blow to me not selling[12] it shows how unpopular my work has become with the N.Z public – oh me! Life is not easy. Sometimes my courage goes & I wonder if I have strength or courage to carry on. It all seems so hopeless – painting ones youth away & all for a public that doesn't want you –

I have been hoping Sis would send some message about the pictures at the Art Gallery – something to show that she has a little appreciation for what we have been doing. It is from her and people with the true artistic sense that one looks for encouragement in these efforts – surely some of the pictures must appeal to her. I do so admire and respect that brave little band of enthusiasts out there, who

[11] The Franco-British Exhibition of 1908 reflected the growing alignment of France and England that had begun with the Entente Cordiale of 1903-4.
[12] The exhibition was arranged at McGregor Wright's Art Gallery.

have worked so splendidly for the interests of the Gallery. I see by yesterday's paper sent me from London that the £600 Leader has been stolen – Hurrah! What luck some galleries have. Tell me all about it in your next. . .

[169] To Rachel Hodgkins, 24 April 1908

Rijsoord. April 24th. 1908

My darling Mother

You see from the above address I have flitted from Veere and taken up my abode here. It grew so unbearably cold . . . & to the misery of cold was added the discomfort of spring cleaning in a very virulent form . . . chaos everywhere & not a corner to be quiet in so I packed up & come back to Dordt on Easter Saturday & on the Monday came over here. . . . You may remember I spent a summer here once with Miss Richmond. It is a regular artists' place. . . . The food here is excellent, very plain & plentiful . . . & there is a cosy little sitting room with a cheerful stove always burning & the kindest old Vrouv fussing round & looking after ones comfort. All this for £1 a week . . . . Models here are good & much cheaper than at Veere . . . . There are several people here – dull & worthy – 2 art students from Paris, sickly tired out looking girls rather depressing to see. Then there is a large fat party, grossly stout & plain, with rude brusque manners & a scandal loving nature, quite odious, to come in contact with in a small house where you cant get out of her road. She has been here all the winter & is by way of being an artist . . . .

. . . . Easter hens laid no good eggs for me – on the contrary I got news that my 2 pictures had been rejected by the R.A. which doesn't help to make one any prouder of oneself. The Academy is as uncertain as the weather in its favours – & if one has no friends to push & shove your work it fares badly with outsiders. Of course it is a great disappointment – but it is no good caring too much. If my pictures dont sell in Wellington after this next little show I think they had better be put up for auction – it is no use lumbering up McGregor Wrights with them. . . . I want you to tell me honestly if you want me to come back . . . . I wake every night & think that when the morning comes I must pack up & go back to you for fear you may be ill or lonely. I often hear how well you are looking & how cosy you & Bert are in the little house. How did you ever come to have such an Ishmaelite of a Daughter?

[170] To RACHEL HODGKINS, 26 MAY 1908

Pension Noorlander, Rijsoord. May 26th

My darling Mother

. . . . Your daughter has been working very hard & she was a teeny bit seedy for a few days last week & missed the mail. . . . Pupils do not roll up as quickly as I could wish. The season has started badly – the weather no doubt is to blame. . . . Mr. Garstin says despondently you must be dead before you can make a living at Art . . . . A man from Leeds where I have 2 pictures at a local Exh: writes to say he greatly admires my work & would like to possess one – would I take £15 for a £42 picture – or would I prefer to take £10 for a £25 one – it is all the same to him. Beggars cant afford to make terms & these times you must accept any paltry offer anyone likes to make you & be thankful. This is all the business that has come my way this week – I'm forgetting my first pupil – a Dutch lady – & so lovely a creature I shall never be able to do anything but look at her. She wrote from the Hague & said she wld like some lessons – I arranged to meet her in Dordt – but when the day arrived I was seedy & unable to leave my bed – she obligingly came here – into the room sailed a tall graceful black swan or heron of a creature with the prettiest of faces & loveliest manners – she was like Lydia only more so. I had been expecting a Dutch Vrouv of homely aspect & wasn't putting on any airs myself. She was quite captivating & I felt the injustice of only being a woman – oh to be a man – but I forget – I was in bed – to business. She seemed to think I was all right – & of course she didnt know what a toothache I was having in the pit of my stomach & how Spartan like I was underneath my winning smile & engaging little ways. We parted mutually pleased – but since then it has been the very divil to meet each other & now after a whole week of hide & seek we have not yet managed to have a lesson. . . .

It is such a pretty time of year now, full of blossom & wildflowers and other excitements of that kind. Today is Ascension Day, a great holiday in Europe & little Rijsoord is rather a noisy & roystering place at such a time. Keep well dear & write to me soon & love me always

Your loving Frances

[171] To RACHEL HODGKINS, 12 JUNE 1908

Rijsoord. June 12th – 08

My darling Mother

. . . . Its hard to believe you are 70 dear. . . . I shall be back with you before your next birthday . . . . I would like, if funds permit & you are still well, to have 2 or 3 months in Italy on my way back . . . . It would be a good spec to bring out some small Italian sketches & perhaps have a show in Melbourne on my way out.

. . . So far I have had a very poor start to my class – only 1 pupil, the lady from the Hague. . . . The weather was so awful last summer that people probably are "off" Holland for this year – also millions are flocking to the Franco-British Exh. which seems to be a very stupendous & marvellous affair. Gertrude tells me the French pictures are as perfect a collection as one could see – far excelling the British section in artistic excellence, arrangement, frames, colour scheme etc: What a clever old King we have to bring all the entente to pass between the two countries. I hope they will treat him kindly in Russia where he now is on a visit to the Czar. The Labour Party is furious at him for exchanging any courtesies with a "common murderer" etc etc as they call the Czar. . . .

We have had a fierce burst of intense heat – 3 days of real *hell* fire & at night an infuriated universe – I never saw such lightning – like a mailed army in battle or a sea full of green snakes. The thunder raged & rolled & roared from every corner of the sky. . . . I am expecting Gertrude over tonight for a fortnight – which will gladden my heart. It is a long time since I have had a friend with me. . . . Be sure & push on sales all you can for me. I would sell my back hair if anyone would make a bid. I shall get along for [the] present on the Leeds sale. It is rather hard luck having to take £15 for a picture that started at £42. Mr Paterson told me to hang on to it, even for 5 years, he was sure I would have a success with it – but times are too pressing & precarious & you must sell when you can.
[Postscript] Tell Bert I go fishing in the evenings – but so far have not caught anything – but then I have only been at it a week.

[172] To Rachel Hodgkins, 15 June 1908

Rijsoord. June 15th

My darling Mother
    It has been so delightful having Gertrude Crompton with me – you can't think how I appreciate a friend after the lonely winter. We have done a great deal of painting in the 8 days she has been here though the weather has not been too good (it never is quite right for artists or farmers). We have spent a lot of our time in the boat away from the rather noisy little pension & we are now writing our sundry letters to our respective Mamas in a shady little back water in among the rushes. We have brought our lunch with us & fishing rods & hooks & Puck the yellow dog & it is all very peaceful & quiet. . . . I am . . . waiting for pupils but in vain . . . . it is easy to understand if you read the lists of Sketching Classes in the Studio the wonder is that anyone gets any pupils at all – it is the straw to which so many desperate artists are clinging. . . . It is to be hoped something will sell in Auckland[13]. . . . Mr Lindner has been back in Dordt for a few days. I went

---

[13] Her paintings had been sent to the Auckland Society of Arts Exhibition.

over & had lunch with him one day & he came out here to see my work which he liked I think. He has promised me a letter to a well known London dealer which might help me along a bit. It is a drawback not being on the spot to place your work when you get the opportunity – you are apt to be overlooked & forgotten if you don't keep pegging away in your own interests. Mr Lindner told me of a new Society now being formed called the Allied Artists[14] & which he advised me to try & get into – you pay a guinea subscription & can send 5 pictures to be hung in a group & there is no jury but you are elected a member by practically paying for your wall space. It at least gives artists not in the swim a chance of having their work noticed which is something in these days when it is almost impossible to get into any Society unless you have enormous influence behind you. Mr. Lindner & a lot of good men are members & the Albert Hall has been taken for the first Exh: I unluckily applied a week too late & the lists were closed but I have joined for next year. Gertrude has finished her letter & enlivened the proceedings by catching a fish – there are only very little ones in this river, a small kind of bass & sometimes eels. . . .

. . . . Gertrude & Puck are clamouring for lunch & I am rather ravening myself. My dearest love to you all from your loving Frances.

PS I cant tell you where my Policy is. What do you want it for – I believe it is locked up with my papers in Wellington. *Be sure* & get Bert to see the AMP people about my premium. . . . we must keep it up whatever happens. It is the only thing I have to face OLD AGE with. It expires in 1912.

[173] To Dorothy Richmond, 2 July 1908

Pension Nulaander, Rijsoord. July 2nd

My dearest Dolla

Just a few lines to follow up my last rather despairing letter & to let you know that the tide has turned . . . . I think I have been tested to my utmost and this last six months has been a pretty thin time, the blackest of winters & springs. . . . It wld have been heart rending to give in just when things are in the balance. My people of course understand nothing at all about the difficulties of making a career or the uphill struggle there is for folk without money & without influence & my dear Mother clamours for my return. I have promised her I will go back next Spring, but she does not realize what it means to me but I feel I owe it to her & she is past 70 now & is beginning to feel the weight of years. It is no use

---

[14] The critic Frank Rutter organised the Allied Artists Association on the model of the French Salon des Indépendants. In the first exhibition, in July 1908, there were over 3000 exhibits. Rutter later wrote *Revolution in Art: An Introduction to the Study of Cézanne, Gauguin, Van Gogh and Other Modern Painters*, London, 1910, and *Evolution in Modern Art*, London, 1926. He was one of the first important critics to notice FH.

grieving over the inevitable & I must just make the most of the time left to me to strengthen my position as much as I can. Gertrude Crompton has been with me for a fortnight. She is a very Rock of Ages, so strong & stedfast – I had decided to go back & stay with them in Yorkshire & try & beat up a sketching class there . . . . then came the joyful news that I had won this prize at the Franco British[15] which filled my heart with new courage & I think that night, for the first time for many months I slept & waked without my pet Bogey Poverty sitting at the foot of my bed. I know quite well that I wouldn't starve, one has too many kind friends for that. It is the dangerous havoc to ones nerves that is the trouble. Dear Grace had stocked me with paper & paint at the beginning of the winter so I did not feel pinched in that quarter. . . . My Sketching Class has been an utter frost. So many big guns are teaching these days that there is small chance for the small fry. . . . My Mother begs me to go to Italy and leave this sad ugly country where there is no colour. . . . maybe I shall end up in Paris for the winter, that is if the Gods are kind & generous. I cannot face a big city with insufficient means – one must be comfortable. I should dearly love to get some oil lessons under a first rate man. That kind dry old stick Moffat has been a real trump to me & is going to introduce me to some of the right sort when I go to Town. . . . *Dont* pass this on to anyone. It cant help matters to let people know I am not prospering. . . . Thank you so much for the kind words about my piccys. You are the only one who has said a good word for them. . . .

[174] TO RACHEL HODGKINS, 6 JULY 1908

Pension Norlaander, Rijsoord. July 6th.

My darling Mother

I expect before this reaches you you will have heard of my good fortune in winning 1st. Prize at the Franco British in the Australian Section of Women's Art – or rather a ½ share in the 1st. prize. I believe if I had been an Australian I should have had the full prize . . . . This prize money has saved the day. . . . Twice I have been quite without any money to carry on . . . . My friends here cheered & sustained me throughout & had faith in me & this has kept me afloat. . . .

I must tell you the man from Leeds backed out of his bargain at the 11th. hour refusing to pay commission. I had asked him to pay the commission as the price was so greatly reduced – it was rather despicable but a sign of the times, or I am told a good example of the way they do business in Yorkshire. Anyway it left me up a tree. . . . You cant think how different I feel – the physical side of poverty, the mind acting on the body is what breaks one up. *Now* I feel I could fight an

[15] For *The Window Seat*, the painting of Maud and Una Nickalls, now in the Art Gallery of New South Wales. FH shared the prize with the Australian artist Thea Proctor.

elephant single handed. . . . I have authorized [Gertrude] to receive my award & do the polite & politic for me at the Prize giving. She has nice clothes & charming manners and will do it a great deal better than I would. I am sorry you dont like my pictures I have sent out. You must remember I cant send out the more attractive ones – it is better that they should be shown on this side. . . .

How glad I am, so very glad to be able to tell you of this good news. I know it will gladden your heart – as it did mine. Much love dearest Your loving Frances

[175] To RACHEL HODGKINS, JULY 1908

Rijsoord. July

My darling Mother
    . . . . Yes its time Madam you said something decent about your daughters pictures, your last letter cut into me a little – I daresay it came at a crisis when everything seemed pretty well stripped to the bone & nothing left over but things are right again now and I am £30 to the good and the prospect of 2 pupils coming along in August. . . . You must be in evidence & advertise your wares if you want to sell & this little mudflat where I am now is not exactly the place one wants to stay in longer than is necessary. . . . At present there is a party of Americans here, all very noisy & over dressed who were got here by mistake I think. . . . They tickle your ear for a little while with their apparent smartness but very few of them touch your heart. . . . Having finished all my work here & re-inforced with my £30 I am leaving here on Sat: . . I have been very lonely since Gertrude left and perhaps a little weary of painting. I wish I could lay down my arms for a bit & drop the fight. One's whole soul gets engrossed in the struggle. I long so passionately for success and recognition, not a cheap popularity quick to arrive & quick to vanish, but something more genuine & abiding than that, something that may yet come & place me securely & firmly on the side of the sheep & not of the goats! . . .
    . . . . In my next letter I hope to have more to tell – I have been leading the life of a hermit crab for so long I feel my wits are much in need of a little burnishing.

[176] To RACHEL HODGKINS, 29 JULY 1908

English Pension, Laren, N. Holland. July 29th.

My darling Mother
    Behold I have jumped from the South to the North of Holland . . . . this is a dry sandy Holland without waterways & windmills & just now very parched & hot. I dont find it half so picturesque as some of the places I have been in – but it all depends on what you are after. Here the boers houses, large barns, cavernous

& dark where the cows & the horses & dogs & the winter fodder & the man & his wife & his family all live together under one large thatched roof. If you remember Israel's & Van der Velden's pictures you will get a very true idea of a North Holland interior. Artists have been coming here for many years, ever since Mauve lived & painted & died here 40 years ago.[16] Nearly every farmhouse has an artist in it either painting in it or hiring a room where he sleeps & works for the summer months.

The simple primitive charm of the place however is fast disappearing & the rich people from Amsterdam have found out that the air here is bracing & fresh & they have come along with their ugly villas & hotels & all the other sinful outrages of Arcady . . . & the artist is wrath & sore & presently will trek off elsewhere in search of some unspoilt corner he can call his own. . . . Artists do not destroy & knock down & build up in sacrilegious fashion – this is a terribly hideous & progressive age & soon there will be a dead level of vulgar smugness over the land & one place will be exactly like another. . . . It would have been less lonely and more comfortable for me if I had come here for the winter but I did not know about it in time. I imagined myself the only English woman in Holland & never dreamed of a little colony up here in the wilds. . . . The peasants charge 1 franc (10d) to paint in their houses either for a morning or an afternoon. Landscapists have the best of it after all in this respect – Nature levies no toll. . . . There is an Australian lady artist living in one of the farms, who has been here for 10 years (and looks it) she comes here for meals & is an odd piece of humanity in a rugged uncouth way. I was entertained at overhearing a conversation about me through the window – unknown voice outside – "Whats her name?" 2nd ditto "I dont know but she comes from NZ." "But she has no accent!" "Oh! but they dont have accents now-a-days" ! ! . . .

[177] To Rachel Hodgkins, 12 August 1908

Laren, N. Holland. Aug 12th.

My darling Mother

. . . . It is rather a staggerer to hear I have £32 to pay on my insurance. I dont know where it is coming from. Heaven help poor Frances. . . . If the auction is successful, better pay this debt off or at any rate part of it. It is a bad business having an auction it looks so like failure & bankruptcy – but Hélas what can one

---

[16] Jozef Israëls (1824-1911) was called 'the Dutch Millet' because he painted humble people, peasants and fishermen, and their environment. He was a member of the Hague School, the Dutch equivalent of the Barbizon School, dedicated to painting direct from nature. Petrus Van der Velden was associated with this group of Dutch artists, which included the three Maris brothers and Anton Mauve, all of whom FH cited in 1913, along with Arthur Melville, as watercolourists from whom she had learned a great deal. (See Letter 72)

do. Dont press me to come back till I have had another try in London dear theres a small stubborn dogged voice somewhere deep down which tells me things will right themselves & that I may yet come into my Kingdom if I can only hang on – keep on keeping on – like the Suffragettes but the difference between them & me is great – they have funds & I have none. I am really proud of what I have done without much money . . . . I cant see that things will be much better in Wellington – I might get a teaching billet in some school, but that means death to my painting. . . . Somehow I am more hopeful about the future than I have been for a long time. . . . Whatever you do mother dear dont on any account let the impression get about that I am hard up & not prospering – remember it will spoil my chances when I come out again – tell people nothing but the bright stories. . . .

Girlie tells me she is playing diabolo[17] a lot. I do it but not very well. A female Hodgkins never played *any* game well. Yesterday, a little lady here broke the record & her nose at the same time . . . . Oh such a hot oppressive week we have had – my room faces East & the glorious orb of day wakes me much too early in the morning to please me. The peasants houses are full of fleas & flies and there is a dusty monotony about the dunes that scares you off them till the sun is down. I have found a pretty model & a baby & I take them to the pine woods & there endeavour to paint idylls – it is so hot & dry under ground & overhead that every twig & blade rattles as you pass. . . .

[178] To Rachel Hodgkins, 2 September 1908
at Tanfield House, Bedale, Yorks. Sep: 2nd

My darling Mother

Here I am safely settled at Tanfield & enjoying a little taste of home life once more. It is a very different little world to the one I have just left & one that requires quite a different set of wits – and clothes – neither of which let me add are at all adequate to the occasion. They are a very gay irresponsible merry making lot of young people & if it were not for my more staid & serious Gertrude I should bolt. Gertrude is 33 & her 2 younger sisters 24 & 26 respectively & the young brother 20 fresh from Cambridge with his two friends & they spend their days in various ways, strange & unfamiliar to me. Shooting & cricket & racquets & fishing & flirting in a gay & flippant & elegant fashion that has very little in common with the work a day serious side of life that is my lot. . . . To be in earnest or serious about anything is dull & boring – & conversation must be kept up at all costs & flippancy passes for wit more often than not. The girls are pretty with

---

[17] The game 'devil on two sticks': a double cone is tossed into the air and caught on a string attached to two sticks held in the hands.

dazzling English complexions of which we never see the like in our windblown little island. . . .

A nice thing happened the day before yesterday. Some friends of the Cromptons came to call, just at [the] time when I was showing my sketches. They showed such delightful sympathy & appreciation a *very* rare thing in this set of people – & the same evening sent a message round to Mrs Crompton to know if I sold my pictures & if so would I quote a price for the large Dutch picture of a bridge & barges. I instantly quoted £15 though it was worth twice that amount, & I believe I should have got it, but I wanted the money badly & was frightened I might lose the chance. The next morning the chauffeur arrived with the cheque & the request that the picture might be forwarded at once as they had friends coming to lunch & wished to show it them – now isnt that a very nice & prompt & princely manner in which to buy pictures. . . .

[179] To RACHEL HODGKINS, SEPTEMBER 1908

Tanfield House, Bedale, Yorkshire.

My darling Mother

. . . . Maud Nickalls has sent me a most handsome supply of new paints which always has the effect of making me rapturously greedy & happy . . . . I have lost my heart to a fine subject in the melon house – large fat green melons hanging from the roof, with the pretty little Hazel Crompton posing for me in a large hat – quite a fine thing, but a scorching hot place to do it in . . . . Yesterday a party of us made an expedition up to the moors . . . we took our lunch & trained up to the foot of the hills, then walked till we came to the purple heather, which spread for purple miles as far as the eye could reach. It was grey & misty (as it nearly always is in this little island) & I wondered what they would have thought of a little real New Zealand blue. . . . I leave here on the 17th. for Manchester & then go right down to Devon to spend a fortnight with my painting friend Miss Thorp then to the Lindners for a week end & so to London. . . . Oh! dear I meant to have written you a longer letter dearest but this is a frantic house in which to get 2 quiet minutes to yourself. . . . More on Sunday. Your loving but chivvied Frances

[180] To RACHEL HODGKINS, 15 SEPTEMBER 1908

Tanfield House, Bedale, Yorks. Sept 15th.

My darling Mother

. . . . I am so relieved to hear of another sale. I hope it is a legitimate one & no family or Richmond contrivance to raise money for me. I am eternally grateful to my dear kind Dolla for using her influence with the N.Z Academy on my behalf. . . . In two days time I shall be on my very cross country way to Manchester there to spend 4 days with the Patons. They are very artistic people with a large circle of artist friends & I thought perhaps he might be able to advise me about the possibility of having a Show of all my surplus stock now in London, in Manchester. It is more or less of an art centre & not so over done as London. . . . It is always helpful to talk over ways & means with a practical minded man who is willing to help lame dogs over stiles & give them a push into the bargain. . . . Gertrude is starting off the same day . . . to give some sketching lessons to 3 or 4 wealthy & fashionable young ladies who are much too fine & precious for their Mammas to let mix with a common herd at a Sketching Class. They pay of course, a good deal more but against this you have to take all your smartest clothes & play the part of a "real lidy" at the same time as you are doing your best to be an artist. Gertrude does it with more ease & grace than I could of course for it is her world, & they do not expect the same class of art as *I* would give them. The Cromptons are all as poor as church mice who have inherited beautiful properties with hardly a penny on which to keep them up. It is amusing to contrast Gertrudes poverty with mine – the varying degrees of the same complaint! The maid making her pretty blouses & turning her out like the Princess in the Psalms "all beautiful within" & packing for her & starting her off on her little journey equipped & a[s] pretty as a pink, unharrassed & calm! I draw a veil over my proceedings . . . one dress on tother one off & a mousetrap for odds & ends. Gertrude is thinking of having a Show of her watercolours next month in London – no doubt she will do awfully well – her work is slight & attractive, not very strong in any way but the sort of slick clever little sort of picture that attracts a certain class of buyer – people say it is modelled a good deal on mine – I dont know. She has a far better business instinct than I have & never *never* lets a chance slip by. I would like you to know her. She is a very human & loveable woman & has been a real rock of defense to me. . . .

[181] To Rachel Hodgkins, 10 October 1908

Rock Farm, Beer, S. Devon. Oct: 10th

My darling little Mother
    . . . . My plan was, you remember to be in London this week & there to try & raise the wind which wind when raised was intended to blow me over to France, first to Moret[18] for October & Nov: & then Paris for a winter's hard grind at the Studios. Beer, however has proved so attractive, that I have settled to stay on & complete my series of children. . . . I was taking my last walk last Sunday with

---

[18] A well-known sketching ground near Fontainebleau.

Miss Thorp, miserable because I had to go the next day, & hating the thought of London . . . after these tranquil times in this blessed little haven no more blackberrying, no more junkett or Devonshire cream, no more pink cheeked babies to paint. It was running away from the blessings of Providence. Miss Thorp said "Chuck it & stay, London can wait & you wont spoil your chances by adding ½ doz good sketches to your collection." So I settled to stay & felt happy again. I took train next day to the Lindners in Dorset, not very far from here, & was met at the station by the motor & whizzed 8 miles along a switchback road & in 5 jiffs was walking into the Lindners front door in a fur lined coat & a motor veil & thinking what a pity it was we had to stop – motoring spoils you for humdrum life. Art is insipid & flavourless after such sport. . . . Dear old Moffaty bought one of my pictures, a small one, but the compliment was bigger than the cheque & my heart swelled within when he said he wanted one. . . . I spent 4 days with them, & then back here to work. . . .

. . . . I never thought I should rave over anything in England but I do love this funny little place – it is 3 miles from everywhere & absurdly primitive in its habits & the villagers talk broad dialect with a rich buttery accent & mostly all of them might have come from Southern Spain so bronzed & swarthy & darkeyed are they. The Armada must have sprinkled a fair number of black eyed ruffians along this coast judging from results. . . . Since writing this last night a welcome letter from you has come & it is a great relief to my mind to have it my dear. My pleasure was rather dashed by the stupid little clipping you enclosed reporting my prize at the Franco British. Why cant people take the trouble to report things accurately? As I was fortunate enough to win the First Prize why can't they say so in plain language & at least quote the correct title of my picture – The "Window Seat" is surely not in the least like a "Water Seat" . . . . I have had so much success lately that I am feeling more hopeful of something turning up which will make it quite possible to give me another winter on this side & very possibly also to help to clear away some of that frightening insurance bill. . . . Did I tell you in my last of the offer I have had from a Manchester dealer to show some of my work there early in the year – their idea is to hold a Show of Dutch work & that I should form part of the scheme. . . . Did I mention my Franco British picture has had 2 special invitations to Leeds & Bristol. This is all my news this week I think – am working very hard & painting Beer to bits – you see I take kindly to Beer and am also getting Stout – all 'ale to you all – & adieu adieu soon to meet again I hope and I say, tell Bert to hurry up & get a motor car. I am sorry my writing is so bad . . . but life is too short & full. . . .

[182] To Rachel Hodgkins, 8 November 1908

3 Cheyne Walk, Chelsea. Nov: 8th.

My darling Mother

I have now had a whole week of London, going it hot & strong & hard, night & day & enjoying it hugely . . . . First & foremost Mr. Paterson has seen my work & likes it & it is practically certain he will show it again for me possibly 2nd. week in Dec: a good time to catch people buying Xmas presents. . . . Since my last letter I have sold a picture for £10 to a Leeds man – this & the £16 Dr. Fell has sent from NZ will go a long way to helping me through the winter. I know I shall not be able to live as cheaply in Paris as in Holland, but against this my chances are better. . . . Did I tell you I had received a special invitation to send 3 pictures to Brussells to rather a swagger water colour show there – all expenses paid – also Mr John Baillie, who is now in a most sumptuous gallery near Bond St has asked me to contribute a picture to his Children's Exhibition opening Jan: 1st. This show is to consist of pictures of babies & children & ought to be rather charming. . . . I had a wonderful day at the Franco British. The Nickalls took me bore me off at 10 o'clock in a taxicab & gave me a magnificent time. The crowd was so great that it was difficult moving about . . . . The N.Z court was small but very nice though rather apt to be overlooked. I was disappointed in the native wood exhibit – it was a very mean looking one indeed & hardly did our beautiful timber justice. It was on a revolving stand, small panels, with nothing to show it off to advantage. The Kauri Gum made a fine show – I believe the King was very much struck by the size of the trout. . . . I only got the most hurried glimpse at the pictures – but oh my dear the French dresses! they wld make an angel weep with joy & jealousy – loveliest of colours, most impossible of human figures, but so exquisite in design & colour & material that one longed to be re-created in order that one might wear such ravishing garments. How Sis wld have gloated – any artist would. Miss Richmond tells me that Sis has some *wonderfully* clever work at the Academy – she thinks that Sis & Girlie should come home & study in Paris. What fun! . . . Yesterday I found myself on the top of [a] bus beside who do you think Miss Annie Black – mutual recognition & smiles. . . . We had a long talk & I promised to go & see her if I have time & meet her husband. A funny thing happened I asked after Grace Joel & she was telling me all about her & giving me her address when I looked down & there in the street was the little lady herself – Joel all over, but much better dressed & more prosperous looking. More recognitions – she looked up & caught my eye & we waved to each other. In this great big London it really was rather odd! . . . It is bitterly cold. The distress among the unemployed is great. To think thousands are starving & homeless in the richest city in the world. . . . I'm a hot socialist when I see these wretched starving creatures – I see nothing but red when these beautiful exotic women pass in their costly motors – Its mean & cruel. I feel as though I had hardly [the] right

to wear the warm squirrell coat that Miss Winthrop has given [me]. Rags &
Velvet – that is what London is. . . .

Part Ten

1908-12

Settled in France

Frances Hodgkins arrived in Paris at a momentous time in the development of western pictorial ideas: the period between the fauve exhibitions and the advent of cubism. Her exposure to the art of Paris was eventually of great importance in the development of her painting, but her immediate purpose was to learn to paint in oils. Tantalisingly, in the letters written at this time FH was no longer listing artists seen and describing her responses as on her first arrival in London. Her paintings provide some evidence of the artists she was looking at. By about 1912, the naturalistic watercolours in the manner of the Newlyn and Dutch artists had given way to the modified French impressionism of works like Barges on the Seine, Summer *(Plate 1)*, The Convalescent. *Instead of using traditional washes FH built up her forms with long strokes of paint, sometimes laid down in dancing arabesques. In interviews given in Australia in 1913 FH described how it was the impressionism of Manet, Monet, Pissarro, Degas and Sisley that impressed her when she first arrived in Paris; later she appreciated the post-impressionists, Gauguin, Cézanne and Van Gogh; she spoke enthusiastically of Paris and its receptivity to new ideas compared to the conservatism of London. The other painters FH saw during her four years in France cannot be precisely known, but she visited galleries such as the Bernheim-Jeune where contemporary work was on show and may have become aware of Matisse, Picasso, Braque, Bonnard and the other French artists whose influence appeared later in her work. She attended the futurists' conference in 1912, was dubious about the extreme position advocated by those artists, but did not reject it: 'We have got everything from the old masters so far; we cannot go on getting it from them indefinitely. What the final result will be I cannot say. The futurists think it will end in pure abstraction, but that is so far ahead that one cannot view it with anything like seriousness.'[1]*

FH had to find an exhibiting context for herself in Paris. There were four main public salons held annually, similar in scope to the Royal Academy in London. Three of them were held in the spring, the most conservative being the salon of the Société des Artistes Français, where FH had work accepted in both 1909 and 1910. Painters influenced by impressionism chose the salon of the Société Nationale des Beaux-Arts and Hodgkins exhibited there in 1911 and 1912. She did not exhibit at the unjuried Salon des Indépendants, which had been founded by progressive artists in 1884. The juried Salon d'Automne, founded in 1903, was held, as its name implies, later in the year and placed before the public paintings made during the summer that were smaller, more experimental and less carefully worked up than those presented for the spring shows. It was not until 1924 that FH exhibited at the Salon d'Automne. As well as the salons, she built on her success of 1906 with the watercolour society, showing again with the Société Internationale d'Aquarellistes in 1910 and the more exclusive Société Internationale de la Peinture à l'Eau in 1911.

In 1912 she had the satisfaction of having two works accepted at the New English Art Club, and in 1910 and 1911 showed with the International Society of Sculptors,

---

[1] Interview in the *Mail*, Adelaide, 28 June 1913.

Painters and Gravers in London. In England during this period modern painting from France gained wider public acceptance, particularly through the two controversial exhibitions organised by Roger Fry in 1910 and 1912, for which he coined the term post-impressionist. Cézanne, Gauguin, Van Gogh, Matisse, Braque and Picasso were well represented in these exhibitions, the second of which also included, among other English artists, Duncan Grant and Vanessa Bell.

On her arrival in Paris FH settled into lodgings in the rue Vaneau on the Left Bank, near the Hôtel des Invalides.

[183] To Rachel Hodgkins, 24 November 1908

85 Rue Vaneau, Paris. Nov: 24th

My darling Mother

I am afraid it will seem a very long gap between this letter & my last. It was hopeless trying to write before I left London. . . . We had a vile crossing. I sat on deck & Miss Thorp went below & neither of us was spared. . . . [We] had settled down in comfort to enjoy a hasty meal in the train when in came a sprightly-looking young man of 20 or so of charming appearance. He appeared distressed that we should be deranged by his presence – far from it – we were enchanté etc etc – Tourjours la politesse! . . . [He] explained that he had been a page to the Russian Empress & brought up at Court, had left it to fight the Japs, & was now on his way to join the diplomatic service in Paris – how he hated the nobility & aristocrats & wished to lead his own life unhampered by family convention. . . . He gave us his card – Comte Antonin Borch – & after he had helped us with our baggage we said goodbye & the last we saw of our charming little boy he was standing in the mud, bare headed, bowing like a courtier to two dishevelled seasick weary middle aged British women. . . . The next day I spent looking at studios – the first thing I did was to run into Rosamond Marshall. She has a lovely little flat & is living like a little Princess in the greatest comfort & luxury. She wants me to spend a month with her from the 5th. Dec: to 5th Jan: – I dont know yet if I shall. Miss Thorp is a much better mate for me. She is a worker like myself & very serious about art. Rosamond is not. This pension is very nice & cheap. I have a small room at the top of the house & the sun streams in all day, when there is sun. Miss Thorp has a beautiful big room lower down where she has a fire & where we sit in the evenings. I have decided to work in a studio in the mornings & paint out-of-doors or out of windows in the afternoons. It has been gloriously fine since our arrival & we have been working in the Luxembourg Gardens. . . . I hope to get a lot of good from a winter's work here. . . .

[184] To Rachel Hodgkins, 9 December 1908

85 Rue Vaneau, Paris. Dec: 9th

My dearest Mother

No letter from you for such a long time You haven't forgotten me have you? I always feel specially in need of letters about Xmas time . . . . Did I tell you in my last that I had joined the Studio of M Beronneau[2] where I work 3½ [hours] in the morning from the nude in oils. I find it most puzzling & difficult to submit to having my work swept ruthlessly away in the same way I treat my pupils! It is quite beautiful to see him work, his strength & certainty & the delicate way his big rough hands handle the brushes & re-make a wobbly knock-kneed daub into a living breathing piece of human flesh. It will do me an enormous lot of good & I wish I had done this sort of thing years ago when I had youth & strength – it is fatiguing now & a real exertion. This pension is 20 minutes walk from the studio & this part of it is very good for my health. . . . It seems a most curious thing to find an attractive & refined little thing like Rosamond not yet 30 living alone in Paris, where such things are not generally done. Her little mother of whom she is very fond lives in St Andrews but their tastes are different – Rosamund loves Art & her mother loves gardening & they both think it is a pity to let either interfere with the other's life & as there seems to be heaps of money they can manage to do this sort of thing with comfort & pleasure.

. . . . I am painting every afternoon with R. We have the lovliest arrangement – a partially dressed model lying on a white cover against a white wall – sort of "After the Ball" idea if it turns out as nicely as it has started I am going to send it to the International in London next week. How shall I ever settle down in Wellington after Paris? Who will pose as a "nood" for me?

You will be glad to hear my little Mother of the nice commission that is coming my way shortly. The Head Mistress of St Leonards in St Andrews is retiring & it is proposed to give her a present for which the girls are subscribing – they propose to ask me for a picture. . . . How I come to be asked is through Miss Abernethy one of the House Mistresses who has 2 of my pictures. I am so pleased I feel I could jump over the moon with joy if there was one which there isnt. Likewise I have had an excellent notice from Brussells about my pictures where the paper says I have scored an artistic success with my "spirituelle washes" – I hope some of their ill gotten Congo Gold may come my way – And added to this I have sold a small picture in London for £7.7 so things are brightening I hope & soon I hope to have amassed sufficient fortune to return to N.Z & retire on my means & live happily ever afterwards with you.

Christmas is close at hand & I wish I were going to spend [it] with you all. I

[2] Pierre Marcel-Beronneau (1869-1937). The reasons for Hodgkins's choice of this teacher remain obscure, apart from her desire to avoid the 'babel and sordidness of the ordinary art school'. (Letter from Gertude Crompton of 3 December 1908.)

dont know what we shall do – Rosamond proposes we should dine with her & help eat the plum pudding her Mother has sent her. I send you on a letter from Gertrude with a description of her show. . . .

[185] TO RACHEL HODGKINS, 17 DECEMBER 1908

Paris. Dec: 17th.

My darling Mother

Only a short little line this week just to send you word that that prize of £20 I told you of last mail has fallen to my happy lot whereat I know you will rejoice with me.[3] It is an American Club, The Students Hostel, it is called & the scholarship is endowed by a rich American lady . . . . On the whole I think it was quite a smart thing of me to have done for the Americans are a clever lot & I am very proud to have one of my pictures hung in the permanent collection among some really first-class work. . . . There is no very special news from this quarter – I have been working morning & afternoon at the Studio & finishing in between times some pictures I am sending off to London tomorrow & am now feeling very tired physically but mentally much cheered & refreshed by this piece of unhoped for good luck. . . . How black it was last Xmas Tide. I nearly gave up trying! This prize is a much coveted one in the Latin Quarter among the women students & it has been so pleasant to know that everyone is unanimous about my winning it. . . .

[186] TO RACHEL HODGKINS, 27 DECEMBER 1908

85 Rue Vaneau, Paris. Dec: 27th. 08

My darling Mother

You are always specially in my thoughts at Christmas time . . . . It is hard on us both that we are separated . . . . but N.Z. will never satisfy the artist side of me I fear . . . . I am longing for a letter from you with news of the Elections & how it fares with Will. Of course he will get in again . . . . The Suffragettes are working fiercely against the Government in England & a good many seats have been lost through their influence. So many of my friends are ardent Suffragettes but on the more Constitutional lines – the militant ones are endangering their cause by their ill judged tactics.[4] There is no doubt about them being in profoundly & deadly

---

[3] The Whitney-Hoff Prize, awarded to the best watercolour submitted to the exhibition at the American (Women's) Student Hostel in the Boulevard Saint-Michel. FH's painting was *Le Bonheur*, a watercolour of a mother and child. There was no mention of the prize in the previous week's letter.

[4] The militant branch of the suffragette movement was the Women's Social and Political Union, founded in 1903 out of impatience with the failure of a moderate approach. It advocated violent methods such as stone-throwing, window-smashing and the use of bombs.

earnest. So many of them are splendid women & if these chosen few could be granted the franchise I am sure it would work nobly. For the majority of women I can't see that it will answer. I tried to go to some of the meetings when in London but never succeeded in getting in – the crowd was so great. . . .

[187] TO RACHEL HODGKINS, 2 JANUARY 1909

Paris. Jan. 2nd.

My dearest Mother,

 . . . . My heartiest congratulations to Will on his victory. By now I hope he is covered with more glory & lustre & has attained the coveted portfolio.[5] I saw in an English paper that N.Z should be congratulated on Sir Joseph Wards new Ministry. . . . Hurry up & tell me the great news so that I may lose no time in referring to "my brother in law the Minister of Lands" It might help to sell my pictures. . . . Lord how busy I've been this last fortnight – I wonder I'm alive to tell the tale. The American Club which awarded me the Prize recently has offered me their Studio free in which to teach a Watercolour Class if I care to form one. . . . No one but myself seems to have any doubt about pupils rolling up. We shall see. I am to get £1 for each pupil a month & to visit the Studio twice a week & give criticisms. This would leave me ample time for my own work. In the meantime I have been monstrous busy in all sorts of ways. I show 5 pictures at a rather important ex: at the Grand Palais opening next week.[6] My hair is grey – no greyer – with my various French correspondence. . . . I went to an "At Home" last Sat: evening at the house of a charming Russian artist & his wife. It was a Bohemian gathering, very picturesque, artistic literary, musical people of all nationalities from pole to pole . . . . I longed to paint some of the women looking like rich Velasquez against tapestry backgrounds – sleek black heads, white sparkling faces, fiery eyes & great intelligence. A lovely little woman about 25 was introduced to me. She wore trailing velvet draperies, scant & clinging with a huge fur toque & her blonde hair tied up with turquoise ribbons which hung in a ravishing manner in loops over her peachy cheeks – you never saw a more alluring thing – she nearly kissed me when she was told I had painted "Le Bonheur" – the prize picture – I wish she had. This adorable vision was Madame Benezech, famous in Paris as the first lady avocat! She pleads specially for women. *No* jury could possibly withstand her – though she is innocent of wiles & guiles except of a most womanly & loveable kind. She has a baby – & incidentally no doubt a husband & next week I am going to see her. We talked a long time & she never

---

[5] In the 1908 General Election, the Liberals were once again returned to power. Will Field did not become a cabinet minister either then or during the rest of his long career in parliament.

[6] Either the Salon d'Hiver de l'Association Syndicale des Peintres et Sculpteurs Français, or the Sixième Salon de l'Ecole Française, whose exhibitions ran through January and February at the Grand Palais.

once smiled at my execrable French. She was very interested to hear about the women of N.Z. I met a lot of other interesting people – some were freaks – mostly men with beards & mushy French faces – but no doubt everyone was more distinguished than they looked. The less said about my own appearance the better. I try not to be small minded about my clothes but it is hard to keep even decent on my small means. . . .

[188] To Rachel Hodgkins, c.15 February 1909

at 19 Quai Conti, Paris.

My dearest little Mother

. . . . I came over to Rosamond for a week or so & am painting a picture for the Salon, the subject is a table laid for dejeuner, Rosamond making the salad – figure of bonne in background. I have had some good notices about some work exhibited in London. I send you one . . . . How do you fancy your daughter painting like Sargent? I might believe it if another paper had not likened me to Arthur Melville – two poles cannot meet. My little show here opens on the 20th.[7] & then my Class after that. An artist friend is designing me a gorgeous poster. . . .

[189] To Rachel Hodgkins, 20 April 1909

Paris. April 20th.

My dearest Mother,

I missed last weeks mail – not very well & couldn't manage a letter – you must forgive me. In the meantime your letter has come announcing Bert's new engagement. I am of course rejoiced to hear it for his sake & hope he will have much happiness & that the new bride will be a family friend as well as a relation. . . . It makes for you & me a convulsion like an earthquake – as far as altering our plans is concerned & naturally it is a bit of a shock to me though of course it was always on the cards that this would happen sooner or later. Alas! that I were a man with a man's freedom of action. Before I go on to discuss my plans I beg of you if this reaches you in time *not* to have an auction of my work. I am much upset at the thought of such a thing after I particularly requested that my pictures be sent to me to put in my show. Besides I dislike the idea intensely, *specially* as I am coming out at the end of the year – a pretty sort of advertisement for me! Unfortunately I value my work more than the people in NZ seem to & it is very embittering to me to have my work sold for what it will fetch – even to pay my

[7] An exhibition at the Holy Trinity Lodge, rue Pierre Nicole.

bills. I am not in a position to send out any money just at present to reduce my insurance – my own bills & running expenses are as much as I can meet – but I am sure my three brothers between them will not let my policy expire for want of a helping hand. It does not seem very much for a sister to ask when so much is at stake. I shall not know I suppose for some mails yet when Bertie intends marrying. I hope he will delay it till the end of the year. You see I have had to make my summer plans, & have also signed an agreement to hold a show[8] of my summers work in London the 2nd. week in Nov: which, if I cancel it I must pay £30 which naturally I do not want to do – & cannot. I am making the most of my opportunities – my work is beginning to be known & wanted, my class is prospering beyond my dreams & altogether things are just beginning to look rosy . . . bearing fruit in fact as I hoped & believed it would some day if I could only hold on. If you were younger & stronger Mother dear I should say come to me & let us make our home on this side where all my chances lie & my future – but this is not possible. Such is life – What I propose to do is to hold my class in Montreuil during the summer – have my show in Nov: & come out to you in the next boat sailing *early* in Dec: . . . I shall possibly try a show in Melbourne also – so you mustnt expect to see me much before the end of January. In the meantime you will have to keep an eye open for a wee huis or an apartment – you will find it difficult to get anything small enough I expect – & not too far out of town. I am not great at climbing hills & I am sure you are not. I wonder how much of your little legacy you have left! not much I expect. Do tell me everything quite plainly when you write. I must try & get a Gov: appointment at the Art School if possible but no doubt there will be no vacancy – just because I want one – Get Will to sound the authorities about this & just what chances there are of a billet. One artist here says the Gov: should make a billet for me & encourage their artists to remain in the Colony. . . . I have plenty of pupils in prospect – two old professionals coming to me for a month to get hold a little of my style etc. . . . Varnishing Day[9] at the Salon this week. . . .

Time is pressing & there is more than enough to be done. Put a young kitten (black) into training for me. It is long since I have lived with a cat.
[Postscript] If Mrs. Malcom Ross or anyone else puts any more announcements in the paper about me or my doings please remind her that my public name is Frances not *Fanny*

---

[8] At the Ryder Gallery, London.
[9] Vernissage: the formal opening of the Salon des Artistes Français, at which FH was exhibiting two watercolours.

[190] To Rachel Hodgkins, 9 May 1909

85 Rue Vaneau, Paris. May 9th.

My Dearest Mother,

A nice cheerful letter from you arrived a few days ago I am so very glad you are all so pleased with Berts fiancée . . . . I am relieved to hear also that they are not to marry till the end of the year – it will leave you less time alone before I arrive. If possible Dear, try & settle into a house before I come so that I can go straight there on my arrival. I am interested to hear they are building flats, they are so much more suitable for small families & their small space economises labour. . . .

. . . . Did I tell you how well my pictures are hung at the Salon, also they have two small numbers pasted on them which means there is a chance of my receiving an honourable mention but this I shall not know for certain till the end of May. I am not in the R.A. . . . .

. . . . Have you been reading anything nice lately? I seldom get much time for reading – but I have managed to enjoy three American books that were lent me a few weeks back.

"The Fruit of the Tree"
"The House of Mirth"
      By Edith Wharton

"The Common Lot" by someone else whose name I have mislaid. The first two I particularly liked – try & get them if you can. Edith Wharton, Americans tell you is their finest novelist. . . .

[191] To Rachel Hodgkins, 25 May 1909

Montreuil-sur-mer. May 25th

My darling Mother

Here I am at Montreuil enjoying the quiet country life & good strong air after the stifling heat & noise of Paris. . . . The Studio has a tiny bedroom upstairs – a sort of balcony arrangement very convenient for an artist living alone & the whole thing is very compact & commodious. . . . I did very well indeed in Paris before I left – quite a rush of pupils towards the last . . . . If I went back to Paris I should charge £1 a lesson . . . . It is a pity this good luck did not come sooner so that I could benefit by it & make up for all the past dreary years of hard work – I sever every tie when I leave here in Nov: & once dropped they can never be taken up again. I see myself selling 10/- pictures in NZ. like poor Mr. Sheriff – horrors! Perhaps I might win fame & glory by painting Lady Ward – no doubt we shall rub along all right, you & I and the cat!

. . . . I am feeling rather a lame dog myself today – the heat has been awful –

not a breath of wind to blow away the mosquitoes & a storm brewing. In the evening we walk on the ramparts, which run all round the old town. It is shady & cool under the trees. Long ago Montreuil was on the sea – now it is high & dry 12 miles inland with a tiny river flowing where once there was a wide estuary. . . .

. . . . A great friend of Daisy Fitchetts is coming to me here – an Australian girl – nice & very ugly.[10] Did I tell you I saw a weird & familiar little figure in the Salon one day, it turned out to be Miss Joel. I was with friends & she had passed in the crowd before I could stop her. . . . I love the large freedom of living among strangers – knowing no one's private affairs & no one knowing yours – going about without a label in fact. . . .

[192] To Rachel Hodgkins, 10 June 1909

Montreuil-sur-mer. June 10th.

My darling Mother

I have had a nice bright letter from you this morn with good news of the family and an especially good account of poor Frank. . . . So Bert is to be married in November – and furnishing again. . . . By all means accept all the sticks he can give you – we will want it all when we start housekeeping. I dont suppose I shall have much to spend when I return. I am sorry to hear times are bad out there, a bad look out for me! I am still going on prosperously, feeling quite famous in fact, in my small conceited way. Have just sold a 15 guinea picture in England which helps to keep up ones self esteem! . . .

. . . . Sissie's letter was startling – red hot from the heart no doubt and quite convinced – if not convincing. Strange that she should get into communion with Father through the mediumship of the Reynolds whose spiritualistic tendencies he used to ridicule! I dont scoff at all & though I dont believe I am enormously interested in all I hear about psychical phenomena. . . . The great thing is that Sis is happier & has found a living faith. I hope it calms her & not excites – let me know further about it. I have had a dear little letter from Girlie – to think of her being 15! my ears & whiskers what an age I feel – tell her I have some more stamps for her, & not to forget to send me some good N.Z ones to exchange. We will collect together. I hope you have sent my pictures home my dearest and *not* had an odious auction. I must consider my prestige a little bit. I am glad Miss Richmond is looking well & doing well – brave dear woman – she doesn't care a snap for the world. I *do*. I *do*. I *do*. I must tell you of an amusing jaunt we had on Sunday. We took a train to the little village of St. Josse to see a pilgrimage to kiss the sacred relics of the good St Josse & to dip in the holy pool & be cured

[10] Bessie Gibson (1868-1961) worked in Paris from 1905 to 1947, when she returned to Australia.

of all ones devils. . . . [We] followed the crowd & squeezed into the little chapel & up to the altar to kiss the sacred relics, religious fervour ran high, music, gutting candles, incense, the madonna faces of some of the women, devout & rapt all helped to carry one on with a wild sort of surge towards the altar. I was suddenly swept on & found myself almost in front of a priest, a fat, bloated, sensual, pagan beast who only wanted a few vine leaves to turn him into Bacchus – he was holding out to the struggling crowd a large waxen leg & foot – the good St Josse's, which each one kissed & passed on but not till they had dropped a penny into a golden coffer held under their noses by another priest.

I clutched my little Tiki-man, & decided it was good enough for me & wedged out of the crowd followed by an ugly look from the fat Satyr at the altar. It was not a pretty sight at all. What pagans we all are! . . .

Effie Spence, no doubt, with the eyes of faith, would have seen wonders. . . .

[193] To Rachel Hodgkins, 18 June 1909

Montreuil, Sunday. June 18th

My darling Mother

Just a little line though I have really very little to tell you – My girls have all gone off bicycling for the day to Etaples and I am having a quiet go at letters & stockings and thinking of my sins and of what a long time it is since I've seen you. It will be 5 years by the time I am back again – & yet I feel younger today than I did that first eventful year I came Home 9 years ago – 40 is a much more comfortable age than 30 – at my ripe age one finds one's limitations & keeps within them which greatly simplifies life. . . .

[194] To Rachel Hodgkins, 5 July 1909

Montreuil. July 5th

My darling Mother

. . . . We are all very excited about the aeroplane which is to fly across the channel tomorrow. What wondrous times these are – To think of flying! Leonardo da Vinci invented a flying machine of sorts but it has taken from then till now to produce a Wilbur Wright. It is not too impossible to believe that we may yet wing it over the seas to New Zealand. . . .

[195] To Rachel Hodgkins, 24 July 1909

Montreuil. July 24th

My darling Mother

I am leading a very busy & strenuous life, at it from morning till night & making money hand over fist. I feel as if I had sadly neglected you this past fortnight but you must forgive me dear, my leisure moments have been something a little less than scant these last few weeks. I get desperately tired & used up at times but the excitement of it all keeps me going also the feeling that I am in a responsible position & that I must always be top sides of circumstances & equal to the occasion keeps one up to the mark – but this God like attitude is a little difficult to preserve. I have now a very large party – Imagine me sitting at the head of a table of 15! We have a room to ourselves where we have our meals & we are a very cheerful party – tomorrow a young man comes I hope he wont disturb the sweet accord. The less said about the weather the better. My nerves will not stand many more wet days. . . . It is a great strain teaching so many & some days I condemn them all to perdition – there is nothing that takes it out of one so much as a class & being in a responsible position for the wellfare & success of everything. I give way every now and again to an instinctive craving to sneak away & sleep – I dont sleep too well of nights. . . . [I have] received the good news that I have sold my Salon picture & 2 others – amounting in all to £70. . . . I am reaping a late harvest with the work I did 3 years ago – it is nice to sell off ones old work. . . . Best of all I have had a letter from a dealer man in Manchester asking me for some work. When the dealers come after your work it is a pretty good sign. I have 3 pictures very well hung at the Allied Artists at the Albert Hall. Poor Gertrude is in great distress. She has lost her little Aberdeen terrier or rather it was stolen from her while she was sketching in the Park – poor girl – she is broken hearted & has searched London to try & recover him but these dog thieves are so clever it is almost impossible to pit your wits against their villianies. . . . It is a mistake to get too fond of a pet – one gets too harrowed when anything happens to them. It must be an awful thing to have to break yourself of the habit of scratching someone's ear. . . .

[196] To Rachel Hodgkins, 10 August 1909

Montreuil. August 10th.

My darling Mother

. . . . The latest thing in Montreuil art circles was the Exhibition of my pupils work held in my studio. It was a great success. . . . We asked far more than the room could hold & everybody came who was asked & many who weren't & they all said nice things about the sketches, which were really very good indeed though

I say it as shouldn't. I gained 2 new pupils on the spot . . . . I think I told you about the Manchester dealer. Well I sent him ½ dozen sketches & he has sent me a cheque for £52 – not so very much but one cant make terms with these gentlemen when one is practically unknown. . . . He bought all the work of the last 2½ months so I am cleaned out of pictures for the moment & will have to work like wild horses for the next 2 months if I am to be ready for my show in Nov: . . . The rival lady artist who has a class here takes life very easily & lets her class look after itself, the consequence is she gets few recruits & it must be rather riling to her to see them all come into my fold. While I am toiling round in the baking sun on the hot cobbles looking after my flock *she* is painting comfortably in some cool shadow. She gives criticisms twice a week & talks for 2 hours on the various methods of putting on the paint – but her pupils judging from their work would thrive better on a little more practice & not quite so much theory. . . .

FH did not return to New Zealand in December 1909 as planned. She spent a second, even more successful winter in Paris, becoming the first woman to teach a class at the Académie Colarossi, one of the best of the private academies in Paris. With the coming of the summer sketching season she moved with her class of pupils to Brittany. The letters documenting this ten-month period have not survived.

[197] To Rachel Hodgkins, 28 July 1910

Concarneau. July 28th.

My darling Mother

Since my last letter I have moved from the Hotel into a room in the village – in fact have gone to live with the old lady who keeps the crow & the parrots & the cats about whom I told you in my last. She has one room over the shop which has been occupied by an artist for the last 20 winters . . . . I got so tired of seeing my pupils at every meal as no doubt they did of me . . . . It isn't luxurious but I haven't one doubt which life I prefer – this or the Hotel – tho' I do love comfort right down in to the very bones of me. Still it is necessary for me to seize all the quiet & rest I can in between teaching times & this I can do here more easily. I eat at a little café where I get large platefulls of soup & sardines & crabs & veal & bifteaks very raw & red & nearly always green peas stewed with onions & lots of sugar which taste much better than they sound – all washed down with copious quantities of red wine & very sour cider. . . . Mr. Owen Merton[11] has his meals

[11] Owen Merton (1887-1931), born in Christchurch, had already spent two years studying art in England, returning to New Zealand in 1906 when he had met Dorothy Richmond. His watercolours have affinities with the work of Hodgkins. He left New Zealand permanently in 1908, married an American art student and moved to America during the First World War.

there also & next week there will be some more of us & then we are to have a little private room to ourselves. . . .

[198] To Rachel Hodgkins, 3 October 1910

Concarneau. Oct 3rd.

My dearest Mother

. . . . I have been very busy getting off my 6 watercolours to Paris.[12] Did I tell you I had been asked to send up 4, then 6 . . . & the fear of death was upon me in case I couldn't get them finished, having ordered frames etc. . . . & now they are off to frame – (& fame) I hope. I am thinking of sending out a few smallish pictures to you to see if you can sell them. What do you think. I would like to raise some money to pay you back for your loan on my insurance & also to meet the next (& final) premium. . . . I am doing my utmost to raise funds for the voyage – at present I have not much more than will take me further than Paris. I wish you were content dear to wait till my Insurance is paid – then things will be easier – at present it is impossible to move one way or the other. I have decided not to go back to Paris just yet. . . . It doesn't seem worth while building up my connection in Paris if I am to go back to NZ – it is a big grind for nothing. . . . I feel unsettled & dont really know where my interest lies – So until some more money comes in I must stop quietly here. I have been told I can have the same position at Colla Rossis, & it would be as good as anything – with an assured support – but if I take it up again my painting suffers, if you teach you *cant* paint. Besides I was not too well all last winter in Paris & I am not sure I want to risk another year. I spent all I made & did not save a penny. Paris is so expensive. Some friends think I am making a mistake not to take advantage of the opening I made for myself last year. Perhaps I am . . . . I half expect Gertrude Crompton . . . . She is on her own now, earning all the money she can rake in. Of course she has always her 2 homes to fall back on, & I still look upon her as a rich woman. . . . I wish you could meet Gertrude – she is really a splendid woman. She is really 4 years my junior – tho' her fine mass of grey hair makes her look older. I can still pass as a *dark haired* woman. Gertrude is fine steel all through – brains – grit – & feeling – she has stood by me thro' thick & thin especially the thin.

I hear from Owen Merton that he is installed in Paris in a Studio & working at Collarossis Atelier – in love with everything & enjoying his young self to the full. . . .

[12] Four works were exhibited with the Société Internationale d'Aquarellistes, held at the Galerie Georges Petit.

[199] To Rachel Hodgkins, c.15 October 1910

Grand Hotel des Voyageurs, Concarneau

My dearest Mother

Let me tell you it is not at all warm here – Its very cold indeed – but brisk & healthy . . . the wind blows keen & salt & I am feeling a lot fitter than in the hot weather – It has been raining in bucketfuls & the full moon has brought the waters all but up to the doors. . . . It has been a week of excitement for me – each post has brought me in some good news from Paris about my pictures – flattering press notices[13] – kind letters – requests for lessons etc & I am feeling a little happier than usual. . . . Aren't you willing I should stay & follow it up? Don't you want me to find myself permanently & definitely in an established niche in the Art world. I wish you were as *terribly* ambitious for me as I am for myself. It wld. help a lot dear – Mothers are generally the most unselfish & self denying angels – you are & have always been so to me & I hate to ask you to stretch your generosity a point further & say Stay a little longer & do what you *can* – I see & feel deeply yr. point of view as well as my own – You know that – & it is no use going into it again – I feel that Fathers heritage to *me* should work out its true fulfillment – I have a long way to travel yet but I am further on the way each year – & who knows when I may find myself – there! You know what I wish to do – I have told you so before – & it may be a matter of "very few months" as Owen Merton says before I get the recognition I am working for. Then – & not till then do I think it is good policy to leave this side of the world. The R[oyal[W[atercolour] S[ociety] elections are only annual – in Jan. It is not an easy Society to get into . . . one is elected on ones merits. . . . It is the Blue Ribband for Water Colourists – And I dont care to be anything short of this – I am not leading a selfish indulgent life at all – I work fiercely – the economies I practice might surprise you. I am glad there is one member of the family who is well dressed & hatted & booted & spurred – & most awfully glad I am to hear that Sis is so gay & popular & dashing – Hasn't she always had the Grande manner? What real *genius* to give a party for 300 souls! Ye gods – I tremble at the thought of such a thing. But I have always been a scared owl where Society is concerned – I am only happy when I am with artists – with a smudge of paint on my nose & my palette on my thumb – I fear no man when I am on my own ground – but dress me up & take me out calling I jibber with fear –

. . . . I am the only woman artist left in Concarneau. . . . A lot of men are turning up for the winter & settling into their studios. As I said in my last letter – I'll try & be good – if I can't be good I'll be careful – can't promise more!

I would send on the press notices – but they are in French. I will only give you my word for it they say I am a deuced clever woman or words to that effect. It has

[13] This was the first time her work had caught the attention of the Parisian press.

been a tempestuous week. I go for walks by the sad sea walls – when it is too dark to paint – They are never sad for me I love them so & the gulls & the big sky overhead. Its grey moments are too big to allow for sadness really. . . .

[200] To Rachel Hodgkins, 22 December 1910

Hotel des voyageurs, Concarneau.

My dearest little Mother

Three days till Xmas! Most glorious weather . . . a whole week of it a delightful surprise like the currant in the seed cake. Camellias are blooming out of doors & I am expecting the first snowdrop to pop up any minute. . . I am boisterously well . . . it is so much more soothing to live among simple peasants than wild eyed people of both sexes clamouring & grovelling after fame & filthy lucre – what I was doing with indifferent success last winter – one wants both courage & capital to compete against the relentless competition & sordid toil & moil. When I have some money to speculate with I shall go back again & will find it a very different affair I know. Supplies lately here have been falling very low & I have been scanning the horizon anxiously for cheques sales etc. . . . Two days ago however I had a letter from Taylor to say some man had called & bought a 15 guinea "motif" but he – Taylor – the wretch had collared it in payment of my framing bill which was £20 odd.[14] How I swore & ground my teeth – & the day that might have smelt of newmown hay or lavender – or violets reeked instead of brimstone.

The next day however was a little brighter – news came of a picture sold in Edinburgh for a paltry £5 – not much but better than a poke in the eye with a burnt stick as Gertrude Crompton wld. say. The day after – or this morning to be quite accurate – has been brightest of all as I hear I have sold another "motif" in Paris for £10 – so that leaves me £15 to pay a few debts & get square again tho' not enough to start on my return journey to N.Z. I am afraid. What a blessed gamble it all is. Mon Dieu why do we do it?. . .

[201] To Rachel Hodgkins, 28 February 1911

Concarneau. Feb. 28th

My darling Mother

This is Shrove Tuesday – Mardi Gras – & I should by rights be eating pancakes. Everybody is out in the streets – masquerading – singing & dancing & getting very drunk. It is the prettiest sight – I wish you could see it. The gay Celt

---

[14] FH had probably incurred framing expenses in London when she exhibited in March 1910 with the Royal Institute of Painters in Water-colour.

comes out in the stolid Breton on occasions like these. The sun is shining & the wild music of the binyou[15] players blowing themselves purple in the face in the Place under my windows is very tantalising & seductive. Some of the costumes are lovely – the favourite disguise is a pierrot – Troups of them – arm in arm flit about noiselessly playing all sorts of pranks – but always most gallant & polite – even when drunk. . . In the evening I dined with some artist friends at the rival Hotel & afterwards went on to see the Bal Masque in the Salle de Venise . . . Coming home at midnight we found an impassioned Pierrot embracing a tree & singing to the stars & emploring the tree to embrace him as quickly as possible. . . . It does perk one up to see gay colour & some good sunshine – longing as I am always for both things. . . . I hear I have been very well hung & reviewed in Paris at the Water Colour Show[16] – also I hear I am elected a member of the Women's International Society[17] now holding an Exhibition at the Grafton Galleries in London. This means another 2 guineas – How the money flies! . . .

I am so glad you are still lingering on enjoying the nice quiet life with Jean & Willie. Will you go to Percy when you return? He sounds in great spirits & prosperity . . . .

No letters survive for the next eight months at the end of which the Canadian artist Emily Carr studied with FH at Concarneau. FH returned to Paris for the winter.

[202] To Rachel Hodgkins, 27 November 1911

Paris. Nov. 27

My dearest Mother

. . . . My Class is a real going concern now & a great success. I am refusing pupils on account of lack of space. I can only take 16 altogether – 8 in each class as the Studio is not large. Also I have several private pupils at a guinea an hour. Not bad is it – the first month in Paris & practically no advertising. My group of Water Colours at the Petit Gallery brought me a good deal of notice. Tomorrow I am giving a lesson in Pastel. . . . We have already had one big fall of snow & I expect we are in for a pretty sharp winter . . . . Fogs too – we are having – dark at 3.30 – after that we can hardly see the model. . . . I have had all yr. letters re

---

[15] Biniou, a kind of bagpipe peculiar to Brittany.

[16] The Société Internationale de la Peinture à l'Eau, with whom FH was invited to exhibit in February 1911. Membership was limited to 25 artists who invited other artists to exhibit. The president Gaston La Touche, along with the artists Lucien Simon and Henri Martin, was mentioned by FH later as a desirable restraining influence on the 'over extravagance' of some modern painters. (*Mail*, Adelaide, 28 June 1913, p.9.)

[17] The Women's International Art Club, an exhibiting society founded in 1900, held its first exhibition in Paris that year and thereafter arranged annual exhibitions either in England or on the continent.

the Training College appointment & by this time you will have received my reply. Under no circumstances could I accept it & I am so sorry you have been to so much trouble over it. I regret that you have even let it be known that I might be willing to accept a post like that. I am [not] coming out to NZ in an humble spirit willing to accept any old post they care to offer me. I shall no doubt be able to form a private Class of my own failing a good appointment at any of the Art Schools as Painting Instructress where I should have scope for the work in which I have specialized. You see I have gained a considerable position in Paris as a teacher along advanced & modern lines which very probably will not be either understood or appreciated in NZ. where conventional & academic methods are popular. . . . You say in yr. last letter that you expect & hope to have me out for Xmas. Do you forget dear that until my insurance money comes to me that I cant make any move in your direction. To take this long & expensive journey – why!? I havent enough money in my purse tonight to buy a railway ticket to Versailles if my life depended on it. All that I earn by my pupils between this & then must go to reducing debts & bills on this side before I have any over for steamer ticket etc. What you have paid for me in premiums I will faithfully refund when we meet . . . .

I am looking out urgently for news of the elections & sincerely hope there will be good news of Wills return. They must be pretty fagged out – he & Sis – with the long strain & excitement. I see that they will carry total prohibition if 60% votes are obtained. Heaven forbid – it will ruin the Colony. You say in yr. last that I will not tag on to Colonial life after staying away so long – you surely dont expect & want me to settle down into a Maiden Aunt do you & throw up career & ambition & lose the precious ground I have gained – you are much too dear & unselfish for that I am sure. I am coming out merely to see you & Sis & the children to be with you for a while & then to return to my work like any man of business. To make you happy I must be happy myself. I *want* to see you *badly* & feel I must come soon at no matter what sacrifice. But *do* realise Mother that its on this side of the world that my work & future career lie. I grieve sometimes that you do not understand this more. Xmas will soon be round. I cant bear to think of it. The academies close for one day – some not even that. If I have pupils I will keep going all the holidays. . . . I think it wd. be a good move to stop in Melbourne & have a show – also to tour New Zealand on my return having shows in the different towns. I have a lot of stuff. . . .

. . . . Next week I have to spend 2 days on the Hanging Com: of an exhibition of American Women's Art. There is always plenty to do – But no time for my own work. The days are so short. . . .

[203] To Rachel Hodgkins, 14 December 1911

Paris. Dec. 14th

My darling Mother,

.... I am to get possession of the large new Atelier on the 24th & by the 26th. Dec will be in full swing with what promises to be a monster class if they all come. It is working under high pressure at present & the strain is pretty awful. I am up at 6 – a scuffle to light the fire take a bath – breakfast & get the room ready by 8.30 follows as you may imagine – knowing me of old. I dont get rid of them till 4.30. After that I am played out – but not finished. I have a lot to do at the new Studio – get rid of the traces of the carpenter – the late tenant – get the walls white-washed & some bits of furniture moved in & so on. There are so many pupils in a hurry to start that I shall go straight on the day after Xmas. . . . I wd. like to send you all nice presents – but I can't. All my hard cash is layed out in Studio rents & grabbing concierges & coal-merchants & gas companies & bread & milk emporiums. But I am buoyed up by the feeling that things are going well & that my Classes are a success . . . .

A nice N.Z. girl came to see me today – a Wilding[18] from Chch – She wishes to join after Xmas – She told me she knows Miss Richmond.

.... Thank Will for sending catalogue – it is most interesting – many of the names quite new to me. I have just passed it on this very minute to Mr. S. Thompson[19] who was at my door with a message. I am writing behind a screen in the corner – the other 3 corners are fully occupied. My pretty little Studio is so squalid & dirty with muddied feet & charcoal ends – N'importe! It is no good worrying. I am going to dine tonight with my pretty amusing friend Mabel Harrison – the one bright spot in the day – it has been a bad sort of day. I started off by breaking my large mirror – an old Empire one which serves as [a] good property for posing models etc. This made me cross – it also hurt my bare foot on which it fell! this maddened me. The fire wouldn't burn & when it did it was so fierce the model went to sleep with the heat . . . .

Isn't it nice that my pupil Miss Kemp has won the £20 prize at the Student Hostel that I won 4 years ago – And Miss Bridge has an Honorable Mention for a Water Colour – I am very proud of them. . . .

[18] Cora Wilding (1888-1982). After studying with FH she returned to New Zealand, painting with Margaret Stoddart and Rosa Dixon. A member of The Group, the informal painting and exhibiting society set up by progressive artists in Christchurch in the late 1920s, she wrote *Murals for New Zealanders* (1946), reflecting an awareness of the social responsibilities of the artist.

[19] Sydney Lough Thompson (1877-1973) was born in Canterbury and first visited Paris in 1900. He studied at the Académie Julian in 1901, and in 1911, after six years' teaching and painting in New Zealand, returned to Paris. For the next twenty years he and his wife lived in France, based in Concarneau. Thereafter he moved between France and New Zealand, winning great popularity in his native country with his poetic evocations of Europe. From the 1930s on, his paintings were increasingly seen in New Zealand as expressing 'imported' values. Where FH continued to meet the challenge of modernism, he remained committed to an impressionist-based idiom. He died in Concarneau.

[204] To Rachel Hodgkins, 29 December 1911

17 rue Boissonnade, Paris. Dec. 29th.

My darling Mother

. . . . I shall remember this Xmas all my life the amount I have crowded into it . . . . I finished work at 4.30 on Xmas Eve. At 9 o'clock I went off to a party at the Phillips Foxes[20] with Mrs. Molesworth Miss Henderson & Owen Merton in a taxi – & made merry till I couldn't lift an eyelid to see the time o'day. We were mostly Australians of high & low degree. . . . Owen M. played an accompaniment which marked him as a musician. He tells me he has a piano now & is keeping up his music. He really is the best of boys. What do you think he did today – Whitewashed my big Studio in a most stunning & splendid way – & saved me no end of money & trouble – we put a deep golden ochre dado round the room which looks very effective & pleasing against the cream walls – not to say stimulating. It is a gorgeous Studio – as big as any ones – & I hope to do so well in it & make the school attractive. I was to have started on the 26th. but couldnt manage it . . . . My latest outlay has been on a prosaic stove & piping – the room is so big it will take a lot of heating – & then stools & easels – pop goes every sou I have! . . . I feel so sad I cannot send you something nice for Xmas or stretch out & give you a kiss & a hug. But when the school is well on its legs.– we'll see! Its a big venture – single handed – but I got drawn into [it] like a vortex & I wld. have been a fool to not have seized my chance. I hope I shall not find out too plainly that fool rhymes to school. I don't think so. Do you realise you have a little daughter in Paris with a big following & one of the biggest Private Classes in the Quarter.

I have now partly got over the shock of seeing the telegram announcing the defeat of the Gov: Party. It is hard to realise all it will mean to the Fields. I fear it will be a serious blow. . . . I see it is a narrow squeak over Prohibition. Was the Labour Party very strong?[21] . . .

For the summer of 1912 FH took her class to St Valery-sur-Somme, where she had worked with Norman Garstin in 1906. No letters survive from the first eight months of 1912, which was clearly a difficult time for mother and daughter as each came to terms with the necessity of living apart. When the insurance policy matured FH was able to afford the voyage to New Zealand.

[20] Emanuel Phillips Fox (1865-1915), born in Melbourne, studied under Bouguereau in Paris in 1887 but developed an authentic impressionist technique before his return to Melbourne in 1892 where he helped found the Melbourne School of Art; returned to Europe in 1902.

[21] The 1911 election marked the end of twenty years of Liberal rule. Will Field subsequently transferred his allegiance to the Reform party which had been formed in 1909 under William Massey to represent conservative interests and now became the Government. Four Labour members were elected, only two of whom represented the newly formed Labour Party.

[205] To Isabel Field. 11 September 1912

St Valery s. Somme, France. Sept 11th.

My dearest Sis

I am homeward bound at last! I have got a berth on the "Otranto" sailing 3rd Oct from Toulon – a bare 3 weeks from now – I want you awfully to come to Melbourne & meet me if you can. *Do* try – it would be lovely to see you there on my arrival & we could run the Show together & make a big thing out of it with your prescence gracing it. I am sure you want a holiday & spree away from yr. family. For my own sake I want you to come badly – I feel horribly shy coming home after all these years & will want your support. . . . I am in the throes – Another week here polishing off pupils – they have rallied round me to the last & we depart hence en masse. The weather is doing its awful utmost & we might as well be in an Aquarium.

Two of my pupils – the sporting sort – are going up in an aeroplane tomorrow if it is calm enough – They have to pay £4 each.

There is much to be done before I sail – it frightens me – but I will worry thro' somehow I expect. Send me a line to Colombo or Freemantle or Adelaide & say you will cheer my homesick eyes with a sight of yr. dear old self.

Your loving sister

I arrive Melbourne about 7th or 8th November I fancy.

I shall be most *awfully disappointed* if you dont come. I am sure you wld. enjoy it. I know I should

Best love to Mother

[206] To Rachel Hodgkins, 20 September 1912

Paris. Sept 20th

My dearest Mother

. . . . I am up to my eyes . . . . I left St V. 3 days ago – much toasting & feasting & kindness all round, & now I am at this Hotel till I sail. Letters from Winnie [Brotherton] yesterday & the Customs Officer, H Halford, assure me that Duty can't be evaded & that I shall have to pay down £60 on arrival with a rebate on all unsold work. . . . Well! it is very annoying & obstructive of them but it can't be helped. I flew round to Phillips Fox & he advised me to risk it & get Halford to guarantee the loan – for after all it is only that . . . . If the pictures sell its all right – if they dont the deposit is withdrawn on taking pictures out of country. . . . . It is not possible to draw back now that my pictures are all packed & ready. I have spent too much. It is very riling all the same. New Zealand is never any use to me! there are no privileges attached to belonging to our little island – I have long ago learnt the truth of this. For a Colonial like myself to have to pay to exhibit in her own Dominion is a little too stiff. . . .

. . . . Make Sis come over if she can – I am sure she would love it & I know I should. My pupils have all bought small pictures & this enables me to act more easily. Madame at the St Valery Hotel refused to be paid because I had brought her so much business! which was lucky for me. My young American Croesus has 3 pictures in the Autumn Salon & he is mad with joy & can't do enough for me to show his gratitude. . . . He drives me about to do my shopping & helps no end in various ways. I have been out to dinner every night since I arrived & am dropping to pieces with sheer fag – & long for a deck chair & sky & sea & nothing else. People are wondrous good & kind.

[Postscript] Excuse bottles in enclosed photo. It is only local colour & is inseparable with life in France!

PART ELEVEN

1912-14

Antipodean Triumph

[207] To Isabel Field, 8 November 1912

84 Park Rd., "Delgetti", South Yarra. Friday.

My Dearest Sis

. . . . I am *so* very sorry you cannot come. I have been dreadfully lonely &
wondering what had become of you all . . . . I am distressed you are feeling so ill
& tired – you will have to take a holiday when I get over – shall I take you away
from the children or the children away from you or run off with Will? I'll do
anything in my power to help.

I have reached Melb: at a bad moment, Cup week & not a thing doing – my
luggage not thro' the Customs & my pictures Heaven knows where – rumour says
2 cases are missing . . . . The chief difficulty will be the Duty on pictures. . . . Aunt
Jane has come nobly to the rescue & placed £100 in the Bank to be used if
required. . . . It is iniquitous that I should require all this coming into my own
country[1]. . . . I have secured a nice Room for the Show from the 20th. right in the
centre of Collins St – Centreway it is called. The Theosophical Soc: are tenanted
there & it will not be a bad place for WaterColours once the Besant & Blarelok
monuments are removed & their sacred aura replaced by mine! It is white, light
large & square – will need some veiling of the 2 windows a few formal pot plants
& some comfy chairs. . . . I have had shoals of letters – cards – invitations &
telephone calls from people – known & unknown – everyone is wondrously kind
& friendly. . . . I am going up to Castlemaine for the week end – Winnie will not
be able to leave her Mother – I hear she is a *slave* – a perfect wonder of brains &
energy . . . . I must fly – I have to be on the wharf in ½ an hour to face the Customs
Officer. . . .

[208] To Rachel Hodgkins, 15 November 1912

"Delgetti", South Yarra. Friday 15th.

My darling Mother

I have been through a busy & tedious time with the Customs & only yesterday
after endless delay & obstruction & red tape could I regain possession of my
pictures & put them into the hands of a framer to fix them up for the Show. £135
had to be paid into the Customs – £100 by Aunt Jane – the balance by the
Customs Officer himself . . . . All the time I have not been "leaning" up against
my cases at the Customs Shed & arguing with officials I have been doing a million
other things all bearing on the great Show, being interviewed – returning calls
trying to keep cool (the heat is awful or rather *was* until yesterday – today it is

---

[1] A reference to her Australian origins. FH told the reporter of the *Daily Telegraph* in Sydney that she liked
to think of herself as an Australasian (14 April 1913, p.8).

raining & we steam instead of bake – that is the only difference). . . . I spent a week end at Castlemaine & found [Winnie] & Aunt Jane wonderfully well – & of an energy! I arrived at 8 p.m. & we sat up half the night talking . . . . Aunt J. sitting straight & bright-eyed in a hard chair as wide awake as a 2 yr. old, I in the last stage of weariness with a pain I daren't mention

. . . . I escaped as soon as the first train wld. let me the next morning – loving them both dearly & full of admiration in my heart but oh! so tired! They are 2 wonderful women. I am now very busy indeed getting ready for Thursday 20th. I am not having an official opening – the time is too short to approach it suitably, but I think lots of nice people will roll up & make it amusing. I had tea with Mrs. Kirkpatrick today & she had asked some people to meet me & they are all coming & their friends – & they I gather are the crème de la crème! ! . . .

[209] To Rachel Hodgkins, 26 November 1912

Delgetti, Park St, South Yarra. Monday 26th.

My darling Mother

This week has been a strenuous one & agitating as well – so please forgive the gap in my letters – all time & energy was used up in preparation for Show Day.

It duly came off & was opened by Mrs. Kirkpatrick & was quite a nice function. The Press let themselves go over my work & the Argus gave me what I am told is the best notice any artist has ever had from them. It sent the public driving in & the gallery has been full nearly all the time – & it is creating wildest excitement – much discussion & disparagement but on the whole strong support & approval. The artists are with me to a man – in varying degrees – according to their lights. . . . Mr. Bernard Hall the Director of the Nat: Gallery was my first visitor & has been several times. There are rumours that a picture has been selected by him for the Gallery, but it is not officially chosen yet – so don't breathe a word abroad dear will you.[2] He has a coldblooded Academic mind about art – & can't be relied upon – still he has rather overflowed about my work so I am hopeful. . . . It is all so new to Melbourne & people confess they are dazzled & confused – don't know whether the influence is good or bad – & can't trust themselves to buy till they get accustomed. The Art Critic of the Argus was most amusing – I must tell you – we talked for a while – Then he said, Are *you* the Artist? What, a little thing like you! Why I thought you were a giant with a Sword! Well anyway Bismarck with fierce moustachios! Everyone says it is the best show ever held in Australia – which is gratifying. . . .

---

[2] There is no record of a picture entering the National Gallery of Victoria at this time; the gallery currently holds four works. There were apparently few sales from this exhibition, in spite of the critical acclaim.

FH arrived home on Christmas Day 1912 and went to stay with Isabel. After visiting Willie in Masterton she once again went to paint in the village of Ohinemutu on the shores of Lake Rotorua.

[210] TO WILL FIELD, 1 MARCH 1913

Lake House Hotel, Rotorua. March 1st.

My dear Will

How very kind to send that wire. Its most awfully good of you but I have enough for a fortnight with my ticket home & thats as much as I shall want I fancy. Luckily the weather is good so I am having two good goes a day at the Maori, but have not yet got anything worthy of them. My hand & eye are out & I can't get on to the colour a bit. I find them as facinating as ever & if I lived in N.Z. I should settle alongside this sympathetic Lake – I love it. The Maori has a strong sense of race & ancestry about him very interesting to feel & in this classic spot, Mokoia & the Lake as a background it is quite easy to lose ones heart to him. There is a young blood I have been introduced to – no not rubbed noses, who has a £1000 a year & a motor car which I fancy he keeps under his bed there is no garage & the house is a shanty. He is only 26 but most comely. The conversation consisted in guessing my age. He gallantly put it at 32 – the women said 35 – I will let you know further if anything else transpires. Nobody at this hotel but two nicish English men – one a prospective sheep farmer & a student of the Maori – his love. I suspect him of being "Mere Mere" in the Dominion & like to watch him wriggle when I mention the articles. . . . What fish butchers the men are here. They can only talk of the gross *weight* of what they catch – no sporting instinct at all. . . .

No more now, the mail closing. Saturday night & the shops all open, am going into village to see the beau monde. . . .

On 28 March 1913 FH left Wellington on board the Moeraki *to arrange an exhibition in Sydney. She had already written to George Rich to enlist his help and went to stay with him and his family.*

[211] TO RACHEL HODGKINS, 3 APRIL 1913

Belton, Mona Road, Darling Point [Sydney]. Thursday

My Dearest Mother

Here I am safe & sound . . . . Arrived in Sydney at 3 oclock . . . . great excitement – Judge George – (the future Sir George) having just been appointed to the High Court amid public & private rejoicing that very day. . . . He is a dear kind fellow – & has been every sort of a trump to me astonishingly kind & thoughtful in the midst of his own triumphs. Thinks of everything – the handsome Betha does not fash herself. I can't fathom her – she is mysterious. That one so fine to look at can give ear to so much parish pump stories as she does is beyond me. I believe she *prefers* Maggie G's company to *mine*! The Judge doesn't. Well I lost no time in getting to work. The Judge placed his Associate at my disposal all yesterday. He took me to Horderns[3] – I nearly swooned when I saw the Show Room – not an inch of wall space – show cases & stands thick everywhere – & fixtures. I said quite definitely I couldn't show my pictures there – then the heads of the firm were called into solemn conclave – they were keen to keep me – & put their heads together & have decided to erect a tempory wall & clear a space in front of it – & with this I must rest content tho' it is far from satisfactory. I am fixed to open on Monday 14th. the Chief Justice & Lady Cullen to open it I believe . . . .

[212] To Percy Hodgkins, c. 17 April 1913
at Belton, Mona Rd. Darling Pnt. Sydney.

My dear Percy,
   I have kept an eye open for all news concerning N. Territory & send on a paper with an article from a medical man's point of view that will interest you; it is a side not to be ignored. I sound every man I meet – some know nothing – care less – one or two . . . [say] it is not a climate for New Zealanders – if it is to be peopled Queensland will supply the population – *and* the money. I give you this for what it is worth – cattle ranching seems to be worth something. This is all I can gather at present – both hands very full at present with my Show. Life is a swirl. It is a great success my dear! The crowds blowing in out of the streets – papers eulogizing – trams full – lifts overflowing – trumpets blowing & lots of butter at 2/6 a lb! Society in their best flocked on Monday to the P.V. Sold two skinny little pictures for £5 each . . . . next day £90 worth flew off the walls & the 3rd. day another £60 – today nothin' doin' *but* the Nat. gallery have ordered 5 or 6 to be sent up to the gallery on "appro". I await results.[4] Folk say nobody – not even the great & only Longstaff[5] has ever had such a show or made so much talk. Horderns' have behaved nobly – the firm bought one picture & young Samuel two for £70. They have been so decent & civil & are *delighted* with results, tho' their faces were pretty long when they first opened the cases &

[3] Anthony Hordern and Sons' New Palace Emporium, where FH's exhibition was to be held. She exhibited 76 watercolours ranging in price from £3.3.0 to £70.
[4] The Gallery bought *The Window Seat*.
[5] Sir John Longstaff, popular Australian painter of portraits and historical pieces.

saw a few ultra-ultras[6] with broken glasses. It is such a comfort to be on a business footing – backed by business men. It is all spoon fed & playful compared to Melbourne . . . . I wish you could be here before I leave Sydney – it is an enchanting spot . . . . The Judge owns a launch & we spin round the Harbour when nothing else is doing. Vice Royalty honours me with a visit this afternoon . . . . Hope things shape well & that you are hearing the right sort of news from Darwin. . . . Good luck dear boy & love to Ouida

FH was now planning an exhibition in Adelaide.

[213] To WILL FIELD, 19 APRIL 1913

Sydney. April 19th. 1913

My dear Will

A hurried line to ask you to be so kind as to send me *by return* quickest possible route a Water Colour (unframed) of Venetian Sails – which Percy had & wh. is now reposing (I think) on the chest of drawers in Granny's room at The Terrace.

It is a large drawing – bright red sails. . . .

Go on to Adelaide about the 30th. I think & want to have it with me. Show goes well. Crowds of people & interest increasing.

Will write when there is anything new to report.

Love to Sis

Yrs. Frances

Sold all my old work I brought over.

[214] To WILL FIELD, 19 APRIL 1913

On second thoughts please send "*Goose girl*" with "Red Sails"

You will find it tucked away behind picture on table in drawing room I think – if not there in basement with other pictures. It is unframed.

Yrs. in haste

Frances

---

[6] The Sydney critics called the work 'ultra-impressionist'.

[215] TO RACHEL HODGKINS, 17 MAY 1913

Sydney. May 17th.

My dearest Mother

. . . . I am perishing with cold & very impatient to be off to Adelaide – I may go any moment, am only waiting for the Art Societys Room to be free. Was much surprised to hear Mrs. Tudor Atkinson's voice thro' the telephone on Wed: I met them at the Art Gallery & then to tea with them in town . . . who wld. have thought of meeting them of all people on their way to England. It is really part of their charm – their unexpectedness. I do hope a fortune lies ahead of them – she said she was in search of the other end of their rainbow & was going to help Tudor find it if possible. She is a fine creature & says more good things in ½ an hour than most of us in a lifetime. . . .

Jack & Jill[7] have a lunch party for flappers today & a launch party tomorrow. . . . They live in a constant racket, dances – theatres – taxis – pictures – pianolas & gramophones – and flirtations – as their mothers & aunts were before them so are they. The trivial is upper most all the time. . . .

[216] TO RACHEL HODGKINS, 23 MAY 1913

Belton, Mona Rd, Darling Pnt, Sydney. May 23rd.

My Dearest Mother

Why this big silence? No letter for a fortnight – I heard from Willie that you were bright & well otherwise I should be anxious. . . . There is such a mix up with the customs I am not at liberty to move my pictures from here till things are straightened up. It appears my bond to remove my pictures from Australia in 6 months expired on the 16th. May. Not having worn the wretched thing on my watch chain or round my neck & having received no notice of it falling due I overlooked it by 2 days. The Customs thereupon crashed down upon me – threatened to seize pictures – *did* seize deposit of £107 & converted it into revenue & furthermore peremptorily ordered me & my pictures to Melbourne without delay. Fortunately for me the Judge [Rich] is in Melbourne & he has written to the Comptroller, the Comptroller has written to the Minister & I hope with their help & God's infinite mercy I may escape jail. All I know at present is an assurance from the Minister that he will stay proceedings for a week till the matter is gone into. Pretty nasty isn't it? & just when I was feeling rather bucked up & pleased with myself. Business men say it will be all right & that the Customs underlings always go on like that & make it d—ishly uncomfortable for private people when they can. Of course my agent Mr. Halford has behaved most meanly

---

[7] The children of George and Betha Rich.

in not reminding me that date was due. It looks as if it was a regular trap to get my deposit & make me liable for the £200 bond. Naturally I am very worried & have not had exactly a happy week & can of course make no definite plans for Adelaide. . . .

[217] To Isabel Field, 30 May 1913

Sydney. May 30th.

Dearest Sis

Hows yourself and family?. . . I had hoped to be in Adelaide by now – if not on my way back to N.Z. – but for this bad luck with the Customs. . . . [Horderns] are very keen to have another show of mine in 2 years time or less – I suggest that you get enough work together by that time & we'll have a joint stock show & show them what N.Z can really do if it likes.

I have just completed a deal with them today letting them have 10 pictures cheap for £105 – rather depleting my Adelaide show I fear – but a bird in the hand etc. This makes £305 I have received from them – minus commission but not Customs Duty wh. still has to come off. I am sending £100 to the London Bank for a sinking fund – have sent Brother Willie his £42 – & tomorrow £60 good money goes to Aunt Jane who is waxing anxious. I am very sorry that I cannot show you all my pictures Sis dear – I am afraid a lot of the best have gone. Its queer how they all like my old stuff best – its easier understood – but there's no comparison which is really the right stuff – a few people *do* know however. I suppose you have seen the A. G. Stephens article.[8] He is the leading literary prophet over here. He is a fat bearded giant not unlike King Edward VII but he is reputed to consider himself more like Jesus Christ. I wish he had referred to Father with less condescension – it was ignorance of course – I wrote & asked him to change it – but it was too late. It seemed mean to accept so much praise for myself & so little for him – I have learnt to be pretty wary with my tongue – Sydney society swarms with voracious ladies of the Mrs. Malcolm Ross type – you know them as surely as you know a blackbird about to find a fat grub, tummy, tail & eye quivering for a spicy morsel. . . . There has been a rush on Hordern's Gallery by the artists – since my appearance there – I have started the vogue!

. . . . None of the little cousins over here can hold a candle to your girls – either in looks or brains – Jack Rich is the flower of the flock I think – He is a bright boy with a charm of manner. . . .

---

[8] This was reprinted in both *Otago Daily Times*, 3 May 1913 and *Otago Witness*, 28 May 1913. The headline was 'A DUNEDIN GIRL WHO CONQUERED PARIS'. See E. H. McCormick, *The Expatriate*, p.153, for a discussion of the text.

[218] To Rachel Hodgkins, 14 June 1913

South Australian Hotel, North Terrace, Adelaide. Saturday 14th.

My dearest Mother

I arrived here yesterday morning early after an uneventful but deadly cold journey. . . . Arrived in Melbourne on the King's Birthday everything hermetically closed – went to breakfast at Menzies Hotel & found the stately Betha breakfasting late at 10 oclock and making ready for her departure that afternoon at 5. I eat solidly – the first food since Sydney at 11.30. . . . Then Betha & I went out to look at what shops had no shutters up – this needless to say was not my suggestion – Betha's mind dwells lovingly on a shop window – Diamonds or dusters – it doesnt matter what. Back to lunch with . . . the dear little Judge who always is good sport. . . . After lunch we walked in the gardens – then goodbye to Betha who was travelling in semi-state in a reserved compartment. . . . She has been a great social success – the various Excellencies taking special notice of her. She really is a superb creature with a cool suave manner as soothing as a suede glove. . . . Tuesday & Wed: mornings I spent with the tricksy Customs people. . . . It is a rotten Act . . . & is to be repealed at the end of the year if this Gov: is still in. I can't tell you the difficulties & obstructions that have beset me. Not so much because I am not a good business woman – simply the silly twisted nature of the regulations. So far I have paid £75 into their hands. I am standing out *not* to pay 25% on my catalogue prices (wh I don't always get) but to be taxed on *one third* of the value as per trade prices. This is considered a fair proposition by business people – but not by the Customs – so far. . . . Business people say I am the first victim – & they hope the last. I am very weary of travelling Shows – it is a very tedious job after the first excitement wears off. . . . Write soon theres a dear little Mother. I feel dreadful lonesome at times – in spite of friends. . . . Mr. Gill of the Art School showed me round yesterday & I am getting things in train. The Art Societys Room is very good – the best I have struck so far – tho' the walls a bad colour. I shall have to cover them with brown paper.

Adelaide is a sweet place, very quiet & unexciting – I wish you lived in Australia dear – the climate is so much kinder. Are there any letters for me? I fear I shall not be back in Wllgtn before the 1st. week in July. This Show business is a slow affair. I hope Adelaide is good for £300. Love to you all & much to your dear self Yrs. Fanny

The Art Gallery of South Australia bought At the Window *and the exhibition was a financial success (sales totalled over £300 according to the* Mail*). After the exhibition FH went straight to Dunedin, arriving on 14 July 1913. She stayed with old friends, the Rattrays.*

[219] To WILL FIELD, 22 JULY 1913

Craighall, Eglinton Rd, Dunedin. Tuesday 22nd.

My dear Will

. . . . I have the use of the big Art Gallery. It is a handsome room – too large for my purposes – a vile pink colour – & very cold . . . . I have worked hard & have lost no time & the Show opened yesterday – Monday – in a howling gale of rain & wind. About 40 people came – the other 150 rang up during the evening to explain why they couldnt come. The Mayor Mr. Willie Downie Stewart, made a very nice speech & Mr. Theomin also – & many old friends were there in mackintoshes & damp feet. Mr. Jim Roberts bought the first picture after a determined bargain – I am not used to these methods of doing business but Mr. Neilson who is selling for me says it is the custom to "make offers". Everyone seems pleased over my work tho' surprised. Dr. Scott did not come to the opening – but came down during the morning. I was much shocked at his appearance but thought him looking better yesterday.

. . . . He moves heavily & when tired his speech is very slow. . . . He can laugh & say sharp things as well as ever but you can see the queer frightened look in his eyes. Being a doctor he knows so well what it means, poor chap.

. . . . It is nice seeing old friends. Everybody is so kind. This is more the real home coming. People are pretty poor down here & I don't expect great things – there is an awful lot of mud & the distances terrify me & to make matters a little more difficult I am doubled in half with rheumatism with the damp – clothes & boots are always drying beside the kitchen fire. . . .

P.S. If this doesn't arrive too late, will you please see Mr. Fisher Minister of Customs & put in a word on my behalf about paying duty on pictures. I have sent him in a petition to that effect but think a word from you will help a lot. It seems I must pay £1 on each picture as I have been away from N.Z longer than 5 yrs. Perhaps he will strain a point in my peculiarly deserving case & make me exempt from payment or at least make some concession

[220] To RACHEL HODGKINS, 31 JULY 1913

Craighall. Thursday.

My dearest Mother

Just a line dear to tell you the Public Gallery has bought *3* of my pictures for £80.[9] They raised the money by subscription. I was very sad & blue the other day when I wrote. It looked like a hopeless failure. But this is good & I feel much bucked up. . . .

---

[9] *Dordrecht, Holland* and *Fishing Boats,* both c.1908, and a later, more 'modern' work, *Summer* (c.1912).

. . . . It is still fiendishly cold & I hate it & feel very nipped. Can't we fly off to the Islands dear? Do lets. How is the Richmond-Merton show doing? I wanted to see it – so sorry they couldn't wait for me. I would have helped sell for them. Such a lot of people I am seeing – parties packed into every corner of the day.

. . . . Must fly to yon wee gallery.

Love to you all

Fanny.

Sold 6 pictures – up to £150 I fancy. 3 of the Wellington lot Will sent on

FH returned to Wellington for her last Antipodean exhibition which began on 25 August 1913. Opened by the Countess of Liverpool, the wife of the Governor, it was a social and artistic success with the National Gallery acquiring The Hill Top.

FH sailed from Wellington on 21 October 1913 to return to Europe. In Sydney she visited the Rich and Rolin families and called on Horderns' who had had six shows since hers but 'none so successful'. They were arranging for a cubist show from Paris and expected her back in two years when their new gallery would be built. When she left Sydney aboard the Otway *there seemed no reason why she should not return to exhibit in Australasia, combining business with the pleasure of seeing her family and friends. She had one more exhibition at Anthony Horderns' in October 1918 while living in England. It was not as commercially successful, her 'post-impressionism' winning the approval of only the more advanced critics. The* Otway *called at Melbourne and Adelaide where FH renewed her acquaintance with Peter Waite (1834-1922), a wealthy pastoralist and philanthropist. The Waite Agricultural Research Institute at Adelaide University was founded through his benevolence, which extended also to individuals and other institutions such as the Salvation Army.*

[221] To Rachel Hodgkins, October 1913

Otway, off Freemantle.

My Dearest Mother

. . . . I had a nice time at Adelaide – we got in early & I found Mr. Peter Waite waiting for me in his car as soon as we came alongside the wharf, with an arm full of roses. He had left home at 7 oclock & it took him 2 hours to run down from his place in the hills. He drove me up to Adelaide an hour's run & dropped me at the Queen Adelaide Club where Mrs. Downer had arranged a morning tea party for me of 9 ladies whom I had met before. More roses & a dash for the special train & back to the ship by 12.30 & off again. Mr. Waite has presented his beautiful home & estate in the hills to the city of Adelaide to be turned into a School of Agriculture after his death. The town is ringing with his name. It is a princely gift. . . . I dont know why the old man has taken a fancy to me. He said "don't be frightened to let me know if you want help lassie" The family is determined not to lose sight of me, which is nice of them. . . .

No more now dear. It is very cold & rocky, I shall go to bed – mighty fine place bed on a night like this. It will be a long while before I hear from you dear. Hope to have a letter a week after I reach Naples 27th. Nov.

Shall be glad to get to solid work again. Go up to Perth in the morning & lunch with Judge Rich. . . .

[222] TO RACHEL HODGKINS, 11 DECEMBER 1913

Hotel Windsor, Capri. Dec 11th.

My dearest Mother

Installed at last in my winter quarters & started on a strenuous Spartan life. I think I am going to like it. . . .

I left Rome midday with my big new trunk, great comfort, reached Naples 7 o'c dined & slept at same Hotel, arose at 6, paid my bill, tipped the multitudinous minions tuppence each, & drove behind my big box down to the Quai, where I was surrounded by brigands of every hue & shape, was taken by two of them in a small boat & landed on ship for Capri. Men of Italy I have tipped every one of you, if I have overlooked any man among you let him stand forth or for ever hold his peace. . . . Capri is full of Germans. This Hotel is full of them too – dreadful horrors who eat with their fingers & guzzle like animals. It was lovely sailing across the Bay of Naples, Vesuvius rising from the blue mists, & every pleat in the hills along the coast visible as the sun grew stronger. We made Capri at 11 o'clock. It is just a goat island, precipitous & craggy – with Capri in the cleft of two high peaks, Ana Capri on the hill top above us – I landed as I had embarked at Naples, brigands in boats etc. But this time I knew a thing or two & managed better. . . . No one can help loving Italy & all its queer primitive innocent (?) ways. I wonder indeed why people live anywhere else. My room overlooks all Capri – is flooded with sun, has wide green French windows open night & day, & a narrow balcony over hung with vine leaves which are vividly & marvellously bloody red – this 2nd. last word slipped out by mistake, dont take it in the bad sense of that bad word dear. . . .

[223] TO RACHEL HODGKINS, 19 DECEMBER 1913

Pension Faraglioni, Capri. Dec 19th.

My Dearest Mother

The Bank forwarded me a welcome letter from you this morning full of exciting things written at the height of the Strike.[10] Not having seen a paper since I left Australia I dont know what has happened & am trusting to your next to tell me the sequel. Tucked away on this quiet little island the outside world seems so unreal I don't feel "me" at all, it is all so strange & foreign & unlike anything I have ever done before. It is going to be good for painting & as soon as I can get focussed & really on to work I am sure I shall be happy, but at present I am trying to adapt myself to the strange surroundings. I have had to change my Hotel & I think for the better. I couldn't endure any longer the rough Germans & their beastly table manners. . . . I am very stiff in the joints today as I climbed up to Monte Solaro yesterday, the highest peak in the island. Tiberius lived in Capri at the wickedest part of his wicked life & built 12 villas on the various eminences, one for every month of the year. Monte Solaro is where he used to be carried on a litter to consult the Stars. It is a dizzy climb & needs a good head to steer round the narrow ledges. There is nothing between you & the deep blue ocean. I went with one of the despised Germans [a Baroness] who flew over the rough stones & boulders like a pigeon leaving me panting & very annoyed long behind. However I got to the top in time to see the sunset & I sat as long as I dared at the foot of a little shrine to the Virgin (conquered gods) & wished the stones could speak & the unutterable German would be silent. How much better it would be. These great pagan ruins, devoid of ornamentation mere quarries of stone, are very satisfying by their sheer simplicity – no beautiful tiles or frescoes, just a shell of stones like a great altar to the gods & the blue realm of the Mediterranean below. We had to descend very cannily – loose stones & night coming on quickly – luckily we got over the worst of it before it was quite dark . . . . When we got to Anacapri we had hot black coffee & found a belated carriage which took us down the hill for a franc, the little pony going like lightning, round & round the winding road, black as pitch only one light between the two towns & that the Shrine of the Virgin in a nitch of the rocks high up on the face of the cliff. . . . [The Caprisians] never molest or worry strangers & one can roam all over the island alone. The only drawback is the poor milk. It comes from the mainland & is pale blue. But the wine is good & included in the bill. . . . Have you read Wells' "Passionate Friend"?. . .

[224] To Isabel Hughes Field [Girlie], 6 January 1914

Hotel & Pension Faraglioni, Capri. Epiphany Jan 6th.

My Dearest Girl

I am sending you a little lace collar which I think will look very sweetly on you.

---

[10] The 1913 Waterfront Strike was the most violent industrial dispute in the history of New Zealand, involving arson and riots and the enrolment of thousands of special police.

It is made here & is called Irish Crochet! . . . I am looking forward to a nice long letter one day. I know you are a busy pair you & Lydia but do try & write once in a way my dears. Remember how much I want to hear the family news & it is so easy to slip out of touch if we never write. Just write a scrap. I don't mind how short it is & say what you are doing & how you all are and how behaving & how Granny is, very especially & if Mother is planning to come to Europe & lots of little bits of news like this.

. . . . A new young man has arrived an artist of quite the nutty style, black hair thrown backwards grey sombrero, & melancholy face. He has gone forth to paint this morning. From my window I can see the corner of Ischia rising out of the sea, dead black on the horizon. Ischia is Capri's rival in beauty.

. . . . Many big hugs & love

from your Auntie

Tell Lydia when I have saved some more sous I will buy her a collar if she likes it.

[225] To Rachel Hodgkins, 25 February 1914

Siena. Feb. 25th.

My Dearest Mother

Today is the first of Lent – How different from yesterday the last day of Carnival Shrove Tuesday. Of course it was Festa for all the Town. I joined the populace & walked up & down the Corso the principal street & got a good deal of confetti down my back. . . . About dusk the churches began to fill up for the Ave Maria. . . . It was very impressive to kneel in the dimly lit church among the strange unknown figures, peasants & fine ladies, the rich & the very poor, infinitely more human & corporate than ever you feel an English service to be – the candles on the altar gleamed like the peasant's idea of Heaven & you could see their fixed gaze through & beyond in a rapt ecstacy which gave their faces an almost sightless look. It is literally the gaze of blind faith. One by one the lights went out & we went home. The carnival went on till the Ashen Dawn & then, or just before there was a great burst of bells from every quarter of the earth it seemed, loud & quick & deep & full of portent slowly growing fainter & fainter till the echo of the last echo died away on the silent Dawn & a cock started crowing & it was Ash Wednesday. I took the day off & had quite an orgie of churches & beautiful altar pieces & towards 5 o'clock more vespers & candles & solemn Gregorian chants which sink into ones soul very deeply. . . .

. . . . My three septuagenarian British ladies whom I told you of turn out to be militant suffragettes, full of zeal for smashes & burnings & bombs – I can hardly believe it – they are so mild. They are very full of Christabels book "The Great

Scourge" which is making a big sensation.[11] Well, after all, the evil it deals with is a women's question & it has been left to a woman to drag it out into the pure daylight & combat it – one cant help but admire her splendid courage tho' militants & military are tiring & bewildering no matter how much one sympathises. Causes work in awful badly with Art & I find even the presence of the mildest militants disturbing. I found one of my old ladies reading the "Rosary" & almost weeping over it.[12] Curious the inconsistent mind that can get sentimental over such poor trash & yet lash herself into fury over sterner things. Do get a life of St Catherine of Siena dear & read it & we can compare notes while I am here. The history of Siena is immensely interesting – they were Ghibellines you know & always at war, for centuries, with the Florentines, fierce fighters & killers. Today they are the gentlest of Gods creatures & I find it quite the nicest town in Italy to paint in. The children don't bother you & you can go anywhere unmolested. . . . I watch eagerly for your letters, dear & rejoice so that you keep so well & spirited. You are so wonderful you know dear little Mother. . . .

[226] To Rachel Hodgkins, 17 March 1914

Siena. March 17th.

My Dearest Mother
    . . . . Life in Siena is uneventful once you have seen all the sights tho' the country just now is lovely enough for anything with the almond blossom in filmy freshness standing out from the old stone walls & the brick buildings like ballet skirts round an old brown negress. There is no end of course to the treasures in the shape of old pictures & bronzes & relics that one can see if one gives up time & energy to it but travelling round dark churches with a taper really is only a luxury for the leisured maiden ladies who have no other ties. It would never do for me. In contrast to the leisurely English ladies are the Americans who do it all in one gasp. People come in motors & stay one night look at the Cathedral & squiff off again next day with that weary whats the good look that motorists seem to wear. . . . When next you are in McGregor Wrights will you ask him dear if any of my small pictures are sold. If they are make him give you the money. Say I said so. I put them there for you. No more now, my fingers feel all bones & very stiff. I am getting a nice lot of work together to bring out to Australia next year. I must bustle into bed now before my bottle gets cold. . . .

[11] *The Great Scourge, and how to end it*, London, 1913, by Christabel Pankhurst, daughter of the famous suffragette. The scourge was venereal disease, the author pointing out the dangers of marriage to women when 75-80% of men in England suffered from some form of the disease.
[12] Florence Louisa Charlesworth Barclay, *The Rosary*, 1909, 1915, 1950.

[227] TO RACHEL HODGKINS, 5 APRIL 1914

Siena. April 5th.

My Dearest Mother

Your letter with the sad news of Dr. Scott's death has just come & I must say I feel very sad. The world will not seem quite the same place without him. He really has been a big influence in our lives & I owe him much. . . . His sun really set when his wife died & everything since then has been a mere carrying on of his duty. . . . The news of his death has cast a gloom over a very perfect day – the best we have had so far – in the true sense of leaving nothing to be desired for the moment, dappled sunshine upon all, fragrance in the air, blossoms round the feet, peace & deliciousness to all the senses. The world as God meant it to be with no marring note but this sad letter with the news of a good friend's death. . . .

I am slogging in at the Spring blossom & I have found a most seductive garden full of cherry & almond blossom where I work undisturbed by what I call the "inconveniente" that is, the small boys in the street, Spawn of Satan, sons of Belial, every Mother's son of them! It is really a find this garden. I do wish you were here my dear little Mother to bring your book & enjoy it with me. There is no pale milkiness about the sunshine now – but hot & sparkling like golden wine – light that makes you shut your eyes & shade your hand & the blue in the sky really talks so rampant is it. . . .

I heard from the Richs on their arrival at Naples – they are now in Rome & we hope to meet at Florence on my way to Paris in about a fortnight's time. I rather want to put in a week or two in the market place of Verona which I hear is splendid for colour. I must not delay in getting to Paris. Studios get snapped up about this time & it is very necessary I should get a good one for next winter. . . .

I am going to have asparagus for dinner tonight, the first fruits of the Spring, presented to me by the old padrone of the gardens. . . .

[228] TO RACHEL HODGKINS, 29 APRIL 1914

Hotel Riva S. Lorenzo & Cavour, Vérone. April 29th.

My Dearest Mother

. . . . Florence is a treasure house, so lovely in herself, so full of gems, like a rosary of exquisite prayers in marble, bronze, paint, & glass. Every corner of the street there is something to delight the eye & feed the spirit & every step you drink in deep draughts of beauty & inspiration. I think I have never seen anything so sweet or more freshly lovely than Botticelli's two great pictures "Primavera" (Spring) & the "Birth of Venus" I am sending Girlie prints of them for I want her to love them too. The swiftly gliding Flora in the "Primavera" is the most winsome thing you can ever wish to see, pursued by a lusty Zephyrus blowing the roses out of her hands. Oh! my *so* lovely! Then theres Donatello in bronze with his beautiful young David going forth to do battle with Goliath, a nude stripling, with his shepherd's hat engarlanded with flowers & nothing else but his sling with his five stones in it. A young & very cocksome David & well he may be with his sandalled foot on the great head of the champion. I made a mistake in saying he was "going forth". He was already back before Saul & trying not to boast too hard.

If only burgling were not so risky & dangerous a game how I would like to walk off with a few things I saw in Florence. Michel Angelos great giant David doesnt stir me one half so much as the smaller bronze Donatello with its suave & easy grace. Michel Angelo is a super-man & too big to take to your heart in the same way as the lesser & more human artists. He is Titan. The great Ghiberti gates in bronze are to be seen in front of the Baptistry. Far back in the mists of antiquity I remember drawing replicas of these same gates (& hating them so) under Mr. Hutton's dirty guidance.[13] I was 4 ½ days in Florence & of course only saw a fragment of all its beauty but I didnt want to linger too long, easy and pleasant as it would have been to stay and steep ones self in the art & history of the place. . . . Betha is excruciatingly funny – quite frankly can't see beauty in any of the old masters, is buying copies of cheap & vulgar madonnas & comparing the shops unfavourably with Anthony Horderns. She is travelling with a party whom I consider awful outsiders. I mean they should not be her sort. Better alone any day than in the wrong company – I would like to hear Jacks opinion of it all. I expect he is getting a lot out of it – he has his Father's keen eye & brain.

I came on here in a crowded train, a long job it was from 2.25 till 10, very hot, a disgusting journey, & I couldn't have stood it a moment longer. . . . Italian trains are always over crowded & stifling – windows closed tight & corridors crowded. No wonder that what happened did happen. In changing trains, at Modena, at which place the train switched into three, one part to Venice, one to Milan & the rest on here. Two minutes to have a cup of coffee & when I got back to my seat I found to my dismay my precious bundle with all my painting kit in it was not there, & no time to go after it. Arrived at Verona I wired to Venice Milan & Bologna but no trace of it yet & here I am after 4 days, still waiting & very anxious as of course I am unable to work & this place has so much gorgeously fine material on which I am longing to spread myself. All my winter's work was rolled in a case & if I lose it it will be a bad business. Things are apt to get lost in Italy for months. If I do not hear of it tomorrow I shall go on to Milan, put the matter in the hands of Cook & leave him to find it & forward to Paris & I

[13] David Con Hutton was the drawing master and later director of the Otago School of Art from its inception in 1870 to 1908.

shall go straight to Paris myself. I can't buy another outfit here even if I were inclined to go to that expense. . . .

[229] TO RACHEL HODGKINS, 21 MAY 1914

Paris. May 21st.

My Dearest Mother it seems a long time ago since I wrote last you must forgive me dear I have been so very busy since I arrived. I last wrote from Verona telling you of the misadventure over my pictures. Failing to hear any news of them I packed up & hurried on to Milan where I spent 5 hours in an agitated search thro' the left luggage office & interviews with Thos Cook & the British Consul & in their hands I had to leave the matter as there was nothing else I could do. . . . I am feeling very low in my mind indeed over the loss of my sketches & all my painting kit tho' I still have hopes of recovering them. . . . This is not the only blow – On my arrival here I found a letter from my London agent Taylor informing me that the 2 cases supposed to have been sent from Wellington by Curtis have never turned up. These cases were paid for by me before I left NZ & were to be sent off soon afterwards. Will you please get either Will or Bert or Percy or all three seperately or together to go & make a row about it & find out what has happened. . . . My luck has deserted me & I am feeling quite miserable. . . . Among those pictures there were some meant for exhibition in London. I started studio hunting the day after I arrived – an awful job. I find rents & rates up a lot . . . . After a long hunt I have found two Studios close together, one to live & paint in & the other for pupils, both £45 rent & rates. . . . I take possession 15th. July & pay 6 months in advance so this year will be a heavy one. . . . Mr. Griffiths[14] . . . gallantly placed his cosy little flat at my disposal & here I am very comfy indeed – such pretty things, Chippendale furniture & good English rugs & big easy chairs . . . . I find pupils almost panting for me which is gratifying. How odd isn't it? I am starting a Summer Class almost at once & go to a tiny little cliff village near Boulogne-s-Mer next week where I have had the luck to take over a studio cottage from some artists for the summer. . . .

. . . . What books have you read lately? I have been going back to Thos Hardy & loving him immensely. They are so full of meat his books & human! . . .

[230] TO RACHEL HODGKINS, 6 JUNE 1914

Equihen, Boulogne-s-Mer. June 6th.

My dearest Mother
   I have exchanged the roar of Paris trafic for the roar of the English Channel.

[14] Mr Griffiths had joined FH for private lessons in Siena in March.

Imagine me perked up high on the cliff in my little cottage. It is rather a neat little place, the last house in the village, with the Studio in a cabbage patch further up the hillside. If only it would get warm. . . . The sand dunes stretch inland & are patched with little pine woods, very windblown & tortured in shape, lots of goats & cattle tended by shaggy little goatherds, purely pastoral subjects of the kind I am very partial to.[15] I have to face the horrid fact of my lost bundle – it has gone I fear for good & all. The search is now abandoned as no trace of it can be found. It is very disheartening. I am trying to face it like a man but it [is] rather a staggerer. I don't feel much in heart to begin all over again. The money loss is so great. I have had to get a new outfit. I so hate the sight of my new tools – they have no virtue in them. Betha & party arrive in Paris tomorrow. I shall probably run over to London & see an oculist about glasses – I feel my eyes & have headaches, probably I have strained them in Italy where the light is so strong.

It is a reign of Terror in London just now with the wild women. Everything is closed. Destruction of Churches & pictures is their great game carried out with an appalling amount of fervour.[16] It has become a matter between them & their God (?) & nothing now will stop them in their mad course of self immolation. It is very horrible to read of these daily brawls & fights between men & women where physical violence is resorted to & the women at Death's door from starvation & torture. . . .

[231] TO RACHEL HODGKINS, 22 JUNE 1914

Equihen. June 22nd

My Dearest Mother

I will just shoot you off a short line tho' I have nothing really to tell you dear. We have had fogs & now storms, today is a raging gale the sea hammering on the cliffs & a big surf, no boats out, nothing doing for the poor fishermen & next to nothing for the poor artists. Such wild weather. June has been a bad month. I have no pupils, no one will come near the sea in such weather. . . . So Aunt Jane has sent the bulbs for Father's grave. I am sending you a draft for £3 thro' the Bank. Use some of it to pay the man's expenses dear & also send Frank some fruit or whatever you think best. I wish I could send you twice as much. No news of my pictures. I have written to the New York Herald & Paris Daily Mail which are widely circulated in Italy, & asked them to insert paragraphs. I have also doubled the reward. I think about it night & day & sometimes I wake up at night & my subconscious mind almost projects clues & messages on to the white wall so

---

[15] Equihen was a popular sketching ground with English painters, particularly Sir Herbert Hughes-Stanton RA (1870-1937), who was staying at the inn when FH was there.
[16] 1907-14 was the most violent phase of the campaign for women's suffrage. Among other attacks on art works, Mary Richardson on 10 March 1914 took an axe to Velazquez's *Rokeby Venus* in the National Gallery.

intensely am I willing & directing my energies towards their recovery. It hurts me to think of my lost time & chances, all gone by a stroke of ill luck, a whole batch of work gone in a flash. Far, far worse than having your best R.A picture cut up by a Suffragette. *That* would be an advertisement some artists might even envy one. . . .

[232] To Rachel Hodgkins, 10 July 1914

Equihen. July 10th.

My dearest little Mother

It is always such a relief & joy to me when your letters come telling me you are well. . . . I have been having rather a fiendish time one way & another. My pupils hate this place & cant find subjects, idiots, & have persuaded me much against my inclination to go off to Concarneau & throw up the cottage. . . . I am now packing once more & will be off in a couple of hours. It is 6.30 – a lovely pearly morning. I can almost see England it is so clear. An aeroplane has just passed glittering like a silver bee. Three companies of soldiers are passing along under my window singing. I can almost touch their caps they are so close. They are on fatigue duty from Boulogne & are making for the sands to cross to Hardelot. I hate going. I really love this place & my little cottage & the simple quiet life . . . . A rival group of students have asked me to stay & take them on but I can't break faith with my old pupils. . . . No more now dearest. I [am] off to get a bowl of hot coffee at the Hotel. I have been up since cock crow, I had a brain fever day yesterday finishing pictures. A coy sun – & two little devils of babies to finish. Will write from Concarneau

[233] To Rachel Hodgkins, 29 July 1914

Atlantic-Hotel, Concarneau. July 29th.

My Darling Mother

I hope you have lost the horrid cold dear you mention in your last letter. Have the woollies arrived yet from Paris. You must guard against chills & take furious care of yourself dear. . . . We are rather a dismal little band. I have a bad cold & dreadfully off work like everyone else with this persistent rain & want of sun. I am giving 2 lessons a day never-the-less for we are all perturbed & anxious over the war alarms & feel that any moment things may happen & we may have to disperse. This morning there was a stampede of Germans & Austrians from this Hotel. It was difficult to keep calm in the midst of such a fuss. Mdme. the Proprietress wringing her hands & crying that the season was ruined & that the Hotel must be closed The maids weeping & people flying off in motor cars hot foot for Paris. The situation is this Austria declared war on Servia yesterday. France mobilised her army last night – men marched out of Concarneau at nightfall, everyone rather panic-stricken fearing a catastrophe of the gravest, that the Hour has come & Germany is going to strike at last altho' it is Russia's next move that will decide the issue. As artists we all feel our present insignificance in the scheme of things. Why work? Who wants it? Who cares? England is working passionately for peace & if only Time can be gained War may yet be averted, or rather localised. All this talk of Peace & here we are at each other's throats. What a little distance we have advanced in civilization really – the more we change the more we are the same.

Last week the burning questions were Home rule & the Caillaux trial. Some blood has been shed in Ulster & the Nationalists are lusting to fight & Redmond is far from obsequious & Civil War seems in dead certainty – unless this greater & more fatal issue abroad will prevent the lesser peril. . . . News has just come thro' that Mdme. Caillaux is acquitted. The French have a quaint idea of Justice but this is fantastic – can we then all murder our enemies?[17]. . .

[234] TO RACHEL HODGKINS, 31 JULY 1914

Atlantic-Hotel, Concarneau. July 31st.

My Darling Mother

I want you not to be alarmed about me whatever you read in the papers. I shall be out of harm's way & with friends. . . . It is all very shocking – we may decide to stay on here, it is as quiet as anywhere tho of course prices will go up & living will be dear. Already bread has gone up & the bakers shops taken over by the Government. My only fear is about money. . . . I have taken the precaution to draw out £50, or rather I have written for it but whether I get it or not remains to be seen. The French banks have stopped payment at all the country towns, here as well & consternation and panic is everywhere – general stampede of nearly everyone but artists & English people who keep cool thank Heaven. One of my pupils Mr. Bailey an American, left for Paris last night. He is rather a coward & will possibly bolt for America. Rumour says there is red revolution in Paris today & that Jaurès the Socialist leader has been assasinated.[18] Everyone is hording their gold. Germany has declared a state of war & the worst is feared No doubt the first plunge they make will be over the frontier to Paris. I am manfully doing my best to stand firm – we all are. . . . Mr. Griffiths has gone to a neighbouring village for

[17] On 16 March 1914 Henriette Caillaux, wife of the Minister of Finance, shot dead Gaston Calmette, the editor of *Le Figaro*, who had been running a campaign against her husband. The trial polarised the public, Mme Caillaux's acquittal being a triumph for the liberal left view that subconscious forces, especially in a woman, can lead to acts for which one may not be held accountable.

[18] Jean Jaurès was assassinated 31 July 1914.

a spell & is cruising round the countryside looking at places for next year. I shall be largely influenced by his advice. He has a practical mind & is my very good friend

It's impossible even to dream what may happen. The world has never before been faced by such a calamity – it confounds us all. So much for communicalism which we have been taught to believe governs the world. . . . I pray that things will be straightened out before this reaches you & that we may all be going our gentle ways in peace once more

[235] To Rachel Hodgkins, 4 August 1914

Concarneau. 4th. Aug. 14

My Dearest Mother

This is a record of events in Concarneau since the Declaration of War on Sat 1st. Aug.

Saturday was a day of suspense & agitation, nobody could work. We hung round the Mairie & Post Office waiting for news. Being Saturday the Port was full of fishermen, all very drunk. About 5 the town crier announced the fateful news we were all waiting for. Declaration of War by Germany & General Mobilisation of the French Army. Women wept & fled to their homes with their aprons over their heads. Next came the order that persons wishing to leave Concarneau for Paris or the sea ports must go at once, that night, or not at all – general exodus, Hotels emptied of all but the permanent visitors, artists etc. Mobilisation was to commence next day & trains would only be available for troops. Simultaneously the telegraph was cut off & no letters came in or went out. Lights were to be out by 8 o'clock, all buvettes closed, no drink sold. Next morning early we were warned to register ourselves with the Police, have our photos taken & not attempt to leave Concarneau without permission from the Prefêt at Quimper. During the day Concarneau slowly emptied itself of sailors – blind drunk most of them, escorted to the station by cheering friends & weeping women. Tough, hard & very fit the men looked – all under 27 years of age. Later on in the day, orders for all men under 47 to hold themselves in readiness to mobilise in 2 days time, caused a fresh outbreak of tears & consternation. Practically the whole male element of Concarneau has been drawn away. Nobody but grey beards & youngsters remain. Civil & military life in France are insepa-rable & all men between 23 & 47 are soldiers & patriots, ready at a moments notice to leave their work & sacrifice everything for their country. . . . Nobody wants war, France least of all, & there is no enthusiasm shown, but a grim determination not to be humiliated or bullied by Germany – I have heard many men say "Well! it had to come, the situation is intolerable Better fight & get it over – Germany's attitude is unbearable"

One hardly dared wake on Monday morning for fear of fresh shocks. Everyone was asking What is England going to do? Will she hold aloof? The English Colony [were] looked at rather suspiciously Were we going to abandon France to her fate as once before? Why doesn't Asquith act promptly & resolutely? France looks to the English Fleet to save her from the German claws. We know the English Fleet has sailed under sealed orders which speaks for itself – but no further news – we are told England must have its "week end" undisturbed – Monday they will decide. The Government has commandeered all horses & motor cars. The farmers brought in their nags yesterday, many of them spavined, boney old crocks, patiently walked off to their new duties, their owners paid by Gov: cheque. Silver & gold is scarce people refusing to part with what they have. Everyone seems to be living on credit – like myself. We hear the Gov: has issued some small paper money 5 frs. & 20 frs., which will relieve the pressure if only it would find its way down here. Anyone in a motor car is instantly spilled out of it on to the road & the car borne off by the Police. These lighter touches never fail to give great pleasure to the crowd. Nobody ever really enjoys seeing someone else in a motor car! Since Sunday – two days ago, no news from the outside world – gloom deeper than the deepest has settled on us – no letters, no papers, rain in torrents our beautiful tunnyboats "all gone like butterflies" the black sardine boats deserted, fish market closed, banks closed, sardine factories closed, no life anywhere & this is what is happening ditto ditto, over the length & breadth of France – while her brave sons go forth to fight those abhorred, accursed sons of Belial over the frontier, Messieurs les Allemands.

The German Fleet is nestling in the Baltic round Kiel but when she comes into the open things will happen – & those things will be coloured carmine. . . Personally I feel *sick* with apprehension – I do –

Le Faouet, Morbiliau [Morbihan] Aug 16th.

I don't know if you will ever get this probably not. It is dreadful to be cut off like this but things will improve when mobilisation is complete & the trains running again. They say it will take 31 days, 15 of which are passed – one or two letters have come in but nothing from N.Z & no news from the Bank of money sent as requested. In the meantime I am mewed up here stranded for want of cash & powerless to move. I motored over here from Concarneau, spent my last £2 in getting here – Mr. Garstin who was here with his Class wired to say this was a quiet little asylum & at such awful moments of suspense & terror it would be some satisfaction to be together, & so I thought so after seeing off my own girls by motor to St Malo, a risky & expensive journey for them poor dears . . . & armed with passport & a safe conduct I made a dash along a road infested with officials who stopped me every 100 kils or so. . . . I was thankful to get out of Concarneau. The desolation there was utter . . . all the pleasant things gone, its lordly boats & all that queer bustle made by man & machinery. "A Berlin" every able bodied male lusting to get to the frontier & use their "white arm" as they call their bayonet on all that German cochonnerie gathered round Liège. Heavens what a hammering the Germans & Austrians will get. They will be beaten to their knees of course. It will be a hideous fight but we will win please God. Italy has come in with us which completes the belt of steel & will end the war quicker. We get very little news here & are dependent on what filters thro' from the censor. . . . Well to continue my tale – when I got here I found the Garstin party in a flutter having been told by the Consul at L'Orient that it would be wiser for them to go. So he & Mrs. & the 17 virgins, all very young & frightened poor dears, went off in a great hurry, I assisting to poke things into bags & tie on labels. Mr. Griffiths refused to go & leave me stranded, besides he hadn't any money either so here we are in the queerest plight, waiting [for] news & money to make a move. This was a week ago & we have reason to think that the Garstin party are bottled up in Jersey half way across the Channel. The Nickalls have written begging me to go to them which I shall do as soon as I get to London, until I make some plan for the winter. The future is dark & precarious for us all & for artists – there will be nothing doing for long to come. I feel so useless. All my English friends are making shirts & bandages. If possible I shall make a dash for Paris, get my winter clothes get rid of my Studios which will be required for Hospitals I expect & then get over to London, but of course this may be quite out of the question if the Germans come on towards Paris. At present everyone is full of joy & hope & courage at the unexpected way the Germans have been repulsed & kept in check but of course we know things are not going to be all our way. The Russians are not expected to come on till the 3 or 4th act & by that time many ugly things will have happened. England has behaved grandly. It makes the blood surge in ones veins to think of it. All the same the weight on ones soul is very heavy. We have kept hoping against all outward signs that this mad folly would come to an end & that the human race would regain its common sense but here it is & oceans of blood must flow & we are standing breathless before a possible tragedy the like of which the world has never seen. We shall need all courage & fortitude we are capable of. I am so anxious for news of you dear – God send you are well. I won't cable to you – every penny now is precious.

Your loving Fanny.

[236] To Rachel Hodgkins, c.September 1914

Le Faouet, Brittany.

My Darling Mother

. . . . The papers are wonderful in the things they don't tell you. The thin trickle we get from Paris is just enough to show us the awful gravity of the situation, that things are not too rosy with the Allies, that the British Force has had severe losses & that the Germans "avance toujours". The tambour no longer beats in the Place & the one eyed butcher has ceased to read us the news from the Marne. . . . Everything is still & hushed, like the last chapter in the Book of Ecclesiastes. We are expecting a convoy of wounded & beds & bandages are in readiness. Yesterday a man with his wife & daughter arrived in a motor from Roubaix near Lille. He is a spinner & has a factory there. He said the Germans were there making women dig trenches at the point of the bayonet. I never saw man so broken. He had lost everything. At first we refused to believe the frightful tales of brutality that the papers published but it is a war of ruthless rancour & hatred, no quarter given, especially towards the British soldiers whose participation in the war has inflamed the Germans to mad dogness. Now it is war à l'outrance. If one's heart didnt beat so sickeningly at the horror of it all one could get some high thrills at the stupendous play of force & genius & passion unrolling itself along that Chinese wall of human flesh & blood, each unit hoping to hurt the other all it can. We are hating our enemies in the good old healthy way – consequently we love our friends better which is a change for the better. Anyway we are done with smugness & hypocrisy & the common danger will purge the world of much materialism & self interest – & the Empire will be strengthened & purified Some people think the horrors of war are not too big a price to pay. Certainly for the moment life is much simpler. Why look forward to a tomorrow which may never come. . . .

. . . . Money from the bank arrived after a month on the way. I am living from day to day, painting small pictures & doing one's little best to keep going. I shall probably be ruined, but so shall we all. I have 2 studios on my hands for a year which will drain me badly. A letter dated July 3rd. has just come from you for which I am thankful. It is so long since I heard, ages ago, in fact a month. It is extremely tiresome that Curtis is such a fool. My agent wrote asking him *where* my pictures are *not* what he was to do with them. If they are not forthcoming I will sue Mr. Curtis for their value. I am very annoyed – I have had pestilential luck this year & can't survive many more losses.

We are all very proud of N.Z & Australia rushing to hurl themselves into the fray. If only they could be *here now*. There may be an overplus of men too late. The German game is to stake all on this one great hazard, if necessary to sacrifice 50% of their army to secure a victory. The Russians are flowing out like a river in the direction of Berlin & will soon have reached the inner line of the German defences – things will happen soon that will haunt the Germans to their dying hour. As they have meted out the cruellest punishment to poor gallant little Belgium I hope Russia will give them something a little worse than worse, or as I heard an Englishman say "the father & mother of a belting" Much love dearest. So glad you keep well you dear you

Your loving Fanny.

It is so splendid to hear of the English troops in action, as steady as rocks, in the hottest of hot corners fighting like nailers. I feel such a superfluous woman. Even the children are more use than I am. They help to get in the harvest. I have seen women ploughing & thrashing.

PART TWELVE

1914-18

St Ives in Wartime

The war had a decisive effect on Frances Hodgkins's career in that it severed her ties with France and removed the possibility that she might become a French artist. Though she was to return to France after the war, she remained committed to London as an exhibiting centre and to an identity as a British artist. She settled down in the artists' colony at St Ives in Cornwall and, partly in response to the wartime ban on coastal sketching, concentrated on portraiture and figure compositions. Though she continued to paint in watercolour she took up again her earlier resolve to use oils. By the end of the war she had painted, among others, the large and ambitious oil The Edwardians. *She continued to submit work to the Royal Academy, where her pictures were hung in 1915 and 1916, and resumed the links established in 1910-11 with the more cosmopolitan International Society of Sculptors, Painters and Gravers, exhibiting there 1915-19. Her work was also hung in the National Portrait Society in London, where it was praised in 1916 by the influential and progressive critic Frank Rutter. An important friendship began in Cornwall in 1917 when FH met the young Cedric Morris (1889-1982), who was at the beginning of his career as an artist and whose earliest known work is a 1917 gouache portrait of FH.*

[237] To Rachel Hodgkins, 30 September 1914

Kenn Pier Farm, Somerset. Sept. 30th

My dearest Mother

I am safe in England at last for which you will be thankful I know. . . . The war is dragging on, today the 18th. of continuous night & day fighting on the Aisne, but the prospect for the Allies is full of hope . . . . Those terrible days when the Germans were before Paris are gone never to return tho' we won't feel quite comfy till the last barbarian is driven off French soil back across the Rhine. . . . It makes one glow to see the way heroism & sacrifice have come out on top, voluntary heroes every one of them. The gentle folk have all lead the way & it is said there isnt a man who hasn't volunteered or a woman either, for work of some sort, Red Xing or whatever comes along. Dear Jack Rich was waiting to be attached to some regiment when last I heard, & is probably at the front by now. I am expecting a letter any minute from Betha. The casualties have been heavy for poor England. The French losses have never been published, we only know roughly 1 killed to 3 wounded – & the wounded are in scores of thousands. It was saddening to pass trains full of poor bandaged crippled men on the way through France, all going West, the eastern trains full of reservists cheerful & clamourous for cider & cigarettes on their way to Paris. It was quite an easy [journey] tho' very long & hot, many changes & delays & waiting at way side stations to let the wounded pass. We thought it best to come to England. We heard rumours that Southampton might be closed & mines were being laid & there would be a certain risk in crossing if we left it any later. . . . St Malo was a melancholy sight, hundreds of vessels interned & idle in the harbour wounded soldiers everywhere & the gay little town silent & still as under a spell. The sea was like a bath tub, only a sprinkling of people like ourselves at a loose end, & a few French & Belgian refugees & lots of children being sent for safety's sake over here. . . . . At Southampton we parted company – Mr. G. going on to a place in Dorset, I coming on here a six hours journey, to Gertrude Crompton at her little farmhouse where I shall be till I can settle on some winter plan & abode. London is out of all question on a dwindling purse, people are too busy with the war & the terrible necessitous future to think about classes. Luckily for us artists we carry our machinery in our heads & if we survive we can start again being self contained so to speak, but it will be years before things are again at the stage where we left off. You will have read of the destruction of Reims Cathedral The whole world is full of rage & pity at such a dastardly act, eternal shame & dishonour on the wicked race who has done it . . . . There is a little baby in a village close by with its arm cut off by these arch devils. The mother is distraught. Think of the undying hatred & horror these awful acts must sow in these poor peoples hearts, no reprisals can ever give *them* back peace or joy for all they have lost. . . . There are mercifully a few light touches to relieve the awful hours. Have you seen the Punch cartoon of William with a halo & surplice, behind a lectern, usual eagle etc, saying "Let us prey" really rather good, grim but "honourably the stomach rises" as the Japs say when they are amused. The Kaiser so rumour says, is sending a fleet of Zeppelins to destroy London, his intention is to spare Westminster Abbey & Buckingham Palace as he intends being crowned in one & sleeping in the other. . . . Spies still continue to be caught & hanged. . . . They say your hair would stand on end if you only knew what highly placed people are suspected. . . . All we know is that the Allies right wing has been strongly reinforced. We know the Canadian & Indian troupes are there & I suppose pretty soon the Australians will be in the field. It makes one gurgle with joy to think of it – One is so blood thirsty these days – When we hear of a German cruiser being sunk *we* say How splendid. How utterly wrong the Kaiser has been in all his calculations. . . . In my own poor miserable heart I don't know what any of us are fighting for or where it will all end – Clearly none of us are fighting for the same cause. I am reading Cramb on Germany & for the life of me much as I loathe them I can't [help] seeing their case – but its seditious to hint at such a thing aloud.[1] Read it for yourself. . . . I feel very safe in this peaceful orchard, the deep peace of this place is very soothing – Gertrude is very comfy, has 3 rooms & her own furniture, & nice kind people to look after her, busy farm life all round her,

[1] J. A. Cramb, *Germany and England,* John Murray, 1914, the text of a series of lectures given in March and February 1913, in which Professor Cramb described the thwarted imperialist ambitions animating modern Germany and warned that a conflict between England and Germany was almost inevitable: 'So long as England, the great robber-state, retains her booty, the spoils of a world, what right has she to expect peace from the nations?' (p.14.)

apple orchards & lots of subjects at her door. . . . Am so glad the woollies have arrived & that they please you. . . . Such delicious weather, gentle sweet west winds rural England at her best

[238] To Rachel Hodgkins, 15 October 1914

Rock Farm, Beer, Devon. Oct. 15th.

My dearest Mother

It has been a black week. The fall of Antwerp a great blow. . . . The misery & horrors are too awful – Belgium is a mere skeleton of herself, two thirds of her population are flocking to England, penniless & starving. . . . We live from day to day . . . normal life is quite upset ones centre of gravity queerly shifted. I envy the people with something definite to do. Of course we can all knit & push open cottage doors & cheer women up a bit, but the real work falls only to the trained workers – women are tumbling over each other in their desire to find jobs & hundreds of incompetent ladies have to be sternly with held from injuring poor wounded soldiers & put to scrubbing floors in the Hospitals instead. Still it is a fault on the right side. Any woman who can say "Avez vous famm?" is allowed to snap up a Belgian refugee & cherish them. One smiles at these things in order not to weep for the tragedy is heart breaking.

A text over my bed says "The Lord is good to all & His Mercies are over all His works." How is one to believe in this? How is one ever to believe in anything ever again? What are the Belgians to believe in or put their faith in. This war is revealing to us a greater realization of pain if it fails to make anything else clear, but where is our great faith in brotherly love, charity, honour & truth & the other Christian virtues in this hideous welter of cruelty & sin. To think of it is [to] get weighed down by the horror of it. To keep busy is the thing one can do so little & I curse my sex daily when I see these great healthy lumps of men going off to their training ground on Salisbury Ground. . . . The papers reach us about 11, & we spend most of the day reading them. The Times is full of solid information & takes a lot of careful reading with a map. I have heard from Betha she seems well tho' heartbroken at leaving Jack who is with his Regiment at Liverpool waiting to go to the front. . . . Poor little Rosamond Marshall has lost her brother. Nearly everyone one meets has red eyes & a catch in the throat but most wonderfully brave & resigned. I am knitting scarves & have offered my services as Secretary to one of the Red X hospitals near Clevedon if wanted. I can write tidily when put to it. . . .

[239] To Rachel Hodgkins, 23 October 1914

Chelsea, London. Oct 23rd.

My dearest Mother

Yours of the 10th. Sept came this morning & was very welcome. These troubled times one can't hear often enough. I have been in London 3 days. Of course its wet & foggy. I looked up Betha the first thing . . . . I am glad she has decided to go home. . . . [She] told me when she refused her consent to Jack's enlisting he said "Come Mother think of your Grandmother"[2] and even when this coercion failed he said "Well Napoloen was Captain at 19 I really *must* go" & he cabled his Father for permission. The Judge cabled "Ask your Mother" Neither parent had the courage to say yes & yet the Judge must be full of pride at the boys spirit & judgement. If Jack is spared he will be a fine man & have a career. . . .

The news continues good, quite inspiring in fact. My temper was very short last week but I feel better now we have sunk 4 German destroyers. . . . If you want a study in contrast stop & look at some of the big West End shops displaying their latest winter fashions together with enlarged photographs of the war pasted on the windows just high enough not to obscure the contents of the window You can get a taste of the savour of pain & the latest novelties in velvet & fur at the same moment. I suppose it is only human that pretty oval faced girls should prefer what is soft & cosy & elegant to ugly cruel pictures of blood & hatred – Betha won't look at a war picture. They possess me I can't get past them. In their stark & terrible way they tell so much. I found my landlady was German. It was a shock. I nearly backed out but didnt know where else to go – she is naturalized. . . .

I am going down to the Nickalls next week for a few days. They are on night duty at their Red X hospital this week but want me to go down to them all the same. Then I think I shall go down to St Ives in Cornwall where I can live cheap & quiet for the winter, & come the worst it is a prudent spot to be in well out of the way of Zeppelins etc. . . .

No more now dear. I have lots to do. Have found my pictures & am fighting the agents over a preposterous bill for storage. They have not been straight at all & have denied all knowledge of cases for 5 months then sent me in bill for storage! . . .

[240] To Rachel Hodgkins, 19 November 1914

St. Ives. Nov 19th.

Just a short line dearest Mother to say I am well & busy fixing up a Studio with the aid of an old man hired for the purpose, white washing & scrubbing out &

---

[2] Lydia Phillips, the maternal grandmother of Rachel Hodgkins, Lydia Rolin and Betha Rich, was a lively family heroine who, according to legend, had danced at the ball on the eve of Waterloo.

sticking in a few sticks that I have picked up for a few half crowns in the village. It is [a] huge barn that will do very nicely for a Class not pretty – but useful. It gives on a yellow sandy beach & at high tide the waves beat against the walls & sometimes the window – for this commodious loft – studio – pigsty – barn I pay £10 sterling a year – & no suppliments as in Paris where you first tip the concierge, postman, policeman & dustman before installing *yourself*. The weather has been very vile – blizzards for nearly a week . . . the only thing I know to equal it in fury is Central Terrace in a buster. I have been to tea with the Moffat Lindners who have a very lovely artistic house. . . .

[241] TO RACHEL HODGKINS, 8 DECEMBER 1914

St Ives. Dec. 8th.

My dearest Mother

. . . . The Studio is ship shape & any moment I may break out into paint. . . .

Today, contrary to all meteorological forecasts is as mild as Spring. People looked quite young & jolly walking along the Fore St this morning – flaming posters at every step – Three German cruisers sunk – Kaiser *very* ill – & in very small type serious Russian reverse. . . . The cowl has blown off my chimney out to sea, the stove smokes. The plumber will not work till the high gales abate. This day being quite calm & beautiful he brought his ladder – but never mounted it being Thursday & half holiday from 12 o'c. The ladder was removed. He tells me my window *often* blows in in Easterly gales. I think he is a liar. To warm myself I take sharp walks up & down the sands below my window – nobody but the seagulls & black masses of kelp looking like dead crocodiles in the deep dusk. . . .

There has been a strikingly touching little speech by a Maori member on the war & New Zealand's duty to the Mother Country, much copied by the English papers – very fine it was – like a little bit out of a collect. I am thinking of you all this week, this week of weeks. I hope Otaki will have sense & grace to return the right man. There will be many thrills as well as much hard work for Will & Sis. Good luck to them. . . .

[242] TO RACHEL HODGKINS, 6 JANUARY 1915

St Ives. Jan. 6th.

My dearest Mother

A very dull tho' peaceful Xmas is happily over. . . . I eat my dinner alone . . . a slice from the landlady's goose, afterwards walked on the moors with Miss

Henderson[3] & then carols till all was blue. . . . The weather was atrocious, one long blizzard. The rain & sea came in my Studio & I spent some time swabbing up the mess. On New Year's Day, Mr. Garstin came over from Newlyn to see me. He talked very fervidly of the War & its horrors. He is writing some lectures on Disarmament & the Prospect of Peace – but he might as well preach the Sermon on the Mount & expect people to follow it. . . . I wonder if any of you went to the Great Universal Intercession Service agreed upon to be held in churches of every denomination in Britain France & Russia & throughout the Empire – the funds to go to the Red X & St Johns. I went to the celebration here, in the little ivied all over church. I thought it too penitential & abasing – not human or national enough & came home very gloomy & lugubrious instead of consoled & strengthened as surely we were meant to be – after due humiliation & prayer. When I go to the Anglican services I always wish I had been born a Catholic.

It is a steady drench & soak of continuous rain wh. adds to the gloom & sense of tragedy in the air. Everybody is busy in some way or another. Last night I went to a tableaux & concert entertainment for the Red X – sat in the front row with Miss Henderson & applauded heartily. It was got up by artists & the tableaux were mostly R.A. popular pictures, The Black Brunswicker & Cherry Ripe etc. & a stirring patriotic one for the end up.

I start teaching next week with three pupils & more to come. But for the War I should now be in Paris with forty & three I expect. I have one local pupil – a nice woman who is going to be a great help to me in many ways – she has a glorious collection of old china & has given me carte blanche to borrow it when so disposed. She is having a tea party for me this week – 30 people – oh dear! I have been reading a good book – Sinister St. by Compton Mackenzie in 2 vols – excellent – be sure & get it – I seem to get very few letters from you dear – things are so dislocated & uncertain. . . . My little capital is slowly melting. I have hardly earned a stiver for ever so long . . . . Some people are making their fortune by the War – but I am not one of them. . . . Jack Rich is still quartered at Edinburgh. I dread the day when he goes to the Front. I write pretty often but don't get many letters. He is so busy. It might so easily have been Geoff. It is not good to be too much alone these days – one wakes in the night & hears the wind & rain – & straight one is in the trenches visualizing all the lurid & ghastly things one has read in the paper before going to bed. . . . The submarine menace is a new horror.

You will think I have got the blues tonight dear, so will stop & go to bed. . . .

[3] A pupil.

[243] TO RACHEL HODGKINS, 14 JANUARY 1915

St Ives, Cornwall. Jan 14th.

My dearest Mother

It has been almost possible to forget the War so quiet has it been this week & except for the long casualty lists there has been nothing at all dramatic from the Front. . . . I have been almost festive – quite a number of people at the Studio saying pleasant things & another pupil to the good. The lady of the china collection gave a tea party on Saturday. The Studio was so crowded by the time I arrived I could hardly squeeze in & when in there was hardly room to light a cigarette. Much the most interesting person there was a Submarine man, wounded of course but not badly, a large cheerful person who pulled everybodys leg & lapped up muffins & compliments with equal relish. . . . A lady with a face like St. Augustine's Mother recited some bad poetry in a sobbing voice & upturned eye – about the War. The S.M was heard to say it made him sick & wouldn't help recruiting. People who do *real* things are so simple in their mode of speech. He was next heard to remark that he hoped a few German shells would fall in St Ives & rouse up the lazy Cornishmen. This cast a slight shadow on the sun of his popularity – but he didnt seem to mind. I saw him later in the evening at the Art Club take a black bottle from a locker & retire with it while yet we were listening to a humdrum lecture on Burmah by Sir Somebody Something ex Governor of Rangoon. A large breezy soul, entirely undismayed. . . . He came to the Studio one morning & told thrilling tales – & incidentally was most intelligent over my Water Colours. . . . Prices are rising alarmingly – coal & bread are the big items. I am eating N.Z butter with a Wellington brand on it & S. Australian honey, both about 3d. cheaper than the local product & much nicer. . . .

[244] TO RACHEL HODGKINS, 28 JANUARY 1915

St Ives, Cornwall. Jan 28th.

My dearest Mother

At last the good news of Will's victory![4] Hurrah! I am delighted. . . . I have been having quite a flutter. Jack came down from Edinburgh by the night train & it was barely light when I met him & brought him up here. He looked white & tired but a good breakfast of porridge & cream etc soon restored him. We cruised round the village & then to call on two pretty Americans in their Studio who tuned up the gramophone for us & were cordial. We lost no time in getting our photos taken for 4d. a dozen. I send you the results. Jack then bought an expensive Kodak & a yule tide log at the pastry cooks consisting of almond icing

[4] In the 1914 general election, at which the Reform party was returned to power.

& pink cake & an enormous box of chocolates & so home to tea. Next day, very cold & blowey to Penzance & Newlyn. We consulted a Fortune Teller who gave us rather unpleasant characters. She told me my only talent lay in arranging flowers & driving horses. Both of us are to live to a great and undistinguished old age; rather depressed we went & had a large & expensive lunch at the Queen's Hotel on the Parade. We afterwards visited the Art Gallery & freely criticised the pictures, bought a piece of copper work for Betha, took photos of the Newlyn streets, tea & train & home. Next day we arranged [a] motor trip to Land's End & Lizzard. The weather was bad – a violent storm & terrific sea running & it didnt seem possible that we would be able to go – but Sunday morning broke fine & sunny tho' biting cold & up came the car at 9 o'clock & off we flew with hot bottles cushions 6 rugs bottle of wine & ditto stout for refreshment by the way – we had a glorious run to Land's End, about 2 hours, & Jack was delighted. The sea had calmed down & was a vivid green & blue – no boats in sight save one little tin pot steamer carrying guns & puffing up & down. The Coastguardsman told us she had secured a German grain boat the week before & towed her in to Falmouth. We scrambled about the rocks & took some photos & then on to the Lizzard for lunch. . . . From here we drove inland over the icy moors & fetched up about 6 half frozen at Launceston, still in Cornwall where we dined & spent the night at the White Hart. Next morning the country was white with frost & it took some courage to start – the roads were like iron & ice everywhere – we had to abandon the moors & take another route up & down the red Devon coombes, the ploughed lands silvery white & the trees crystalled & cracking like pistol shots under the weight of frost. We got some good photos but the cold was hardly bearable – our faces weren't worth looking at by the time we got to Exeter. Jack was in merry mood. He is an extravagant young dog & lets his money flow about a little too free. We went to a super swanky Hotel & had cold pheasant & what not & dallied so long in the warm smoking room we had no time to see the Cathedral, shame be it spoken. Our faces had lost that hatchetty look & the world seemed a better & brighter place after our good meal. We dashed to the Station & off Jack went in one train & I in another. The final & most dramatic act was the writing of the cheque for the car! Jack is a lovely spender! What his careful parents would say I daren't think. His arguments are so disarming – "I am sure to peg out before long so why not see life while I can." I quite agree & so wld. the little Judge were he here. Jack's last words were "When I come home wounded we'll have another motor trip." He is an endearing lad straight as they make them & with high principles & stiff convictions on several subjects that make one feel very confident in him. He looked little more than a child & yet there he is with the power of life & death over 50 stalwart men & very much master of his Fate – this is within limitations as far as anyone can be these stormy times – I wish he & Geoff could know each other. It was great larks flying round the country in the depth of winter in an open car with a dashing young subaltern. Everyone thought we were mad – but it ended all right. . . .

It is rather flat coming back to work. Snow is in the air & it is a black east wind & very vilely cold. . . .

[245] To Rachel Hodgkins, 4 February 1915

St Ives. Feb. 4th.

My dearest Mother,

. . . . The war has entered upon a still more deadly aspect – submarines have got round this coast 1200 miles from base & are menacing our merchant & traffic routes. Spies have been very active in Cornwall & the St Ives people are feeling very sick because they were so nice to a young German Count who took a Studio here last year. After war was declared Studio was raided charts of every cove, road, track, rock, tides & currents were found & copious diaries. The Count himself escaped – we heard there was a german submarine in Newquay Harbour 2 days ago – about 30 miles from here. . . . It is mild & calm. I had a dish of Spring rhubarb from the Scilly Islands yesterday 2d. a bundle – so good – coal & bread still rising. . . .

[246] To Rachel Hodgkins, 17 February 1915

St Ives. Feb 17th.

My dearest Mother

. . . . Today is Ash Wednesday – Last year I was in Italy & it was so spring like & lovely – here squalling gales & grey skies & a terrible black menace in the air. Tomorrow is the day the German Blockade of England commences. The British flesh doesn't creep very easily – but I fancy people are uneasy & anxious. Bills are posted up in the town today offering £1000 to the fishermen who will help destroy mines or submarines or bring in any news of enemy ships – a big premium for bravery. . . . You can imagine it is not easy to paint in the circumstances. And yet I am – I drive myself to it but the feeling of insecurity weighs one down with depression & dark doubts. It is rather lonely too – I have no friends here as in Paris. I find I am too modern for people down here & I am conscious of the cold eye of distrust & disapproval by the older members of St Ives. It is not an inspiring atmosphere tho' I love it for many other things. I will go a long way before I find another Studio like the one I have now. . . .

[247] To Rachel Hodgkins, 25 February 1915

St Ives. Feb 25th.

My dearest Mother

It is a most perfect day – I wish you were here – It is not often I feel like sharing this climate with anyone. . . . I had meant to work hard this week but outrageous Fortune is against me & I have been 4 days chiefly in bed with a chill. I think living alone is rather depressing in a climate like this. I am considering whether I can stand it much longer. If a few more pupils wld. roll up I would go to [a] nice boarding house I know of who wld. take me for 30/- & where I at least wld. eat my food in human society. This place is very nice & Mrs. Pond a treasure tho' a desponding one. She *never* will smile. The sun shone hot & bright on my bed this morning I said How lovely & she replied Yes but its very black in the front. "All is lost" is stamped indelibly on her weary face – that weary Celtic look poets rave about – most depressing I find it. . . . I hear from Paris there is nothing doing in the art world. In fact charitable people are instituting canteens in the Latin Quarter & Montmatre to supply hard up artists & students with free meals . . . .

Dear old Mr. Peter Waite of Adelaide wrote me such a beautiful letter the other day saying how sorry he was I had lost my sketches in Italy & enclosing cheque for £50 to help a little to make up for loss. It was so touching. I won't touch the money for I am not so reduced as that but it will give me great moral support to know it is there if things get worse – as they are bound to as far as I can look into the sinister future. My ill fated profession is going to feel the pinch pretty badly. Why was I so prodigal last year, travelling about as tho' I had endless resources – Still I don't regret it. It was the first, absolutely the first time I felt happy & secure & sure of myself. I was in full flight & full of aspiration! The war has put much that might have been quite out of reach. . . .

[248] To Rachel Hodgkins, 28 April 1915

St Ives. April 28th.

My dearest little Mother,

. . . . A short line from Jack this morning before he left for the front. Really gone this time & I fear his days are numbered. . . . This latest aspect of the War makes one sick at heart. These poisonous gases are hellish . . . . Life here is calm enough. Coal is down 2d. Rates up. . . . The country is a sight to behold – mostly yellow as the yoke of an egg with gorse & cowslips & King cups & smelling like pudding – so gorgeous & gay.

These warm young Spring days make you long for the ending of this hideous war, so the world could be happy again.

I am very busy in a pleasant way. Not such a rush as sometimes. Did I tell you I have a picture in the R.A. A large one.[5] I don't know where placed. No flies on the R.A this year! A kind thoughtful action like this puts you in a good frame of mind! It is nearly 10 years since I have hung on their august walls. Have I my lucid moments or have They?. . .

[249] To Rachel Hodgkins, 15 May 1915

Tree Inn, Sithney, Cornwall. May 15th.

My Dearest Mother

. . . . The war news stupefies one – It is impossible to escape depression. You look at the apple blossom & wonder if the war will be over by the time the apples are red & rosy. An old gipsy woman at the door yesterday said to the Landlord "As sure as you have fifteen & tuppence in your pocket the war will be over in June." And the old man slowly counted out the exact sum. I did not see it myself but I like to believe it is true. . . .

How proud the Dominion must feel at the glorious way the New Zealanders fought at Sari Bair Beach in Gallipoli. It was magnificent. I have sent you papers with glowing accounts of their doughty deeds. The losses are appalling. The Times today gives the list of officers' casualties, British, Canadian & Australasian, as 1,400 odd! *in ten days* on all the Fronts. These are days of "pure killing". We will never be able to forget it. The material desolation or the awful personal loss. No news of Jack for 10 days. The last letter was from the trenches under shell fire cheery & full of courage. He says the food is good & plenty of it. I got a farmer's wife to bake him a currant loaf & I sent this off today with a lb of good butter which I think will warm the cockles of his heart bless him. He said he had been in the trenches for five days & had only seen one live German – tho plenty of dead ones lying in the No Man's Land between the trenches – 60 metres apart.

. . . . I think the Germans really believe they are going to triumph . . . And the worst of it is they have every reason in supposing so . . . . One hears the Officers in "Kitcheners" Army are a drunken & dissolute lot. One knows they are not all gentlemen. I heard there was a notice put up in some barracks "Temporary Sub-Lieutenants are requested to behave as Temporary Gentlemen". This sounds like high treason – I had better drop it. When I go back to St Ives next week I am going into new lodgings. A change of landladys is sometimes desirable. . . . I have been offered a sweet little Georgian House of 6 rooms & a small garden for £15 a year. It is rather tempting. It would mean a servant of course – But how much nicer than rooms & hideous furniture at 25/- a week. The war, or the effects of

---

[5] FH's pictures at the RA were: 1903, *Fatima*; 1904, *Vegetable Stall, Dinan*; 1905, *Market Day, Dinan*; 1915, *Mardi Gras*; 1916, *Gypsies*.

it, may last another 3 years, one feels the longing to sit tight at a time when this
malign force abroad is sapping & snatching lifes' resources away.

I had a visit from a most beautiful & attractive woman the other day at my
Studio – The Ranee of Sarawak. I don't know if you have ever heard of her. She
is the wife of the White Rajah of Sarawak in Borneo. A serene Highness in every
sense of the word. She has written a book on her life in Sarawak wh. I am told
is worth reading. . . . I am asked to tea with her next week. Miss Winthrop & Miss
Stafford[6] are coming out for the day tomorrow – Mrs. Long, the landlady, says she
will make us a chicken pie. She is a tall toppling body with a lean hatchett face
& her cooking is not her strong point. Every time she brings up my dinner she
says "Another poor soul put to rest". . . .

Jack Rich was killed in action 17 May 1915.

[250] To Rachel Hodgkins, 17 June 1915
> 7 Porthmeor Studio, St Ives. June 17th

My Dearest little Mother

I see there is a mail your way tomorrow so a line to say I am well & busy, which
is the nearest one can get to happiness these sad days. . . . Give my love &
congratulations to Muriel & Bertie on the newly born. Tell them to be more
patriotic next time. Two sisters rather run in the family. But, please, *boys* in the
future for La Patrie!

Poor N.Z. such a lot of her brave boys have gone. . . .

I am still without any details of Jack's death. Today I had letters from his father
& Mother. Poor Betha – she was suffering torments of anxiety when she wrote,
wh. was 3 weeks before Jack was killed. He had cabled for his father's birthday on
the 28th. April, "Hodgkins looking after me" wh. of course made them think him
wounded & they both wrote full of gratitude & anxiety. . . . Oh it is all so heart
rending – where is it to end? Every house is full of sorrow & mourning. If only
we women could go off & make shells or bullets – I believe they will soon. They
are doing all they can to release men & do their jobs.

I have given up my rooms & come down to the Studio to sleep. This will be
a big economy . . . . I have got a gas cooker installed & am doing my own chores,
with extreme disrelish let me tell you – but I feel it is a wise precaution to save as
much as possible for pupils are dropping off & many who are expected are not
coming. . . . Tomorrow is Waterloo Centenary! Two nights ago, on the 15th. 100

[6] A portrait of Miss Eva Stafford along with five other works was exhibited with the International Society of
Sculptors, Painters and Gravers in the Grosvenor Gallery, London, in October 1915.

years ago the Duchess of Richmonds Ball & our Great Grandmother possibly hob nobbing with Becky Sharp & Rawdon & Dobbin and all that push. I felt ghosts were about. To lose dear Jack in Flanders, her great great grandson, just a century-all-but-a-few-weeks after![7] Jack was a true Phillips – on the female side.

[251] To Rachel Hodgkins, 22 July 1915

St Ives. July 22nd.

My Dearest Little Mother

. . . . The shock of the week was being turned off a nice little rocky retreat we had found for ourselves far from the madding crowd – and we hoped the Constables eye. . . . No such luck. He found us out and out we had to go – sketching is strictly prohibited within sight of the coast which means it is practically prohibited everywhere . . . . I discovered this nice little cove over an old mine . . . very private & secluded, walled in, & almost invisible to passers by. . . . For 2 blessed weeks we posed our models there & crossed ourselves piously thinking how lucky we were. Then pounced the Sargeant himself & turned us out of our Eden. I am very low in my mind to know what to do. It is such a bore to have to work indoors when the sun shines. . . . I am now searching for a garden where I can have my model groups – but even gardens are at a premium.

I have now 10 pupils – one just crossed from Paris & an old favourite – Bessie Gibson from Brisbane, come to England to say goodbye to a brother just off to the Dardanelles. . . .

. . . . I heard from [Judge Rich] again today – poor restless little man, without news & aching to hear any scrap of news – But there is none – I am still pestering the War Office for news & have written to the Colonel of the Regt. in the Judge's name & hope soon for an answer.

I had tea with the Moffat Lindners on Sunday . . . . The Julius Olssons were there. He is a bloated A.RA & is spreading himself, large & pink, having just sold his big marine [picture] to the Sydney Gallery.[8] I don't coalese with RA. people, tho' I tried my best to charm! . . .

[252] To Rachel Hodgkins, 16 August 1915

7 Porthmeor Studio, St Ives. Aug 16th.

My Dearest Mother

. . . . The weather is gorgeous and my girls have been painting imps up on the

---

[7] FH is combining family history with Thackeray's account of the ball before Waterloo in *Vanity Fair*. Jack Rich was the great grandson of Lydia Phillips.
[8] *The Night Tide* by Julius Olsson (1864-1942).

moors or in gardens or any mortal thing that turns up in the way of a willing model. I have been hard put to it keeping my Class together, converting landscape painters into figure dittos, pushed into it against their will, but liking it hugely once they start. Three girls went off today bubbling over with enthusiasm, one of them with a picture of mine under her arm wh. she bought for 10 guineas – a welcome windfall to me. I wonder when I shall live by painting & selling only. How delightful. It is so tantalizing to be within sight of so many beautiful things to paint, rocks, pools skies paddling children & bits of coast – I tried my best blandishments on the Sergeant from time to time promising not an inch of coast line to be included but he is adamant & threatens to confiscate my painting gear if I dont look out. He says the Cornish artists "worry him awful" they are so "teasy". I told him it was very worrying to the poor artists to be so treated. At times it seems so callous & selfish & somehow so petty, as if my little world at the end of my nose, or rather paint brush, were all that mattered, when men are dying every minute for my safety. And yet it seems our lot to go on earning our bread as if nothing mattered & our own private welfare was of first importance. It is a queer jumbled up world at present. The year drags on & we make no real progress. The Russian affairs look very grave. If they capitulate now it will go badly with the West – Heaven forbid – I think the Czar wld. sign a peace. . . . I heard the other day we had taken 68 enemy submarines since the war broke out & have established a pretty effective blockade. When one knows that not a single transport or a packet of stores has been lost it is really wonderful. . . . Judge Rich tells me he has heard from the C.O. of Jack's Regt. & the Capt. of his Company who both said he "had behaved with the utmost gallantry on all occasions". He was killed instantaneously. . . . Everybody is making sandbags now splashed with brown, blue & black paint, a dodge of course borrowed from the enemy, to baffle the enemy guns. . . . Did I tell you I have a kitten, a very ugly yellow one called Rufus, of a good amiable character but of no pedigree. I take him out on the sands & he is exactly the same shade, like a nicely done piece of toast. He follows just like a dog – indeed I am training him not to be too much of a cat. St Ives cats are all rakes & look as if they fed on lids of sardine tins & blue bottles – but they keep the mice from eating us up. . . . I have ordered the nice winter coat for you such a nice comely shape & shade I think. I am sure you will like it. . . . I do wish I had thought of it sooner so as to keep you cosy & warm dear. Be sure & wear it yourself dear. Remember you & I are the ones who must *keep* things for ourselves. All the others have protectors who clothe them in rich attire. I am cutting down exs all I can. Food is so dear. I eat meat once a week & then it is tough & nasty. I have found an eating-house where they will give you a slice off the roast for 6d. . . .

[253] To Rachel Hodgkins, August 1915

[St Ives, Cornwall]

Dearest little Mother

. . . . It appears Jack was caught by a machine gun on his return with two of his men, from a dangerous piece of work, taking re-inforcements to advance trenches. . . . His Captain said he was continually seen to stand up & cheer his men on till ordered to lie down & seemed certain to win distinction by his fine courage. . . . One of my protegées brothers has won the R.SM at the Dardanelles. She is my favourite model, the one in the R.A picture & comes of a poor but honest family of a very sturdy Cornish stock. I took round some flowers & found the family in decent black, granny, widow & four little ginger tops, very solemn in the front room. The fact that he was slightly wounded out weighed the honour, wh. they scarcely seemed to realize. I said in my excited way, "How splendid to have a hero son." "So Lady 'Ayne says" said Mrs Kitchen calmly "but I make it out like this miss Willy 'ad to do it & he done it" which after all is the simplest form of heroism robbed of all tiresome psychology.

Laura Knight,[9] the Newlyn painter & her husband are here painting, she is painting nude children bathing, with all St Ives looking on, the horrified & the un- together & even the Sergeant himself not knowing whether to interfere in the interests of public morality or not. The mother of "Frankie" who was being painted together with 11 others told me "lor miss to see 'er paint the parting in the boys' 'ed & down his back would frighten yer" Next day she went a step further – tapping Mrs. Knight on the shoulder she told her, fair & square if she didnt instantly put bathing drawers on all the 13 boys in her picture she would go for the Sergeant. Mrs. Knight realising the situation & anxious to avoid trouble gave 2/- to the biggest youth & told him to clear off & buy pants but whether she altered her picture or not is doubtful. . . .

[254] To Rachel Hodgkins, 16 September 1915

St Ives. Sept 16th.

My dearest Mother

. . . . I have a little more time than usual on my hands, since last writing a new

[9] Dame Laura Knight (1887-1970), who had arrived in Newlyn with her husband Harold in 1907, became one of the most successful, wealthy and popular British artists of her day. Her work was accessible because it was figurative, naturalistic and dealt with recognisable and appealing subjects: children, ballet dancers, circus performers, gypsies. Feminist art historians find particularly interesting her pictures of women performing men's work during the Second World War, while her *Self-Portrait with Nude* of 1913 appeared on the cover of *Looking On*, a 1987 compilation of feminist texts. Somewhat scorned by the avant garde, which included Frances Hodgkins, she may be reassessed as a fine painter and intelligent recorder of her world. Her autobiography, *Oilpaint and Greasepaint*, appeared in 1936.

edict forbidding *all sketching* in Cornwall has been issued which came like a thunder bolt, scattering my pupils & placing me in the novel position of wondering what I would do next. A fine of £40 if one is caught with an easel or a camera – Some conscientious coast watchers even confiscate strangers field glasses & spectacles, but these are the rabid ones. We have protested & made all the fuss we dare . . . . By keeping out of the eye of the Sergeant, who has promised not to run me in more often than he need, & sending my painting kit stealthily over night, I am able to work in the Weir Lewis' garden round their lily pond, but it is nervey work & any moment may be stopped. A Concentration Camp & food allowance is what they should do with us seeing they are depriving us of our daily bread & butter. Mrs. Weir Lewis keeps on having lessons in a methodical & sensible way & pays me 4 guineas a month for helping her acquire a good imitation of the Hodgkins style. . . . An old pupil, with an unfortunate enemy name & appearance, but loyally British, who came down from Bristol to do a little work, I am helping along with lessons & assisting her to show her sketches, wh. are very able & attractive.[10] She is hard hit & hardly knows where to turn. . . .

. . . . I have taken a large empty studio next door & am rigging it up for winter Classes starting next month. It is £10 rent like this. I hope to fill it – with luck. . . .

[255] To Rachel Hodgkins, 29 September 1915

7 Porthmeor Studio, St Ives. Sept 29th.

My Darling Mother

The weather has broken at last & is now wintry & wet, & I am finding it hard work keeping warm in the Studio. I am having the sea windows cemented up for the winter to keep out the draughts . . . . If possible I shall try & light my room with gas . . . petrol is so dear & going up still higher & I use so much with two lamps especially as I paint a good deal by lamp light. . . . A few hardy souls are still dipping in the foam, in spite of wind & rain. As I write there are two girls in front of my window bobbing about like corks in the surf, peacock waves breaking over them & the rain coming down. Such is youth! The Zepp raids over London were real & earnest. The lakes & ponds in the Parks have been drained dry these many months so as not to be a landmark. But there is still the Thames, which is an indestructible guide it seems. The great fact is that no one seems to have been scared into panic. It must have been a fine & appalling sight to see over your beloved London a silver slug dealing death & destruction, out of reach of the

---

[10] The friendship with Amy Krauss, who became a successful potter and occasional painter, lasted until FH's death.

helpless mortals below. What a sensation. Fancy children being born into this new age – and there will still be children who will skip the train age & be born into the Zeppelin-airship age – who may never know what it feels like to lumber over the map of Europe in a train!

Now I have to go to a silly tea – & back to paint by six o'clock. I have a night piece in oil[11] on the go, which promises well. . . .

[256] To Rachel Hodgkins, 9 November 1915

St Ives. 9 Nov.

My dearest Mother

Since my last letter I have been on a 4 day's trip to London. After thinking about it for a long time I made up my mind quite suddenly & went the next day, and now I am back again feeling . . . rather like a gorged Python who has eaten a rather fat missionary. . . . . I was very spartan & never entered a shop or bought a thing, came as I went in country clothes & only one hat to my head & that one St Ives. . . . It is the smart thing to be shabby – to wear last years clothes . . . . I *never* felt more at home in London. . . . Khaki everywhere – I listened in Trafalgar Square on Sat: afternoon to war battered soldiers recruiting. It was a slow business – in ½ an hour they got one man aged 39 for the Finsbury Rifles. Australians & New Zealanders were extolled & rammed down the slacker's throats. What *will* the Colonials think of *you* – I heard again & again. One woman, with a pair of old boots & a service cap on her arm (her dead sons) got up on the plinth of Nelson's Monument & cajoled, exhorted & foamed, begging men to join – but many walked away. . . . I went the first morning to the International in Bond St and found my pictures very well hung, 4 on the line. They looked their best on the vieux rose damask walls & I wished it were my lot never to show anywhere else but in the gracious Grosvener Gallery. I was in town too short a time to see many people. People I looked up were away, recruiting or doing some war work or other. . . . The change has done me good. This is a very relaxing climate & I was feeling enervated & lifeless. I supped on Sunday night at Hampstead with the Robt. Lynds.[12] They had a little party of literary people all interesting who talked in a golden-silvery way of their own rather flashing & brilliant. I kept up a poor end of the conversation but then I was expected to be a looker on. This particular little group are born conversationalists – the men (the husbands) were rather silent, both being writers, the two pretty wives shining. I kept wondering what we

[11] The first mention of working in oil since the lessons in Beronneau's studio in 1908. There is no obvious 'night piece' among FH's early oil paintings. The earliest known, *Loveday and Ann: Two Women with a Basket of Flowers,* now in the Tate Gallery, dates from this time.
[12] Robert Lynd (1879-1949), journalist and essayist with the *Nation* and the *New Statesman,* and Sylvia Lynd (1888-1952), literary editor, poet and novelist, author of *The Chorus,* 1915, and *The Swallow Dive,* 1921.

would all do if Zepps came – would we die as a quintet or how? In any case it would be good company & I wondered how their wit would stand the test. If they would die the death with a neat epigram etc. . . . .

[257] To Isabel Field, 16 November 1915

7 Porthmeor Studio, St Ives, Cornwall. Nov 16th.

My Dearest Sis

Bertie's letter with news of Mother's illness[13] has just come. It is dreadful to hear of the poor darling suffering so. . . . . Bert says your care & devotion pulled Mother round and that you never spared yourself night or day. Remembering other family crises & how you rose to the occasion & helped us all in our trouble I am not surprised. . . . . I catch at the hope that Mothers health & vitality will resist this attack grave as it sounds and that strength will come back with the warm spring days but oh! how terribly prostrated & weak she must be after the pain. I feel rather dazed. We have just passed thro' the fiercest storm for over 40 years. It began to blow about 10 at night – such a night. The Studio rocked like a baby's cradle & at dawn looked like a drunkard's home. The sky light blew in & of course floods of rain. About 4 o'c a fisherman came round & begged me to shelter in their house but I stuck it out, made a cup of cocoa & went to bed again. . . . . Tiles rained down in the courtyard & windows & chimneys crashed & banged. One man's Studio close by was blown clean down & half out to sea . . . . Poor Gertrude Crompton's only brother is killed & leaves a broken Mother to mourn him. . . . .

[258] To Rachel Hodgkins, 10 January 1916

St Ives. 10.1.16.

Darling Mother

You can imagine how glad I was to see your dear handwriting once more. I feel ever so much happier about you now . . . . But you must not strain your eyes by writing to me, much as I love getting letters . . . . Shingles is very prevalent – no doubt the anxiety & worries caused by the war have much to do with it. . . . I am so glad the jacket is a success. I thought it rather nice & comfy myself. . . . I am working hard – immersed in portraits for the Nat: Portrait Soc: in Feb: to which I am asked to send, & I hope for the same good luck as at the International – but you never can tell – what you think damgood they may think quite the opposite. Mr. Lindner & his little girl Hope are posing for me against his great Studio

---

[13] Mrs Hodgkins, now aged 77, suffered a painful attack of shingles in the head and eyes.

window – open, with the wind tossing her brown hair, the sea beyond. They wear such jolly tweed clothes, he snuff coat, check waistcoat & orange tie with black spots – & his jolly pink face & white curls – same colouring as Father – you may remember he always reminds me of him, a young edition – very dapper. Hope in grey tweed, berry red buttons & bright blue Tam, white stockings. This is a 4ft.x3ft. canvas in oil – and so far it shapes well[14] . . . .

I am sad about my little cat. He has been ill of a mysterious ailment, probably distemper, for 3 weeks & I seem unable to cure him. He is thin as a ribbon & so pathetic he wrings my heart. . . .   Poor little beast, he is such a wise little cat follows me as far as I like to take him, even carries messages like a carrier pigeon to & fro from 2 studios where he is on friendly terms. . . .

A diversion here – Coast watcher, in khaki, six ft. tall with a couple of dogs & a revolver, just looked in to say I have too much light in my window. He tied up dogs & looked at cat (I consult all comers) . . . . The Judge writes always – so sad – He feels it more as time passes – I am helping him with Jacks biography for a reference book. No more now dearest, to bed early tonight. I work like a nailer these days. I feel I have the thin end of the wedge rammed in now all right. Friends say my work is much stronger now than ever – I feel it is – perhaps the war has vitalised & fortified – who knows. No new pupils yet, but booking up for summer. Much love & much thankfulness that you are well again. *Keep* well wont you. . . .

[259] TO RACHEL HODGKINS, 10 FEBRUARY 1916

7 Porthmeor Studio, St. Ives, Cornwall. 10.2.16

My Darling Mother

It is *so* cold now. We have caught it at last – wild storms with big seas running. It is like a noisy cab rank below my windows – the shingles being hurled about by the high tides. If I am here another winter I must try & get shutters rigged up to keep out the cold & noise at night. It is quite likely I may be here for several winters the monotonous way the war drags on. I am working hard at my portraits. It is some relief in one way, not to have pupils – it leaves so much more time & strength for work. . . . I am giving some private criticisms to a woman artist here wh. brings in a little. I had a letter last week from the Judge's London Solicitors saying they had heard from him that he wished to make a payment into my Bank as he was certain my profession was suffering severely. They wished to know what amount I would like – I gladly accepted the offer & asked for £15.0.0. which was promptly paid. I know how sincerely the Judge meant it. He had written about

[14] The painting underwent considerable modification. Called *Mr and Mrs Moffat Lindner and Hope,* it is now in Dunedin Public Art Gallery.

it several times and I am certain he will be glad I have accepted his generous help. He never forgets that the artist has to struggle for his bread & butter. I don't feel the same hesitation about accepting help now as I used to. I am in a better position & my earning powers are greater. This bad weather won't last for ever & soon business will buck up and things get busy again. My painting is as strong again as it was a year ago. Mr. Lindner whose opinion I value, says my old work is not worth looking at compared to it. Certainly I am gaining recognition at last – & high time too. I am waiting for the verdict on my last portraits sent to London. I should hear any day now. I sold my possum furs the other day for £3 & was glad to be so clever as to convert them into a commodity I was more in need of at the moment. What do you think of that? I am half way on with Jack's portrait . . . . It is in oils & rather like the dear boy I think. All my work is in oils for the moment. . . .

[260] To Rachel Hodgkins, 11 March 1916

St Ives. 11.3.16

My dearest Mother

Yesterday was Show Day, *and* snow day . . . . *Thats* over thank goodness & the pictures in their cases & off. I am so tired. I would like to go off now for a change – but it is too cold to leave your own bed & fire – besides where to go? Friends are all working & don't want you. . . . This afternoon I went into the country to tea with a friend just back from France & brought back an armful of daffs. It was very cold & muddy but I enjoyed it after being in the Studio so much. She took me to see a dear old man called Hudson a naturalist who is convalescing in a cottage near her. He is rather a celebrity in his way & has written much about the fauna of Cornwall. He knew much more about NZ than I did & corresponds with the Agricultural Dept. etc. Such a fine head, like Geo Meredith – sad & noble. I brought home his book on these parts[15]. . . . The wind has dropped & there is a love of a moon – such a night to go Zepping. . . .

[261] To Rachel Hodgkins, 29 March 1916

7 Porthmeor Studio, St. Ives, Cornwall. 29.3.16.

My Dearest little Mother

. . . . I told you in my last I had met a NZ man from Gallipolli, wounded, who knew Willie & had played golf with him in Masterton. . . . It was Mr

[15] W. H. Hudson (1841-1922), the Argentine naturalist, is better known for his novel *Green Mansions*, 1904, and his autobiographical *Far Away and Long Ago*, 1918, than for *The Lands End*, his account of Cornwall.

Beresford Maunsell, nephew of the Dunedin family of that name. . . . very nice, quiet fair typical New Zealander longing to get home again. He has a riddled lung poor chap but is getting on all right & I think a few spoonfuls of St Ives air will brace him for the voyage. . . . I dined with him . . . as the guest of some gay & pretty ladies, friends of the Moffat Lindners . . . . 4 of us – a pretty little Anglo Indian grass widow called Radcliffe chaperoning a lovely tall girl, neice of Oscar Wilde, so like him I could swear she was his daughter – her name Wilde. Of course the only thing I wished to talk about was her uncle – but with an effort controlled myself. She had a great trumpet shaped mouth & langorous blue eyes & looked as if she got up late & didnt mend her clothes. But *so* attractive. They saw me home in the moonlight through a lovely wood, the grounds of the old castle wh. is now the Great Western Hotel. It was quite haunted & enchanted & I was very entertained. . . . I have been hard at work getting ready for the next International in April – lost to the world, frowning if anyone comes to the door & making myself thoroughly disliked. You have to keep your neighbours at bay with a big stick if you want to work. The Portrait Soc: did so well it has kept open another month. Think of that as a war performance. I am lucky to be in such a good show. Invitations to show pour in now. "We hope you will send as we want to have things by all the best women artists of the day" sort of style – pleasant & *so* different to what it used to be. Very handy thing to make a hit. I am still uncertain where to go in the summer – must make up my mind soon & get out of this & try & let my Studio while I am away – it should not be difficult in the summer. The first warm day I shall sow my nasturtium seeds in the tubs – & paint them (the tubs) bright yellow with azure blue bands – what do you think of that? One must keep up one's spirits – & colour does cheer one in this drab old courtyard. . . .

[262] To Rachel Hodgkins, 13 April 1916

[St Ives] April 13th.

My Dearest Mother

Only a line this mail as I am not up to anything more ambitious for the moment. I had hardly posted my last letter when quite suddenly I got a bad quinsy & had to go to bed where I have been for the last 9 days . . . . I had been going it rather too hard & I suppose got run down anyway it caught me in the middle of my work for the International & has smashed that up all right.[16] People have been beyond kind & everything from old Brandy to aluminium saucepans has been showered on me. . . . The Lindners instructed the Dr. to get me well & send in the bill to them. They believe I am going to make such a lot of money one

---

[16] FH showed with the International Society in both May and October 1916.

day with my oils that a little help now shouldnt come amiss. . . . It is almost worth while to have been ill to get well again – it seems so good to be alive with friends & a brain full of work. . . .

With the approach of summer FH left St Ives to look for a suitable village for a summer class. She first spent a few restful days with Miss Winthrop in Exeter and then four days in London, where her pictures were 'all well displayed & not looking too awful'. Basing herself in the small town of Evesham, she explored the nearby villages on a hired bicycle, finally settling on Chipping Campden in Gloucestershire.

[263] TO RACHEL HODGKINS, 22 JUNE 1916
Noel Arms Hotel, Chipping Campden, Glos. 22-6-16

My Dearest Mother
. . . . After a hot climb up the Cotswolds I found this place as dear a little grey town as you could wish to see & *such* a nice Inn & landlady who understands our temperament & feeds us well & simply. It is on the very top of the Cotswolds (not so very high – but they think it is quite a mountain) & you see great views over 12 counties when it is not too hazy. I am so well, feeling happy & pacified & cheerful about the Class wh. I hope is going to be a good one. I have one pupil, a nice elderly man, not unacquainted with wealth. . . . I gather he escapes from his family for a few weeks & pursues his hobby – then is pounced on & brought back to the fold after a little gentle coasting on the extreme edge of Bohemia. . . .

[264] TO RACHEL HODGKINS, 6 JULY 1916
Noel Arm's Hotel, Chipping Campden, Glos. July 6th.

Dearest Little Mother So glad you have had that nice little trip to the Farm[17]. . . . What a lovely place Sis must have made of it – her magical "touch" – and plenty of patience & a pretty big backache as well. . . . The poor farmers are having an awful time getting in their hay – heavy thunder showers doing their worst. I am painting babies till the hay dries & they can get on with the ricks – but they (the babies) all seem to come out like Winston Churchill. . . . Hearts are

---

[17] The homestead at Waikanae, north of Wellington. Since the time of his marriage to Isabel in the 1890s Will Field had gradually been acquiring land in the area. By 1923 he owned 3000 acres of coastal plain, with interests in flaxmilling as well as farming. A keen tramper and lover of the native bush, he was a founding member of the Scenery Preservation Society in 1903, a forward-looking group in those entrepreneurial days, and was responsible for the preservation of stands of native bush in the Waikanae district.

lighter since this fine news from France last Sat: now they have let drive in real earnest & there will be no mistake this time please Heaven.[18] I am sending Girlie a little washing silk blouse given me by a friend – I never wear things that want washing (how nasty I hear you say) so post it on to Girlie to make use of. Did I tell you of Mr. Waites last kindness? He wants some more sketches or says he does & is depositing another £50 at my Bank for me – isnt he a grand old friend. He & the Judge between them keep the kindest watch over me. The best friend I have in England is an Australian. . . . The Nickalls have just lost a beloved sister. There is no end to their losses since the war. I think this sister has died from a broken heart at the loss of her two sons. . . .

[265] To Rachel Hodgkins, 22 July 1916

Chipping Campden, Glos. 22.VII.16.

My Dearest Mother

. . . . I have now a thriving class, and lots more coming in Aug: luck isn't it? Not much time to spare these days. I am on the go early & late, but it agrees with me to be busy & out of doors. I have a cold bath at 6.30 get my letters & answer them before breakfast, when we all assemble to discuss the order of the day – then out till 1.o'c, after lunch a siesta & again to work after an early tea – dinner at 7.30. Gorgeous hot weather now starting with early mists & clearing off the hills clear & blue by 10 – then a real scorch, very good for the bones, which have got a bit stiff with so much damp & cold. I am nicely brown now & feeling very fit & hard. . . . Have you heard poor Alice McGowans boy is missing believed killed – too awful for her poor girl. . . . A girl who was coming to me has written she has lost 2 brothers in the Big Push, & yet writes so gallantly & bravely. . . .

[266] To Rachel Hodgkins, 5 August 1916

Campden, Glos. Aug 5th.

My Dearest Mother

. . . . I have a big party round me & I am teaching both morning & afternoon . . . . They are rather a dull lot of human beings, & I think to myself that any Art School Master wld. be good enough for them & curse secretly at having to lay out so much strength & energy in such unpromising material. . . . The best of them are doing war work & have no time for anything but helping the stern prosecution of the war – so I have to put up with the duffers & be as patient as I can. I have great contempt for the pampered well fed English woman whose

---

[18] The disastrous Battle of the Somme began on 1 July 1916.

physical wellfare is her only thought. . . . I am for ever listening to complaints about the beds & the cooking, & the Town clock, & the motor cars in the court yard, & the escape of gas & cold hot water in the morning, tough toast & bad butter – I sleep in a hot attic myself . . . & I am up at 6 & on the go all day, talking & painting & looking for rooms for the latest new comer & happily go to bed so tired out I sleep like a log like the weary maids in the other attics beside me . . . .

. . . . A nice & unexpected thing happened yesterday. I got a letter from an old school friend Dolly Murdoch (now Darling) from Oamaru asking me to paint her a £5 sketch – she had seen I had a picture in the R.A. Such are the sweet uses of advertisement. I was rather touched – she was one of Miss Dick's[19] girls. . . . .

[267] To Rachel Hodgkins, 9 September 1916
Noel Arms Hotel, Campden, Glos. Sept 9th. 1916

My Dearest Mother

A short line to say I am well but very busy finishing off pupils who depart tomorrow . . . . I feel very tired & brain fagged – nothing left in the reservoir so to speak – but next week I can relax . . . perhaps go blackberrying & gathering mushrooms. . . . I stay on till the end of month finishing my pictures for the International then back to St Ives – & Ginger, who I hear is fat & arrogant & grown too big for his basket. . . . The country is looking sweet now – the horrible greeness has gone. . . . I am on a large picture of bathing boys. There is a pool in one of the fields, rather public, & I have to dodge the villagers & especially the Superintendent of Police who suspects I have some stunt up my sleeve not quite quite. I bribe the boys to bathe at 1/- a head & buns all round – I have to go like the wind for fear of being caught, but I have nearly finished now. The pool is really rather a mud hole & full of rats, but it has a lovely old ruined gateway near it & makes a perfect setting for a pastoral. . . .

By the beginning of October 1916 FH was back in St Ives. Anticipating another bleak winter, she spent some of her savings on shutters, carpet and curtains for the studio, but the old building continued to resist her attempts to make it warm and comfortable. No letters survive for the winter, during which she once again spent some time with Miss Winthrop in Exeter.

---

[19] Miss Jessie Dick, principal of Braemar House, where the Hodgkins sisters received their secondary education.

[268] To Rachel Hodgkins, 22 February 1917

St Ives. Feb. 22nd.

My Dearest Mother

I am afraid it is some time since my last but I have had rather a trying time combatting a chill which got hold of me as soon as I got back. The sudden change from the warm house to a draughty studio in this polar like cold was bound to be risky. Luckily it was no worse – I stopped in bed for 4 days, rolled in a blanket & Sarah Couch came in & lit the fire & kept my hot bottle filled. One morning the water in it was frozen. . . . The submarines are giving our boats a hot time . . . . I found all St Ives shuddering at a sight they had seen that very day I got back, a big grain boat, torpedoed 4 miles out, in sight of the shore, gunboats, seaplanes airships, & patrols all on the scene & our life boat to the rescue. It took 5 minutes to sink & then the sea was as if there had been no ship there. Almost every day the black ball goes up which is a warning submarines are about & there is frequent firing which means there is a fight not far off between patrols & sub. . . . I have been sitting tight & wondering what on earth to do to raise the wind. . . . I took to going to bed at 7 o'clock to save light & coal – which is not gay. I lived on a hot splosh I concocted of potatoes, onions, herbs & a dash of salad oil, a first rate savoury mess if you are hungry & *very* nourishing & staying – but dull, like going to bed early – finally came the last shilling, & like a gambler I laid it out, as my last throw, on ½ cwt of coke – then sat down to face the unwelcome job of writing to Miss Winthrop to tell her that I was stuck & that she was right there were no pupils. Well that very next morning a letter came from a woman in Dublin, unknown to me, but she knew pupils of mine & had heard I was selling sketches at war prices & would I send her some at 5 gns. to choose from! Isn't it uncanny the way these things happen when I am hard pressed. But I don't like sailing so close to the edge of all things these days, when you must have hard cash to buy anything. . . .

A big WaterColour group I painted last summer of my Class & exhibited at the International has evidently attracted attention. I am going to have it reproduced in "Colour" that new Art magazine, with my advt:[20] A man came into the Studio yesterday with Louis Sargent & said "I want to tell you Miss Hodgkins that I have watched your work for some time & I consider you are the first woman painter in England" – What about Laura Knig– ? I said. Oh hang Laura Knight – she is not in it – It struck me as being rather comic that the best woman painter etc: the day before yesterday could not pay her washing bill & had to wash her own clothes. However I said nothing about this. Perhaps my day will come – I wonder. I have friends here, the Lindners, Meades, who would give me a fat fiver in a

---

[20] The picture reproduced in *Colour* was *Summer Joys*, a study of a woman and child in the shade of a green umbrella.

minute if I was really up against it, but it never does to let these things be known if possible. They are the ups & downs of 2½ years of war & there must be plenty of others fellow sufferers – if one only knew it. By the time this reaches you I will no doubt be rolling again, otherwise I wouldnt tell you. . . .

Isabel's eldest son Geoffrey arrived in England to join the New Zealand Expeditionary Force. FH was in the Oxfordshire village of Burford trying to organise a summer sketching class.

[269] To ISABEL FIELD, 17 JUNE 1917

The Swan, Burford, Oxon. June 17th.

My Dearest Sis

I have just heard from Geoff that he is safe in England, or rather a letter written at sea & posted from Salisbury Plain two days ago so I expect he is in camp by now & very glad to be off the ship at last. . . . I am not very far away so if he gets leave I want him to join me here for a day or so, if not I will try & run up to Town & meet there – of course we must meet somehow. I am longing to see him & hear all his news. He sounds in great form & very keen. You will live for his letters. . . . I had 3 days in Town on my way here wh. I wont forget in a hurry. I had gone down to the City by Underground to the Bank for some of the money that Will had sent & hurried back to the Grosvenor Gallery for the P.V of the International when bombs were heard. Fancy missing them by ½ an hour. They fell quite near Threadneedle St & made ghastly havoc in crowded parts at the most crowded time of day. An infant school was bombed & many children killed. You can imagine what people felt like. Pictures had no attraction & a lunch I was asked to at the "Rendezvous" fell flat – we were too jumpy & excited for food.

I spent most of the afternoon at the "Grosvenor" wh. was filled with a very smart well dressed crowd. I saw Mrs. Asquith, Lady Diana Manners, Lady Curzon & other celebrities – all of whom had their portraits on the walls. I met a good many people I knew among artists. One of my WaterColours hung in the centre of the WaterColour Room Augustus John had the opposite wall – I had 7 things hung altogether – well hung. In the evening I dined with 2 men – steady! one of whom was a canon, no less a personage than Dean Farrar's son-in-law, one of them, there were many, & all parsons, (what a horrible family atmosphere). Anyway this one was charming, & just back from Salonika, Egypt, Mudros, & other places where he has been organising Y.M.C.A work, huts etc. Most interesting. Afterwards, by way of contrast, & because we all wanted an antidote to the day's awful happenings we went to see "A little bit of Fluff" at the Criterion, a screaming farce, really funny, wh. made us rock & restored one's equilibrium. I had forgotten how to laugh. The next day I came down here, having had 3 days in London & spent no more than my nights lodging & breakfast – thanks to friends. I had no difficulty in resisting fashions. They are so ugly except for the very few who are beautiful & slender. I sat in the Park on Sunday morning & thought I had never seen so many ugly women in my life – old & young looking as tho' they were in for war babies in maternity gowns of horrible cut

I wrote Will a short line when the money arrived in answer to my despairing cable so I won't touch on it again. I know you will all understand how it was without my saying more. It won't happen again I hope. I hated having to ask for I know the pinch must affect you as well – war is impartial & we all suffer alike. The unexpected happens all the time – this morning comes a 3gn. cheque for a picture sold – & the cheering news of pupils. So I must pull up my socks & go & look for rooms. I am writing to Mother so will keep Burford for her. This is just to say that I am in touch with Geoff & hope to see him before long. I wish I could be the Fairy God mother & give him a good time dear boy anyway I am nice & close in the same tight little island for the present at least and these days we must take short views of life & live in the present – and for others if possible – it is the only way, of that I am convinced tho' I am very far from living up to it myself – alas. Much love dear Sis I will write as soon as I have seen your Geoff. My dear how brave you are

Your loving Frances

[270] To Geoffrey Field, c.27 June 1917

Porthmeor Studio, St Ives, Cornwall. Sat

My Dear Geoff

Yours just come. So glad to get in touch with you but am rather sad you have only 4 days leave. But we must have the jolliest spree we can in the time. This is what I suggest. You see I am back in St Ives – Burford didn't do, so I came back here & am not sorry. This is a ripping place in summer as you'll agree when you see it. Well, suppose, the moment you are free you get on board the first train for St Ives. . . .

 . . . . I'll get you a room close to my Studio & we can have meals together & I'll show you round . . . . We'll leave London till another time – first time you are back from France. . . .

[271] To Isabel Field, 9 July 1917

St Ives. 9th. July

My Dearest Sis

Geoff has been & gone, all too quickly, & now he is in France as plain Private Hughes Field doing his gallantest.

It was lovely having him tho' it was for such a short time. He looked splendid, so plump & fit & brown as his own hat . . . .

He was in great spirits & loved everything from the journey down to the cream & even his Aunties cooking wasn't half bad. . . . We got a day at Land's End & sat on the most enderly rock in England in the sunshine. In his heart I think he was comparing the cliffs with Kapiti as I did long ago when first I saw them – the thick carpet of wild flowers struck him & he said "Wouldn't Dad love it" One night we dined at the Lindners & saw their lovely house his first English home. . . . Dear Mr. Hartley, the etcher, said to him "Oh young man what would I not give to be in your shoes" and he certainly did look a happy young warrior. . . . I am getting busy now, have 2 private pupils . . . . Best of all I have received my first commission to paint a portrait. . . .

[272] To Hannah Ritchie,[21] 11 July 1917

7 Porthmeor Studio, St Ives, Cornwall. July 11th

Dear Miss Ritchie

It is nice to know you & Miss Saunders have not forgotten me.

I am not at Burford which I hope will not be a blow to you. I went there in June & hated it found it so stuffy & dull & not at all the charming spot I had expected to find it. It lies in a fold of the Cotswolds & was not bracing – wartime has affected it & the village life & farming activities had all but ceased. So I came back here, secretly very glad to get back to beautiful St Ives – anywhere inland stifles one after this vast & splendid colour & air.

If you feel like the long journey I do hope you will come. I am sure you would love it – it is worth the effort I think. There is fine bathing as a set off to painting & a variety of every sort of subject. If you share a sitting room I think you could live for 25/-a week each. My terms are as usual £3-3-0.

If you cared about roughing it I know of a small cottage studio – 2 bedrooms, studio, sitting room – kitchen – 10/- a week. I should suggest your going to an Hotel for the first night & looking round – if you do decide on coming. It would

---

[21] Hannah Ritchie had studied with FH at the summer school in Concarneau in 1911, and in 1912 had returned to the class at St Valéry-sur-Somme bringing her friend Dorothy Jane Saunders. The two women were art teachers at Manchester High School for Girls and wanted to join the summer class that had been planned for Burford.

be a great pleasure to see you again. Let me know & I will give you any information I can – I wish it were not such a long & expensive journey – but if you have been in Manchester all the winter I am sure a spoonful of sea air will be all to the good – Kindest regards from

Frances Hodgkins

[273] To RACHEL HODGKINS, 17 JULY 1917

7 Porthmeor Studio, St Ives. July 17th

My Dearest Mother

. . . . Luckily things are looking up with me. Have just finished a very successful portrait of Mrs. Hellyer wh. everyone likes, especially the husband who has just been down for the week end & now insists on my painting him as well as a large group of the children – wh. will mean £100 in my pocket if I pull it all off. Have already a cheque for 25 gns. So I am off on Friday to stay with them for a week or 10 days at their cottage down the Coast, where they are now. They are pleasant keen people, nicely well off just come into a fortune & know how to spend it. . . .

Luckily I have this on, otherwise it would have been awkward about the Class. There is a disgusting rumour that no more sketching permits are to be issued & our own perhaps cancelled. . . . It wont break my heart if the Class falls thro'. I am very fed up with pupils hard boring work & not worth the candle as things are at present. Six girls have written asking me to go to Manchester & teach for a month – free of expense. But portraits are better pay so I will stick to them – I feel confident of a success in the line I have struck. . . .

[274] To GEOFFREY FIELD, 30 JULY 1917

7 Porthmeor Studio, St Ives, Cornwall. July 30th.

My Dear Geoff

Thank you for the p.c & papers, most interesting. . . . Did you get the parcel all right?. . . Write as often as you can dear boy you can guess I am anxious all the time – I feel you are in a hot corner, somewhere near Nieuport I take it. I am just back from Port Isaac, where I have been for a week painting that portrait I told you of. Had a ripping good time & loved the rest & change. I was miles away from shops, right in the country, so could not send papers to you. . . . I am sending you a currant loaf, Cornish variety – wh. I hope you will receive before it is too dry & stale warranted fresh for a month. . . .

Your affectionate

Aunt Fanny

[275] To Rachel Hodgkins, 7 August 1917

St Ives. Aug. 7th.

My Dearest Mother

These two cards came from Geoff today, which I send on in case Sis has not heard so recently. They tell mighty little but it is a comfort to see his fist & know so far he is all right. New Zealanders are in the thick of it in Flanders . . . .

I sent Geoff a parcel & papers yesterday. It is a comfort to know he gets them safely. I wonder if he is in the trenches yet.

Well I went to the Hellyers at Port Isaac & had a great week. Luckily it was fine so I was able to do a big portrait group of them in the garden in the hammock, round the tea table, sunshiny effect, which came off happily & they were awfully pleased. It was all very cheery & comfy starting the day in a leisurely & Christian like way, breakfast at 10.30 etc. I painted for 3 days then a day off & we had a run round the North coast of Cornwall up as far as the Devon coast & back again ending up at Tintagel where we dined at King Arthur's Castle & sat round the Round Table (not the original board but a good imitation from the Tottenham Court Rd.) & looked very out of date in the baronial halls, not so marble as Tennyson would have us believe. . . . This left me with 2 days to finish the portrait wh. I didnt do, but have brought it back to the Studio. "Some" trouble it was getting it back to St Ives, in a crowded August train, but the guards & porters of the Great Western are darlings & do anything for you . . . . Everyone is looking fatter & on the whole happier since we've had potatoes – got 32lbs. for 2/- from the Club allottment. Not bad is it?. . .

[276] To Rachel Hodgkins, 20 August 1917

St Ives. Aug. 20th.

My Dearest Mother

No news from Geoff since the last cards I sent you. I wish he wld. write. If I don't hear pretty soon I will write to the W.O. I have written often to him, just a line, day by day, to let him know we are all thinking of him. They are all heavily in it out there now & the fight now on is reckoned the biggest of the war. . . . I am pretty busy now – 5 pupils, who have all to be looked after. It is not so trying as when there were only two, who were both fond of me & hated each other. . . . It is wonderful how well & pain free you have been comparatively speaking. I hope always I will keep as well & as young tho' I am beginning to suspect rheumatism myself, specially in the feet. St Ives is a damp place for that. I keep fit & hard by Swedish exercises rigorously every morn & night. To paint one must be physically strong. Much love from

Frances

[277] To Isabel Field, 28 August 1917

St Ives. Aug. 28th.

My Dearest Sis

I send on Geoff's last letter came yesterday, in case any of yrs. may have gone astray. A month since I had heard from him & I was getting anxious, in fact I wrote to the Officer of Records (N.Z) in London to find out if he knew anything of Geoffs whereabouts, in the meantime his own letter turns up. He says precious little – but the main thing is that he is well & fit & still ducking shells. . . . He doesn't seem to be getting my letters or parcels – but I expect they will reach him in a bunch. . . .

A short line from the Judge this morning – I have just sent cheque for £25 to cover insurance rates to Sydney on pictures.[22] Have insured for £400 – almost hope they will go down & have done with it. . . .

Unable to get to St Ives for the summer painting class, Hannah Ritchie sent sketches she had done at Ludlow for criticism. The following letter was accompanied by several demonstration sketches, in which FH copied Hannah Ritchie's motifs, illustrating her recommendations about how they might be improved. Now lodged in the Auckland City Art Gallery, these sketches are unique records of FH's teaching methods.

[278] To Hannah Ritchie, August 1917

St Ives, Cornwall. Friday

My Dear Miss Ritchie

Your sketches came this morning & yr. letter & cheque yesterday for which many thanks.

I find your Drawings most vigorous & spirited & for 10 days out put quite astonishing. You will see I have said a lot of rude things about them for I know you want an honest opinion. At the same time I want you to realise that I appreciate their good qualities & see in them much that I like.

What I wd. like to see in yr. work is a finer & subtler sense of colour & more attention given to the design (wh. has nothing to do with drawing) of yr. sketch. To place it better on the paper, give it a little more thought & judgement, space it so that you give full advantage to the chief object of the sketch, such as a bridge or Tower, keeping all the rest of yr. composition subordinate to it, both in values & colour. Place with distinction – I specially liked the Castle & I think you should get something very good out of it.

---

[22] Judge Rich was helping to organise the exhibition at Anthony Horderns'.

Why not do it again on a slightly larger piece of paper leaving room for a large breezy sky, just enough foreground for the wall to rest on. Make it look immense & impressive –

Do you use black?

I find using pure paint & only mixing them with black when you want deeper tones keeps purity & unity throughout.

viz:

blue –   with black
r. madder   "
vermillion   "
Viridian   "   & so on –

Drop cobalt & vermillion – I think it such a sickly mixture & becomes a habit & monotonous. Transparent Viridian, lemon yell: & aurelion are my colours for greens. Viridian is indispensible & is absolutely pure. You will find viridian & rose madder make exquisite greys for skies etc –

I think you wd. get more style into your work if you used charcoal a little more freely & left less for your brush to do. Try to be a little freer & more spontaneous, not to labour yr. colour; leave it fresher & the colours more separate

Yr. backgrounds are too heavy – the older I grow in Water Colour I realize *the* great charm is freshness & lovely colour. *Don't* reproduce – Get the character & essential spirit of the place in the simplest manner –

I think Ludlow must be rather facinating. I rather envy you yr. bridges & ruins – tho' the leafy trees are an awful problem. Simply do not paint them their full strength. It is not possible. Vary yr. greens & try black instead of blues. Don't let anything I say depress you. You have a fine bold talent & I shall hope to see some of yr. later work in a lighter vein – pure colour etc. You should do well

The diagrams I have made are merely colour notes in elementary stage – just another chord of colour for you to try. Maddertons Viridian in $\frac{1}{2}$ studio tubes is good & cheaper than others.

Hope this is all legible – Have had to write quickly – a busy day Yrs. very sincerely & good luck to you

[279] To G. V. F. Mann,[23] 23 October 1917

The Wharf Studio, St Ives, Cornwall. Oct 23rd. 17

Dear Mr. Mann

Some time ago Mr. Justice Rich wrote to say that he had spoken to you about some pictures which I proposed sending out to Sydney

He mentioned that you had kindly promised to interest yourself in them,

---

[23] Director of the Art Gallery of New South Wales, 1912-19.

receive them on their arrival, get them through the Customs duty free, look them over & select a few with a view to submitting them to the Council of the National Gallery. This will be very kind indeed if you will do all this for me.

This encouraged me so much that I decided to send a collection of 35 pictures in all, 4 oils, the rest Water Colours, all painted since my return to Europe, with one or two exceptions. The 3 cases were despatched by S.S Barambah on the 19th. Oct & I send you the bill of lading in order that you may take possession on arrival . . . .

I find my Agent has put the selling prices on the labels on back of each picture, which I hope will not prove a difficulty with the Customs.

Will you kindly let Mr. Justice Rich know of the[ir] arrival, so that he can make the necessary arrangements for showing them at Messrs. Horderns' Gallery after you have finished with them.

You will see that I have priced them low, considerably less than English prices. I know it is not the moment for anything but easy prices & in England sales are all but legendary – except for posthumous portraits

I am painting mostly portraits now – this will be my line in future I expect. Portraiture has a big out look

The War has produced nothing very remarkable or exclamatory in Art – Nevinson & Epstein perhaps are the most significant & personal

I send you Frank Rutter's first quarterly in case you may not have come on it. Also 'Colour' with a badly reproduced Hodgkins.

I shall be anxious to hear of the arrival of my cases. Though well insured I should hate to lose them

Did you hear they put a bomb thro' No. 9 Room of the RA the last Raid but one. Is it a blessing in disguise I wonder?

Thanking you in advance for your kind help & interest

[280] To Isabel Field, 23 October 1917
The Wharf Studio, St Ives, Cornwall. Oct 23rd.

My Dearest Sis

Just a word to enclose [with] these 2 cards, which make a rough sort of diary, in sequence of dates if nothing else. I am hoping so for a letter from Geoff, but there is tough work for our New Zealanders on foot just now & one never knows between the morning & the night what news the post may bring us. They have done most grandly the papers are ringing with their prowess.[24] May Heaven spare your boy & send him home again to you. I guess how anxious & weary you are tho' I have not heard from you. Do write like a dear. I feel horribly sad for you

---

[24] 640 New Zealanders died in one day during the attack on Passchendaele ridge on 12 October 1917.

all at times & far away, but one has to put iron bands round the heart & not show ones feelings. . . .

I moved in here last week & am so much more comfy & warm in this smaller Studio, facing the East & out of the bleak winds from the sea. It is such a rest not to have the waves nagging at one night & day. I can breakfast with the sun on me & have all the mysteries of the harbour unfolded to me, & can keep my eye on the British navy at the same time. . . . Fancy I got a commission (5 gns.) to paint a portrait head of Mr. Lindner's pretty neice & was asked if I could do it in 3 days – starting the day after I moved in here – I took it on feeling it wld. never do to turn away work, no matter how untimely. They were very pleased & I was very tired but you can now think of me as a warmer & less harrassed woman. . . .

[281] To Sylvia Lynd, 6 December 1917

Wharf Studio, St Ives. Thursday 10.30 AM

My Dear Mrs Lynd

I have just watched your train go out. I was on the way to the station but fell in with the mason on his way to mend my roof and masons are so coy these days you have to handle them with care, so back I came with him. I had two of the biggest apples, pears & 8 walnuts from an Essex orchard, sent me yesterday, which I thought your daughters might like to eat in the train. I am afraid you were awfully tired & did feel for you & do hope you are none the worse. . . .

Let me know where you are & later, when I have got over this destructive fit, I'll send the group for yr. inspection.[25] I think I can do it from memory, better than from the original – at this stage.

It will be duller than ever without you.

The mason appears to be sliding off the roof so no more

Much love from

Frances Hodgkins

If it was you who sent those heavenly violets thank you *so* much

[282] To Rachel Hodgkins, 7 January 1918

[St Ives] Jan 7th.

My Dearest Mother

A white world today – heavy snow falls & squalls and horribly cold – impossible to work or keep warm. This is a draughty old loft & the roof flaps about in the wind but I expect it is Paradise to some of the dugouts in Flanders.

---

[25] FH was painting a portrait of the novelist and her two children.

I wish Geoff would write. Hoping for a card by every post I heard nothing for Xmas nor have had acknowledgement of parcels. . . . I dined Xmas night with some friends at one of the Hotels & had a very plain tho' nice dinner severely rationed . . . . My presents were all food – tea, biscuits, oat cakes, jam & apples – & ½ doz eggs – rare birds these days. Two pairs of silk stockings from Mrs. Hellyer leavened the lump. The rest of me is threadbare – goodness knows when I will get another outfit we are warned to prepare for a tight time – short of starvation. . . . Submarines are about a lot on this bit of coast – 5 vessels torpedoed during Xmas week – quite close in – one boat just off the Porthmeor Beach – in our very mouth so to speak – crews of 30 & 40 shivering half clad men have been landed on the bitterest days, some wounded. . . .

I am glad to hear Miss Richmond has done so well with her pictures. But what a depressing thought that in order to make sales one must "go back" to ones former style. Wellington is *not* an artistic centre. Neither I, nor my work was ever popular there so I am not greatly surprised that my sketches were unappreciated. They were not meant for exhibition, those little ones I sent out. . . .

I will be glad to see my two pupils back next week. They are my props & mainstay. Too cold for more dear – porridge & to bed – my hot bottle lost its morale last night & burst! Reduced to a brick now. After the war catch me liv[ing] in a climate any colder than an English summer. Am reading Vanity Fair for the umpty umpth time. I had a book of modern History for a Xmas present & a very choice sonnet to my eye brow by the local Poetess – too shy to send it you[26]. . . .

[283] To WILL FIELD, 30 MARCH 1918

Wharf Studio, St Ives. March 30th.

My Dear Will

Very many thanks for yours of the 17th Jany with £5 for Geoff. It is awfully good of you. It helps a lot towards the parcels. . . .

Don't send any more money, unless I ask for it. Am doing much better now. Portraits are a paying "stunt" and I have made quite a bit by the last set. . . . Told yesterday Mr. Lindner stakes his reputation that my future *is* certain. Hope so. I have never doubted it if only I can live long enough. What I want is a small & tidy income so that I need not have to fight for daily bread. Truly living is a fine art these days. Yesterday I sold a 12gn. baby. Item: Paint more babies! In fact keep the cradle full to quote an old friend of yours. Where the shoe pinches me is that I haven't any more business sense than a wild foal in the field – tho' dont say I said so.

---

[26] See *Portrait of Frances Hodgkins*, p.91, for the text.

The other day 3 nice girls, all from NZ, blew in to the Studio – Miss Denniston of Peel Forest – Barker – ditto & Beatrice Wood from Chch, a bright fair haired girl with a fluffy dog in her arms. She wanted me to paint her a sketch of herself for her Dad – William Wood – which I did![27] She was awfully pleased & sent a cheque for 8 gns and has dunned her Father for the balance of £12.12. She is a masterful young person – of the nice sort, & I would like to adopt her. Now, *she* is endowed with a business sense, inherited no doubt from that big family of miller & merchant Woods I used to know as young men in my youth in Chch. . . .

Have had a hamper of food of all sorts from potatoes to Allenby's Food for Invalides, sent from Norfolk by a kind woman who was here & had her portrait painted the other day. Have not seen so much to eat for a long while – was able to make Geoff's parcel quite attractive. . . .

[284] To Will Field, 14 April 1918

St Ives. April 14th.

My Dear Will

Another week has gone by & still no news of Geoff. . . . It may be of course that [he] is too pressed & harrassed to write to me. Without fearing the worst one must face the possibility of one of several nasty things happening – one hears so often of men gassed losing their memory temporarily. This new mustard gas the enemy is using affects the eyes more than the lungs. This is just a hurried line to let you know I am fully alive & aware of the horrors our dear Geoff is up against & that you & Sis may rely on me to act at once if I get any news that is disquieting. I would give much to hear of him being in hospital with a clean shrapnel wound, & safely out of that hell over there. The men who are back from it are certain it can't last much longer at this awful pace. . . . I hear from Judge Rich that my pictures have reached Sydney after 4½ months and in another ship – something spirited must have befallen them. Love to all. I am all hopes fears & alarms but it is no time to despair. If ever there was a time to rouse our souls it is now. Our men are fighting to the death for us. We must be strong. It is the real crisis. I am thinking of you all & loving you I can say no more. Yrs Fanny

[27] Beatrice Wood, later Mrs T. E. Y. Seddon, took lessons from FH.

[285] To Will Field, 2 May 1918

St Ives. May 2nd.

My Dear Will

I am still without news of Geoff. Nothing from the H.C. . . . This ghastly doubt is worse than anything. I did beg Geoff to put my name down in case of trouble. . . . The hard lot of poor parents & relatives who can't get news is very cruel. I do pray you & Sis are better posted in news, good or ill, than I am. . . .

The R.A opens on Monday. My big portrait group is chucked. It was a bit too much for them. It would have been wiser to have kept it for the International where they are nice to me. . . . The weather is lovely – But I am too harrassed by the absence of all news to enjoy it. The most trying state of all. Friends only add to the tension by words of comfort. I have been to the Hellyers for a week of rest They are good to me.

Still without news of her nephew FH moved to Porlock in Somerset for her summer class.

[286] To Geoffrey Field, 11 July 1918

Castle Hotel, Porlock, Somerset. July 11th.

My Dear Geoff

It was indeed a surprise to get yr. letter & I could hardly believe my eyes – I had long ago given you up & had written very sadly to yr. people & feared to hear from them. Why didn't you send a card dear boy? Surely you knew how anxious I was especially after that heavy fighting when the NZ's got it so hotly. I wrote twice to the High Commissioner, but evidently my letters were lost, they deny having had them, & then I tried all the NZ hospitals, enquiring everywhere, but no news. . . .

[287] To Rachel Hodgkins, 25 August 1918

Porlock. Aug 25th.

My Dearest Mother

I am writing this in the summer house, rather earwiggy & damp. It is pouring wet, & Sunday morning & one can't take the usual walk – I have two new pupils, both young energetic things of over 65, & they pursue me everywhere asking questions, with their last horrible sketch to criticise. One is a Post Impressionist and the other a Pre Raephaelite, and as neither of them wld. go to church, which they should have done, I left one drawing the village street from the drawing room window, & the other the staircase from the landing, then I escaped by the side door up here. . . . I get very bored by pupils & fear I begin to show it – the temptation to tell them to go to the d—l is great. But they pay my hotel bill – a big item nowadays. Fancy £3.3 a week for a country inn. . . . There are a lot of hunting people here now – mostly hard faced women with straight backs & lean figures – who rise at daybreak & groom their horses & talk horses at every meal. They don't call it huntin' in war time, only hackin'. . . . hacking, I take it, is riding someone else[s] horses, not your own, that someone presumably being engaged in fighting for his country. Don't know but it may be this – I am much too shy to ask questions. Sir Joseph[28] has consented to take Miss Woods portrait back with him & it has been removed from the walls of the Grosvenor Gallery & handed over to his Secretary. . . .

[288] To Rachel Hodgkins, 18 September 1918

Wharf Studio, St Ives. Sept 18th.

My Dearest Mother

Just a quick line to say I am back in the Studio since last Sat: I returned sooner than I meant as the Hotel at Porlock closed suddenly & we all had to pack up & clear out. I am thinking the large helpings of beef & mutton & rice pudding paid me better than it did them poor beggars, for they went bankrupt and have had to sell out. . . . The day before I left Porlock I heard from the International Socty that they would give me a wall to myself – for my Water Colours at the coming show next week. This caused some flutter, but luckily most of them were finished, so I sent them to the framer & begged him to do his best. It will be a scratch lot of frames as I can't afford much in fact I am doing it on credit. There will be a smash if some of them don't sell! But its a big chance & one not to be lost. They are small pictures mostly at easy prices – all babies & Mothers & children. Sort of Infant Wellfare idea if you can stretch the point so far – as attractive as I could make them. I gave the Mothers (5) and their offspring (numerous) a tea party at the Hotel before I left – Such fun – They were so nice & blushing & shining over it all got up regardless. Dear women all of them with husbands fighting & one a prisoner who had never seen his beautiful baby. One of them brought me 2lbs of black berries & another broad beans, so broad they might be marrows. I found afterwards kind Mrs. Cox the landlady had given me the party for nothing, as I had given her a sketch of her child & she was grateful. My pupils all enjoyed themselves & loved Porlock, and as times go it was really quite a success. I know

---

[28] Sir Joseph Ward was leader of the defeated Liberal Party, but shared power with Prime Minister W. F. Massey during the wartime coalition government.

I feel great – the change & good food did wonders – I could not have done what I did, teach & paint, except for those big helpings aforesaid. I have made up my mind to go out for a hot lunch every day now cost what it may – it means health – I can't thrive on my own cooking – it is so poisonous. . . . An old friend from Paris is coming next week for some lessons – Miss Wallis, a well known Canadian Sculptress[29] – a dear – She [is] over on leave. . . . How are you dear? Forgive me not writing sooner. Have worked like a navvy. Think of 24 Water Colours in 2 months! . . .

[289] To Isabel Field, 2 November 1918
Rosehill in the Fern, Camborne, Cornwall. Nov 2. 18.[30]

My Dearest Sis I have just written to Geoff and sent some Mirrors & a Weekly Press sent by Willie & told him we'll lunch together on Xmas Day unless he is too busy sweeping up Berlin. The inevitable end is near . . . & unless something extraordinary happens we will have peace very soon & the boys coming back to us. . . . We are indeed a dam fine race – tho the flue is trying to reduce our numbers. People are dying right & left & [it] is specially bad at St Ives – where the inhabitants don't flush drains etc as often as they might. I marvel I have escaped. . . .

. . . . I am delighted to hear Bert has moved to the Terrace – Mother will have them within smiling distance now. What a wonder she is keeping so well & active. There is an old lady of 83 in this house, whom they call the youngster she can thread her needle almost in the dark & is astonishingly agile & erect – she is darning & mending my rags for me & you simply can't give her too much to do. The Cornish are a powerful virile race – tho' I have no love for them. They are so hard & narrow beyond name – the number of illiterate men & women who can't read or write would make a New Zealander stare. . . .

Sunday Nov 9th Tomorrow at noon we are to hear if Germany surrenders or will fight on. A whole week has passed. . . . Miss Wallis' sister died of flue & there was a great upset poor dears. I have lost many acquaintances at St Ives. I hear the worst is over down there & that they have left off dying. I hope it won't work out your way, tho' it appears to spread like a prairie fire – I don't know what my plans are – I feel very unsettled & utterly unlike painting. Fancy trying to ponder a picture at such a time. . . .

---

[29] Katherine Wallis (1861-1957) studied at the Académie Colarossi, exhibited at the RA as well as in Canada, Paris and Dresden. She was known for her studies of children and animals.
[30] FH was holidaying at a farmhouse as a paying guest.

The war ended with the signing of the Armistice on 11 November 1918.

[290] To Will Field, 28 November 1918

Wharf Studio, St Ives, Cornwall. Nov 28th

My Dear Will

I think you and Sis have a picture of mine called "April" in a white carved frame. I am writing to ask you if you will be so kind as to send it to Mr. Peter Waite in Adelaide . . . . As you know he has been so generous & fine to me and I naturally wish to give him something he will appreciate.[31] He finds my modern work out of character & keeping with his house – which is easy to understand. There are quite a number of people who still prefer my earlier period – I hope to convert them in time.

. . . . I am pretty busy – pupils here and at Newlyn. I am climbing steadily I hope. Times are thick & thin by turns – Wonderful what ones lives through! . . .

---

[31] Peter Waite had recently sent FH £100 to rent a studio in London.

UPPER: At work in an aloe grove in Tangier with Absolom in attendance, 1902.
Alexander Turnbull Library.
LOWER: Dorothy Richmond painting from the model in Stanhope Forbes's studio,
c.1902. Courtesy of the Atkinson family, Wellington.

Collection Villard, Quimper

ABOVE: Frances at work on the beach at Concarneau, c.1910. RIGHT: Inscribed on the back 'Lest you forget, FMH', this photograph was probably given to Dorothy Richmond, c.1907, after Frances's return to Europe.

RIGHT: Frances Hodgkins, c.1914. Auckland City Art Gallery.
BELOW: Frances with two of her pupils at St Valery-sur-Somme, 1912. She wrote to her mother: 'Excuse the bottles in the enclosed photo. It is only local colour & is inseparable with life in France!'

ABOVE: With Hannah Ritchie (left) and Jane Saunders, c.1925. The two art teachers from Manchester are the subject of *Double Portrait*, c.1922 (Plate 2).
BELOW: Hannah Ritchie and Jane Saunders.

RIGHT: The painter Katharine Church (Kitty), b.1910, with a portrait of herself by Frances Hodgkins. Kitty married the writer Anthony West in 1936 and they are the subject of *Double Portrait, No. 2*, 1937 (Plate 5).
BELOW: John Piper and his wife, the critic Myfanwy Evans, c.1940.

Duncan Macdonald of the Lefevre Gallery and his wife Lily, 1948.

Lucy Wertheim, ardent admirer and generous patron of Frances Hodgkins, who ran the Wertheim Gallery 1930–39. Auckland City Art Gallery, photograph Lafayette.

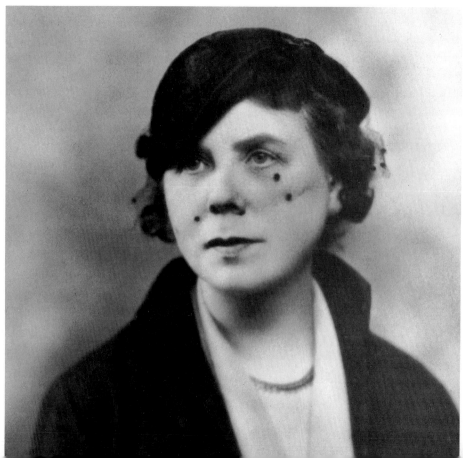

ABOVE: The potter Amy Krauss.
UPPER RIGHT: With David Brynley at Corfe Castle, 1940s. Alexander Turnbull Library, photograph Celia Keating.
BELOW: Frances on holiday in Northumberland, August 1939. Photograph Jane Saunders.
LOWER RIGHT: With Dorothy Selby in the Croft garden, late in 1940. Alexander Turnbull Library.

Frances Hodgkins at Corfe Castle, 1945. ABOVE: Inside the studio with *Zipp*, one of her last oil paintings, on the easel. BELOW: Outside in the village by a van selling pots and pans. Alexander Turnbull Library, Felix H. Man Collection.

PART THIRTEEN

1919-27

'The Terror of These Distracted Years'

In The Edwardians *of 1918 Frances Hodgkins had made a valedictory painting. The First World War signalled the end of the Edwardian social order with its wealthy leisured class who had provided a source of patronage for artists, who in turn reflected its values. Gone too were the legions of domestic servants so poorly paid that even an artist like FH could make use of their services. FH was affected by these changes and the decade after the war was the most difficult period of her life.*

The fragility of her economic situation was linked to the strength and ambition of her position as an artist. She was now confident enough to take the risks, artistic and financial, that were necessary for a modern artist in Britain during these years. The new role of the artist had been proclaimed by Clive Bell in his book Art, *published in 1914. Artists would earn their place in society, not by painting the portraits, possessions and ideals of wealthy connoisseurs, but by drawing from within themselves autonomous arrangements of shape, line and colour, which might or might not refer to the physical world, but which would inspire and redeem the viewer with the purifying release of aesthetic emotion. While stopping short of Clive Bell's quasi-religious claims for art, Roger Fry shared his ideas about the absolute importance of formal qualities. Fry's critical writing, of which a collection,* Vision and Design, *was published in 1920, was influential in developing a public for modern art in England after the war. FH recommended this book to the New Zealand artist Edith Collier early in 1921: her own work reflected an increasing interest in formal concerns and the influence of developments in Paris.*

FH spent lengthy periods in France throughout the 1920s, passing regularly through Paris on her way to sketching grounds in the provinces. Though there are important landscape drawings from these years, she continued to paint mainly figures, notable works being Double Portrait, *1922 (Plate 2), which looks to Matisse in its simplification of form and use of patterning, and* Lancashire Family, *c.1927, where forms are more solidly modelled in a close tonal range, suggestive of Picasso's neo-classicism of the 1920s. In* Red Cockerel, *an unusual still life of 1924, and* Three French Children *(Plate 3) the faceted shallow surfaces are a personal adaptation of cubism.*

She enjoyed the continued support of Frank Rutter and other critics, and was noticed by influential artists, one of whom, Charles Ginner (1878-1952), is mentioned in a letter of 1921. He was an associate of Harold Gilman and Spencer Gore, an original member of the Camden Town Group of 1911, one of the artist-initiated exhibiting societies set up as progressive alternatives to the Royal Academy and the New English Art Club. FH's friendship with Cedric Morris deepened. In 1918 Morris had begun his life-long partnership with the artist Arthur Lett Haines (1894-1978) and in 1919 the two men moved to Newlyn for two years. FH stayed with them on occasion in Newlyn, though their names do not appear in letters written at this time. Her friendship with so unconventional a household is a measure of how far she had moved from the proprieties that ruled Dunedin. Cedric Morris admired her original-ity, courage and wit and liked her work because it was more modern and challenging

337

*than anything being done in St Ives or Newlyn. Morris and Lett Haines were based
in Paris 1921-6 and FH visited them there on occasion.*

*At the beginning of December 1918 FH decided to take the gamble of renting a
studio in Kensington, a building in a garden behind a row of terrace houses. She
retained the St Ives studio.*

[291] To Rachel Hodgkins, 30 December 1918

The Studio, 1 Eldon Road, London W.8. Dec 30th.

My Dearest Mother

. . . . I have had no milk nor butter since coming to London . . . nor can I get
my clothes washed no laundry will look at a new customer, so, dear, I have been
very over worked & weary I can tell you washing, cooking, charring, painting
teaching & going out to tea & dinner – too much altogether – I can't keep it up.
In between the acts I get some painting done, but very little – you can't get any
help at all – women ask £1 a week just to light yr. fire – the coal question is fierce.
I have struggled along with a smoking stove & insufficient coal till I am desperate
now I have decided to make a clean sweep of the stove & get a gas one instead &
make my landlady go halves. . . . Still these worries will all smooth out in time.
I was warned of the great difficulties of life in London & I took it on with my eyes
open so don't complain. There is lots of good food in the shops for the rich, but
the price of everything is staggering to my modest purse. . . .

I have hoped in vain to hear from Geoff this Xmas, but not a sound from him.
It is very disappointing. . . . I have not seen any of the distinguished visitors Foch,
Haig or Wilson – the crowds in the trains & buses are so great it takes nerve to
face them. I have already had my handbag & ration book & purse stolen & I can
tell you it is no joke losing yr. ration book these days. . . .

The Sydney Show seems to have started well & the first week about £130
worth, 7 pictures, were sold. One I believe was bought by Mdm Melba's sister.
Mr. Waite wrote that he had met Melba at Gov: House in Adelaide & told her
about me & my show & she had promised to go herself and see it when she got
to Sydney. I am greatly relieved that, at least I have paid expenses & Judge Rich
will not be out of pocket – *awful* thought – I am hoping for further news &
further sales. I wish the papers wouldn't make me out a sort of freak artist – I am
really a very sober minded thoughtful sort of person with nothing slapdash or
offhand about my work – every stroke I put down comes from real conviction &
is a sincere *aspect* of truth – if not the whole truth. If I can only live long enough
the world will have to acknowledge me – I am horribly stubborn & I haven't lived
these long years of privation & hard work for nothing. . . . I have been so cold &
uncomfortable altho' I seemed to start off in this Studio fairly well – it wasn't so
cold then – & I was excited & pleased with everything. May Hosking is going to

pose for her portrait tomorrow – & Mary Ellis née McKenzie next week. Tell Sis I am looking out for that cake of hers. . . .

[292] To RACHEL HODGKINS, 30 JANUARY 1919
Studio, 1 Eldon Road, Kensington. Jan 30th.

My Dearest Mother

Snowed up & 9.30p.m the pipes frozen & I have just finished carrying water from the house thro' a sort of black lagoon of choking fog & sleet. I have now got into large warm gouty slippers & turned the gas on full & hang the expense . . . . You have to be as strong as a horse to stand this climate. Later on, when I have attained affluence, I shall cease to live in cold studios I hope. . . .

Morning.

Still foggy & dark, no pupils so I have a half holiday – rare event. The postman has brought [a] letter from you & delicious chocolates wh. I found with the milk on my snow bound doorstep. I am making a pig of myself. They *are* good. . . . I must stop now & cart my pictures across London in a taxi to the Grosvenor Gallery – Portrait Socty. I have been pegging away, very close at it, & must now have a rest from painting for a bit. So many invitations now blow in, asking for work – it keeps me busy. I could do with less admiration & more sales. . . .

[293] To RACHEL HODGKINS, 18 FEBRUARY 1919
Studio, 1 Eldon Road, Kensington. Feb 18th.

My Dearest Mother

. . . . I think I told you how I had scrapped my old coal stove in favour of gas – well the gas played me false – no pressure & jolly little heat & gone up in price 10% since I got it laid on. I froze – the temperature of the Studio was never more than 40 – pupils wouldnt come model wouldn't sit – oh the misery of it – I nearly threw my demented self into the Thames. The agony of getting up in the morning & facing a dull cold world with a yellow sickly fog – it broke ones spirit. I saw trouble years ahead of me. I called on the plumber & flung myself at his gouty feet and begged him to come & put back my stove. The devil smiled & said "I thought you'd be along presently Miss that gas stove aint no good for 'eating purposes but I wasn't going to throw cold water on your little plan". Plumbers are all they are made out to be and worse – a scurvy lot. Well that little item has added 30/- to my already mountainous bill. I have got the stove back however & that is the main thing. Now there is a coal & wood famine – I have been to 6 places this morning after coal – finally got ½ cwt. from a hawker. . . . Meanwhile I have to suspend my Class – the Tube & train strike has blocked me so – but that is over. What next I ask you?. . .

[294] To Rachel Hodgkins, 12 April 1919

Polperro, Cornwall. April 12th.

My Dearest Mother

You will be all in great spirits when this reaches you, with Geoff home again, or very nearly so. . . . I am feeling pretty rotten & have left London having let my Studio for 6 months. I am a broken winded old bronchic having just struggled thro' a savage attack of flue – just – I would rather die than go through another 3 weeks like the last . . . . However I got away from London – & that is the great thing. . . . It has been an experience – a dear one – & has shown me I am not strong enough for it single handed – work has suffered. No doubt of it that more money is to be made in London if you can play the game & have the strength for it. An income is what is wanted. . . . I let my Studio for 2gns. wh. will keep me in rooms & give me a rest from housekeeping & foraging for myself – also freedom for work. My work has attracted a lot of notice & the press is showing itself less hostile (or assinine) towards it. Frank Rutter of the Sunday Times has defined my place in the Art world with some emphasis & being an authority the other papers are taking their cue from him – & about time too.[1] Please ask Will to have it put about in the N.Z. papers broadcast. The best notice I am sorry I can't send as I have only 1 copy – it places me 3rd. among 4 big women painters of Continental fame – Mrs. Swynnerton (English) Mary Cassett (American who lived in France 30 yrs. ago), F.H., and then "wonderful Mdme. Mutermilch" a Polish painter now in Paris.[2] The élite!

I am sorry to have to record this myself. Tho' I can't help feeling a twinge of pride – I have worked! Lately I have felt so "off" that I felt my swan song had been sung – the most pleasant side of it has been the letters from friends who have known me & my life. I hope, from this point on, my life may not be so arduous. It must make a difference. I hope to have a big Class in July at Ludlow in Shropshire. . . . I am sorry to be such an egoist – we can't help it. . . .

. . . . This is a tiny fishing village, to which I have often wanted to come – facing South & not nearly so bleak as St Ives. . . . Miss Jenny W[imperis] blew in one

[1] FH exhibited with the Women's International Art Club in March 1919 and in his review Frank Rutter called her 'one of the most richly gifted and personal painters of either sex we have today'.
[2] Annie Swynnerton (1844-1933), co-founder of the Manchester Society of Women Painters, known for her allegorical paintings. Mary Cassatt (1844-1926) settled in Paris in 1868 and exhibited with the Impressionists, painting scenes of domestic life, especially mothers and children. She stopped painting in 1914 because of failing eye-sight. Marie-Mela Muter, formerly Mutermilch (1886-1967), settled in Paris in 1902, studied at the Académie Colarossi and became a member of the jury of the Salon d'Automne; she is best known for her portraits, including one of Roger Fry (1922).

day – a pathetic little figure of lonely un-wanted old age – with a loving warm heart for all her old friends. . . .

[295] To Isabel Field [Girlie], 19 May 1919

Polperro. May 19th.

My Dearest Girlie

By this time you will have Geoff home again – you will all be in the seventh Heaven. . . . Doesn't it sound like a miracle his coming through it all safe & untouched. . . .

This is a lovely place for rambles & rock climbing – tho' the walks are all rather too climby. I have never seen such masses of primroses & bluebells as this year. . . . On Sundays, when it is fine, we generally take a Cornish pastie and go for a long walk. The two Australian ladies who are sharing the sitting room with me are demons for long tramps & nearly kill me if I go out with them. I nearly always prefer resting on the shady side of a hedge – they prefer to get through a hole in it & cut across the next field wherever they see a board Trespassers will be prosecuted or This Path way is closed. What I like is to sit in a green glade & listen to the 2 notes of the cuckoo & the screech of the gulls & the break of a wave between or the wood pidgeon saying

> Two sticks across
> And a little bit of moss
> That will do – That will do-o-o

But the Australian ladies are so intensely practical & have their heads so full of common sense that there is no room for painting or poetry or nonsense like that. But they are nice all the same & if they had continued to live in N.Z where they were born instead of emigrating to Australia they would be nicer still. . . .

[296] To Rachel Hodgkins, 28 June 1919

Ludlow. June 28th. Peace Day.

My Dearest Mother

I must send off a line dear on this great & exciting day come at last! The news came through quicker than we expected & by 4 o'c the bells were hard at it & flags out & all creation in the streets. We bought flags & paraded with the crowd & then went off & did an evening sketch. Two girls are with me now, who were at Concarneau when war broke out. They reminded me how cross I was because they *would* sketch in the evening, while I went to & fro from the Mairie reading the bulletins . . . . Did I tell you that Bee Wood is working up a class of 6 or 7 at a small village in Oxfordshire & that I have promised to go on there on Aug: 4th. & give them lessons till the end of Sept: when I go back to Town. . . . Who knows by next July I may be back in France with all my girls & pals as in the good old days – Fills one with vim to think of it. . . .

[297] To Rachel Hodgkins, 12 July 1919

Ludlow. July 12th.

My Dearest Mother

. . . . In about a fortnight I shall be moving onward – to my little village in Oxfordshire, where I really long to be, for nice as Ludlow is, it is large & in this hot weather very fatiguing – my poor feet *ache* at night. People always wonder how I can walk all the morning after my pupils & stand all the evening at my easel. I dont always feel very walkative or workified I can tell you – but one goes on & gets through somehow. I shall die standing like Queen Elizabeth. . . .

[298] To Rachel Hodgkins, 10 August 1919

Park Farm, Great Barrington, Oxon. Aug 10th

My Dearest Mother

I made the journey from Ludlow quite easily in spite of my fears . . . . I am stopping at a delightful Farm house, one of those old cool stone houses, flagged floors & thick walls so delightful in summer & deadly cold in winter – it is a 500 acre mixed farm, with fine old barns & a great rick yard where they have now started to thrash corn – I have my meals with the family & jolly good meals they are – the poor farmer always contrives to have the best on the land I find. It is splendid harvest weather – tho' bad for roots I gather. We are sunning ourselves in summer. My party of 7 are housed in rose covered cottages, with tiny windows & narrow staircases, but are loving it all and as cheerful as 7 birds. Such nice girls – the kind I like all keen on my teaching – which always seems to me such a joke. . . . By the end of the month we shall be 12 in all. The farmer family is large – quite patriarchial – Granny & Auntie & Step Mother & Dad & Nell & Geordie & Tom & 2 collie dogs & 5 cats & kittens & Fanny the maid and I am so at home with them all that I begin to wonder whether I am a Bartlett or a Hodgkins. I have breakfast sent up on a tray at 7 and by 8 I am in the Rick yard – working very hard to get as much work as possible before winter comes. It is such a haven after Ludlow . . . . It is so soothing to be wakened by the hum of the cream seperator, & no sound louder than the wood pidgeon & if there is any brawling it is done by the brook. We are 8 miles from a station, so you can imagine the deep peace of it.

I have had 4 letters from Judge Rich this mail. The pictures are not selling & he is going to send them back as soon as an opportunity occurs. He says the

London Correspondent of the Argus has said some handsome things about my work – this & the notices I sent him have impressed him. He sounds nervey & tired & anxious & as he says Nothing matters now – which is hardly fair to Betha. Poor dears. I shall not be able to send you the Daily papers dear as usual, until I get back to Town . . . but you shall have the Sunday one wh. I get by post. . . . I am longing for the good time to come when I shall be able to send you more than I do – but it is not yet. Frames cost so much & drain me of every copper. . . .

[299] TO RACHEL HODGKINS, 20 OCTOBER 1919

Studio, 1 Eldon Rd, Kensington W8. Oct 20th.

My Dearest Mother

I have been back a fortnight and bar colds am feeling well, tho' rather as if the octopus had got hold of me again. London clutches you like that. I managed to get up from Barrington – in spite of the railway strike, which was an ugly bit of real warfare tho' without bloodshed – I managed to board the only train running on the Midland line, worked by Volunteers & I stood for 60 miles & came safely thro' with luggage & self intact. . . .

I found two nice welcome letters from you dear. . . . [I] was cheered by Sissie's Coney coat & the motor car. Wish I could see her in both, bless her. I notice sighs & motors are inseparable. All my motoring friends sigh over them! Something always goes wrong.

I came back to Town to find I had made a bit of a hit at the International with this last lot of work. Also, & this is good mark you, I have had my first visit from a bona fide dealer – which is what I have worked, wanted & prayed for since long enough. This is in the shape of a flattering invitation to hold a one man show, Feb & March, at the Hampstead Art Gallery, just opened & about to show a brilliant set of one man shows. The brilliancy I hope may not end when mine commences! I had a 2 hours interview, here yesterday. The Show is to be well done – they say they are going to spend £100 over each show – Wolmark[3] is now showing – then comes Walter Bayes, Lucien Pissarro[4] – and I follow on. It will be an advertisement & if it is nothing more I shan't complain – fame must preceed gain. This doesn't prevent me from being exceedingly hard up & insolvent. . . . I can only send these 2 cuttings. The more important ones I must keep by me – one paper

[3] Alfred Wolmark (1877-1961).
[4] Walter Bayes (1869-1956), painter, teacher and critic, and Lucien Pissarro (1863-1944) had both been original members of the Camden Town Group. Pissarro was the son of the impressionist Camille Pissarro and had settled permanently in England in 1890. His daughter Orovida was also a painter. FH exhibited with her at the Leicester Galleries in February 1935.

calls me a "refreshing tonic amid a sea of sedatives" Love to all Dearest & your dear unselfish self. You do write such brave & sweet letters

Your ever loving Fanny

[300] TO RACHEL HODGKINS, 18 NOVEMBER 1919

Wharf Studio, St Ives. Nov 18th

My Dearest Mother

I am back here again having found 2 nice quiet tenants[5] for my London Studio – I turned it over to them & with the first instalment of rent in hand caught the train for St Ives – just in time to avoid the sharp frosts & winds – hardly felt down here, tempered climate as it is, compared to London. . . . St Ives feels very different coming back to it on a short visit – I can easily spend 3 months & be well employed with models etc and stray sitters among my friends. It is so light & blue & bright & the herring season at its height & everyone doing well & making money. The old Studio has changed landlords & wonderful to relate it is to be done up, inside & out, & made snug & watertight for me – it seems too good to be true. The Gov: Inspector came round & decreed the old place must either be pulled down – or restored. I have been busy seeing old friends & dining several times over & meeting the same people at different houses as is the way of St Ives. The first week end Mrs. Hellyer bore me off to their lovely new house at Carbis Bay. She is now a widow, beautiful & not yet 40 facinating – & such a house to facinate in! Much reduced in wealth by her husbands sudden death so there will be no more pictures by Frances Hodgkins bought alas. . . . The Director of the Carnegie Institute I told you of has seen my "Seaside Lodgings" at the International & written specially inviting it to America.

. . . . I enclose you a letter from Miss Williams[6] who grows more & more like a character out of Jane Austen every day . . . . She is unique among my friends . . . but so true & gentle & unassuming – her only weakness is what school girls call a "pash" for me – I love her for it. . . .

[301] TO RACHEL HODGKINS, 4 JANUARY 1920

St Ives. Jan 4th.

My Dearest Kind Little Mother a whole bunch of N.Z letters came a few days ago

---

[5] Cedric Morris and Arthur Lett Haines, who were living in Newlyn but retained this foothold in London. They may have been the first tenants mentioned in Letter 294, renewing the six-month lease.
[6] Madeline Williams, a pupil from the St Valéry summer school of 1906.

. . . I am delighted about Lydia's engagement[7]. . . . It is thrilling to think of seeing them, him & her, so shortly. It is nearly time to pack up & go back to Eldon Rd. worse luck . . . . That was indeed a 'rather nice idear' of yours to sell the old piano and I was very grateful & touched to get that little fiver you sent me – *very* glad of it dear & many many thanks. I have sold & pawned every stick I have, bar bed and table to keep the wolf from the door. It simplifies life – Thats one way of looking at it. As long as I can pay for paint & canvas I would part with anything. I have hung on so long by the skin of my teeth I suppose I can hang on a bit longer. People always think I am well off. Thats my secret – and pride – if life is not so very full of meat & comforts it at least does not lack variety or friends or experience. But I am glad Lydia has preferred John to Glory. And so I hope will dear old Girlie. I have far more boy friends now than ever I had at their age. I have grown younger with [the] years I think. Who do you think descends on me tonight the McLarens. I am rather dreading it – I am so *busy* & preoccupied I have no time for any outside distractions. Well I must do what I can for them – but this is the artists biggest time of the year. I was amused to hear the other day that Mrs. Laura Fox (née Hooper) was in Penzance. She met a friend of mine who told her I was here. [Mrs Fox] promptly offered to come over & see me. My friend said "Oh! you can't go & see Miss H. without an appointment – She's very busy & lets no one interfere with her work you know she's a GENIUS!" Well! said Mrs. Fox You *do* surprise me. All I can say *is* that she showed no trace of it at School! . . .

[302] To RACHEL HODGKINS, 24 FEBRUARY 1920
12 Bedford Gardens, London W8. Feb 24th.

My Dearest Mother
    . . . . I have been extremely busy – moving from Eldon Rd. here & launching my little Hampstead Show – which is now well on its legs, blessed by most perfect weather, fairly well patronized & a few sales, £42 worth in all – well covering the framing expenses. . . . You will see Frank Rutter has written a nice little foreward for me. He has been extremely nice about it all. . . . The first person I knocked against, (knock is hardly the word for so frail a thing) was Miss J Wimperis looking – I cant say how old – it was pathetic – when I get that age I shall hide in the mountains. I am going to have tea with her tomorrow – oh! how piteous it is to see her so alone & so frail – I am glad she is provided for. . . . I may spend a week or two with the Nickalls at Boxley Abbey, & then to Miss Winthrop. I crave a rest & a degree of comfort. But no one has any servants & visiting friends

---

[7] To Captain Noel Pharazyn of the Royal Field Artillery. After the wedding the couple were to return to England.

isn't the easy thing it was. I wonder where Lydia will live. Hope she will turn up soon. . . .

[303] To ISABEL FIELD, 14 MARCH 1920

12 Bedford Gardens. March 14th.

My Dearest Sis

At last Lydia has arrived & we have met. . . . at dinner at their Hotel – Lydia looking like a darling little peach, so happy, with that enchanting air of being absolutely at home wherever she finds herself. They make a delightful pair, he seems the right mate for her – very much in love and appreciative. . . . They told their story in unison – Lydia most sprightly, he coming in with the few more solid facts necessary to holding the narrative together – man-like more construc-tional. . . . [We] met again next morning at Buckingham Palace – for the hero's investiture. I may mention we tried not to be damped by the news of Noel's possible departure for the Black Sea at an early date. I found Lydia sitting in the *centre seat* of the *front Row* of the Throne Room exactly opposite & quite close to The King & his retinue. She was keeping a seat for me, guarded by boy scouts & Court Officials. This I think is a good augury for her future life. She has a distinct affinity for the right spot. Lucky instinct! . . . Noel looked very gallant, golden & unconcerned and we thought made the best bows of any . . . . I have been very busy winding up my Show – I am relieved it is over – I have sold £90 worth – out of which I keep about £15 – the rest goes on frames & commission – huge items in a modern picture show. . . . However I have come out of the Show with honours as far as a good Press is concerned – some kudos I hope & some useful propaganda work for a future & more important Show in the West End. I have made friends & extended my teaching connection & altogether have come out of it without any broken bones. . . .

If Noel *does* go to Constantinople of course I'll stand by Lydia & see that she is not left alone. They are the plucky sort bless them – but it will be rough luck if he has to go . . . .

[304] To RACHEL HODGKINS, 15 MAY 1920

4 Barnom Terrace, St Ives. May 15th.

My Dearest Mother

. . . . [Lydia] is a great joy to me & is happy & gay making friends with everyone & seeing the funny side of life, playing golf hard & writing innumerable letters in a very practical & dutiful way. I admire her so much – she's so intelligent & amusing. . . . She is a little angel of kindness & consideration to me & I shall horribly miss her when she goes. One thing I am determined she must not grow too plump & spoil her daintiness. She certainly has put on flesh since she arrived. I am feeling a crock, so queer & tired & rather fussed about myself but I expect its only that bad old fool time that overtakes one in mid career – Lydia is a dear & saves me in every sort of way – she bought a bottle of port wine yesterday & today I feel pints better. . . .

. . . . Lydia will have told you of the amusing weekend at Newlyn – with the 2 painters in their Futuristic abode.[8] Her slightly mad admirer, one Mirams, is motoring down on Sat: & whirring us off on a 3 days tour to Lord knows where & back. He smothers her in – no – only cakes – last week & the week before it was cakes – this week it is to be dried fruits & nuts. She is a killing child – all his letters are sent on to Noel & copies of hers to him as well. I have never known so candid a soul. . . . She is forging links with [Noel] all the time in her wise little way – learning Golf, reading books he likes, keeping a vigilant eye on her cash book & acquainting herself with life generally or life as we drowsily live it in Cornwall . . . .

[305] To Rachel Hodgkins, 9 June 1920

Porthmeor Studio, St Ives. 9.6.20

My Dearest Mother

I have been treating you rather shabbily about letters since Lydia has been here – but she is a great hand at letters & gets through prodigious screeds . . . in that charmingly ready & natural way in which she does everything. It springs from her joyous young zest of life & a real happiness. No shadows – no doubts all in the sunshine. . . . I feel she is a real loss to the Colonies. There isn't scope enough for her free spirit in this cramped old England. She must have lots of children & I don't see how a soldiers wife is going to achieve that. She is not one scrap artistic. The Lord in His mercy has seen to that. She has the nesting fever on her very badly just now & has gone off to Town to find a little flat & see what she can make of housekeeping on a tiny scale until Noel wants her to join him. I think it is a good move. She will learn a lot of useful tips about life in general & I think she is too sensible to do anything rash, having *the* coolest corner in that very clear young brain box of hers. Here in St Ives there is nothing to attract unless one paints or plays golf. I shall miss her sadly. She is so bright & pat & alert. I only wish I could have made it gayer for her. But money is tight & I cant live up to her money spending pace at all – not that she's the least extravagant indeed she is more than conscientious, its only that I always have lived more frugally than she is accustomed to. . . . Lydia sat for her portrait – I am only half satisfied with it

[8] The Bowgie, home of Cedric Morris and Lett Haines.

– but its a picture and already a woman has been in & asked me to do something similar for her of herself to possess & pass to her children. I persuaded Lydia to brush her hair back straight & show her serene young brow. Popular opinion does not favour the style – but I love it. Yesterday we were locked in the Studio for a final sitting (Lydia left this morning) when a letter from Sis at Rotorua was poked thro' the door – to Lydia's huge joy – Much enjoyed by us both – So glad Sis got off to see the Prince & take the Baths.

. . . . I must buck up & get my Studio colour washed & my pictures onto the walls & try & get rid of some of the creations to the summer visitors. I badly want to get over to France & rub off some of the rust of ages. . . .

[306] To Rachel Hodgkins, 9 September 1920

St Ives, Cornwall. Sept 9th.

My Dearest Mother

A rush of work has demoralized me as to letters – I have had a crowd of pupils and I prosper in a way I have not done for years. Selling pictures also – Have been able to bank nearly £200, besides paying about half that in debts – so I progress. But its been hard work – I believe I shall get back to France in a month or so – the South of it. It takes some skill to keep all going – my curious household has to run itself – and my vast Studio gets chaotically dirty & unswept – I get in a villager to clean up when I can bear it no longer. I had Miss Mary & Emmy Richmond & Mabel Atkinson to tea yesterday – most delightful to see them – we did talk. . . .

Sunday – Today is the most perfect of all the year – I have been sitting on The Island – picking daisies & watching the rock pools fill with water from the rising tide – A thing of beauty today – I have been sending long long thoughts to you all wondering what you are about & hoping all is well. No news yet from Lydia – I am sending you 'Punch' – its such good cheer. . . .

[307] To Rachel Hodgkins, 1 October 1920

St Ives. Oct 1st.

My Dearest little Mother

. . . . I hope to be in the South of France by the end of the month, with luck – and am extremely busy winding up & making ready. My class is now reduced to 3, all of whom will follow me South – useful to grease the wheels, but rather in the way – I am longing for a large new region all to myself – I have sold so well this summer that I am full of hope it may continue and enable me to do without pupils in future. No news yet of Lydia – I hope Sis hears long & often. I have one very bright N.Zealander, from Wanganui, Collier[9] by name – who is coming on wonderfully – I'll make something of her I feel sure – Also an Australian from Brisbane[10] – sterling good girls both of them. Addicted to me & my works – the Queen can do no wrong. . . . I'm buoyed up with the thought of France. . . . I hear Miss Richmond is so well & has 50 pupils – I don't know whether to rejoice or commiserate. . . . I hope little Peter is well over the mumps & the Berties also well again.

Much love dearest Yr. loving Fanny

[308] To Rachel Hodgkins, 26 October 1920

St Ives. Oct: 26th.

My Dearest Mother

. . . . The die is cast. My old Studio is let & the furniture sold – I got £50 for it, a big advance on what I gave for it, current prices being good . . . . I might have kept on the Studio & farmed it out, i.e. let it, for 25/- a week, but its risky business with strange tenants, so I decided to give it up & burn my boats definitely turning my back on St Ives – a wise move I think – it is no great catch being down here – if I came back to Cornwall another year it will be to Newlyn. . . . Meanwhile I shall wander for a year in the South & gather material for a show in London in 1921. I have never failed to do well with my foreign work. . . . I have banked enough to keep me for a year with care & economy.

England is a miserable country to be in just now – prices high & coal scarce – Strikes in the air, & this tragic Irish question growing more acute & ominous every day – I am not quite certain where I am going to – I have changed my mind several times already . . . . I rather funk travelling. I have forgotten how – I have forgotten all my French too – I have just filled in my passport and now I am going round to the fried fish shop to meet 3 friends & sup. . . .

[309] To Rachel Hodgkins, 12 December 1920

St Tropez, Var, France. Dec 12th.

My Dearest Mother,

I have been in France a little over a week & most of the time has been spent

---

[9] Edith Collier (1885-1964), born in Wanganui, studied at the Technical School there and worked in England 1913-21, with a period of study under the Australian artist Margaret Preston (née MacPherson). By 1920 Collier had developed a modern approach to picture-making, exhibiting with FH at the Women's International Art Club in 1920. After her return to Wanganui in 1922 she gave up serious painting. Discouraged by the unsympathetic reaction to her work, she was easily absorbed into the role of beloved maiden aunt in her large extended family.

[10] Probably Bessie Gibson.

in recovering from the horrible journey. It was formidable – a long 24 hour sit in an over heated train, crowded & stuffy, after a Channel crossing which had reduced me to rags & sea sickness in spite of much whisky & a 4/6 dose of the infallible Mother Sill (or Sell). . . . We could not get to the pet corner of France we hoped for – off the beaten track & only linked up by omnibus train – which are the devil – so we had to take another route . . . . No time for any fun in London – or more than one or two friends but I did manage to see a performance of Mr Gays 'Beggars Opera' pretty much as it was originally played witty, sparkling & naughty. So pretty, such loveable roysterers & home we all came, I am sure, smiling & happy & well pleased with our evening. . . . You remember the airs – "How happy I could be with either" – "Over the hills & far away" & "He so teazed me – He so pleased me you'd have done what I did do" I for one, would certainly have done so, so engaging was Captain MacHeath, Highwayman. . . . I was more than glad to leave England. The dark sad cold days, hideous prices, depression & all round difficulties – it is a country to be out of. Hardly one of my friends can afford to live in their own houses – But let me keep to facts. We got to Paris, where we spent the night & had extensive troubles – mostly because of our own stupidity, so I'll say no more. . . . We spent the night in the over heated train. My feet blistered on the hot brass. My head like a baked apple. At dawn I said "What a horrible night" & a French gentleman opposite said "I dont know why Madamoiselle complains seeing she has slept like an infant all night." It was not true. So much for rapprochement. The French are in the worst of humours with us. They complain bitterly of our high priced coal. They certainly use too much of it in heating their trains. . . . As we got further South the colder it grew & we ran into floods, deluge of rain & when we were finally dumped at our station you couldn't see where the sea ended & the floods began. It was Sunday afternoon at 5 o'c. No one in sight. We asked for a porter – the ticket lady said Is it not indeed sad that our only porter is so ill? We said we thought it much sadder that two English ladies had to carry their own luggage. At last a boy with a Murillo face, found a donkey & removed our luggage across from one platform to another. An hour's wait. A little folding of the hands in sleep – for me at least, on the grass green couch in the waiting room, then on again thro' the rising floods, by a sort of tram . . . rain coming down like a shower bath thro' the top, at last, nearly dead & wishing we were, tipped out into deep puddles & complete darkness at 9.45 we reached St Tropez. A six course dinner solaced us – much wine – & bed for about 2 whole days – awoke with horrible colds, a sort of plague which is plunging round & round the house, as soon as you get well you get worse again . . . . St Tropez being off the track & unfashionable, is comparatively cheap. We are being done extremely well for less than 2gns. per week including wine. The Exchange is still high, well over double normal. My pupil pays me £1 a week & two more will do the same after Xmas, so I am all right. . . .

. . . . I am posting by this mail a little woollen cape I thought rather sweet &

which I think will look so cosy over your blouses dear. Not much warmth in it I am afraid – but a little French touch I felt you would like . . . . The French do understand every nook & cranny of a woman's mind. . . .

[310] To Rachel Hodgkins, 21 December 1920

Cassis, nr. Marseilles, France. Dec 21st

My Dearest Mother

. . . . We moved here from St Tropez a week ago – an hours journey by train. It suits me better – I am well pleased & contented. There is great stuff on all sides. . . . This place is off the beaten track, not very far from Marseilles, on the coast, much frequented by artists on account of the landscape. . . . Winston Churchill his wife & suite have been here lately, he for a fortnights painting. Perhaps you didnt know he had talent in that direction?. . .

[311] To Rachel Hodgkins, 4 February 1921

Martigues, Bouches du Rhône, France. Feb 4th

My Dear Darling Mother

. . . . Martigues is called the Venice of France. A rather grandiloquent name for a very dirty little fishing village, on one of the indefatigable mouths of the Rhône, a few miles to the westward of Marseilles – its as filthy as its picturesque. . . . We have many people at the Hotel . . . . No English, but many Americans from that great & free country they are so fond of talking of. They are amazing people, even if they were belated in their assistance to the Allies. Who else but an American could converse like this Say! do you think that Roman Catholicism has benefited mankind – any? Whilst you are bracing yourself to some decision she is in stern chase after another problem. . . . In an unguarded moment I showed them my Cassis Drawings. They are now silent, or rather not quite so verbally keen on waving the Stars & Stripes. . . . I am sending off my Cassis set of drawings to Mr. Frank Rutter to see if he can arrange to show them in London & possibly have them reproduced in a portfolio. I have many requests for them in that form. . . . What about Lydia? Why doesn't the child write? A nice letter from Girlie just come. . . .

[312] To Edith Collier, 18 February 1921
Hotel Moderne, Martigues, Bouches du Rhône, France. Feb: 18th.

My dear Miss Collier

Very many thanks for the postal order for £5 – safely come. It was good of you to send it so quickly – I do hope you are not running yourself short. You had better wait till you get out to N.Z before sending balance (£9.15)[11] Better send draft to me c/o my Bank NSWales 29 Threadneedle St EC. This will be quite all right. I am glad you are going to stay on a little longer. I am certain your fate will bring you back to England, as mine did. It will help your work a lot getting away from it, thinking over it from a distance & sorting out values & generally consolidating what you have absorbed. It was a tragedy your pictures missing fire like that & lying all this time at the P.O. This may explain your Father's attitude. It was too disappointing. But don't mind the buffets or knocks. They are inseperable from the artists life. Its an uphill tug all the way & its only the stout hearted who win through. I am glad you are working hard – we came here a fortnight ago – very cold weather – no fires – cold floors & an icy wind. But its milder now & the dear sun warming us through. A young American from Paris is having lessons – very keen. By the end of the month there will be 2 more pupils & then we move on towards Spain. I am doing Mothers & Babes as a corrective to Cassis mountains. If I show in London before you leave I'll let you know. I hope to show at [the] International & will send you tickets if I do. I wish you could invest in Roger Frys "Vision & Design" (25/- alas) to take back with you to NZ. I am told its good. It will give you something to think over. Best of luck & courage

Yours very sincerely
Frances Hodgkins

[313] To William Hodgkins, 28 February 1921
Martigues, Bouches du Rhône, France. Feb: 28th. (?)

My dearest Willie

I was so sorry to hear from Mother that Jean had retreated into a private Hospital. This must have meant a little anxiety for you. I hope by now she is happily well again. . . . When I read in yesterday's New York Herald (published in Paris) that "one of the leaders of Art in Great Britain Miss Frances Hodgkins was now in Martigues" etc etc I realised why & how Americans get on in life.

---

[11] Almost certainly payment for FH's watercolour *Belgian Mother and Child*, now in the Sarjeant Gallery, Wanganui.

They feed on the society paragraph – self supplied. I gave one of them, a woman, a lesson this morning, or rather a general talk on Art, for which I was paid 60 francs – an hour's talk. She took down every word of it. They absorb culture as they swallow ice cream soda & the more they pay the better they are pleased and uplifted. I asked her how she would like her lesson. "Waal – she said I guess you can talk some – Then talk!" We strolled round the village – the first thing we came to was a weeping willow in front of a tall cypress. I said thats a good study in optimism & pessimism in tree life. She said that remark was well worth 2 dollars. . . . Some pupils from England are joining me for 6 weeks & will be here in a day or so. . . . Miss Cadell, Gibson my Anglo American pupil who is shaping finely. . . . One likes to think one can be of help to the young & in-earnest. And its only the young who can keep you young – & who are worth teaching. We draw in the cafés in the evening – Such types – largely Spanish in certain quarters. Such beauty & bearing. We go to some of the humblest places. You come away feeling you have spent an evening in the company of princes. . . .

[314] To Rachel Hodgkins, 14 April 1921

Martigues. April 14th.

My Darling Mother

. . . . I have been showing my work to a critic from Paris – a sympathetic personality. He says I must have a show in Paris. But these things cost much money – And I have none – I wish Mr. Auctioneer Percy would collect all my pictures & have a sale & send me the proceeds. There must be quite a number knocking about that would fetch a few pounds. What about that old Dutch woman at the window that Sis is storing for me? It should fetch something. If you only knew what a God send it would be to me to have something in the Bank for a rainy day. . . . The reason I don't send out more work to NZ. is that it has become a bit too modern & I find it very difficult to return to my earlier & more easily selling style. . . .

[315] To Rachel Hodgkins, 19 May 1921

Hotel de l'Europe, Douarnenez, Finistère, Brittany. May 19th

My dearest Mother

A long silence on my part must have made you wonder but the truth is I have been on the tramp for nearly a month exploring Brittany for a good spot for my Summer Class. . . . We are now settled at this place – not many miles from Concarneau where I lived for so long. . . . I have spent all my money so hope pupils will roll up quickly. . . . Miss Cadell is still with me. We are both stoney broke & unable to pay for our next weeks washing. Try & make some sales for me dear. I don't mind how cheap Percy sells my pictures for if he will only sell them. I nearly pegged out with congestion of the lungs at Martigues before I left, but I am all right again now & I think this climate is going to cure the wheeze I've had all the winter. The winds were too cold for me. . . .

[316] To Isabel Field, 23 September 1921

Tréboul, Finistere. Sept 23rd.

My Dearest Sis

I have been thinking how nice it wld. be if you & Will – or Girlie – could take a trip to Europe to see your little daughter. I wld. gladly go out to NZ & take care of the little Mother & Peter. . . . The worst of it is it needs so much hard cash. My last voyage out I paid out of my insurance. Now I have nothing in hand. If you wd. pass the hat round & wd. raise my passage I wd. come in the clothes I stand up in & wd. spend a year in NZ while you had a thorough good long holiday. I could live quite happily at the Farm but 1 day in Wellington wd be too much for me.

Do think it over dear old girl – I do realize, as time goes on that you must make this big effort to see something of the world. Life will have new thrills you cannot dream of & think of Lydia's joy. I am anxious to see the little frail Mother again & keep thinking a lot about you all out there. So let us swop spheres for a year & see what we can each make of the others. I have not been making much of a success of my year – the strain to keep up with the times is exhausting – and I don't need to be told that you are facing similar difficulties in degree if not in kind. My great panacea is change of environment. It gives one a fresh impulse & new courage & heart. . . .

I have not written to Mother for goodness knows how long. I have not had much of a time just lately & everything has been difficult & wrong. In all my teaching experience never have I had such an atmosphere round me as this year – Quarrelling, nerves, jealousy & a thorough bad feeling all round. A very clever elderly lady, of great intelligence & experience, joined the Class, tired everyone out with her vitality & ended by making so much mischief & trouble that the Class broke up & we migrated over here – leaving her in possession of the Hotel de l'Europe – looking rather surprised – but thoroughly unrepentant. I have had to placate her – keep her going – on my last visit she scornfully called me the Christian Peace Maker – a nasty thing to be I admit. She says herself never in her life has she had such teaching or help as from me – its what she has been needing all her life etc. But she spoils everything by being so uncharitable & hard on people who bore or don't interest her. She is very advanced in Oriental wisdom & is striving after ONENESS with all her might – but here on this human plane is making a sorry mess of it – as so many of these yearning & mystical souls seeking after harmony – do. All this – And my other worries about the future, immediate & pressing, have not made it a very comfortable time. I have been painting flowers & have sent them to dear old Anne Winthrop who is always a great ally in time of need . . . . It is perfectly true things do lighten – overnight sometimes – but the night mare of not knowing where to go is rather appalling – if you are not feeling in good form – if I could only have £60 a year to keep a roof over my head I could get along all right & find the 3 meals a day & paints & paper. I gave up my old rat infested Studio in St Ives & sold up last year – So I have not even that to fall back on. . . . The irony of it all is – That with £600 a year you cannot find a Studio in Paris or London! . . .

. . . . If you decide to act on my *excellent* suggestion I will try & hurry up with my Show. . . . I wonder if the sketches have turned up safely & [if] there will be any sale for them. . . . Do be very frank & honest with me & tell me what people say about them. It is best to know what is being said & I am strong enough to hear the *truth*. I seem to have wandered away from what I sat down to say – that is *do* make use of me, your sister, now when I can be of use to you and make up your mind to have this great trip – not to lose any more time but to look steadily in the direction you want to go and make a shot for it. I expect you sometimes envy me my freedom – but believe me it is not easy the way bristles with difficulty on all sides one sees the sham & the shoddy the false & the vulgar, in Art, thriving & on top. If you have ideals & are sensitive – then you are dedicated to a life of Poverty & suffering – If you are born so – then you just go on enduring the racking struggle – on the surface – but within & above & beyond you lie the rewards of the spirit

Well say the word dear Sis & I'll come along & look after that lovely garden of yours at the Farm & paint flowers & Maori babies & be with the little Mother while you & Will dash off to Europe on a second honeymoon. . . .

[317] To Rachel Hodgkins, 31 October 1921

Tréboul. Oct 31st

My dearest Mother

I have been in too low spirits to write home & have been waiting for my affaires to improve so that I could write something cheerful. For the last 2 months I have been without money and have stayed on here in the hopes of my flower peices selling in England also building on help from NZ. But nothing comes. Anne Winthrop could do nothing with my flowers – lots of compliments but everyone too hard up to buy. . . . I cannot stay on here any longer living on hope & credit so have literally had to send round the hat & beg fivers from my friends. This has not been nice for me & I am loaded up with a debt wh. I shall find it difficult to repay. However! There it is. I have been working like a horse & now have plenty for a Show in Town. In my next letter I shall be in a position to say when my Show is to be – not for some months to come as the Leicester Galleries are full for some time ahead. Mr. Charles Ginner, the artist, is making enquiries for me & hopes they will give me a Show free, on what he will be able to tell them of my work. Thats for next year. Meanwhile I must live – I am having pour parlers with Manchester to see if I can run a Show there pending my London one. But I am not hopeful. Pictures are a glut & the only sort that sell is the old fashioned conventional stuff. In my despair I have allowed my name to be sent in to an Artists Benevolent Fund for helping those who are hard up, thro' sickness or non-sales. This takes time. I am quite prepared to have them say Oh! she's a New Zealander. Let her own country support her. But I hope this will not be so – if they will only give me my rent how happy I should be. Otherwise it will be quite easy to founder in these troublous times. My friends are working for me & apart from any merits of my own, I think my case is a deserving one. They say the better the work the more they pay. Mr. Von Haast says I shld. have a pension, as poets get. Ask Sis & Will to put this before Mr. Massey. Sis with her wonderful powers of charm & persuasion could do much – if it was only £50 a year! What is that to a very rich & powerful little country. In the future Sissie's grand children will live to see Art put on the rates, like music is now in Germany. I am crossing to England on the 4th. four days from now & expect to go to the Nickalls in Kent for a week or so. . . . I am so glad Sis is getting letters from Lydia, I also have heard. The letter several months old. She has invited me to go out to Anatolia & visit them. . . . It is sweet of her to want me I appreciate *that* very much. . . . I have no further news to recount. I have been too full of my own troubles to read or think – hardly sleep or eat – in my endeavour to get out of this mess – and after all I have had to come down on my poor friends! Luckily for me they still have faith! . . . Percy will speed up things for me & do all he humanly can to raise the wind & send Home some cash to a much pressed and sorely tried little sister. You will see the prospects for *next year* are bright enough. I shall take care to be early in the field with my advertisements for my Summer Class – & hold it in England. I attribute my troubles this summer to the fact of being late with my plans – now I am paying the price. Meanwhile get Sis to work the oracle with Mr. Massey. My long life has taught me how strong is the personal element & when one is well known & much regarded one can achieve results for people who in the press of life wld. be overlooked. Dont let N Zealand wait to put up a memorial tablet in my memory – let her help me *now* whilst I am working at work that I hope will live after me. All my friends ask Why doesn't your country help you? Canada helps her artists – Australia I think does – little Belgium supports her artists. See that I am not left to exist on the charity of a Benevolent Fund. Mr. Massey well knows the conditions of life in England – the high cost of everything especially rent & rates. I will make N.Z proud of me – if she will pay my rent – Thats a fair offer!

It has been a marvellous summer – only 2 days rain. The drought is causing much sickness & misery – villages have to pay 1 franc for a bottle of water. Prices are rising. Butter very dear & nasty – the poor cattle suffer. I am still wearing print dresses & working out of doors. But England is cold & I expect I shall get bronchitis as soon as I get there. . . .

[318] TO RACHEL HODGKINS, 20 NOVEMBER 1921

Topsham, Exeter. Nov. 20th.

My dearest Mother

My last letter was written from Tréboul before leaving for England. It was not a happy letter dear. I am so sorry to have teased you with my worries which seemed to crush me, but as one feels so one writes! Now that I am back in England among friends things are a lot brighter & plans are arranging themselves & soon I hope I shall have good news for you about Shows. I travelled all night from Brittany reaching Paris by 7 o'clock, just time for hot coffee & a wash then a dash across Paris with the milk cans, to the boat train to Boulogne & by 4 that afternoon was in London. . . . Dear Ann Winthrop has been so kind – the atmosphere is rather too charged with bridge parties & teas – but I wriggle out of them as gracefully as I can & go for walks with the dog. I have had an awfully kind letter from Willie with a £5 cheque wh I dont like taking at all these bad days of narrow means. Lydia, the dear, has also sent me the same & that grand old man Peter Waite £10 to buy something 'warm'. I have banked all this. . . . I will write as soon as plans mature. . . .

[319] TO RACHEL HODGKINS, 27 DECEMBER 1921

London. Dec 27th.

My dearest Mother

I have come to anchor for a few days in London in a friends Studio lent for 10 days. I have been moving about & changing my address, like one suspended between heaven & hell, on the endless hunt for a place to house myself in. I have at last fixed on Burford, a small town about 20 miles from Oxford & 2 hours from London. You may remember I was there once before, or rather in the next village, Great Barrington, and liked it, & found the Cotswold country very paintable & the air splendidly bracing. I have been staying with the Parkinson's who have a country place near Oxford & they motored me round & we found a fine old stone wool barn in Burford which would make a good Studio – light large & *dry*, for the enormous rent of £10 a year. In Burford itself I have friends & 2 former pupils so I shall not be lonely. In order to be close at hand & fix things up on a business basis I put up for a few days at my dear old Farmhouse in Barrington. The weather was warm & dry & I walked into Burford & back every day, 7 miles, and I have now settled up definitely, and go down to Burford next week, set up my goods once more, & establish myself. I shall try & make it boom. My friends think it is a sound move. Burford itself is booming & people are buying up the old houses. One, Horniman, the rich man there, is starting a boarding house, 14 rooms, unpicking an old timbered house & modernising it. This will be handy for my pupils – I intend to make them come to me in future. I am spending some of the welcome £10 Will sent me, on advertisement. It has just reached me! . . . It has saved the situation. I have been marking time staying with friends. I long to settle down again & start work & earning once more. The weather is so wonderful & bright it gives one hope & courage merely to see the sunshine & clear skies. It really has been a Merry Xmas, I think, for the millions, food is plentiful & prices down – by next year they will have levelled up still more & most people look forward hopefully to 1922. I do too. . . .

[320] To Rachel Hodgkins, 13 January 1922
Studio, St Lawrence's St, Burford, Oxon. Jan 13th

My dearest Mother

Please address your next letter to Burford from now onward my new home. I simply cannot believe that I am settling down in England after shaking the dust off my feet only a year ago. Perhaps I have found that in spite of her faults there is no better place than the old country – France showed me that & cured me of restlessness. I was so nearly down & out. . . .

Whoever sent me the £20 telegram at Xmas has saved me from black ruin & disaster and I thank them with undying gratitude. I shall be in a position, I hope, this time next year to repay in full. . . . The telegram reached me just in time to get it cashed at the G.P.O and with it I payed my year's rent, advertised in the "Studio" & "Colour" laid in a stock of painting material, all heavy items. Now I feel I shall be safe & can ride out the storm. I shall be pretty busy trying to make ends meet for a while, but living here is primitive & as cheap as you can get anywhere. My great assett is my improved health & spirits.

. . . . [The Studio] is a lovely old barn. I have bought 8 old chairs for 10/- . . . an old counter for a table, an iron bedstead & various adjuncts including a black kitten, young of Mrs. Plosh of Park Farm, Barrington. It takes plenty of nerve to climb my ladder – a handrail will be necessary if visitors are not to break the neck in the semi-darkness of a winter afternoon. . . .

No more now Dearest. It is too cold. You must walk seven miles at least if you want to get thawed – so I am off – I go [in] the afternoon round by Grt. Barrington by the low road & back by the High. . . .

[321] TO RACHEL HODGKINS, 25 JANUARY 1922

Studio, Burford, Oxon. Jan 25th.

My dearest Mother

Just a line to let you know how I am getting along in my new quarters. . . . All work is scratched so to speak for the moment. Icy blizzards & all clogged up with snow & biting E winds. . . . I am keeping well & fit & thanks to the splendid help from home not too anxious. I am more sure every day that I am making a bid for the best & good times will come for me yet. . . .

. . . . Today my old friend Gertrude Crompton is marrying her Quaker mystic poet. A great Adventure for a woman of 43. It will be a tight pinch. Neither has a sou except what they make, he by his lectures & she by her painting. Now she has taken on a male burden to cook for & tend & be buffer for. Well! marriage is the only way for some. But I prefer single blessedness – or unblessedness. . . .

[322] TO RACHEL HODGKINS, 12 FEBRUARY 1922

Studio, Burford, Oxon. Feb 12th.

My darling Mother

. . . . We have been having a bad dose of flue – I am all right, in fact have never felt brisker & better, in spite of the frightful cold. I sob with pain over frozen fingers & toes, especially when I try to thaw them at the fire, real trench toes. It has been a long hard frost on a snow bound country killing all the flue germs I hope. For a week every shop in Burford was closed except the chemist – whole families succumbed. Side doors were left open & one entered & helped oneself to potatoes & fish & anything one fancied. We had quite a fire too, one day – a dynamo & petrol shed caught. I was passing at the time 9.30a.m & did my share in yelling for help. At long last a small hose on a wheel barrow was brought into action & after much excitement & bucket carrying flames were got under & Burford saved. Medieavel isnt it?. . . I have been keeping warm (?) decorating my barn. Wonderful what one can do with about tuppence worth of powder colours & a big brush to make things look merry & bright. I am playing the artful spider game – ensnaring flies into my parlour – I see I shall have to record everything I do, small & great, if I am to fill a sheet. It is impossible that anything should ever alter at all in Burford – wh. is a kind of Cranford & lives in its past. Yesterday I had tea at the Vicarage. The Vicar's sister "Miss Fanny" is deaf & a little like Miss

Matty. I looked at her sketches of Corsica. Mrs Cobb was the other guest slightly more antique than either of us – I was very grateful to her. She was so enthusiastic over the sketches & kept saying What an admirable bit of blue distance Miss Fanny –. She asked me if, when I got tired of painting did I not like hunting up the tombstones of my ancestors.

This is enough for today – Next week I'll tell you some more. Life in Burford is too thrilling. Tonight I take high tea with two other maiden ladies (I shall soon be one myself) the invitation is worded "Please come at 7.30 – We go to bed early". . . .

[323] To Rachel Hodgkins, 5 March 1922
                                        Studio, Burford, Oxon. March 5th.

My dearest Mother
    . . . . Life jogs on placidly & except for my feud with Mr. Smith the dustman, in which I don't know yet whether I am bested or worsted, nothing has happened worth recording. Mr. Smith is an influential man in Burford & it would be unwise to quarrel with him. He is my neighbour & he keeps a brown lurcher dog which he is fond of shutting up for the weekend in a shed opposite my Studio – I suspect without food or water and it is one long howl till Monday morning. I have tried my refining influence on Mr. Smith – vainly. It is useless to complain to the policeman because they are pals. Anyone who has not been in Burford for 300 years is nobody. . . .

I am busy trying every sort of dodge to collect money – I am competing for a prize poster for 100 guineas offered by one of the daily papers for the Womans Exhb. in July – "Modern Woman 1922" I simply must win it. . . .

[324] To Rachel Hodgkins, 25 March 1922
                                        Studio, Burford, Oxon. March 25th.

My dearest Mother
    . . . . I may say that we have only had *one* gale this winter, it commenced in Jany and has not stopped yet! . . . It has been too uncomfortable & miserable for words & I shall remember March 1922 for a very long time. . . . We have only had one real Spring day – a fortnight ago I walked out to the Bartletts [at Barrington] for dinner & had a tremendous gorge of a farmhouse meal enough for a fortnight, & walked home slowly, very slowly, in the evening, with a ½ lb of butter & a bunch of violets in my arms. . . .

Your birthday is a short 3 weeks, and mine in five. This will not arrive in time – but my thoughts will go out to you dearest, from my barn to your basement, which will be gay with flowers I hope, and the day will pass happily & peacefully . . . . It was a dear little room I remember, & warm & one did not feel the wind so much downstairs. I am so relieved to hear Sis is improving in health & the fear of an operation passing over. I was very anxious. So the great young Peter is off to school to train for farming. This will be the 4th. farmer in the family of this generation. . . .

I have been busy with my posters – but waiting for warmer weather to enjoy work. Fingers are too stiff & clumsy to do much. This week I send off one of them (poster not finger). Hope I shall have luck. There is a fine field for poster work. Pictures are out of fashion & no one buys them. If you have a crisp bright idea put it into a poster. . . .

[325] To Rachel Hodgkins, 13 May 1922

Studio, Burford, Oxon. May 13th.

My dearest Mother

I am sitting out in the sunshine – How long will it last?

Spring is tardy in these parts. The winter nearly finished me but now I am pulling my exhausted self together & trying to forget all the little things of life that have annoyed me so much of late. At the moment my special affliction is church bells. The Oxford Bell Ringers are performing. . . . You would think all Burford is being married. I said to Mrs. Search my neighbour in the Lane "Why is this?" "Oh just an 'obby Miss" They started at ½ past 2 and now it is 5.30. It is about time they went back to Oxford.

. . . . I think I was in the throes of Posters when I last wrote. I have not heard the result of the G.W.R competition but I *have* heard the Posters sent in are so good & numerous that they are to be exhibited in London. The Oxford Folk Dance Socty. has asked me to design them a Poster. I went over to Oxford on Sat. to a Musical Festival & saw some Morris Dances on the beautiful lawns of one of the Colleges – I made sketches & notes. I forget whether I told you I had a day in London. . . . [Mr. Gibson] met me at Paddington rushed me round in a taxi from gallery to gallery seeing all the best Picture Shows, then a jolly good lunch, his own work, more Pictures & back by the evening train – tired but stimulated. . . .

[326] To RACHEL HODGKINS, 12 JUNE 1922

Studio, Burford, Oxon. June 12th.

My dearest Mother

. . . . We have had weeks & weeks of this hot dry weather which the newspapers call a drought and which I think is like Italy without the heavy train fare. . . . I think I told you of the 2 energetic spinster Americans who came for a week's lessons. . . . Then followed 2 Manchester Art School teachers[12] very keen & serious minded & earnest – terribly so for the state of the temperature. . . . So you see the sky is clearing & I am passing out of the shadows into sunlight. . . .

There is a lot of talk in the papers about the poverty of the Artists & their bad prospects. . . . One jolly day last week I took a day off (it was Whit Monday) & went for a picnic with the Kettlewells to see some Country Dancing in one of the villages. . . . I was introduced to the daughter of William Morris, Miss May Morris – I told her my sister in NZ had Morris papers carpets chairs etc from her father's factory – was it Kelmscote? I forget. She asked me to go & visit her at Kelmscote where she lives. A faded gentle lady – with no sign of the parental virility & force – or magnetism. . . .

. . . . The G.W.R. Poster Competition results were published today – & as was expected rank outsiders have won the prizes. To be quite correct I hear that just over 3000 entered for it! vastly to the amusement of the G.W.R. . . .

[327] To JANE SAUNDERS[13] AND HANNAH RITCHIE, c.24 JUNE 1922

Studio, Burford, Oxon. Saturday.

My Dear Miss Saunders & Ritchie

You must forgive me for not writing sooner to thank you for your letters & the interesting Eustace Miles Letters[14] & the Roger Fry Pamphlet.

They are the Law & the Prophets of Diet & Art & both speak with deepest conviction & a touch of righteous fanaticism. Certainly they are two subjects to be treated jointly? As far as my own food is concerned I hardly know which satisfies me most, the savoury mess or the dish of herbs; but some day, when leisure comes, I foresee myself designing & plotting & planning a meal as deliberately as I do my pictures – meanwhile I "catch" my food rather as people catch trains & buses & thats all there is to it – except frequent twinges of indigestion.

Since you left the weather has been – well you know what it has been without

---

[12] Hannah Ritchie and Jane Saunders.

[13] Known at first as Dorothy, Miss Saunders later adopted her middle name, Jane, and this has been used throughout to identify the letters addressed to her.

[14] About vegetarianism.

my enlarging on it. You had the cream of it. I have been hard put to it keeping my small band interested & happy & directing their thoughts from packing up & departing by the next train. Burford is a deadly place for stranded artists when it rains. I have had them all very heavily on my chest. A friend living at Taynton, 1½ miles away, has let me have the run of her house & garden while she is in London – so we have been tramping out there in the wet with our lunch & tea & painting flowers – of every description – a lovely rose garden with torrents of blossom from every tree. My non-conformist conscience won't let me send you off a bunch of buds – but when she returns I'll get some for you & post them. Of course I shall be delighted to have Miss Ritchie's sister in Sept: & will do all I can to help her. Those are the sort of pupils one prays for – I would like to see some of her work so as to "realize" her better when she comes. So, if you can, do bring some in Aug: when you come – I was sorry Miss Ritchie did not see V. Bell's work.[15] I see Marchand[16] has a Show at the Independent. Two of my party are running up for the day to see it . . . .

[328] To Rachel Hodgkins, 27 July 1922

Burford. July 27th.

My dearest Mother

I have been terribly slack writing to you. Do forgive me – It has been an utterly miserable month – the weather just gruesome – floods of rain & so cool, never a blink of sun. It has been maddening! . . . Now its the end of July, generally my best month, with one pupil in hand. So I feel a trifle flat & no wonder. It is charming weather now, fine and calm & cool and I am getting over my resentment. . . . Someone on their way home from the allotments has thrown 2 large onions & a bunch of carrots in at my big loft door. Yesterday I had a basket of rasps & logan berries given me which made 2 nice pots of jam. . . .

I have no news to recount – Life is dull & sleepy – I know I am in a backwater but it won't be for ever – With returning health & energy I'll shoulder my way out somehow. . . .

I am busy working out Poster ideas & other stunts – "Colour" has reproduced a Drawing of mine on the first page[17]. . . .

---

[15] Vanessa Bell (1879-1961) was associated with Roger Fry, Duncan Grant and Clive Bell in the application of post-impressionist ideas to British painting and the decorative arts.

[16] Jean Marchand (1882-1941) was a French painter championed by the British post-impressionists.

[17] *The Cinema*, a charcoal drawing of three children.

[329] To Rachel Hodgkins, 13 August 1922

Studio, Burford. Aug 13th.

My dearest Mother

. . . . The 2 Manchester girls came for a fortnight & worked indoors. I have promised them I'll go to Manchester in Oct for a month & give a short teaching session. I am to stay with them. They are to try & find me a Studio & we hope, by starting in a quiet way, I may work up a connection, possibly arrange for a Show. Anyway it is a cork to cling to & will get me out of Burford for the winter. Later on it may be possible to run a Class somewhere in the S. of France. I don't mean to stop for ever in Burford dear, only to use it as pied à terre, to come back to, & store my belongings. . . . No more now dearest. I must go on with the noble sport of attracting passers by on the way to see the Church – into my Studio. I have hung the little room downstairs with small pictures for sale & put posters & other bait on the door. So far I have bagged one man for Sept: & it looks as tho' I had sold a picture. . . .

[330] To Hannah Ritchie, c.17 August 1922

Studio, St. Lawrence's Street, Burford, Oxon. Thursday

My Dear Hannah

. . . . August is a poor month for London galleries, but I am glad you saw the Tate, really worth a visit since the moderns are housed there. . . . How would it do to send a p.c to Mr. Frank Rutter, whose address you have, & ask if there is to be an Allied Artists Exh. this Autumn – Then you could perhaps send a group of Drawings. They hang each artist seperately in groups. As you know it is a modern Independent Show & is held at the Mansard gallery. He is always on the look out for young progressive spirits & asked me some time ago to recommend the AAA wh. is the London equivalent of the Paris Salon Indépendents. . . .

[331] To Hannah Ritchie and Jane Saunders, c.5 September 1922

Studio, St. Lawrence's Street, Burford, Oxon. Tuesday

The bonnie heather sprig & yr. two nice cheery letters has just come & I must send you a line while the morning is fresh & before the business of the day gets its clutch on me. It is difficult to stand clear of things & get detachment for either work or letters.

I have been up all night ? battling with a bat. It wouldn't depart by the window nor the door – neither would it lie down (or up) & sleep & let *me* sleep. It got among the rafters. Well! day dawned & it is still here but invisible. . . . The white heather has come like balm of gilead. . . .

Don't worry not painting – Run wild on the moors & fill lungs with great breaths of that lovely clean strong air. It will put force & life into you worth more than gold. I read the Walenski[18] article with much interest. He is far & away a more enfranchised critic than Roger Fry. He wrote for the Athenaum, but was possibly too strong a personality for the Editor's taste (so I was told) & he was turned down & Roger Fry took his place. I met him once – a turbulent young Jew. He has said a few polite things about my work & one or two very rude ones about my hat. Still I don't bear malice. He is an independent & iconoclast. . . .

FH stayed with friends in London and no doubt visited galleries before going to Manchester. She asked for and received financial help from Hannah Ritchie to cover the expenses of this journey.

[332] TO RACHEL HODGKINS, 1 NOVEMBER 1922

Manchester. Nov 1st.

My dearest Mother

This will reach you about Xmas time – I hope you will have a happy & cheery time dear. . . . I am now in Manchester giving a short course of lessons at the Girls' High School – which is the 3rd. most notable Girls' School in England. It is not a very big class – but it may grow. The two young Art Mistresses are pupils of mine & it is through them that I have been invited to give this course. Theirs' is a wholetime job for wh. they get big salaries. They live in a cosy flat a tram ride out of Manchester. I have had splendid weather – clear frosty days – not the usual fog & rain that Manchester is noted for. Yesterday we walked in Derbyshire – Took train into the country & then tramped over the bleak peaks – black as well as bleak – you never saw such dreary country – I have met a number of nice people, literary & theatrical, who are living hard but satisfying lives. The boom year is not yet for artists – but we are not standing idle. You would have been amused to see me one day conducting six School Mistresses (Maths: Classics, Literature & 3 Art mistresses) round the galleries. There is an amazing show on in Manchester now, a collection of Theatre Designs & Models, a European Collection got together by Gordon Craig, Ellen Terry's genius Son, & destined for the S. Kensington Museum. It is now touring the big cities – & is open free

---

[18] R. H. Wilenski, Special Lecturer in the History of Art, University of Manchester, wrote a number of books on art (*Dutch Painting; Modern French Painters; The Modern Movement in Art*) and championed the British avant garde painters of the 1930s.

to the public, who take advantage of it & pour through the galleries on one's heels. Well I discovered the English Teacher was a Miss Hackeridge, neice of the little Dunedin Artist[19] – Father's old protegé – I hear he has recently died. He was a nice little man I remember. She came & had tea with us on Sunday.

This is a dear little flat, all complete – gas fires books galore & a gramaphone – my friends are both vegetarian – and cook their food deliciously – I am always hungry & could eat most of the meals twice over. It has been a nice holiday & rest & I am going back to Burford next week much refreshed – and perhaps a little thinner.

I hear my horrid little stove is emitting suffocating smells & weeping buckets of treacle. This being so I should like to remain in Manchester. . . .

[333] To Hannah Ritchie, c.19 November 1922

[Burford] Sunday

My Dear Hannah

You are an extraordinary generous pair & kind beyond the dreams of kindness.

Just as I set about inhibiting a desire for China Tea comes a parcel of it – and figs – a delicious bon bouche to have kept up your sleeve & sent after me to make it more absolutely nice. I am enjoying myself – Thank you ever so much. . . .

I have ordered the 'New Leader' & am reading it instead of going to Church! much better for me.

Today you are caravaning with Miss Nicholls – I hope it is as mild a day as with us – foggy rather – I shall start a landscape of the valley if tomorrow is fine. . . .

[334] To Rachel Hodgkins, 22 November 1922

Burford. Nov 22nd.

My dearest Mother

I am just back from Manchester & feeling more full of hope & cheerfulness than when I went – Everyone was so kind to me . . . . I have promised to go back after Xmas for 3 months if a Studio can be found for me – all expenses to be paid by my two kind pupil friends – rent coal etc & I am to live with them at their flat. I should do well – relieved of financial worries – and secure, or temporarily secure at any rate, for a time. The enemy has been sleeplessness – I have been dreading another winter in Burford – I can stick it till Xmas . . . . My first act after my return was to get the stove set right. It has been dealt with & now gives out a

---

[19] Robert H. Hawcridge (1866-1920) worked in Dunedin as an illustrator and lithographer, taught at the Dunedin School of Art and exhibited at the Otago Art Society 1890-1904.

glorious heat . . . . Another good friend has offered to be responsible for my coal bills – & has given me carte blanche with the coal! So I am in clover so to say. I must make good with my painting & justify all this benevolence on the part of my kind friends. Of course it makes all the difference in life to me – having unstinted warmth. . . .

I must not write a long letter tonight dearest. This is strictly speaking a "coal" letter, all about fuel, plenty of it without considering how fast it goes! Think of it! This is what makes the world go round. The well-off ones *must* help the poorer these difficult times & no one is proud or stiff about accepting help. I am grateful from the bottom of my soul. So I end up on a cheery note wishing you all the best & brightest for Xmas & the New Year – and for your own dear self continued good health & spirits for a long long time to come

Your loving Fanny.

[335] TO HANNAH RITCHIE, C.25 DECEMBER 1922

Studio, Burford, Oxon. Christmas 1922

My Dear Hannah

. . . . I feel overwhelmed by your & Dorothy's goodness to me – I am afraid certain personias are denying themselves many things this Xmas in order that I may partake. It is very splendid of you & I am full of thanks & gratitude – Your energy & go are most exhilirating . . . . Let us agree to hold over the Studio question till I arrive on the scene – I am so susceptible to environment that I almost dread your taking a room I might not be able to work in. The Plymouth Grove room *may* be quite the place . . . . The Goupil closes on the 28th. I believe there is a Daumier Show somewhere in the King's Rd (?) wh. should be thrilling – if it is still open

The Henry Lamb[20] portrait might be anybodys – it looks quite prosy – but that was intentional without doubt to keep within a traditional boundary. . . .

Real cold now – but the Stove glows –

A Happy Christmas to you both (will you share this letter) and lots of cheer and deep down thanks from me for giving me so much pleasure – and best of all – hope –

---

[20] Henry Lamb (1885-1960), another member of the Camden Town Group, is remembered for his portraits, particularly one of Lytton Strachey (c.1912), which hovers on the borders of caricature.

[336] To Hannah Ritchie, c.10 January 1923

Studio. Sunday

My Dear Hannah

You are two bricks to slave so hard on my behalf – I *am* grateful. . . .

. . . . I know you are up to the eyes in work & time is short & you must decide this week so I leave it to you to do what [is] expedient & best & if you fix up with the P[lymouth] Grove room I will gladly fall in with all the plans – *I am out to please & be pleased remember.* There is to be no repining – ever – it is to be Art without Tears this time – to a large extent I have lost my terror – thanks to you – & time I hope will prove that it pays to put me on my legs again & make me a busy useful woman again whose best work is ahead of her. You two girls have had the courage & imagination to do what other richer friends could have done twice over without turning a hair – one of them writes to say she is sending me an old rug for my Manchester Studio – wh. will be something to shake out of my window anyway. . . . I hope Dorothy will not cut her holidays short. Don't let her Hannah if she is really having a good time in London. I will come when you are ready for me. I have made several good beginnings of gypsy women & children (I am trading my old clothes for sittings) & I hope to finish them after the New Year & have them ready for Frank Rutters Show if it ever comes off. I suppose you will be able to raise models for me – at the start – I expect I will get some good ones thro' the missions?

What Manchester needs is a running series of good shows – John – Brangwn – Orpen[21] – the young moderns – even Laura Knight (in an interim) to tone it up & give it a habit of mind towards good modern work. . . .

I have seen no one for days. The air is full of decay & damp – mental & physical. I am scratching along as best I can

I enclose todays S. Times criticisms. You may see the "Independent" Show in Grafton Street – I believe the Jap: Show at the B.M. is still on – And the Goupil. . . . How jolly for you having the School Studio done up. Pitch pine of course limits one's flights. I think you have chosen a nice proportion of yellow & grey to white – you can always add a line of orange or ochre. . . .

You dont mention rents of Studios. I hope they are not ruinous. . . . I will hear all news when I come. Life is a scrimmage now

I shall be *more* than grateful for a fiver [to settle] up here before I leave [I hope to be] paying "divvys" by next Xmas. I hate breaking into yr. Xmas cheques you are real pals. . . .

---

[21] Augustus John (1878-1961), Frank Brangwyn (1867-1956) and William Orpen (1878-1931) were all associated with the Royal Academy. John and Orpen were graduates of the Slade School and exhibited with the NEAC, Brangwyn was noted for his decorative, richly coloured murals.

FH arrived in Manchester at the beginning of February 1923 and set up a teaching studio within walking distance of her friends' flat.

[337] To Rachel Hodgkins, 17 March 1923

Manchester. March 17th.

Very many happy returns of the 14th. dearest little Mother & all loving wishes for continued good health & strength to enjoy the many more birthdays you may be spared to see. I had hoped to send you a nice book but I can't manage it this month – petty cash is pettier than usual. It is splendid news to hear of Willie's promotion up into the sun – Auckland is a real catch I should say – I am so glad[22] . . . . I am still in Manchester but am soon returning to Burford. I feel I could have done much here if I had money to splash about. If only Mr. Waite *had* remembered me in his will – what a different life it might be for me. The world would then hear of Frances Hodgkins & her works. No I had not heard of his death, but I knew he was failing fast. He felt very strongly that I was following a difficult & unpopular line in my Art & said so frankly. He could not understand my recent work. At which I am not surprised. I must write to Miss Waite. He was a good friend to me & if he lacked the magic touch of vision to see that I am worth helping so much the worse for me. My two teacher friends are going to Paris for their Easter holidays. I am joining some artist & dramatic friends in the country for a fortnight. One of them, Margaret Nicholls has a caravan – and I have a room in a Farmhouse hard by. The others of the party are at a cottage not far off. They consist of F. Sladen Smith, playwright, W. Grimmond artist & scenepainter, & two others of the "Unnamed" Society, a young Dramatic Group which is making a "name" for itself, writing, acting, & producing their own plays – having high standards – these small Art Theatres are served by artists, musicians, poets, playwrights all working together for a common end & harmonising their contributions.

It is a vital little group & they want me to come back in the winter & associate myself with them.

I have no recent news of Lydia.

. . . . I think I have got through my winter marvellously all things considered and am most grateful to the two nice girls who have showed me much kindness

---

[22] Willie was now manager of the Bank of New South Wales in Auckland.

[338] TO RACHEL HODGKINS, 2 APRIL 1923

Rainow, Cheshire. April 2nd.

My dearest Mother

This is written from a tiny village, about 800 ft. up from Macclesfield, where the black smoke & factory chimneys are seen in the valley below, and I am sitting on the step of the Caravan belonging to my friend Margaret Nicholls who is inside cooking dinner in picturesque attire. This sort of country reminds you of Wuthering Heights. . . . High, wild, lonely – with the reluctant Spring coming on slow slowly, the black charred trees turning palest green & the wan sun hardly through the thick mist. Higher up the hill, on the real top, the group I told you of have their cottage, the Blue Boar – a jolly place where they week end in turns. I have been going up there to paint their portraits. . . .

We go for long tramps, talk a lot, work, at least *I* do – have given some lessons, & booked a few of the members for my Summer Class in Burford – So I have not lived in vain. . . . Peggy the mare is nibbling my ear & breathing soft nothings down my back – she noses round for tit bits & has a happy life doing nothing & growing fat. . . . Have you seen Willie?

[339] TO DOROTHY SELBY,[23] 26 APRIL 1923

Studio, St. Lawrence's Street, Burford, Oxon. April 26th.

Dear Madam

Please excuse the delay in writing. Your letter was waiting for me here on my return from Manchester last night.

I shall be most pleased to give you some coaching in the summer, or as soon after May 14th as you like. My Season starts then.

My terms are 4 guineas a month a course of 12 demonstration lessons, or I can give you the course in a shorter time if desirable

I can book you a room in village (if you will kindly write by return) or, there is an excellent boarding house, most comfortable newly opened & run on modern lines – tariff 3 guineas –

The best way to get to Burford is by the 4-45 train from Paddington-Oxford & catch bus on here. It takes luggage.

It there is anything more I can tell you about material etc please let me know

Yours truly

Frances Hodgkins

[23] Dorothy Selby, head of a large secretarial college in London, was an amateur painter who wished to join FH's class. She was a close friend of Elsie Barling (1883-1976), who had studied with FH in Burford. Elsie Barling was an art teacher (her most notable pupil was the painter John Craxton) and professional painter, who was to share some exhibiting situations with FH. The three women remained friends until the end of FH's life.

[340] To Hannah Ritchie and Jane Saunders, 1 May 1923
Studio, St. Lawrence's Street, Burford, Oxon. May 1st

Dearest Friends

You are ever so much too good & kind to me – its *endless* kindness in four dimensions. The postman has just left two packages of all my best loved food the nice "foody" food of Eustace Miles which makes all the cheap stuff sold here in the shops seem "foodless". You have sent me such *heaps* & *acres* of good things – there is a Pyramid in front of me. Never in the memory of man has my birthday been honoured – I am not used to it – *You must spend no more on me.* You have piloted me safely through the winter of 1923 & launched me for the summer & *now* you must think of yourselves & begin to horde a bit for the future –

I mean this.

I have paid off 3 of my enemies & begin to feel lighter-hearted – (and they are also no doubt)

A pupil wrote today that she has her first picture in the R.A & is so bucked that she enclosed £5 for a long coveted Drawing of mine. Nice isn't it?. . . .

Amy Krauss suggests coming for the summer with a crate of Pottery & her wheel & setting up business & teaching – I am finding her a shop front – It will be invigorating for Burford –

. . . . I shall make a pig of myself over the black olives – I adore them.

[341] To Hannah Ritchie, c.June 1923
Studio, St. Lawrence's Street, Burford, Oxon. Monday

My Dear Hannah

By now I expect you are both back again. If it has been as cold & wet in the Lakes as it has been in the Cotswolds I am sorry for you. It will have quite knocked the bottom out of your painting, but otherwise I hope you have had a good time & enjoyed it all. I got the p.c – what tremendous *big* country. I can't see you tackling it in Water Colour – I am intensely curious to see what you *have* done with it.

I have been very busy – this time it really has been "the goods"

There has been a succession of friends & pupils almost ever since I got back – a trickle more than a stream – but it has kept me busy & out of mischief (I get so bored here I don't know what to do with myself). The Wolverhampton people were very nice – very rich – had a car, son at Oxford, and were not difficult to teach, as they knew next to nothing about art, but were just out to be mildly thrilled & have it poured into them painlessly. It was horrible weather so they took a room for the fortnight & did flowers & still life . . . . They bought £25 worth of Water Colours much to my joy and intend returning to me later on.

. . . . Miss Krauss comes next month. She has got a shop – discovered where to get clay for nothing – where to build a field-furnace – and seems likely to make a good thing of it. . . .

. . . . I sent yr. portrait[24] & the Rowbotham girls to the NEAC but no luck. Did you send? It is a fraudulent affair I think. They take our 5/- without any intention of hanging any but the chosen few. . . .

[342] TO HANNAH RITCHIE, 15 SEPTEMBER 1923

Studio, St. Lawrence's Street, Burford, Oxon. Sunday 15th[25]

My Dear Hannah

. . . . I have put off writing till more tranquil times. You can imagine I have been pretty thoroughly occupied & confess to you I am tired out & used up – I go into rooms tomorrow for a few weeks to recover. I wish I could sit on the top of one of your hills & lose myself . . . & cease from instructing & simply "be" – I am at the dead end. . . .

I have had some *very* intelligent pupils & some powerfully unintelligent ones – I think they have all enjoyed themselves. . . . My love to you both – You *must* be with me next year in France. There is no one quite like you in my affections & esteem. . . .

[343] TO RACHEL HODGKINS, 3 DECEMBER 1923

St Paul du Var, A(lpes) M(aritimes), France. Dec 3rd

My Dearest Mother

I am happy to say that I am back again in France. . . . I have been here 3 weeks, rather wretched ones, as I caught a chill on the journey & I have been on the verge of jaundice – but am better now, very peeved at missing so much valuable time. I simply could not write letters dearest I had the hump so badly. . . .

It is nice to be out of dreary little Burford, where the sun hardly ever shone & the people were so good & dull & learned. I stood it for 2 years – by setting my jaws. Life here is primitive – but one can put up with a good deal when the sun shines – I have 2 rooms, one I use as a Studio, & the other to sleep in – I make my own breakfast & supper & have one good meal at the inn – and for all this I pay something over 15/- a week . . . . Of course it is not luxury – but then I always have to wear a hair shirt – & am inured to economy.

. . . . This is an old old house where I am living – originally a prison in the time

---

[24] Probably *Double Portrait*, dated 1922 (Plate 2). See pp. 388, 566.
[25] Written after two months' teaching in Burford.

of Francis I – the next room to mine, walls a metre & half thick has gentle reminders in the shape of iron rings & chains on the walls. To meet the exigencies of the times it is now being converted into a lavatory. . . .

[344] TO HANNAH RITCHIE AND JANE SAUNDERS, C.20 DECEMBER 1923
[St Paul du Var] Thursday

My Dear Hannah & Dorothy
    . . . . I have been meaning to write for many a day but have been a poor sort of creature with a queer sort of feverish chill hanging about . . . . The truth is I came here too early in the season – for these heights – it is a severe climate & the winter has been a bad one. I happen to be alone in this house except for a young person who comes for an hour in the morning to tidy (?) up. I generally have to tidy up after her – it is a pretty cold house but I manage to keep wood fires going which answer very well except when the wood is green. The chimney too, smokes when it likes. Imagine me at night, (wh. begins at 4 o'c) with 2 lean grey cats sitting up, uneasy, watching me hard – they have found out I like feeding hungry beasts & have told their friends. At 6-30 I descend to the Hôtel for dinner, talk broken English – French – Danish – for as long as I can keep it up & by 8 o'c I am in bed – & thankful to be there out of the cold. It is hardly cheerful – but things will improve later on. St Paul is a great place – if you yourself are great – something like the lakes I should imagine, for range & height & vastness – cultivated every inch of it up to the snows – I am thankful there is no one here to ask me how to render it – *I cant*. . . .
    My show seems to be a fiasco.[26] It has brought no comfort – I have sold 5 Drawings about £28 worth, but when all is paid for there is little left but the advertisement. I was at a disadvantage – in a poky gallery & overshadowed by the Van Gogh show. The Press notices were discrediting & unfair. I can't help feeling morbid. Think well before you embark on an art career – it is a stony path unless you keep on traditional lines – the free lance gets it in the neck every time. *Attach yourselves to a group.* That is my advice –
    The Morning Post grades me as a diciple of Gogh – which is manifestly absurd – I have too much technique of my own to cope with without taking on anothers. What I do share with him is poverty and a touch of ecstacy –
    I do hope you will see the V. Goghs & how they will affect you. . . .
    . . . . To bed now – to sleep & forget my wrongs & all the miseries of life – as a French woman said to me yesterday "Middle Life is a hard joke" with which I agreed – Best of love, luck & a lovely time & dont worry about me will you my dears. If I am up a tree I'll tell you *thank* you –
                    A happy Xmas to you   Frances Hodgkins

[26] Held at the Little Art Rooms, 8 Duke Street, London.

[345] To Hannah Ritchie, 29 December 1923

St Paul. Dec. 29th.

My Dearest Hannah

Firstly let me congratulate you on making a sale at the Show. I cant say how happy it made me to hear of it & I am sure Dorothy is as pleased as I am . . . .

How about the Van Goghs & what do you think of him tell me – He cannot be judged by the ordinary standards. He is apart, alone, not part of any whole like we lesser folk. Curiously I met the Dutch Dealer who arranged for the Show, at tea yesterday. . . . I had a long talk with him & also listened to him talking to another dealer – not such a big pot. Have you ever heard 2 dealers talking? Your ears just lie back & the roof of your head slowly lifts – you realise a little of the big game & guess the rest. He told me a lot of interesting facts about the family Van Gogh – Cezanne & old Vollard[27] & all the rest of them –

The widow sister-in-law owns most of the Goghs & is rolling rich & fat on the sales. He says London has now seen the best – not *all* by any means. He won't let the Leicester Gallery people have his best pictures (other artists) as he says they don't know how to pack or unpack them – & several other polite little things like that he let drop –

Redon[28] is now the man whose work he is "making". He told me he had offered it to Turner of the Independent who said No thank you not those ugly faces! "He will regret it" said this quiet little man. You can now buy the best Redon for £400, whereas Cezanne's *worst* start about that figure –

I would rather not talk about my own show – & I expect you know as much about it as I do – which is very little. It has worried me – I am trying to forget it & get to work & recover from the sense of defeat & futility which swamps me at present. . . .

Secondly I have to thank you for 2 things which have given me intense pleasure in different ways –

To enjoy your delicious tea you need to have drunk French stuff for 2 months. Your tea is quite intoxicating – my word how I look forward to 4 o'c! . . .

The New Leader has only just come & I am going to have a treat. . . .

---

[27] Ambroise Vollard (1865-1939) ran his celebrated gallery at 6 rue Lafitte, 1893-1914. He gave the first important exhibition of Cézanne's paintings in 1895 and was at the centre of progressive art in Paris, showing among others Bonnard, Picasso, Matisse, Derain, Vlaminck.

[28] Odilon Redon (1840-1916), French symbolist painter whose work is marked by the contrast between the sinister, grotesque creatures drawn in black and white during the first part of his career and the brilliantly coloured flowers and mythologies to which he turned during the last two decades of his life.

[346] To Rachel Hodgkins, 20 January 1924

St Paul. Jany 20th.

My dearest Mother

Since my last letter we have had some real winter weather, snow all round, close up, on the hills & a sprinkling on dear little St Paul . . . . I thought it high time to look for warmer quarters & I happily found a room on the sunny side better furnished, a little more expensive but it is well worth it. . . . The wall paper rather like a striped bandbox & makes you feel like a faded old last year Hat – the bed with 10 heavy crochet counter panes & canopy. . . . *But* the view – *and* the sun – they make up the list of blessings. . . .

This is only to let you know I am well dearest. There is little to tell – I have sold a 5 gn. water colour – wh. converted into francs makes quite a little lot & lasts longer here than it would in England. . . .

[347] To Rachel Hodgkins, 22 February 1924

St Paul. Feb. 22nd

My Dearest little Mother

. . . . I hope I am in time to wish you very Happy returns dearest – I long to pop in & give you a hug. . . . I have been indulging in a cold which lasted so long I began to think it had become chronic . . . but am better now & quite on the mend. I have had to work – been going down the hill, by tram & train, twice weekly to Nice where I have started, or rather the Butler girls[29] have started a small Sketching Class for me – I hope to develop it – Nice is a good cache – full of wealth & bored people. I would gladly relieve them of a little of both commodities – It is frightfully exhausting work – a long day – rising 6a.m & getting back late. One day I missed my last tram – got as far on the return journey as Cagnes, where I reckoned on spending the night – but the place was crowded & I couldn't find a bed anywhere. . . . Finally after two hours forlorn searching I consulted the local chemist who took pity on me & persuaded a neighbouring tobacconist's wife to make me up a bed. . . . I rose at 6a.m to catch the early tram back to St Paul – half way up the hill it broke down & I had to walk. What do you think of that for a day's outing. . . . I have been quite definitely snubbed out of showing at the Brit: Em[pire] Exhbn. I have in turn applied to the various authorities concerned – but no notice taken of my letters – the British Art Section is in the hands of a few of the big well known men & their followers & schools & if you do not belong to their Societies you run no chance at all. I think I once told you that the only 2 societies that I have belonged to in England were International &

---

[29] Mary and Peggy Butler, New Zealand acquaintances, known to Isabel Field.

both have gone phut. If it is in your blood to be a rebel & run counter to tradition then you must not expect favour from the Academics – English Art keeps stodgily & safely in a rut of its own – though of course there are many minor Societies fighting for more modern methods & having some fight for it. Of course I am sorry I am not represented or honoured by an invitation to show at the B.E. show. I am staying on here during the summer. It is so expensive moving. Rail fares are up 50% – several pupils are coming out from England to join me in April[30] – they still think it worth 2 days journey to come & work with me!

    . . . . The longing grows very great to see you all again – I am *so* near Toulon & Marseilles & the big liners. . . .

[348] To Rachel Hodgkins, 9 March 1924
                    St Paul du Var, Alpes Maritimes, France. March 9th.

My dearest Mother

    Your letter of Janry: 27 came this morning . . . and made me feel quite close to you all, in fact produced acute homesickness – I so long to cut everything & come out to N.Z for a couple of years. I ache to do it. But how can I manage it?. . . I will write to Willy & consult him – I can't very well dump myself down on them, poor dears, if they have no home & live at a Hotel; it is *home* life I crave for & nothing else can give me what I am in sore need of – a real rest – mind & body. . . .

[349] To William Hodgkins, 12 April 1924
                                    St Paul. April 12th.

My dearest Willie

    In my last letter to Mother I told her that if it could possibly be managed that I should try to come out to NZ at the end of the year – I expect she has passed on the letter to you. . . . As you may imagine I have a very natural longing to see Mother & you all again Mother being so very far on in years I feel I must not delay my visit, if I am to see her alive. Sissie tells me she is wonderfully well & vigorous still – she certainly writes a most firm and characteristic letter . . . brave, & cheerful, taking life as she finds it & making the best of a rather dull business poor dear – her life has not been an exciting one but I dont think it has been exactly unhappy do you? She has a serene & contented nature otherwise she could not have endured the tempestuous Field atmosphere as long as she has. I am beginning to wonder what you all look like after all these years you & Jean &

[30] One of these was Elsie Barling, Dorothy Selby's friend.

Mike – I should immensely love to pay you a visit for a bit if only I can wangle a passage somehow. Are you in a house of your own by now & is Jean stronger again & equal to the burden of house keeping – I would start tomorrow if I had the cash. Do you think I could pay at the other end supposing I had a Show – I am pretty certain I could raise the sum by selling my Water Colours & by teaching. . . . I should bring no modern stuff at all – just good straightforward Water Colours likely to sell at reasonable democratic prices – I am told Auckland is very go ahead & progressive in all artistic matters – I think Chch might also be a good centre. . . .

. . . . There is no money to be made in Europe unless you have private means & can advertise & play [the] publicity game for all it is worth. It costs anything from £50 to £100 for a Gallery for a fortnight add your frames to this & 30% or more to your dealer & there you are! If you *don't* sell you are in the Soup. In Dec: last I had a small show of black & white Drawings at a minor & less well known gallery in London – in this case the guarantee was waived – I sold £35 of Drawings – frames cost me £15 – Dealer kept £12 – I the rest! I have been living down here in the South of France since last Sept: life is supposed to be cheap – but prices have steadily gone up & up . . . . It is my hourly, daily obsession how to keep going – naturally insecurity & anxiety like this don't make for first class work – so you see how I welcome a chance of a trip to N.Z where life is less strenuous & overcrowded & bankrupt than this weary demented old Europe – striving after peace & security but still in a welter of unrest & misery. . . . I am anxious to meet your Mike. How is he shaping now? Has he found his right job yet? I gather he has exceptional ability – but perhaps not quite on the strictly normal lines best suited for Colonial life. . . .

This letter was begun some weeks ago – things happened to prevent me getting it off – pupils arrived – the sun came out after bitter cold winter winds & rain . . . . Now my season is started & I am not doing so badly. Today is Easter Sunday – I am picnic-ing in olive woods away from the holiday mob . . . . This address will reach me till Sept: I am not on speaking terms with the Bank at present. They are asking me for my overdraft of £15. . . . My best love to you all & hoping I may see you all before too long. Your loving Fanny.

[350] To Hannah Ritchie, c.17 April 1924

St Paul. Thursday

My Dearest Hannah

This in answer to your welcome one just come. I have been waiting for certain little plans to mature at this end before writing fully on more or less wobbly matters concerning us all . . . . This is the arrangement I have made for you here in May when you come – I have rented a small pavillion with an orange garden

– walled & private – right in St Paul – just the ideal thing for the summer. There is one large light room – upstairs – The studio – great views – back & front – double bed – fireplace – downstairs 2 small barely furnished rooms – across the courtyard a tiny kitchen furnished all complete – one would have meals out of doors . . . .

I have been living at this darling abode of light & peace for nearly 3 weeks, marvelling at my luck, and hugging myself at my cleverness in snatching it from under the noses of other clamorous people who are greatly envious. It was Providence at work – I pay 200 frs. a month for it which is very cheap as things go. . . . My intention is to hand over the Pavillion to you & Dorothy for the time you are here. . . . I shall probably go down to Nice after you come for a few weeks if I can find a cheap & respectable Hotel in the old Town, to work in the Flower market & old Harbour – returning to St Paul for the week ends . . . . I am keen about your working quite apart & independent of me – you won't need me, or anyone else, to quicken your perceptions when once you reach St Paul – what you require now is time & experience & leisure to work out your own ideas – of course I shall want to see your work whenever you feel like showing it. Since writing to you last I have decided I must go out to N.Z for next winter – perhaps for 2 years or so – I have written to ask the brothers to either finance, or arrange to pay my passage at that end, I shall take all my unsold work & try to sell it – also teach – living with my family as best I can – I feel the burden of responsibility must rest on them for a while & give me a calm period relieved of the necessity of earning. I can't face another winter of this semi-bankruptcy – I can't expect any help from them at this end – they are indifferent – they simply dont care nor have they the imagination to understand. . . . god knows I hate the idea of cutting myself off from civilization for so long – even to civilize my fellow countrymen! But honestly Hannah I can't face another rough winter, without comforts – or anything that makes life worth the living. Well! having made this decision I want to spend the Summer making attractive best-selling pictures – such as flower markets & red sails & blue Mediterranean – they used to lap up this sort of thing in the good old times. So that is the reason why I want to run down to Nice for a few weeks – so if you will sweetly come & occupy my Pavillion for as long as you like I shall be happy. . . . You will see *lots* of me. You will love my garden & the sacred citron tree in the centre of the courtyard – heavy with fruit – I eat my meals beneath its shade. . . .

[351] To Rachel Hodgkins, Easter Sunday 1924

St Paul. Easter Sunday

My dearest Mother
    I am spending today in the woods – above St Paul – with my lunch, sketching

gear & stylo – two English girls and a French novel. So far I have done nothing but eat & smoke cigarettes to keep off the flies – suck oranges & move from the shade of the olives into the scorching sunshine – & back again. It is real wonder weather at last – *blue blue* sky overhead & bells ringing all through the valley from all the tiny hill towers – one to the other.

I wonder what you are all doing this Easter tide?

I am keeping my trip to N.Z steadily in view & working hard getting sketches together so that I can make a start whenever I hear from you that the fare has been guaranteed or arranged at the other end. . . .

FH decided to go north for her summer class and chose Montreuil-sur-Mer where she had spent the summer of 1909.

[352] To HANNAH RITCHIE AND JANE SAUNDERS, c.18 JUNE 1924
Hotel Belle Vue, Montreuil-S-Mer, Pas de Calais. Wed

Dear Girls

Arrived last night Tuesday – 8pm – very much the worse for wear . . . . our train was rushed by Syrian refugees just landed in a Greek boat – one of them, a young girl in the last throes of exhaustion & fear slept the night thro on my knees . . . . I sketched what I saw & hope I have sufficient data for a good picture – "Night travel" –

. . . . No one here yet . . . . the country is very green & stodgy after the brilliant south & the clear cut shapes & shadow forms. In spirit I have been side slipping South all day – homesick for you both & the Pavilion & the dear sun. Here it is grey & a bit cool – but fresh – my head feels clearer & I feel up to business & work . . . .

I do hope you will find work runs smoothly – it should. The stimulus gained by novel surroundings is so valuable even if it is confusing for a while. You could never have got the same thrill in settling down here – *now* you are acquainted with the rare & illusive atmosphere of the South – we all become enslaved in our time . . . .

[353] To RACHEL HODGKINS, 25 AUGUST 1924
Hotel Belle Vue, Montreuil s-mer, Pas de Calais, France. Aug 25:

My dearest Mother

It is a month or more since my last letter dear. You must not imagine I am ill when you don't hear from me. . . . On the whole I have not done badly & still have 5 pupils working with me. I am getting some pictures ready for the Paris Salon in Sept: & feel quite excited to be showing again after all these years – I hope it may be the beginning of a fresh run of prosperity. The village carpenter is making me some frames. I have done a certain number of flower subjects – you get such jolly big mixed bunches in the market for a few sous, & pot plants too – Gloxinias – begonias etc – real beauties – so cheap – it is a wonderful place for flowers. This little inn is mostly filled by fishermen who come about this time for fly fishing – I heard 2 men lauding up the N.Z trout fishing last night at dinner – I am stopping on here indefinitely – until I can arrange to come out to you. No news from Willie as yet. . . . Friends think I must not leave France till I have had a big Show either in Paris or London. To go so far away *now* might be fatal. . . . I am feeling so very much better [and] improved in health – I am living on peptonised food & a very reduced dietary – it is wonderful what it does for me – mind & body. So I am struggling some more – & in better heart. . . .

[354] To Jane Saunders, September 1924

Hotel Belle Vue, Montreuil S. mer. Sunday

My Dearest Dorothy

Your letter just come. . . . This just to greet you in Paris – where I hope you will stay long enough to rest & refresh yourselves after the heavy fatigue of packing & journey – I would *love* to see you here en route but realise it would over-complicate a difficult & exhausting home journey. So *don't* try it – we know each other far too well to misunderstand . . . .

I am stopping on here *indefinitely* – I shall not go South this winter. . . . Try & comfort yourselves by remembering all art is *slow* – dont be depressed. It is only normal to feel all that you feel about yr. work. . . . I knew well you were likely to be up against difficulties – as in mountaineering so in art – there is only a very narrow edge of safety on which we can walk. In Paris see the Tuileries Salon – the best of the Beaux Art is there – walk down Rue Boétsie, Rue Lafitte & try gallerie Bernheim (Boul: Madeleine) for private shows that is all I know. Miss Drey[31] saw very little new work – only at these galleries – She asked for Derain[32] but could see none – Ask for Maria Blanchard[33] at Rosenbergs Rue Boétsie. . . .

[31] FH had met the Dreys in Manchester. Agnes Drey, the sister of the critic O. Raymond Drey, was a pupil.
[32] André Derain (1880-1954), an associate of Matisse of the Fauve period and also of Picasso; by the 1920s had changed to a more sombre palette and traditional approach to landscape, still life and portraiture.
[33] Maria Blanchard (1881-1932), a Spanish born painter who settled in Paris in 1916, known for her paintings of family life.

[355] To William Hodgkins, 25 September 1924
        Hotel Belle Vue, Montreuil-S-mer, Pas de Calais, France. Sept 25th.

My dearest Willie

Thank you so very much for your kind & warm hearted letter of July 5th
. . . . First of all let me thank you for settling my overdraft – it is an immense relief
to me – and I am very grateful – I am now happily free of debt – as each year, since
that fatal Armistice year when I dashed to London & took a Studio & made a bid
for fame, I have slowly & painfully reduced the debts then incurred, one by one,
till I am now once more a free woman . . . . I hope to be able to repay you in full
before too long. My outlook is a more hopeful one. I am making a fresh start –
exhibiting both in Paris & London this Autumn – & may yet be back in the
limelight – & N.Z still be proud of me. The Women's International Society has
invited (wh. means all expenses paid) a group of my work to be shown in London
next week in a prominent gallery – I have sent 10 works into the Salon D'Automne,
Paris . . . . I took them to Paris myself last week – by the night train – arrived in
Paris 11.30 got a bed – the last one at the Station Hotel (Gare du Nord) & by 8
the next morning was at my Agents. It was Heaven to be in Paris again on a clear
Autumn morning. . . . Everything was so lovely the shops a dream after this dull
little country town – one could feast on them even with an empty pocket – I had
just time enough to visit an Exhibition of Modern Art – I stood at a crowded
corner waiting for my auto bus – I asked an elderly Frenchman . . . with his wife
– or daughter, (or neither) also standing there – how long the next bus would be.
I told him my destination – His own swell car drove up – He said "get in we'll
drive you there" – I did – And down the beautiful Champs Elysée, thro' the most
fashionable part of Paris I drove between these two charming people. It was a
gracious & kindly act. A sort of Peter Waite touch – I took it as a happy omen.
My youth had not entirely left me. There was still adventure in the world –

I am jotting all this down, as it comes fresh to my mind – next week it will be
forgotten. I have taken all your good advice to heart. I quite see that a visit to
Auckland would be a hazardous undertaking from the purely business point of
view. . . . I know I should be *quite* out of my element living a conventional Town
life – & you would all be most horribly bored by me. However I shall not be
discouraged from returning to NZ for a trip – with pictures enough to tour the
Colony, create a boom – look up old friends – & see my family & breathe my
native air once more – but this, as you say – will come about in its own good
time. Meanwhile . . . [I] shall continue to work towards it & one day I'll turn up
– in Dunedin for choice, & work up through the Towns spreading "Culture" as
I go! . . .

You have been a real brick to me. I wish I could persuade my hard pressed
family to allow me, between them, £2 a month for *one year only* – money to be
placed at Bank for payment of my *rent only* – I would benefit enormously in

physical & mental health by the *security* it would give me. . . . It would augment my powers. *Security is the root of success.* In France one can live very cheaply. In England, everywhere living is dear & difficult . . . . At this little Inn I am living for the equivalent of 30/- a week – good food, electric light, a studio – chauffage – but of course these are special terms, on consideration of all the people I have brought here. So I am staying on thro' the winter, which is generally a pretty cold & wet one, but I have plenty of work – & the prospect of 4 or 5 pupils from now on till Xmas – Montreuil is easily accessible from England. A certain number of English people live here – Maud Burge[34] (Williams of Wllgtn) bought a house here – gave it up on a whim – but may return to it. She is a nervey changeable charming woman – I hope she will come back.

Well Brother talk this over with the Family – I hate appealing for help – But I feel so firmly convinced that the timely help *now*, as I am struggling back to the limelight, will be of the greatest value to me in every sort of way – moral & material. It will assist me to help myself – make me sleep better – have a quieter mind – & generally keep my end up in a hard & bitter world – £24 a year for 1 year . . . a small certainty to be sent me each month by the Bank. Promises to repay are futile I know. But I *hope* you will not regret it – give me time. I shall try & send out some Water Colours for the Local Shows – as you suggest – & keep my name in front of the people . . . .

I am glad you find Auckland attractive & have a jolly group of friends. Hard work – but a nice life – & from all accounts an almost perfect climate.

We have had the world's worst summer.

. . . . Best of love & thanks again – to you both. . . .

[356] TO RACHEL HODGKINS, 4 OCTOBER 1924

Hotel Belle Vue, Montreuil S. Mer, France. Oct 4th.

My dearest Mother

. . . . I should feel bucked – news has just come that 7 of my pictures have been accepted by the Salon D'Automne in Paris – if they make me an Associé next year I shall be on firm ground & nothing should stop me – it is inspiring to be back in the running once more – tho' it has cost me nearly my last sou – I want the Family to stand by me a little this winter & send me what they can. It is going to be a hard winter – but if they will help a little, say pay my Studio rent of £2 a month, I shall worry through all right . . . . I have had the kindest of letters from Willie. He declines to repatriate me – I think he is right . . . . I am in good form

[34] Maud Burge (1865-1957) had studied with James Nairn and worked in Charles Goldie's studio in Auckland before travelling to Europe for further experience. She worked with Brangwyn and remained in Europe until about 1937. Her watercolours have something of the quality of FH's earlier work in their lightness of touch and skilful evocation of foreign scenes.

– except for my eyes, which are causing me serious concern. I am seeing a Specialist tomorrow at Boulogne. Naturally all this extra expense eats into my narrow winter hoard. Eyes *are* eyes & can't be neglected – so my shirt must go on new glasses – even if I have to walk there & back. . . . Today has been a great day in the Swallow world. They commence their great Southern migration. In spite of a raging storm of rain & wind (a South wind) they commenced to assemble punctually at 10 o'clock. I was told the previous night to watch for them at that hour – but was sceptical. However *there* they were – in their hundreds – lining up close on the telegraph wires, with their heads to the storm, on the trees, on all the ledges & cornices & in the eaves of this Hotel, packed tight, while a certain number of them kept wheeling in the air & scouting for others not yet arrived at the starting place.

. . . . Still a *little* sceptical I waited anxiously till 4 oclock, towards sunset, the storm abating slightly. Sure enough they were all in the air as it struck the hour & by 5 o'c there wasnt a single feather of a swallow to be seen. They flew into the storm – head to it – feathers neat & unruffled – I crossed the road & talked to the old man at the Toll gate (octroi) – who had been there for 40 years. He said they were as punctual as the trains – perhaps more so – he added with [a] twinkle – knowing his trains. . . .

Oct 5th

. . . . Address yr. letters dear, to the Bank – I am none too sure of staying on here – this Inn *may* close – & I may have to look for other quarters. The Manchester girls would like me to go to them – but there is not much doing in Manchester in art circles – It just rains soot & depression. A fact that I was ignorant of till the other day is that Manchester would not be Manchester, The Centre of the Worlds Cotton Trade, if it *did not* rain every day. The damp climate is necessary to keep the raw material moist. . . .

I shall be writing again very soon. Tell me all the news & how you are keeping. You will never know, my dear Family, to what an extent my thoughts are turned your way. It is one of the tragedies of leaving Home – N.Z is too far away – it ceases to be *real*. New Zealanders like myself can not help becoming de-nationalized – they have no country – it is sad – but true – one carries about an exaggerated sense of *not doing* quite the right thing – leaving your Home & your family – Art is like that – it absorbs your whole life & being. Few women can do it successfully. It requires enormous vitality. That is *my* conception of genius – vitality. One is fighting mental inertia *all* the time. One's family, overseas – awaits results – not knowing or realizing the fierce obstacles & difficulties. How can they?. . .

[357] To Hannah Ritchie, c.21 November 1924
                    Hotel du Commerce, St Valery s-Somme.[35] Friday

Dearest Hannah

Just a line to say I am not going to London for the interivew. The Secretary has let me off – I can't make any plans till I know what the A.G.B.I[36] is going to do for me. . . . I am in bed with rheumatism – feeling rotten . . . . I'll leave as soon as I can – you may be sure of that. . . .

I do hope they will fork out generously. I am so sick of this hand to mouth existence – I want to make a fresh start – Moffat Lindner has written to the Sec: on my behalf – a very strong letter of recommendation. He is very concerned at my misfortunes –

No more – no brains – one big ache –

[358] To Hannah Ritchie. c.1 December 1924
                    Hotel du Commerce, St Valery-s-Somme. Monday
Dearest of Hannahs

I waited for this morning's post before writing – No news yet from the A.G.B.I but I have had a private line to say that they have voted me £50 to go on with – for a Show – and more on further application if required – which I think is handsome of them, considering they are mostly old fogies, who hate my sort of work – I heard they didnt like the Drawings I sent in – but Walter Russell & Derrick Williams[37] *did* & would stand no nonsense & insisted on a good big grant. . . . Thank Heaven! *Thank* Heaven! I shall try & put up a really good show & give people the beauty craved for – *not* problems. It only needs this peace of mind to bring me back full circle to my old style & restore placidity – I have felt so crushed & dismal – it had got into my work –

So there now – Sink deep into your armchairs & feel happy about me. . . .

As a matter of fact I had made up my mind that neither of you must send me any more money & my first impulse on receiving your last instalment was to send it firmly & gratefully back to you. But I was ill & feeble minded & in arrears. So I kept it – *deeply* thankful for it – I am still a stiff crock – the chemist has cautioned me – & advises me to go from St Valery – rheumatism is the local curse. A young & beautiful woman who comes & poses for me out of kindness is all but a cripple & is departing for the Pyrenees & mud baths – I had tea with her family one day.

[35] The move to St Valéry, another of FH's former sketching grounds, suggests that the Hôtel Belle Vue in Montreuil had closed.
[36] The Artists' General Benevolent Institution.
[37] Sir Walter Westley Russell RA, RWS, NEAC (1867-1949) and Terrick John Williams RA, RI, RWA (1860-1936).

They made me a roly poly which we eat in our fingers – & washed it down with weak tea. . . .

Apart from the disappointment of not seeing you at Xmas, I think you will call me wise If I *don't* cross to London till the end of Janry – I am still short of pictures for the show – especially Water Colours – I want to have such a strong hand when I see the Dealers that they cant say NO. So I am going south to Martigues near Marseilles . . . for 6 weeks & there I shall work furiously. It is a happy hunting ground & my Spaniards are there. By the end of Janry: I shall be back in London – and after doing my business there I'll come on to you if I may – with real joy . . . .

I shall have the goods all ready by Janry – moreover I want to send Water Colours out to N.Z for the big N.Z & South Seas Exhibition to be held in my birth place next year – I have written asking for a special invitation – Fancy having to do so! My callous family has cast me off. . . .

[359] TO HANNAH RITCHIE AND JANE SAUNDERS, 21 DECEMBER 1924
Hotel Modern, Martigues, Bouches du Rhône, France. Dec 21st.

My dearest Hannah & Dorothy

I got down here yesterday, a long drawn out journey thro' fog, almost as far as Avignon. . . . Quite heavenly to have dropped out of fog & frost into this elysium. . . .

The Hotel is full of artists – all of them English, not much account I should say . . . . I have not started work yet, tho I did a little chap in pencil this morning to break the ice. The strong light is disturbing at first & one feels all to pieces & not *quite* certain the plunge is prudent & *was* it right to have made it? or is it worth all the buffettings?

I am sorry not to see you this Xmas – we must meet in some sunny land some time – let us emigrate to Australia. I am told I could make £5-600 a year in Melbourne teaching – on my reputation – the rest would (I hope) follow. . . . It would be rather jolly to be out there working smoothly & profitably instead of . . . hanging on by your teeth in this old Europe – escaping disaster by a miracle! . . .

[360] TO RACHEL HODGKINS, 15 JANUARY 1925
Martigues, France. Jan 15th. 1925

My dearest Mother

. . . . It is possible I may be seeing you before very long as I am going out to Melbourne – emigrating – some time this year – my passage has been promised me by an old friend – I have faith that somewhere out there there is a place for me and that I shall find plenty of work by my teaching & portraits.

There is nothing for me on this side. My teaching connection for the time being is dead – I am sick of working without profit, barely keeping myself in food & clothes so why wait till I go slowly "bust"? Nearly all my friends on this side have fallen on bad times since the War – I want to be up & doing not down & out and to go somewhere where life isn't such a hard business as it is in my world over here. I don't intend taking any pictures with me, remembering that nuisance of a tax. I am returning to London in a few weeks to wind up my affairs & if opportunity occurs having a Show. . . .

[361] To Hannah Ritchie, 3 February 1925

Hotel Modern, Martigues, B du R. Feb: 3rd.

My Dearest Hannah

Thank you so much for your letter & news, just what I wanted to hear – that one of you had joined the Sickert[38] Class. He will do you no end of good – don't take him too seriously in his "offish" moments. He is a bit of a blaguer – mocquer – but withal a very fine & inspiring influence and Manchester is in luck to get one of his calibre to come all that way to talk to them –

Is he being financed I wonder, or is it his own private spec: . . . Private teaching, from all I hear is in a bad way. Pupils prefer the Slade & other London Schools where they are sure of the traditional sanction to their work when it comes to earning a living –

It is truly a day of sauve qui peut –

I am leaving here Wed: 11th. and going, I hope, straight through to Boulogne, passing the day in Paris, & on to the night boat. This will save my pocket I hope. . . .

[362] To Hannah Ritchie, 20 February 1925

61 Earl's Court Square, London S.W.5. Friday 20th.

My Dearest Hannah

You will wonder not hearing from me. It has been a bustle ever since I left Martigues on Friday 13th . . . . A cold starlight crossing – reached London 11.15 – got here near midnight perishing cold & half dead – bed & hot baths on Sunday resucitated me since when I have been fooling aimlessly round seeing friends & visiting pictures & hearing much depressing talk about the hard times etc – have

---

[38] Walter Sickert began teaching in Manchester in 1925, commuting from London.

seen one very good show at the Lefevre Gallery, Ferguson, Nash, A. E. Rice etc
– really nice stuff – really very jolly indeed – I was quite bucked – I counted 28
stars – Nash's I think[39] . . . .

I have done nothing yet about a Show of my own. My plans are in the melting
pot for the moment. My friends think I am mad to go off to Australia till I have
given London a trial – I had lunch yesterday with an old pupil who told me of a
little plan she & some other old pupils were framing between them with a view
to raising a small fund & investing it for me – enough say to pay my rent –
frightfully kind of them – I am afraid they will not find it easy work . . . . In
consideration of my services as a teacher some people think I have the right to
apply for a Civil Service Pension – & have a very good chance – well – we'll see!

Meanwhile, my friend Mrs. Mayor who has this big fine house is letting me
have a nice big light room at the top of the house for 10/- a week – furnished –
& is willing for me to keep it on indefinitely as a pied à terre & studio – Again
– we'll see! . . .

Tomorrow I am going down to Boxley Abbey Maidstone Kent – to stay with
old friends [the Nickalls] till the 25th. when I return here – & will come on to
you . . . .

Shall try & see A E Rice & her husband before leaving Town.

[363] To Hannah Ritchie, 14 March 1925

61 Earls Court Square, SW5. 14th March

My Dearest Hannah

You will think me a fraud. It would pain me exceedingly if I am upsetting your
plans by not coming at once, or by not giving a definite date for my visit. The fact
is Hannah things are in the *brooding* stage – nothing definite has happened tho'
much is in the air – such as the probable re forming of the International at an early
date. Of course I must be in *that* at all costs – Then there is the big N.Z South
Seas Exhtn. for which I am doing my best to wangle an invitation. It is not so easy.
The Selection Committee is of the usual official kind – the R.A & NEAC faction
will be favoured. You would imagine I should be one of the first to be invited my
Father being the Father of Art in NZ & Dunedin my "home town". It would
change the outlook for me if I could send a group of early popular work & sell
it out there –

[39] The Lefevre Gallery was one of the most prestigious in London, showing modern French work and
supporting British avant garde artists like Ben Nicholson, Barbara Hepworth and Henry Moore through the
thirties when their work did not sell readily. It became FH's gallery in 1932. The changes that took place
in FH's work at the end of the 1920s drew her closer to English painters like Paul Nash (1889-1946) who
used landscape-based imagery. J. D. Fergusson (1874-1961) was a Scottish colourist, member of the
Glasgow School; Anne Estelle Rice (1879-1959), a friend of Katherine Mansfield, was married to the critic
O. Raymond Drey, whose sister Agnes was FH's pupil.

Tomorrow I have tea with the Raymond Dreys –

My pictures have only just been unpacked & delivered – not yet framed. That is the crux – I am mustering all my old fashioned gilt frames & trying to sell them & get some simpler & more modern ones – to suit modern work – This all takes time. It is essential to be in Town & meet people on their own ground. . . . I am glad to hear A[my] K[rauss] has done well with her pots at Lefevres – So glad – She is a good sport. What are you doing at Easter – I could come away with you if you are not on a walking – climbing holiday – or dont want to be alone & together. As I am not off to Australia before the Autumn we have the summer before us. Do let us have a painting jaunt together. . . .

You will be sorry to hear that the Anuity Fund being collected for me has fallen thro', so few people being able to give much – so it has closed at £25

I have your portrait group with me – it wears well. It needs *so* little to both faces to make it a fine thing – I'll bring it with me to finish it – I bequeath it to you both if you like it *when* finished. Some man who buys Mark Gertler[40] & modern stuff is coming one day to see my things – Forgive my horrible Ego – It is nauseating the way I bore my friends –

Did I tell you Miss Barling has 4 good canvases at the WIA.C[41] – in fact the best in the show – my *private* view. She must show in a more modern gallery. . . .

[364] To Dorothy Selby, 27 April 1925

142 Wellington Rd, Withington, Manchester. April 27th.

Dear Miss Selby

Your letter was waiting for me when I arrived here on the 25th. –

. . . . There will be no summer Class this year as I am sailing for Australia at the end of June – for an indefinite time. Art is paying so badly & I find it hard to make a living by it – so I am emigrating in the hope of finding a better opening out there. . . .

If you cared about it of course I could give you one or two demonstrations in my Water Colour methods (the less modern method on which I teach) and look at some of your work – I shall be in Town all June & could easily fit this in. This address will find me till May 28th.

---

[40] Mark Gertler (1891-1939) was born of poor Polish-Jewish parents in Whitechapel and became one of the most progressive British painters.
[41] Women's International Art Club.

[365] To William Hodgkins, 28 April 1925
                    142 Wellington Road, Withington, Manchester. April 28th.

My dearest Willie

Just to let you know that I have booked a passage to Melbourne in the "Jervis Bay" Commonwealth Line, sailing June 30th. arriving M. 6th. Aug. . . . I saw Mr. Campbell at the Bank last week before coming here – & closed my a/c. He is writing to the Melbourne Manager – introducing me – He thinks me very wise doing what I do – he knows all about the difficulty of earning a living at art, told me how artists semi starving came into the Bank trying to sell their pictures. . . . Of course I am sad & mortified having to chuck it all – but Fate is too strong for me – I hope I shall soon find a market in Melbourne & prices that really pay – even if I only do bread & butter stuff – ie teaching – for a time. . . . anyway I go cheerfully & hope to give as well as to receive.

I am feeling worn out with all my worries & shall be glad of the voyage – & sunshine. . . . I have had to dispose of all my possessions & store pictures – a job – now I am spending the last few weeks among friends & pupils – folk very dear to me – not rich or able to do more than keep me for a week or two. Last night I dined with some rich Jews who are giving me an introduction to a brother [on] the "Argus" staff in Melbourne. A portrait of their daughter hangs over the dining room mantlepiece – painted by me some time ago & only now begun to be very much appreciated! . . .

[366] To Dorothy Selby, 6 May 1925
                    142 Wellington Rd, Withington, Manchester. May 6th.

Dear Miss Selby

Just a line to say I shall be delighted to give you some demonstrations when I return –

I will keep Saturday 30th-31st free if either of these days will suit you. . . .

I am making enquiries for a summer Class for you – I have rather lost track of the men who are teaching. . . .

[367] To Rachel Hodgkins, 30 May 1925
                    Cheyne Club, Chelsea, London. May 30th.

My dearest Mother

In my last letter I told you that I had booked a passage to Melbourne sailing 30th. June. It seemed as tho' I might possibly be seeing you all again before the end of the year. Now however my plans are all knocked sideways – and instead of *Melbourne* its *Manchester*. I have been offered a post as Designer in a big Cotton Firm at a salary of £500 per annum – on a 6 months trial. It all happened suddenly & was fixed up in 2 days. . . . Having touched the bed rock of hard times & despondence this good luck comes dramatically. I shall be working professionally for the biggest Cotton Firm – the "Calico Printer's Association" a huge Combine in the biggest cotton city Manchester. I was interviewed by 7 Managers, my designs approved of and 2 of them bought at the meeting. . . . My own work is in abeyance of course – I shall only have week ends. Of course I feel very bucked with life & the prospect of security & a little comfort *at long last*. . . . I shall be able to send you a bit now dearest, tho' I can't be very lavish till I get the *permanent* post. I am keeping my steamer ticket in abeyance for 6 months so that there is still Melbourne if I find I can't do the work & it proves a fiasco. Don't give up hope of seeing me walk in one of these days. . . .

[368] To Rachel Hodgkins, 20 June 1925
                                   Platt Abbey, Rusholme, Manchester. June 20th

My dearest little Mother
    I must send you a few lines in answer to yours of March 30th. which has only just reached me. . . . I grieve to hear the poor eyes are paining you & that you have had a return of those nasty shingles. You must not tire yourself writing me letters much as I love getting them & want to hear how you are. . . . I feel miserable when I hear of you suffering & wish it were possible to come to you & be with you now when you feel your strength failing & need someone with you all the time but alas I am now settling down to my new work & slowly getting used to the long hours & unusual restrictions, rather tedious after going my own sweet way for so long. But for security's sake one has to pay a high price. I can hardly believe that the terror of these past distracted years has passed & that life has eased for me . . . .

[369] To Hannah Ritchie and Jane Saunders, 23 August 1925
                                   Platt Abbey, Manchester. Aug. 23rd

My Dears
    . . . . The great event of the week is that I have gained my way with the CPA & now got a room to myself (& Miss Jones). This act of grace took place immediately after my interview with the Managers when I made my report on the Paris trip[42] – I think I satisfied them. I made a dramatic jesture when I entered the room & flung over a chair the jolly cubistic scarf of many colours –

---

[42] FH had been sent to the Exposition Internationale des Arts Décoratifs.

with the words Thats straight from the horses mouth ready for the consumer. It got across all right & it was easy to go on after this – they were interested & I hope impressed. Colour was much discussed. At the end of the interview I boldly asked for a room to myself – within 10 minutes it had been fixed up – the contents of the room where I had been working with 4 others were shot out, desks, telephone, chairs etc & I was left in possession. The ejected ones took it in good part & hid their feelings. I handed round cigarettes the next morning & no bones were broken & I don't think they bear malice. . . . The future of course is just as unpredictable as ever – one of the older men said to me – Dont worry – you are as safe as eggs – You will be here just as long as you like to stay . . . . Well I hope he is right. . . .

I have seen two Shaw plays – one by myself & one with Agnes Drey. . . . The Play was the 20 year old overdue tabooed Mrs. Warren's Profession. Some squeamish people left the theatre. . . . A woman doctor friend of Agnes talked to us in one of the frequent intervals. She thought it a "dreadful play" I could only say Hell! – by way of reply . . . .

. . . . Keep the eye open for likely ideas for designs etc wont you my two dear Pals – photos – prints p.c or journals anything that might help & prove grist to the mill. . . .

[370] To Isabel Field, 29 August 1925

Platt Abby, Rusholme, Manchester. Aug 29th

My dearest Sis

I hope you will not have to pay duty on the small parcel I am posting you. The blue one piece frock I hope may fit you – Americans were wearing them in Paris in the mornings – looking so smart with white collar . . . . The batik scarf comes from my Firm – made for the W. African trade . . . . Nearly 3 months has gone already. Hard work but I don't shirk that – I am not up to much after the heat & toil of a long day – passive rest and the only real sensation I feel is waiting for my evening meal . . . .

I am just back from 3 weeks in Paris – Paris under new conditions – none of the old "Me" none of the old Paris – I lived like a real lady for once – taxis everywhere – even so I was leg-weary looking for the things I was supposed to see. I was sent over on purpose to see the wonderful Exposition Arts Decoratif, an ultra-modern Show of European & British industrial art – all marvellously well done & displayed – that is all except the British Section, which quite failed to express itself in modern terms, & as a consequence looked old fashioned & dingy beside the faultless order & taste of France – which was beautiful & ingenious & tasteful to the nth. degree. French phsychology expressed itself – its love & glorification of feminine beauty & grace. The Pavilion of Elegance was supremely well done – 200 above life size gold and silver mannequins, clothed in ravishing frocks in exquisite colour schemes. What there was of the dresses was delicious. They had no backs – very little front, up to the knees & no sleeves – but long tails or trains or wings like fire flies. The tailor mades & more ordinary frocks were, of course more discreet. Many high French artists are now designing fabrics – many of the fabrics were groups & arranged in artificially lighted cases (like shop windows) in front of back cloths painted & signed by some of the biggest artists of the day. So art comes at last to serve commerce – and raise & beautify it – even if its only the label for a bottle of relish. . . .

[371] TO RACHEL HODGKINS, 1 NOVEMBER 1925

Platt Abbey, Manchester. Nov 1st.

My Dearest Mother

It is about 6 months since I have heard from any of you. I am feeling anxious – time simply flies. . . . I shall soon hear if I am to stay on permanently. I'll stick to them if they will stick to me – You must not be too disappointed if I lose the post. The qualifications are exacting & the standard a very high one – I have done my best & worked hard. In 6 months one can only hope to be a partial success[43]. . . .

[372] TO RACHEL HODGKINS, 22 JANUARY 1926

Manchester. Jan 22nd.

My Dearest little Mother

It has been a deadly cold winter fog frost & snow – sudden thaws worse than the frost – then terrible cold again which bites pieces out of your flesh. I have had a busy time of it and on Xmas Eve moved from my lodgings to a tiny flat in Wellington Road of all places – my 2 friends have the top floor & I have 2 rooms downstairs – one room as Studio – I have been busy making curtains, chair covers & painting my furniture a cheerful bright colour – to liven the gloom of this dismal climate where you see the sun once every blue moon. . . .

I do miss my letters from you dear tho I have been hearing through Willie & Sis that you are well tho' not equal to writing much. . . .

I have a coal fireplace in my kitchenette – a bath – a geyser – cooker electric light & gas stove – cork matting very little furniture and earthen ware cooking

---

[43] This is the last mention of the contract. FH's silence on the subject, a move in December from comfortable lodgings to a presumably cheaper flat, a return to teaching the following summer, suggest that the contract was not renewed. But see note 47.

pots which I can pop in the oven. As I never eat meat it is not very difficult to make meals – 2 big armchairs & a comfy bed – all the essential comforts of a home. Alas no animals – I long for a cat. . . .

This is to send you my dearest love Your loving Fanny.

[373] To Lucy Wertheim,[44] early in 1926

[Manchester] 8.30p.m

Dear Mrs. Wertheim

I am surprised to find myself still alive. I simply can't go to bed without sending you a line of grateful thanks for the masses of delicious things you left this morning –

I have been drinking the chicken broth in large quantities & have large hopes of being quite all right by tomorrow & well out of the wood . . . .

This morning when you came I was in a state of wretched vertigo of depression & feebleness but I went to bed in the warm front room & have slept all day & am now feeling a new woman. Your good food & soup as strong as wine have put new life into me – I feel I might paint a master piece – I am like a child & make a quick recovery with a little kindness and something nice to eat!

[374] To Lucy Wertheim, 8 April 1926

142 Wellington Rd, [Manchester]. Thursday 8th

My Dear Luce

I was delighted to get your nice letter in transit[45]

I had already had a visit from Hilary & her Nanny & promised to have Tea with her on Wed: . . . They were so good & sweet to me and we had a delicious cosy tea in the Nursery & sat round the fire & talked. Mr. Wertheim came in for a short time before I left

I hope you found your boys both well and that you were not too exhausted when you reached the Cottage.

Am looking forward to the party on the 18th. Sickert comes no more to

---

[44] Lucy Wertheim (1883-1971), the daughter of a Manchester cloth merchant and wife of a wealthy businessman, Paul Wertheim, was an enthusiastic patron of modern artists and eventually, from 1930-9, ran her own gallery in London. *Adventure in Art,* 1947, is her account of those years. Her friendship with A. R. D. Fairburn led, in 1948, to the donation of a substantial collection of paintings and prints to the Auckland City Art Gallery.

[45] Mrs Wertheim was on her way to the family cottage on the south coast where her two sons were staying. Her daughter Hilary had remained in Manchester.

Manchester I gather. He slipped silently away from his last Class without farewells. . . .

Yours

Frances Hodgkins

[375] To Isabel Field, 26 April 1926

142 Wellington Rd, Withington, Manchester, April 26th.

My Dearest Sis

Willie's cable with the news of the dear little mother's death[46] was a shock even tho' I have been expecting it for so long – I cabled a reply meant for you all. . . . I can't help feeling sad and at the same time relieved that the end has come & that her sad old age has not dragged on longer – I do hope she went peacefully & without much pain & that you were with her at the last – I do hope you will write & tell me all about her death & if she remembered me & sent a message – but this I think is unlikely judging from what Willie told me of her failing memory when he saw her in Jany. It is a long time to wait for news. What will you do now? Shall you come to England for a trip or Sydney to Lydia? Get away somewhere Sis dear – right away & get the best rest & change you can – you need it – after the long strain of past years – your freedom has come. On the night of the 22nd. one of my large Water Colours which is on exhibition in a Manchester Gallery fell off the wall & smashed the glass – I was leaving the Gallery at the time & heard a crash – there seemed no sort of reason for it – except the usual reason that applies to about 1000 other pictures that fall anually off the wall – it just happened – I said to [the] Secretary " *That* is a family premonition – death always follows –" Sure enough the first post in the morning brought me the cable – I was – and am alone in the house for this week & one is prone to dwell on these matters – and wonder!

I have had a long bad bout of bronchitis – kept in the house for nearly a month & away from work . . . . I am hoping to get 10 days at the Lakes at Whitsuntide (21st May) which will put some health into me.

I'll write again – this must go tonight if it is to catch first NZ mail – I have written to Willie as well – I am thinking of you all. Have you buried Mother at Karori?

Your loving Sister Fanny

---

[46] Rachel Hodgkins died on 22 April, aged 88.

[376] To Isabel Field, 26 June 1926
142 Wellington Road, Withington, Manchester. June 26th

My Dearest Sis,

It is a great consolation to get your letter of April 7th. with last news of the dear little Mother . . . . her courage never failed – *mine* is always failing – it was curious about the picture falling . . . at the hour of death there often comes a resuscitation of power & vision & in a flash she would be with a child. There is an extraordinary bond between a Mother & child – even when you have lived so long apart. When the last generation goes – oneself is left the representative somehow – & one is lonely – there is no one ahead of one in experience – in meeting life –

. . . . I am sure the strain & tension of nursing Mother day & night must have been awful for you & I am glad the family stood by & helped & that you let them help you Sis dear. I hope you put my name with yours on the flowers for the pretty grave. How glad I am you decided on Waikanae – Dunedin would have been so far away from you all – you have made Waikanae ancestral – it is just right – quite the right thing that she should lie there nearby & amongst you all.

News of Norman Garstin's death has just come . . . . We have lost a good friend & are greatly the poorer for his death. Tell D. K Richmond that he is dead when you see her. Perhaps I shall find time to write to her myself. I am busy. I am just off to Ludlow for 6 weeks some pupils coming along with me. I get temperamental brain storms of fatigue & nerves wishing I could chuck all this uncongenial work. I am out of my class – But que voulez vous? . . .

[377] To Isabel Field, 16 October 1926
142 Wellington Rd, Withington, Manchester. Oct 16th

My Dearest Sis

Whatever do you think of me. I have had a very busy time of it this Summer, with a big Sketching Class in the country . . . a bit of a gamble – took an old Shropshire Farm a few miles out of Bridgnorth on the Severn, a rambling old house in a jolly garden on the Riverbank with 6 rooms & 2 attics – the Farmer's wife to cook & cater for us. I had to keep it filled with pupils & luckily did so . . . . Taking it all round, it was a decided success & I more than paid expenses with a bit over to go on with – the Summer was a blaze of sunshine – really divine for old England . . . . I came back to Manchester last week – to find a letter from you – I have also 2 others to thank you for, which I have not yet answered. You have been a dear writing so fully. . . . Now I am going to look forward to next year when you & Will may come to England. It is not too late Sis . . . .

I expect you will be having a snap shot of dearest Mother's grave – be sure to send me one – it sounds such a lovely spot. I gathered some lavender in the summer which I am enclosing in a seperate envelope – when you are next at the grave do put it there for me – I do so miss her letters – "from your loving Mother" the letters she had written over 25 years – always the same gentle loving letters – filled with faith & loyalty & hope for the best.

You complain of your eyes – mine are causing me trouble too, designing in this foggy dark climate is fatal to them. I hardly ever read – I wear tortoiseshell rims all the time now, while at work & pince nez in the street – I have got to that – we all come to it. Luckily I am fit & well – I attribute it to not eating meat & taking exercise – but I dont dogmatise about vegetarianism – it is a matter of temperament . . . .

You must not allow your beautiful self to get old or ill – come Home – it will beautify & rejuvenate you. We would be good pals I am sure – & we could be idle & happy a bit together & all the better for it. . . . .

[Postscript] I still take my cold bath in the morning – Spartan in this climate – its habit. . . .

[378] To Isabel Field, 3 December 1926

Manchester. 3-12-26

My Dearest Sis

Only 3 weeks to Xmas . . . I have been very busy – I opened a Show of my Paintings on the 4th. Nov and yesterday it closed. It has been a success . . . . Sold over £100 worth – which is considered good for Manchester where there is no great picture buying public as in London. It is mostly the University Set that has supported me. With the proceeds – and greatly helped by the big advertisement & publicity – I am starting a Studio in Town and begin my Painting Classes (night & day ones) at the New Year – I am doing all this in order that I may escape the tedium of textiles – it is hard work but it comes easier to me than the mechanical designing & monotonous life of a designer.[47] I have made many good friends & I believe I shall do well. . . . If you but knew how conservative & old fashioned Manchester folk are you would appreciate what to you must seem a very small success indeed & the prices *very* small beer compared to Colonial prices . . . .

The introduction on the Catalogue was written by a well known London Critic who has always been cordial to my work.[48] One man from Blackham came in &

---

[47] The references to designing in this and the preceding letter imply that FH was still working for the Calico Printers' Association, a year after the presumed expiry of her six-month contract. No records of her work at the CPA have been found.

[48] O. Raymond Drey. The introduction discussed the degree of abstraction in the paintings and concluded, '. . . . she makes each stroke of her brush instinct with life. And in this her genius is akin to that of the great Chinese masters of calligraphy.' (Exhibition of Paintings by Frances Hodgkins, 2 Mount Street, Manchester, 4-30 November 1926.)

said he had watched my work for the last 15 years & he considered *I* was one of the world's women painters – bought a Drawing. I *may* be able to get back into the lime light – friends seem to think I am touching fame at last. Heaven knows! Money would do it for me of course – I have had to be sociable & go out a lot.

I have dined with the Curator of the City Art Gallery, Mr. & Mrs Laurence Howard – with Prof: Alexander Professor of Philosophy (University) whose head is one of the 7 wonders of the world & has just been sculped by the great Epstein. . . . He spoke much of Rutherford the N.Z. Radium man. He also knew Sir Robert Stout. I was the 3rd. New Zealander he had entertained. He was very keen to get out of me *what* went on inside me when I painted a picture. He is writing a thesis on Art. I couldn't tell him much more than that I painted a picture much as a hen lays an egg – that it was inevitable – which seemed to please him . . . . Artists are too engaged "doing" it to analyse their emotions.

. . . . After all I did not send the Lavender bunch for Darling Mothers grave – it was difficult to pack. . . .

[379] TO DOROTHY SELBY, 8 DECEMBER 1926
142 Wellington Rd, Withington, Manchester. 8-12-26

Dear Miss Selby

. . . . It is extremely nice of you to buy a Drawing – and rash – *what* am I to do about it? I have several small figure groups done at Bridgnorth that I think you might like – I will send them along . . . . There was a fair run on my small things & I sold quite a lot towards the last. . . .

I have dined with Profr. Alexander . . . . He would like to know what goes on inside me – or any artist, when they are creating a picture! As well ask the hen *why* it lays an egg – I told him creation is governed by material. He must make his own philosophic abstractions . . . .

Neither of the 2 Art galleries have so far bought – but they are hovering. . . . I do think it is most charming of you to want a sketch these days when there are so many reasons for not buying pictures. Thank you so much.

By February 1927 FH had settled into a studio in Grosvenor Street, All Saints, an area known as the Latin Quarter of Manchester.

Part Fourteen

1927-31

Success in London

Some time in the middle of 1927 Frances Hodgkins left Manchester for good and probably spent time in London before travelling to Tréboul in Brittany for the summer. In June her oil painting Lancashire Family was exhibited with the London Group. Though the work was 'skied', as she later reported (in June 1944), she had gained a place in one of the more progressive exhibiting groups in London. In December 1927 she again had work accepted at the New English Art Club. Her inclusion in this exhibition provided a stepping stone to the sustaining relationships with good galleries that formed the professional background to the last fifteen years of her life. One of her paintings at the New English Art Club caught the eye of Arthur Howell, director of the St George's Gallery, Hanover Square. He began to exhibit her watercolours in group shows in 1928 and 1929. By 1930 he was ready to offer her a contract and finally agreed to mount a solo exhibition of oils and watercolours in October of that year. The success of this exhibition marks the beginning of FH's career as an established artist in London. When Arthur Howell's gallery closed in 1931, the Lefevre and Leicester galleries took over the contract and remained FH's dealers until her death.

The death of Mrs Hodgkins in 1926 had brought to an end the most important emotional attachment in FH's life and removed whatever lingering and unsettling desire she may have had to return to New Zealand. At the same time another attachment was strengthened when Cedric Morris and Arthur Lett Haines returned to London after six years based in Paris. Cedric Morris, who had held his first successful solo exhibition in London in 1924, had recently been elected to the London Group and the New English Art Club and it was possibly through his influence that FH exhibited with those organisations. He may also have helped in some way towards FH's 1928 solo exhibition – her first in London for five years – at the Claridge Gallery where he had exhibited in 1926. It was certainly Cedric Morris who in 1929 proposed her as a member of the Seven and Five Society, which at that time was organising some of the more significant exhibitions in London and included among its members Ben and Winifred Nicholson, Ivon Hitchens, David Jones and Christopher Wood.

FH's career between 1928 and 1931 has been documented in Arthur Howell's book, Four Vital Years. Published in 1951, at the height of FH's English reputation, the book portrays Howell as the perceptive dealer who single-handedly discovered and launched a major talent. This inflation of Howell's role could only have occurred in connection with a woman artist, and an elderly one at that, who concealed her own strength and determination in her relations with him and downplayed the extent of the support she was receiving elsewhere. FH's letters document her relationship with the patron and dealer Lucy Wertheim. Another supporter to appear during these years was the writer Geoffrey Gorer, who was introduced to FH by Lett Haines in about 1929. He and his mother occupied a less flamboyant place in FH's life than Lucy Wertheim, but the extent of their undemanding assistance is revealed in her letters.

FH stopped teaching. These years of concentrated painting coincided with a growing acceptance by the buying public of the kind of modernist work that, fifteen *years earlier, had been greeted with bafflement and indignation. FH was manipulating oil paint with greater confidence, exploiting its opacity, building up a richly encrusted all-over surface, different from her earlier more fluid use of the medium. Her watercolours became more expressive and innovative. Sometimes she used line and wash with great delicacy, in other works she mixed watercolour with black and white and built up networks of brush strokes and dense areas of colour. She was also making drawings, complex, highly finished works in pencil or chalk that revealed an exquisite sensitivity to graphic marking. During this period FH enlarged her content, adding still life to her range and quickly arriving at the combination of still life and landscape which became one of the central themes of her work.*

Her former pupils, now her friends, Dorothy Selby, Elsie Barling, Hannah Ritchie and Jane Saunders, joined her in 1927 for the summer painting expedition to Tréboul where Cedric Morris and Lett Haines were also painting.

[380] To Dorothy Selby, c.27 August 1927

[Post card] Tréboul. Sat. 9-30 p.m.

After all I was asleep when you slipped silently away this morning – I awoke to the rattling of your bus – and at once the house felt lonely – I had at least intended calling out bon voyage from the bannisters – Impossible to thank you enough for the fat wad of notes – *far too much* – how generous! You over value my part of the job. I was very greatly impressed by the progress of the last week – Keep it up – excellent. . . .

[381] To Dorothy Selby, 24 October 1927

Hotel des Voyageurs, Concarneau, Finistére. Oct: 24th.

Dear Miss Selby

Ever so many grateful thanks both for your letter & the Notes. You are too good. To me money is like sunlight – sent by God – its life – grand possibilities open to me – better work, travel – fine thinking – and a fiver in French Notes seems *everlasting* & vast. We artists are the Illusionists!

The current is drawing me towards London and soon I hope you will have the chance of choosing your pet drawing – framed – something you really like, find restful & soul satisfying – I am getting very keen to see my things framed and on Show. I can't go on leading this easy life here in the ooze – for that is what it amounts to mentally – and when the tide is out – physically. . . . Very bad health has kept me in bed for 2 days under the yellow counterpane but otherwise I am fit & well & been working like a fiend for fear the weather will break . . . . The dealer man[1] from NZ has taken with him 5 of the 8 Drawings of Concarneau which I sent him & hopes to tempt collectors in Australia to buy them – I hope he will. My pictures (I hear through him) are on view in Wellington[2] & are creating interest and (you bet) some war hoops – Bye and bye I hope to receive a cheque –

No one comes to the Hotel. It is very dull – And yet I feel this solitude a spiritual necessity the older I grow – I do my best work alone. One fine day a man called Austin Phillips – a writer of fiction – turned up from a village not far off where he has been writing for the last 12 months – a novel on Corsica. . . . He seemed to be in search of someone to listen to him. After 2 hours I gave up – exhausted – I felt he might any moment produce his manuscript & ask me to listen to it. His book is called "That Girl from Corsica"[3]. . . .

[382] To Isabel Field, 15 December 1927

Caledonian Hotel, Bloomsbury. Dec: 15th.

My Dearest Sis

It is Christmas – or thereabouts – and I have not written you a line of greetings. Since my return from abroad I have been extremely busy with arrangements for a London Show. Nothing so far is definitely fixed but I have hopes of a Gallery in the early Spring – January or Feb: It is mostly a question of planking down a guarantee of £50 or so – & *that* is not so easy – there are very few good Galleries & far too many artists wanting them. The gilded (but not always gifted) amateur generally scores.

You will see I am represented this year in the New English Art Club – 2 works – which is, as you know, considered important. Many aspire but few are chosen. I am making a big effort to recover my lost footing in London. It is now a matter of "brute cash" & holding on till I am recognized. Every penny goes to the cause – frames – dealer – etc. Once *really* known sales follow. So back me in N.Z for all you are worth & push sales and send me a cheque as soon as you can. You & Will have been bricks in looking after the pictures in Wellington. Willie told me you were doing your best for me. . . . He told me of your stroke of good luck. It shows your powers are not on the wane. Why don't you take it up seriously Sis and "Come back". It can be done – with your fine colour & sympathetic imagination you might be as strong as ever again. I find it a hard & exacting life – but worth it. So far I have not been eliminated in the struggle for life – but

---

[1] Identified by E. H. McCormick as E. Murray Fuller.

[2] At the New Zealand Academy of Fine Arts (five works ranging from 1916 to 1924).

[3] *The Girl out in Corsica* by Austin Philips was published in 1927. Philips was a prolific writer of poems, short stories and romantic novels as well as a history of the Home Civil Service, *Pariah and Brahmin*, 1914.

London & London fogs & cold would soon kill me off if I stayed on a winter. No more now dear Sis. Best wishes for 1928 – let me say it in handkies.

[383] To Lucy Wertheim, 14 January 1928
                    Hotel Moderne, Martigues, Bouches du Rhone, France. Jan 14th

My Dearest Luce

I have waited to get fairly settled before writing. It has been so *painfully* cold . . . . One feels rather insulted coming so far to be treated so coolly – How are you all? It seems . . . an eternity of days since I left the cosy flat[4] & swooped down here . . . and now I am thinking about getting to work – tho' it is hardly ideal; there is no one here as yet – this is no winter resort – but Augustus John & his Family are at their villa outside the Town . . . . He has identified himself with Martigues in the past & painted that lovely panel series of his wife & children here. I think most of them now in New York. They were better looking in those days. They look terribly sophisticated now, with their big Touring Car & this blight of prosperity over them. A sort of modern Holy Family – not *too* Holy any way –

My show is fixed for early May.[5] You *must* be in town Luce – I am concentrating *hard* on work for it . . . . Chiefly I hope you are rested after the Christmas orgy. *How* you worked & thought of all & every body – even to leaving that noble pot of broth for me . . . . Much love to you all Yours ever Frances

[384] To Dorothy Selby, 21 January 1928
                    Hotel Moderne, Martigues, Bouches du Rhône, France. Jan: 21st 1928

Dear Miss Selby

Most of my friends think I was drowned in the Channel in the Great Blizzard of Boxing Day – so completely have I vanished – I have been wondering if I should leave it at that – and have a posthumous Show at the Claridge – what a lot of trouble I should be saved. . . .

Since I got here it has been a long fight with the cold . . . of course it looks like midsummer & there is the usual mimosa & a sort of saffron colour in the air which deceives one into leaving off a top coat & catching pneumonia by sunset –

Have, so far, done no serious work. Have been too busy looking after myself. . . .

. . . . Martigues is half Spanish – I have a small room in the Spanish quarter

---

[4] Lucy Wertheim's flat in London, regularly made available to FH.
[5] The exhibition, *Paintings and Watercolours*, at the Claridge Gallery, 52 Brook St, opened in April 1928.

where I have models . . . there is no chasing & begging on bended knee as at Tréboul – they are only too pleased to sit & gaze at you with immense eyes for as long as you like . . . .

The St George's Gallery has written to ask me for 2 Water Colours to be sent in by the 25th.[6]

This seems impossible, seeing it is now the 21st – unless you will by a miracle of kindness let them have the framed Water Colour of the 3 Children you fetched from Skillens – or did you?

I have no others framed & available for immediate show – I have written to Skillen to try & rush one or two into frames to send in to the gallery – as Mr Howell wishes to select *himself* – I feel I would like to show the children . . . . I suggest your putting a big price on it £25 so that it won't sell – I am sure you would prefer making a final choice at my own show – at the same time not losing yr. chance of the children – is that right? Anyway I leave it to you . . . .

Always bothering you . . . .

I hope Barling will be prepared – but then, curse her, she always is – the clever pig. . . .

I would call it *Drawing.* . . .

[385] To Arthur Lett Haines, 30 January 1928
        Hotel Modern, Martigues, Bouches du Rhône, France. Jan 30th. 1928

Dear Lett
        . . . . Martigues . . . is no place for Jan: Feb – still it suits me in many ways – it is off the map & cheap & models are easy to get – tho' none too easy to keep . . . I have painted about 4-5 canvases, 1 large one 'Spanish Family' I think is good. . . .

I bow the head in deepest apology to you for not sending the Paris 'Cahiers' as I said – but there was a deficit just when I had most need of cash – since when I have been living on the verge of the purée – my only bit of business this year being a 3 guinea sketch. . . .

Only a few people at this Hotel – 2 Englishmen 1 American exploring Roman remains on a motor bicycle – Augustus John & what appears to be several wives . . . they are at their villa – and sometimes dine here – he looks a dour old dog and soon will look like Rowley Smart if he isn't very careful – at dinner he studies the winelist & doesn't talk much – they stay till Easter. He tells folk here that he is ill & is going into a Sanatorium – with pride they claim at least 17 of his offspring at Martigues –

---

[6] For the exhibition, *Contemporary English Water-colours*, the first time Arthur Howell presented her work in the St George's Gallery. There were no sales.

I hope Cedric is doing some shining work & both of you are well love from
FRANCES

[386] TO LUCY WERTHEIM, 13 FEBRUARY 1928
                    Hotel Moderne, Martigues, Bouches du Rhône, France. Feb 13th

My Dearest Luce
    . . . . I was immensely pleased to have the letter from Sophie Thompson[7] &
to know she liked the Drawing . . . she is a fine critical soul & a real artist herself
. . . . I assume she has not my great job to cope with – earning bread & butter &
rent by art in a terribly over stocked market – also *I* have had to choose between
showing my work in the older established Shows and the smaller exclusive
modern ones with whom I am in sympathy . . . .
    I preferred *not* to show at all rather than exhibit with the older traditional set
with whom I have nothing in common. But chiefly, I have not been able to afford
to exhibit & have had to put my art aside & do other money making jobs – in
order to live. Thats the whole secret of my *delayed* success. But now I am slowly
creeping back – and invitations from the right quarters are coming in – and, I
hope, my Show will make things right for me – I am putting my Shirt on paint,
canvas, models & frames – if the beastly thing is *not* a success Luce, I shall go up
in the air & not come down again. Sophie Thompson is quite right – I am
wayward – what artist worth his salt is not? but au fond – deep in my work – I
am steadfast & steady as a rock – I have *changed* & *evolved* & *experimented* – but
am none the worse for that. My present work is consistent – I shall sink or swim
by it – I think swim . . . .
    I am up to my eyes in unfinished canvases – fiendish little models who don't
turn [up] make life a hell to me . . . .
    . . . . Artists only come to Martigues in their oldest clo' wh. is all I possess
. . . *really* – you wouldn't speak to me if you met me in Oxford Road. I am tearing
up my undies for paint rags too . . . .

[387] TO LUCY WERTHEIM, c.7 MARCH 1928
                                                          Martigues. Wed:

My Dearest Luce
    How *very* nice of you to offer me fents[8] – I should adore a parcel – as you say
it will stem the tide of destruction. . . .

----

[7] A former pupil at the Colarossi Academy in 1910.
[8] Cloth remnants which FH could use for painting rags.

I am specially glad you like the Mathew Smith[9] more & more. It will wear –
I think it was an inspired purchase on yr. part –

. . . . I am rush rush *rushing* to get my work finished. . . .

*FH left Martigues on 21 March and returned to London. Her exhibition at the
Claridge Gallery opened on 23 April and was well reviewed, the* Times *critic
comparing her to Cézanne.[10] There were also some sales.*

[388] To Dorothy Selby, c.24 May 1928

Caledonian Hotel, Harpers St WC.1. Thursday night.

Dear Miss Selby

It was nice of you to write . . . I am sure you must be awfully tired & I am glad
you are off to the country –

. . . . Howell still clings to the "Children" & seems always "just on the point
of selling it" – & won't give it up. He says it attracts – & leads up to talk on
my other work. Perhaps he is right. . . . So you must have the Green Boys –
pro tem . . . .

I am still at this horrible little Hotel – waiting till the Claridge elects to pay
me. . . .

Howell has hung 4 of my things in his Show. Hope they will justify his faith
in them[11] –

It is a good Show – I am sorry Barling is not there. Why I wonder? Did she not
send?

Cedric is on the wings of an incomparable success – selling & selling – over 40
pictures now gone[12]. . . . He is as simple & charming as ever – no swank – Lett
is off to Paris this weekend – they are giving an "End of the World" party on Wed:
positively Judgement Day dress!

Yes let us meet when you return. . . .

[9] Matthew Smith (1879-1959) had studied in Paris and evolved a painterly idiom that combined thick,
luscious brush work with the bold unnaturalistic colours associated with fauvism. After solo exhibitions in
1926 and 1927 he was beginning to receive recognition in London. He was closer in age to FH than other
emerging painters, his career being hindered by periods of psychological distress, made worse by shell-shock
in the First World War.

[10] Quoted in E. H. McCormick, *Portrait of Frances Hodgkins*, p.106-7.

[11] This was FH's second group exhibition at the St George's Gallery, the *Modern English Water-Colour
Society*, May-June 1928. Two works sold.

[12] The exhibition was at Arthur Tooth and Sons.

FH, now in her sixtieth year, moved into a studio in Fitzrovia, the area round Fitzroy and Charlotte Streets, at the northern limits of Soho. Here Walter Sickert had taken a studio after returning from France in 1905 and set up the Fitzroy Street Group, the forerunner of the Camden Town Group. Though no longer the heart of an avant garde challenge to British conservatism, the area was still frequented by artists and writers, and it was also close to Cedric Morris's studio in Great Ormond Street in Bloomsbury, a few blocks to the east.

In New Zealand FH's younger brother Gilbert had been appointed Chief Electoral Officer.

[389] TO GILBERT HODGKINS, 15 AUGUST 1928

[16 Cleveland Mews, Maple Street, W.1] London. Aug: 15th.

Dear Chief

Heartiest Congratulations! I was rejoiced to read in the Evening Post of your new honours. Splendid – I *am* glad. Thank you for sending me the papers – your photograph, I think, is excellent, a most impressive head – and strangely like Father. . . . I am so delighted this recognition has come while you are young enough to enjoy it. . . . Odd how you and I are in the news together, fluttering in the limelight – the same week. Quite a nice sort of article, tho' hardly calculated to start a boom in my work. It is about time they realise I exist and am doing something a little more significant than the usual ruck of artists who come to Europe – even if it is unpopular now people will in time grow used to the strangeness of my technique, a "handwriting" unfamiliar to them . . . . I have won my difficult way by sincerity – it is the only test. The foe, of course, is debt, starvation etc and I have had the rottenest of times during the long struggle – but I hope to survive. I have now got a Studio in London. It is in a Mews – mostly garages & 1 blacksmith, 1 vet: 2 artists beside myself – poor & *very* poor people in the neighbouring streets, mostly Jews & Italians, & a big sprinkling of Germans – I have never seen so many fat boys. The next big street is the sort of London Latin Quarter, a rival to Chelsea – & Bloomsbury. One time the Rents were *very* low – now soaring to fancy prices. I give £80 for one room which does *not* exude comfort – indeed I doubt if I shall be able to winter in it. I can buy all my food in the little shops round about – you can get anything from stewed eels to kippers! & lovely fruit off the barrows – but nothing is really cheap (nor so nice) as in France. . . . I suppose you drive your own car – or do the big daughters drive for you? How is Percy getting along? I would like to hear some cheery news of him.

This is a stupid letter dear Bert but it is the best my dull brain can do tonight . . . . My love to your Family & my loving regards to Percy & Ouida when you see them & I wish you splendid health & a good heart to enjoy your new success.

Ever yours affectionately

Fanny

I lived on lemons until they went up to 5d. each!

[390] To Miss Harmston,[13] 20 August 1928

34 Fitzroy St. W.1. Aug: 20th.

Dear Miss Harmston

Thank you for your letter – I am sorry those 2 Paris addresses came too late to catch Mr. Howell

However I enclose them for future use – Hotel Fleuri – rue Eugéne Carrière 18ième (Montmartre) Hotel d'Oriente rue l'Abbé Gregoire 6 (Montparnasse district) near Luxembourg

rooms 18-24 frs.

very good morning coffee

hot cold water etc

ask for room in front –

If you are writing to Mr. Howell please tell him he can see the water colours of Le Fauconnier[14] at the Gallerie Billiet rue la Boëtie (almost at corner of rue Miromesnil – one of the Directors speaks English). . . .

His work is unknown to me personally but I understand he wishes to have a Show in London . . . .

[391] To Lucy and Paul Wertheim, August-September 1928

34 Fitzroy St W.1. Sunday evening

Dearest Luce & Paul

I got back here from you – a lame duck – and on opening my bag found the big Note you had slipped in dear great hearted Luce (I am sure you had pinched it out of poor Paul's pocket) & before I sleep I must send you all my love & thanks dear generous ones –

My only means of adequate thanks is to beg you to come soon & choose the best of my pictures (I have some new flower ones) & a Water Colour for the Cousin –

So please *do* come –

It was shocking of me to make such a goose of myself this afternoon – and

[13] Arthur Howell's secretary at the St George's Gallery. Howell had asked FH to recommend hotels in Paris.
[14] Henri Le Fauconnier (1881-1946) had exhibited with the cubist painters in 1911. He gained a European reputation on the basis of his ability to disseminate important ideas rather than his own inventiveness.

I was hysterical & weak & should not have attempted to go so far – I was shakey –

I shall try & get into the country for a week or two – that will put the nerves straight –

The reason I refused your lovely flowers was that I *couldn't* bear to have them near me & not paint them – it was tantalizing me too much – *also* it makes me sad to see them die before I have painted them – *also* I had no bowl to put them in.

. . . . Goodnight & very best love & please dont worry about me – you know I have one or two pupils which keep me going & I may get more. The main thing is to get well

Frances

[392] To WILLIAM HODGKINS, 23 NOVEMBER 1928

34 Fitzroy St, London W.1. 23rd. Nov:

My Dearest Willie

I must hurry up with my Christmas letter & good wishes if it is to reach you in time – I shall think of you enjoying a happy cheery out-of-door picnic Christmas Sun shining, nice & warm & jolly – all that it is not here in cold, black, miserable old England – where I have all but died since I last wrote to you. I have been very ill. Following on much pain I had to seek advice – and for $2^1/_2$ months I have been ill with internal ulceration – slowly being cured by dieting & as much rest as I can give myself – I am now to have my remaining teeth out – I am lucky to have escaped an operation – I have been staying in the country with friends & living on milk & sops & come back to London every 2 or 3 weeks to see the doctor, who is quite a famous person on the Staff of the Women's Cancer Clinic & who has attended me for nothing. Naturally my earning powers have suffered. It is an age since I heard from any of you. I hope all goes well with the Family. Have you started to build yet? There is very little news to tell you – I have been too down on my luck to do any work – and now the winter has closed in & the days are so short & dark & sunless – one gets little chance with the brush – I am doing some textiles to make some money – not easy money – and I am doing a design for the B.B.C British Broadcasting Co. for a book on textiles they are bringing out – no cash – only kudos. Have you had any sales in NZ? Forgive this scrap – I am still very much of a crock – write to me soon – & think of me at Xmas time as I will of all of you. Loving wishes to you & Jean from

Frances

[393] To William Hodgkins, 5 December 1928

34 Fitzroy St, W.1. 5th. Dec:

My Dearest Willie

There is just time for a quick line of thanks by this mail for your cheque wh. came last week.[15] Thank you most awfully for it . . . [it] came in the nick of time to help pay some of my bills – you are a great dear to add to it – oh! I *am* a nuisance to you – I am feeling better than when I wrote . . . . Oddly enough I am having a little whiff of luck, even fame – I can even dare hope that the tide has at last turned in my favour – it appears an eminent art critic has been praising my work – & has even asked if he may come & see me. And all because he is reported to have said that he considers me one of the great European Water Colourists (hope he was sober) I have sold

    1 oil   20gns
    1 Water Colour 7gns
    1 Drawing   5gns

and 4 different people have enquired after Water Colours & wish to buy. Friends are advising their friends to buy now – while I am (comparatively) cheap – next year – !

It is very cheering – I can do with a bit of luck. I have had a rough time – & my illness has been brought about by hard work & anxiety . . . . I have had wonderful friends who have never lost faith in me. I have travelled far from the Academic tradition which fetters England & recognizes no possibility of further revelation. There is now a growing increase of interest in the newer outlook & a change of attitude – I believe if you saw my present work you would find it very *simple* to understand – it has grown more & more simple & sincere – I will send you some photographs – photos cost money but now I shall be able to indulge. I am going to Tunbridge for Xmas – to friends – & then on to the Nickalls at Boxley – a quiet Xmas – eating & sleeping. Send this on to Sis – I am writing to her but not this mail – I am in a bit of a rush trying to let this Flat & move into the country where the doctor thinks I will be better in health – & less tired. Dont put anything in the Press about this new turn of luck. Wait a bit. Love to you all & thanks my Dear

Fanny

---

[15] Proceeds from sales. The paintings sent out to the Academy of Fine Arts in 1927, together with some additional works, had been exhibited at the art societies in Christchurch and Auckland and again at the Academy of Fine Arts in Wellington.

[394] To Lucy Wertheim, c.12 January 1929

44 Mecklenburgh Square Basement Flat, W.C.2.

My Dearest Luce

Thank you so much for your letter – it is good of you to write when you are so busy – I have been meaning to write, myself, for days but somehow have never a minute – I am *very* hard at work – & tomorrow I move over to Nancy Morris's[16] Flat in Bloomsbury – where I have taken a small room – I expect to be much more comfortable – with less house work to do – also the joys of a bath! Such bliss after this primitive place – I can't tell you how disappointed I was not to be able to seize the chance of seeing you – but that night I was *dizzy* with tiredness & had a visitor – you must have thought me a wretch not to 'phone back by return – but the messenger had gone too quickly –

I have wanted to tell you how attractive & sweet Hilary looked at Cedric's studio. . . .

I am going in to the country on the 22nd. for a fortnight – to get some landscape – & some country exercise –

Duncan Grant[17] came to see my work the other morning. He is a nice soul – very like his own work. . . .

My dear love to you Luce dear. . . & Au Revoir till you are next in Town – Always Frances

[395] To Arthur Howell, 15 January 1929

44 Mecklenburgh Square Basement Flat, W.C2. 15-1-29.
Please cancel 34 Fitzroy St.

Dear Mr. Howell

I have a double apology to make – First for not answering your kind letter before now – and secondly (and this is more important) for not backing my word and letting you have some fresh Water Colours in place of the ones I took away – since long enough – I fully intended doing so – but, to be quite frank, as they are my original sketches for some oil canvases on which I am still at work I cannot part with on the moment – these dark short cold days work goes very slowly – I am very hard at work and I very much hope that you will be able to give me a Show about April or May – I think I can promise the work will be an advance on the last show – I mean more *attractive* – I am going into the country next week & hope to get some winter subjects – on my return I will come & show you what stuff I (hope to) have

[16] Cedric Morris's sister. FH was anticipating her move in giving the Mecklenburgh Square address.
[17] Duncan Grant (1885-1978), painter and decorator associated with Vanessa Bell, Roger Fry and the Omega workshops, one of the leading painters of the Bloomsbury group.

I am not discouraged at your not selling more of my things – I know you did your very best for me – and I am confident interest in my work will grow. I think you are very patient – An enthusiast like yourself, is needed to push work of my calibre! Faith is essential –

I hope you will have a very lucky year –

With kind regards

Yours sincerely

Frances Hodgkins

Mr. Duncan Grant asked to come & see my Water Colours. The man who came with him, an art critic, asked for the 2 sleeping children. I told him that it was at yr. Gallery – No question of buying it, merely friendly interest

[396] To Dorothy Selby, c.16 April 1929

M.S.B.F. Tuesday

Dear Miss Selby

I went down to Forest Row yesterday & saw cottage – it is rather a duck of a place – and if *you* – *I* – know what is good for us we should jump at it –

It is "humble" and primitive – quite clean dry & otherwise habitable – 1 living room small with large open fireplace 2 bedrooms up tiny steep stairs – you know the thing – larder – kitchen & earth closet in garden – a labourers cottage furnished appropriately by a fairly tasteful woman – but it is quite *tiny* & humble – 3 beds – & a sufficiency of bedclothes – etc

The great catch is Mrs. Woods . . . whose house ajoins but does not overlook . . . who wld. cook clean for us for 10/- a week – or less, accordingly –

The country is superb – & the view from the Cottage S.W. is one great panorama of the Downs – nothing but space & air – too exhilirating for tired eyes & nerves – scattered round are hamlets & cottages & farms – heaps of material for the searching. The cottage is in the Ashdown Forest on a side road – ¼ of an hour from bus to Forest Row – an easy ½ mile on good road –

The Rent is £1 weekly – for May & June – I think more July & Aug: but I gather we could have the place on lease – or for keeps – by purchase. It wd. certainly pay us better to have it on lease should you like it well enough – then we could let it to our friends (& enemies) at a profit (!) when we were not using it ourselves –

But all this is for future consideration –

The fare from Victoria *week end* is 5/10

Bus fare to Red Lion 4d.

Rent 10/- each

Your share of Mrs. Woods (week end) 3/6

Food say 5/-

Please think it all over . . . and let me know by return if possible so that I can write to Mrs. Ormsby & secure it for May June with option of retaining it. . . .

I would love to take the cottage with you but of course could not do it alone. . . .

[397] To Dorothy Selby, c.19 April 1929
44 Mecklenburgh Square Basement Flat. Friday

Dear Miss Selby

. . . . The cottage is now ours – and I shall go down on 1st. and make ready for you. I do hope you may get off for that week end – No *of course* neither of us will slave – What is Mrs. Woods for? I intend to do a lot of painting don't you?. . .

I will order in provisions for week end & we can settle when we meet there –

Mrs. Woods will cook our mid day meal & prepare evening one – I'll see to the breakfast – or perhaps we'll do it turn about. The great thing is peace, *deep* peace for us both

Heals have asked me for a selection of 8 pictures for a Modern Show of paintings in May[18] – so am busy

[398] To Lucy Wertheim, 23 April 1929
[Mrs Wertheim's flat in London] Tuesday 9 30 pm

Dearest Luce Hullo Dear how are you both – *very* tired I expect you were both of you when you got to 82. . . .

How well I sleep here – the Spirit of the Flat is so serene – it always soothes my jangled nerves –

I have had a long day in the dining room – painting the bouquet which look[ed] exquisite against the green curtains – & touches of yellow spring green leaves from outside – I bought 2 white lilies to give it the white note – it just gives it that "kick" as a composition. The black pot was introduced at a later stage – to the picture's enhancement. . . .

---

[18] *Recent Paintings by Living British Artists* at the Mansard Gallery in Heal's department store. Other artists included were: Cedric Morris, Nina Hamnett, John Banting and Christopher Wood.

[399] To Lucy Wertheim, c.4 May 1929
    Romary Cottage, Birch Grove, nr. Haywards Heath, Sussex. Saturday

My Dearest Luce

I found so much to interest me & attend to when I got here on Wed: that I have not had a moments pause to sit down & write. Writing a letter is an event – as one has to walk *2* miles to post it – and, you know, I am no walker. . . . I *should* do some good work here – the bush fires blackened the country side but it is all now gently screened by palest green – & the blossoms so lovely – a sweet moment & I feel great & big with inspiration & will to paint – rain however has damped my spirit . . . .

I am anxious to hear how you are dear Luce – & if the pain is easier – I was so sorry I had to run off before you came – I had a hectic race to finish my 2 big oils of yr. lovely flowers – you must go & see them at Heals Show – wont you? I spent some of the Fiver you gave me on frames & paint. Such a Godsend it was dear Luce . . . .

. . . . This quiet life is the life for me much love darling Luce & billions of thanks for everything – you were an angel to leave me in the Flat alone with the Flowers. . . .

[400] To Dorothy Selby, c.5 May 1929
    Romary Cottage, Birch Wood, Nr Haywards Heath, Sussex. Sunday

My Dear Miss Selby

I am longing for you to be well & get down here. . . . I don't know when I have felt so full of well-being & contentment – tho' in *reality* – life is just about the same – only I feel differently towards it . . . .

. . . . I have done 3 goodish Water Colours – painted out of doors – & tomorrow Monday dash to Town by motor coach (moach) to have them framed for Heals show. . . .

I find, likewise, village is only 5 minutes off – complete with telephone & *every* commodity – a local Woolworth –

So . . . Come! Come!! Come!!!

Better bring rug if you have one – blankets *thin* – nights cold
                    Yours,
                        F H –

[401] To Lucy Wertheim, c.11 May 1929

Romary Cottage, Birch Grove, nr. Haywards Heath, Sussex. Sat afternoon

Luce Darling your Friday night letter just now come – & I hasten to rush off a reply – I'll wire also if there is a chance of doing so – but I am afraid there is no telegraph – or telephone – within walking distance – I am rejoiced you are sufficiently recovered to go to the Cottage – revived anyway in spirit. . . .

I had better wait till after Whitsun to come to Little Belan – it will certainly be wiser for *you* to spare yourself extra fatigue – I could more easily come then. . . . I *promise* to come – & will let nothing interfere with my visit *this* time – I come from my Cot to your Cottage – I am so happy here – painting in the garden – groups of wild flowers – fruit blossom & funny cottage chimney ornaments – I feel peacefully dead – to the world – so relieved to get away from that awful Basement which was ruining health & nerves – & eventually my work – the best work is always done in dark corners, I know, but not in that corner –

You are a great friend to me – your sympathy and *very solid* support on my road to fame (?) is bringing me more quickly to the goal. The money you so generously spare to me is all put into the cause – & is helping on the good work – I *know* success is not far off – I shall owe it all to you & Paul – many times I should have fallen by the way – but for your solid & substantial help – you Darlings –

Now for the Post – I must fly –

Your loving & very grateful

Frances –

[402] To Lucy Wertheim, Summer 1929

Romary Cottage, Birch Grove, nr Haywards Heath. Thursday

My dearest Luce

I got back here this morning . . . from my circular tour which ended rather more lamely than when I started out with you – in luxury & elegance – just a week ago – I have thought of that lovely drive we had together many times since then . . . .

At Wilmington[19] the weather was of the best. I found 3 quite quite pretty girls floating round doing nothing in particular – grand models for me . . . the Cottage is owned by 2 sisters who understand to the last hair the craft of homemaking – two bright girls – who a year ago were nicely well off – keeping horses & a man servant etc. This year they have hardly a cent – owing to a slump in shares – and are gamely tiding over a crisis – keeping the home together by their various exertions – and all so cheerfully – they did me no end of good – tho' I must say

[19] In Sussex, a visit arranged by Arthur Lett Haines.

I have felt it appallingly dull & lonely returning to an empty & poky little cottage – the worst of holidays! I got a fire going as quick as I could – and got rid of that corpse in the barn feeling. . . .

[403] To Lucy Wertheim, Autumn 1929

Flat. Sat: night

My Dear Luce

I am very sorry to hear of the accident to Paul but am relieved to hear he escaped serious injury. . . . It won't add to your own peace of mind when motoring – I am glad you were near him when he was hurt and could coddle him & come to his aid with stiking plaster etc –

It embarrasses me very much to accept the Note from you – I feel deeply that I have no further right to accept anything from you. If I am to believe what you tell me I think you should be practicing economy. Let it begin from now onward – your lavish generosity & expenditure alarms & bewilders me – & [I] fear there will be a crash if you are not careful –

It is no business of mine – but you gave me some of your confidences – and I can not help judging from what I see & hear. Your pace is too rapid for me – I am stodgy & serious minded – needing a quiet life and a contemplative one so you must cut me out of your gay young circle – it is too exciting for me –

Perhaps you are changing from the Luce I knew in Manchester – or perhaps I know you better –

I shall always be deeply grateful to you & Paul for what you have done for me – I feel I must not sponge – or lean on you *any* longer – it is bad for us both –

I intend leading a very quiet winter devoted to work – I believe I have found a toplight room off the Gray's Inn Rd. with bath – gas – attendance etc. . . . I meant to leave the Flat today but have a bad cold – I shall stay till early Monday morning & give Mrs. Lake keys –

Goodnight & Bless you for your friendship

[404] To Lucy Wertheim, c.29 October 1929

22 Fitzroy St, W.C.1. Tuesday

My Dear Luce

I moved into this Studio on Sat: and so am now back in my old slum – where I belong –

When I have calmed down & get used to the place I hope to get to work – but I wonder if I shall ever be in the right mood again to paint. . . .

I hope Paul is all right – & none the worse – and that you are doing jolly things – in jolly clothes – with jolly people –

I am sorry I said naughty things to you – as I did – but I felt badly you were not being fair to me – though you meant so kindly – I was deeply hurt & tried to tell you so – I expect you feel as sore as I do –   Forgive me

Frances –

[405] To Lucy Wertheim, 7 November 1929

22 Fitzroy St. WC.1. Thursday (7/11/29)

My Dearest Luce

. . . . I think that you & I have rather lost our sense of values – *you* just as badly as *myself* and that re-adjustment is necessary if we are to understand each other's point of view –

I speak as the *artist* – not the woman and friend – if I had shown more honest common sense & a sense of humour the situation would never have grown as acute as it did – and I apologise for making a scene & making a fuss over what was not so very venal [an] offense on your part – tho' I thought it was bad enough at the time – I was getting rubbed up & irritable from the moment you made me an offer for 5 of my big drawings – (to be given away as Xmas presents) and I felt such a slump in the value of my work was humiliating & painful and could do me no good. Of course I should have laughed & said I'll see you d – d first or something equally rude & silly – but I took it heavily – and brooded over it – overlooking the generous motive in your heart & your sincere wish to provide cash for me. They are good Drawings which Howell *should* be selling for me at 15 gns. each – but he *isn't*. So I have no real case to argue from – excepting my own belief in the things as good Drawings. Then came yr. visit to Cooling's – which further upset me. You had no doubt forgotten that Mr. Courtauld, 2 years ago, had decided he could not make me a member of the Group.[20] Naturally my pride revolted at what seemed a back door attempt on my part to get in at any price – Mr. Davidson has done me many good turns – and being a close friend of Cedric & Nancy he knows both me & my work. So why press him further?. . . That is my side of the argument Luce – without heat or bias – I now think it d – d silly to worry about anything so trivial – and to risk losing you as a loving helpful & very dear friend – who has been *absolutely wonderful* to me – kinder than anyone I have ever known – who is, in fact, enabling me to carry

[20] The 'Group' was the London Artists Association, which was holding its exhibition in a gallery above Coollings in Bond Street. Mrs Wertheim had approached her friend Angus Davidson, the secretary, suggesting that FH be made a member. In a letter to John Barr, Director of the Auckland Art Gallery, 21 October 1948, Mrs Wertheim described FH's outburst of anger about this as a 'torrent of abuse' and said that 'things were never quite the same' between them afterwards.

on & make good. It does not require to be told that your friends adore you. Of course they do – I can see that for myself –

But I do claim that you keep me in a special watertight compartment from yr. other friends – I am not a good mixer. Friendship is a great luxury – few artists can spare the time – I mean at least the older ones of my generation –

I have the warmest affection for you Luce and you must forgive me if I have failed you in the many emotional crises of the past few weeks – I have never known a woman ride so many crises & survive – that is why I pray you to go slower – it will repay you 100 fold – in the end –

When you can bear the sight of my ugly *earnest* face come & see me – with empty hands – just for a cup of tea and no back chat Dear!

Thank you for the Note – and for the nice things you say of Open Window – Perhaps!

My love always
Frances

I have seen no one for days & am working from 7-2 while the light is good –

[406] To Lucy Wertheim, c.8 November 1929

22 Fitzroy St, W.C1. Friday

My Dearest Luce

My very best thanks for your Note & the enclosed £1 –

It is extraordinary kind of you to send me another so soon . . . .

I am touched & pleased at your doing so – but really from now forward there will be no further need as Mr. Howell is taking a number of my Water Colours & paying for them in installments – which later on may turn into a contract – I told him that you had greatly befriended me – & that no one had ever done so much for me – or ever will again. . . .

I may go South in about 10 days time – to work for a Spring Show – but before doing so am putting on a joint Show (by invitation) of about 10-12 canvases with Vera Cunningham[21] at Dr. Oriakovski's Gallery at 34 Bloomsbury – opening 16th. Nov.

So I have not much time to turn round on – before then –

I should love you to come to tea – but dare not give myself that treat *next* week as I must *concentrate* for all I am worth if I am to get my things off in time. . . .

Better not mention the contract subject to Mr. Howell as it is only, so far in the air – & under offer to me – not yet accepted & clinched –

The offer had a bracing & invigorating effect upon me – I am so glad Paul is better . . . .

[21] Vera Cuningham (1897-1955) RBA, member of the London Group (1927), Women's International Art Club and exhibitor at the Salon des Indépendants.

[407] To Arthur Howell, 5 December 1929

Pastorale, Route St Jeannet, La Gaude, A.M. France. 5 12 29

Dear Mr. Howell

I have been in this astounding place for 10 days – it is such a staggering change from London fog & gloom that I am getting down to it only now. Really it is so lovely up on this misty mountain where the air is like wine – and the wine like champagne – all is lovely all is peaceful not even the faintest whiff of a neighbour to spoil the absolute charm of the place. There is work enough for a life time. So far I have done nothing but look – Faces figures landscapes panoramas and the Basses Alpes waiting to be painted but let me tell you that in my humility I have not lifted eyes higher than the red earth & the broken earthen ware pots strewn about making such ripping shapes turning in the pure clear light – you may hear them clink as you un-roll the Water Colours I am sending along to you by this same post. They are first fruits – and an earnest of better to come – one is bound to work off a certain amount of "pep" – but *whatever* I send you and *however* it is I know you will tell me honest Injun what you think of it. I have shown rare sense coming here and my chances of good work in a land of good & plenty were never greater than they are today – thanks again to you – I hope I shall make good and my dream come true –

This region is so vast & varied & rich that I must work between closest limits & on simplest lines if I am not to lose my head & my way & get out of breath and go completely ga ga – hence the pots in their lowliness – presently I'll get on to faces & figures – which of course have their cash value & one has to pour out largesse before one can get away with it

So please Mr. Howell be very kind and send me the remaining £20 if it is convenient to you I shall be glad of it

It is too funny for words what a perfectly easy matter it is to live for almost nothing at all *compared* to my late London slum

. . . . The coastal prices of course are another affair. . . .

[408] To Lucy Wertheim, c.27 January 1930

Chez Madame Villa, St Jeannet, A.M., France. Monday

My dearest Luce

It is hard to find words to thank you for the kind things you are doing for me – I wonder that I have a friend left in the world – you must forgive my not writing – I have written hardly any letters since I came out here – it takes all my time & all of me to keep warm & alive in this mountain retreat – into which I stumbled – & once here it has been hard to get away from – the winter has been severe – snow is falling now – and it *is* cold – I have been feeling a rotter not writing to you – and now comes your awfully kind letter with the news of 2 sales at Heals – which is comforting to me – I had a line from Mrs. Disher by the same post promising to send me a cheque quickly – an unusual custom with galleries – it is really nice and large hearted of you to buy my Drawings and I am very touched & affected by your generosity to which there seems no end – thank you more than I can say Luce Dear – and for the £1 note which comes in so handy for new paints –

I am not in need of money now tho' it has been a thin time waiting till my contract terms became operative – it has been difficult to comply with the demand for a supply of saleable & attractive Water Colours under the very exhausting conditions of living in St Jeannet & keeping up ones end generally. . . .

I have 2 rooms & do my own work & most of the cooking – I depend on the crazy old Inn for a midday meal. There are a few French artists here – the hardy kind – one *very* good – with whom I have palled up – he is decorating a French Marquise's villa in the neighbourhood.[22] She is sending her car for me on Thursday for me to inspect them. Otherwise I am cut off from the world. . . . In one way it has been good for me – I was in such a nervy & chaotic state of health & mind – in sore need of rest. I have not spoken English for nearly 2 months – and have been looking on life from a new angle – and life is more bearable. . . .

It was bad of me not to write at Xmas to thank you for the Sketch & dear little hanky and letter – I am not as good as I ought to be about letters – or anything else – and the less said of my manners the better – with the warmer weather & coming of Spring I really mean to turn a new leaf – you will see –

Meanwhile dear Luce bear with me –

Too cold to write more – Much love & *much* appreciation of all your goodness & very genuine help for a struggling pal – I hope I am making headway now & really going ahead –

Take care of yourself. What are you busy over now?

I'll write before long – Your loving Frances

[22] Maurice Garnier (1880-1945) was beginning to make experimental sculptural reliefs out of stones, rock and other found objects such as shells and broken glass. He was associated with the Museum of Popular Arts and Traditions in Paris, and the folk element in his work might have attracted FH. 'I think [his work] has much charm and personality', she wrote to Lucy Wertheim in May 1930. 'He is a dear soul & would do anything for a friend of mine I am sure.' Among the papers found in FH's studio after her death and now lodged in the Tate Archives are two pencil portraits of Maurice Garnier. See E. H. McCormick's *Late Attachment* for an account of FH's friendship with this artist.

[409] To Arthur Howell, 4 February 1930

Chez Madame Villa, St Jeannet, AM, France. Feb 4th. 1930

Dear Mr. Howell

Your letter of Jan: 25 reached me here on Feb 2nd. sent on from La Gaude. No wonder you are feeling apprehensive about these long over due Drawings – I dont wonder. Perhaps it was hardly discreet of me to give you the assurance, so confident, that I was sending them along shortly – but I really meant to – feeling so sure of myself & my capacity for prolific production under the spell & magic of my surroundings . . . .

Then it grew cold & I was left with housekeeping etc on my hands and I have been spending a good deal too much time keeping warm . . . . Now I have moved from La Pastorale to St Jeannet – which is next door village and cheerfulness (comparative) has again set in . . . . I have quite a volume of pencil sketches but Water Colours have eluded me

The 3 Water Colours I have sent you are not exactly what I *hoped* to send – you may consider them too elaborate & too "searched" with the "atmosphere" over done – I made them in view of painting oils from them –

. . . . I belong to the troubled & anxious school & only flourish when I am in funds – & solvent – from which I am far from being at present. It pleases me to hear that you are not un-hopeful that I will turn out well in time & that the market is brightening. . . . Let me hear without delay what you suggest for the future – and if I can comply with your terms. It is essential to act at once – as I am au bout de mes forces and must otherwise *immediately* return to London & set about earning – which would be a pity. My London studio is not let & I have to pay rent – which is an added drain. . . .

If you will be so kind as to send me a little money *by return* (in Notes if possible) a cheque is difficult to cash – & so enable me to get on with my work & send you without further delay some really chic Water Colours which will be useful – I should like to make a "stir" if not a storm in your gallery. . . .

[410] To Arthur Howell, 23 February 1930

chez Mdme. Villa, St Jeannet, AM, France. Sunday Feb: 23rd.

Dear Mr. Howell

Your letter of the 14th. Feb: with enclosed cheque and contract Form has reached me safely. . . .

Now as to the agreement between us – I have read it carefully & slept over it and I see no reason why I should not sign it & return it to you with the assurance that willingly, I will send you the required Water Colours for selection in accordance with the terms you have outlined – I cant do more than give you my promise that you will receive the best work I am capable of – as they are painted – and that I will keep faith with you and do my best to make a success of the bargain –

To this I can add nothing – I am sure that you will consider it sufficient – I am extremely grateful to you for what you are doing for me and do not under value the time money & hard work that the launching entails – I think you can count on "the goods"

A certain peace of mind has descended upon me which with the improving weather should produce something rather nice – before long –

Meanwhile, with this letter I am sending you some fresh work – I should like to hear how it strikes you. One of the French artists here wishes to buy one of them –

Following on the "starring" of my 3 Water Colours at the Modern Water Colour Show I hope you have had some bona fide sales[23]. . . .

Of course I shall work hard – I always do –

My work has a way of asking too much from me –

I think I have answered all the points in your letter. So with a final assurance of my loyalty and co-operation in the joint speculative adventure.

By the terms of the contract Arthur Howell became the sole agent for her watercolours for three years, undertaking to buy two thirds of her annual output until a total of thirty-three paintings was reached. In the first year he would pay £3 a painting, in the second £4 and in the third £5. He also had the right to buy additional paintings at the same price and to act as agent for her oil paintings if he so decided. The prices offered by Howell may be compared with those asked for FH's watercolours at her Claridge Gallery exhibition in April/May 1928. These ranged from ten to fifteen guineas, with three smaller works at eight guineas, from which the cost of of framing and the dealer's 33 per cent commission must be subtracted.

[411] To Lucy Wertheim, c.24 February 1930
chez Mdme Villa, St Jeannet, A.M. Monday 22nd.[24]

My Dearest Luce

Your happy cheerful very kind letter spread a glow over my day – which is a cold one – but fine – and I have been out on the icy flank of the mountain – finishing the last of 8 water colours for St Georges Gallery – (dont mention *my* mentioning this) – frozen feet – blue face. How boring it is having to plug away at a thing – past inspiration stage – in a cold wind. . . .

[23] Arthur Howell had bought the three works himself.
[24] FH seems to have made a mistake: Monday was 24 February in 1930.

I may go down to Toulon for a couple of weeks to work on the Quais & in the cafés with a friend – I long for some funny cinemas & low life generally. But I intend to see out this long coming Spring – on this mountain side –

So Cedric is having a Show – & staying at the Flat – well that will be very jolly all round – if Cedric is fond of me as you say I am 100% fonder of him & with more cause – so thats that – the fact that I am working here today – in a state of comparative liberty & independence I very largely owe to the friendship of Lett & Cedric – and I dont forget it –

Letters be hanged –

Why all this fuss about writing – artists have no time for writing – a quimquennial letter – have you a dictionary – I have not – should suffice between real friends –

So there! Mrs. Wertheim dear –

Curse me – but curse me softly. . . .

By the end of February FH had finished a series of watercolours and sent them off to Arthur Howell.

[412] To Dorothy Selby, 6 March 1930
                    Chez Mdme Villa, St Jeannet, A.M. France. March 6th.

My Dear Selby

Thank you *very* much for the Statesmen (3) that have been a godsend – I see you are in Switzerland . . . I hope with lots of snow & the other proper ingredients . . . . I am still here – faute de mieux – having shivered through a long & horrible winter. . . . Well I could grouse on a long time yet – but I'll spare you – besides which I am working *very very* hard & have little time for anything else but my painting – I only just signed my contract last week & am now in receipt of the emoluments there of – only just in time – it has been a thin time waiting about till things got settled. . . .

The Spring should be gorgeous here – *when* it comes – but I feel a bit blasé and weather worn – stale in fact – so am going down to Antibes to a little Hotel there for a week or so to soak in some hot baths & relax a trifle – I think I told you I had a big apartment here – clean & light & all that – but no help from outside. I have one big solid semi demi Italian-French meal at midi – and more or less starve for the rest of the day – what time I make the big mental effort required to produce an all but daily water colour!

In addition to my water colour contract I may have another for my oils on my return. . . .

[413] To Arthur Howell, 17 March 1930

St Jeannet, A.M. France. Monday

Dear Mr. Howell

Your letter of March 2nd. has been rather long reaching me having followed me to Antibes and back here – a long post. Your friendly & encouraging letter pleased me very much. . . .

A few words like these go a long way to strengthen the spirit and help one to bear up against oneself – the enemy – I am cut off from interesting people out here and have to drive hard to stick it out and keep up my end. The French artists are now gone and I am left the Hermit of St Jeannet but presently I shall be moving off – when the present vein is run out – at present the flair is strong and with increasing facilities & under your genial auspices the world is a brighter picture than formerly. I am much happier –

Now to touch on the point of your letter: I shall bear in mind the various sets indicated by you

The nice qualities that you say you like in them such as poise, balance – colour etc are largely the result of slow & deliberate workmanship: Those symphonic schemes are not done in 5 minutes!

Well I'll see what I can do about it –

The *time factor must at all costs be kept out*: quite fatal: As work is finished it will be sent to you – I am glad you agree that this is the right way. Have no qualms about it: as long as I keep my health you will have the best I can do –

I shall hope within a few days to send along a further batch of work to square the £75 you have so far paid out to me – I hope you may find some of them to your taste. What you say of my last lot is interesting – I think I understand. Put them aside – they will probably find their proper place – in time – I can't judge my own work – I am too close to it. *All* of it is done at a venture – ones re-actions vary. They all seem very real & convincing to me at the time – and I send them off in good faith hot from the heart. The cool critical detachment sets in later – to the point of distraction which might end in my not sending any of them!

I think this is all –

Thank you again for the comforting messages –

Whatever you say to me in the way of business is *confidential* & the terms of our arrangement shall be kept private – you may rely on my discretion. I have told friends that my work is to be had from you. That is all –

Thank you I will let you know when funds run out

For the moment I am all right

Yours very sincerely

Frances Hodgkins

Mrs Wertheim's plans for opening a gallery in London were now well under way and she was looking ahead to possible exhibitions.

[414] To Lucy Wertheim, 3 April 1930

St Jeannet, A.M. France. April 3rd.

My Dearest Luce

I am delighted to hear you have a little house in view – now that is very exciting – I do hope it will fall into your hands – it will make you *very* happy – at least for a while – & by *that* time you will be able to sell out of it – at a profit. Shall you live there as well and give up the Flat?. . . You certainly are an enthusiast – and I hope I shall be hearing of you making a start very soon. . . .

Well Luce Dear if blessings & good wishes from me will help fortify you here they are in plenty –

I do hope you will be able to dispose comfortably of all difficulties & get your wish and even make a start next month – as you propose – it would be wonderful –

It is nice of you to consider a Drawing show of mine but much as I should enjoy it I doubt if I'll have stuff enough –

But will see – nearer the time. . . .

It is a funny game – selling pictures – & you'll learn all about it before long – I hope you won't blame me for putting it into yr. head – as you say – but *did* I?

You have a fertile brain & no mistake[25]. . . .

I shall be moving North soon I think. . . .

[415] To Arthur Howell, 4 April 1930

St Jeannet, Alpes Maritimes, France. 4th. April

Dear Mr. Howell

Yesterday I posted you 4 Water Colours – there remain another 5 all but finished which are temporarily in the soup waiting for fine weather. . . .

I expect to be here for another 2-3 weeks and by then I think I shall have had enough of the South – for the present – I feel like doing some quiet work in my own Studio –

I hope to take my oil paintings down to Nice early next week to be packed – it can't be done from here . . . .

Funds are getting low & I should be very grateful for a little money if it [is] convenient to you to send it me – I do hope it is –

[25] Mrs Wertheim stated that the idea of opening a gallery came from a remark made by FH in Manchester (*Adventure in Art*, 1947, p.2).

I am so very sorry not to have sent you more figure work but luck has been against it. The weather has been so cold & rough the peasants are just shapeless bundles of clothes – not at all attractive – but the summer will give me my chance – & my subjects get more variety – of that I am sure. . . .

Ten days later FH posted off 'the last of the Still Life Series'. Arthur Howell was now selling more of her work, in particular to Mrs Elizabeth Curtis (1888-1966), the founder and headmistress of the progressive girls' school, Langford Grove. FH and Howell arranged to meet in Paris on 29 April on her way back to London. While there she saw 'millions of pictures'.

[416] To Lucy Wertheim, 12 May 1930

22 Fitzroy St. Monday

My Dearest Luce

It will take me all my life time thanking you . . . you are far too good to me. . . . I was at the Flat by 12 this morning & got keys & had a snack of lunch – sardine & cheese – & back here to work – but Elton & Geoffrey Gorer[26] came & spent the afternoon (wet) pie-jawing – gone now & I am tidying up before going back to sleep at Flat. . . .

[417] To Lucy Wertheim, c.early June 1930

22 Fitzroy St, WC.2. Wed.

Dearest Luce

. . . . How are you getting along with your Gallery? I hear you have visitors & are very busy. So am I. What a scrimmage it all is –

If you are free Friday *or* Thursday night shall I bring along Maurice Garnier who is over for a few days & goes back Saturday. He would like to see you but we know you are *very* occupied with yr. Gallery & friends & visitors – so will quite understand, (but be disappointed) if you are too engaged to see us. He is trying to fix up a Show – & is now at the Leicester Galleries with his stuff –

I have had a hectic furious week – no work – What a life!

---

[26] Arthur Elton (1906-73), a pioneer of documentary film-making and friend of Cedric Morris and Lett Haines. Geoffrey Gorer (1905-85), another member of the circle, became a noted anthropologist, sociologist and writer after the success of his first book, *The Life and Ideas of the Marquis de Sade*, 1934. He studied with Margaret Mead and Ruth Benedict and went on expeditions to Africa and the Himalayas, later working in America as a researcher on contemporary culture.

Much love always
                    Frances
Yesterday had a perfect day with Lett & Cedric –

*FH accepted an invitation to stay at Pound Farm near Dedham, East Anglia, where
Cedric Morris and Lett Haines had recently begun to live. They arranged for her to
use the studio at Flatford Mill, which was now the property of the National Trust. She
stayed some of the time at the Pound and the rest at the White Horse Hotel in East
Bergholt. She wrote to Miss Harmston on 26 June, giving her new address, and ended
her letter, 'I am full of hope and am just off. Summer will be gone before I can grasp
it.'*

[418] To Lucy Wertheim, c.30 June 1930
                        White Horse Hotel, E. Bergholt, Suffolk. Monday evening

My Dearest Luce
    .... Lett & Cedric were here this morning – told me that you had been down
yesterday – you wonder woman. How do you contrive to be in Manchester &
Suffolk the same week end?. . .
    I promise to give something really choice for yr. Gallery – *the pick of my
summer's work* – so there! I am not yet ready to make terms with Mr. Howell –
after a month's work down here I shall be in a stronger position. . . . Is it all sealed
signed & delivered your Gallery? Cheers when it is – You have been brave! . . .

[419] To Lucy Wertheim, c.3 July 1930
                        The White Horse. Thursday morning

Very Dearest Luce
    A quick line by this post to thank you for yr. letter & cheque – I never dreamed
of getting it so soon or before you had made up your mind *which* picture – Rather
rough on the pocket dear Luce – at this stage of *su*spense & *ex*pense – Shall I keep
it back for a bit? I can easily do so if you wish as I am living quietly & well within my humble earnings –
    By the way better not approach Geoffrey about his picture until I have broken
it to him – I can't very well remove *that* one until I have given him another. Do
you see? I will write to him tonight. He might be horribly huffy – You never can
tell – And the last thing I would do would be to hurt his feelings. They have been
such firm supporters (in the practical way) ever since I have known them – I have
a great regard & affection for the Family –

Look carefully at the *Floral* group at the Bloomsbury Gallery – Geoffrey, himself, nearly as possible bought the pale fawnish one – with vase on table etc –

This morning I do not go down to Mill – I am now waiting for Cedric to take me to see some villages – wh. may suit me –

Yes the Mill is oppressive. But the big Studio & quietness are very helpful to me for the time being while I am finishing my winter's work – I shall move on in about a fortnight or so if I can fix up in a more alluring spot – I *have* to keep calm & broody while I am painting –

Miss Selby, a friend you must one day meet, is coming this week end & then another friend for a week. So I must not budge from here yet – I have to come to town next week with work for Mr. Howell – I'll let you know which day & perhaps you will let me come to Flat & see you. . . .

[420] To Lucy Wertheim, c.9 July 1930

White Horse Hotel, E. Bergholt, Suffolk. Wed

Dearest Luce

. . . . [I] am glad of the quiet & deep peace of this place but anywhere in England is unsympathetic & difficult for an artist – The sea of green everywhere – The red brick – & the stoney paths & stoney stares of the villagers – Oh Lord! But the big free Studio at the Mill is a real catch – & worth a lot to me – I quite like the mile walk thro' fields & over stiles to & fro night & morning – it tunes one up & puts one in the mood – for work – so good for the health also –

I shall crock up altogether unless I lead a dead quiet life – I am so nervey – & excitable – & painting gets more & more difficult the longer one lives in England –

So Lett has at last seen the great little gallery!

Things appear to be shaping well – Splendid – They should in your clever hands – I hope I'll have something really choice for your opening – we must all give our best – as you intend doing yr. best by us Mrs. Wertheim dear. Come down & see me whenever you feel like a day off in the country. But it is rather a hole to get to. . . .

[421] To Lucy Wertheim, c.3 August 1930

White Horse. Sunday

My Dearest Luce

The voluminous letter has come – duly read, noted, and sent on, as you request, to Higham – I have not seen the boys for some time – nor heard from them – but one day Arthur Elton came over to sit for his portrait, returning the next day to finish it – quite a success I think. I know nothing of Cedric's plans or intentions – I hope he is feeling more cheerful than I am over this horrible weather. . . . I have abandoned my plan of coming to London just yet & am sending up my Water Colours by a friend. It is a tiring journey from here & breaks a good vein of work. The Luxury of *you* & the *Flat* must be postponed –

. . . . What is your opening Show to consist of . . . . You can count on 6 fresh paintings from me – let me know when you want them. The frames may stump me rather – as I have none in hand – suitable –

About the colour of yr. Gallery – I think I would follow the advice you quote & keep it white. My preference is always white – & in the winter months it will hold the maximum of light . . . .

Oh! Geoffrey writes to say he is off abroad – & will render you the picture if required in Sept on his return. . . .

Mrs Wertheim visited FH, Cedric Morris and Lett Haines early in August 1930.

[422] To Lucy Wertheim, c.4 August 1930
White Horse Hotel, E. Bergholt, Suffolk. Monday night

Very Dearest Luce

. . . . I loved seeing you – you courageous & go ahead & vital thing!

I am glad you now know my background. . . .

After you had left we sat in the Tea Garden and talked about your Gallery – particularly the naming of it – which we regard of the *first* importance –

To avoid giving the cynical critics a handle to lay hold on is a great point –

We unanimously agreed to ask you as a great favour to reconsider the name of "Young Masters" & call yr. gallery simply The *Wertheim* Gallery –

To begin with yr. main planks & supports (say Cedric – Matthew Smith, Kit Wood[27] – A Robinson? Sickert & myself *specially myself* are mature in art as in years – How can I pass as a young master? See how the critics get you. Think of Wilenski touching it off in his biting way. It will kill the gallery – as it killed the "Young Painters" by ridicule –

Whereas "Wertheim" is a great name in the world of affairs & wealth. It

[27] Lucy Wertheim was particularly interested in discovering and exhibiting the work of young painters. She was a passionate admirer of Christopher Wood (1901-30), the precociously gifted English painter, who, while studying earlier at the Académie Julian, had enjoyed the friendship of Picasso and Cocteau. He had worked with Ben and Winifred Nicholson in Cornwall, 1926-8, discovering the amateur painter Alfred Wallis and, like the Nicholsons, incorporating into his own work characteristics of this genuinely naive painter. The primitivism in the work of these English artists was one of the many influences absorbed by FH.

implies wealthy backing & patronage & *strength*. It is a name that *talks* –

Do consider it Darling Luce. These men do know what they are talking about – It is their world you know. . . .

On 5 August FH wrote to Arthur Howell to arrange a meeting in London. Arthur Howell was on holiday and his secretary replied.

[423] To Miss Harmston, 8 August 1930

Flatford Mill, E. Bergholt, Suffolk. Aug 8th.

Dear Miss Harmston

Thank you so much for writing. I had imagined *you* on holiday, you indomitable person, who never rests nor plays – I don't know how you last out as you do, without visible signs of wear & tear – it is wonderful. Seriously tho' I do hope you are taking a proper holiday . . . before the winter comes . . . .

Perhaps I had better wait till Mr. Howell's return – I am bringing canvases, as well as Water Colours, to show him – & shall motor up. Please send me a pc saying which day I can see him . . . .

It will be better *not* to break my good painting spell

I am in good vein – Such deep peace & I really am in tune with my surroundings – no interruptions, not even a fly settles on me – but sometimes a butterfly –

[424] To Lucy Wertheim, 8 August 1930

Flatford Mill, E. Bergholt, Suffolk. Sat: 8th. Aug.

My Dearest Luce

So *very* glad to hear all about your latest news – Lett came during the day & I read most of it to him. He was also very pleased that things are going so well, & about Matthew Smiths interest. . . . He is quite his old self again & his plumage smoothed down – you two mustn't ruffle up again! . . .

I don't think you need be anxious about the 6 new canvases I am sending you for yr. Show – which I should like you to sell on commission. From now onwards I must keep up my prices. This present line of work is *good* – Lett is much impressed & thinks they will "go". I have got well into the spirit of the place & it is yielding up riches – undreamed of, at first sight – I am glad I have stayed & got so into rapport with the country. . . .

The Note you send me is at once converted into the necessary dope ie: paint – *very* gratefully . . . . It is *grist* to my Mill & no mistake – & the flour –

flower – of the raw grain – will I hope emerge in due course at the Wertheim Gallery. . . .

If you are in Town at the end of Aug: do let me know – I am then coming to London to see Mr. Howell . . . . As I am motoring up I may bring you a few canvases – Don't mention the matter to H—ll (which sounds like H-ll –) The 2 Drawings at Store St I'll let you have for £2-10 each £5 the two – only *don't sell them cheap – Force up the price.* The money is of great assistance to me *now* when I am in a productive & fertile mood. The stream is bound to dry up – temporarily – but while it lasts it is profitable to encourage it – it pays. You can have the big oil for the £10 you have already paid me – in place of Geoffrey's picture, if you prefer it. It is a good one & Matthew Smith spoke well of it – In his bloodless way he was quite excited. The subjects I am doing here are quite different. . . .

This is about enough for the moment dear Luce – I must get down to my Mill – The weather erratic & stormy – but there are lovely bits in between. . . .

[425] To Lucy Wertheim, c.9 August 1930

White Horse Hotel, E. Bergholt, Suffolk. Sunday

My Dearest Luce

Two good letters from you unanswered – I am working hard – which makes me rather tired cross & stupid. Rural England *is* depressing – when you are by yourself. My brain reels trying to reduce this exuberant Nature to pictorial form – it is so gross green & lush – I think I shall have to make for France if I am to get any work. Here I feel lost in a deadening sea of growth –

The large cool Studio is a joy & I have been able to complete my unfinished canvases in peace – But the spirit of the place is disturbed & outraged by the stream of trippers pouring in in their thousands. . . .

The Gorers' place is very interesting isn't it? Geoffrey has a very intelligent outlook on art and on the whole makes very few mistakes – I am glad you have made their acquaintance. They are a vital family. . . .

On 21 August 1930 Christopher Wood fell under an express train at Salisbury station. This was generally considered to be suicide, perhaps related to Wood's taking of opium, a habit he had developed in Paris during his friendship with Cocteau. In Adventure in Art, *p.18, Mrs Wertheim described how she had visited Wood in Paris in July 1930 to buy pictures from him for her gallery. In a distraught moment, he had threatened to shoot himself unless she provided him with an annual income of £1200. His violent death so soon afterwards was most distressing for her.*

[426] To Lucy Wertheim, 27 August 1930

The Mill. Wed 27th.

Luce Dearest

A line in great haste to say that I am coming up on *Monday* 1st. Sept to see Mr. Howell . . . and propose stopping 1 night at the Flat if you can have me. . . . Lett is motoring me & I hope will be in *a proper mood* after the week end. This heat may give him rather a thirst! You see I cherish no illusions about my men pals – nor will I glorify what appears to me nothing but weakness & slack morality. Some things make me *sick* – and I am not afraid to say so. You have your boy Michael to think of & set a standard for – therefore I am relieved to hear in this mornings letter that you now look at the Kit affair in its true proportion –

Of course you are shocked & sorry – who isn't? But what *can* be said in defence or justification? Dont you think he has let you all down? His Mother, his Art, his Group, his Dealer? His friends and you? who backed him. Life was jolly nice to Kit – He had no troubles but of his own making. Thats that. There is nothing more to be said alas. Sob-stuff is out of place –

What must Michael think if you defend such things. Drugs are beastly & abominable – & lead to *depths* of degradation – physical & spiritual. He has not had strength or staying power so his Doom & Destiny have descended on him prematurely –

No – go ahead with his Show & do *your best out of it.* It is a great opportunity for Showmanship – but *No Sentiment* for God's Sake in yr. Gallery. Keep it on a hard business basis of merit & worth. Art will go on just the same without Kit's help – but it is a pity he has gone & left us –

I am not a hard woman dear Luce. But I do hate to hear of your needless suffering – at a moment when you need all yr. fighting strength for what is ahead of you. . . .

Throughout the summer, FH was working on both oils and watercolours, although her contract with Howell covered only watercolours. On 14 September she wrote accepting Howell's suggestion that they mount a watercolour exhibition before attempting to launch her oil paintings. She suggested he lend Mrs Wertheim the oil paintings for her opening exhibition on 7 October 1930.

[427] To Lucy Wertheim, c.17 September 1930.

[Flatford Mill] Wed. Eve

My Dearest Luce

The darling Robe Rose has come – too delicious –

How can you part with it? It is beyond my Dreams – I shall start vamping Suffolk in it –

It fits so well & I look proper smart in it – & shall feel worlds happier wearing it. . . .

It is a lovely lavish present & it makes me feel full of *sex allure*. . . .

Did you get caught in the storm? Don't forget to tell me what Howell says – Much love & blessings – Goodnight to you Frances

Howell decided to risk an exhibition that combined oils and watercolours, and, three weeks before the opening date, he presented FH with a contract. As with the water-colours, he would guarantee to buy an annual number of paintings. The price offered was £10 each. She was to decide whether to date the contract before or after the opening of the exhibition. Howell declared himself 'willing to take the risk of dating it before'.

[428] To Arthur Howell, 23 September 1930

[Flatford Mill] Tuesday evening

Dear Mr. Howell

I have just returned from the Pound, 7 p.m and found & read your letter of Sept 19th.

I am much too tired & confused by over much painting to reply to it tonight but will consider it carefully & let you have a reply within a very short time – I have brought back two, well finished open air still lifes (as you prompted) up to standard – you'll approve I think. . . .

Thank you very much for your letter & Contracts – I note date of show – in haste to catch post

About three days before the opening of the exhibition FH signed the contract, pre-selling the whole exhibition to Howell. She chose not to go to London for the opening on Thursday, 9 October, preferring to see the pictures quietly on the following Saturday. There were twenty-one pictures in the catalogue; the watercolours were priced between £12 and £15 and the oils between £30 and £45. To give FH a rest and a change, Lett Haines arranged for her to stay at St Osyth in a seaside cottage belonging to a friend of his.

[429] To Arthur Howell, 19 October 1930
Old Cottage, St. Osyth, Essex. Sunday.

Dear Mr. Howell,

I send you my new address – you will see I am in Essex, some 15 miles from Flatford – quite different country – as much Dutch as English – a good fifty-fifty mixture – level fields, winding estuary, a *real* water mill, tidal river mud flats, etc. I feel pleasantly anchored – I arrived yesterday – I have eaten a partridge – poached. The weather is perfect and I am sitting under a magnolia tree in the scorch of a blazing sun. I have been wretchedly tired and the victim of neuritis but I believe this place and the salt breezes will soon put me right. . . .

A little season of slacking won't do any harm.

I must look around for something fresh to which I can re-act – touch and see –

Are things still going well? I heard you had sold pretty nearly everything. It is wonderful. Something is really happening at last – and yet this, I feel, is only a half-way stage.

I do congratulate you –

I think you are a fine Producer –

I was much struck by the sense of unity & comprehensive pattern that you had achieved in the hanging. No one, I think, has ever before so successfully bracketed oils & water colours together in so satisfying a way. Every one I know seems impressed – & speaks highly of the effect you have so happily produced –

Well I consider that I am "made" and that my work has at last taken root – work must now start in earnest – & keep up the standard we have set for it. My very warm appreciation & thanks to you both for your generous backing & enthusiasm. You do seem to have spotted a winner – for which I am whole-heartedly glad. It is all such a ghastly risk – And the Times![28] It seems incredible that we have got away with it! Mr. Howell! Miss Harmston! We are a wonderful fine combine!

If I feel equal to it I shall be in Town on Wed: & shall look in some time to filch from you a little more of that £50 – I still am paying debts!
Very sincerely & gratefully
Frances Hodgkins.

. . . . By the way have you noticed the pictures are unsigned – I must see to that before they scatter.

[28] The review in *The Times* was enthusiastic: 'The exhibition . . . ought to confirm and extend the reputation of one of our most original artists.' (11 October 1930)

[430] To Arthur Howell, 3 November 1930

Old Cottage, St Osyth, Essex. Monday

Thank you for your letter, just come, with enclosures – Wednesday is the earliest I can come. Been under the weather, unable to leave the house & so on – very boring – No work – This place too lonely & remote – gets on the nerves – Have to do all my own work – wont do – doesnt pay – depression one of the deadliest sins –

What to do?

Where to go?

yrs. F. H.

[431] To Arthur Howell, 7 November 1930

Old Cottage, St Osyth, Essex, Clacton on Sea. Nov 7th.

Dear Mr. Howell

You have made me very happy by that more than inspired act of yours in paying the Skillen bill[29] it has been such a bogey to me – I do thank you from my heart – I already feel better in physical health, so much does cause & effect play havoc with one & the mind act on body –

You have made my path both smooth & pleasant – and I am grateful for that fine touch of imaginative generosity – prompt & practical – which has done it –

Now to work – No more malingering – I have fixed up to go to friends at Wilmington Sussex. They have a Farmhouse-cottage – warm cheery & congenial – I shall have a Studio in village. . . . This is only a line . . . to let you know what relief joy & comfort your thoughtful act has given me. . . .

[432] To Arthur Howell, 11 November 1930

St Osyth. Tuesday 11th.

Dear Mr. Howell

Thank you very much for letting me know about the Reading Cottage –

But it is this way with me

I simply cannot face living alone in *any* house at the present moment – I am much too nervy & below par – Having had so much of it in the past I know its horrors. . . .

Under the circumstances I think I do wisely to go to friends as a paying guest – at any rate for a month on trial . . . . I shall *not* have to eat my meals alone &

---

[29] For framing, an expense normally borne by the artist.

there will be pleasant things like books music, animals & such like – a nice cheery atmosphere, potentially productive of subjects – ideas & all that – I am much more likely to do the "work of my life" in such a setting – than on my own – one is prone to grow morbid living alone. . . .

[433] To Dorothy Selby, c.17 November 1930
Wise Follies, Wilmington, by Polgate, Sussex. Monday

My Dear Selby

I feel you must have given me up for lost. I have been wanting to get in touch with you so much – to have a talk & pick up threads – but somehow I have been feeling so utterly exhausted with a recurrence of the old trouble (that gastric curse) which has pretty generally made hay of my autumn plans & programme – it has forced on me rigid dieting & a quiet life – any effort reduced me to tears! I had made a considerable effort getting ready for my 2 Shows – when that was finished I cracked up – I kept right away from the Show, in fact have only twice been in London for the day within the last 2 months. I have a wardrobe of unanswered letters. And Howell expecting me to be doing the work of my life! Isn't it maddening to be let down by one's vile body?

But I am getting better – by degrees – and trying to make up leeway – and forget the horrible last 6 weeks. Briefly, I stayed on at the Old Mill rather too long – went from there end of October to Miss Judy Wogan's cottage at St Osyths nr. Clacton on Sea – lent me – in hopes it would brace me. So it did, nearly out of my skin – a darling place in summer but bleak & lonely this time of year – I moped & did no work & considered jumping off the pier at Clacton on Sea – but came down here instead, a week ago – & am staying on with my friends here for a few weeks longer. This village you may remember is Letts ancestral home – and I am staying with family friends of his – 2 girls who half farm a small property here – jolly good sorts – & cheery. It is a problem to know where to put oneself for the winter –

How are you both getting on – I have heard no news of you. One day I hope you will meet me & have lunch or tea with me – perhaps a Saturday –

You sent me a charming letter in October, which made me very happy – it was quite one of the nicest letters I received –

I was glad for Howell's sake the Show went well. He sold the house out – & more in reserve – Mrs. Wertheim also is doing well with the Water Colours of mine that she bought from Howell – So they are making a spot of money out of me!

How are you? Doing any painting? Working disgustingly hard I expect in the City –

Excuse this scrawl –

I felt I *must* write Wretch that I am –
Much love to you both
Frances –

[434] To Arthur Howell, 28 December 1930
12 Primrose Hill Rd. Sunday 9.30

I am just back from country & will call to see you Monday about 5 & discuss frames pictures etc – Have brought 2 canvases back[30] – not bad ones. Thank you *very much* for sending on letters. A happy New Year – yours in much haste
FH –

[435] To Arthur Howell, 14 February 1931
Hotel Moderne, Les Martigues, Bouches du Rhone, France. Feb 14th.

Dear Mr. Howell

This is where I am – in the self same Hotel with the self same people that I have known for years

Les Martigues is an old friend of mine – I find fresh things to paint on every visit –

Let me tell you that it is as cold here as in London –

Today is a blue day – like a cake of cobalt –

I am looking – Tomorrow I will paint –

Mr. Augustus John was here until a few days ago –

I stayed in Paris long enough to see some pictures – I saw some immaculate Matisses: a wall of them; each picture was painted with a different palette –

I stayed in Paris long enough to eat a perfect dejeuner chez Prunier oysters, langoustine – fois gras – seated on high stools at a Marble Bar – of Heaven – all very soulful & concentrated[31] –

Afterwards I saw the fag end of a memorial show of Pascin's work[32] – he who lately killed himself in a manner much more spectacular than did Christopher

---

[30] At the Seven and Five Society's 10th exhibition in January 1931 FH showed two oil paintings, *Pastoral* and *Berries and Laurel*. It is likely that these were the works referred to here. Since *Berries and Laurel* depicted vases from The Croft, Geoffrey Gorer's cottage at Bradford-on-Tone in Somerset, it can be assumed that FH had been staying there. This was probably her first visit: ownership of the cottage was transferred to Geoffrey Gorer on 14 July 1930. Geoffrey Gorer, writing to E. H. McCormick, 3 July 1969, stated, 'I only purchased the Croft in the autumn of 1930, and I think the first time that F.H. stopped there long enough to paint was in 1934.'

[31] E. H. McCormick suggests that FH was entertained by Maurice Garnier during this visit to Paris.

[32] Jules Pascin (1885-1930), Bulgarian born painter who settled in Paris. He was noted for his erotic nudes of young girls and studies of the low life world of brothels and bars.

Wood – a short life and a long death – opening his veins and slowly bleeding to death whilst writing to his wife & friends. He left ½ his pictures to wife and ½ to friend. I met the friend a most lovely thing – and I saw the work of the wife – which impressed me more than did the work of her neurasthenic husband – Hermine Davide[33] is her name. It is the sort of style you would like – Watch for it –

Later I saw a very exciting show of Picasso – Braque – Matisse etc & met some exciting looking people – 1 Princess – 1 Ambassador – who being a Diplomat enjoyed talking – I enjoyed listening to him explaining what Picasso really meant. The Princess tapped him on the arm & said "You know an artist *never* explains" –

I murmured that I thought Leger was only an inspired plumber – un plombier inspiré – and the mot went round the room – my little moment –

By the way Garnier is going to write & ask Dufy if he will arrange a Water Colour Show with you – Garnier will let you know result –

He was very pleased at you keeping one of his Drawings –

Dufy of course produces masses of work – so there is every chance of a Show. Some nasty person called his work "painted riband" which is rubbish. It is slick – but it is not all that slick –

How have the young Moderns taken your present Show.[34] It makes many of them look like a damp squib doesn't it? We won't mention names. It should do a lot of good & clear the air – open windows etc – we badly need some of that ringing clarity of colour into our work – plus du lyricisme –

I do hope you & Mr. Wilenski have backed a winner –

Between now & the end of the show I hope you will have made some sales & told the world

Now please dont bother to answer this –

I'll be sending you along something presently – in about 2 weeks –

I am writing this in a café with the café pen. Hope you can read it. . . .

[436] TO MISS HARMSTON, 14 APRIL 1931
Hotel Moderne, Martigues, Bu du Rh., France. April 14th

Dear Miss Harmston

Thank you very much for your very nice letter – you do write a good letter – as you speak. . . .

I have just posted 4 Pencil Drawings – figure subjects – which I beg you please

[33] Hermine David (1886-1971), a painter, printmaker and celebrated illustrator.
[34] Of Camille Bombois, a French neo-primitive painter.

to un-pack very carefully as they are *not fixed*[35]– I rather hope Mr. Howell will decide to frame them, instead of putting them loose into a portfolio. They are more in the way of being finished *pictures* than just drawings – & would gain doubly by a frame. I have other water colours – semi-ready – & will post them on to you presently. In a day or so I am going from here into the mountains for a month or so before returning to England. I hope to work in oils – unless I hear expressly from Mr. Howell that he prefers me to do more water colours – which let me say, in passing, take as much time, if not more than painting a canvas! Result, charming (?) but hardly so important. . . .

Towards the end of April FH moved to St Tropez from where, during the next six weeks, she posted two batches of watercolours to the St George's Gallery.

[437] TO ARTHUR HOWELL, 8 JUNE 1931

Hotel Sube, St Tropez, Var, France. June 8th.

Dear Mr. Howell

I shall soon be back again, with the bulk of my work to show you. It is now going thro' the uncertainties of finishing touches – no easy path as you know. I have bundles of work & am bristling to finish it – before the weather grows hotter than I can bear. This is a wonderfully nice place – growing hotter & more Bohemian every day – really amusing to paint

I must confess that I have not been working very smoothly or feeling very alive about my work but my present things strike me as more satisfactory: mostly painted directly on the spot out of doors. Speed is no longer my strong point: Eyesight & age are against it: But I am doing my best & taking my own time as I know you prefer me to do. There is no other way – *now*

I hope to "dump" my work in your Gallery very shortly & to leave the merchandising of it in your good hands – I look forward to hearing your opinion. I have met several people who say they want to buy a Water Colour – I have told them to wait till my next show. . . .

I am keen to hear how you have done with Lett's work – I hope really well – and that both of you are tasting the sweets of success – I should like to see him come in to his own & be up & doing. He should have pretty bright hopes – providing he works – most truly he is an artist –

---

[35] A protective coating, generally with a resin base, is sprayed onto pencil drawings to preserve them and prevent smudging and soiling.

[438] To Dorothy Selby, 25 June 1931

Sube Hotel, St Tropez, Var. 25 June

My Dear Selby

I think it is most awfully nice of you to write me the news – a long letter from you is a real gift. How true it is that *really* busy people always find time to write. . . .

. . . . Thanks for cuttings – especially the Lawrence one – wh. interested me most. Old Rutter is *too* prosy – "Mutter" would be nearer the mark. Tatlock[36] of the D.T. knows a lot more than he writes – or dares to write. Fancy Howell taking up his pen. No I have not seen what he said – I suppose you have not kept the D.T. of May 1st?[37] I have written to the Gallery to ask him to send it – but will he?. . .

I am glad Lett did well – and that you liked his things. He should be encouraged – clever Pig –

I do hope St. George's will come thro' this crisis – I can't help feeling anxious. I send him work from here each month – & very hard work I find it. Inspiration is not a faculty to be tapped at will – & sometimes my work proves my point I fear.

But this last batch of a dozen drawings is good I think. Definitely it is summer weather now and one is at ones best. The air is thick with artists – mostly American – Swedish & Russian, Rumanian – not any English – or many French as far as one can see –

St Tropez is very attractive – but to be avoided in July – August . . . . Already the Hotels are packed – Such types – The young & goodlooking approaching as near Nudism as they dare – wh. is pretty near. Lucky for me I have re-found an old friend[38] & her husband who have a villa here – with a jolly garden next door to Signac's villa. She is very keen on painting in an amateur way & arranges & collects still life & flowers for me wh. we do in the cool garden –

I spend most of my day up there. On Sundays we take lunch & spend the day in the Cork Forests – very shady & cool & select – not a soul in sight. . . .

. . . . What do you plan for your holiday? Is Barling joining on with you this year?. . . I intend stopping on as I am doing good work & life down here is simpler & cheaper than elsewhere . . . .

---

[36] R. R. Tatlock, art critic of the *Daily Telegraph*, later editor of *The Burlington Magazine*.

[37] In his article, 'Why Not Scrap the Art Committees?', Arthur Howell urged public galleries to buy contemporary art. Among neglected English painters he mentioned Sickert, Augustus John, Duncan Grant and Matthew Smith, and then cited Miss Frances Hodgkins, who 'held an exhibition in London last October, and sold everything. She is known to be one of our most original artists, and the public were told so at the time by the leading critics. But I think I am right in saying that up to now not a single one of her paintings is to be found in any of our public galleries. Yet she promises to be the finest painter England has produced.' *Daily Telegraph*, 1 May 1931.

[38] Maud Burge.

Jane Saunders (after she has de-janed herself from Hannah the Forlorn) wants to come & work with me but I can't take her on – I am too busy – & no longer equal to such a strain –

There is a Professor from Munich[39] here with a class of Americans & Swedes – who is making them stretch their brains. He is very able – and a good lecturer – young & nicelooking with a charming pyjama-ed American wife – I enclose his Prospectus. His principals are sound – even if one dislikes his sort of art. It may interest Barling – Perhaps you will send it on to her – as I have only 1 copy. Some of his pupils are very pretty & attractive. Some have begged me to give them Water Colour lessons after their course is finished –

No thank you. But I appreciate the compliment. . . .

There is no sign here of bad times – Every villa is taken. Not so in other Riviera places – where every second villa is empty. They give them to you for nothing if you happen to be young & good looking –

I have read a lot about the Five Year's Plan & heard it much discussed. (Duranti the D. Mail correspondent at Moscow is here now staying with red Emma Goldstein the Communist) Who can tell? This weeks Statesman says it is silly nonsense: anyway if it *does* succeed it will show us our systems are antiquated & want scrapping! Fancy forced Labour in England or France! Unthinkable. I have heard some people say they give it a year for *civil* war in *every* country. . . .

. . . . Pity you could not see the Picassos[40] –

Well I hope you will get some painting done this summer & make up leeway. . . .

On 24 June, upon the expiry of his lease in Hanover Square, Howell moved to temporary premises in 81 Gower Street. He wrote to FH on about 20 July informing her that he had made arrangements for the Lefevre Gallery to act as co-agents for her work in the meantime. He asked to see her. At this stage he was undecided about the future of his gallery.

[439] To Arthur Howell, 1 August 1931

St Tropez. August 1st. 31

My dear Mr. Howell

I am suffering from the effects of a really nasty cold – which explains why I

[39] Edmund Daniel Kinzinger, a teacher at the Hans Hofmann School for Modern Art in Munich. He taught the New Zealand-born painter Flora Scales who met FH at St Tropez at this time. Flora Scales's notebooks of Hofmann's theories were important in the early development of the New Zealand artists Toss Woollaston and Colin McCahon.

[40] The Lefevre Gallery held a thirty-year retrospective of Picasso's work in April 1931.

wired to you instead of replying by return to your letter – Which was a bombshell.
Now, happily, I am recovering after feeling at the dead end of everything –

Painting has been difficult – writing worse!

My impoverished brain simply can't get anything on to paper – I have been ordered rest & massage: with good results, and now I am definitely better & hope with luck to be on my way back by the end of the week –

But what a new world to which I am returning! I am feeling pretty sick at the news you have sent me. . . .

I am anxious for further news – I feel one of the family if I may say so –

Lefevres is Lefevres – and naturally I feel elated at the prospect of showing my work in that old powerful firm –

But I am a loser in other ways: I know it: And I drop a tear.

I do grieve sincerely at the going of St George's Gallery – as will many others –

I am bringing with me 8 canvases (size 15 figure French) I hope there will be a frame handy –

I am longing to show them to you – I hope they will appeal –

I shall be putting up at some small Bloomsbury Hotel & will call at 81 Gower St. sometime Monday or Tuesday. . . .

FH put off her return to London after learning that Howell was to go on holiday. She arrived about 20 August, settling first at 1 Gordon Street in Bloomsbury where Howell visited her and collected the work brought back from St Tropez. He was delighted with it. In October FH moved again, to a small studio in Fitzrovia but was driven out by the noise and found another nearby. She was working on oil paintings based on her 'Summer notes'.

[440] To William Hodgkins, 12 November 1931

6 Fitzroy St, London W.C.2. Nov: 12th.

My Dearest Willie

I have treated you rottenly over letters this year but you have no idea what a hectic year it has been. I seem to have been caught in a vicious circle. Of course everything is comparative and I am not the only one having very anxious times. By no means. When did I last write? April? an awful long time ago – I was in France. I stayed there till mid August, more or less in company with Maude & George Burge, who were, owing to bad times, economising (if it was not really so serious some of the richer of one's friends' economies would make one laugh) in one of the less fashionable of the Riviera resorts – St Tropez a famous artists place but now grown pretentious & expensive, tho' still very lovely. Let me see, that was the end of May when I fell in with them – I more or less persuaded them to take a villa which they did, inviting me to occupy the spare room, this however I did not do, but I used to work in their garden vineyard and on their shady Terrace. George is very game & sporting & an excellent manager – did the shopping gardening – and then quite suddenly took to doing quite good water colours in an amazing modern sort of way – making Maude's things look rather washed out – I gave them both "crits" but of course I had no time to take them on seriously as pupils. Later on a young German Professor of Painting turned up with a class & I lived to see both of them taking up art *seriously* & from a most advanced angle – marvellous wasnt it? George assured me it was all my fault, that my work made him dissatisfied with the old stuff. He certainly has much more talent & imagination than Maude. So I left them to it – and Maude tells me she is happier than she has been in years – which is cheering. Of course *now* they will be in the soup with the £1 down to 15/6. The poor dears had had to sell their nice home, motor cars etc – and were hoping to save money living quietly abroad until they had saved enough to go out to N.Z. & settle. But N.Z. is now out of the question. But now they have "found" art they don't so much mind. Well! What do you think of the goings on on this side of the world? It is as bad as may be and the out look is very black – but, on the whole, people are feeling less panicky since the Election . . . . I have had a bad scare & have had some horrid agitations just lately. In August my Dealer wired for me to return to London & confer – I found St George's Gallery closed *indefinitely* my contract still held but on reduced terms. I had to accept a cut – and still another one so now I am hardly earning my keep. Theoretically I am supposed to be in a very safe position – Mr. Howell wrote "You of all people need have no fear for the future" My work has been transferred to Lefevre – an old important Firm generally showing nothing but the best French British modern work. So I have risen in prestige at least. If all goes well I am to have a Show in the Spring – meanwhile I have to continue producing masterpieces (?) against all odds, very difficult & wearing. Most of my recent work is now on view at Lefevres – but whether it is selling or not I dont know. Also there have been Water Colour Shows starring FH which have done well considering the times. This week there is one at Cambridge. These are all held independently of me and are part of the publicity scheme. It no longer seems strange to see my name on sandwich boards FRANCES HODGKINS and others. In Bond St there is a Show case where 3 of my Drawings are shown against [an] Aluminium background very alluring & chic. If times were only normal I should be nicely well off – but as it is things are in a bad way – the picture business is all but at a standstill – many smaller Galleries have closed both in London & Paris – and we artists are in for a bad winter – London is full of Canadians & Americans – people who usually winter abroad – so the Hotels & boarding Houses are benefitting. There is the growing realisation that England is at the crossroads & that the next phase will be an International one: that this is the definite end to the old civilization as we know it – one hears open talk of revolution & chaos – there is talk talk talk, but precious little action on the part of the government – as yet. . . .

It is nice of you to suggest I should try a trip to NZ – there is not the faintest hope of it alas – I am glad you are enjoying your newfound liberty as much as you thought you would – you could never be bored – you possess the real secret of enjoyment – plus health. I got your 2 good letters, also paper with presentation ceremony & yr. speech – most interesting – I showed it to the Burges.

Now I must write a line to Issy. Her last letter was something like yours – a long list of sick & dying friends & acquaintances – very saddening. I keep fairly fit I am glad to say – hard work does not kill one – I hope I shall be spared further financial worries. I shall spend my Xmas with 2 married friends in Devon.[41] I am posting you Pops diary. No money for pewter & such like. Happiest Xmas to you all & hoping all are well

Love to Jean Mike & your dear old self Fanny.

At the end of November FH was informed by Arthur Howell that his gallery was to close and that he was negotiating with the Lefevre Gallery to take over the contract with her. According to his account, they had expressed reservations about some of the pictures he showed them and he urged FH to 'do something like those three pictures . . . with the white house in them', involving more landscape.[42]

[441] To Arthur Howell, c.10 December 1931
The Nook, Bodinnick by Fowey, Cornwall. Friday

Dear Mr. Howell

Please tell me if you are likely to be in Town over the week end as I propose sending up 3 Water Colours which I would like you to pass judgment on with a view to their going to Chicago on appro[43]. . . . It seems to me rather important that I should be represented in Chicago by my best work & through yours or the Lefevres courtesy

The alternative is through the Wertheim Gallery – & this I do not desire[44]. . . .

The weather here is soft grey & mild – I am embarking on landscape now – if only to show you I do not flout your wishes!

[41] Gertrude Crompton and her husband lived in Fowey in Cornwall, not Devon.
[42] *Four Vital Years*, pp.84-8.
[43] For the Century of Progress Exposition, better known as the Chicago World Fair, which opened in 1933.
[44] Lucy Wertheim was keen to take over FH's contract with Arthur Howell and there had been some negotiations between the two dealers. See *Four Vital Years*, p.90.

The 3 Drawings I propose sending you now are still life groups – I have to get eye & hand in in this very difficult light – oh! so very difficult. . . .
[Postscript] Did Miss Harmston get the cream all right?

[442] To Dorothy Selby, 21 December 1931

The Nook, Bodinnick-By-Fowey, Cornwall. Dec 21st.

My Dear Selby

A happy Christmas somewhere to you both and my love & thoughts for the New Year. . . .

I enclose you a picture of The "Nook" which is my temporary home. The large white house on the right belongs to Sir Gerald du Maurier which he uses as a stage setting only in the summer – But his rather beautiful son-daughter lives here, Daphne,[45] & is [a] rather disturbing feature in the extremely homely little village

She *will* wear male attire – very attractive but theatrical – wh. she is *not*, I believe, only merely literary. In my boredom I try to read her Cornish local books . . . .

I am working very hard – searching for subjects; bad light, cold hands – depression all the seven devils as usual –

My contract may end any moment.[46] The general position seems gloomy & mine in particular not much better. One bright patch – two Water Colours bought by the Contemporary Society, chosen by Col. Ivor Churchill recommended by Sir Michael Sadleir[47] –

Also a set of Water Colours invited to Chicago – selected by Tate Gallery –

I forget if I have written since I came down here – I stayed some days with my friend Gertrude Crompton at her house built on an exposed & very steep cliff – her Folly I call it – so bleak – winter – no trees – no flowers – no grass will grow. Why *do* very practical minded people with great souls loving all humanity build houses on remote & isolated windswept rocks? The storms are *too* awful – all windows are sealed. Do you remember you & Barling falling into a rocky Hotel by mistake – near Tréboul – well this is mild compared to it. So I searched round & found Bodinnick up a creek, over several ferries & *quite* ungettable after dark – & here I am. The Nook is neither of the "Rookery" or the "Cosy" sort but suits my needs – no other fool could stand it –

I expect to be back soon after New Year. . . .

---

[45] Daphne du Maurier (1907-89), author of *Rebecca* (1938) and other popular novels, as well as books of local history. She was the granddaughter of George du Maurier, author of *Trilby*.

[46] FH received payments from Arthur Howell through the Bank of New South Wales until 20 January 1932. (Letter from A. J. McNeill Reid to FH, 16 April 1932.)

[47] Michael Sadleir (1888-1957) was director of Constable publishing house, a bibliographer and novelist, author of *Fanny by Gaslight*.

It is too cold to work out of doors – Besides which the colour is so dark & sodden with damp. Bracken is bright red – black ships on the river[48]. . . .

[48] Bodinnick is on the river Fowey, just above the village of Fowey. Surprisingly large ships sail up the narrow river to pick up cargoes of china clay brought down from St Austells. Two such ships (as well as her landlady's parrot) appear in Hodgkins's *Wings Over Water* in the Leeds City Art Gallery.

PART FIFTEEN

1932-9

The Firm

In spite of the closure of the St George's Gallery, 1932 began well for Frances Hodgkins. She returned to London and in February exhibited six works with the Seven and Five Society. She met Duncan Macdonald of the Lefevre Gallery for the first time on 6 February and on 11 February was given a contract. For a guaranteed annual income of £200 (to be paid quarterly) she was to offer all paintings, oils and watercolours, to the Lefevre Gallery, who reserved the right to reject work they considered unsuitable. They would cover the cost of framing and pay £10 for oil paintings and £5 for watercolours until the sum of £200 had been reached. If they bought more than £200 worth, FH would receive, in addition to the contract price, half the profit made on the sale, but would bear the cost of framing herself. Lefevre shared the contract with the Leicester Galleries. Given that England was in the grip of the Depression, FH could be considered fortunate to have this contract and the financial security it offered. However, if she was to 'earn' her salary as she interpreted that obligation, the number of paintings required annually was unrealistic.

During this period FH made the last of her long continental journeys – to Ibiza, Spain and France – and also travelled constantly within Britain. As always her vision was renewed by a change of place, and though her letters emphasise the initial period of hesitation, the paintings that emerged are confident responses to each new environment. To oil, watercolour and various graphic media she now added gouache, and produced in this underrated medium some of her most interesting paintings.

Her relationship with the Seven and Five Society, with whom she exhibited 1929-34, provides a barometer of her artistic allegiances. As originally constituted the society welcomed a range of attitudes and this suited FH, whose strongest artistic need was the freedom to respond intuitively to the present moment. Under the chairmanship of Ben Nicholson, the society laid down in 1934 that only non-figurative work would henceforth be acceptable and FH resigned. The push towards the geometric abstraction favoured by Ben Nicholson went against her own inclinations. The 1935 exhibition of the Seven and Five Society was the first entirely abstract exhibition held in England. It was also the last exhibition of the Society. FH found a more sympathetic context within the 1940s resurgence of the romantic English landscape tradition. Partly a response to the threat of the war, this was a swing away from the internationalism of the avant garde during the first decades of the century. Typical of this swing was the career of the painter John Piper (1903-92), a member of the Seven and Five, who became a friend and supporter of FH at this time. After favouring abstraction, he returned emphatically to representation and, with his wife, the critic Myfanwy Evans, articulated the British neo-romantic position. In 1938, an unsuccessful attempt was made to revive the Seven and Five Society, with Piper urging the re-election of FH together with the younger painters Paul Nash, Graham Sutherland and Robert Medley. The other artists involved were Henry Moore, Winifred Nicholson, Ivon Hitchens and the ceramist W. Staite Murray.

In February 1932 FH returned to Cornwall. A vivid picture of her at this time is given by the painter Winifred Nicholson (1893-1981), who, with her three *children, stayed for a while at Par near Fowey: 'I took my father to see her ... and she gave us tea in a little funny dark Cornish room. My father was ... rather stiff and stern and English and generally didn't like painters very much ... but he admired her .... I remember we had sardines and Cornish cream and jam for tea – all mixed up. ... Afterwards on the way home he said she had a Shakespearian sense of humour. ... I had a funny pony-cart which I used to pack the children in and sometimes I went to see her. And sometimes she came to see me. There was a copper-mine in between on the way ... and she admired this copper-mine with the orange coloured earth cut away into funny queer bits and she said it reminded her of New Zealand and she loved it. ... We used to talk on these pony rides together and I had been having a certain amount of emotional difficulties just then [Ben Nicholson had left his family the previous autumn and gone to live with Barbara Hepworth], and she told me that all women had and that's why there were so few good women painters. But she said after one was sixty one could get clear of emotional relationships and the difficulties of making them work, then one could really settle down to painting. She felt she was free from them after sixty and detached from other human beings.'[1] FH liked Winifred Nicholson's work and continued to take an interest in it: 'I want ... to see Winifred's Show – & see what she has made of the modern problem, stood up to it, or ignored it.' (Letter to Duncan Macdonald, 24 June 1936.)*

[443] To Karl Hagedorn,[2] 6 March 1932

The Nook, Bodinnick-by-Fowey, Cornwall. 6-3-32

My Dear Karl

I found time, after I saw you, to look in at the "National" to see yr. drawings – and very good they are too – I spotted them at once, well hung & honoured as they should be. The person who can do work like that can do better still given the right mood & place & I see you going far on those lines. . . . I think you have got onto something very sound – even lovely later on when you decide on letting yourself "go". . . .

. . . . Bodinnick is limited – & I am here till I exhaust the mood. There have been some perfect days when I have spent 6 hours outside in the woods – sheer enjoyment –

Have just been invited by Tooth's to give them a show – how they all come round you when you have no need of their favours – It was nice seeing you both again – All luck   Love from F.H.

[1] Interview with June Opie, 1969.
[2] Karl Hagedorn RBA, RI (1889-1969) had met FH in about 1923 when she was dividing her time between Manchester and Burford. They met again in London after the Hagedorns moved there in 1927. A textile designer as well as a landscape painter, Hagedorn exhibited at the Royal Academy and at the New English Art Club in the 1930s.

Dorothy Selby joined FH in Cornwall for a fortnight's sketching holiday.

[444] To Dorothy Selby, c.25 May 1932
[Bodinnick] Wed morning. 8 A.M.

Now look here D.S. this simply won't do – You are really a dreadful woman – & if you were still here I would give you a good hard biff –

These are definitely not the times to scatter fivers about on stray mantlepieces – of course I love you for it – but you *must* take them back & bank them for our next holiday together. It is quite lovely of you to give them to me – & I know you understand me well enough not to be hurt – (please dont dare to be hurt) at my sending them back. You see I am *quite* safe for another year – & perhaps for ever – in any case I would like to know what I did to earn or deserve them while you were here – I purposely refrained from cutting in & offering advice – it was not the moment. Indeed it is I who owe you thanks a hundredfold – you do me more good by coming – that is thanks enough from you – than I can possibly tell you. It is not everyone who would care about a fortnight in the wilds with a vague & irritable Water Colourist like self – I simply loved having you & thank you for coming *and* staying. . . .

[445] To Dorothy Selby, c.29 May 1932
40 Belsize Park Gardens N.W.3. Sunday 8.30 p.m.

My Dear Dorothy

Just back from Cornwall – after all I stayed out the week – weather too good to leave – allowing me to get some 2 or 3 really nice things, also to finish my first batch in comfort. They are on the wall now – 11 of them – & I must confess look rather jollier than I imagined. The Hagedorns came in for a P.V. after I had lunched with them today – and were very complimentary – think them far away best work I have produced – let us hope my Dealers may agree. . . .

Thank you for your charming letter. I have spent quite a little while trying to see matters from your point of view – but with no success – indeed your argument hasn't a leg to stand upon. Quite frankly do you wish to deprive me of the great pleasure of asking you to share future holidays – I promise you I will tell you when I feel like accepting fees – but at present I *dont* feel like it, [n]or am even capable of helping you in the way you so kindly say I do. What you need more than anything is the time & opportunity to get at it – & keep at it till you have got it! This is one of the secrets. Besides these are levelling times – we are all in the same boat – but that is another side of the question & irrelevant. I thank you from my heart for your generous gift – & consideration for me. Take back the lucre &

come sketching again another time – *that* is your best way of thanking me . . . .

I am thinking of taking some motor bus rides into E. Anglia & seeing about a place for the summer. . . .

This is a marvel Flatlet – the whole house is electrically run – seems sur-charged with power – very high power – I feel rather un-canny – kettle boils as you put the plug in – bath ditto – everything bright clean & labour saving . . . .

[446] To Dorothy Selby, c.14 August 1932

[King's] Lynn, [Norfolk] Sunday

My Dear Dorothy

This place complete wash out – Won't do in any way – from our point of view – Hannah [Ritchie] admits she has made a mistake . . . depressing waste of mud flats on all sides – & flat flat landscape – a lifeless outlook. We have jogged round for 2 days & have decided against staying – she halfheartedly & *I* very emphatically – and are leaving Tuesday morning for Bridgnorth my old love. . . . I am tingling with impatience to get settled – & at work –

On reaching Bridgnorth I'll either wire you – or send you card to reach you Wed: morning – I hope to find rooms all together in the Town nr. river – & promise not to put you up a hill by yourself as last time. . . .

Till Thursday then – at Bridgnorth –

Love from Frances

The summer at Bridgnorth in Shropshire was as productive as the winter in Cornwall. The paintings were those of gardens by the river Severn like Pleasure Garden, Sabrina's Garden *and* Pleasure Boat, Bridgnorth. *On returning to London FH took a studio in Lambolle Road in Hampstead, within walking distance of the studios of Ben Nicholson, Barbara Hepworth and Henry Moore at The Mall Studios in Tasker Road. She then left London to spend the winter in Ibiza, possibly at the suggestion of Maurice Garnier.*

[447] To Karl Hagedorn, 3 January 1933

Hotel Balear, Ibiza, Balearic Islands. Jan 3rd

My dear Karl

Thank you very much for your cheery letter and very good wishes for the New Year. . . .

As for cursing yourself because you did not see me off I would like to know what more could you & Nelly have done for me that ghastly night than you did for me? No one alive could have prevented me from doing foolish things that day – the supreme act of folly was my travelling when I was so down & all to pieces – when I was at last on the IBIZA Boat I broke in agonised sobs & only Nelly's second pastille calmed a bad attack of hysteria – friends meeting me thought I was a very bad case indeed – but I quickly pulled round . . . . Naturally I am worried about the Studio but even under the present conditions I would rather be here in sunshine than alone in the Studio – it was getting me badly. The SHOW[3] is the THING – I must set London talking – they expect it of me – my Dealers – & it is a rotten bad thought to fill ones mind – but down here I forget all about it & think only of the jolly things I see round me & the awful urge to get at them. . . .

Now about the Studio – I think your suggestion a very sound one & am quite willing to act on it – in fact I instructed Ross to accept £60 – but am willing to let it go at £50 to get it off my hands –

It is very kind of you to say you'll act for me – I am very grateful. . . .

[448] To Dorothy Selby, 10 January 1933

Hotel Balear, Ibiza, Balearic Islands. 10th. Jany

My Dear Dorothy

At last I write – I have done lots of work – which means very few letters – days are getting cool and are very short. Your saucy yellow hanky was a delight – I love yellow – thank you so much – It looks so bold & full of life and fills me full of kick and makes the sun look like the moon. . . .

I am still reacting pleasantly to Ibiza in the painting way and find heaps to do – all very lovely I can hardly believe it. Weather much colder – but fine today – houses very cold & we seek bed – or the cafe in evenings – to keep warm – twice weekly a 6d. Cinema to help kill time – & keep us from dwelling on the badness of the food – its scarcity – the discomforts *of life – and how infinitely preferable in every way is life in London & what fools we were to come away & so on* you know how one goes on. . . .

---

[3] Planned for the spring of 1933, FH's first solo exhibition with the Lefevre Gallery, *New Watercolour Drawings*, eventually took place in October-November 1933. FH shared the gallery with Ben Nicholson and Barbara Hepworth and 32 watercolours were listed in the catalogue, the subjects drawn from Bridgnorth, Ibiza and Cornwall (*Four Vital Years*, p.118).

[449] To Karl Hagedorn, 29 January 1933
Hotel Balear, Ibiza, Balearic Islands, Spain. Sunday Jan 29th.

My Dear Karl

Best thanks for your letter & all the news . . . .

Awful turmoil here – climatic – freak storms – short & wild, lamb like intervals – then wild cat fury again high seas – no boats out – deluge of rain – all the time almond blossom bursting on the trees in spite of dirty looks from the skies – & now blue skies & warmth again – & we bask again – and forget

I send you P.V. ticket for 7 & 5 and hope you'll go if you can fit it in & it interests you – No new work from me.[4] Disgusted letters from Ben [Nicholson] – He writes he is making paintings – 8 in 4 days – ribbons of rubbish I should say – at that high speed. He is far from being divorced by his lawful wife on the contrary he has been spending Xmas with her in Paris & he writes of how much he loves being with her again – at the same time missing Barbara "more than he can say"

Well! Well.

I have got off my first batch of Aquerelles to Lefevre – they are mainly Cat & Dog subjects, something novel for me – I must say, in this clear ivory light every common object looks important & significant – I wonder what you would make of subjects here – things appear in stark simplicity minus all detail – nothing corked up (bouchée) or hidden as in grey, or brown light of the North. Of course, later on, this intense sun light will convert colour & form into absolute negation but at the moment there is complete lovlieness. The pale coloured flat roofed houses without windows give a blind restful feeling, of immense space. There is a special breed of Island dog which goes so well in the landscape – long legged fleet fawn & white hounds which really *look* & *are* dogs – not the inbred animal as we know it in England – something out of something else – but pure dog – doggey – unfriendly but not at all mauvais – and happily nearly always in good condition & cared for. I can say that of all the IBIZA animals – mules – horses – asses dogs cats & caged birds by the dozen – A kindly people I think –

It seems hard to remember that I recently lived in the Lambolle Rd. so completely do I feel absorbed into this setting – the one thing calculated to bring me down to Reality is Rent day . . . .

I hope a tenant for the Studio will soon materialise – strain being felt. . . . I have been drawing rather heavily on resources since I left but I shall soon be square and solvent again, and really quite affluent if the Studio quickly lets – No extras or temptations here – you can have a Vermouth for 2d.

---

[4] FH exhibited six works, oils and watercolours. The other exhibitors included Ivon Hitchens, Christopher Wood, Cedric Morris, Ben and Winifred Nicholson, David Jones, Edward Bawden, Henry Moore and Barbara Hepworth.

Last night we celebrated – for what I forget – on olives & Xeres wine at the least disreputable Bodegan & the wine Bill was exactly 7½. . . .

Nearly all foreigners here are Germans –

I met an elderly artist last night – German, who has lived here for 7 years, on £20 a quarter allowed him by his divorced Australian wife. He dresses well – smokes cigars – drinks good wine and seems to enjoy life & is looking out for & hoping to find an heiress of 33 who will marry him.

Another pair of Germans are a young couple the wife who looks like a boy & the husband who looks like a woman – been here also 7 years – he teaching a little of every language – In fact all the Germans I have met prefer to speak English among themselves – Isn't that strange?. . .

[450] To Dorothy Selby, 2 May 1933

Hotel Balear, Ibiza de May 2nd de 1933

My Dear Selby

You must wonder why I give no evidence of myself – in reply to the letters & papers & Press Notices which have poured in on me – thanks to your kindness. My very warmest thanks for them all –

My work has been pressing on me – I have been straining to complete contract work; not been too happy over it – got over tired: had to go away from here to other side of Island & get it off my mind! came back – same thing happened all over again & finally I have had to postpone my Show until Autumn. This has all been distressing me – of course I am in disgrace in St James's – & have caused some inconvenience – but there it is – I am in a very nervey depressed state & for the moment am not painting – But hope soon to get back my balance & sense of proportion – Fact is I live too close to my work. IBIZA is so *crowded* with refugee Jew Germans that there isnt a spare room for a Studio to be had in Town. IBIZA is the place to learn to speak German!

I have a smallish badly lit room where I paint & sleep – not ideal. . . .

I was so *very* sorry to hear about the cooks illness & know how distressed you must all be about it. . . . I feel so heartless not writing sooner – but truth to tell I have simply not felt equal to a letter –

Do please convey my sympathy & good wishes for her recovery to health to your butler – don't forget – My grammar has gone to pot but my heart beats true. . . .

Everyone here is hard up – Germans feverishly investing, buying, building. A war scare – air – tightening up of passports etc. . . . I was at Palma the other day to see oculist – saw the British Fleet – 70 ships strong. My hairdresser said nervously – "They may take these Islands as they "took" Gibraltar." Absurd isnt it?. . .

There are more writers (of all nationalty) than painters – I know a fair number of nice people whom I enjoy talking with – we meet in the cafés when we can – Swiss, Czechoslovakian Russian – Belge – young Eric Tattersall, very English & easily possessing the world's most perfect manners – He writes – but I think cooking is more in his line. Geoffrey Gorer & his mother are at Madrid & may come here. . . .

This is a poor letter – I am feeling rather rotten – & cant disguise the fact – I am picture-weary – Too much of it –

How lucky I am to have you as friend. . . .

[451] To Dorothy Selby, 5 May 1933

[Postcard] Ibiza

Sorry I wrote so gloomily yesterday – Had a bad fit of the blues – Brighter today.

Am going off for a week to St José, a tiny village on the N. side of the Island. . . . I shall rest & sun bathe. . . .

By mid-July 1933 FH was back in her Lambolle Road Studio.

[452] To Dorothy Selby, 3 September 1933

Studio, 7 Lambolle Rd, NW3. Sept 3rd.

My Dear Dorothy

I hope Mevagissey is turning out to be the goods & giving you some fun[5]. . . .

I am all alone in my Studio – that is with 2 deserted cats who share my fishbones – absolute stillness: I have really got down to work & have finished the bulk of it –

I have not seen a soul for days – Barbara [Hepworth] stole softly to the door this morning to ask me to supper tonight to meet Herbert Read Poet[6] – Ben is with Winifred –

On his return he & Barbara go to Dieppe there to meet Bracque & persuade him to have a Show in London –

---

[5] Dorothy Selby was on holiday in Cornwall with Elsie Barling.
[6] Herbert Read (1893-1968), poet and critic, author of *The Meaning of Art* (1931) and *Art Now* (1933). A friend of Moore, Hepworth and Nicholson during the 1930s, he was an important advocate for their ideas about abstraction. He was later involved with Unit One and one of the main organisers of the important 1936 International Surrealist Exhibition.

No chance of my joining you I fear – I have, as usual, only more so, no prospects. It is not likely I shall get a rise in salary until after Show –

Is Barling doing some nice work? Does she work in oils?

A shilling pot of Coverine & plenty of sand is about all the young modern requires nowadays – plus a wire pot cleaner for scraping purposes – Surface is the idea –

Has Barling read a translation of Ozenfant's book?[7]

He that is teacher of painting at this newly formed Mediterranean School near Nice. . . .

Thank you for your joint pc – I delayed writing till this urge to paint & finish had spent itself –

I have seen some silly films at my Hampstead Cinema – they amuse and rest me – but I have discovered one real actor – at last – Leslie Howard – and English – Watch out for him. He is an intellectual & most subtle actor – I really got a thrill – I hope he wont let me down. . . .

Havent heard how Hannah & her lady German doctor are getting along – Hope lady doctor hasnt eaten poor Hannah – Silence – one feels somehow that savagery must be latent in *all* Germans – seeing how they rally to that arch Savage Hitler –

Love to you both. . . .

[453] TO ARTHUR LETT HAINES, 28 NOVEMBER 1933
Studio, 7 Lambolle Rd, NW3 Tuesday

Dear Lett

The Lefevre Gallery is very willing that I should show 2 paintings[8] – will you call there tomorrow morning to choose them. . . .

[454] TO ARTHUR LETT HAINES, 11 DECEMBER 1933
Studio, 7 Lambolle Rd. NW3. Monday

My Dear Lett

I am most grieved to hurt you: this you must believe, but quite definitely I wish

---

[7] *Foundations of Modern Art,* 1931. Amédée Ozenfant was associated with Le Corbusier in the development of a post-cubist doctrine known as purism, which rigidly excluded ornamentation.

[8] Lett Haines was organising an exhibition of contemporary British art at the Anglo German Club in mid-December. It was hoped that an exhibition of contemporary German art would follow. The exhibitors included Edward Burra, Vera Cuningham, J. D. Fergusson, Mark Gertler, Charles Ginner, Barbara Hepworth, Augustus John, Henry Moore, Cedric Morris, Paul and John Nash, C. R. W. Nevinson, Ben Nicholson, Stanley Spencer, Matthew Smith and Edward Wadsworth. Duncan Grant and Epstein declined the invitation on political grounds. FH was invited to exhibit.

to withdraw my support from your Exhibition for this clear reason that I do not wish to identify myself with a movement aimed at benefitting English art & artists at a moment when such atrocious cruelty & hardship has been shown to Germany's own cultured classes

I saw for myself, in Spain this year, the sufferings & privation of exiled artists – it shocked me profoundly –

I blame myself for not getting more exact information & facts from you when we met – it satisfied me to know that the Contemporary Art Society was backing the enterprise and, more particularly that *you* were in charge of the selection of pictures and *naturally*, of *course* I was with you – I am sorry Lett – I cannot go against my conscience –

I am sending you a wire – this is to confirm it

In haste

Love from Frances

[455] To Duncan Macdonald, 28 February 1934

Studio. Wed: Evening

Dear Mr. Macdonald

I will turn up at the Gallery Friday morning – *honest Injun* complete with canvasses –

Please send both boys, if you can spare them, round about 10.30 or so – then no need for taxi as you say –

I am contrite being so disappointing but am feeling terribly under the weather & temperamental

It will be a great relief to talk over the canvasses with you

It sounds most terribly attractive meeting Rebecca West at your Flat at luncheon[9] – but I simply *cannot* promise to come feeling as I do at my very lowest ebb of intelligence. . . .

[456] To Duncan Macdonald, 2 March 1934

Studio [7 Lambolle Rd, NW3] Friday 8AM

Dear Mr. Macdonald

It pains me *extremely* to break my word to you about coming down this morning – but I *must* have a few more quiet hours to finish my canvasses – I find that working yesterday in artificial light I got too much blue in my colour – so am

[9] Rebecca West and her son Anthony had bought a watercolour by FH. The other luncheon guest also owned a work. The luncheon was therefore something of a business occasion and FH had never enjoyed this side of the artist's life.

now at work putting it right – I shall serve you much better by bringing you work you can be proud of, rather not ashamed of, than by keeping a charming rendezvous for lunch for which definitely I am in the wrong key – my mind is stuck on my work. Dont be angry with me, poor old Mother Frances is doing her best for *you* & incidentally for herself –

I send you 2 canvasses to go on with – the rest will follow – as sure as tomorrow's Sun will rise – even before. The work is good – I know it – but I find I have been working too much under the cursed blue light – & colour has got a trifle heavy – Hence the apparent procrastination –

I know you will see my point –

I simply *hate* failing you –

I shall ring up for boy the very moment I am ready – I *must* not make date or hour – it baulks me – I am that sort of idiot –

Yours Frances H

After exhibiting with the Seven and Five Society in March 1934 (seven works) FH gave up her Hampstead studio and moved first to Lanteglos near Fowey in Cornwall and then to Somerset.

[457] To Duncan Macdonald, c.1 July 1934

The Croft, Bradford on Tone, Taunton, Somerset.

Dear Mr. Macdonald

Shall I find you still in London when I return to Town in about a weeks time from now?

I do very much hope so – I have a lot of work for you to cast an eye over – a kindly eye please –

I feel I cannot bear any more of the country –

I have worked – till I stopped working – not so much inspired as conscientiously gouging subjects out of, first, Cornwall & now Somerset

I am in Somerset not so much for Somerset's sake as for the good reason that Mrs. Gorer offered me the use of this cottage while Geoffrey was abroad

It was rather a godsend. It has helped me to save pennies. The house keeper[10] has the Billionaire's Standard of provisioning – or I might be saving many more –

I have had a deadly – frightful – time since end of March – cursed with an unperceiving eye and unresponsive English landscape – sheer bad luck – I have been many times on the verge of ordering in coffin from the village wheelwright.

---

[10] Mrs Annie Coggan was the wife of a neighbouring farmer who helped to look after the cottage.

Comical little dramas!

How absurd they are –

I hope you wont find my work too dull – I am not Exhibitionist –

Cross patch was what you called me – very apt then – but no longer applies. . . .

[458] To DUNCAN MACDONALD, 10 JULY 1934

The Croft, Bradford on Tone, Taunton, Somerset. 10th July

Dear Mr. Macdonald

What a very nice letter – thank you so very much – nice royal letter. . . . It made me feel I could do anything from 1-100 canvasses after reading it. . . . Can I say more?

It is difficult for me to explain away to you in mere words how grateful I am to you & Lily for extending to me such a real & understanding friendship –

. . . . Sympathy can be both whip & spur. Up went my spirits like a red baloon and I came to life again just as I was practically buried . . . .

I shall be very glad to see you all again – I must see the Braques –

My days here are not too sadly numbered. Might you be at the Gallery on Thursday [July] 20th? if I called with some of my work – I have quite a little mound of canvasses to overwhelm you –

I have been eaten alive by the too tedious character of this country – so backless – formless. Doubtless there is a right spot if only I could strike it –

I go out into the fields every day, among the red cattle, strike an attitude and paint a composite picture – a sort of wish fulfillment of a picture – I have a fond hope you will like some, if not more of them –

Water Colours did you say? Hardly – There has been a drought – But I hope to do some in September in a more fecund spot –

It gave me great pleasure to hear you had presented an FH canvas to the Hon Margaret Thesiger – Which can it be I wonder?. . .

FH was back in London in the middle of July and worked in at least two studios before once again taking refuge in the country, this time at the village of Corfe Castle in Dorset, where her friend from St Ives days, the potter Amy Krauss, had settled. This visit heralds a connection with Dorset that was to last for the rest of FH's life. Corfe Castle is situated in the area known as the Isle of Purbeck, not in fact an island, but the peninsula that forms the southeast corner of Dorset, surrounded on two sides by the English Channel and on the third by Poole Harbour. Corfe Castle is a historic site, the ruins of the ancient castle rearing up on the hill immediately behind the small village, a dramatic landmark that became a motif in several later paintings.

[459] To A. J. McNeill Reid,[11] 20 December 1934

Highlands, Corfe Castle, Dorset. Dec 20th. 34

Dear Mr. Reid

I cannot give myself the pleasure of a visit to The Gallery as, actually, I am at Corfe Castle Dorset so this is to convey the good wishes of the Season and my most cordial greetings to yourself & Dr. Honeyman – Mr. Macdonald I gather being still in Canada –

I had hoped to send you some work to herald this letter – but now it is the other way about –

It seems a long gap since I sent you anything and you have heard nothing from me for so long my silence & absence must be becoming suspicious – I slipped out of London during one of the fog intervals without a word to say whither I had flown

I was feeling very much under the weather both physically & otherwise but have picked up wonderfully since coming here and am now doing quite good work under the spell of the place & general atmosphere of calm & simplicity: boredom, of course for anyone but a fool artist waiting believingly for inspiration

Corfe cannot in any way be called stimulating –

I could leave it without regret

But I am making it 'do' –

And marking time till we get some weather worth calling good weather when I can get about & explore the neighbourhood. I have a Studio –

Mr. Francis Newberry,[12] now a very aged man has let me have the use of his – a large one time Chapel[13] – central heated – very convenient. The high walls are hung with canvasses of a long past Academic School – not so convenient –

A quaint galère to find myself in!

As soon as the holiday rush is over I shall send what Paintings (still lifes) and Water Colours I have finished – by carrier – and still later I shall hope to turn up in person –

I do better in every way by remaining out of London – I hope I am now in for a steady flow of work. . . .

[11] Senior Director of the Lefevre Gallery.
[12] Francis Newbery RWA (1855-1946), a genre painter, director of the Glasgow School of Art.
[13] An eighteenth-century Methodist chapel. John Wesley reputedly preached from the steps, because there were too many people to fit inside the building. The 'Wesleyan Steps' appear in later paintings of the courtyard outside the chapel.

[460] To A. J. McNeill Reid, 11 January 1935
Highlands, Corfe Castle, Dorset. Friday Jan 11 35

Dear Mr. Reid

Your letters caused some flutter in this dovecote – I was away with friends when your first one came, so, in case you were thinking of me as a person of no manners this morning I wired you a definite answer in favour of holding an immediate Show at the Leicester Galleries[14] –

Rather against my will be it said but of course I cannot protest if you and the Partners are built on my showing with Mr. Brown. . . .

As you say the pictures *must* come out of cold storage and quickly. . . .

I can't promise Water Colours – They are not my strong Suit – at the moment. If I want to make those nice ones you like I must escape abroad & hide away in some quiet corner – it is the only way I can do them –

I expect this is what I shall have to do in order to balance that terrific deficit which haunts me[15]. . . .

I am in danger of forgetting I am primarily a Water Colourist – if you want me at my best & *most profitable* & *prolific* encourage me to return to them. . . .

[461] To A. J. McNeill Reid, 12 March 1935
Highlands, Corfe Castle, Dorset. March 12th. 35

Dear Mr. Reid

. . . . Naturally I am concerned about the adverse balance you tell me of and which looks as if the profits of the Show had been nil – I hope this is not the case. . . .

I am very much in the dark as to how many pictures were sold. Halfway through the time I heard eight had gone and thought that this was not too terribly bad seeing that arch genius & Prince of Salesmen Mr. Macdonald was not in command –

Now what's to be done about it? I can only suggest that I make tracks for Spain & paint Water Colours[16]

These I can only do in the Sun –

---

[14] The exhibition, *Paintings and Water-colours by Frances Hodgkins*, opened 29 January and ran through February 1935. See *Four Vital Years*, p.119, for catalogue. The exhibition attracted very favourable critical comment, notably from Frank Rutter of the *Sunday Times*.

[15] 'You are, at the moment, owing us £280 for pictures which we have not yet selected.' Letter from A. J. McNeill Reid, 7 January 1935. Out of thirteen pictures sent in they selected only seven. FH had begun her contract with Lefevre's in arrears because of money owed to Arthur Howell.

[16] The exhibition had consisted primarily of oil paintings.

It seems a great pity that you should have qualms about the ultimate success of our efforts – since you have worked so hard to make my work known –

If one can judge by the critics the Show has been, at least, a reputational success

Don't you consider that you have put the roof on the house & nothing short of an earthquake should bring it down?

I hope to be in Town within a few days. . . . I am very anxious to hear what you & Mr. Macdonald have to say about future plans and I hope I won't get a shock –

Anyway it is good to hear you don't mean to 'drop me'. That would be finis

[462] To Dorothy Selby, c.March 1935

Highlands, Corfe Castle, Dorset. Wed

Dearest Dorothy

Just a quick line of thanks for your very welcome letter full of comfort for my soul & nice things I like to hear. . . .

The great Sickert's letter pinned on the wall of the Gallery helped cheer things up –

Did you see it when you went the second time? I had any amount of praise & a wonderful Press – but this will not help to make things easier for me if the sales were poor – I wonder how many really sold –

I now need a long long *rest* from painting – I am near breaking point. . . .

Elsie's 2 friends "Norman & David"[17] – I at last know their names – were here last week end – took Amy & self to a Film at Swanage – cheery friendly pair – I had no real talk with them. It was rather a scramble – how d'you do & goodbye. . . .

Absolutely no news – My brain congeals into lumps in this social atmosphere. . . .

I can't stay long in London – too expensive – but we'll meet –

FH moved back to London during the summer, taking a studio in Camden Town.

[17] Norman Notley (1891-1980) was a singing teacher, a former member of the English Singers, who specialised in the performance of English madrigals and contributed to the revival of interest in early English music. David Brynley, his companion, was also a member of the English Singers and wrote an autobiographical novel *Seth* in 1955. They owned a cottage in Corfe Castle and eventually retired to it.

[463] To Duncan Macdonald, 18 June 1935

No 2 Studio, 4 Albert St, NW1. June 18th. 35

Dear Mr. Macdonald –

This evening I have received a letter from my Banker giving me a sharp reminder that I am overdrawn to the extent of over £20

This can only mean that my quarterly salary has not been paid in by you. This is really too bad –

I cannot believe that you have made any alteration in the terms of the contract without first telling me

Can you reasonably expect me to preserve the state of mind conducive to good work under such circumstances?

I am now worrying about the payment of this overdraft and how I can go abroad and how I can do more and better work. I can only remind you that Mr. Reid himself realizes that happiness is the keynote of my best work, and yet you permit such things like this to happen: goodness knows I have been struggling enough lately without this additional worry

Naturally, of course, I dont wish to make a break with your Firm but I must work peacefully – and yet each time we meet you fill my mind with doubt, with the result that it takes days, sometimes weeks, to re-integrate my vision[18] –

This really won't do –

Surely it is better to assist me to extend my ability rather than fill my mind with useless doubt about my work – I paint as I do, because it is my point of view & it seems to me to be futile to go on discussing why I do this & that

What does need discussion is how & where I can get the necessary atmosphere in which to do plenty of good work. I must have something definite from you about what you want me to do –

I am feeling ill & distraught and have worked up a terrible neurosis over the whole business – my strength is dwindling & I feel I cannot go on any longer living "rough", keeping the Studio clean and myself decent, at the same time producing first class work for you!

My own firm opinion is that I need to go abroad & have much more time for Water Colours – I would like to be freer to do more Water Colours. It seems foolish to keep me bound to a contract demanding ten oils a year – Were it not for this I could have produced no end of good Water Colours which would surely be more profitable to you & myself –

I fancy I have set too high a standard for myself in oil and am finding it hard to live up to it. It also operates thus: that you dont like what I am doing –

I can't get the class of subject for Water Colours here in England – In addition,

---

[18] Duncan Macdonald had expressed reservations about some oil paintings he had been shown during a recent studio visit.

I can find abroad someone to look after me & supply meals for considerably less cost than in England – And there is the sunshine –

So please Mr. Macdonald write me your definite plans as to the future – Meanwhile I am finishing the paintings and will send them to the Gallery in a few days time

Most miserably & unhappily yours
Frances Hodgkins

A cheque for £50 was posted on 21 June. In a letter written the same day Duncan Macdonald explained that the cheque had been delayed because Miss Miller, the secretary, was under the impression there was some discussion about the contract pending between the Lefevre and Leicester Galleries. He defended himself against FH's criticism, protesting that she had imposed on herself the need for ten oil paintings and that she should not invite criticism of her work only to reject it when it was honestly given. Soon after, with amicable relations restored, FH paid her first visit to Wales, in the company of Cedric Morris. In mid-September, she set out for Spain, settling at Tossa de Mar, a village on the Costa Brava north of Barcelona, one of the many continental places which, first frequented by artists and writers, later became popular resorts. Like Ibiza, it was at this time a refuge for German people threatened by Nazism, the hotel being run by a German couple.

[464] To Rée Gorer,[19] 23 September 1935
Casa Steyer, Tossa de Mar, Gerona, Spain. Sept 23rd.

My dearest Rée

I got here on Tuesday 17th. nearly a week ago after a very bad crossing – one of the worst, battered & bruised but not ill & for a few days quite terribly seedy, bumps swollen arms ankles – high temperature and aches!! As well as Blisters! But I was *not* rushed to a Hospital at Barcelona as was another woman here –

Now I am quite recovered & normal & glad I've come –

Summer is still raging –

Tossa is not all it is painted. . . .

The food copious & wholly German – You never know when or where an anchovy or a pickle will crop up. . . .

One of the loveliest sights is the fishing boats lit by huge lamps, setting out after dark – their phantom shapes splashed in silver & blue like the fish they are going to dazzle. . . .

I was quite startled to find *how like* my picture (I mean *your* picture) is to this

[19] Mother of Geoffrey Gorer. She had helped finance FH's journey, choosing a picture in return.

place – Colour especially – I felt as tho' that last bit of painting had something both sound, sane, & SPAIN too, in it. . . .

> Lovingly Frances
> (transformed)

[465] To Dorothy Selby, late November 1935

> Casa Steyer, Tossa de mar, Gerona, Spain.

Dearest Dorothy

I enjoyed your good letter so much thanks so much for the catalogues & cuttings – most interesting and your comments as well – I am glad you are keeping well & fit & getting lots of exercise. My one means of keeping warm is by walking – I climb daily to a point on the hills above Tossa where one can see the Pyrenees 60 miles to the North. It is getting horribly cold here –

We still eat our midday meal outside – and the November wasps buzz round – it is very pleasant – But the snag is the long evenings. I have developed a sort of technique how to spend the evenings –

There is the BAR where one can herd with noisy Germans, one loud voice against another, but cheerful – painters & writers & so forth – I sometimes go –

Usually I sit near the stove in the small dining room unventilated but nice & warm where one can read the paper & gossip a spot

I paint during the morning – dividing my time inside & outside the Studio – this is the very charming part of a place like Tossa. So small & simple one can step into the old streets and have a look round – make a quick sketch & back to the Studio – repeating this little stunt perhaps 2-3 times during the morning – no fatigue – no complications –

I am mildly happy here as regards work. Subjects have come slowly – I still think it rather a middling sort of place . . . only very so-so for landscape – but a good deal better now that the River has come down from the mountains & is slowly filling up the dry riverbed. . . .

[466] To Rée Gorer, 7 December 1935

> Tossa de Mar, Gerona, Spain. Dec: 7th 35

My Dearest Rée

It seems years since I came to Spain or, since I corresponded with my friends. . . .

When I first came the country side did not appeal to me & I collected a lot of notes & sketches, casually, without bothering much about what *might* come through – it is only this last 6 weeks I have settled down to serious work . . . .

I hear from Mrs. Coggan that Geoffrey has left for the U.S – which is news. . . .

I have learnt the technique of Tossa and got a way of living that suits me, and am not being either under- or over fed – a room to paint in – I am not worrying – (NB, the spells of indigestion which I was born to are sad material things & you know how important they are but they don't kill me – they just fizzle out!)

The only *real* thing I grieve over is that middle age tho a happy time, lasts so short a time!

I have not been out of Tossa since I came. It is a terrible place to get away from. The motor bus leaves so early – 4.30AM – So I have not been to Barcelona – I funk the journey –

There is plenty of material here to paint. I am working up courage to start on figures – The life of the village is rich & dramatic. The little shops at night, enchanting like Dutch interiors gone Spanish – and the gilded altars in the village churches, vulgar & gaudy, but in the dim light, like a Rembrandt – one could go on, "likening" things for a long time – but I won't bore you. . . .

I am sending off 2 Water Colours of Tossa one for you & one for the Dear Geoffrey

I hope they will reach you before Christmas

[467] To Duncan Macdonald, 10 February 1936

[Postcard] Gerona, Spain.

Dear Mr. Macdonald

Have just posted from here parcel containing 9 Gouache Paintings to be followed by others in a few days time. . . .

[468] To Duncan Macdonald, c.15 February 1936

Casa Steyer, Tossa de Mar, Gerona, Spain.

My Dear Mr. Macdonald

I scribbled a line to you from Gerona when sending off my Paintings. Now I am back again in Tossa finishing a second lot ready to follow in a few days time

This will complete my winter's work. There will be a few I hope that will appeal to you. May I suggest that you await to see the full set, series, suite before making up your mind about them

You will see that I have put a large amount of Frances Hodgkins into them, even into the joyless marrows, and I do hope that you will not say this woman's work is not worth a penny a day to me. I am sure you will realise that I have had to adapt myself to local conditions & do the best I can – I defy *anyone* to paint lovingly & buoyantly through a Spanish winter, or be incited to imaginative heights

The Water Colours I intend for you are still in embryo, and may remain so for some long time yet if this cold weather continues. I have just returned from a few days motor trip & feel very fit & fresh & rested and almost recovered from the shock of that malicious abhorrent & hateful woman's (you wot of) Show of my early work – she is a d—d nuisance

It leaves me with a blank outlook as regards my real show with you for I suppose it wont do to have another one, at any rate till the Autumn.[20] What do you feel about it?

It must have annoyed you –

But why make a mountain out of a molehill – for she *is* a molehill – a selfassertive one

I shall be moving on from here at the end of the month on the long trail homewards – quite happy to leave Spain feeling as I do all the time that my spirit is out of place. There is a nice Spanish Proverb which says If you desire to bring back the wealth of the Indies you must take with you the wealth of the Indies – in other words nothing for nothing.

I was lucky to see a Picasso Show[21] in Barcelona (good) a most purifying experience. All my energy was torn from me – (Bad). . . .

It would make life look a little more complete if you write me a line

Upon her return to England FH went to stay with Amy Krauss in Corfe Castle.

[469] To Duncan Macdonald, 23 May 1936

Red Lane Cottage, Corfe Castle, Dorset. May 23rd. 36

My Dear Duncan

I am back again, at last, & very glad to be back. I came on here, non stop, with all my stuff . . . portfolio uncontrollably bulging –

Plenty of work ahead for me

I am looking for a quiet corner where I can settle down & chrystallize the after glow of my Spanish memories – before they grow dim –

. . . . On the whole I have had a good time in spite of a diabolically cold winter & political disturbances.[22] I have not done so badly I hope you'll agree

---

[20] Without consulting FH, Lucy Wertheim had mounted an exhibition in January 1936 of the oils and watercolours she had bought earlier either from FH herself or from Arthur Howell.

[21] Organised by ADLAN (Friends of New Art). Picasso's work had been suppressed during the dictatorship in the 1920s.

[22] The Spanish Civil War began with a military revolt in July 1936.

My one wish is for you to see them

At the moment I am looking them over, how one's eye changes in the Northern light . . . .

[470] To Rée Gorer, 20 August 1936

The Cottage, Llangennith, Swansea, [Wales] August 20th.

My Dearest Rée

At last I write, a long time in doing so do forgive me. It seemed as if I would never get here being held up in Dorset finishing work I brought out of London, finally on here, where I have been lost in a thick sea mist for 4 days out of 5, but at last today, joy, the sky is clear & cloudless and I can see the landscape nicely spaced below me fields farms chapels & a lovely 5 mile stretch of golden sand with Worm's Hd at one end – tremendous big views, more Cedric's kind than mine, still I see heaps of jolly things if I can walk for them & climb for them. . . .

I am expecting D Selby & presently we may move on to a tiny fishing village in Pembrokeshire, not far off, at present infested by trippers, but later on will suit us as being rather more of a pocket edition of what we want than this vast panorama, great as it is –

I saw Macdonald before leaving London – He rather hopes I'll be ready for a Show in the Autumn but leaves it to me to do my best. . . . He has Pricilla Preece[23] up his sleeve. Do you remember the shy girl painter sponsored by Roger Fry & D Grant? Shy? A pose – I saw her at the Gallery – most attractive creature. Well! she may look like a poem but she paints like a pudding – the suet variety – I think Macdonald may run our shows conjointly. . . .

That happy bright week I spent with you past like a dream –

[471] To Duncan Macdonald, c.12 November 1936

Red Lane Cottage, East Street, Corfe Castle, Dorset. Wednesday

My Dear Duncan

I feel happier now that I have sent you off some work for your approval . . . .

I am so very sorry to have kept you waiting for it so long do believe please how grateful I am to you for not jogging me or otherwise showing impatience, for I must admit that I have been quite a gruesome long time over these gouache things, the nasty stuff proving just a bit too difficult for my technical subtleties.

---

[23] Patricia Preece (1906-1971) had studied at the Slade and in 1936 had her first solo exhibition at the Lefevre Gallery, with a catalogue preface written by Duncan Grant. She became the second wife of Stanley Spencer.

Still I have enjoyed the experience wh. has had its value & I hope you won't think that I have wasted my time & your money –

I haven't forgotten that you want some larger sized oils and as soon as this last set of gouaches is finished I will get to work on them – that is next week –

As to a Show? Have you any plans – I must say the project of an early Spring Show wld. be a powerful stimulus.[24] Heaven knows I need one –

I am back here from Wales – the attraction here being the loan of a warmed Studio – Corfe is the place for quiet ones!

I have been working moderately hard, moderately successful in a landscape of steep valleys speedy rivers & castles looking like their own mountains but it takes a long long time to acquire a little idiom & rhythm in paint – if ever – Such nice gentle people I was among at Solva,[25] mostly bird watchers & such all terribly poor. . . .

Hoping to see you soon, I don't quite know when I shall be in London it would be a pity to disturb this good vein of work, energy & industry etc which is on me & wh. may happily result in your giving me a Show. I do hope so –

FH sent ten gouache paintings to Lefevre's soon after this.

[472] To Rée Gorer, 21 December 1936

Studio, West Street, Corfe Castle, Dorset. Dec: 21st. 36

My Dearest Rée

I hope this rather large sized Christmas card will not startle you & Geoffrey, who I devoutly hope will be by your side to support you when you receive this parcel

I have long wished to give you & Geoffrey one of my Gouache Paintings and at last I have selected two I like most & send them off in the hopes that they will please you as well if not they can be changed for others when I come to London next month . . . .

FH was troubled with bronchitis in January 1937 and found it difficult to work: 'I take out my brushes, look at the little brutes, give them an airing & put them away again – that is about the note of it.'[26] By February she was working on oil paintings,

[24] The exhibition *New Paintings and Water-colours* took place in October/November 1937.
[25] The fishing village in Pembrokeshire mentioned in the previous letter. Nearby was the village of Middle Mill, subject of several landscapes. Solva was like the Cornish fishing villages, tucked on slopes around an inlet, even more remote, being at the westernmost tip of Wales.
[26] Letter to Rée Gorer, 26 January 1936.

six of which were dispatched to the gallery before she sought a change of scene by moving in mid-March to the Gorers' house at Bradford-on-Tone. In April she spent a week with Lily Macdonald at her home in Conduit Street in the heart of the West End. Duncan Macdonald was away in Italy combining business with a sulphur cure for sciatica. After the visit FH fell ill again, this time with laryngitis, and was nursed for three weeks by Mrs Gorer at her house The Elms in Highgate. Towards the end of May FH moved to Worth Matravers, a tiny village high above the Channel three and a half miles south of Corfe. The nephew of Amy Krauss, Dr Peter Davis, wrote: 'I remember my aunt telling me that, when Frances Hodgkins really got going on painting, she would stick at it for several days, and no one was allowed to disturb her at Worth. Food was just left at the door.'[27]

[473] TO DUNCAN MACDONALD, 20 MAY 1937.

Sea View, Worth Matravers, Dorset. May 20th 37

My Dear Duncan

. . . . Has Duncan Grant spoken to you about 1 or 2 Paintings he would like me to send to a June-July Show of 15 Painters at Agnew's

The idea being that pictures should be chosen by the artist – which, of course is out of the question as regards myself. But I hope, at least, you will allow me to indicate the 2 I would wish to send should you be willing viz: the 2 square Welsh landscapes – painted this Spring[28] –

I feel it will be better to send something fresh that has not been already seen in London – Do you agree?

. . . . It was not encouraging to find my two pictures of an early vintage hanging on the landing of the 4th floor at The Peace Congress Exhn in Grosvenor St – Better not have sent –

But I *was* delighted to get your Roman postcard & to hear you were having such a princely time – but all too short

Are you better? I do hope so –

You must all be glad the Coronation is over – such an ant heap of red white & blue – people & vehicles – trying for the temper & glaring to the eye.

[474] TO RÉE GORER, 23 JULY 1937

Sea View, Worth Matravers, Dorset. Friday

My Dearest Rée

My Fate has fixed me in Worth. I hope you & Geoffrey will come here one day

---

[27] Letter to E. H. McCormick, 20 February 1967.

[28] Probably oil versions of the Middle Mill gouaches of 1936.

when I get fixed properly. Rather than continue a homeless wanderer I am settling down here in a somewhat negative mood, neither liking nor disliking the place, but thankful to have it & call it a home

I started life here with a Studio Shed in the garden & 1 room – now I have spread over ½ the Farmhouse & occupy quite a good little 3 roomed flat which I am decorating & simplifying to a labour saving level of bareness – with E[lectric] L[ight] & anthracite stove in the offing – to be installed before the winter –

The house is a one time Vicarage, of the starkest kind – It never has had one single debonair touch – It over looks the Channel. The mornings are very lovely & I want to paint even before I have finished breakfast. Sunsets splashed yellow & black – Not very exciting landscape –

It has been a very horrid time for weather hasnt it?

I am ashamed not writing before

I have been busy & ill by turns –

Some days I feel wonderful – then every five minutes life comes to bits & has to be put together again –

I continue the treatment – My weight is now down to 9 stone – all to the good – But I *appear* the same – which is not so good –

At the moment I am nearly buried under a great stack of canvasses I am retouching or repainting for my Show – I paint with fearful slowness – Eyes!

I am having 3 weeks in Brittany from the 29th. When I come back I shall hope to see you & Geoffrey either here or in London. . . .

[475] To Duncan Macdonald, 28 July 1937

Sea View, Worth Matravers, Dorset. July 28th.

My Dear Duncan

I feel nothing but abject words of apology can excuse the long delay in answering your most kind letter, as well as acknowledging receipt of the 2 cases which were slow in descending upon me as the S. Railway only delivers at Worth once weekly[29] –

However I have had the canvases unpacked, in my Studio for over a week and of course I should have lost no time in telling you that I think you did quite right to send them back

I am thankful to have the chance of scrapping some & re-painting others. Some I feel it is hardly worth while spending further time over representing as they do some of the essential ME of a particular mood and as such best left alone –

---

[29] Duncan Macdonald sent back some oil paintings 'because I cannot see them doing you a great deal of credit in a "one-man" Show'. (Letter to FH, 8 July 1937.)

I shall have to work my quickest ever if I am to be ready in time

This is only the briefest note to tell you that I am off to Brittany (Tréboul) tomorrow for 2-3 weeks. . . .

When I return about the 25th. I hope to spend a few days with the Wests.[30] I feel very much like going to see them they are indeed a charming & friendly couple and I am glad they have invited me. . . .

[476] TO DUNCAN MACDONALD, 20 SEPTEMBER 1937
                    Sea View, Worth Matravers, Dorset. Monday Sept: 20th. 37

My Dear Duncan

. . . . Dont please feel anxious about me and my work. We will be ready for you by the end of October . . . .

I think they look very well, 100% better than the ones you sent back to me. . . . they seem to me to look fresher & simpler & easy to look at with the paint going on very well, that is the paint going on as I like paint to go on – What more can the artist say?

I do think it is too much to expect the artist to corroborate tall statements as to her being "our finest painter" but still I shall have a very good try. . . .

I had the happiest long week end with the Wests & have painted 3 quite attractive canvases inspired by objects observed by me out of the corner of my subjective eye, when *really* looking for black berries – you'll see!

They are 2 delightful Dears Anthony & Kitty – I loved my visit to them. . . .

My love to you both & please go on believing in me

                    Frances

[477] TO DUNCAN MACDONALD, 10 OCTOBER 1937
                    Sea View, Worth Matravers, Dorset. Sunday Oct 10th. 37

My Dear Duncan

. . . . I know only too well how anxious you are for the success of my work, which you back so warmly & I hope from the depths of my heart it will prove a lucky gamble for gamble it is – the only *certain* element about it is that we are both doing our best – alas it is something higher than "best" required of the artist to produce a work of art – in these last hectic days before a Show one is aware of the truth of this statement. . . .

---

[30] Duncan Macdonald had brought Anthony West and his wife the painter Katharine Church to visit FH at Worth Matravers.

[478] To Dorothy Selby, c.23 October 1937

Sea View, Worth Matravers, Dorset. Sat –

Dearest Dorothy –

I hope the Lefevre gallery has sent you cards for the P.V. of my Show on Wed: 27th[31]. . . .

I am not very excited – I have been bustled into getting ready & have had a lot of work to do – but you won't see any brand new work I think – & I myself don't know what is being shown. . . .

Personally I am feeling tired out & not at all in the right frame of mind for a walking on part at a Picture Show –

It needs will power wh. I lack at the moment –

So you may not see me on Wed: . . .

Weather almost perfect for weeks – but today a change . . . .

I have been getting up at 5 the mornings are lovely. . . .

No news – my days are uneventful – but busy – it is only my one strong interest that keeps me alive –

Worth is really Ultima Thule. When the house alterations are finished & a bath fixed up etc I hope you will pay me a visit – but it is a place for fine weather – it is too bleak for words other times

Queer fate that has landed me here!

Goodbye. I wonder what you'll think of my Show. . . .

[479] To Dorothy Selby, 30 November 1937

Worth Matravers, Dorset. Nov 30th.

My Dear Dorothy

I am back again in Dorset & winter closing in . . . .

. . . . I shall never, willingly, have another full dress Show – it is too great an ordeal repercussions go *on* & *on* (as is meant of course) I hope they have sent you "Ferns & Eggs" by now & that you have become good & lasting friends with them. . . .

They played tricks with my pictures changing them, withdrawing some – adding others – sending off 2 to America. The walls never seemed 2 days alike nor to run with the catalogue numbers titles appeared simply silly in some cases. I came away on the Wed: before closing day, just as the gallery was filling up & some freshly framed watercolours had come in – I felt depressed – tho' Macdonald was gay & eloquent & (elegant) in that light falsetto way of his (very attractive)

---

[31] See *Four Vital Years*, p.119, for the catalogue of the exhibition. Among the 63 works were oil paintings, gouaches, watercolours and pencil drawings. Landscapes from Spain, Wales, and England predominated, with some still life and one figure study.

I felt rather that the Show had fallen flat on a blasé London – I have no news of how it finally ended – they will let me know some time in their own good time. Did you go back again?. . .

There was quite a good article by Geoffrey Gorer, illustrated, in last weeks Listener (17th Nov:) spoilt somewhat by bad reproduction[32]. . . .

Amy [Krauss] & May Wilson accompanied by the shy spectacled gingercoloured nephew went up to see the Show – returned elated & thrilled – but exhausted

Jane Saunders, from Manchester, also went up by night-train, returning even more thrilled & elated – *& exhausted*. . . .

The shy nephew has a crush on me, *on my painting* – he gets more pleasure from it he says, than from any artist *living or dead*. Tall order! Nice to think it can set him sweetly dreaming thus – He little knows!

He has written to say that he is dedicating his play written round Gaugin as Hero to *me* – embarrassing rather as I do so heartily dislike Gaugin. . . .

You were very lovely to me – I felt your greathearted help & strength in the real sense of the word

[480] To Rée Gorer, 24 December 1937

Worth Matravers, Dorset. Christmas Eve 1937

Cheers! Dearest Rée the great Chair has come timed to perfection for Christmas Eve – towards 10 o'c, by Southern Railway, just as I was off to bed – Thick fog outside – I opened the door to see what looked like a box as large as a cottage attempting to get into *my* Cottage & finding it the very deuce of a job. . . .

Today I unpacked it – no Her – my dearly loved Cinderella has turned into a beauteous Princess clad in dove coloured velvet

Like the Prince I was transfixed, & have remained so all day – in fact we have spent almost the entire day together in each others arms so to say in front of the fire – It is a chair in which to dream – oh! much more than that – a support, a tonic, a prop, a very real succour which cuts down through everything to ones very soul – Say – like a good picture – It has magic qualities – it makes one think, for instance, that some of my worst duds may be finished pictures one day . . . .

---

[32] The article was warmly enthusiastic: 'Frances Hodgkins . . . is a genuinely individual painter who has slowly evolved her own idiom to express her own novel vision. . . . [She] looks at the objects she depicts – flowers and fruit, landscape and animals, implements of farm and household – as though she were seeing them for the first time, without meaning or association; nothing for her is too common or mean, or too rare and exotic.' It included a proto-feminist discussion of FH: '. . . . European painting has been almost exclusively a masculine art and has therefore naturally developed a set of symbols and attitudes adapted to men; such women as have painted have either adopted the masculine attitude, or they have produced paintings corresponding to the male stereotype for women – pretty and tasteful and superficial. Frances Hodgkins is a serious woman painter, as Emily Brontë or Jane Austen or Edith Sitwell are serious women writers. Like these writers she has a contribution to make to the world which no man could provide.'

It looks good & right & dignified in this little room where not so long ago the small window was lit with oil candles & a horn lantern –

The draughts still remain –

All my thanks & here is my love & my Salutations for 1938 wherever you are –

Frances . . . .

[481] To Jane Saunders, December 1937
[Worth Matravers] Sat? Sunday? Monday? I dont know?

Dear Jane I am still here at Worth – my Christmas in Wiltshire was a sad fiasco owing to a serious outbreak of foot & mouth disease on my friends farm. . . . No Christmas party for us.

You sounded terribly tired & afflicted to the very marrow with too much of everything. I think it is *brutal* the way they work you . . . . One thing is certain that *you* have surmounted all your worries & thrown a lovely Christmas party with or without the housekeeper – being a genius – unshatterably plucky *and* an artist – You moan after a quiet shell – but you never creep into it I notice like I do. And now to come to the real point of this note wh is to thank you for a very lovely & unexpected present of a red scarf . . . the magic of your clever fingers began to work directly the parcel was handed in to me – I absorbed it all – pink paper, twine printing – size – space – giving pleasure making one feel well & happy & nice . . . .

I would love to hear from you when youve time & strength

[482] To David Brynley, c.30 January 1938
Worth Matravers. Sunday

Dear David

Your letter gave me very great pleasure. It made me happy as a child to know you like my pictures & find them "mystic" queer – incomprehensible – magnetic despite which you simply *must* possess one – I am glad beyond words you fell – And I am proud I have tempted you

Your letter was delicious –

Such a letter helps cover the scars which I have all over my body from the people whose heads you want to knock together – the blighters –

Why of course yes I'll sign the picture & will make an earnest journey for the purpose as soon as I get back from London where I am off to for a week on Wednesday – this is just a line to go ahead – to say that at the moment I haven't a second – but should adore to come & see you as soon after I get back as is right for you – I'll phone –

I have been feeling frightfully groggy – or rather a prettier way is to say I am as frail as a Paul Nash Water Colour – but am reviving in this good quiet spot – blessedly healing – but dull –

Hoping we shall meet very soon

Please do let us

> Frances The Artist

Early in June 1938 FH told the directors of the Lefevre Gallery that she did not wish to continue working under the terms of the contract made in 1932. This had been for only one year and had continued informally thereafter. Her relationship with the gallery was now under discussion.

[483] To Dorothy Selby, c.18 June 1938

[Worth Matravers] Saturday morning

Herewith pyjamas. Have not laundered them locally – result might be fatal –

Was glad to have yr. card & letter & to hear you found a seat without much jostling

I simply loved having you –

You did me a world of good & *cheered* me up It was very lonely without you

Mist lasted all next day – then bright blue – clear & lovely – great storm clouds about today – very electric –

At last a letter, this morning, from Macd – They wish to keep me –

I am to meet the Directors & discuss things from a business basis – what this exactly means remains for me to find out –

Anyway my opinions have been sympathetically received by them & are under consideration etc etc. . . .

How I wish you were nearer & you could drop in more often. Come again won't you?

Did I half enough thank your sister for the terribly good cake?. . .

In taking the risk of severing connections with the Lefevre Gallery, FH was supported by the Gorers, with whom she was staying when she wrote the following letter.

[484] To Duncan Macdonald, 25 June 1938

The Elms, Fitzroy Park, Highgate, N.6. June 25th. 38

My Dear Duncan

I thank you for your letter of June 16th. I have considered all your suggestions most carefully. Under the present contract I find that the annual amount of work which I have to supply is excessive, it means constant over work and gives me no time for relaxation

My health has suffered from my efforts and I am faced with fears of a complete break down and incurring a debt I might find it impossible to pay

I should like to suggest a modified contract calling for, say:

6 oils

10 gouaches

10 Water Colours per annum

As I do not feel I can easily complete the existing contract I am returning your cheque for £50

I should like to make it clear that I wish you to continue having my work but since you cannot increase the money, which, with the greater comfort & materials it would give would make work easier the solution seems to be either a smaller annual output, or else the pro rata selling you suggest

I am in town for a few days at this address. . . .

[485] To Dr Honeyman, 6 July 1938

Worth Matravers, Dorset. July 6th. 38

Dear Dr. Honeyman

. . . . I much regret the delay in acknowledging [your letter] sooner. I have been giving the whole matter a good deal of thought

In regard to the two suggestions you put before me I think the first offer in which you guarantee £200 annually with percentage selling appeals to me most & is, I think, extremely generous on your part –

I am willing to agree to these conditions and to continue to give you all my work on sale, or in the event of selling to other dealers to do so through you. . . .

There is one other small point. I should like to continue showing at the 7 & 5 and to select any of my pictures in stock that I wished – this of course would not affect your commission – also I beg you *not* to show my pictures at the Women Artists – it displeases me very much –

[486] To Dorothy Selby, 27 July 1938

Worth Matravers, Dorset. July 27th

My Dearest Dorothy

We last met at the Highgate House – I wonder did you go to the State Garden Party last week? Did you find it a little terrifying, as did some of my artist friends who were there –

The prescence of Edith Sitwell is always rather discomfiting she can be so black & sinister looking –

I was safe away in the wilds – Kimmeridge, a tiny fishing village on this coast – where I made numerous drawings – in pencil – and am now back at Worth, & am going to make them into pictures – the same old hat trick – you know! . . .

I have renewed my contract for a further 2 years – By the new terms I shall have more money & a larger outlet for my work – I give them less work – but on the other hand I am in arrears – so for the next 2 years I don't stand to benefit, except morally, I consider I have won. The Gallery now realises I have the Gorers, very solid behind me – their one wish is that I should be unworried and rested – and not over worked. . . .

Have you been to the Leicester Gallery –

Do you prefer Watts to Hodgkins? If Watts why not Alma Tadema[33]

I hope it will be a very happy & blessed & peaceful holiday for you both

Love from Frances . . . .

[487] To Dorothy Selby, 7 October 1938

Worth Matravers, Dorset. Oct 7th

My Dearest Dorothy

I was glad to get news of you in the Crisis week[34] & I have meant to send you news of myself but things have been happening with such rapidity culminating in Peace or what looks like a very shaky peace but even 6 months of Peace seems worth having no matter how dangerous it may be. . . .

Have you been able to visit any of the galleries or to think about pictures . . . .

---

[33] Both George Frederic Watts RA (1817-1904) and Lawrence Alma-Tadema RA (1836-1910) belonged to the flowering of the Victorian classical revival. Their superb draughtsmanship and mastery of traditional oil technique did not prevent a total reversal after their death of the high reputation they had enjoyed during their life-time, Alma-Tadema in particular becoming a symbol of outdated artistic practice.

[34] The Munich crisis during which Neville Chamberlain and the French Premier Daladier agreed to Hitler's demand that the Sudetenland become part of Germany. The Munich Agreement was signed 29 September 1938.

Do try & see Piccasso's Show[35] – you may hate it – but at least go & see it – Graham Sutherland[36] at Bruton St should also be seen – He is in the making – coming on fast. Do you recall our seeing a canvas by him at the Cambrian Hotel Solva of blessed memory – we thought it a crib from Cedric –

No news here – Have had to spend £20 on a new tin roof to my Studio – if that is news! Mrs. Gorer & her friends the Hansards collected me last Sunday in their car & lunched at Swanage –

The Gorers burrowing in trenches in their nice garden Geoffrey says let them stay – next time an air raid there will be no warning – His mother comments He has a nasty way of sometimes being right – so his word goes. . . .

[488] To William Hodgkins, 15 October 1938

Worth Matravers, Dorset. Oct 15th.

My Dearest Willie

I very much want news of you all. I ought to have given you news of myself but things have succeeded one another more rapidly than usual lately . . . . I don't think anyone who has been through [the crisis] will ever forget it . . . . Even now a fortnight afterwards there is only one thought uppermost in our minds thankfulness for peace . . . of course now we are beginning to think more coolly of the awful price that has been paid and that we are now in face of a changing world & very painful it is. Dictators suffering from dementia are *not* to be trusted. England is salving her conscience by pouring out money to help the Czechoslovakians who we have all but smothered out of existence in order to avert world war. . . . Many people think war may come sooner than we think & this time (Oh Lor!) there will be no warning we shall just be bombed to bits unless of course by that time we have strengthened our air defenses . . . .

I am still in Dorset in my little lost village on the coast near Swanage opp: the Isle of Wight. I often feel very lonely – especially in the winter & wish for the proximity of shops & a cinema. The European situation is too acute to venture abroad so here I am & must make the best of it – tho' I am often very dull & wish I were back in France – or Spain. I have had to go slow & not work quite so hard in fact I felt so fatigued & over worked some months ago I gave up my contract . . . as I found the work too much for my strength & eyesight. However my firm were very considerate & generous & refused to give me up & have made terms easier for me & reduced the amount of the quota of work I am supposed to supply. . . . But for the critical state of the art world I should break my contract

[35] Exhibition of *Guernica* and related studies at the New Burlington Galleries in October and afterwards at Whitechapel Gallery.

[36] Graham Sutherland (1903-80) evolved a semi-abstract pictorial language based on natural forms and landscape.

which is an exhausting one & I am tired of it and would like to make more money than I earn now. As contracts go I suppose I have one of the best & most coveted in England – but they can last too long & exhaust the artist.

. . . . Another bit of news is that Peep Bowes only daughter has been married . . . they sent me an invitation . . . . As Alice was supposed to have artistic leanings I sent her a picture – or rather an auto-lithograph, a new process which a group of 20 artists, myself included, has just produced & exhibited at the Leicester Galleries with very great success. My lithograph was one among a set chosen by the Brit: Museum. I find it interesting & remunerative as a side line to my other work. I hope you are *very* well & Jean too. . . .

[489] To Dr Honeyman, 23 January 1939
                                        Worth Matravers, Dorset. Jan 23rd. 39

Dear Dr. Honeyman
. . . . I was delighted to receive an invitation to send to the New York World's Fair and am proud & happy to contribute an example of my work . . . .

I very much appreciate the courteous suggestion of Sir Kenneth Clark,[37] and, of course, yourself in suggesting that I should indicate a choice but I would rather leave it to you, if I may, as I distrust my judgement when it comes to giving an opinion of my own work – Pictures, once painted, are forgotten or, at least, cease to interest me – much – and I am all for the latest newly conceived – which I invariably consider my life's greatest masterpiece

I should like to show you the 5-6 fresh canvasses I am bringing up to the Gallery, before making your final decision – I said tomorrow Tuesday in my wire to you but it must be Thursday, or Friday. I am sorry to alter the day – I want to have them photographed – signed, christened – and then packed. . . .

[490] To Dorothy Selby, 14 February 1939
                                        Worth Matravers, Dorset. Feb 14th.

My Dearest Dorothy
Are you thinking I am *never* going to write again? The winter has been so awful that I have not been able to pull myself out of the pit of depression – and you know how dangerous it is to be there – supine refusing to make any attempt at climbing out. . . . I have never passed a more miserable time & this is really the only reasonable excuse I have for my long & grumpy silence do forgive me – it is only last week that I had zest enough to eat your delicious Bittermints it was

[37] Director of the National Gallery 1933-45.

very sweet & lovely of you to send them and the handky – I started to write, but words seemed inadequate so I refrained. . . . Normally I would have gone abroad – of course –

. . . . Mrs. Gorer has persuaded [me] to go on a motoring trip through France to the South of it – leisurely – stopping at places off the beaten track & having, incidentally some good food & wine – on the road –

. . . . We should be away from 2-3 weeks – barring no surprise attacks or crises – I feel impelled to go – it may be my last chance. . . .

They are all growing very war minded down here – Amy deep in ARP[38] . . . .

I am terribly lacking in courage & am consumed with morbid worry

I have been quite busy painting a picture for the Worlds Fair (NY) invited by Sir Kenneth Clark – painted at intervals during the cold weather. . . .

FH travelled with Mrs Gorer as far as St Tropez and remained there with the intention of doing some watercolours. She hoped that Dorothy Selby might join her.

[491] TO DOROTHY SELBY, C.4 MAY 1939

The Croft, Bradford-on-Tone, Taunton, Somerset. Thursday

My Dearest Dorothy

Thanks so much for your letter, came yesterday sent on from Dorset. . . .

When we meet we must fill in the gaps. How vexing to think we *just* missed at St Tropez. Did you sail across the Gulf from Beauvallon? That seering shrivelling black wind that blows in Provence is just sheer bad luck – you escape it or you dont. . . . I don't suppose you sketched much? on the move? I snatched a few Drawings –

I felt a terrific strain all the time – once alone – at St Tropez – Mussolini grabbing the ground I was sitting on – that sort of jitters – cowardly – contemptible – but I feel it still, only worse – even amid these peaceful green fields

When Geoffrey Gorer asked me to take charge of his cottage & keep it "warm & human" while he was absent in America (he has gone to work for Rockefellers) for at least 3 months I packed up & came over – here I am – comfortable & regaining my health, which is by now, almost rude thanks to Mrs. Coggan's care & cooking . . . .

Come when you feel like it & for as long as you like – just wire & take a train – I shall be overjoyed – so *Come*

The garden is paradise – of course Mrs. Gorer will "evacuate" down here if the occasion rises, wh. god forbid – it wont – we are in the melting pot & melt we must if form & order is to re-emerge

[38] Air Raid Precautions.

A cri du coeur from E[lsie] B[arling] from Langharne – She is annoyed by mud & rain. I havent any good counsel for her – Wales *is* Wales – I hope the sun will come out. . . .

[492] To William Hodgkins, 5 May 1939
The Croft, Bradford-on-Tone, Taunton, Somerset. May 5th.

My Dearest Willie

You will have had my p.c from France. I got back to England 2 weeks after writing it, disappointing, doubly so, having to come back once down there in the sun, but our time was much over shadowed by this awful war scare . . . .

The only thing is to go on hoping for a sane settlement – we can still hope – the guns have not yet gone off! Ones spirits go up and down according to the latest news – for instance the news that Chamberlain was going fishing to Scotland for Easter gave us confidence – only to be soon followed by the Albanian bombshell – and so on. But enough depressing talk.

Are you feeling jittery in NZ? . . . I liked the Tourist Guide you sent me it gave a very clear idea of Tauranga. It looks a nice place and you sound happy & interested, with just enough serious work to fill in time, against a pleasant background of friends & outdoor life very much to your liking & so good for you. Do wish I could see it . . . .

. . . . I am sending you 2 numbers of the New Statesman & will wait to see how you react before following up with others. It may prove too "left" for your taste. It has been my dope for donkeyest years. There was a letter of appeal in a recent number from a visiting lady to NZ to send out "left" literature to N.Z friends – who would welcome it.

I didnt quite make out in yr. last letter whether you disliked Katherine Mansfield as a woman or a writer? Surely *not* as a writer? Did you know her?[39]

---

[39] The only mention of KM who, during April and May 1916, had lived in Zennor, Cornwall, only a few miles away from FH's studio in St Ives. There is no record of the two having met, though it must be assumed each was aware of the other's existence. In 1951 the singer David Brynley supplied E. H. McCormick with the following impressions: 'At one of [our] parties [in the 1940s]. . . our late friends, Phillip & Lady Ottoline Morrel & Mrs Thomas Hardy were present. They were admirers of Frances who loved meeting them at our house. . . . Frances was greatly impressed by Lady Ottoline's beauty, warmth & intellectual awareness. On that afternoon, I remember, they talked a great deal about Katherine Mansfield whom Lady Ottoline helped so much.' (Letter, 4 June 1951.) 'I gathered that Frances was not an admirer of Katherine Mansfield – but her judgement might possibly have been tinged by envy because of the extravagant praise which was lavished, particularly in the early days, on Miss Mansfield. Frances certainly did not consider her to be a writer of the first magnitude. Frances was intolerant of purposeless suffering, about which Katherine Mansfield so often wrote, & yet in this there is a paradox – for Frances herself, particularly in her later years, was preoccupied with loneliness & frustration. However, Frances did make full artistic use of her own personal experiences, something which she felt Katherine Mansfield was incapable of doing. That is about all I can say on this subject.' (Letter, 2 July 1951.)

So you have met Oliphant Shaw! He wrote & told me he had met & liked you & Jean & asked me to meet him when he got home again. He is a dear man – with a charming gay philosophy of life – very fond of the ladies, & an exquisite fly fisher – I have seen him casting – like a poet. . . .

[493] To William Hodgkins, 22 July 1939

Studio, Corfe Castle, Dorset. July 22nd.

My Dearest Willie

The Air Mail brings us a lot nearer together. Yours of the 27th. June has just come, 22nd. July, & would have reached me sooner but for change of address – that is pretty quick. This is only a line to acknowledge it

I am rather in a rush at the moment finishing some work & trying not to lose my head over it. There is plenty to rattle one these days – Your letter has plenty of sad news in it –

First things first – The great thing is that you & Jean are well and Jean getting over her dental troubles . . . .

. . . . It is often very difficult for one to see old friends – much less write to them – like Issy Rattray – I simply can't keep up with my overseas letters. I think an artists life is a *very* hardworking & busy one – there is no rest this side the grave – and also a very lonely one you haven't the time for friends – of course I am ageing & find life a strain – or rather the strain is to concentrate. . . .

. . . . There are about 8000 Territorials in camp just outside Corfe – the weather has been *infernal* – rain unending – but the men, or boys, look cheerful & tell you not to be afraid, Hitler is only bluffing – everyone is bluffing, that the whole affair is one thoro' Bluff. Let us hope they are right. They say the organisation in the Army is a marvel of efficient organisation & preparedness – so different to the last time –

Mr. Nash is very much in the limelight & has raised a wapping big loan for you –

My head is not very clear tonight & I ramble on – but I felt I must send you a quick line to let you know I am O.K. and going for a holiday on the E Coast, up in Northumberland where some old Manchester friends have a caravan & cottage. I gasp for some bracing E Coast air – & hope to bring back some useful work –

All my love to you

Frances . . . .

PLATE 6: *Pembrokeshire Landscape*, 1938, gouache, 537 x 762 mm, Auckland City Art Gallery.

PLATE 7: *Flowers and a Cat*, 1941, gouache, 305 x 410 mm, Dunedin Public Art Gallery.

PLATE 8: *The New Rick*, 1942, gouache, 565 x 435 mm, Dunedin Public Art Gallery.

[494] To Dorothy Selby, 7 August 1939

c/o The Vicarage, Whittingham, Northumberland. Bank Holiday

My Dearest Dorothy

. . . . I am enjoying my visit very much & doing quite a lot of painting in the farm barns & in Jane's very pleasant Studio. She has a caravan in a wood on the Vicarage estate, which is, together with the house large & rambling . . . . The present vicar, Anglo Catholic is more of a village priest, childless – hardworking. He & his wife live in the front of the Vicarage looking out on a landscape which stretches as far as the Border I should say, with the graceful feminine looking Cheviots half encircling the view. . . .

Jane's girl friend aged 40 has gone off to Italy with a younger girl friend aged 20 . . . .

One of those infatuations difficult to explain & disastrous in its reactions –

Jane, however, is behaving well – having done all she humanly can to save the situation has now faced up to it & is looking brighter & happier than I ever remember her, also much more understanding & companionable & *generally adult* than formerly – a bit of an actress perhaps, a hang over from the Drama vibrations. . . .

It was lovely seeing you, & seeing a lovely film with you – And the funny bear! And the whole charming day you & your sister made for me. . . .

I wish you were here – It is so divinely simple & smooth going – Jane's old Housekeeper cooking delicious vegetable meals – all fresh from the garden – great dishes of raspberries & cream – birds in the wood & a hedgehog on the Lawn – giving an exhibition of its tricks –

Even the rain doesn't spoil it – I make the most of it – feeling it is a lull before a crash – & to be cherished –

[495] To William Hodgkins, 1 September 1939

Corfe Castle, Dorset. Sept 1st 39.

My Dearest Willie

I must write you a quick line All is confusion – we have been very near war for six vital days & *now* it *is* war. Germany is bombing Poland – I am filled with hatred of Germany and filled with hatred of Russia, but even now, at this flash point I still hope for a solution and still dare hope for the miracle to happen

DONT WORRY ABOUT ME I beg you not to worry – I can't help wishing I were with you all – or you with me – I am well enough thank goodness, & young enough to go and fetch my own gas mask. Enclosed snap bears out my words. Only a world crisis would persuade me to send it you – as snaps go it isnt too frightfully bad. I came back from my Northern holiday feeling very fit & braced for any emergency – spent a few days in lovely weather with the Anthony Wests in Wiltshire. He is one of the numerous offspring of H G Wells, parentally acknowledged his Mother is Rebecca West – he inherits the literary gifts of both parents – a formidable heritage – but he is equal to it & is making a reputation – very happily married to a young heiress to Lyles' sugar wealth – they, like everyone else are knocked sideways, & when I left them were preparing to receive expectant Mothers & Blind People evacuated from London – also darkening dozens of windows. I have been busy doing the same with my Studio windows – & not too sure that the Studio will not be comandeered to lodge soldiers, as it was in the last war – by Dorsetshire Yeomenry. Here everyone is calm & very busy getting their spare rooms ready for the children arriving from London tomorrow – no one grumbling – all resigned philosophically – only the older women fearful & afraid –

I am boarding in a Cottage in the village. So far no rations – food plentiful. I have no hoard – only 2 pots of Raspberry jam in the cupboard. . . . I have given friends your address in case anything happens – I'll write again – This is written in desperate haste to let you know I am well & keeping cheery. You do the same – All my love to all Let Sis know my news Frances

PART SIXTEEN

1939-47

'They All Want Frances H Now'

Frances Hodgkins was seventy when Britain declared war on 3 September 1939. She continued to live in Corfe Castle but the village was not the refuge St Ives had been in the First World War. Dorset's proximity to the Channel meant that towns like Swanage and Wareham were targets for enemy bombing, while the open heathland in the Isle of Purbeck became a training ground for artillery. The narrow streets of Corfe Castle, situated in the gap in the Purbeck Hills that gave access to the coast, became a thoroughfare for tanks and military convoys. Geoffrey Gorer's cottage in Somerset was a quieter place, apart from being close to the flight path for German bombers on their way to Bristol and Wales. FH moved between the two villages, with occasional excursions elsewhere. Rural life remained her theme: farm implements and machinery, barns and outbuildings, farmyards, ponds, animals, trees and hills. The war seems to make its mark in an elegiac note that comes when the machinery stands idle or broken, compared with the purposeful throb of the threshing machine that can almost be heard in the Cotswolds paintings of 1919. When forced by the weather she worked indoors and made still life paintings of objects that lay to hand.

[496] TO WILLIAM HODGKINS, 28 SEPTEMBER 1939

Corfe Castle, Dorset. Sept: 28th.

My Dearest Willie

I hope my letters are getting thro to you alright. So far we are having a quiet war, no visitors from Germany – yet – & we are all comparatively cheerful at the same time not deluding ourselves as to what may soon be coming to us. . . . It is no use being frightened and taking things too much to heart after all long faces & worrying do no good to anybody.

I suppose this horror will go on for years – The ghastly tragic boredom of it *and* the waste. What am I doing? I dont know – dont ask me – I just look at it! the work I am doing my damdest to finish for my London Firm before the crash comes. The Lefevre Gallery I am glad to say has neither closed down nor packed up – but is running a very good Autumn Show to mitigate the gloom. . . . Schoolchildren & Mothers arrived by mistake on the first day of evacuation, instead of Mothers & Babies. Nobody was expecting them & there was a terrific thunder storm at the time of arrival. I have never seen such lightning . . . the children are very nice & not much trouble – but all lousey – wh. has caused some fuss – some peoples war work seems to consist in combing hair. Still, c'est la guerre! The Mothers find Corfe dull – I dont blame them, & mostly have gone back to London – to their husbands leaving the children where they are – It creates an awkward situation. *When* the raids start in earnest they will regret not stopping where they were at least as safe as one can hope to be. . . . The next batch of evacuees will be housed in hostels camps etc run on communal lines – a much better arrangement than billetting in small houses or even large ones.

I live in fear of my Studio being taken from me. I believe the vicar has his eye on it – that would be a minor catastrophe. Our major catastrophe today is Russia's treachery[1] – & its serious implications. . . .

I dread the winter – the weather now is lovely, the evenings of course, rather dreary & sinister. We sit in darkened rooms, gas mask handy a list of do-s and donts pinned on the wall what to do in a raid etc. We sleep sound – the friend with whom I am staying is an ARP Warden – so I leave everything to her – I am of no use whatever – being ½ blind but well thank goodness & still going strong. . . .

[497] To William Hodgkins, 28 October 1939

Corfe Castle, Dorset. Oct. 28th. 39

My Dearest Willie

A quick line to you to let you know that I have just finished reading your letter of *Sept 28th* most welcome & comforting. . . .

You are a jewel of a brother.

Thanks so much for kind thoughts of help & sympathy jolly good of you. *But don't worry.* As it happens I am very well, so well I hope that I am not going to be ill – and am really pretty comfortable, quite well fed, no food shortage to speak of, I heard the one & only Baker complaining today of a possible scarcity of almond icing for Xmas Cakes & the butcher said firmly '*No miss NO cats meat.*' Neither can I wangle more than cwt anthracite for my Studio stove – wh. I keep going night & day – You cant call this hardship can you?

I am warm enough & able to get on with my work & finish it & am under no compulsion to do new stuff. I feel less unsettled than I did. So far it hasn't affected me unpleasantly like some of the poor people I know who are completely ship wrecked. All the musicians are right on the rocks, and I imagine mostly all the painters too. One hardly likes to ask after friends. My young friends of the Tudor Farmhouse I told you of are living in a caravan 40 miles from here. Their house was filled to the roof with Barnardo kids. He wrote to me – "Personally" he said I feel that some good will come out of it even if it is only the destruction of London and a few Art Dealers –

Now he is skinning rabbits for a living helping on a righteous war by peaceful means. . . .

---

[1] The Russian invasion of eastern Poland on 17 September 1939.

[498] To A. J. McNeill Reid, 12 November 1939

Studio, West St, Corfe Castle, Dorset. Nov 12th. 39

Dear Mr. Reid

Thank you for your letter of the 9th. inst received yesterday

Of course I am naturally sorry that my contract has come to an end and will fizzle out ingloriously in a bankrupt (myself) show in the New Year

C'est la guerre and it is no good worrying

A larger issue in this dreadful business is that the Lefevre Gallery should escape damage & destruction

I have read with intense admiration that you are keeping your Gallery open so helping to mitigate the London gloom as much as symbolising the permanence of art

This is a very grand thing to do, and must be enormously appreciated

I can well understand you wishing to terminate the contract owing to the difficult times and the news in your letter did not surprise me. What does shock me is the size of the *deficit* caused, of course, by the rejection of the six paintings after very nearly a year –

This is a hard blow –

I will do as you suggest & send you a selection of Water Colours, Gouaches, etc also some smaller paintings and by the Spring if you put on a Show and I am not utterly on the rocks I'll come up to London & give them a blessing

Meanwhile please store my 6 paintings pending my fixing for their removal elsewhere –

I do not want them to leave London

I think this is all there is to say

The only sensible thing I can do is to go on & keep the paint flowing as you I hope will go on showing

[499] To A. J. McNeill Reid, 26 November 1939

Studio, East St,[2] Corfe Castle, Dorset. Nov 26th. 39

Dear Mr Reid

I have sent you a Parcel of Water Colours 12 in number, together with 3 Pencil Drawings which I hope will go some way to liquidating my debt to you. . . .

---

[2] FH's studio, the old chapel, was in West Street. Amy Krauss lived in East Street.

[500] To Dorothy Selby, c.27 December 1939

[Studio, Corfe Castle, Dorset]

Dearest Dorothy

Happy New Year to you – and all the best in the coming year, Health, Safety and Peace – I wonder where you spent your Christmas – Mine has been quiet. . . .

The frost has held up work at Studio – could not get warm – It is specially important for me to finish the work I have in hand as they have honoured me with a Room at the Venice International (a Biennial Show) in the Spring, no desperate hurry, but pictures have to be got together – Reid Lefevre are very pleased that I have been asked to represent Britain, one of the artists that is – & mean if possible to run a London Show of my Water Colours & Gouaches – conjointly –

They are also much impressed by the Newton Paragraph in the S. Times[3] – wh. was the direct means of selling the picture – I wonder what they asked for it? I wonder! ! "a good Hodgkins of the finest Period" etc. I hear them!

All quite hopeful signs – I expect they regret having stopped my Contract. . .

It was lovely of you to send the Bitter Mints – there wont be many left for AK. . . .

Last – but not least – your letter & proffered subscription just what I want & would greatly enjoy & value – *but* I must think it over – my lazy mind wont work – this cold weather – I take N[ew] S[tatesman] already & have a sub: running at the moment –

What about Time & Tide for 6 months – we might share it – I wld. post back to you – or vice versa? Penguin Specials & Oxford 3d Pamphlets are quickly read & extremely interesting & valuable – I thought of the Left Book Club – but can't tackle a big book every month – So if Time & Tide suits you it suits me & *many* thanks to you both for the thought – [a] truly blessed one. . . .

[501] To A. J. McNeill Reid, c.18 January 1940

Studio, West St, Corfe Castle, Dorset. Thursday Jan ?

Dear Mr. Reid

The enclosed cuttings from N.Z, I think, will interest you & please as well as surprise you as they do me. . . .

The 2 pictures have been bought by a NZ woman unknown to me who is said

---

[3] Eric Newton singled out FH's *Road to Barcelona* as the outstanding painting in an exhibition of British watercolours at the Lefevre Gallery, praising its colour 'which made everything else in the room look pedestrian and tentative'. (*Sunday Times*, 17 December 1939.)

to have a genuine liking for British modern abstract Art & like a good sport buys them by the brace[4]. . . .

From what I gather the only other British work sold is an Augustus John –

My pictures have made *thunder* in my circle out there, as you may judge from the inspired cutting written I am sure by the office boy. Who else would imagine the Artist paints to please the multitude –

I fear there will not be much left of the 75 guineas by the time commissions, freight, exchange[5] etc is deducted – but remains the Honour & Glory for the artist and warm assurance that her work has not been in vain –

The Reproduction of the Drawing[6] explains itself – It was offered to the Auckland Gallery last Autumn by the joint owners while on a tour of N.Z. . . .

[502] To A. J. McNEILL REID, 6 MARCH 1940
Studio, West St, Corfe Castle, Dorset. Wednesday

Dear Mr. Reid

. . . . By the time you get this you will have had from me a roll of 4 Gouaches

I do not claim them as "stunners" merely the best I can give you with hands swollen to twice their normal size with chilblains, that painful but humorous complaint which never in all the years have I had –

It makes me feel waspishly towards all the world. Do you blame me?

. . . . I am quite willing to go & collect Geoffrey Gorer's picture, please tell Mrs. Gorer, if she can't arrange otherwise. I'll try & write to her about it.[7] What about "Wings over Water"[8] (I think bought by Contemporary Soc) Can't you get it?

As to Mrs. Curtis I gather she has a lot of early 1930 Water Colours & a Painting of that period not I think my "finest period"

Don't count on more than 4-5 new Paintings from me – I can send you two canvasses at once 25 x 30 size – landscapes – farm peices – and the others to follow. *Please tell me the latest date for sending to Venice* – I have practically re painted all my canvasses on smaller scale – a decided improvement. . . .

[4] The paintings were *Bridge at Ponterwyd* and *Ruins* (gouache, 1937) in the British section of the Centennial Exhibition of International and New Zealand Art held at the National Gallery, Wellington, November 1939-April 1940.

[5] From 1934 to 1948 £NZ125 = £Stg100.

[6] *Flute Players*, presented by Angus Wilson and Odo Cross.

[7] Mr Reid was arranging to borrow pictures for the Venice Biennale. Geoffrey Gorer lent *Quarry Farm* (oil) and Mrs Gorer *In Cornwall* (oil), later renamed *Wings over Water*, the version now in the Tate Gallery.

[8] This is the version now in the Leeds City Art Gallery.

[503] To Dorothy Selby, 10 March 1940

Studio, West St, Corfe Castle, Dorset. Sunday 10th. March

My Dearest Dorothy

I have been trying for weeks, months to write to you but I have been a slave to the dreadful inertia of the winter. . . .

I am now beginning to shake off the sloth and come to life again. . . .

My London Show opens 4th. April.⁹ This is a surprise – Not much time for preparation. . . .

A.K has been staying with EB – about a week. . . . She is troubled with rhumatism in her hands & has to keep them out of clay & her feet off the wheel for a bit – real hardship for her. She does so love her pots & her work. Warm weather will put her right I am sure. . . .

I suppose you *never* find time to paint. . . .

It has been a grim & terrible time – I try to forget each day as it passes – I am not one of those who find a spur to work in wartime, tho I remember feeling so in the last war. . . .

[504] To A. J. McNeill Reid, 10 March 1940

Studio, West St, Corfe Castle, Dorset. March 10th. 1940

Dear Mr. Reid

Many thanks for your letter. I am grateful to you for giving me a push in the direction of the calcium cure for chilblains . . . .

You sound extremely hard working and enduring –

Enjoyment will, I hope, come later on with the *Prize Money* 25,000 lire¹⁰ –

By the way who keeps this Vast Sum? if won? or do we share it

. . . . We certainly dont want too big a dose of Water Colours –

A few more good oils are urgently needed – if the proportion is to be kept and the walls to look as brilliant as possible –

What about a Painting "Spanish Shrine".¹¹ Can you trace it? and get it if available?. . .

I shall remember what you say & shall aim at being in London round about the end of the month but I begin to feel quite funereal at the thought of a "personal appearance" Isn't it retiring time for veterans? I think so –

⁹ *Gouaches and Pencil Drawings,* 4-27 April 1940; 32 gouaches and six pencil drawings are listed in the catalogue, the work going back to 1932. (*Four Vital Years,* p.120.)

¹⁰ Awarded for the best foreign picture in the Venice Biennale.

¹¹ This painting, the result of the visit to Ibiza in 1932-3, is now in the Auckland City Art Gallery.

[505] To William Hodgkins, 18 March 1940

Dorset. March 18th. 1940.

My Dearest Willie

I have been wanting to write to you for days & weeks past & must not put it off any longer – or you will be wondering if anything has gone wrong on this side. It has been such a frightful winter, absolutely downed me, bout after bout of snow & ice, frozen pipes everywhere, broken arms & legs quite common, not my own thank goodness. . . .

I'll tell you all my woes first, with accent on the coal shortage, a major misery let me tell you – I burn anthracite & keep my stove in night & day – but I have just not had enough to heat the big Studio – what I do get is stone & dust. Don't remind me that there is a war on – we are beginning to know it – *However we dont lose faith.*

I am well, most thankfully – and more hopeful in spite of what *must* be ahead of us, more hopeful of what will come out of it all. . . . How are you all?. . . .

I was absolutely delighted to hear of the sale of my 2 pictures at the Centennial Ex[hibition]. Betty Rhind,[12] dear girl, was the first to tell me the good news – then came your letter with Bertie's enclosures. . . . I found the news from NZ a spur to work.

Two things happened early in Dec: first the staggering news that my contract reluctantly stopped – nasty shock. By almost the same post came an invitation from the British Council to represent British Art at the Biennial Exhibition in Venice in April – that is to fill a large sized Room in the British Pavillion, the other painters being Duncan Grant, Wadsworth & Munnings[13] – each with a Room of their own – a very considerable compliment to your sister one is assumed to be either eminent or dead – perhaps a bit of both – before you can qualify for this honour – it is a very important Exhibition. Under the circumstances it was felt that refusal was out of the question as a great effort is being made to promote good relations in the Arts sphere of the two countries. I went up to London on one of the blackest days leaving here in the dark. I found my Gallery sandbagged & gloomy, the staff of glamorous young men all gone, only 1 Director, and I female typist, Secretary, & not a soul in the only 2 small galleries open. (Things have brightened up since then, however, that was the panicky time, shows are going merrily now & sales comparatively numerous at smaller inexpensive prices) I had a very good lunch with the Senior Director at a French place in

---

[12] Betty Rhind, a former pupil of FH, was represented in the New Zealand section of the Centennial Exhibition.

[13] Edward Wadsworth (1889-1949) was initially associated with Wyndham Lewis and the Vorticists, a member of Unit One in 1933. Best known for his hyper-realist paintings of maritime subjects. Alfred Munnings (1878-1959) was the great painter of horses and idyllic country scenes, President of the Royal Academy 1944-9 and vociferous opponent of modern art.

Jermyn St, full to the teeth of officers – we had to wait ½ hour for table – a scrumpscious meal – hors d'oeuvres rather skimpy. Then I made my call on the Brit: Council and heard more particulars, arranged for the 25 pictures to be collected from their various owners etc, private collections & Public Galleries, all pictures painted within the last 10 years and sold through my Dealers.

By this time it was pitchy dark & foggy & I only just reached Waterloo for my train at 4 30 reaching here 9 o'c & only my flash to guide me home . . . . I can't tell you the horror of the Black Out & the effect on your nerves – the want of ventilation at night is very trying – perhaps the nastiest part of it all. Since that day I havent been again to London but on April 4th. I am opening a Show of Water Colours Hitler permitting, & shall have to be there! This show will liquidate my debt to the Gallery. From now on I get no fixed salary, but sell to them on commission basis – so I am not utterly stranded. They are very good friends – Besides which I have a timely legacy of £100 coming to me from a grateful pupil who died lately . . . . I have made another rather surprising sale lately though, in this case also I dont get a bean of the money. The RA organised a big Red X charity show of United Artists – not much of an artistic success but they raised over £4000 – 50-50 between Red X & artist. In my case the Dealer scoops I having been paid for the picture some years back.[14] I am selling pretty well – I owe this to my Dealers. . . . I must stop full stop – No time for more – Send this on to Sis – I have had a wonderful sweet letter from her . . . Love to all write & wish me luck & No Bombing.

Frances

[506] To Betty Rhind, 18 March 1940
[Postcard of Franz Marc's *Blue Horse*] Corfe Castle, Dorset. March 18th. 1940

Dear Betty

You were the first to tell me the good news of the sale of 2 of my pictures to the "Mother of Mrs Harry Atkinson".[15] It was kind & thoughtful of you thank you so much. It gives me great pleasure to know who has bought them and that they are now in a true art lovers collection. Could I wish for a better setting than the enlightened Richmond Atkinson group? How is your own work going?. . . [Postscript] I saw that you had sold your flowers in the C.E. . . .

[14] FH received £10 for her share in this painting, *Jar and Melon,* and chose to put the sum towards the repayment of her debt to the gallery. (A. J. McNeill Reid to FH, 2 March 1940.)

[15] Mrs Joshua Shields. Her daughter Connie was the wife of Harry Temple Atkinson, son of Sir Harry and half-brother of Tudor, who is mentioned in Letter 80, 6 November 1901.

[507] To A. J. McNeill Reid, 24 March 1940

Studio, West St, Corfe Castle, Dorset. March 24th.

Dear Mr. Reid

. . . . I am desperately sorry to tell you that I have abandoned the 4 paintings promised you for this week, as temporally hopeless, they simply won't march –

I am certain that you would be as dissatisfied with them as I am. I have looked at them too long – the *vision is lost* and in their present state [they] are not likely to please you or any one else –

If, by a miracle, I finish them I'll bring them with me when I come but I am dubious about this not feeling at all in a good painting vein – very much in need of a complete change of scenery – I dont generally give in to this form of weakness – the thumb & first finger of my right hand have gone on strike. . . .

I shall be in London on the 29th. & will be at the Gallery Monday morning if that will be convenient for you –

I hope I am to be given the inner gallery not the front Room which is not so flattering to Water Colours. . . .

[508] To Isabel Field, 26 March 1940

Corfe Castle, Dorset. March 26th.

My Dearest Sis

. . . . I was delighted to see your handwriting again which in spite of the stiff thumb is as firm & legible as ever. . . . These days it is quite a feat to be able to manage a letter at all . . . . I am thankful for [Willie's] letters. If I was not so busy I would be unbearably lonely & homesick for you all – I feel if this horrible war lasts very long I shall be a neurotic old introvert if you know what that is – but I must stick to tin tacks as I am in a bit of a rush & feeling rather hot & bothered having to go to London for the P.V of my own Show opening April 4th. I have written Willie all my news up to date & asked him to send it on to you – I am very interested in what you tell me about him and his way of life – his letters are full of enthusiasm & interest, above all affection & loyalty for his millions(!) of friends – past & present – young old & decrepid whose names I forget but whose faces sometimes haunt me when I think of my girlhood in NZ and how completely I have lost touch with that past life – it was inevitable. In gaining a public I have lost my friends. Artists are terribly lonely people – the serious ones I of course mean. Be glad none of yr. family inclines that way. . . . It is hard to believe your Peter is 33 & married. . . .

Don't laugh if you receive by post a many coloured shawl – which the Cornish fisherwives wear – also artists. I bought it from an artist friend who is having a very sticky time just now – & for fun, and also because I think you'll like its gay

Victorian colour reminding you of antimacassar days of long ago. Anyway it will keep you nice & warm the point of the shawl should touch the ground behind – worn with a black dress it can look pretty good – *not* to be displayed as an antimac – not on any account.

Also about the same time you *may* receive a Christmas present. I have forgotten what it is, but it was meant to reach you late in January – but was never posted. . . . I found this parcel today all done up & nowhere to go, so am sending it along –

Bye Bye Sis Dear I have no time for more – keep in good heart Mothers are such terribly important & valuable people to their family – and beyond – Give my love to Will – I hope his health is better – Keep well

All my love
Frances

If you hear that cabbages are 1/6 you can believe it but only during the Easter holiday.

[509] To Douglas Glass,[16] 29 March 1940

Studio, West St, Corfe Castle, Dorset. March 29th 40

My Dear Douglas

I hope you are not having hard thoughts of me not writing. I should have answered your Christmas greeting before now & thanked you as I should like to thank you for your welcome & honoured card which has been ever since on my mantle piece . . . . I wonder where you are – I hope you are well, as I, thankfully am, more or less . . . . I had a card from May Smith[17] and she mentioned that you had plans of returning to N.Z.

I am glad she is out there – for a few years it won't do her any harm in many ways I envy her and wish I were younger & could make the venture. Europe is a good place to be out of.

I am writing this hurried note to tell you I am having a Water Colour Show at Lefevres opening 4th April & am hoping that you will be there to wish me luck. . . . I wish I lived nearer & could get you to photograph my paintings.

I am one of the 4 British artists exhibiting at the Venice Biennale International this summer a roomful each – 25 pictures – a lot of eggs in one basket!

Love to you both & hoping to see you & best of luck to you

Frances Hodgkins

---

[16] Douglas Glass, whom FH had met in Ibiza, was a New Zealand-born photographer.

[17] May Smith (1906-88), artist and textile designer, was born in India, studied in Auckland and London, and met FH in Ibiza. She returned to New Zealand in 1939, settling in Coromandel in 1967. Her most innovative work was done soon after her return from England e.g. *Characterisation in Colour* (1941), Auckland City Art Gallery.

[510] To May Smith, March 1940

Studio, West St, Corfe Castle, Dorset. March 1940

May Dear

It was lovely of you to send me the Maori card at Christmas with the sweet words on it very welcome & warming this dreadfully cold winter. I am glad you are out of it

You could have knocked me down with a feather had there been one handy. I had no idea where you had got to and am very glad to know that you have gone back to NZ for a time. I wish I were there too down in the Sunshine and all those little islands lovely but different to our dear Baleares of blessed memory.

I can believe how lonely you feel sometimes without your friends but I am sure you will benefit in health in that wonderful climate. The views from your windows must seem to challenge all that is going on in the world on this side.

I am sure you will find peace & some good work to do nothing *you* can show them can be futile or tedious. Good luck to you –

I am still in Dorset – it is not wildly exciting – but I have a Studio and when I want "picturesque" I go out & look for it. . . . Kitty Church has just had a highly successful show [at Lefevres] sold 13 small priced paintings & put herself on the map . . . . Pictures, cheap ones, are selling like hot cakes. So *thats* one good thing to be said for this war. . . .

So far no hardships other than blackout & coal shortage – but unbearable strain & anxiety & boredom

Love to you dear May & be well & happy

Frances

[511] To William Hodgkins, 4 May 1940

Corfe Castle, Dorset. May 4th. 40

My Dearest Willie

I am just back from London where I went for my Show . . . . It has been a terrific success both aesthetically & commercially speaking with a total number of 40 pictures sold at close of Show, which was sold completely out. I had an extremely good Press – glowing praise – from the left and from the right.[18] Prices

---

[18] Reviews appeared in the *Sunday Times* (Eric Newton), *New Statesman*, *The Times*, *Spectator* (John Piper), *Listener* (Myfanwy Evans), *News Chronicle*, *Jewish Chronicle*, *Architect & Building News*. See *Portrait of Frances Hodgkins*, p.129. FH valued most highly John Piper's writing, which she called 'a prose poem': ' Probably no living painter has such extraordinary powers of arranging colours in original and telling ways . . . . At first glance her paintings seem to have such a strong life of their own in colour and pattern that the subjects appear to be of little importance; they seem as independent and as self-sufficient as fine Persian rugs or early mediaeval windows of pattern-glass. It is an added delight to recognise at second glance Wales, Shropshire, Dorset and other places, and to find the temper of each to have been deliberately noted. There is nothing accidental about this painter's vision.'

were low – So many who wanted the pictures were young ones who would be debarred at prices we all agreed should be asked – but there is a war on and who knows where it will lead or how develope? It is now very close to us – within the space of my 3 week Show the ill starred Norwegian business began & ended – even it didnt appear to be a damper on the sales

Before hanging my own Show I had the pleasure of seeing the 26 pictures for Venice collected together before being sent off in a specially constructed travelling van. They looked good – Alas they got no further than Paris news has just come that the French & British Gov:s have called off the show on account of the political situation, i.e. suspicion of what Mussolini may be up to in the Mediterranean – isn't it all a B-Bore.[19] The British Council now propose showing the pictures in London charging a fee & giving the proceeds to the Red X which I am sure no one will mind at all – but what a sad washout for the artists

. . . . Now I am going to rest and take a bit of care of myself . . . . My legacy has come at a perfect moment – and no death duties. I am thinking of retreating to Wales for the summer. I have sent you a copy of the New Statesman & Spectator with notices of my work. . . . I dont want you & Sis to miss them – also a Listener.

On my side I have to thank you for the Waitangi Number wonderful photographs. New Zealanders always look so happy & smiling & prosperous. . . .

I daren't talk about the war – it is too near . . . . As one gets nearer to it the more of a growing mystery it becomes – like Death. . . .

[512] To Dorothy Selby, 4 May 1940

West St, Corfe Castle, Dorset. May 4th.

My Dearest Dorothy

I hope you are in the country this lovely Sunday morning amidst the lambs & blossom. H. Ritchie writing from a Westmoreland dale says all the lambs up there are given bags to lie on on the hill side & actually *do* lie on them

I dont know when I have found Spring so magical and lovely as now – by contrast, no doubt with the long dull winter. . . . I am wasting my time here – I feel lazy *and* apprehensive – *must* get a move on & retreat into Wales, starting at Bridgnorth & exploring a few addresses I have in those parts – on & about the Severn. Anyway about the end of July I'll be expecting you – let us hope you will get a good long peaceful spell. . . .

. . . . I am so glad you are quite contented with your 'Elevator'[20]. . . . I like to think that you have it & that from the first blush you liked each other! May

---

[19] Italy entered the war on 10 June 1940.
[20] A gouache from the April exhibition, now in the Auckland City Art Gallery.

PLATE 9: *Green Valley, Carmarthenshire*, 1942, gouache, 373 x 524 mm, Dunedin Public Art Gallery.

PLATE 10: *Abandoned Cottage, Cerne Abbas*, 1943, gouache, 380 x 520 mm, Private Collection. Mentioned in Letter 574.

PLATE 11: *Broken Tractor*, 1942, gouache, 381 x 571 mm, Tate Gallery.

PLATE 12: *Spring at Little Woolgarston*, 1946, gouache, 364 x 500 mm, The Museum of New Zealand Te Papa Tongarewa, Wellington.

Wilson drove me to some woods near Studland now being felled we made sketches & eat sandwiches. Very jolly – I enjoyed it. . . .

[513] To A. J. McNeill Reid, 6 May 1940
Corfe Castle. Monday May 6th.

Dear Mr. Reid
. . . . I have to thank you for the 3 Photographs which I am delighted to have – It is good of you to send them – They take the place of my spiritual offspring of which I am now bereft to the fantastic number of 40 (?) Whatever made them go off like that with a whoop?

Is there a catch some where? Did you let them go very cheaply?

I have been defending myself rather hotly in certain quarters for selling for small prices, prices which of course I don't control. No one can question the fairness on your part of reducing the prices to meet the demand mostly from young people who otherwise would be debarred from buying. . . .

But I am sure we both agree on this point that from now on prices should go up and remain up – This refers specially to the oils which I hope will not prove quite such a "problem" as you fear –

I am at work on 3 paintings at the moment which I'll send on to you as soon as finished. . . .

I note with gratitude that you & Mr. Brown propose reducing my debit Balance which will be very helpful & welcome[21]

[514] To Myfanwy Evans, 15 May 1940
Studio, West St, Corfe Castle, Dorset. May 15th. 40

My Dear Myfwany
. . . . I have been intending to write for so long but put it off from day to day, not lazily, chiefly because my pen is always so distant from me & my brush so near and my eye for ever turned to something on an easel.

Not that I have been working – far from it – muscular rhumatism has kept me indoors wasted my time & torn my nerves to ribbons aided by the nasty news & the awful aura of Hitler approaching us. I mention the rhumatism to give verisimilitude – But quite privately it has been damnably crippling, & playing havoc with my poor joints. I am told the attack goes as suddenly as it comes –

I was made so very happy by what you & John wrote about me and I owe you

[21] 'There is still a debit balance against you of £120.2.6d, and while we may not feel it possible to wipe the whole of this out we both agree that something at any rate can, and will be done.' (Letter from A. J. McNeill Reid, 30 April 1940.)

very particular thanks – it gave to my show all the success I could hope for it and how jolly & right & apt the Braque looked, cliff to cliff my opposite number – by a reverse process we seemed to arrive at pretty nearly the same concept[22] – you wrote deliciously about the Show – I tried to chant the words – ecstatically – like poetry they were best said aloud. I like to think my Spring has not flowered without anybody seeing it

The show I think was a democratic success, popular like the Old Vic is popular – of the people – as far as I could see there was nothing high brow about it – with the one exception of the N. S article[23] – the homliest people spoke to me & said how much they liked it. There was no Duncan Macdonald. There was no Blah! Mr. Reid made it sensational by the number of pictures sold. . . .

Goodness & Beauty must persist dear Myfanwy, & Love is the keynote. When shall we meet again? Soon I hope – All my love

Frances . . . .

[515] To William Hodgkins, 26 May 1940

The Croft, Bradford-on-Tone, Taunton, Somerset. May 26th. 40

My Dearest Willie

These are dark days[24] – Shall we win through this time? By the law of average its about time our side got an innings – battles rarely go *all* one way. Nothing has ever made me so sick at heart as all this treachery – it is pure cold horror – No I don't for a moment despair. . . .

At least and at last, we are united with Labour pulling its weight and every ounce being put into War Effort.

Today is the day of prayer. Thought is a powerful thing – May such a wave stand as a bulwark against the evil forces against us

I have moved over here to the Croft from Corfe Castle not because it is any safer. No place is safe but it is rather more away from it all than on the S. coast where the coastal gunfire rattled my big studio windows – very worrying. Geoffrey gave me the use of the Croft for the summer & I shall stay here so long as the Gov: doesnt fill it up with evacuees. . . . I have dispensed with the

---

[22] The two illustrations accompanying Myfanwy Evans's *Listener* review of 18 April 1940 were FH's *Kimmeridge*, a view along Kimmeridge beach in Dorset to the cliffs at the far end, and Braque's *La Mer près des Falaises* which had similar subject matter, including two boats painted in a simplified 'childlike' manner. By 'reverse process' FH meant Braque's return to figuration after the cubist years, compared to her own move away from figuration towards a greater degree of abstraction.

[23] Raymond Mortimer's article in the *New Statesman*, 6 April 1940, began with a theoretical discussion of three approaches to painting, according to whether the artist was most interested in representing facts (Hogarth, Frith), capturing appearances (Velazquez, Monet) or constructing a separate object out of both facts and appearances (Poussin, Cézanne). FH belonged to the latter group.

[24] Written two days before the surrender of Belgium.

Housekeeper & am doing my own work & cooking in a sort of a fashion. . . .

Forgive me if I dont write more. In the face of the horror which is doing its best to engulf us all it is not easy to write – whatever one says or does seems immaterial in a world which changes imperceptibly from hour to hour. Perhaps these are the birth pangs of a new world order – what will the offspring be like?

My work is interrupted my gallery writes Goodness knows what will happen to all the Art Exhibitions in the light of the past few days' events in France. . . . [Postscript] I need *nothing* only the help of your will power –

[516] TO GEOFFREY GORER, 26 JUNE 1940

Croft. Midsummer 26-6-40

My Dearest Geoffrey

It is so pleasant in your garden, scented & radiant, just a trifle untidy, naturally you not being here, & weedy & brown, especially the macrocarpa hedge after the winter's frost, like myself rather wizened, now recovering, showing signs of green at the roots. The hedge has been my sorrow – minor one, but real, like a band of rusty iron round your home oh! so ugly. . . . I live mostly on garden produce, eating my way locust like through the garden – Mrs Coggan supplies a meal once a day & this arrangement fits in very well & suits us both

I have removed all your pictures from the walls, in handy piles for evacuating them in case of danger, & danger is pretty real & close let me tell you . . . .

I intend to stay here, put, till I hear otherwise from you. Have given up all idea of sketching in Wales. I have no great taste for sketching in war time – exposing myself to a 5th. Column scare. . . .

[517] TO WILLIAM HODGKINS, 28 JUNE 1940[25]

The Croft, Bradford on Tone. June 28 40

My Dearest Willie

I hope you have had my letter telling you I have moved away from the S. coast into Somerset. Air raids have started and we are told by various eminent people of the wireless that . . . we must try & be brave etc & stay where we are & when we see German parachoutists coming towards us we must scatter broken glass in front of them – so on & so forth. . . . Enemy planes have been over Bradford 2 nights this last week, chased from Wales, & missing Taunton Station – we heard the bombs, 4-6 miles away – awoke us – but we went to sleep again. . . .

[25] Written six days after the French surrender at Compiègne. For the next eighteen months London and other cities were subjected to intensive bombing, which reached a peak from September 1940 to May 1941.

My Dear this is the bloodiest war I am sure you are as heartsick & as stunned as I am and now comes this last shock of France's collapse & betrayal and, to us, mortal peril. . . .

There are 2 French women refugees in the village – their anger is terrible to see – they tear their hair – they have torn up their French passports – the younger woman tore off her bracelet & raffled it for the British Red X. Poor beautiful France she is "stripped to the bone & left with only her eyes to weep from" Her desolation is complete. My grief is deep that I shall never look on her immortal beauty again. This is Power! God help us!

I do the housework – my cooking my shopping, a spot of weeding in Geoffrey's imaculate garden, all for escape from thought not much good for the mind – but its escape. Practically no painting. . . . It was cheering at this difficult moment to get Helen Simpson's brave book on NZ women[26] I read it with greatest interest & pride and am letting some of my friends read it before returning it to you – thank you for sending it – I am grateful. What grand heroic scale pioneer women they were. . . . I like the illustrations so much. How green were the English roots planted in NZ soil & how green they remain. I wish I could fight as those women fought. Goodbye Dears – you must not worry – send this to Sis.

[518] To William Hodgkins, 27 August 1940

Croft. 27th. Aug 40

My Dearest Willie

I must really pull myself together & get off a line to you or you'll be wondering what has [be]come of me. . . . I got tied up fast with muscular rhumatism, laming me, & other troubles, very awkward as war conditions were getting more active every day the doctor said bed for 2 weeks & diet – an intensive one – which lengthened into 6 weeks before I was up again – a woman from the village looked after me & now she & her husband have taken up their abode here & I am glad to have them – it keeps strangers out for unoccupied rooms are snapped up for evacuees & God never meant me to look after little boys & girls. . . . I do wish you were not so remote & that I could come back to NZ & escape the terrible conditions which begin to weigh heavily upon me – since the night bombing has started & goes on without intermission night after night. . . . I am rather worried about the fate of some of Father's watercolours – now alas rather discoloured – which I have had with me these many years and I feel should be sent back to NZ.

---

[26] Helen M. Simpson (a niece of D. K. Richmond), *The Women of New Zealand*, Department of Internal Affairs, 1940, one of the New Zealand Centennial Surveys. FH was mentioned: 'The work of . . . Miss Frances Hodgkins has received the seal of the highest authorities. . . . her later work is little known in her own country; nor is it likely that it would be very popular if it were known better. It shows, nevertheless, the marks of genius and of the true artist: it has never ceased to develop.' (p.164.)

At the moment they are in air tight packets in my Corfe Studio & I am wondering
if I should send them to the High Commissioner or to Bk. N.S.W to forward to
you or Sis – I think they ought to be offered to one of the Art Galleries as valuable
& interesting records of early NZ life. He was a wonderful what they now call
pedestrian artist who painted as he strolled taking Nature as he found her – Also
he was the ideal "Sunday" painter as they are called in France. Looking back &
remembering, what a lovely temperament his was and how little of his serenity &
happy outlook on life has come my way except of late years when I have learnt a
little wisdom & philosophy. My aspect of the family talent, or curse? has taken
the form of a deep intellectual experience a force which has given me no rest or
peace but infinite joy & sometimes even rapture. How then could I come back
to NZ to settle down in my declining years among my Grandmother friends of
my youth Ethel[27] for instance who writes me she is an Aunt of 2 Grandfathers and
grt. grt. Aunt to great great nieces & nephews Can you beat it she says. The same
old Ethel gay amusing satiric & not easily impressed. Do write Hodgkins (how
I hate that horrid name) wish we could meet & have a good laugh. . . . I do miss
Lily – She always laughed at my jokes & so on. My mind keeps going back to
those early days. I must keep off the War.

   . . . . I do believe there is tremendous *will* power at work & absolute confidence
& belief in our final victory – it may take years. Take this story – Down the road
a bomb fell near a cottage – blew out of her bed the farmer's wife who was
eventually dug out with her mouth full of dust.

   This will teach me not to sleep with my mouth open – she said smiling. . . .

*In July 1940 Alex Reid announced the closure of the Lefevre Gallery and offered to
cancel FH's debit balance of £111.16.6. The Leicester Galleries continued to sell her
work on commission. At the end of October FH visited Mrs Elizabeth Curtis, a patron
from the Arthur Howell days, whose school, Langford Grove, was now housed in a
former stately home at Eywood, Herefordshire near the Welsh border. FH was invited
to take over the art teaching for the winter term but declined. The school's art
department had created a minor sensation in the art world in 1938 when an
exhibition of the work of pupils aged between nine and sixteen was held at the
Zwemmer Gallery.*

---

[27] Ethel McLaren, the subject of an early portrait.

[519] To Dorothy Selby, 21 November 1940

Croft. Wed 21st. Nov

My Dearest Dorothy

. . . . Let me tell you of . . . my visit to Eywood. It took some getting there –
all day journey & then a long drive thro endless parks & gates almost into Wales.
The house was in semi darkness excepting for the vast Hall where Mrs. C[urtis]
was receiving & speeding various guests – small girls dressed in fancy dress flitted
around the whole scene like a surrealist picture of a girls school in a stately home
of England – the last word in incongruity. When I came down for dinner I found
a good many people round a log fire in what was meant to be the drawing room,
draped windows chandeliers, a lot of ormulu & fairly awful pictures & statues you
know the sort of junk the Victorians gathered round them. The room dominated
us all – *except* Mrs. Curtis who has a towering personality who really looked
gorgeous in a sort of very becoming fancy dress & leopard skin furs. She talked
gently – no one seemed to hear or answer her – we all sat round a round table &
eat a very good & lavish dinner & were gradually introduced to each other – most
of the guests seemed to be leaving at 5A.M so retired early. I sat between John
Pudney, Herberts son in law, on the News Chronicle staff – with his Press
Photographer doing a little publicity work – and a nice fat handsome woman –
wife of one of the Euston Rd. painters who had been bombed from her flat but
still smiling – I found the general attitude was to ignore the Raids & concentrate
on evacuation, schooling & maternity centres –

Mrs. J. B. Priestley is running such a place in a nearby village. They came the
next day, she & her big fat J.B pipe & all . . . there are 4 of his daughters at the
school – one a fine looking girl – the others not so attractive. She seems to have
an uncanny gift for painting – running, like so many of them before she walks –
but still –

I thanked him as one in millions for his broadcasts. He said No need to thank
me *you* have given *me* as much pleasure as you say I have given you I have 2 of yr.
pictures. The older girls staged a rather dull little Greek play for his benefit –
dressed in white sheets with homemade paper masks very ugly – slashed with em.
green & crimson. J.B said seems to me the girrls are getting a lot better looking
than they were – & winked. . . .

I came back cheered but worn out & am now paying for my gastronomic
excesses which is a bore & very depressing – Bournemouth has had it badly – also
Swanage & Poole but so far Corfe is safe. . . .

[520] To Geoffrey Gorer, 14 January 1941

Croft. Jan 14. 41

My Dear Geoffrey

Let me make hay while the sun shines & send you a brief line of reassurance just in case letters are lost. . . .

All well here bar the usual colds. . . . I have fortified myself with another load of logs, the 2nd. load this winter – nothing like the comfort of a good inspiring log fire. When the black out is up it keeps the blue devils away better than anything I know. . . .

Times are too awful for comment, still there is a hopeful aspect in peoples' willingness to "endure the unendurable" and cooperate – at last –

For instance we are going to help put out each other's fires to which end a bucket of sand is placed at yr. front gate this morning, (we already have 2 inside & out) & mop, brooms, rake etc handy – a ladder might be a help – bath is kept ½ full – the cottage is fairly cluttered with candles, matches torches & so on

So you see I am here still. You don't mind do you? I hope not It seems meant to be so – a little place of refuge – a bit lonely – I wish the evacuees were more of an acquisition . . . .

I get plenty of sprouts, roots etc from the garden, potatoes of course, wh. I cook in my own sweet way, good olive oil in place of bad butter – occasional eggs – a daily pint of milk – for cat & me – Mrs C[oggan] is dotty on rabbits. I am *not* partial. . . .

[521] To Geoffrey Gorer, 18 January 1941

Croft. Jan 18th. 41

My Dear Geoffrey

Very many thanks for what you have paid into my Bank it is most extremely kind of you. . . .

I write under rather a strain. We caught it fairly badly 2 nights ago in an all night raid on Swansea – planes were noisy & near guns loud & continuous, about 7 o'c there was a big bang wh. even Mrs Coggan heard. I pushed her under the stairs, protesting. *What* is it? she said. Nancy [Coggan] was here too – A Bomb Mother & dashed out of the door she was dressed for a village dance. I sheltered under the kitchen dresser. So it went on, at intervals till 1.30 when we had hot drinks & felt lucky to be alive. . . . The big bang was a Land Mine laid quietly down at the end of [the] village. Result now there is a baby at the Croft – a screamer – with Mother & Grandmother. They were bombed out of Barry's Farm London evacuees & were brought here scared stiff poor wretches we have done our best for them. I cannot see how to carry on & therefore am ready for any change. It is all rather confusing. No damage to the Croft though it had a good shaking. . . .

Will write again in a few days when things have settled down. It is urgent that I should start earning again – I have several commissions as well as 2 good offers from Manchester Firms for textile designs – also prospect of a Spring Show in London (?) I may decide to venture a few weeks in Corfe & take a chance & return here later on. . . .

On the night of 22 December 1940 the new school in Manchester where Hannah Ritchie and Jane Saunders were teaching had been bombed. FH received accounts of the event from both women.

[522] TO JANE SAUNDERS, 15 APRIL 1941
Croft, Bradford on Tone, Taunton, Som. April 15th-41

My Dearest Jane

. . . . Sorry I had to break off into silence after yr Blitz letter (the saddest I have ever had I think) & one of the most courageous. . . .

After that I fell ill again with tummy trouble which recurs & ill fits me for work, letters or anything else useful & helpful. I had to be X-Rayed . . . . The diagnosis, by the way, was on the whole not alarming, but I have to watch out for further development in a certain area

Friends from round about & in London came down to have a look at me & see what the trouble is – John Piper, grand fellow, one of them, stopped to do 2-3 days sketching round about cheered me up not the sort of "Cheerio" stunt but some sense & inspiration & faith to prevail – interviewed my Doctor much to his amazement & told him I was one of King Georges subjects of importance & my pictures hang beside Rubens (!!) in the Nat Gallery – (*no impression created at all*) but you wouldnt expect it from a young athletic County practioner. Still I think he has done his best for me – now he says get away for a change & if needs be consult a specialist – so I am going down to that rather Hellish bit Corfe Castle where AK still remains God Bless her unbombed & unscarred. Depends on conditions how long I'll be there. . . .

Yes I like the Renoir because he has glamour in his touch – & a warm human affection that comes to you through the paint – in lesser hands, say the Euston Roaders[28] how cheap it wd be. Thanks for it – It is not the grand class of Renoir but it is Renoir – the 1 & only. . . .

[Postscript] Please send me if you will a few grease crayons to try.

---

[28] The artists associated with the Euston Road School were William Coldstream, Victor Pasmore, Graham Bell and Claude Rogers. They rejected as elitist the modern emphasis on abstraction and believed that realism based on careful observation of ordinary life communicated more widely.

[523] To Dorothy Selby, 21 April 1941

Red Lane Cottage, East St, Corfe Castle, Dorset

Monday morning – sitting in the sun – Dearest Dorothy your 2 letters on breakfast tray this morning, quick work, sent on from Croft . . . . I slipped down here in an empty 1st. Class carriage, trains waiting for me at every change & so to Corfe where AK was large as life, waiting for me, wonderful!

I came on Thursday 17th. determined to follow yr. good advice & break the vicious circle, which may, or may not be in my own power to break – we'll see!

I felt in such trouble halfway on my journey I nearly wired to Mrs. C to come & fetch me – I took Genasperins & arived ½ doped but in my senses, & luggage all there – I quickly recovered as I always do with a little good food & kindness. The house felt *very cold* after the well warmed Croft & I crept to bed early with hot bottle, which, Oh! Lor! burst in the night – almost as bad as a Raid – however I made a sort of raft of the pillows & waited for day break! When Amy to the rescue with several be-ribboned bottles in reserve – I chose a pink one & continued my sleep! I think I have slept away 2 whole days & now feel very good & free of pain –

E[lsie] B[arling] came Sunday morning (yesterday) . . . . very trim & à la mode as usual turban (Red) & costume Brown

Shell burst over us yesterday while sitting in the garden we scuttled into house EB and all

[524] To Geoffrey Gorer, 26 April 1941

Corfe Castle. April 26th. 41

My Dear Geoffrey

At last I am writing to you having meant to write much earlier after receiving your very welcome letter & the second large & generous cheque which is a great help & standby. You are often in my thoughts and they are very grateful thoughts when I realise how different my outlook, if not my prowess, has been since knowing you & your lovely Mother. . . .

And youve been so ill – We were so sorry. Mrs. Coggan was certain you were not getting enough, or the right sort of food. What you need badly is a sight of your own little house & garden. . . .

It has been an unhappy winter. After a severe fight against the spirit of the evacuees I managed to subdue it & prevent it from poisoning me (someone said to me if you let them they'll evacuate you out of your senses)

They came mid Jan & are still there & will be till the bitter end – They are very comfortable & the Croft is ideal to hide in & rear their baby in safety. As for me life was arduous, wearying & seemingly futile – the main preoccupation being food & warmth. I wasnt a free agent at all. The house forced us to live & do things the way *it* wanted. You will realize this. Poor little Croft!

Being ill, or far from well, my scale of values went wrong. Also I was lonely – too cut off – I found it hopeless trying to paint. The atmosphere was entirely wrong – also space & light limited – actually I had not much strength for decent work. . . .

One day, bitter cold, in late March John Piper blew in – in advance of a first order little Picture Show – 1741-1941 starting with Constable & ending with FH. He straight away borrowed *my* painting of *you* painted 10 yrs. ago & still in good condition. I hope you dont mind. . . . It now hangs (for 3 weeks) in Bishop Fox's (Taunton) schoolhouse in honorable company – an excellent show – & drawing droves, well! lots, of people. . . .

John took back to London several earlier Gouaches to frame & sell. He said No more low prices! No more "promising Painter" stuff. Ask a big price & stick to it. He's right. I am not, I fear a financial genius, but am reasonably prudent and I am going to be very careful from now on – everything is scarce & dear from "mending" to leeks & lettuces – luckily the Croft is growing a lot of stuff to eat – there was a spate of caulliflowers nearly ready when I left Bradford a week ago for a short visit here, Corfe Castle, which stands where it did not a stone out of place – nor a window broken in my Chapel studio.

I am torn between Croft & Corfe –

[525] To John Piper, 15 May 1941
                    Croft, Bradford on Tone, Taunton. Thursday May 15th.

My dear John
 . . . . I am very happy to get [your letter] and it is good of you to write while you are in the critical act of falling down stairs, your hands (wrenched) on a pump, the Army closing in and blowing up, a pet millionaire with a Mill I hope paying fabulously for 2 FH's walking off stage –

It takes genius to do this sort of thing – How brilliant you are. A wizard with a sound heart & a Myfwanwy there with the cushion a major crisis indeed. Dont you go & do anything rash, I couldnt bear to think of you *not* painting. . . .

I cant see how any artist with an authentic idea behind his work can be expected to do the stuff say that Julian Trevelyan[29] is doing so contentedly – of course you are recalcitrant – why should you do it? I think it is [a] most unreasonable demand

I am sure Julian is a good fellow but why this care free attitude to art which civilized people possess – in England? All so idyllic –

[29] Julian Trevelyan (1910-1985), painter and graphic artist, who was associated with the British Surrealist group and exhibited with the Lefevre Gallery.

Second Wordsworths all around recollecting & writing odes in tranquility[30] –

No more of this – Let me tell you some real calamitous news & how I went to Clun & back a daring journey these times. But let me first say that I should adore to come to Fawley[31] for a bit if you are both sure I shall fit in at this moment of destiny. . . .

. . . . Travel by train is just H—!! I sat on my suit case nearly all the way to Clun. Something very like a free fight to get on the train at Taunton –

I lost my Painting kit – not yet recovered – but traced – I think to Crewe! or Edinburgh! I loved Clun & the lovely valley from Craven Arms every step of it surely it is good enough for any painter. I was elated by merely coming to see it. . . . but was saddened by the loss of my painting gear. Each day and 3 times a day I met the bus – Finally I bought a copy book & made naturalistic Drawings – after 8 days of lovely air & sunshine tho' cold wind I left, feeling rather more sane than I did & determined never again to move from the spot to which I have returned. . . .

I may add that the planes up there were very fairly noisy – en route for Liverpool

My landlady wld. come in & stand at the foot of the bed say The Lord has been very good to me and fade out again

Did she mean how marvellous of the Creator not to wipe humanity out of existence for its hideous wickedness & cruelty – she was so kind & comradely I hadn't the heart to vex her with silly questioning. . . . .

Postscript

My pictures to me always seem so unrecognizably different when praised by you:[32] Something which will prolong their existence & promises to survive chaos & destruction is given them and I feel that your word will come true & my work will stay there for ever & fear no neighbours. I assure you I do feel the importance of working & taking my hand at the Pump

[526] To Hannah Ritchie, 3 July 1941

Newbury District Hospital, Newbury, Berks. July 3rd.

My Dearest Hannah

I am in a nursing Home in Newbury, Berks, under treatment and don't know

---

[30] Eric Newton had written of FH's 1937 exhibition, 'Relying as she does on the immediate crystallisation of an experience, her work has none of the serenity of emotion recollected in tranquillity. One could call her at best, unashamedly romantic: at worst undisciplined, even a little hysterical. But experience with so fierce a pressure of steam behind it can afford to be a little hysterical.' (*Sunday Times*, 31 October 1937) Was this review still rankling, four years later?

[31] Fawley Bottom Farmhouse at Henley-on-Thames, the Pipers' home.

[32] Probably a reference to John Piper's review in *Spectator*, 2 May 1941, of the National Gallery exhibition *Six Water-colour Painters of Today* which included 10 pictures by FH.

how long I shall be here. I have been over 2 weeks already & have suffered considerable pain – I am very well looked after and am within 5 miles of friends[33]

I am writing this to explain why I could not send you anything for your Show, nor shall I be able to as far as I can see in the future – so I must ask you to accept my resignation with regret on my part[34] – I have done no work this past year –

I enclose £1 for the current year Please tell Jane –

I am so distressed by the thought of what you both have to go through. I wish you could be out in the country painting before this lovely weather is over –

[527] To Dorothy Selby, 14 July 1941

District Hospital, Newbury, Berks. Monday 14th.

Dearest Dorothy

I have had a sleepey week end too muddle headed to write you a line Those divine things you have sent me – which I crave – you are a darling – thank you *thank you*. . . .

By now I have seen the Specialist from Reading – who looks no fool & one who knows his job

He is to operate on Friday 2.30 this week then some days of discomfort and *then* 3-4 weeks recovery – then, they promise, return to health & work. . . .

In fact they seem to think it will be quite a cheery affair. . . .

A.K paints a *perfectly disgusting* picture of herself in her garden in front of rows of ripening peas & potatoes against background of raspberries – Not decent is it?

. . . . Wish me luck Dorothy – you and yr. sister – Angels of goodness to me – Frances

FH underwent major surgery for duodenal ulceration, the construction of a by pass round the ulcerated area. Because the operation was always risky and involved a long and stressful period of recuperation, it was undertaken only to relieve intense pain. The following letter was written in pencil in lines slewed at an angle across the page.

[528] To Jane Saunders, 28 July 1941

Monday 28th July

Dearest Jane

I doubt whether I am alive or *dead* I have been through a weird experience which I shall do my best to forget – operation itself perfect as a dream

[33] FH was staying with Anthony and Kitty West when she was taken ill.
[34] From the Society of Modern Painters, Manchester, of which Hannah Ritchie was the treasurer.

I was blacked out beautifully – without pain what has followed has been ugly violent – & long drawn out to the point of exhaustion I am terribly low hysterical & suffering from shock.

Hope it will be a final success & give me a few yrs. of hard work. . . .

[529] To Jane Saunders, 5 August 1941

Newbury Hospital. Aug 5th

Dearest Jane

You are a dear friend during this duress in Hospital with my mind vague & wandering. I have been living in the past with you & by gone things – dearer to me than the present moment. What a rambling old life I have lived – some sort of crazy pattern! & mostly blind instinct – cruel kind or otherwise – Forgive!

Well! I have come thro' for another chance. May I make good – I talk like an old Penitent – so boring – I hope I shall live to see you free from school still young enough to enjoy it – & *not alone.* Somehow I have thought of you since I saw you as partially with yr pal E[35] & comfortably learning together. Have you got to the caravan yet?

Now I am cured & free of pain but of course have to get strong & fattened & up to work.

The Anthony Wests who live nearish here on a model Dairy Farm too pretty to paint, are cherishing me for a week before I go on to Corfe – first to AK – then? It will be nice to get to my studio & bench

Sweet of you to say you wd come & nurse me I wish you could. But I am still too feeble to ask you to come to see me. I must do as you say husband my strength. . . .

Jane why not paint?

Do some more of those semi abstracts I liked – Get keen

Much love & be happy

[Postscript] Inadequate letter – but more sane – some sense of clarity. Of course you work too hard – it wouldn't be *you* if you didnt – but paint a bit for *my* sake

FH left the hospital round 22 August and, after the week with Kitty and Anthony West, was driven by Amy Krauss back to Corfe. She stayed with Amy at Red Lane Cottage in East Street until she was well enough to look after herself.

---

[35] Elizabeth Shaw.

[530] To David Brynley, 31 August 1941
[Postcard of Picasso, *Nature Morte,* Musée d'Art de Catalunya] [Corfe Castle]

It was lovely of you to send me that great armful of exciting books to pass my time so happily. Thank you so very much – I hear that you are not often in Corfe but if you are & have the time I should love to see you . . . .
[Postscript] This is not my pet Picasso
All Picassos are pets?

[531] To Dorothy Selby, 4 September 1941
Studio, East St, Corfe Castle, Dorset. Thursday 4th. Sept

My Dearest Dorothy
I am sorry to be so long writing you from Corfe, as I promised. . . . I was kept more or less in bed or anyway the house for a week which rather mortified me but it was meant for my good tho' I was *aching* to get to the Studio especially as the Leicester Galleries proposed opening a Show of my work on Sept 20th. & John Piper was coming down to choose work for it[36]. . . .

[532] To John Piper, c.8 September 1941
Studio, East St, Corfe Castle, Dorset. Monday

My dear John
Two letters on my breakfast tray this morning – one from Dr. Paul Cave (what a name for a Radiologist) presenting his bill of £6 for my Gall Bladder X Rays – The other the nicest letter I am ever likely to have on this earth telling me of all the nice things you & Mister Brown have fixed up for me with the ultimate glory & honour of the inner Gallery thrown [in] – Its too much greatness. . . .

Talking of titles I feel mine to be banale & inadequate – if Myfwanwy and you have some silver words up yr. sleeves give them to me. I am glad you find you have a surplus of things to choose from. . . .

Among the everyday worries of life here I dont know who I *am* – but somehow contracted into a ball of anonymous worry and there will be much fumbling before I start again to paint – Rest I must –

How generously thoughtful of Sir K Clark to jog the Secretary of the Civil List – I was touched – it will be a help if he sends some money sometime but I am not in need

Much love
Frances . . . .

---

[36] *Paintings and Water-colours,* an exhibition of 32 works, including some pencil drawings. See *Four Vital Years,* p.121-2. Subjects included Tréboul, Worth Matravers, Solva, Llangennith and Kimmeridge.

Nevertheless I'll send the 4 gouaches along when finished – they can go into stock if not wanted

[533] To William Hodgkins, 12 September 1941
Studio, East St, Corfe Castle, Dorset. Sept 12th. 41

My Dearest Willie

I dont remember whether I have written since getting back here (by road) from Newbury & how ever since I have been sitting about in the garden with my feet up enjoying the late summer sun & slowly getting better & stronger. . . . I am passing through a stage of hunger when *any* sort of food is nice – if only they would give it me!

I have had a most lovely surprise within these last 3 weeks. The gift of butter, marmalade & tongues & potted meat, 3 parcels, came quickly & safe through the Bank sent by Issy & Frances Rattray. Did you ever know anything so kind? I was bitterly disappointed I was not allowed to start eating them all at once . . . .

A Show of my work is fixed up for opening next week at the Leicester Galls & looks like being a great success. I haven't anything to worry about as it is all being done for me by a young group of friends, writers & painters backed by Sir Kenneth Clarke director Nat: Gallery – who thinks I must have a Civil List Pension for no other reason I can see than that they like my painting & dont like the idea of my being in want during the time I am forced to put aside my work. The Leicester Galleries are very keen on my Show & are giving me their best Rooms – it is to be hoped Hitler will be too occupied where he now is to bother about dropping bombs on my pictures. . . . The gallery takes no *commission* usually it is 33%. . . .

What I should love more than anything would be a lb of butter please to help the wheels go round. Am I greedy?. . .

[534] To Eardley Knollys,[37] 16 September 1941
Studio, East St, Corfe Castle, Dorset. Sept 16th 1941

Dear Mr Knollys

I am truly contrite not to have written this letter long ago when you sent me delicious grapes with a nice letter of good wishes when I was ill in Newbury Hospital enduring a soul destroying cure.

[37] Eardley Knollys (1902-1991) was proprietor of the Storran Gallery, Knightsbridge, 1935-40, a dealer with a good eye who developed a collection of modern French paintings and became a buyer for the Contemporary Art Society. He admired and collected FH's work. His own early ambition to be a painter was eventually realised and he held his first solo exhibition at the Minories in Colchester in 1960.

Your grapes were the very nicest things I had ever tasted.

I ate them – nurses standing by – admonishing me NO pips – no skins

At that moment grapes seemed the one thing in life that had a quite real meaning. . . .

I like to think of the happy chance that caused me to visit the Storran Gallery & to meet you . . .

[535] TO JOHN PIPER, 16 OCTOBER 1941
Studio, East St, Corfe Castle, Dorset. Thursday

My dear John

I have heard from Kitty [West] a letter all buoyancy & go she seems to have a sweet & pleasing babe[38] if tiny and she is having a lot of fun falling in love with the doctor. Pas serieux voyons! . . .

I am looking forward eagerly to tomorrow's Spectator & your verdict on the Show, a rebuke I hope to the would be crushing Times.[39] Who expects the Times, anyhow to beam with pleasure at the sight of my pictures? I shall be surprised if you dont include the big *oils* as part & parcel of my progress & maturity.[40]

I look for severity as well as gentleness & wisdom & wit in all you write – I can only make a feeble guess at all that you have done to make my Show a living valid thing what time I have been eating my heart out down here because I can't see my own darling Show. . . .

I have had many letters – very few notices – nothing of value excepting R Mortimer's distinguished notice & Erics love sonnet in the Listener.[41] No flattery can be laid on too thick for me to swallow and I am sure dear old Mr. Sickert is feeling the same about his silly old etchings. . . .

[536] TO JOHN PIPER, 19 OCTOBER 1941
Studio, Corfe Castle. Sunday

My dear John

A line just to say I think you have got me right. What more could anyone ask?

---

[38] Caroline Frances Rebecca, born 2 October 1941.

[39] *The Times* devoted most of the review to Walter Sickert's etchings, which the Leicester Galleries were showing at the same time. FH was dismissed in one sentence at the end: 'Miss Hodgkins often achieves rich and strong colour effects, but the general impression of her pictures, even though it is usually possible (in the fashionable phrase) to "read" them, is on the whole one of confusion.' *The Times*, 30 September 1941.

[40] 'What John Piper said actually on seeing my big canvases was Frances those are a knock out' (letter to Jane Saunders c.19 October 1941). *Kimmeridge Foreshore* and *Spanish Shrine*, two big oils, sold from the exhibition, as well as several gouaches.

[41] Eric Newton. See Introduction, p. 9.

IT IS and this I think sums up what you think of my work

They ARE by reason of their (overpowering?) reality

Most people who have written to me after seeing them remain speechless.

Myself I should say that I, my medium and my subject act & react to produce new & vital creations &, if possible, acheive a perfect balance –

How few of us see how the difference between this & that matters – It is too subtle –

Thank you for an important & inspiring piece of writing. In a world running counter to all ones preaching, teaching, these few spots of goodness matter greatly – How beautifully you say what I'm groping after & your phrase of the song does please me very specially[42]

Early in November FH was well enough to leave Amy Krauss's care. She moved into two small rooms adjoining her studio in West Street.

[537] To Peter Watson,[43] 14 November 1941

Studio, West St, Corfe Castle, Dorset. Nov 14th. 41

Dear Mr Watson

I must thank you so much for your letter and for letting me see the three photographs illustrating John Piper's article which you are publishing in HORIZON

You do me an honour and I am very happy indeed about it

I specially like the two prints in the more recent idiom, preferring them to the Drawing of Sabrina's Garden with its concession to clarity & coherence of an earlier date

The original painting of Sabrina's Garden with its 2 wooden figures is, incidentally my favourite of that vintage 1930-40. I wish I could send you a print but I think the Leicester Galleries ought to have one

Another painting I am rather partial to is Wings over Water shown at the National Gallery & now at Leeds Art Gallery –

But unquestionably my high spot is the Man & Chicken[44] & it takes a John Piper to say so – and see. . . .

---

[42] 'There is in result no sign of the effort that has gone to the creation of these works; no sign of the years of toil that have allowed this . . . apparently songlike expression to have its full effect. Her vision is primarily a vision of colour, yet as every painting here shows (and the final clue is given by three or four drawings in black and white) she draws with originality and power.' *Spectator*, 17 October 1941.

[43] The owner of *Horizon*, an arts magazine edited by Stephen Spender and Cyril Connolly, of which the first issue had appeared in January 1940. Watson was a liberal patron of the arts, helping, among others, the young artists John Craxton and Lucian Freud set up a studio in 1942.

[44] The works illustrated in the *Horizon* article were the recent paintings *Llangennith College Farm*, gouache, 1940, and *Houses and Outhouses, Purbeck*, oil, 1940. The latter included a man plucking a chicken.

[538] To William Hodgkins, 10 December 1941[45]

Studio, West Street, Corfe Castle, Dorset. Dec 10th. 41

My dearest Willie

At last a letter from you. *So* glad to get it & hear all is well. . . . I have been very thrilled & excited receiving 2 parcels, close together through the Bank . . . .

It is wonderful to get the food I need . . . .

I am now living next door to Studio in Courtyard & furnished 2 small rooms, one up – one down – bedroom & kitchenette . . . . Terrible news from Japan just come I feel too agitated to write more – will break off & write more later In much stress of mind

Yrs. lovingly Frances

[539] To Jane Saunders, 23 December 1941

Studio Cottage, West St, Corfe Castle, Dorset. Dec 23rd-41

My Dearest Jane

I hope they sent you the Christmas Horizon with John Piper's article – long deferred.

It pleases & flatters me – I think he has done it very well – made a nice little frame for me – given away no secrets or skeletons.

Because I enjoy Horizon so much myself I hope that you do too & will be glad to have it for a 6 months trial. I can only hope that we will both be alive to renew our subscriptions by then. Horizon will go on expanding *if it doesnt drop out altogether meanwhile* & charming & amusing & irritating – a little of all sorts for everyone who has wit & sense to enjoy it – I like its impudence & crispness –

This is only a scrap for the New Year with all the best wishes one can send & are possible these tragic times. . . . I have had to go slow & quietly – I have now a tiny cottage 2 rooms 1 up & down – a few cupboards E.L. & heater – a tub – but my own I am free

I pay £8 a year rent – it is part of this studio – & a wall one yard thick separates it – very handy & convenient for my work – easy to run with the help of a kind neighbour in country and I wish I could ask you along – but stress is everywhere everyone anxious & overworked.

Dont try to write letters to me or strain on your leesh more than you can avoid –

Love dear Jane & all possible good wishes for a far far happier time ahead

Frances . . . .

---

[45] Written three days after the attack on Pearl Harbor.

[540] To A. J. McNeill Reid, 22 March 1942
Studio Cottage, West St, Corfe Castle, Dorset. March 22nd 42

Dear Mr. Reid

No need to say how delighted I was to get your letter with the stirring news of your return to St James's – this is only a short line to assure you of my sincere appreciation of what you have done these last two horrible years

I am certain you are now doing the right thing in re-opening your Gallery which many of your friends think should never have closed. . . .

I am glad you are putting on a Show soon – There seems to be plenty of business – *no need* for the French assets – There are lots of young British painters coming along & who need a little petting – & as for the more mature ones, say Sutherland, John Piper and the fully mature say (very modestly) myself I would, in your place feel very inclined to put my shirt on them –

I do want very much to be represented in your inaugural Show & am painting you something especially for it. . . .

I am not yet very robust but I have regained my health in a marvellous way and I dont think my painting has suffered in any way – perhaps the contrary

Friends have been wonderful. Kitty & of course Anthony have been darlings & helped me through difficult days after the operation. I can never forget what they did for me – It was ideal at their Farm on those hot September days – I lay out all day in the garden in sight of their beautiful herd of cows, whose milk did the trick & built up my strength –

I never thought you could possibly find time to write – I was sure you felt sympathy. It must have been heartbreaking to you to close the gallery that fateful week when Norway fell. . . .

[541] To A. J. McNeill Reid, 15 April 1942
Studio Cottage, West St, Corfe Castle, Dorset. 15th. April 1942

Dear Mr. Reid

Thank you for your letter of the 10th which reached me Monday morning. Miss Selby did not come, being ill, so your news of the Water Colour Show was fresh to me.[46] I have delayed answering it for 2 days while I looked through my portfolio. The cupboard, really, is pretty bare – and it does not give me much time to brush up what I have got. Ah! Well I must do my best. The Lefevre Gallery must be served. If you can give me till next Monday 20th. I can send you some mounted gouaches . . . .

These Gouaches, baby gouaches, there are 10-12 of them all the same size 14

[46] This was to be a group show at the beginning of May.

x 10½. I call them "Flotsam & Jetsam on Kimmeridge Beach" I am rather partial to them myself & have kept them in reserve meaning to work in oil from them – but at the present time I am not really feeling tough enough to tackle them – my eyesight is troubling me – I am getting some new powerful glasses from a Bournemouth occulist. . . .

The oil I am painting for you will be sent later

In April 1942, FH was granted a Civil List pension of £150 a year.

[542] TO JANE SAUNDERS, 3 MAY 1942

Studio, West St, Corfe Castle, Dorset. Sunday May 3rd 42

My Dearest Jane

It was good of you to write – I am sorry not to have sent you my news from time to time . . . .

. . . . [I] am really much better – times of course when I feel a worm . . . this tiresome & horrible winter slowly passing . . . but this morning I saw the cows climbing up the hill a good sign – the wind in a nice quarter at last. My chief grouse is bronchitis. . . .

Try not to be unhappy Jane Dear. It is hard not to be when one is over worked & ill. I hope this septic trouble will soon clear up . . . . I wish I had a place of my own to ask you to. My cottage is not much larger than yr caravan. . . . I get behind the chimney on raidy nights & trust to expert excavation to dig me out. . . . I try to focus on my work – my cherished escape, but life is all very difficult & addling in spite of the Pension of £150 p.a. which strange to say has a depressing effect on me – *all* artists should have at least that sum with 50 years *before* them to enjoy their freedom & make proper use of it. Let me know if things get sticky I can always send you a fiver – I mean this. I now get a midday meal at the Inn – 3/– a time – but worth it – good food well cooked – plenty of vegetables.

AK very kind & generous with odds & ends & bits & pieces (literally) from her garden produce – sometimes a fresh egg from someone else – & best of all N.Z butter once in a while – now of course, drying up in this calamitous war wh has spread nearly to antipodean shores – now at the stark mercy of invasion – I am very unhappy & afraid of what may come to them. Here, at Corfe, it is hardly a healthy spot – the enemy uses it as a land mark – (we hope he will not destroy his land mark). . . .

[543] To A. J. McNeill Reid, 10 May 1942
                    Studio Cottage, West Street, Corfe Castle, Dorset. May 10th. 42

Dear Mr. Reid

Before answering your letter of May 4th. I have kept it for a few days in order to think over your suggestion about a Show in Nov: so as to make sure I could be ready in time – its alarmingly short time – at first I thought I could not possibly be ready by then and produce worthy work, or at most, worthier than last time, my aim, as you know, being to do higher things as time goes on – and as time goes on I compete against myself more & more which increases the difficulties & all that –

However I am going to have a shot at it starting almost from zero (meaning nothing so far painted) & with luck & some fine weather I may have some success. . . . Now I shall pack a bag & close the Studio & get out of doors & attack Dorset from a fresh angle – somewhere Studland way – not far away but different as well as varied & very lovely. . . .

I should think it likely that the major part of my work will be in gouache, 2 sizes – uniform sizes as much as possible – to be in your hands a month before Exhibition –

I think this is all of importance for the moment and that you can safely book me for November. Of course in the inner Gallery?. . .

[544] To Isabel Field, 29 June 1942
                    Studio, West Street, Corfe Castle, Dorset. June 29-42

My Dearest Sis

You will, I hope, by now have had my p.c & will know I have not altogether vanished from this Earth. You are all much in my thoughts need I say? *Not* how jolly to be in NZ away from this d—d grim old war but oh! Poor Dears how will they defend themselves. You can't all climb Mnt. Cook & freeze or shelter in Ruapehu Crater & burn – but what rot I talk the Japs will never get so far S. or will they? the evil Devils

 . . . . I was in a very poor state but now feel MUCH better and am building up reserves again – weather turned warm, even hot some days & the fruit, gooseberries, strawberries, mostly ripening nicely. I have even coped with a little gooseberry jam made with sugar the Rattrays sent me . . . . Everyone you know grows vegetables – bores you stiff talking of them. . . .

Girlie will be wondering about her wonderful cake which she sent me. . . . easily the worlds best cake in the Mrs. Beaton class, a sort of classic. . . .

Don't forget to tell the others Bertie, Muriel, that I have had their parcels &

that I shall be writing – The Family has been splendid to me. I think of you all very often – you are always at the back of my thoughts in fact . . . .

. . . . Willie tells me Peter is in the Air Force & now in Canada. Let me know if there is any way in which I can be of use if he should, later on, go abroad from there

[545] To William Hodgkins, 30 June 1942

Corfe Castle, Dorset. June 30th. 42

My Dearest Willie

So many thanks for your welcome letter of May 16th. come yesterday by air mail. It was good to hear that you are all well & flourishing & facing up to the enemy so near your gates. . . .

. . . . I go to Swanage by train weekly to change my book & do shopping – alas it is in a nasty mess after a recent raid & many shops no longer there –

I am now receiving my Pension – with one hand & giving it back in Income Tax with the other! Fantastic?. . . After a search among the ruins of Swanage I unearthed a willing accountant who is assisting me assess my claims etc. As a sister of a Banker & the daughter of a lawyer & the sister-in-law of a Distinguished Politician I am a hopeless idiot over business. Oh! by the way you appear to think that the Pension is a reward for hard work & determination – *Not at all* – it is given me on the recommendation of the Director of the National Gallery, Prime Minister & the King – because, solely, I am a good Painter and on those conditions I accepted it. No amount of determination or hard work made a good picture – Talent, or Genius, is required or both. Incidentally I *have* worked hard – made sacrifices & lived a life dedicated to my work – *stayed the course* – I would call it concentration – plus a good dash of selfishness – justifiable in my case I think. Did I tell you my old Firm Lefevre Gallery has opened again after 2 years – I am booked for an Autumn show in October. By the look of things as they are now the outlook is not very hopeful – but as you see Art survives & rises from the chaos. It is true that I sold well at my last Show (the Blitz one) but quite half the pictures belonged to Dealers. "Spanish Shrine" the picture reproduced in Listener was sold to a private collector & materially did not benefit me.[47]

Now I am free to sell on 33% commission on sales. It will be interesting to see how it works.

I am putting a postcard of Coventry Cathedral into a seperate envelope – painted by a friend of mine just after the Blitz.[48] He is one of the official artists working for the Gov: . . .

[47] Illustrating Eric Newton's review, 2 October 1941. It was sold to Sir Michael Sadleir.
[48] John Piper.

[546] To Jane Saunders, c.30 June 1942

Corfe Castle. Tuesday

My Dearest Jane

I was so glad to have your letter of May 12th & to hear better news of your health & general well being. How like you to get round most of your difficulties. . . . That garden of yours sounds stunning – its congenial work, trivial if you like, but awfully rewarding even if your poor back does ache like H—!

Where as painting reduces one to tears & misery – peaks of ectacy – depths of disillusion, depending on how deep you go in search of truth & how long you can stay *alone*. To attain to all this you have to be pretty self contained & strong minded & *very selfish* IS it worth the sacrifice? You say you fear you are "unbalanced tempermently" – from the Manchester High School point of view you may be – but I prefer to call it vision imagination, & rejoice in it. Some wise person said the other day that all art talk is arrant nonsense – half believing it to be true I'll shut up – anyway I have no time for letters – nor have you. . . .

[547] To A. J. McNeill Reid, 5 July 1942

Studio, West St, Corfe Castle, Wareham, Dorset. July 5th. 42

Dear Mr. Reid

So many thanks for your letter of June 25th. in which you express the hope that my summer plans are satisfactory & my work for the Show is going well – Quite frankly I am feeling at my unhappiest over the prospects for the Show & very doubtful indeed whether I can, after all, manage to be ready in time, things being so mixed & difficult

As you see I am still here – I don't think it wise to plant myself away from everyone. Wales is difficult of access these times & cut off from here. . . .

I have been to Studland for a week – It rained – There was a savage raid on Poole one night – I sheltered in the back passage together with other guests. I returned here without a single sketch. The barbed wire had beaten me –

I pour out this feeble story to you in order to explain my difficulties & just why I think it only fair to you to ask you what I should do about it & whether you can conveniently let me postpone my Show till later on

I certainly consider it advisable – to call if off *now* & not leave it to the last moment for you to find a substitute –

I am desperately sorry to fail you, as well as disappoint myself

I am living a primitive sort of life, of necessity, much in need of someone to look after my food & comfort leaving me free to work. As domestic service is non-existent I have to do it myself –

Excuse these boring details – I am faced with the prospect of spending the rest of the Summer in Corfe & the picture is not inspiring – I know there is heaps to do, staring me in the face in fact, but stalemate has set in – & stalemate is as bad as bombs! . . .

When I have any work good enough to send you I will do so – I have 1 packing case left, which happens to be your own – I hope to fill, & return, to you

Very regretfully

Frances Hodgkins

[548] TO DOUGLAS GLASS, 16 JULY 1942

Studio Cottage, West St, Corfe Castle, Wareham, Dorset. July 16th. 42

My Dear Douglas

I wonder if you are still at Brixham. I write to ask because if so I would so much like to break my journey to Wales for a few days & have the pleasure of seeing you & Jane & the son. . . .

Drop me a short line to say if you are willing & able to find a room in either Hotel or Inn not too far away from you & Jane. I dont like too much walking. . . .

How often I have wished you were somewhere handy to take photographs of my paintings – I value the 2 prints you have sent me – trees – 2 hands – Dont hesitate to say you can't find a room. I expect Brixham is crowded out like everywhere else. . . .

[Postscript] Is painting in Harbour allowed?

[549] TO ISABEL FIELD, 23 JULY 1942

[Postcard of *Winter Landscape, Frejus,* by Matthew Smith] Corfe Castle. July 23rd. 42

. . . . Don't use this address from now on. May be moving off somewhere inland. All this area being turned into a gunnery school etc already 400 of neighbouring farmers have gone. The Bank is my safest address. Have been working out of doors doing hay making scenes & getting ready for my Autumn Show. Have made quite a bit of money for the Russian Fund from sales of pictures I have given. I watch news from Pacific hoping the Japs are nowhere about.

[Written beside Matthew Smith's picture] This landscape is rather like yr. part of the world dont you think? Not so red. Much love. . . .

[550] To Douglas Glass, 30 July 1942
Studio Cottage, West St, Corfe Castle, Wareham, Dorset. 30th July 42

My Dear Douglas

Many thanks for fixing up room for me at the Globe Inn. . . .

A request or command? from the "dear Lord Director Sir Kenneth Clark" to be interviewed for a Penguin book complete with 5000 words & illustrations keeps me here . . . (curse it) but failing any further hold up I hope to be eating with you Sat night next week. Mrs John Piper is writing the Penguin – Fairly enterprising in wartime dont you think.

I am sending you a small cheque[49] what was meant to be your wedding present. Buy something for yourselves – that you fancy – Don't thank me. You know perhaps that they have given me a pension not a very big one – but it will keep me from starvation & it is nice to have something coming in regularly. . . .

[551] To Jane Glass, 26 August 1942
Studio, Corfe Castle, Wareham, Dorset. Wednesday 26

My Dear Jane

I came safely through – luggage & all – and arrived to the tick at Corfe – in drenching fog & rain, steamy & hot & heavy, all the way full trains tho & not overcrowded – masses of Canadians – cheery & interfering with no one – no murders or suchlike.

I eat your delicious sandwiches at Templecombe & thought I had never tasted anything so good – I kept losing my hat, leaving it in rack – but it was always returned to me – 3 times. I found poor bereaved people here burying their dead after the double Raid on Swanage –

I miss your bright company & your pretty ways you were very sweet & good to me. . . .

Don't forget my thanks to Robert Graves for giving me the run of his square strong white house – his books, vegetables, fires above all peace[50] – My love to you

---

[49] £5
[50] Robert Graves had a converted farmhouse near Exeter. He spent the Second World War years in England, returning to Majorca in 1946.

[552] To A. J. McNeill Reid, 1 September 1942

Studio, West St, Corfe Castle, Wareham, Dorset. Sept 1st 1942

Dear Mr. Reid

I am just back from a 2 weeks visit to Devon & find waiting for me your letter of Aug: 20th.

I am afraid I am going to disappoint you. I regret to say that I have done nothing much to signify in the way of painting – conditions only grew worse – I could not fix my mind on work, finally gave up functioning as an artist and returned to Corfe –

I had 2 or 3 lovely days, some rain, a few raids of an intimate sort, much too close – I have not much to come & go on in the way of nerve when the All Clear goes –

However I'll do my very best it goes without saying to let you have what you ask for – 2 paintings & 3 or 4 gouaches as quickly as I can

By the way will you keep an eye on my Gouaches & report any sign of cracking – Miss Browse writes that her cousin's picture "Methodist Chapel" is in a bad state. In a world war what doesnt crack?

How does the artist stand in a case like this? I have offered to re-paint it for her if she supplies me with a photograph

[553] To Dorothy Selby, c.16 September 1942

[Dolaucothy Arms Hotel, Pumpsaint, Llanwrda, Carmarthenshire]

Dearest D

I am here & *really resting* brain and body, wishing you were here or likely to be coming for a spot of mountain air & a spell of sketching before old winter sets in. We are over 400 ft. up & the air is like wine flavoured with conifer pine – rather too many conifers.

Very pleasant & friendly & comfy here – old Farm turned into Inn unpretentious – clean – good food & nice folk. Rather expensive – 5 gns – but for war time not excessive. No staff – Mother & Daughter & handy man – Thats all – Try & come if you possibly can before it grows colder –

To me it is paradise after Corfe. Fine country which will be better still in week or so – harvest in full swing. Cant I tempt you?

[554] To William Hodgkins, 22 October 1942
[Dolaucothy Arms Hotel] October 22nd. 42

My Dearest Willie

Strange that your letter of Aug 25th. has come so quickly – it is a great relief to hear all is well in Wellington & the Earthquake a comparatively harmless one flinging chimneys about but nothing much worse. Glad no one was hurt. Nasty things, I cant stand them – any more than bombs & bits of shell that ocasionally drop in gardens of people I know who don't complain for fear they may be evacuated. One woman did complain and the officer said Oh! thats all right it won't hurt you unless, of course, it *hits* you.

You will see that I am in Wales – in a green valley with a big G . . . reminding me in some ways of NZ. The weather is just filthy, but it is quiet & off the beaten track, real country where the people speak their own vernacular. The Gov: ban on the Welsh language has now been lifted & you hear lighthearted tongues wagging like mad – I cant get *my* tongue round a single word. . . .

While the weather was good I painted like mad – Did I mention I am booked for a London Show in the Spring – January – or Feb.

About the pictures you say Leach still has I am quite willing (but not enthusiastically) to let one or all go for the Red X. I wish for no thanks or kudos knowing too well what you all, or nearly all, think of my work and I grow sick of hearing from intelligent people that they wished I hadn't "changed my style". How do they expect progress except thro' change? As to M. Ferguson she should know better being a cultured travelled woman with a clever husband. As to her friend (& once mine) Kathleen Hosking it makes me sicker still when I think of the *unenlightened* disapproval of the thing she doesnt take trouble to understand. I might say to K. Hosking that all great Art at one stage or another requires the help of Braille to explain it to the semi blind and the wilful blind – Art *is never* easy.

So do what you would like to do with the old pictures – I expect they look pretty funny after all these years. They were painted in my experimental days – which were hungry lean hard ones. The tide had begun to turn after my return to NZ. in 1913 but when Dr. Scott had died I received no further interest or help from my native land – curiously there has always been a Dr. Scott in my life round the corner, when I needed support & faith – come to think of it the doctor who looked after me this last illness was a Dr. Scott.

I must stop drooling on. I want you to know as soon as possible that the letters & parcels have reached me but dates are too vague to quote from memory. Memory! mine is getting very blurred – let me remind you that the Red X Fund for Russia has had £100 from me in pictures. Tauranga sounds a good place to be give my love to Ethel Lees, and Jean . . . .

FH's acquaintance with Eardley Knollys, now agent for the National Trust, was renewed when he stayed at the Dolaucothy Arms.

[555] TO EARDLEY KNOLLYS, 31 OCTOBER 1942

Dolaucothy Arms Hotel, Pumpsaint. Oct 31-42-

Dear Eardley Knollys

If I may so address you. I am still at the Inn, but depart in a day or so; before leaving I must send you a line to say how grateful I am to you for introducing me to Mr. Morgan who has made it pleasant & easy for me to come & go about the Estate without the suspicious eye challenging me. . . . I have done masses of work in between showers of torrential rain, in and about the woods & river of Dolaucothy and have even seriously made pictures of the funny chimney orna-ments, which do so lend themselves to decoration – I love them – tender silly unarranged things, receptacle for old & faded letters – I always fall for them – & always shall

I think that you like them too so I am daring to send as a token of my friendship as well as a "Keepsake" from Dolaucothy, forgetmenots & all, a gouache group from off the kitchen dresser in the House of Mr. Morgan, who I may add is looking a sick man & more & more like the manservant in The Cherry Orchard every time I see him, which generally is Sunday when he wears Sunday black in the true Chekov tradition. . . .

By the way you will find the slipper if you hunt for it[51] –

Please let me know where to tell Styles (framer) to send the picture. It will not reach you for a little time but sometime before Christmas I hope when you will consider it no more than a card of greeting Salut – it will make me happy if you will

I think quite often, at least twice a week of the chance or accident which blew me into this very green valley . . . now browning & falling to the autumn gales – and so, at last, met you –

It can be gloomy & grey but not the temp gris clair of Cezanne. . . .

Let me say, once & for all, from the heart how much I thank you for all you have done for an artist friend – Never shall I forget it.

Yours sincerely

Frances Hodgkins

---

[51] A reference to one of the ornaments, a china shoe, depicted in the painting, which is now called *The China Shoe*. It remained in the possession of Eardley Knollys and was included in the exhibition *Frances Hodgkins – the Late Works* at the Minories, Colchester, in 1990-1.

[556] To Dorothy Selby, 22 December 1942
Studio, West St, Corfe Castle, Wareham, Dorset. Tuesday 22nd 42

Dearest Dorothy

The Barley sugar has come – so consoling & beneficial & delicious – like any baby I do love it so – Thank you so much for sending me something I do really like & enjoy – it goes far to mitigate the austerity food we are patriotically stuffing ourselves with this skinny old Christmas tide. . . .

My own work is suffering – these dark mornings & short daylight give one no chance. . . .

I did happen to have a fatalistic sort of feeling that nothing really matters; in any case it was late to protest either to *you* direct or to Myfanwy Piper.[52] She promised to let me know what she had written but I have had no word since *Aug:* when she came to see me here – and am feeling somewhat hurt – I dislike intensely my private life being brought into any sort of prominence – and letters will very soon dry up at their source if letters are handed round without given permission –

How I envy you at the French Pictures. I have been too long without seeing the jewels & gems of the Nat Gallery

I go out very little even down & up the street excepting to lunch at Inn – one never knows when planes swoop – & machine guns splutter round you – I have had some acute panics like everyone else – Much love to you both & Happy New Year

Frances

[557] To A. J. McNeill Reid, 18 January 1943
Studio, West Street, Corfe Castle, Wareham, Dorset. Jan 18th 43

Dear Mr. Reid

The long awaited Roll of my recent Gouache paintings promised you was sent off on Saturday from here and will, I hope reach the Gallery safely & meet with yr. approval –

I am extremely sorry for the delay – Bronchitis is mainly the cause of it . . . . I am by no means ready yet but barring a further break in health, I could manage a late March date. Can you fit me in approximately with the show of French work you spoke of?. . .

I have sent you 9 Gouaches & could complete another lot of 11 & let the framer have them as quickly as possible. You may remember that I said I should like to include 5 Oils bringing up the catalogue number to 25. . . .

---

[52] Dorothy Selby did not receive in time a letter asking her not to give private letters to Myfanwy Piper (Evans), who was preparing to write the essay on FH for the Penguin Modern Painters Series.

I think it is a very good idea to expand your shows & space them over a longer period. I am glad Mr. Macdonald is back with you to aid & abett you . . . .

I felt I had won a war by the time I stuck on the stamps & left it to its fate. . . .

[558] To Duncan Macdonald, 21 February 1943

Studio, Corfe Castle, Wareham, Dorset. Feb 21st 43

My Dear Duncan

. . . . By now the 6 gouaches will be in your hands – making 15 in all, that I have sent –

I cannot promise any more – nor oils either, so will you & Mr. Reid decide the best thing to do – To put on a small compact Show of 15 gouaches (*no back numbers from the cellars please*) this show must be contempory & recent & fresh – I am sure you will agree –

The alternative is to postpone Show till later in Season when I hope to have more both oils & water colours – with which to make a more important show. . . .

. . . . I am sorry I cant come to London just at present it would give a great deal of pleasure to see you & Lily again – the greatest possible pleasure – but while this awful tension goes on I prefer to wait till things are much more smoothed out before I leave my little most unpeaceful village. Meanwhile my love to you both. Hoping my, or our, brave little Show will be a lively & successful one

Keep up my prices – I beg you. . . .

[559] To Dorothy Selby, 15 March 1943

Studio, Corfe Castle, Dorset. Monday 15 March

My Dearest Dorothy

So glad to hear from you – By rights I should be in London for the P.V of a small show opening tomorrow 16th March at Lefevres[53] – I expect you have cards. . . .

After a week in bed I am convalescing after a sharp go of bronchitis, which hangs around, alarming me – otherwise I might be tempted to make a dash for it & see some nice French pictures for which I am aching – and aching. . . .

[53] *Gouaches by Frances Hodgkins – A New Series of Gouaches Painted during 1942-3.* See *Four Vital Years*, p.122. FH's 15 gouaches were well spaced on two walls and on the third wall was a small exhibition of modern French painting, *Picasso and his Contemporaries* ('Never before have we done all the School of Paris with an English artist. And who better than yourself to be the first in line?' Duncan Macdonald to FH, 22 February 1943.)

[560] To Myfanwy Evans, March 1943

Corfe Castle. March 1943

Dearest Myfanwy

I return the Penguin or is it the Pelican?[54] with my thanks finding greatest pleasure & surprises in reading over week end & keeping it longer than intended. Does this matter? I do hope not –

First of all please let me congratulate you I think it is very good – It is excellent. I call it uncanny the acute way you have unravelled the tangle of my life story & made it into a really lovely little grandiose Book

Not quite quite me – but near enough as may be – Pleasantly salted with malice – as it should be. Very readable – very credible – really d—d good by your leave –

As far as pictures can ever be described no one could do it better. It may, of course, prove difficult to know where word becomes pictures & vice versa. Between us, your words & my painting go well together. To my greatest regret you left out that little Fairy bit about my age & birthplace – What a pity – It was so much to my liking – it was exquisite I thought so truly Myfanwy[55] –

On the subject of age you are dead right. I regard myself as a mature veteran not old, but ageing. In some ways finding my years more a privilege than anything else – Oh! the Drums that I have followed

I cant resist enclosing a letter for you to read, come into my hands recently, written by Dolla Richmond whom you wot of (She was Nelly Sickerts friend went with her on the famous I'll-look-at-Dolla-talk-to-you-honeymoon to Dieppe)[56]

It is a good description of where I stood in 1900 the year of our Lord – As a start off in Europe it could hardly be more happy or propitious. Family advice about this time ran rather like this: Don't paint for Eternity, enjoy success while you have it. Little fool I never knew what success was, or when it wasnt failure – Heaps of magic in my life – Not much glamour – Difficult for the poor Biographer –

I am now madly keen to see the illustrations. You have done some wonderful sleuth work hunting up the vintage pictures. To my sorrow I have been so little use to you – you'll agree that the Lady on Sofa in white fluff is pretty degraded art – emulation carried just *too* far[57] –

Thats about all I think – I won't weary you further –

There are just 1-2 minor corrections otherwise it is in every way satisfactory & right enough approximately speaking.

---

[54] MS of the essay destined for The Penguin Modern Painters.

[55] 'This refers to my first letter to her, saying that since no one knew where or when she was born she was probably a fairy' (footnote to letter by Myfanwy Evans).

[56] See Letter 86, 7 March 1902.

[57] *Reverie*, 1908, the watercolour referred to in Letter 184, 9 December 1908.

My gratitude
My admiration
& thanks
      Frances

[561] To Eardley Knollys, 4 April 1943

Studio, Corfe Castle, Dorset. 4.4.43

Dear Eardley Knollys

I was just going to call Stiles a Lame Dog and something else besides when comes your charming & graceful note saying that you are at last in possession of your very own gouache specially painted for you and above all that you like it, to have and to hold for so long as you fancy; keep it; enjoy it for a while & pass it on in the impermanent way of all art. . . .

[562] To Katharine West, 4 April 1943

Studio, Corfe Castle. 4 4 43

Dearest & Amazing Kitty thank goodness that you have safely got over the Great Accouchement introducing Edmund Anthony. . . .

Time flies – I better hurry up with my letter if it is to reach you before Edmund Anthony sets out for College. Your letter telling me of the great event nearly knocked me over with – an Anderson Shelter which arrived on my doorstep, as a present, just about the same moment as the postman & yr. letter. The shelter is likely to be very handy if I can ever find man & boy to put it together – it is no chimney ornament I can tell you[58]. . . .

All this trifling has exhausted me – Also coping with Duncan . . . newly arrived from U.S.A & full of beans (Boston). He is now wholly on his knees at my feet in brown boots – & some marvellous letters have been written – I fancy he has drawn Lily into helping with the letters. To my extreme sorrow I was not fit to risk the trip to London to see my show – in spite of the mild winter there has been a bit of bronchitis, very obstinate, one or two deathbed scenes with kind Amy holding my hand. . . .

I most terribly miss seeing all you inspiring people acheiving brilliantly all sorts of wonders – the thought of you all brings inspiration & re-birth & will to live & create & enjoy – I am feeling fair crazy with the burgeoning Spring just outside my side door & I am starting a series of local landscape which in winter is a scabrous patch of junk. . . .

---

[58] The Anderson shelter was an early form of protection from air raids, designed to be installed in the gardens of private houses.

I have read Myfanwy's Penguin . . . . I think it is very well done, a clever piece of co ordination of masses of material, inclined to be monotonous but thanks to her, very readable & I hope controversial. She has kept the artist well in front of the human being – I think I have been very well served. . . . I hear the local Bookseller at Swanage is booking orders –

Did I hear you murmur "eggs" *Please* don't send any more – I have plenty to eat & soon now there will be salads. . . .

The editor of Vogue *magazine bought one of the gouaches from the exhibition and was eager to publish an article on FH, including photographs of the artist and her studio. Duncan Macdonald passed on the request for photographs to FH. Later correspondence (Letter 583, 8 June 1944) reveals that Myfanwy Evans was to write the text, though FH apparently did not know this when she replied to Macdonald's letter.*

[563] To Duncan Macdonald, 11 April 1943

Corfe Castle. April 11th. 43

Dear Duncan

I think that Lady Septugeranium (incorrectly spelt I know, but best I can do) Artists should be allowed to doze off against a Sunset sky, their latest master piece unfinished at their feet, and on their tombstone the words:

> She knew many Dealers
> and bore with them patiently

Dont you agree?

How am I to answer your letter of 9th. April? I have been staring at it over the week end praying for inspiration. I am bitterly & furiously grieved not to see my own little Show. I wanted so very much to see how a grouping of 15 of a family told as a unit on a wall – was it monotonous? *and* was there that universality I ever strive after, apparent between the Ecole de Paris & FH?

This in all humility

For the answers to these problems I should have to come to London. How I wish I could. But I dare not risk it much tempted as I am and longing to meet you both again. . . .

I do rejoice that you have done such good business, in a small way, and that the cupboard is bare. Would you like a few more to put in it?

I have had quite a lot of letters – Sylvia Lynd wrote asking for a portrait of herself & 2 babies that I painted of them in my Studio at St Ives 25 yrs. ago – offering 20 gns. for them. Having seen my name mentioned with the "great &

famous" she thought how nice to have a Frances Hodgkins to boast of! Well she cannot have it – It is destroyed & rightly so. . . .

Of course I see the considerable publicity value of a Vogue article (illustrated) Before consenting I shall have to find out what restrictions there are about photographing in this ultra restricted area – 1st. Line & all that implies. Supposing you allow me a few days to make enquiries

There is nothing glamorous about my poor old chapel Studio. . . .

My congratulations & warmest thanks to Mr. Reid & yourself.

Always sincerely
Frances Hodgkins

Will let you know how I stand as to photos as soon as possible

[564] To Muriel Hodgkins, 24 April 1943

Corfe Castle, Dorset. April 24th. 43

My Dearest Muriel

Your cable telling me of dear Bert's death reached me yesterday Good Friday April 23rd. It was a sad shock – and I keep wondering what sudden illness has carried him off and I have been very near to tears thinking of you all & the sad blank in your happy Family circle this Easter tide. . . .

It has always been such a comfort to me to know how happy you have made Bert & what a grand unselfish wife you have been & what a success you both have made of married life. . . . My warm love to you and the girls . . . .

I hope this will reach you safely, also the cable message I sent off today in reply to yours. It was so kind & thoughtful of you to think of me. The dear Bert is very much in my thoughts & I think of him always kind always unselfish with a brave honest outlook on life & very loveable & true – Bless him –

Affectionately yours
Frances

[565] To Duncan Macdonald, 22 May 1943

Studio, Corfe Castle, Dorset. May 22nd 43

My Dear Duncan

I have very great pleasure in thanking you for your letter & statement of account which you have sent me and I do most warmly congratulate you & Mr. Reid on your very great success in selling my pictures, in the teeth of the French Masterpieces too – it is just amazing[59] –

---

[59] The exhibition sold out. After framing costs and 33 per cent commission were deducted FH received £290.17.10.

. . . . I never lose sight of the fact that pictures have to be *sold* – They are never *bought*

I am sure you will agree that results have justified the top price of £25 that you so boldly & triumphantly aimed at –

Indeed I am quite as pleased as you are. It will be good to have a nice cheque, even if it is plucked away from me by the Income Tax Fiends leaving me with 2 feathers to fly off with. . . .

As regards the mystery Water Colour sent by Mr. Reid it reached me a day in advance of your letter giving me time to take it in & reconstruct its past history & parentage –

It is obviously unfinished and as you say so truly "I never saw one like it myself before". Its title is Shrine of St Francis Tréboul – Brittany – 1922. I painted it several times – The subject facinated me. So far as I can recall it is the original Sketch of a Water Colour exhibited at Claridge Gallery[60] & bought by Mrs. Robert Little, Tunbridge. Round about this time Mr. Green or Mr. Stone paid a visit one Sunday to the Bloomsbury Studios & invited us to send to his new little Gallery in Chelsea. Cedric Morris persuaded me to send – I did so – I sent several Water Colours one of which they framed & exhibited – I don't fancy the frame was ever paid for – I was so often abroad in those days that I became very careless about the fate of my pictures. They were a continual expense & bother to me – of these sketches the "Shrine" might easily be one – I myself think it is a bad bona fide Hodgkins of that period and I wish Mr. Reid luck with it. At first sight I thought of asking Mr. Reid to let me finish it & improve it but on second thoughts I decided to leave it as it is & not mix 2 vintages – I will sign it & date it and return it during next week I hope

I need a little more time to finish the Gouaches I have for you – April-May months in spite of the idyllic weather conditions have been distracting & dithering beyond words – I have done much less, and less well than I hoped –

. . . . I gather the Penguin Book is on the way – I have seen the proofs, the text, but not the illustrations – very good I think. I shall be sending you several letters from people wanting pictures – the same price & size as the recent show – just as soon as I have answered them. . . . If I succeed in pulling off a good oil Painting that pleases me I will let you have it but it is not so easy getting them packed – will do my best –

Thanking you again for your most marvellous help & enthusiasm without which my little pictures could never have gone off with such a bang!

Admiringly & affectionately
Frances Hodgkins

[60] *Shrine of St. Peter* was exhibited at the Claridge Gallery, April-May 1928.

[566] To William Hodgkins, 1 June 1943

Dorset. June 1st. 43

My Dearest Willie

I am covering odd pieces of paper with jottings – I can't call it a letter – I am very tired & suffering from strain & noise – a bad form of fear – the deadliest sin in war time. . . .

I have posted you 6-8 bundles of Listener – Picture Post dating from Feb, posted every 2 weeks. Hope you have had them.

I have written erratically because I have been so busy – but I *think* I have acknowledged all yr. generous gift parcels of food excepting the last one sent by Jean for which I have a special letter of thanks – warmest sincerest thanks, heartfelt. The only really 100% good food I get is what you send – N.Z tinned goods are supreme – especially the meat – cheese etc. Cheese a bit mouldy if it is delayed in the post – but good. American sardines are the latest delicacy (!) we are sampling – price 5d. Even the cats wont touch them. . . . You will notice that food is uppermost in my mind – my baser side – not hungry but just bored – your gifts are like corn in Egypt. . . .

Well it has been a joy of joys seeing Peter for the first time grown up – It is odd to think of him as a parent 37 years old. He looks such a nice brown boy, honest brave eyes – merry smile like his father – most endearing – smiling his way along. He turned up here one day recently, out of the blue – I was prepared to see him yr. letter having warned me he was on his way over. It was sheer good luck his being stationed at Bournemouth an hrs drive from here – He came again another day & had lunch with me at the Inn[61]. . . .

. . . . Forgive me if I don't write oftener. There is always so much to do – very little of the domestic side goes a long way to tire me – but I have to face it for there is very little outside help – I am always in arrears with the London Dealers who sell my work for me . . . .

---

[61] In a letter to his wife, 8 May 1943, Peter Field described his visit: 'I am feeling in high good humour after spending one of the nicest afternoons possible with Aunt Fanny. . . . She is a marvellous conversationalist & incredibly witty and entertaining. She took me to see a very old friend and admirer of hers, a Miss Krauss who makes pottery. . . . two more delightful companions one could hardly wish for. . . . They have lived their lives never taking the easy way out, profiting by their mistakes, & keeping pace with every new idea & movement & in some cases twenty years ahead. Keen analytical brains sifting the dross from the gold . . . . There is something so wholesome that it is just like a tonic to be with them. To be with Fanny is to understand her pictures, at last I can appreciate them. I can see what she is driving at . . . . They might be compared to an account of the subject, you can't see it at a glance, you have to read them – it is writing in colour and form. After all the earliest writings were in pictorial form & now we have it again from a highly trained hand and eye . . . . '

[567] To William Hodgkins, 5 July 1943

Corfe Castle. July 5th. 43

A quick line dearest Willie to thank you for your letter of 14th. May . . . . 3 big letters in one envelope . . . . It is comforting to hear from Muriel that she was satisfied that Bert had all the attention & skill humanly possible. If only the poor chap had eased off earlier this attack might have been averted. . . .

July 26th. Here letter broke off Without warning of any kind the roof of my poor old Studio did a slide into the court yard below[62] – happily with no injury to self or pictures but with great inconvenience. You never saw such a mess in your life – I had a near miss large peices of ceiling kept falling – since then the Studio has become more derelict & the rains have done their worst. No labour, no building materials obtainable till after the war – all I have to protect my belongings are a few tarpaulins. I have salved all my painting gear & canvases & now live crowded into my tiny next door 2 roomed cottage *very* uncomfortably – but safe – and dry. I am going off presently to another Dorset village Cerne Abbas. I feel I can do with a little peace & quiet. I feel pretty wan & tired – Too many letters from admirers to answer, from Dealers, photographers from "Vogue", from Mothers wanting me to paint their children – etc etc. If I had wanted to be a fashionable painter now is my chance – I find it terribly tedious. My Dealers have a waiting list – All my contemporary work is sold out. There is a Penguin Special coming out shortly – illustrated. . . .

I tried sending you & Jean a fiver the other day – I hope you got it. You have been so good & generous sending food. . . .

. . . . a busy tiring ill spent day, mostly speaking, wasting time & energy over utterly unimportant things – "Picking up your Rations" as they say being the nastiest. But there it is – we are all in it – and lucky to be alive

I have no recent news of Peter. . . .

[568] To Duncan Macdonald, 5 July 1943

Studio Cottage, Corfe Castle, Dorset. Monday 5th. July

My Dear Duncan

I hope that you won't do anything so unjust and so unkind as to send the Editor of Vogue or her assistant to take shots at me against the background of this Studio under its present conditions

Nothing will induce me to consent – the whole idea is repugnant to me & artistically speaking it is a mistake – more, a *crime*

---

[62] The collapse of the studio roof was first reported in a letter of 26 June 1943.

I am going away till the Studio is restored & made safe meanwhile it is locked. . . .

Pchycologically – or perhaps pathologically I have an intense aversion to being photographed now – it is too late –

I am dead off my Studio – I must get away from here for a bit – further inland –

I wish I was as optimistic as you are about the gouache & the Studio roof getting finished in "due course"

In "due course" then I shall send them on to you –

Despairingly
Frances Hodgkins

[569] To Dorothy Selby, 9 July 1943

Corfe Castle. July 9th.

Dearest Dorothy

How noble of you to spare me a stocking – thank you so much I return it to its mate. . . . I should like it very much if you can get me a similar pair at 8/11 each, or if not these the ones at 13/11. . . but for heaven's sake don't tire yourself hunting round London for stockings for me much as they are needed – my legs are a scandal –

I enclose cheque for 30/– . . . *nothing darkish please* – I send my Clothing coupons. You will see I am not much of a shopper –

I have had a nasty shock – The stone roof of the Studio fell off, suddenly, 2 Sunday evenings ago, gave me a fright . . . .

Heavy tank traffic helped to loosen the heavy stones & they just slid *off* the roof in one piece into the garden . . . .

. . . . David & Norman made a lightning descent to pick up belongings for their new flat at Marble Arch – I lunched with them & heard gossip –

Wonderful & beautiful weather record hay harvest – ricks going up like magic – blazing sunshine for days on end – then warm rain & storms to cool us down

The war rolls on – .

I grow more & more eminent – it is an ominous sign – Have been asked by Bournemouth art lovers to open their Show & make a speech – for £5 I don't think –

I'll take yr. advice about underwear & send sample

Storm brewing – No more Love & thanks Frances

[570] To Dorothy Selby, 7 September 1943
                New Inn, Cerne Abbas, Dorchester, Dorset. Tuesday Sept. 7th

Dearest D –

I am here – since Sat: In between showers it is a sweet wee place – Some haughty houses – mostly empty – in purist period dignity, a few Inns – duck ponds & that's about all – but enough – set in brownish landscape, brooded over by a mysterious giant cut in the limestone over the village . . . .

Now about Sat. On hearing from you when yr. train *gets to Dorchester a car from here will meet you*. . . .

. . . . The tarif for car is 12/– I know you wont mind. . . .

Cerne Abbas is complete Anti war & will be a real rest & tonic for a tired worker – such as *you* & *me* etc – we make our beds – & are otherwise handy & helpful to each other. So matey! I came here – despairing – tired out & hopeless – but a few good nights' rest & wholesome food here worked miracles. . . .
[Postscript] Towel – soap – candle – matches – are scarce –

[571] To Peter Field, 16 September 1943
                The New Inn, Cerne Abbes, Dorchester, Dorset. Sept 16th. 43

My Dear Peter

It is good to get your cheerful letter sent on from Corfe – and to hear that things are turning out well with you as you hoped they might when last we met . . . . The last authentic picture I had was of your Mother expecting to speak to you on Sunday morning . . . she sounded elated & happy in her letter and I hope you were able to hear each other across the world. . . . Shortly after yr. visit to Corfe I had the rotten bad luck to have the Studio roof collapse . . . . Finally a mason was found who would tackle the dangerous job of relaying the stone roof – in the meantime, until the Studio is habitable once more I have come here, intending to go on to Wales if I can find accomodation . . . . I have been on the point of writing to you and asking you to come here on yr. next leave; it is rather a darling little village . . . the perfect English scene – over all there broods a mysterious Giant cut in the chalk hill by the Romans & still quite alarming. They could draw in those days! It is a tremendously vital giant – really the God of Fertility – & looks it[63] – So goes the legend –

. . . . I'll give your message to Kraussie – She always asks for you. . . .
                Much love Peter Dear Frances. . . .

[63] The giant has an erect penis.

[572] To Duncan Macdonald, 5 December 1943

Studio, Corfe Castle, Dorset. Dec 5th. 43

My Dear Duncan

Many thanks for your letter. About the pictures for New York I am afraid I am not much help to you. I feel that I cannot produce more work than you & Mr. Brown want from me and if some are sent to America you will have to have patience *or* do without –

If you send the cream of my latest work abroad you wont have it in London –

Mr Thwaites[64] did approach me. I sent him on to you –

If he likes to buy a few of my pictures out right for a high price say £100 each I'll sign them for him – But I am not inclined to send them out on speculation these risky times especially as he says the English Moderns in America are without reputation prestige or market value

Sad but true! He adds –

I am not wholly inactive but I work against difficulties and the work goes slowly. There are about 5-7 gouaches that go to Mr. Brown, as promised, as soon as they have my signature – This is the best I can offer under the present dull circumstances

I am afraid I must postpone the pleasure & honour of collaborating in the NY scheme (quite simply have not got the goods required – cupboard *very* bare)

Yours Frances Hodgkins

Enclosed from Mr Thwaites – I don't want them back

[573] To David Brynley, 21 December 1943

Corfe Castle. Dec 21st. 1943

My dear David

There is no apology abject enough from me to you which could explain & throw light on the mystery of my long silence regarding the handsome gift, or loan, of a signed copy of that rare & daring book I like so much the Ubiquitous Man – weeks & weeks ago – I must have got embedded in work & forgotten how time was flying[65]. . . .

[64] John Thwaites of the British Ministry of Information had been asked by the Nierendorf Gallery in New York to arrange an exhibition of about five leading English artists. When first approached about the exhibition in mid-October FH had expressed interest but insisted, against Mr Thwaites's wishes, that he work through her dealer. The other artists he approached were John Piper, Graham Sutherland and Henry Moore (drawings).

[65] FH had borrowed from David Brynley an autographed copy of Julian Huxley's *The Uniqueness of Man* (London, 1941). She had found it so interesting that she asked if she could keep it. On hearing this, Julian Huxley sent a second copy to David Brynley inscribed 'Cast your bread upon the waters and it will be

I am tremendously proud of my copy – the author's signature adds to its lustre – give him this message that I hope next time he & Mrs. Huxley pass this way they will knock at my Studio door. I should be enchanted – if happily I am there

He belongs to the world. I heard a cosmic voice on the air the other night say that she "loved Julian Huxley because of his accuracy –" so nice & abstract – I thought

I think I am going to dine with the Newberys on Christmas night

Your heart would bleed if you could hear the sad stories of the poor old people being turned out this week end from Kimmeridge to make room for the billions of Canadians pouring in to this part of England[66]. . . .

[574] To Jane Saunders, 4 January 1944

Studio, Corfe Castle, Dorset. Jan 4th 1944

My Dearest Jane

. . . . I have kept you waiting long enough for a reply to your urgent, ardent, wholly delightful letters, both yours & E's – they warm the cockles of my heart.[67] Of course you can keep "Roots" Jane. I am glad you like it I think it is rather a pet. I give it to you for Christmas 1943, with my love. I know you will use greatest discretion & not let it get about that the Artist gave it to you – My dealers might have something to say about that. My prices have risen and are still rising. Unfortunately for me & my Bank a/c I have not been able to fully benefit by this happy state of affairs – owing largely to health & nerves & lack of comfort etc etc – the major root of all our present ills is of course the war & the war climax so close at hand & menacing – I fall into a regular vertigo of fear & horror when I allow myself to dwell on what is happening out there in the black void – let us keep to the point which deals with pictures not battle fields. Will you tell E . . . that if she really wishes to possess the Abandoned Cottage I will accept £5.5 for it & please not to tell friends how much she paid for it. . . .

I think you & E have got a small section of the cream of my work, such as it is. They are vintage pieces – 1943. . . .

P.S. I like the Mathew Smith handkercheif so very much. . . . It is so pretty . . . just large enough to cover the little nude when she takes her rest & allows Matthew to squeeze out some fresh rose madder & emerald green. . . . I know the model of the nude. Her name is Eve – wears tailor mades in real life – very orthodox

---

returned to you, if not buttered, at least autographed.' Huxley owned several paintings by FH and visited her at Corfe shortly after this. (Unpublished memoir of FH by David Brynley, 1951.)

[66] Preparations for the Allied landing in Normandy which began on 6 June 1944.

[67] Jane Saunders's friend Elizabeth Shaw wished to buy one of FH's paintings as a gift for Jane and FH sent three gouaches and a drawing to choose from.

[575] To Jane Saunders, 12 January 1944

Corfe Castle. Jan 12-44

My Dearest Jane

.... It is extremely nice of Elizabeth to send so lordly a cheque and I feel touched and more than pleased that my 3 pictures are so valued & enjoyed. ...

.... Forgive if I return the cheque. I am not in need of it. So do, I beg you both, use it for the Holiday fund, it may come in handy . . . please don't argue there's a dear and be glad I am alive to have the happiness of returning in kind some of the many kind turns you have done me in the past. I don't forget.

I like to think your enjoyment of the pictures is 2 fold & that you have a pal to jointly agree about it – or disagree. I feel myself blessed in being able to pass on a little bit of magic, the magic which runs about the world & is above rubies & beyond price – strictly speaking this is far from the truth but it is a pleasant ½ truth. ...

[576] To Duncan Macdonald, 31 January 1944

Studio Cottage, Corfe Castle, Dorset. Jan 31-44

Dear Duncan

.... You enquire about possible oils – I should prefer to send you 2 recently painted Gouaches and leave the oils till later on when I have time to look them over & get them packed

I think that you will like the Cerne Abbas Gouaches; it so happens they are rather more heavily painted than usual and some art ignoramus might mistake them for oils. ...

The price I leave to you – I think not less than £50. What do you think? I have a horrid fear that my powers are growing dim. So make the most of what I can send you –

It is all to the bad that I am alone down here in this deadly conservative milieu. I feel an out cast.

.... My special love to Lily & thanks for the Christmas card. ...

[577] To Eardley Knollys, 4 March 1944

Studio, Corfe Castle, Dorset. March 4th. 1944

My Dear Eardley

I am sorry to be so long in replying to your very kind letter. I have been so busy painting after your inspiring visit, all too brief, and your flattering words which I drank down thirstily feeling happy & honoured. It is a gorgeous thing to recapture some of the glorious movement & rhythm which moves one both in music & in art. Why? All because one feels happy; lame explanation but it serves.

It was good of you to collect the picture & store it for me till I can decide what to do about it. If any good it ought to have a career in the Galleries I expect it is pretty grimy after [Manchester] & London fogs – & needs conscientious cleaning. 1928 is about the date I fancy – I can't recall it – more than it being rather architectural in design – title 'Lancashire Family' Don't let it be troublesome to you if it is, ask Lefevre or Leicester Galleries to take it away –

I hope your house & occupiers have escaped serious damage and are standing up well to the everlasting damnation bombs come back to us again – I hope it wont be very long before we can put aside anxieties of this sort

The picture you mention owned by Mrs. Dugdale dates from a sumptous short period at St Raphael. I bought hundreds of melons in the market to paint in my room – melons give intense satisfaction. . . .

[578] To Dorothy Selby, 20 March 1944

Corfe Castle. Monday 20th March

Dearest Dorothy

Your big budget of cuttings was flung into my letter box this morning as I was struggling into garments –

I read them as I ate my breakfast. How odd that you should send them – They came in answer to my prayers – I had been mourning the fact that I had missed the poison letter in the Times.[68] So could not make sense of Osbert Lancaster's "Observer" letter – I gathered there was quite a bit of hot air about, over the appointment.[69] The only comment I have heard down here is that Munnings is a rough diamond – which puts it mildly. I suppose he was thought to be an improvement on Augustus John who would have made an excellent even ideal P[resident] RA *sober*. But after his fiasco with the Queen's portrait was he to be trusted to receive, or be received by Royalty? The whole business is sickening. A nasty messy disgusting tale to go out to the world in the name of art – it gives one a very bad headache indeed. . . .

This is a patchy letter – My hands are so cold – work at a standstill – it was a joy to get the 2 cards, especially the primitive gouache – lovely! I almost wept with happiness – it seemed to glow within me how I wish to see it. I shall one of these

---

[68] The letter (11 March 1944) attacked the Council for the Encouragement of Music and the Arts for organising exhibitions 'designed to carry on the baleful influence of what is known as "modernistic" art. This is a subversive movement which, with its several "isms", has been for many years endeavouring to undermine the traditional glories of painting and sculpture.' There were 12 signatories, among them Alfred Munnings.
[69] Alfred Munnings was appointed President of the Royal Academy.

days. But not now – I am all on edge waiting for the finale, the great bubble which *must* burst soon.

No news of nephew – AK had a letter from David [Brynley]. He wrote very emotionally after a bad nights raiding – He told Amy he had to keep a check on his emotions – it was really too agonising – singing to & comforting poor people who had lost sons. I dont wonder they saw something in David to remind them of their boys –

I wish you were out of London – Give my love to your sister All my love & thanks again for items catalogue etc a real thrill

Frances

[579] To Dorothy Selby, 13 April 1944

Corfe Castle. April 13-44

Dearest Dorothy

The turkish delight was heavenly!

Where on earth did you find it – & having found it how angelic of you to pass it along – I had forgotten what a delicious sweet it is, wild honey and camels' milk? Was it John Baptist who fed on it ? – with locusts if so He did not do so badly. . . .

[580] To Duncan Macdonald, 20 April 1944

Studio, Corfe Castle, Dorset. Tuesday April 20th 44

My Dear Duncan

Of course I should love to give you something nice for your coming Show[70] – I will do my best – A day's work is needed before they are ready for the post. . . .

There are 3 gouache – And 2 small sized oils – It may prove not so easy to get them sent by rail – I must see –

I am filled with wonder & admiration at your amazing recovery from the Blitz. And it's grand to hear continuity of "the Lefevre" is assured & safe[71]. . . .

I am in darkest ignorance as to what pictures you now have of mine; such being the case it is not possible for me to send to Bristol[72] which I don't specially wish to do, being very stingily endowed with the Group spirit – As you say what do I gain by sending – Not much – In answering Edward Wolfe's letter will you please

---

[70] A Group Exhibition of FH, Ben Nicholson and Graham Sutherland.
[71] The Gallery was bombed on 23 February and moved to new premises in New Bond Street.
[72] The London Group were exhibiting there.

tell him that I have no available work & have done nothing of importance for some time – owing to health reasons etc. I shall be writing him a line myself –

All these letters have become a bogey to me & I simply can't "cope" any longer with them –

So when you ask if I am happy? NO I am not – or well? Not so bad – I am bored to death when I am not painting and angry with my stupid self because I fail to add to my artistic stature by not answering all the charming letters of recognition & appreciation that come to me & alas receive so little response from me –

Enclosed letter from N. York is one of 2 letters from the same Firm[73] – I expect you know it – As far as I can see at the present rate of production I will not be showing outside London for some years yet – if ever.

I will write again after I have posted my gouache Paintings & listed them etc – I hope you will find them to your taste & fancy –

Meanwhile my very best wishes for the new & brilliant venture ahead of you
Love from Frances

So glad to hear you liked the Leicester Gallery gouaches to the point of envy – I thought I had given you the pick of the basket – Please frame the new ones similarly[74]

[581] To Myfanwy Evans, 28 May 1944
Studio, Corfe Castle, Dorset. May 28th. 44

Concerning the Penguin books will you please Myfwany be a dear and tell me how & where I stand[75]

I ask because having ear marked a certain few pictures in the £100 class, with difficulty, I can bear up better if I hear that a picture is no longer acceptable as barter between Publisher & Painter. The point is, am I no longer a potential Penguin? So what?

How very good indeed they are the 4 elite, elect Aristocrats – I am the happy possesor of all 4 – It should be a raging success and everyone in need of the solace of Art should have a copy – But will they?

It would be less sad to know if my Book is not to be published, definitely yes or no –

It is raging hot here and very uncomfortable with one little stupid scare after another. Where did I read "Like what you get or be a neurotic"

---

73 The Bucholz Gallery, New York.
74 FH had sent three big gouaches to Leicester Galleries, which sold quickly.
75 The first four books of The Penguin Modern Painters series had now been published. The artists were Duncan Grant, Henry Moore, Paul Nash and Graham Sutherland. On the cover future publications in the series were announced. FH was not mentioned.

Am living on a petty plane full of troublesome jobs and doing little painting – So when you can spare the time do just drop me a line to say how you are – and what is expected of me in regard to the token picture. I do dislike this uncertainty & the intolerable sense of sin & frustration caused by an unfinished creative act. It is cumulative & in the end kills the artist

Accept my love

Frances

I especially liked Geoffrey Grigson's tribute to the terrific meaning behind Moores work and its unity. I liked it very much.

[582] To Eardley Knollys, 6 June 1944

Studio, Corfe Castle, Dorset 6-6 44

My Dear Eardley

I owe you a letter in reply to yours of May 23rd . . . . concerning the price of my dusty old picture painted quite 15 yrs. ago in the purlieus of Ancoats (Manchester) a squalid & slummy spot but the real thing for picture making.[76]

I have the dimmest idea of what the picture is like – I remember about that period I had artistic yearnings to paint Lancashire Mill Girls: some of them were raging beauties

I loved painting piled up family groups This must have been one of them – It was shown at the London Group & skied Later it was lent to the 2 scalliwag young men at 3d. a week, who finally vanished to S Africa. I missed their pleasant company but I missed my picture more – This leads up to your unearthing it for me at Paddington of all places and restoring it to me –

I am telling you all this in order that you may think twice about buying it – Do you really like it so much?

Is it quite your cup of tea?

I should very much like you to have it – I had thought of offering it to Mr. Lane[77] to complete my part of his bargain or failing this show it in the Spring of 1945 at my Show in the Leicester Galleries. I wish I could come up to London & have a look at it –

The "number of pounds" would be £50. I dont know what Messieurs the Lefevre Galleries will think about it if ever they find out –

I now possess the 4 advance Penguins. I must say I think they are very good indeed and the quite delightful writing sets one thinking, dreaming, educating –

And now for the next new ones – Graham Sutherland rings the bell How well he understands the secret of ornament & object – Chirico's secret

[76] *Lancashire Family.* See Letter 577, 4 March 1944.
[77] FH was to contribute a painting towards the publication of the Penguin book.

As for myself precious little work – This hot sunshine makes one lazy – Are you eating strawberries to the noise of Battle – I am – To my shame – but no cream –

[583] To Myfanwy Evans, 8 June 1944

Studio, Corfe Castle, Dorset. June 8th 1944

My Dear Myfwany

I was very happy to get your letter. It has cleared the air. . . .

You are a large hearted woman – if you are feeling neglected I am feeling an out cast as well as a bit of a dam fool for caring whether I appear with the first 4 Penguins or the last four

I have been wholly miserable for one reason & another and have searched my conscience – I appear to have behaved like a bounder and no wonder you felt annoyed. I suppose it is not too late to make amends to Vogue? If possible it should be done. It is as long ago as last July that you wrote to me I think we were both on holiday, you in Cornwall & I in Cerne Abbas – I remember we were both hectic & oppressed with affairs – I meant to answer the letter & was quite enthusiastic about it but there was some hesitation in my mind about the "early photographs" & "following Sickert" which puzzled me – So my reply never got written & to my grief I realised too late that I had let you down & thus lost you a useful bit of work plus cheque – Do forgive me –

I have a very real & valid excuse in the state of my health which for the last 2 years has been, on & off, rotten – loss of memory is my chief physical trial at present –

As to the Penguin Book I am so glad to hear that you mean to let me see the illustrations soon – I can't help feeling fussy about them because, admittedly my work does *not* reproduce well –

I do realise dear Myfwany your endless difficulties in the way of writing about me truthfully & intimately. It is painful to go too near the bone and as you say "disgruntling all round"

Is it possible that I have been writing "chatty" letters? Through the same fruitful source I heard pretty things about you & your babies "Myfanwy is marvellous" A perfect Douanier Rousseau. Why wasn't I there to admire you?

How monstrous it is that you are working so hard without help enough. Shall we ever be back to normal? Yes!

Indeed I do wish we could meet – I see no chance of London yet – The ban in this area is rigid. I have tied myself to a date in the early Spring 1945 at the Leicester Galleries –

You will bear in mind what I feel about Vogue – without being abject I would like them to know I am penitent[78]. . . .

You have been sweet to me –
My love Frances

[584] To WILLIAM HODGKINS, 21 JUNE 1944

Corfe Castle. June 21st. 44

My Dearest Willie

Things again not very pleasant. . . . What new horror will they invent?[79] This is just a line to say all well – so far – A parcel just come – containing cheese & jam – how good of you to bother to send . . . . Feeding myself & running my small cottage under great difficulties . . . . I reached point of saturation so came to the "Grey Hound" where I now am, for company's sake as much as anything – I get 3 good meals a day. I have taken the greatest pleasure in sharing my precious cheese with the Soldiers & their wives at the Inn – it is only a small Hotel with a few stuffy noisy bedrooms (convoys of tanks etc make hellish noise passing up & down, in & out of the village) For a shilling there is a hot bath – you have to ask the landlady for the plug & key of bathroom – But it works – & the water is good & hot. . . . I live from hour to hour – day to day – this new Pilot horror makes us feel rather desperate, especially at nights – overhead both day & night doing their damnedest to keep one awake & guessing – you no doubt wonder why I stay? So do I! . . . Friends here are good to me & the country is lovely – & this bit of coast line in Dorset the loveliest in the world – banned now of course. I am in fairly good health – and am feeling the benefit of regular meals – and rest. Most of us are looking rather wan – one needs to be pretty strong headed to survive a 4 yrs. war such as this war. Dont be anxious about me – I am alright so long as you continue to get papers from me – I am glad you enjoy them

Have plenty of work to do for the Galleries – I am deluged with invitations commissions etc – They all want Frances H now.

Sorry letter so scrappy – & vague – You ask me to say what I would like you to send me to eat. Here are a few items I fancy: Barley Sugar, Shortbread, Jam – preferably quince, Meat – now & again. *No more cheese* . . . .

---

[78] Myfanwy Evans was not to write about FH for *Vogue* until August 1947, three months after her death. In September 1945 Jane Stockwood wrote an appreciative account of FH in 'Vogue's Spotlight'. The article was illustrated with a reproduction of a gouache, *Parrot with Poppy*.
[79] The first V1 guided missile fell on London on 13 June 1944.

[585] To Dorothy Selby, 26 June 1944

Corfe Castle. June 26th. 44

My Dearest Dorothy

. . . . How vile it all is this devilry. Please come down here if things are nasty not that it is safe or quiet, far from it, but at any rate it is not so bad as London. . . .

I owe you a letter for the very interesting one you sent me after seeing Cedric's Show.

I wrote him. He wrote back. He thought he might come to the Greyhound & get some rest & change – He wasnt down cast over his Show. Said it "was alright". . . .

The village is stiff with troops mostly Canadians & the motor traffic is terrific. A big chunk of Greyhound wall is knocked off. I dare not advise you one way or another – one can only be guided by events – The planes overhead bringing back wounded from Normandy have scared all art out of me – I simply cannot paint. This lovely weather makes it easier. The sun has been pouring down on us & we are literally cooked

I have heard from Mrs Piper – she is sending samples of my illustrations – Curious you running into each other – was she rather cross?

AK blows in once a week or so to see if I survive, how I am etc. She swops my sugar ration for strawberries & salads, or rather did before I moved into Inn. . . . Putting on weight – but nerves steadier – company is good for one. . . .

Eardley Knollys suggested that he buy and renovate the studio in Corfe Castle, leasing it to FH in return for a picture a year. Mr and Mrs Newbery, the elderly owners, found it difficult to make a decision and asked the advice of their daughters, Mrs Sturrock and Mrs Lang.

[586] To Eardley Knollys, 5 August 1944

Studio, Corfe Castle, Dorset. August 5th. 44

My Dear Eardley

This is in reply to the lovely greedy Braque with the hors d'oeuvre of 3 emasculated oysters, more oyster than oyster making the mouth of this hungry exile water[80] – and here is Mrs. Shurrocks green ink letter which I found waiting me on my return . . . .

---

[80] Braque painted several still life groups including oysters during the 1920s and there is a later work of 1937 with three oysters.

I am sure that you will understand her anxiety that her parents should be spared suffering or distress – they are so very old & frail. I strongly feel that we should negotiate through the sisters – or sister – when one, or both, are here in Sept-October. . . .

Oh! My lovely pictures![81]

Aren't I clever?

These two you have so nobly sent me are my Swan Song – the Family highly stylized aiming at musical unity & a sort of colour combination missing in the Prints. Red Cockerel is the better painting. Thank you so very much for them – They are extremely good photographs.

Love Frances

Have left Pissarro's letters with Margot to return to you & brought away with me Samuel Palmer that massive & holy man.[82] The more one reads of their private lives the more one sees the raw deal that is theirs from all but cradle to grave. . . .

[587] To Dorothy Selby, 13 August 1944

Corfe. Sunday 13th.

Dearest Dorothy

You will be as sorry as I am that Mrs. Hobbs[83] cannot find a room for you in Sept. . . .

I called on AK. to see what could be done – She would offer you a room but has really her hands too full, without help of any kind, to make it possible –

I quite agree – she knocks herself out with work – garden, kitchen, pottery etc – she is looking wilted! . . .

It is imperative that you should get out of London & away from those foully wicked Doodle Bugs. . . .

[588] To Eardley Knollys, 20 October 1944

Studio, Corfe Castle. Oct 20th. 44

Dear Eardley

I was distressed to hear you were ill, but not too tediously so to judge by your high spirited letter. . . . gay & good as a POEM – I read it aloud . . . .

---

[81] Knollys had sent FH photographs of *Lancashire Family* and *Red Cockerel*.

[82] Samuel Palmer (1805-81) transformed the English landscape into visionary paintings celebrating the mystery and fecundity of nature. He was influenced by William Blake and himself influenced Graham Sutherland.

[83] The landlady at the Greyhound Inn, remembered for her kindness. She cared for FH during her last illness.

Well you'll find me here with or without new pictures – all depends
I have 2-3 high-powered gouaches – also ditto oils. . . .

By now I had hopes of news from the Newberrys – All I know is that one of
the Sisters may be here shortly . . . .

I am sorry this is not a very helpful letter – No dearth of news – plenty of it
– *today* a Wedding – yesterday Mary Spenser Watson[84] gored by a Bull – etc &
so on! one grows dangerously hardened under the over shadowing horror of War

Best thanks for a very lovely letter – and love

Frances

*In November it seemed that the Newbery family were prepared to sell the studio to
Eardley Knollys. Grateful for his efforts on her behalf, FH gave him a recent oil,*
Courtyard by Night, *now called* Courtyard in Wartime.

[589] To Katharine West, 12 January 1945

Studio, Corfe Castle, Wareham, Dorset. 12th. Jan 45

Very dearest Kitty

You will be on the point of wondering what has happened to me when your
letter came telling me the worst possible bad news of you & Anthony – it was an
awful shock to me – just heartbreaking – I had heard a tiny rumour some months
ago . . . I did not take it seriously – but, oh! Dear! it is only too true – confirmed
by your sad letter – your very very sad letter. Kitty *what* has happened between
you 2 lovers & pals if ever there were such? It is all incredibly wrong & rotten that
this should have split your lovely home & family life – it seems only the other day
you wrote so happily of your life with Anthony & how well it was working with
the babies as a centre of devotion & care. . . .

I can see you are not daunted or baffled by things – Have you seen much of
the Pipers? Have they been a help? His pictures are having a phenomenal furore!

It was sweetly kind of you to send me the Turkish Delight. . . .

I am not too happy or successful here in Corfe . . . . All the good painting
stuff lies just beyond my walking powers – & in the battle zone. Oh! this cold!
this vast draughty old barn of a Studio, so little fuel, & no E.L. every sort of
discomfort. . . .

I should like to hear from you Kitty but don't feel I am a nuisance. I should
hate [you] to feel that you *must* write to Frances. . . .

---

[84] Mary Spencer Watson (b. 1913), daughter of George Spencer Watson RA, was a sculptor in stone,
terracotta and wood. Taught to carve stone as a child in the quarries of Purbeck, she studied at the Slade and
the Royal Academy schools, and was still exhibiting in 1992.

. . . . I wish we could meet sometime – a very special joy wld. be to see your babies & you together – I am sure they are 2 beauties. . . .

[590] TO DUNCAN MACDONALD, 16 JANUARY 1945
                              Studio, Corfe Castle, Dorset. Jan 16 44 [45]

My Dear Duncan

With frozen chilblain fingers I am writing this to say that I am doing all in my power to prepare for your Feb: show[85]. . . . I realize your enormous difficulties with the frames & you I know will realize *my* difficulties such as the very short notice . . . .

In answer to your Enquiries there are 2 wooden panels (oils) 25-30 which you might like to have together with 2 large sized Gouaches, begun some time ago, not yet completed – Also some period Drawings in black & white –

All these could make one parcel to go by rail if I can succeed in getting them packed. . . .

(I am not tough enough to tackle parcels) there is no one in [the] village who can lend a hand – hence this fuss & worry –

Another point, an important one – You will agree with me Duncan that there is no point in my showing with Graham Sutherland & others if my senority is not respected & my prices equal to, or exceed theirs – The money value is acute with me at this crisis and unless I am to materially benefit by the grouping together why then all this Showmanship?

I feel that I have suffered an unfortunate set-back through illness and that for me now, shows are too exacting & exciting –

I must from now on work within my powers –

Finally I need a Secretary – he or she – even if I drove them mad –

It takes me longer to write a letter than paint a picture – Which is silly. . . .

When I saw Graham[86] some weeks ago he spoke of going to France – afterwards to contribute about 4 works to your Group – Not many but much. . . .

[591] TO PETER FIELD, 17 JANUARY 1945
                                     Corfe Castle, Dorset. Jan. 17th. 45

My Dearest Peter

I am delighted to hear from you again. I had heard of you via NZ with a thrill of pride, only a few days ago, followed by the saddening news of your Fathers

[85] Macdonald asked for new oils or gouaches, and also older black and white drawings, to be included in a group exhibition.
[86] FH first met Graham Sutherland, a friend of Eardley Knollys, in October 1944.

death which was as surprising to me as to yourself. . . . It seems right & proper that you should hurry home. Hope you will. It will prolong your Mother's life I am sure, if you do. . . .

This is just a short line to make contact with you as soon as possible on your arrival in England. Here's my warmest love & admiration. "Some lad" as your all-but octogenarian Uncle Willie said in his last letter mentioning yr. decorations.[87] Willie is wonderful. He has buried his wife.

. . . . Come if you can to see me. If you do there will be an NZ cake waiting for a HERO. My love Peter Dear

Frances

The Newbery family finally refused Eardley Knollys's offer for the studio.

[592] To Eardley Knollys, 22 January 1945

Corfe Castle, Dorset. Jan 22-45

My dear Eardley

I have been on the point of writing to you for an age. It has taken me all the fire of life, which never goes out, to keep alive the fire in my two stoves which on the contrary go out much too often. The Studio . . . is closed till I can get more fuel god knows when & how. . . .

Let me say once again how awfully sorry I am that we have had this set back to your compassionate scheme to tidy up my grubby old Barn & make it habitable & comfortable –

I am now waiting for the break up of the frost to get on with my work. Duncan is crying out for it – he talks of staging a Group consisting of G. Sutherland myself & perhaps 2 others – Nash & Moore – (Talking of Moore can you tell me where a friend of mine could buy one of his Drawings. . . .) She is fanatical over his shelter work. . . .

[593] To Duncan Macdonald, 4 February 1945

Studio, Corfe Castle, Dorset. Sunday Feb 4th. 45

My Dear Duncan

Very many thanks indeed for the cheque you have sent me also the heartening letter that came with it[88]. . . .

---

[87] DFC and bar.

[88] £54.17.6 for three recent gouaches, including *Mangolds, Purbeck.* The letter contained the first mention of an exhibition of old and new work by FH – this eventually became the major retrospective of November 1946. There was also the welcome news that the group show was postponed from February until April. It was to include, at Graham Sutherland's request, the 'newcomer' Francis Bacon.

This is just a line to say that tomorrow I hope to get off 2 Paintings – by Registered Post – In the same packet I have enclosed a few:

Black & White Drawings, water colours etc all early work – & interesting to the collector, otherwise of no great importance. Should you feel inclined to have some of them framed & try your luck with them I hope you will do so – if not let me have them back again –

I find these flash-backs very disturbing but I suppose they are inevitable. . . .

[594] TO DOROTHY SELBY, 4 MARCH 1945
Corfe Castle, Dorset. Sunday March 4th 1945

Dearest Dorothy

Thank you so much for your letter. . . . What a monstrous winter we have had. . . . I seem to live in a world bordering on hysteria . . . but Spring is in the air & there is hope in the word – plenty of yellow daffys – I would send you some if I could concentrate on string & paper etc to parcel them up. . . . My news is practically nil – I have cancelled my show – and await the verdict of the Leicester Galleries.[89] I feel physically unable to do another stroke of painting till I have had a change & rest. Since I saw you last I have never ceased to seek some place to go to – with no success

Yes I have seen the 2 latest Penguins & am hoping that mine will soon be out. . . .

Have you seen a 2/– booklet of Childrens Art (Tomlinson) get it if you havent – awfully good – Tried to buy one for you – but was baulked. . . .

[Postscript]   More hellish rockets – curse them! . . .

In April 1945 Eardley Knollys drove FH to a remote Welsh valley, Llangurig in Montgomeryshire, and she settled in at Clockfaen Hall. The letter she wrote from there was in pencil, barely decipherable.

[595] TO EARDLEY KNOLLYS, 25 APRIL 1945
Clockfaen Hall, Llangurig. April 25-45

Dearest Eardley

I can only think of Suckling's indecorous lines Out on it! For 3 *whole* days I've

---

[89] A solo exhibition arranged a year earlier.

loved – might, perhaps have loved thee more Had it been fine weather –
Inconstant Lover.[90]

I am writing this in garden – Sun has gone to the heart like wine – I hope
you are resting & drinking it in in deep swigs of joy & gratitude for such
blessings. . . .

This place won't do at all for me – *not at all.* I have no hesitation in making
up my mind about it – But I have satisfied a curiosity – that is something. . . .

So far have done no work – beyond lifting up my eyes to the hills in despair
– wondering how to get away – & where to?. . .

I do wish I hadn't lost my small sketch book – with my Corfe Castle Notes –
the village is in hue & cry after it – it may yet turn up. . . . I keep thinking back
on the happenings of that lovely drive thro ravishing bloom & blossom. . . .
Deepest thanks

[596] To Jane Saunders, 3 May 1945

Studio, Corfe Castle, Dorset. May 3rd-1945

My Dearest Jane

Scarf & letter just arrived – what a lovely Birthday present. . . . . I remember
with shame that I have never even acknowledged that most intriguing, fascinating
& useful Christmas box of 4 months ago. . . . What joy unpacking it! I keep it
more or less intact, displaying the unusual colours from time to time – I get ideas.
I exploit you as a creative worker in colour to all who are interested – there is
Ozenfant a scientific colourist working in London during the war & I believe
Winifred Nicholson nee Dacre practices it – writes about it etc. . . . In case the
enclosed is new to you [you] may care to read what she has to say[91] – it might be
worth a trial – I think there is a lot of sense in what she has to say – I personally,
hate all rigid systems – but then I am a rebel –

. . . . I am overjoyed to hear you are selling so well . . . . It is not everyone who
can sell ½ dozen pictures at a time – splendid! I am glad – These are boom times
in the Art world artists like Piper, Graham Sutherland, myself etc especially Piper
– He is 1st favourite

Moore is good – Have you got a Drawing yet? I, alas, am in the hands of the
Dealer & they are the ones who get the bawbees – My highest price for an oil
painting is now £160. There are 4 dealers who show my work – *not* counting our
friend Mrs. Wertheim – What a bore the woman is! . . .

[90] Suckling's lines are: 'Out upon it, I have loved / Three whole days together; / And am like to love three
more / If it prove fair weather.'
[91] 'Liberation of colour', *World Review*, December 1944. Drawing an analogy between music and painting
Winifred Nicholson argued that colour must be detached from objects and studied scientifically, just as
sound has been detached from objects and made into the art/science of music.

Forgive my silence. It sort of fell on me – About Christmas time I felt pretty rotten, work was a martyrdom. . . . *couldnt write letters* . . . . Sounds feeble minded – it was! Your lovely Christmas box cheered me up. . . .

. . . . I have had some out of the ordinary nice visitors – Graham Sutherland & pretty young wife came for week and said he had come to call on Sir Joshua Reynolds.

I have just got back from a 2 weeks visit to mid Wales – high up in mountains – very bracing. I feel better but a bit tired – 3 perfect days – & then 6 days snow. I was motored there by a friend in the Nat. Trust who knows his Wales like his pocket – Accomodation nil – but I had an attic in a guest house. . . .

[Postscript] Later – Anthracite come – feeling better – warmer –

The European war ended on 8 May 1945.

[597] TO EARDLEY KNOLLYS, 28 MAY 1945

Studio, Corfe Castle. May 28th.

My Dear Eardley

Your letter was a bombshell not quite fatal but alarming enough –

Don't write me any more letters like this one or I shall not let you have one of my up to date Gouaches – So there! of course I am proud & pleased to be so greatly honoured it is rare to reach Star Power during one's lifetime . . . .

I would come joyfully, to your party if I could – believe me Eardley I am immensely conscious of all I shall miss at your dazzling Party given in honour of a dilapidated artist from the Slums of Dorset

At the moment I can't write any more. My Muse has returned to me – I found her waiting for me on the doorstep faithful wench, which goes to show how futile it is to travel over mountains in search of material when it lies at your own pavement, for the seeing. I am weary after quite a stupendous onset, but much less weary than if I had not achieved it –

. . . . Thank you from the Heart for your warm & helpful support – Dont hate me –

love from Frances

P. S. Have I made it quite clear that Frances Hodgkins very regretfully cannot be present –

[598] To Myfanwy Evans, 12 June 1945

Studio, Corfe Castle, Dorset. 12.6.45

My Dear Myfwany

Thank you so much for your consoling letter with statement as to how I stand in this belated & laborious appearance of my Penguin Book, which, however, has moved a stage further, thanks to you & very soon, now I hope will be selling on the Book Stalls.[92] Do believe me I have no black looks for you, on the contrary I am full of pangs & sympathy & admiration for your energy in poking up the poor photographer-printer to get on with the job "with all speed"

I have been through the list of coloured prints several times and as far as my memory permits I think it a fairly characteristic selection of my work between the year 1916-1945. The list might be strengthened by addition of 2 extra works of the 1945 class – either Purbeck Series – the two newest oils recently at Lefevres *or* these 2 – Lancashire Family, *Red Cockerel* – both good I think, owned by E Knollys who I am sure would let you have prints of them – He has very good prints I know. I hope No.13 (Mrs. Gorers) – is still life before open window with shells. Well I leave it to you – My private preference is above [Red Cockerel]

I should like to know if my Book is included in the main group Sutherland – Piper – or something slightly different *with other women*[93]. . . . I am working, though not so fiercely hard as your John – I am so very glad you have the K & A babies while Parents go on holiday – All is well again – Disaster averted indeed –

What a marvellous thing has happened to us all everything feels quite different now the bombing & fighting have stopped – the very air is different – the trees & sunshine *know* –

[599] To Duncan Macdonald, 19 July 1945

Studio, Corfe Castle, Dorset. 19 July 1945

My Dear Duncan

Thank you for your 2 letters – Thank you also for your compliments. I am glad you find my face both ugly & beautiful. Lots of people think compliments in a letter vulgar – but I dont – I like to have them pinned down on paper in black & white – You pay very sweet ones –

This must be only a very short letter – letters take me 2 days or more to write – my hands are stiff for both painting & writing

[92] *Frances Hodgkins* in the Penguin Modern Masters series was not published until 1948, the year after her death.

[93] FH was the only woman included in the first 14 books in the series. Myfanwy Piper was the only woman writer.

I am writing primarily to ask you for a cheque – something I can put in my Bank to give me the security I need & without which I am unable to work

I am not feeling specially happy or a great success: letters of congratulation have poured in on me from both friends & strangers – among them a list of Sales from a legal minded friend which I enclose[94] – I hope it is true that the prices he quotes are due to me –

Mr. Rothenstein[95] himself has written to me – He was very pleased to secure my earliest oil – history-making for me – but regretted extremely missing the Drawing of Seated Woman. Now *why* couldn't he have it? It is *mine* you know & has been in yr. cellars many a year – I hear of it in Edinburgh – & other places – attracting attention – When showed at Heals long ago Tottenham Court Rd. it was skied. Another oil picture – Island Ferry is also mine – painted when you were in U.S. It was painted for the Bloomsbury Gallery & returned to St James' Gallery unsold – & with a damaged reputation –

All this data I will leave to your Accountant to deal with

I was formally invited some weeks ago to contribute work for Paris.[96] I have accepted the invitation – Sir Kenneth Clark is lending 3 Gouaches – I hope you wont spoil the unity of the display by including a "man called Bacon"[97] as you did to the recent Show at which I was not mentioned curiously enough! perhaps as well –

I can't enlighten you as to the buyers of the 2 [Purbeck] Courtyards – I ask you –

Well now what about this "man called Goeze"[98] – infelicitous name – ? I have already declined Cecil Beatty.[99] It would be a faux pas if Mr. Goetze had to put someone elses head on my body – so let him come – do let me know when to expect him – & what exactly does he aim at getting –

This is a preamble – leading no where –

You pant after my pictures – I pant after your large cheques & please try & arrange for them to be quarterly & punctual –

---

[94] Eardley Knollys had supplied the following list after visiting the April group exhibition:
'List of 10 pictures by Frances Hodgkins
   Lefevre sold Nos 3-5 and 6 of your oils at that Show, 3 & 6 were 160 guineas each & 5 was 150 guineas (bought by Godfrey Winn)
   They also sold gouache 8 for 50 guineas
   Now this adds up [to] 520 guineas = £546
   I suppose they make you pay for frames
   They ought to owe you at least £300 or more on this show alone –'
In a letter of 7 May 1945, he urged FH to make inquiries of Lefevre's.
[95] The director of the Tate Gallery.
[96] For an exhibition of contemporary British art.
[97] Francis Bacon's *Three Studies for figures at the Base of a Crucifixion* had been shown in the April group exhibition.
[98] Walter Goetz was to write an article on FH and Graham Sutherland, and had asked Duncan Macdonald to obtain permission to send a photographer to Corfe.
[99] Cecil Beaton took photographs for *Vogue*.

We both know all about the rise in prices – You are both superbly good decorators –

Try & believe how difficult my life is – & how my nerves are harried & torn – the awful discomfort & lack of ordinary decencies – I am asking you for money in order that I might clean up this old ruin of a place –

Do you wonder I dont press you & Lily to visit me – or even a Mr. Goetze –

If I am teazed much more I shall get on board the 1st. boat to N.Z. that will take me. So there!

Painting & all that pertains to it is anathema to me at present

I must rest & recover balance –

When I have anything to give you – I'll shout! Love to you both . . . .

In his reply (23 July 1945), Duncan Macdonald stated that he too had nerves, as well as ulcers that, in the opinion of his doctor, could 'easily have been brought on by irascible artists'. He reproached FH for listening to 'mischief makers' who 'cannot know the Lefevre Gallery business'. The gallery had so far received payment for only one of the four works sold at the April exhibition and had earlier offered to advance FH money if she was in need. He also suggested that she should not pass judgement on Francis Bacon's painting without seeing the work. He countered what was probably her deepest grievance, the failure of the Tate Gallery to secure Seated Woman, *by stating that the Lefevre Gallery owned the work, had been trying to sell it, in Edinburgh and elsewhere, and that it was still for sale. He enclosed a cheque for the recent sale (mentioned in a letter of 12 July) of two oil paintings and two gouaches.*

[600] To Duncan Macdonald, 25 July 1945

Studio, Corfe Castle, Dorset. July 25 45

My Dear Duncan

I have already posted you a Receipt of your Firms cheque for £259-3-4 without waiting to enclose this note of thanks to you for sending money so quickly – I was certain that Water would gush forth as soon as you struck the Rock –

I am sorry my letter to you was so ill-worded & clumsy –

I think you know that I don't think much about money *as* money but I just start a temperature when nothing but an ugly overdraft stares me in the face

I note all you say in your letter and welcome the information that you have given me: it greatly helps to clarify my muddled outlook as regards the monetary position. . . . But time passes – I am writing this whilst waiting arrival of photographer & fittings – it is a lovely hazy warm day – ideal for outdoor work – I have booked lunch at the Inn for them – they should enjoy their outing – I hope they will – I'll help all I can even to Smiling –

Thank you for Catalogue & price list – the rise in my prices is right & timely – I hope they will continue to rocket –

As to the "Bacon" contribution I quite agree these vague generalisations are a mistake – We will see what happens as time goes on – when I have seen the pictures in the flesh – the sadistic-macabre-cum-Dali School of thought is not, frankly, to my taste – And is doodling really worth while? I have dabbled myself in my Day –

I am not trying to answer your letter – I try to forget it & having read it through 3 times I shall now destroy it – It is not one of your nicest – but you say you do not wish to be nice – & could be nastier

Later. Wed: Evening –

They have come – & gone – arriving 11-30pm departed 6 o'clock

A tall man in bright blue[100] – a pretty blonde – a Wagnerian like couple – rather unscrubbed – took copious photographs – said they were satisfied – wangled a sketch for his book – so Home – I wangled nothing but a bad headache –

When I have finished the 4 Gouaches I will send them along to you – By then you will no doubt have had a surfeit of Frances Hodgkins & her irascible ways – remember this: please

that I do have the faults of my qualities –

Again my thanks Yours very sincerely Frances Hodgkins

[601] TO EARDLEY KNOLLYS, 3 SEPTEMBER 1945

Studio, Corfe Castle, Dorset. Sept 3-45

My Dear Eardley

. . . . At the moment I am rather fussed with life & its entanglements wondering how I am going to get out of my present predicament without going to law about it – I have been coerced into being photographed not without some pressure from my Firm, Lefevres.

results deplorable –

I faced a demon photographer who has taken some far from flattering, or useful, photographs of myself – reducing me to a state of nerves & hysteria from sheer fear that they may get into circulation before I can stop them –

What a silly story it makes! Who cares? But I do – It is a caddish & hateful thing to happen to an artist who is also an ageing woman – there is the rub[101]

[unsigned]

---

[100] The photographer Felix H. Man.
[101] Felix Man's photographs are now valued as a record of the artist's old age.

[602] To John Rothenstein, 7 October 1945 [102]

Studio, Corfe Castle, Dorset. Oct. 7th 1945.

Dear Mr. Rothenstein, – This is the letter that should have been written two months or more ago, rather late, indeed *very* late and I am filled with remorse that such an important event for me as the acquisition of my earliest painting should go unacknowledged by the artist. My excuse must be for not replying earlier to your letter, is that I was in Wales painting at the time.

Please accept my apologies.

I was absolutely overcome by the high honour paid me – and I greatly appreciate the recognition of my worthiness as creative artist.

In reply to your request for the date when *Two Women with a Basket of Flowers* was painted I think 1915 St. Ives is sufficiently accurate – I remember Mr. Moffat Lindner liking it so much that he bought it as soon as it was finished and from then on it hung in his beautiful house among the Elite – Sickert, Steer, etc.

It would be interesting to know how it came to the Tate Gallery – and when.

It gives me intense pleasure to know that my picture is enshrined in glory at Millbank. I hope I shall soon see it. I was delighted with the copy of 'Windmill' and the excellent reproduction. It gave me a thrill – a nostalgic one. . . .

Thanking you for the warm sympathy and interest you have shown my work.

Yours sincerely,

Frances Hodgkins

In reference to the Drawing of a Woman that you mention I believe it belongs to me. I shall verify this when I am next at the Lefevre Gallery. If this should be the case I would like to present it to the Gallery.[103]

[603] To David Brynley, 2 November 1945

Studio, Corfe Castle, Dorset. Nov 2d. 1945

My Dear David

Thank you so much for writing – I loved your letters both yours & Normans. It is good of you to write in the teeth of so much doing – now and so much ahead – Things are moving – You are wise to cut down concerts to their minimum & get busy on frames . . . . Well I am glad that the dear Norman has at last got his hearts desire [to have a painting exhibition]. Not to be wondered that he is more than a little bit thrilled – Who wouldn't be? One of my theories is that a good picture will *out* like MURDER – This faith has kept me from despair –

As for your portrait I enjoyed doing it & when it was finished it seemed to be DAVID all right – so I left it. . . .

[102] Quoted in John Rothenstein, *Modern English Painters*, v.1, London, 1952, p.132.
[103] *Seated Woman* was eventually bought by the Tate Gallery in 1948.

In fact it was a minor tour de force & only Frances Hodgkins assisted by David Bryndley both geniuses of the 1st. magnitude could have produced it – dont you agree?. . .

FH's brother Willie died in 1945 and her Christmas message was written on a card to Isabel.

[604] TO ISABEL FIELD, NOVEMBER 1945

Studio, Corfe Castle, Dorset. Nov

Fondest love from Fanny Do wish I were with you this Xmas – nothing I should like better but circumstances are just too difficult for us all – am longing to hear from you all about Tauranga & what is being done – how you got through the journey. . . .

I hope you are well – a doctor said to someone the other day everyone is 6 yrs older in years, in wear & tear & strain most are 12 yrs older – Dear Willies food parcels built me up a lot & his kind & faithful letters still more – He had a rare gift of friendship hadn't he?

I am very busy with work for the Spring shows. . . .

Good of you to send me a cake am keeping it for Xmas. . . .Much love dearest Sis take care of yourself, at least as much as you can

Fanny

[605] TO LORNA STYLE, 17 DECEMBER 1945

Studio, Corfe Castle, Dorset. Dec 17th 1945

Dear Lorna Style

Thank you for your letter. If you can send the Maori Girl[104] along by Post rolled & registered I will gladly sign it for you – or if you prefer to bring it do so –

I don't remember painting it – probably about 1900?. . .

I am very interested to hear you are working with Cedric Morris – How wise of you! Tell him I hope he will come & visit us soon. . . .

---

[104] Now in the Auckland City Art Gallery, prominently signed and dated in red.

[606] To Duncan Macdonald, 15 January 1946

Studio, West St, Corfe Castle, Dorset. Jan 15 1946

My Dear Duncan

I was delighted with the p.c from you & Lily. . . .

It was a real knock out. On first sight of it I had a jealous stab – it was so clever – Said I – Duncan [Grant] shaking a fist at poor little Frances. . . .

This is only a feeble line as the snow begins to fall at dusk to say how glad I be that you are off to St Ives for 2 good weeks – indeed you deserve twice as long again & again. . . .

For some occult reason my painting wits have deserted me – or slowed down – but I will not bother you with a letter now – these lines are merely to thank you for the microscopic cheque which wont buy me much more than a bag of coal – as things go – we must do better than that –

I am desperately sad that I have no work for either you, The Leicester Gallery, or anyone else. For 3 months I have done no work bar a pretty feeble portrait sketch of a young boy friend – which will cut no ice. . . .

I am glad Ben & Barbara went home happy & successful – a success in their own right – which is at it should be – no concessions. . . .

[607] To Eardley Knollys, 27 January 1946

Studio, Corfe Castle, Dorset 27th. Jan 1946

My Dear Eardley

Do you think you could come and see me as soon after receiving this as you possibly can?. . .

Myfanwy has written me an important letter about a new art Magazine she is to edit coming out in the Spring, she wants new work from me, about six paintings for reproduction – I have nothing fresh, absolutely nothing . . . .

My point in writing to you is to ask you to get in touch with Myfanwy and if you are willing show her the ones you have got of mine unless of course she has already seen them

Naturally I am keen to be included in the Pavilion more especially as I don't seem to be in a very secure position in the Art world just at present or any other world – and of course for many other reasons – what John & Myfanwy say goes. It is an honour to be invited to support them

I have been cherishing the blessed hope that I should be well & fit enough by now to paint a portrait of you, and also Mr. Raymond Mortimer . . . .

[608] To Eardley Knollys, 6 February 1946

The Elms, Fitzroy Park, Highgate, NW6. Feb 6th. 46[105]

. . . . Eardley there is a wonder woman here called Hodgkins I seem to know her & not know her

I am going to ask Mrs. Gorer to have a Show of her pictures of 1930-45 in place of the show that was planned for this year –

(I am seeing myself today in rose colours – tomorrow there may be a freak storm of revulsion)

I must see those pictures in the National Gallery before I die

Lovingly & gratefully & quite crazy

Frances

[609] To Eardley Knollys, 12 March 1946

The Croft, Bradford-on-Tone, nr. Taunton, Somerset. March 12th 1946

My Dear Eardley

I would really have written sooner but for a bad touch of nervous breakdown – now happily recovering & settling down here for an indefinite stay – if all goes well & the Croft is not wanted by its owner –

I came here yesterday – from Corfe where I have been stopping since my return from the Gorers – an enchanting drive over icy roads to get here. . . .

[610] To Jane Saunders, 25 March 1946

Studio, Corfe Castle, Wareham, Dorset. 25-3-46[106]

My Dearest Jane

I am so very sorry to have been so long writing. I have been suffering from a bit of a break down and my work, of necessity has slowed down if not actually stopped.

One good thing however has emerged from the battling which is: the re-appearance of Old Man Penguin not far off publishing point –

I have even seen your double portrait & you are likely to receive an early copy – or so they say – of course the whole thing is sadly out of date & the script inaccurate & I think insincere – but I am told there are other publications of greater importance in the air – we must wait & see

[105] FH was staying with Rée Gorer, who had a fine collection of her paintings.
[106] Written at The Croft, Bradford on Tone. Two of the last works by FH are gouaches painted at The Croft in 1946. One is of the cottage and its garden, the other, a spring painting, is of the garden with the flowering cherry and pear tree in bloom.

I wish we could meet. You said something about Easter in your letter at Xmas – I feel it might be rash to entice you to come & see me until I am much less unsettled in my mind & have some definite plan for my future – the good people at Dartington Hall have been urging me to go and spend the rest of this very cold winter in a community group but I lack the herd instinct – in fact hate it.

Frankly Jane Dear I am feeling my years. . . .

Much love ever Frances

P.S.   The scarf you sent me was so warm & pretty I wear it these bitter days. Forgive my loss of memory in forgetting to thank you

Dorothy Selby joined FH at The Croft for Easter weekend. Afterwards FH sent her a postcard of Stanley Spencer's Magnolia.

[611] To Dorothy Selby, 22 April 1946

Croft. E. Monday

How good to spend a brief hour enjoying things we treasure. I came back happier than I have been this long while & you felt as I do that I am sure of

Thank you for coming & gladdening the outlook & come again when the spirit moves

All love Frances

[612] To Zika Ascher,[107] 27 April 1946

Studio, Corfe Castle, Dorset. April 27th. 1946

Dear Mr Ascher

I must apologise for not writing sooner to thank you for your letter & suggestion which I much appreciate and had it been possible I should have been very glad to have made a design

I am, however unfortunately unable to do so as I have been troubled with my eyes and am obliged to limit the amount of work I can at present undertake[108] –

I greatly admire the two squares you have so kindly sent me and say I may keep

---

[107] Zika Ascher was a refugee from Nazism who had come to London in 1939. He founded Ascher Textiles and began in the early forties to commission the best modern artists to submit designs for printing on fabric using the silkscreen technique.

[108] In 1983 the Redfern Gallery, London, mounted an exhibition of Ascher panels, squares and designs. The artists represented included Matisse, Moore, Picabia, Derain, Calder, Nicholson. FH was represented by *Ibiza*, a silk square, a design based on a watercolour c. 1933. Proofs only were made of this design, not a full edition.

which I do so with the deepest pleasure hoping it may prove an earnest of things to come –

I hope later that I may have the opportunity of meeting you and if I may will let you know when next I am in London

[613] To Dorothy Selby, 10 June 1946

Studio, Corfe Castle, Dorset. June 10th-46

My Dearest Dorothy

How good you are writing – Your letters have kept me from despair I miss you badly – I keep asking myself where am I? where are you? Did it ever happen that wild wet drive in the rain, to catch a train, to where? We were packed – I, pressed, against Mrs. Coggan . . . it was a nightmare – it would not have been *possible* for you to crowd in – I put all this down in order to test my failing memory – oh Dear! Dear! isnt it all a sad affair? The zest of life has left me – which means no work – no pictures – no cheques –

I am glad that Victory Day bores you as it does me. . . .

. . . . Amy is back again . . . I enclose her letter – *tear it up when read* – it is interesting as bearing on another case of mental strain etc.

Congratulations on a new cousin-in-law and now good night & Bless you. I shall have to borrow some courage from you – who have so much. Thinking it over & which is the best way out –

I'll leave this problem unanswered till next letter –

Shame on me for not writing sooner

[614] To Eardley Knollys, 1 October 1946.

Corfe Castle, Dorset. Oct 1st. 46

My Dearest Eardley

Ready by 3 o'c Friday 4th. if not seeing you for lunch – is this right?

No time for more –

But thanks for your letter & Catalogue, latter in rare good taste in wh. I learn a little news of all my past bequests hitherto unknown to me.

The world is so addled & muddled & fuddled the less said the better –

Oh! isn't he a bore – you know whom![109]

I come in faith

why is the way

ahead so black?

love Frances

---

[109] A probable reference to Duncan Macdonald, who had visited FH on the weekend of 14-15 September to discuss the retrospective exhibition of her work. She had given him three new gouaches.

[615] To Eardley Knollys, 10 October 1946

Studio, Grey Hound. Oct 10th.

Dearest Eardley

I have had an interlude of vetting since we parted on Friday 4th. and I am feeling better definitely better in every way. . . .You have been a darling. I don't know if you will ever want to see me again sad & bad for me if you don't. Let me tell you about the woman called Symonds who lives on a hill over Swanage – she is a genius. She took charge of me – took me in hand – & for an hour & ¾ stabbed at my feet with knives forceps files & God knows what else in the way of coloured solvents *etc*

She was just an ugly kind old English spin to look at – but so wise & quick & certain. . . .

Anyway I feel wonderful –

I tell you all this so as to explain a little why I disappeared & was put once more on my feet – without pain

Friday 11th.

Very nearly Friday again since I sat waiting – having taken you too literally as to time of your arrival – do forgive me – the unforgivable. . . .

[Postscript] You may have heard from the (Oxford) Sutherlands[110] whom I ran into at the Grey Hound – they thought rather poorly of my appearance I gathered & said they had kept awake at night thinking of it! So I write this line in haste to assure you that I am on the top grade & tomorrow will be out with my hoop!

In November 1946 the France Hodgkins Retrospective Exhibition *opened at the Lefevre Gallery. Eric Newton wrote the foreword to the catalogue. Twenty-three oil paintings, forty-one watercolours and gouaches and seventeen drawings were shown ranging from 1902 to 1946. FH went up to London with Amy Krauss to see the exhibition just before it closed at the end of November.*

---

[110] Dr Oliver Sutherland, brother of the painter, keeper of the Ashmolean Museum.

[616] To Duncan Macdonald, 15 December 1946

Studio, Corfe Castle. Dec-15-46

My Dear Duncan

Thank you for the cheque[111]

I enclose receipt

and will write in a few days – I hope –

Yours ever

Frances Hodgkins

Frances Hodgkins died five months later on 13 May 1947 at Herrison House, a mental hospital near Dorchester to which she had been admitted on 22 March. Some combination of bronchopneumonia, heart failure and possibly stroke ended her life. During her last illness she was at times 'confused, disorientated and deluded',[112] at others lucid, recognising her friends, but urging them not to remember her as she was then.[113]

Her death was announced on the BBC nine o'clock news on 14 May.[114] In accordance with her wishes, she was cremated at Weymouth on 17 May, her funeral being attended by John and Myfanwy Piper, Dorothy Selby, Amy Krauss, Duncan Macdonald, Eardley Knollys, Anthony West, David Brynley and Norman Notley. Obituaries appeared in The Times, Art News, Manchester Guardian *and* The Burlington Magazine.

Though there were no possessions of any value in her studio, FH had a considerable sum of money in the bank when she died. An unsourced press clipping in the Tate Archive states that she left £2863, a figure confirmed by later events. Her will laid down that her estate be divided equally among her brothers and sister, or their children if they had predeceased her.

Frances Hodgkins's ashes were placed in the Field family grave in the Waikanae cemetery near Wellington, New Zealand. Her name appears on the headstone with those of her brother-in-law, sister, nephew and mother.

---

[111] £219.14.8 for five gouaches and one pencil drawing sold during the exhibition.

[112] Letter from Dr Sinclair, the superintendent of Herrison House, to Sir Julian Huxley, 9 April 1947.

[113] Letter from Jane Saunders to Hannah Ritchie, c.April 1947.

[114] Letter from Amy Krauss to Isabel Field, 14 May 1947.

Bibliography

BOOKS AND CATALOGUES

Barr, Jim and Mary. *When Art Hits the Headlines, A Survey of Controversial Art in New Zealand*, National Art Gallery, Wellington, 1987. (Exhibition catalogue.)

Bell, Clive. *Art*, 9th ed., London, 1928.

Bell, Leonard. *The Maori in European Art, A Survey of the Representation of the Maori by European Artists from the Time of Captain Cook to the Present Day*, Wellington, 1980.

Collins, Judith. *Winifred Nicholson*, The Tate Gallery, 1987. (Exhibition catalogue.)

Cross, Tom. *Painting in the Warmth of the Sun, St Ives Artists 1939-1975*, Cornwall, 1984.

Eastmond, Elizabeth, and Merimeri Penfold. *Women and the Arts in New Zealand. Forty Works, 1938-86*, Auckland, 1986.

Entwisle, Peter. *William Mathew Hodgkins and his Circle*, Dunedin Public Art Gallery, 1984. (Exhibition catalogue.)

Entwisle, Peter. *Treasures of the Dunedin Public Art Gallery*, Dunedin Public Art Gallery, 1990. (Exhibition catalogue.)

Entwisle, Peter, Michael Dunn and Roger Collins. *Nerli*, Dunedin Public Art Gallery, 1988. (Exhibition catalogue.)

Evans, Myfanwy. *Frances Hodgkins*, Harmondsworth, 1948. (Penguin Modern Painters Series.)

Fox, Caroline, and Francis Greenacre. *Painting in Newlyn 1880-1930*, Barbican Art Gallery, 1985. (Exhibition catalogue.)

Fry, Roger. *Vision and Design*, ed. J. B. Bullen, London, New York, 1990.

Grimes, Teresa, Judith Collins and Oriana Baddeley. *Five Women Painters*, Oxford, 1989.

Harrison, Charles. *English Art and Modernism 1900-1939*, London, 1981.

Holme, Charles (ed.) *Sketching Grounds*, London, Paris and New York, 1909.

Howell, Arthur R. *Frances Hodgkins, Four Vital Years*, London, 1951.

Hubbard, Eric Hesketh. *A Hundred Years of British Painting 1851-1951*, London, 1951.

Hutchison, Sidney C. *The History of the Royal Academy, 1768-1968*, London, 1968.

Jeffrey, Ian. *The British Landscape 1920-1950*, London, 1984.

King, Julie. *Sydney Lough Thompson at Home and Abroad*, Robert McDougall Art Gallery, 1990. (Exhibition catalogue.)

Kirker, Anne. *New Zealand Women Artists*, Auckland, 1986.

McCormick, E. H. *The Expatriate*, Wellington, 1954.

McCormick, E. H. *Late Attachment*, Auckland City Art Gallery, 1988.

McCormick, E. H. *Letters and Art in New Zealand*, Wellington, 1940.

McCormick, E. H. *Portrait of Frances Hodgkins*, Auckland, 1981.

McCormick, E. H. *Works of Frances Hodgkins in New Zealand,* Auckland, 1954.

Mellor, David (ed.) *A Paradise Lost, The Neo-Romantic Imagination in Britain 1935-55,* Barbican Art Gallery, 1987. (Exhibition catalogue.)

Morphet, Richard. *Cedric Morris,* Tate Gallery, 1984. (Exhibition catalogue.)

Nunn, Pamela Gerrish. *Victorian Women Artists,* London, 1987.

Penguin Modern Masters Series on Graham Sutherland (by Edward Sackville-West), Henry Moore (by Geoffrey Grigson), Duncan Grant (by Raymond Mortimer), Paul Nash (by Herbert Read), Matthew Smith (by Philip Hendy), John Piper (by John Betjeman), David Jones (by Robin Ironside)

Platts, Una. *Nineteenth Century Artists, A Guide and Handbook,* Christchurch, 1979.

Smith, Bernard (with Terry Smith). *Australian Painting, 1788-1990,* 3rd ed., Melbourne, 1991.

Rothenstein, John. *Modern English Painters,* v.1, London, 1952.

Spalding, Frances. *British Art since 1900,* London, 1989.

Turner, W. J. (ed.) *Aspects of British Art,* London, 1947.

Wertheim, L. *Adventure in Art,* London, 1947.

Yorke, Malcolm. *The Spirit of Place. Nine Neo-Romantic artists and their times,* London, 1988.

CATALOGUES

Aspects of New Zealand Art 1890-1940, National Art Gallery, Wellington, 1984. (Essays by Anthony Mackle and Ann Calhoun.)

Echo, Works by Women Artists 1850-1940, Tate Gallery Liverpool, 1991. (Text by Maud Sulter.)

Emily Carr in France, Vancouver Art Gallery, 1991. (Essay by Ian M. Thom.)

The First Fifty Years, British Art of the 20th Century, National Art Gallery of New Zealand, 1981. (Introduction by Anne Kirker.)

Frances Hodgkins, 1869-1947, A Centenary Exhibition, Auckland City Art Gallery, 1969. (Essay by Ian Roberts and David Armitage, biographical material by E. H. McCormick)

Frances Hodgkins, 1869-1947, Whitford and Hughes, London, 1990. (Essay by Avenal McKinnon.)

Frances Hodgkins and her Circle, Auckland City Art Gallery, 1954. (Introduction by E. H. McCormick.)

Frances Hodgkins – the Late Work, Minories Art Gallery, Colchester, 1990-1. (Essays by Liz Reintjes, Rosemary Pawsey and Lindsey Bridget Shaw.)

New Zealand's Women Painters, Auckland City Art Gallery, 1975. (Introduction by Anne Kirker and Eric Young.)

The Origins of Frances Hodgkins, Hocken Library, 1969. (Essay by Una Platts.)

The Paintings and Drawings by Frances Hodgkins, Auckland City Art Gallery, 1959. (Introduction by Colin McCahon.)

Under the Spell, Frances Hodgkins, Nellie Hutton and Grace Joel, Three Women Artists Influenced in the 1890s by G.P. Nerli, Hocken Library, 1987. (Introduction by Rosemary Entwisle.)

SELECTED ARTICLES, REVIEWS, ETC.

Art New Zealand 16, 1980. Articles by Gordon H. Brown, Anne Kirker, E. H. McCormick, E. A. Sheppard.

Ascent, Frances Hodgkins commemorative issue, Christchurch, 1969. Articles by Melvin Day, Shay Docking, Anthony S. G. Green, June Opie, E. H. McCormick.

Brown, Gordon. *New Zealand Painting 1900-1920, Traditions and Departures*, Wellington, 1972. Exhibition organised by the Hocken Library for the Queen Elizabeth II Arts Council.

Collins, Roger. 'A New Look at an Old Story, Frances Hodgkins in France', unpublished address at the Dunedin Public Art Gallery, 17 November 1991.

Dunn, Michael. 'Frozen Flame & Slain Tree', *Art New Zealand* 13, 1979, pp.41-45.

Evans, Myfanwy (Piper). 'The Life and Art of Frances Hodgkins', *Listener*, November 1946.

Evans, Myfanwy (Piper). 'Frances Hodgkins', *Vogue*, August 1947.

Fairburn, A. R. D. 'The Wertheim Collection', *Year Book of the Arts in New Zealand*, No. 5, Wellington, 1949, pp.2-9.

Frankel, Margaret. '"The Pleasure Garden" Incident at Christchurch', *Year Book of the Arts in New Zealand*, No. 5, Wellington, 1949, pp.11-17.

Gorer, Geoffrey. *Bali and Angkor*, London, 1936, Appendix II, 'Modern Painting'.

Gorer, Geoffrey. 'The Art of Frances Hodgkins', *Listener*, 17 November 1937.

Gorer, Geoffrey.'Remembering Frances Hodgkins', *Listener*, 19 June,1947.

Kirker, Anne. *The Last years of the 'Seven and Five' Society*. Unpublished thesis presented for the degree of M.A. in Art History at the Courtauld Institute of Art, London, May 1979.

Nunn, Pamela Gerrish. 'Frances Hodgkins. The "Arrival" in Context', *Art New Zealand* 56, 1990, pp.86-89.

Piper, John. 'Frances Hodgkins', *Horizon*, London, 1941, pp.413-6.

Pound, Francis. 'The Stumps of Beauty & the Shriek of Progress', *Art New Zealand* 44, 1987, pp.52-55, 104-5.

Stephens, A. G. 'Frances Hodgkins, a Dunedin girl who conquered Paris', *Otago Witness*, 28 May 1913.

Brief Chronology

1869   28 April, born in Dunedin, third child and second daughter of William Mathew Hodgkins and Rachel Owen Hodgkins (née Parker).

1890   Begins exhibiting with art societies in Christchurch and Dunedin.

1893   Taught by G. P. Nerli.

1895-6 Attends Dunedin School of Art.

1896   Begins teaching private classes.

1898   Death of W. M. Hodgkins.

1901   Leaves Dunedin for Europe.

1901-3 Travels and paints in England, France, Italy, Morocco, Belgium, Holland. Exhibits at three London galleries and the Royal Academy.

1903   December, returns to Wellington.

1904-5 In New Zealand.

1906   January, leaves for Europe.

1906-8 Paints and teaches in England, France, Italy, Holland.

1907   March, first solo exhibition at Paterson's Gallery, London.

1908   November, arrives in Paris and is based there until the end of 1912, spending the summers teaching and painting at sketching grounds in the north of France.

1910   January, teaches watercolour class at the Académie Colarossi.

1911   c. October, opens own school for watercolours in Paris.

1912   October, leaves for Australia. November, exhibits in Melbourne. December, arrives in Wellington.

1913   Exhibits in Sydney, Adelaide, Dunedin and Wellington. October, leaves for Europe.

1914   Travels and paints in Italy and France.

1914-18 Spends war years based in St Ives. Exhibits with International Society of Sculptors, Painters and Gravers, and the National Portrait Society.

1918   December, takes studio in Kensington.

1919-20 Moves between Cornwall and London. February 1920, solo exhibition at Hampstead Gallery. November, leaves for south of France.

1922-3 Settled in Burford, Oxfordshire.

1924   Paints and teaches in France. Exhibits at Salon d'Automne.

1925   c. April, books passage to Australia. May, appointed fabric designer with the Calico Printers' Association, Manchester.

1926   Death of Mrs Hodgkins.

1927   Leaves Manchester. Works in Brittany July 1927-March 1928.

1928-30 Works in London and France.

1929   March, shows for the first time with Seven and Five Society.

1930   March, signs agreement with Arthur R. Howell of St George's Gallery. Solo exhibition in October.

1931   Returns to south of France. St George's Gallery closes.

1932   Signs agreement with the Lefevre and Leicester Galleries. October 1933, first solo exhibition at the Lefevre Gallery.

1932-7   Lives and paints in Great Britain and France. Travels to Ibiza (1932-3) and Spain (1935-6).

1937-8   Lives at Worth Matravers, Dorset.

1939-47   Alternates between Corfe Castle, Dorset and Bradford-on-Tone, Somerset, with excursions elsewhere. Invited to be one of four artists representing Great Britain at the 1940 Venice Biennale.

1946   November, Retrospective Exhibition at the Lefevre Gallery.

1947   13 May, dies at Herrison House, Dorset.

Index of Recipients

Index

Entries in bold type indicate FH's opinion of an artist's work.

577